Windows Vista™
Secrets®

Windows Vista™
Secrets®

Brian Livingston
Paul Thurrott

Wiley Publishing, Inc.

Windows Vista™ Secrets®
Published by
Wiley Publishing, Inc.
10475 Crosspoint Boulevard
Indianapolis, IN 46256
www.wiley.com

Copyright © 2007 by Brian Livingston and Paul Thurrott

Published by Wiley Publishing, Inc., Indianapolis, Indiana

Published simultaneously in Canada

ISBN-13: 978-0-7645-7704-8
ISBN-10: 0-7645-7704-2

Manufactured in the United States of America

10 9 8 7 6 5 4 3 2

1B/SQ/RS/QW/IN

For general information on our other products and services or to obtain technical support, please contact our Customer Care Department within the U.S. at (800) 762-2974, outside the U.S. at (317) 572-3993 or fax (317) 572-4002.

Library of Congress Cataloging-in-Publication Data

Livingston, Brian.
  Windows Vista secrets / Brian Livingston, Paul Thurrott.
      p. cm.
  Includes index.
  ISBN-13: 978-0-7645-7704-8 (paper)
  ISBN-10: 0-7645-7704-2 (paper)
  1. Microsoft Windows (Computer file). 2. Operating systems (Computers). I. Thurrott, Paul B. II. Title.
  QA76.76.O63L5955 2007
  005.4'46—dc22

                                     2006032941

To Margie Livingston and Stephanie, Mark, and Kelly Thurrott

About the Authors

Brian Livingston is editorial director of the weekly *Windows Secrets Newsletter* (**http://WindowsSecrets.com**) and author of the weekly "Executive Tech" column (**http://BrianLivingston.com**) for Datamation. For 12 years, from 1991 to 2003, he was a contributing editor of *InfoWorld Magazine*, writing the weekly "Window Manager" column and (from 2001 to 2003) the *E-Business Secrets* newsletter. He has also been a contributing editor of CNET News.com, *PC World*, *PC/Computing*, *Windows Sources*, and *Windows Magazine*. The business model of WindowsSecrets.com, which is supported by voluntary reader contributions, earned him the Internet Entrepreneur of the Year award at the 2006 Internet Content Summit in New York, sponsored by MarketingSherpa (**http://bri.li/060508**).

Paul Thurrott is the news editor of *Windows IT Pro Media* and editor of the SuperSite for Windows (**http://www.winsupersite.com**). He writes a weekly editorial for Windows IT Pro UPDATE (**http://www.windowsitpro.com/email**); a daily Windows news and information newsletter called *WinInfo Daily UPDATE* (**http://www.wininformant.com**); and a monthly column called "Need To Know" in *Windows IT Pro Magazine*.

Credits

Contents at a Glance

Part VII: Home Office/Power User

Contents

Chapter 2: Installing and Upgrading to Windows Vista...45

Chapter 3: Vista Compatibility 75

Part II: Understanding the Windows Vista User Experience

Chapter 4: What's New in the Windows Vista User Interface 95

Chapter 5: Where's My Stuff? Finding and Organizing Files 125

Part III: Security

Chapter 8: Windows Vista Security Features 215

Chapter 9: New User Account Features..233

Part IV: Digital Media and Entertainment

Preface

Welcome to *Windows Vista Secrets*, the latest in the bestselling *Windows Secrets* series! We've rewritten this book from the ground up in response to this major release of Microsoft Windows. We hope you enjoy combing through this book as much as we enjoyed digging through Windows Vista to find these nuggets of valuable information.

—Brian Livingston and Paul Thurrott

Web Sites Supporting the Book

For updates and new information, please visit these sites:

http://WindowsSecrets.com/vista
http://www.winsupersite.com/vista

Icons Used in This Book

The following icons are used in this book to help flag to your attention some of the most important or most useful information in the book.

Secret

The Secret icon marks little-known facts that are not obvious to most Windows users. This information may be written down *somewhere* by Microsoft, but not in a way that it's easy for users to find.

tip The Tip icon indicates a helpful trick.

cross ref The Cross-Reference icon points to chapters where more information can be found.

caution The Caution icon warns you about possible negative side-effects or precautions you should take before making a change.

Read This First

◆ ◆

In This Chapter

The new Start menu

Windows Aero

Flip 3D

Programs Explorer replaces Add/Remove Programs

Put some gadgets in your Windows Sidebar

Instant Search and the Search pane

Internet Explorer 7.0 catches up with the competition

IE protected mode and phishing filter

Support for RSS news feeds

Encrypt entire drives with BitLocker

Use Easy Transfer to a new PC

Parental Controls

New games

◆ ◆

In this preliminary chapter we give you a crash course in some of the major new features of Vista. Give us 15 minutes and we'll show you the biggest changes in the operating system—before you may have to grapple with them yourself.

The Value of Vista

We waited more than five years for Vista. As you may recall, Windows XP was released with much fanfare in October 2001. But instead of the next Windows version shipping in just a couple of years, as originally expected, Microsoft lost its way in the development process. Vista didn't make it to consumers until early 2007.

Was it worth the wait?

The short answer is, "Yes." We believe Vista is a major advance on Microsoft's previous operating systems. If you're buying a new PC today, we don't hesitate to recommend that you get Vista rather than requesting XP or another, older operating system. (If you're upgrading an older PC to Vista, by contrast, be sure to first read our tips in Chapter 3.)

In 2001, Microsoft executives widely claimed that XP was "the most secure operating system we have ever delivered." In fact, XP and its new Web browser, Internet Explorer 6.0, were full of maddening security holes that previous operating systems didn't suffer from. ActiveX exploits, drive-by downloads, and many other kinds of weaknesses were quickly exploited by black-hat hackers. Microsoft has been issuing patches for XP and IE 6.0 ever since.

The Vista OS and the new IE 7.0 browser are welcome steps toward changing that. Will they never need patching? We'd hardly say that. But Microsoft has added "hardening" features to Vista that should make remote exploits more difficult for hackers to carry out. Besides improved security, XP users who switch to Vista will also find enhancements in desktop searching, Windows Sidebar access to applets called *gadgets*, PC-to-PC content transfers, and even new games—mahjong and (finally!) chess.

Unlike the first chapters of most books—which are filled with boilerplate thank-yous and personal musings—we really do want you to read this chapter. Instead of filling our first few pages with acknowledgements of names you've never heard of, we've moved the credits for our valued sources into the chapters they helped us with.

In these pages, we aim to give you a crash course on Windows Vista. In other words, read on and you can learn the most important new features of Vista in the time it takes to sip a nice, hot cuppa Joe.

Learn Vista in 15 Minutes

It's impossible to cover all the new features of Vista in a single chapter. Many features warrant their own chapters because there's a lot to say about them or we found secret information that isn't in the Help text you get with Vista.

Other new Vista features, although important, may be so straightforward that they don't have any particular secrets. If not, we haven't devoted any further space to them in this book.

But even features that don't have hidden features may be important for you to know about when you turn Vista on for the first time. Exposing those features to you is the purpose of the following overview.

The New Start Menu

In Vista, the Start button is no longer called Start, and the Start menu looks completely different from the menu you may be used to in Windows XP. However, it's still there at the bottom of the screen, and you may find it a bit better organized.

The old Start button has been replaced by a lighted sphere that displays the Windows flag logo. Instead of submenus that fly out to the right of the main menu, Vista displays your most recently used programs in a primary window (see Figure 1).

> **tip** If you don't like the new look, you can get the old Start menu back by reverting to the familiar XP submenu system. Right-click the Start Button, click Properties, select Classic Start Menu, and then click OK.

If you click All Programs, the Start menu switches to a display of collapsing folders. You can expand each folder to show you all available programs, but the Start menu keeps the list within the primary window.

Secret

What Happened to the Run Menu?

One thing you won't find on the default Start menu is the Run option, which generations of Windows users have employed to start programs that may not appear on any menu. The omission isn't a problem — if you know the secret. Simply type the name of the program you want to run (such as **notepad**) into the Start Search bar just above the Start button and then press Enter.

Windows Aero

You'll see a slick new look to objects and applications in Vista — *if* you have a version of the operating system that supports it and hardware that's modern enough to render it.

The new Aero interface gives translucency to the chrome that surrounds most application windows. This enables you to see what lies beneath a window, whether the foreground app is stationary or you're dragging it to a new location.

> **tip** If the translucency of window chrome irritates you, you can switch it off. Click Start⇨Control Panel⇨Customize the Color Scheme and then turn off **Enable Transparency.**

Perhaps more important than translucency is the new *live thumbnail* effect that Aero adds to the taskbar at the bottom of the screen. Hover your mouse over a button that represents a minimized application, and you'll see a miniature picture of what's in the app at that moment (see Figure 2). This can be helpful in deciding which of several minimized applications to switch to.

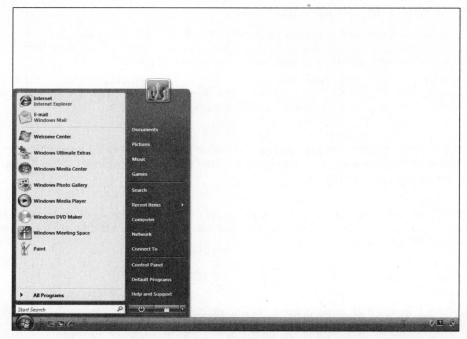

Figure 1: The new Start menu. A primary window contains your most recently used programs and a column of buttons that open windows on common tasks.

You can see the Aero interface (formerly code-named Aero Glass) if you have Vista Home Premium, Business, Enterprise, or Ultimate Edition, and your video board supports the advanced features of Microsoft's new Windows Driver Display Model.

Secret

Can Translucency Help Productivity?

Translucency may seem like an unimportant feature, but a source within Microsoft's Usability Labs tells us that the bold colors of the window frames in Windows XP were found to distract the eye from whatever material was in the main application window. Lightening up the window colors — by making them partially translucent — was found to improve how quickly a person could work with the content within applications.

**cross
ref**   For more on the Aero interface, see Chapter 4.

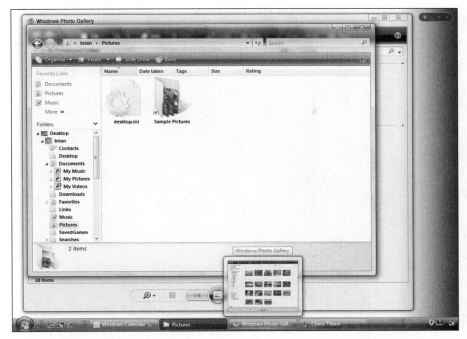

Figure 2: **Aero and live thumbnails.** Besides the slick new look of translucent glass windows, Aero almost instantaneously displays small images of your open applications when you hover your mouse over the taskbar buttons.

Flip 3D

Many Windows users know about Alt+Tab. You can hold down the Alt key and press Tab repeatedly to switch to any application that's currently open.

The Aero user interface adds a powerful enhancement to task switching. Alt+Tab still works—even better, in fact, because now thumbnails of each application are displayed, not just titles. But you'll probably abandon Alt+Tab in favor of Windows+Tab, called Flip3D, which shows you a revolving set of windows at an angle so you can see exactly what you're switching to (see Figure 3).

One of the windows that's shown in the Flip 3D view is always your Windows Desktop. That makes it easy to minimize all of your applications. Simply hold down the Windows key (either the left one or the right one), and then press Tab until the miniature window that looks like your Desktop is uppermost.

tip

You can reverse the order that Flip 3D cycles through your open windows by holding down the Shift key in addition to Windows+Tab. In our tests, the Desktop window has always been displayed as the bottom-most application when we pressed Windows+Tab. To minimize all applications and display your Desktop, therefore, hold down the Windows key, then press Tab, Shift+Tab, and let go of the Windows key.

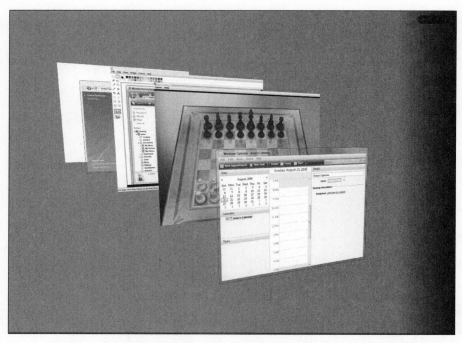

Figure 3: Flip 3D. Holding down the Windows key while repeatedly pressing Tab cycles through miniature windows that show you what's in each of your open applications and your Desktop.

cross
ref   Flip 3D is also discussed in Chapter 4.

Programs Explorer Replaces Add/Remove Programs

Legions of Windows users have become accustomed to using the Add or Remove Programs dialog box in the Control Panel to uninstall applications that they no longer want taking up space on their hard disks. So, in its frustrating way, Microsoft has renamed this feature to make it even harder to find than it was before.

To reconfigure or completely remove an application, you now use the Programs Explorer (see Figure 4). This applet also enables you to turn on or off many of the built-in features that come with Windows Vista, such as the Indexing Service.

Fortunately, the Programs Explorer is still available through the Control Panel. You just need to know to look for it in the Ps instead of the As.

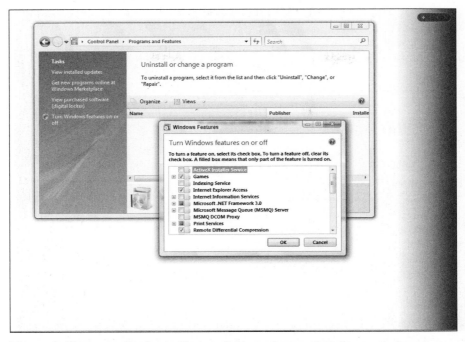

Figure 4: Programs Explorer. You need this applet to uninstall unwanted programs and enable or disable various Vista features.

Put Some Gadgets in Your Windows Sidebar

Apple users have long been able to take advantage of the Mac OS X Dashboard, and Windows users have been able to download Yahoo Widgets (formerly Konfabulator Widgets). Those things are still available, but now Vista has its own little tools, known as gadgets.

Vista gadgets live in the new Windows Sidebar (see Figure 5) — which you can move to the left or right side of the screen by right-clicking it and selecting Properties. Or you can put Gadgets on your Desktop by dragging the little context menu that appears when you hover your mouse over a Gadget.

Using the Properties dialog box, you can configure the Windows Sidebar to start every time Windows starts or only when you want it to appear. If you configure it to require manual intervention, get it back by clicking Start➪All Programs➪Accessories➪Windows Sidebar.

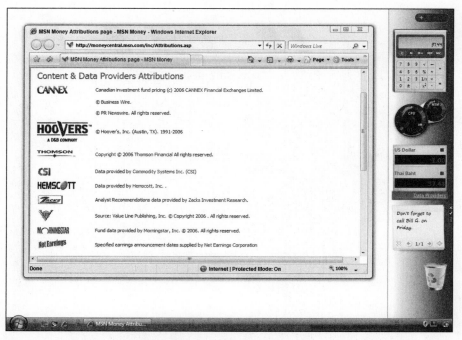

Figure 5: Windows Sidebar with gadgets. In this view, the Windows Sidebar holds five gadgets: Calculator, CPU Meter, Currency Converter, Notes, and the Recycle Bin. The main window shows the data providers you can choose for near-real-time updates in various gadgets.

<table>
<tr><td>cross
ref</td><td>The Windows Sidebar is discussed in detail in Chapter 6.</td></tr>
</table>

Instant Search and the Search Pane

An interactive Instant Search bar is now a feature of every Explorer window in Vista as well as Vista's Start menu. This may not slow the progress of third-party desktop search applications that are increasingly being promoted as Windows downloads from the major search engines. But Microsoft is, in fact, trying to build into Vista advanced search functions to render such downloads unnecessary.

Figure 6 shows the results of **.jpg** entered in the search bar of the Start menu. Pressing Enter opens the more-capable Search pane. In this pane, you can refine your search or organize the results by file size and other attributes.

<table>
<tr><td>tip</td><td>The Instant Search bar can be a handy way to search within a particular application window. Vista's search function becomes context-specific in many such applications. Figure 7 shows the Vista Control Panel in its classic view, which is somewhat cluttered with applets. Figure 8, by contrast, shows the result after you enter **options** into the Control Panel's search bar, which selects just those applets with that word in their titles.</td></tr>
</table>

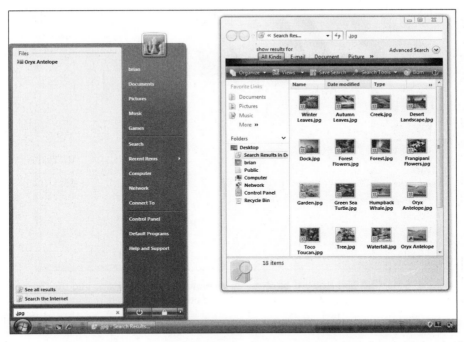

Figure 6: The search bar and Search pane. Entering a string into the search bar in the Start menu and pressing Enter opens the Search pane, where you can refine your search.

Figure 7: The Control Panel's classic view. In this configuration, every Control Panel applet is shown, which looks quite busy.

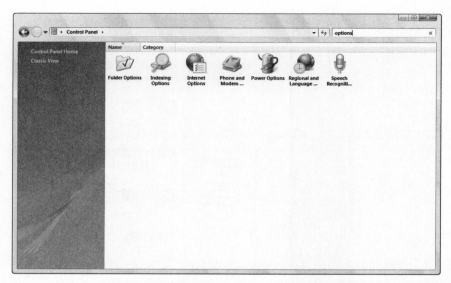

Figure 8: Selecting just options applets. By entering the word **options** into the Control Panel's search bar, only those applets with that word in their titles are displayed, making your choice easier.

cross ref You can read more about searching in Windows Vista in Chapter 5.

Internet Explorer 7.0 Catches Up

IE 7 won't win any awards for innovation, having not quite caught up with features its free competitor, the Mozilla Firefox browser, came out with two years ago.

But the improved security of IE 7, plus the addition of long-requested features such as tabbed browser windows, make Microsoft's new browser a solid component of the OS rather than the backward stepchild that IE 6 became. (Users of Windows XP can and should download and install IE 7, if an upgrade to Vista isn't immediately possible.)

Besides the tabbed windows, IE 7 has (thankfully) copied several other features from Firefox, Opera, and other non-Microsoft browsers. These include the ability to add Internet search engines of your choice to IE's search bar and a default Shink to Fit setting so Web pages will fit your printer's paper size.

However, IE 7 has also gained a few new features that other browsers may themselves need to catch up with.

◆ Pressing Ctrl+Q or clicking the Quick Tabs tab on the IE 7 toolbar tiles all of your open tabs into a convenient thumbnail view (see Figure 9). When you have a lot of tabs open, Quick Tabs can save you a substantial amount of time that you might otherwise spend clicking at random to get back to a particular site.

◆ Page Zoom is another handy feature. When you're viewing a web page that's just too small or too large, hold down the Ctrl key and press + to make the page 10 percent larger, – to make it 10 percent smaller, or 0 (zero) to return the page to its original size.

These special keystroke sequences work exactly the same way as they do in Firefox, except that IE 7 scales both images and text. (Firefox 1.5 scaled just text.) The keystrokes work whether you use the symbol keys on the main keyboard or the numeric keypad.

◆ There's also a small Page Zoom button on the extreme right of IE 7's status bar. You can click it once to scale a Web page to 125 percent, click it again for 150 percent, and click it a third time to go back to 100 percent.

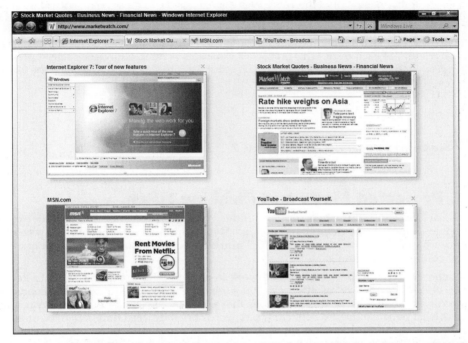

Figure 9: Quick Tabs. Press Ctrl+Q in IE 7 and all of your tabbed windows are tiled, showing you a thumbnail to help you switch to a desired Web page.

Fit the Full URL on Printouts

Secret

Sometimes, you want to print out some Web page you've found, so you can recommend the site to a friend later. But if the Web address (URL) is a long one, it's likely to be truncated in the footer of the printed page. That's because IE, by default, uses a large font and cuts off any of the URL that doesn't fit on the same line as today's date.

continues

continued

You can make URLs print in full almost every time by clicking Tools➪Internet Options. On the General tab, click the Fonts button and then select a Web page font that's more compact than Times New Roman, such as Vista's Cordia New. (This font, which is similar to Arial, also becomes the default font for Web pages that don't specify a font.)

If that doesn't print the entire Web address, give URLs a separate line. To do so, pull down the Printer toolbar and select Page Setup. Enter **&b&u** in the Header field to devote the full header to the URL (aligned to the right). Then enter **&d&b&p** in the Footer field to print the date on the left and the page number on the right at the bottom of each page. (This procedure eliminates printing each page's title, represented by **&w.** A Web page's title takes up space that's best devoted to printing the full URL, in our view.)

cross ref   See Chapter 17 for more discussion of IE 7.

IE Protected Mode and Phishing Filter

Internet Explorer 7.0, when running under Windows Vista (not XP or earlier operating systems), operates by default in *Protected Mode*. This means that dishonest web sites that a user happens to visit cannot trick IE 7 into changing Windows system files or other crucial configuration details.

A separate feature, but one that can work in concert with Protected Mode to keep users out of trouble, is Microsoft's new *Phishing Filter*. IE 7 regularly downloads from a Microsoft server a list of web addresses that appear to be fraudulent. These sites may get on the list because they're collecting passwords or credit card numbers from gullible consumers, they're downloading spyware to people's computers, or for other reasons. In any case, IE 7 doesn't display known phishing sites, instead warning the user about the identified problems with the site.

The features just described are only two of the several Microsoft has added to Internet Explorer. Others include protection against cross-site scripting attacks (in which one site takes over a window used by another site), ActiveX suspension (which disables the most dangerous ActiveX controls), and Windows Defender, which guards against spyware.

It's too early to say whether the new IE security features will add up to an adequate level of safety for Windows users, or whether third-party security products must still be added to Windows. It's likely that Microsoft's own programs will play second fiddle to third-party developers, who concentrate specifically on antiphishing and antispyware research. Read the comparative reviews of security add-ons in respected computer magazines to learn which products provide the best security — and then invest a few bucks in any independent downloads that are top rated.

cross ref   For more discussion of security in Windows Vista, turn to Chapter 8.

Support for RSS News Feeds

IE 7.0 includes an easy way to subscribe to news feeds, regularly updated information that sites publish in the format known as Really Simple Syndication (RSS).

When a surfer visits a site that publishes one or more news feeds, a square broadcast icon on IE 7's toolbar changes from grey to orange. Clicking the icon takes you to a page that explains the content of a feed and provides a clickable link that subscribes you (see Figure 10). This is a big improvement over previous news feed buttons in other browsers, which formerly displayed raw XML code when clicked.

After you've subscribed to a news feed, you can read it using IE 7's Favorites pane. This subwindow is accessed by clicking the yellow star in IE's toolbar and selecting Feeds. The latest news items can be sorted by date or title or filtered by categories provided by the author of the feed (see Figure 11).

IE's native feed handling isn't as capable as a dedicated reader's, such as NewsGator, or an online news aggregator's, such as Bloglines.com. But the addition of RSS support in IE is certain to make this form of communications popular with a much larger chunk of Internet users than had discovered news feeds prior to Vista.

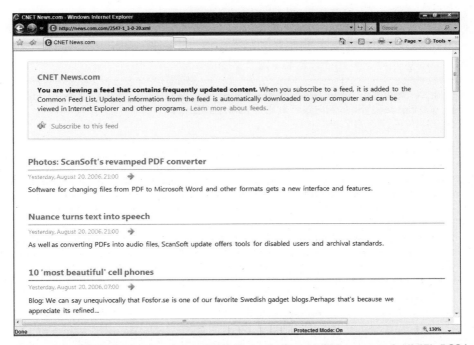

Figure 10: Subscribing to a news feed. If a web site publishes a news feed, IE's RSS icon turns orange. Clicking the icon leads to a page with a link allowing you to subscribe to the feed.

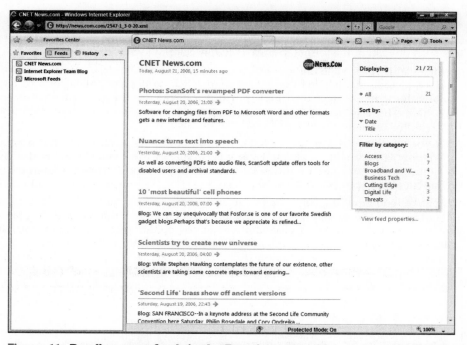

Figure 11: Reading news feeds in the Favorites pane. After you've subscribed to a news feed, you can read the latest posts in IE's Favorites Center.

Secret

There's No Support in IE 7 for Secure RSS

Unfortunately, IE 7.0 shipped without built-in handling for secure news feeds. These are feeds that users can access only by providing a username and password. (For additional security, such feeds may also be encrypted before being sent across the Internet.)

This lack of support means companies can't use RSS to deliver information privately to authorized employees who use IE. Also, publishers can't use RSS to distribute premium content to paying subscribers who use IE.

Dedicated news aggregators, such as NewsGator, *do* allow users to enter a username and password to subscribe to secure RSS feeds. You only need to do this once; the aggregator securely stores your password and periodically uses it to access and download the info you requested.

Sources within the IE development team tell us that support for secure RSS was left out of IE 7.0 to keep the project on schedule, but that it's a high priority for release as an upgrade. Watch for a download that will add this feature to IE.

Encrypt Entire Drives with BitLocker

Screaming headlines in recent years have made the public aware of stolen laptops and desktop computers that contained the personal records of thousands of millions of individuals. These thefts might not have exposed anyone's personal data if the hard drives in the stolen computers had been encrypted and protected by strong passwords.

Various third-party solutions have long been available to encrypt sensitive data folders and entire hard drives. With Vista, Microsoft now enters this market with BitLocker Drive Encryption.

BitLocker has some advantages over competing encryption products because, integrated as it is into Windows, it can check the integrity of a computer system before the Windows user interface is ever loaded. BitLocker can tell when a hard drive has been moved to a different computer—as would be the case if a drive had been stolen—and can defend against brute-force attacks.

BitLocker also integrates with Microsoft's Active Directory domain service scheme. The remote storage of digital keys that can unlock or restore data if a user forgets a password is a difficult and labor-intensive chore for IT administrators. BitLocker handles this by using Active Directory to escrow the keys securely, while still being able to help an authorized (but forgetful) user access crucial data that's stored in a password-protected drive.

BitLocker is available only in Vista Ultimate Edition, which can be purchased separately or upgraded to from the Home and Business Editions, and Vista Enterprise Edition, which can be purchased separately or upgraded to from the Business Edition.

---

cross
ref   **You can read more about BitLocker in Chapter 8.**

Use Easy Transfer to a New PC

Moving all of your old files and templates from one PC to another—not to mention duplicating all of the settings and preferences that you spent hours perfecting in your old copy of Windows—has been a royal pain for years.

Microsoft provides a better solution to this problem with its Easy Transfer utility in Vista. The program accepts files and preferences from Windows 2000 and Windows XP machines, as well as machines running Vista.

You can select just data files to transfer to the new PC or transfer entire clumps of e-mail messages and contacts, Internet settings, and complete user accounts as well (see Figure 12). No information is deleted from the old PC, so you have plenty of time to confirm that the data has been transferred correctly before erasing anything on your obsolete system.

The transfer requires that you install an Easy Transfer program from Vista to the older computer. Also, both the new system and the old one must be capable of exchanging data through one of the following methods:

- A local area network
- A USB Flash drive or external hard drive
- Recordable CDs or DVDs

Microsoft is also promoting the use of a USB Easy Transfer Cable. This procedure, like the other methods just listed, also involves installing to the old computer the Easy Transfer program, which can be found on a CD that's included with the cable. You then plug the provided cable into both machines and start the transfer from the new machine (see Figure 13).

Don't Pay Big Bucks for a Cable

As far as we can tell, an Easy Transfer Cable is just a USB printer cable with a computer-style connector on both ends and firmware in the middle that helps Vista recognize the cable as a Plug-and-Play device. We've seen such cables advertised for $45 USD. Connecting the Ethernet ports of both machines — using a crossover patch cable (about $6 at Radio Shack) to create a simple 2-PC local area network — seems like a cheaper and faster alternative. You may still need the Easy Transfer program, but that should be a simple download.

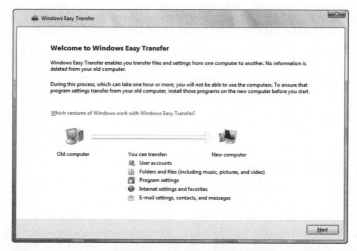

Figure 12: Vista Easy Transfer. Files, settings, and user accounts may be transferred from Windows 2000, Windows XP, or Windows Vista machines to a new machine.

Parental Controls

Vista adds a new Control Panel applet to the mix: Parental Controls. Assuming that you're the first person to password-protect this feature, you can ostensibly dictate the times that other users can log onto the PC, the ratings of the games they may play, the names of any programs they are prohibited from running, and the nature of the web sites they can surf to (see Figure 14).

We say *ostensibly*, because this is exactly the kind of feature that every teenager in the world will be looking for a way to hack around.

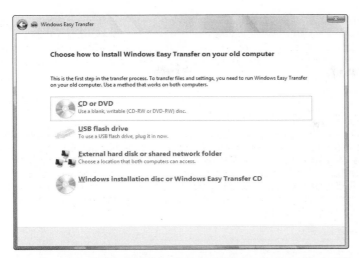

Figure 13: Compatible transfer methods. Both the old machine that will transfer its data and settings and the new machine that will receive them must be capable of exchanging information through a network, recordable CD/DVD, Flash drive, external hard drive, or a special cable.

For one thing, gaining access to the master password gives any user the ability to change the restrictions at will. When the master password is set, the responsible adult is asked by Microsoft to also set a password hint. Most adults, fearing they might forget the password, will set a reminder such as *my date of birth*. This hint, as implemented by Microsoft, is visible to anyone using the system. Thanks, Dad, now I can adjust the parental controls any way I like.

The Parental Controls system might be useful if you'd like to kick your kids off your home PC at, say, 9:00 p.m. so you can surf the Web without competition. We're not sure it's foolproof even for that, however.

Secret

Don't Assume Too Much

If you think Parental Controls on your home PC are going to effectively bar your kids from seeing whatever they want on the Internet, you're fooling yourself. The average teenager has access to dozens of PCs that you don't control — even cell phones can download web content today. You're better off training your kids what not to install from the Web, like free offers that actually contain spyware. That's a much bigger threat to your household's security than uncensored Internet access itself poses.

New Games: Mahjong and Chess

No major version of Windows is complete without the inclusion of a new game. Vista takes this important principle to a new level. Not only are there entirely new games — including Mahjong Titans and Chess Titans, which represent respectable challenges for serious players of either game — but all of the old Windows games have been updated with photorealistic and 3D imagery.

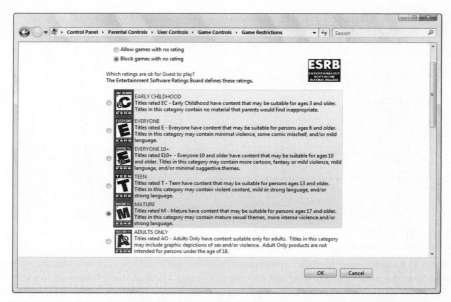

Figure 14: Parental Controls. The Parental Controls feature of Vista enables you to subscribe to the evaluation systems of several different organizations and attempt to restrict computer games to those that bear an age-appropriate rating.

That old standby, Solitaire, for example, is much improved. Not only are the cards more crisp and vivid than ever before, when you move a card from one pile to another, the exposed card turns itself over in a smooth animated effect. Right-clicking an eligible card moves it to the home position. And, if you have many eligible cards (such as when you've succeeded in placing all the cards in columns), right-clicking the green felt background of the game moves *all* the cards home.

All of the new Vista games benefit from enlarging their windows to full-screen. Watch closely when you do this, and you can actually see the objects in a game become richer and more realistic when they have more pixels to render themselves.

Thinking of Cheating at Solitaire?

Secret

Unfortunately, Vista's new Solitaire code seems to have broken one way that ne'er-do-wells have cheated at the game for years. This scandalous behavior was first revealed in *Windows 3 Secrets* all the way back in 1991. As that book explained it, you could click Game⇨Undo when playing a Draw Three game, and the last three cards you turned over from the deck would go back on the pile. If you then *held down the Shift key* while clicking the deck, only one card at a time would turn over, allowing you to pick up a crucial card that wasn't originally on top of the stack. Whether by omission or design, that trick no longer works, and you'll just have to win at Solitaire the good old-fashioned way. (You can still, however, undo the turnover of your last three cards if you suddenly see a move on the board that might benefit.)

Figure 15: The Queen is lost. The new Chess Titans game is an example of the photorealistic, 3D effects that Vista is capable of with Aero-compatible hardware. In the position shown in this figure, White has sacrificed a Knight and prepares to exchange two Rooks in order to gain a Bishop and a Queen. After the Black Bishop captures the White Rook, and another White Rook takes the Bishop, the Black Queen is pinned and cannot escape without exposing her King. With the loss of the Queen, checkmate quickly ensues.

tip   Want to get better 3-D rendering? If you think the special effects in Vista's new games are spectacular, you ain't seen nothin' yet. If your hardware supports it, you can get even better 3-D effects by manipulating a little-used control. In Chess Titans, for example, pull down the Game menu and select the Options dialog box. If the pointer called Graphics Slider isn't all the way to the right end of the range, push it there with your mouse. When you click OK, you'll immediately see the playing pieces become sharper and smoother. We can't guarantee that this extra rendering effort will make your computer opponent a little stupider, but it's worth a shot.

cross ref   Chapter 14 contains more discussion about games and Windows Vista.

Windows Media Player 11

Windows Media Player 11 (WMP 11), a key part of Microsoft's campaign to make Windows the centerpiece of users' digital entertainment collections, is notably changed in Vista from earlier Media Player versions.

The so-called Media Library, for example, now provides additional views of digital files, including genre, year of release, and ratings (see Figure 16).

Ripping CDs to digital files has been enhanced in WMP 11. Two new audio formats appear for the first time: Windows Media Audio Pro and lossless WAV (see Figure 17).

The Pro format, strangely enough, digitizes sound at only 64 kilobits per second (64 Kbps), about half the bit rate of the older Windows Media Audio format. Lossless WAV, by contrast, is so high quality—with a bit rate in the high hundreds of Kbps—that ripping a single CD to disk produces files that total approximately 600 MB.

Hard drives are cheap these days, so whether you really want or need the extra tonal range that comes from lossless ripping may depend on whether you've already filled up most of your disk space.

If you happen to have more than one CD drive installed on your PC, WMP 11 will rip files from all of them at once. That won't make feeding your discs into the CD trays any more fun, but it will get it over with faster.

Figure 16: The Windows Media Player 11 library view. Version 11 provides a variety of ways to organize, play, and view your music and video collection.

In case you decide to reverse the process, and burn your digital files to CDs, WMP 11 has added new forms of support here, too. A disk-spanning feature calculates the number of CDs needed—if your collection exceeds the capacity of a single CD—and automatically burns your playlist over multiple discs.

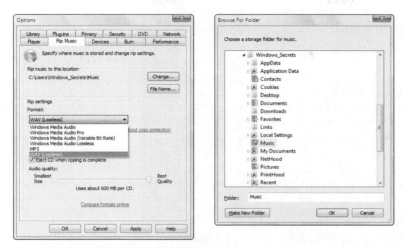

Figure 17: WMP 11 rip formats. Microsoft's new player supports even more formats to store CDs you've digitized.

URGE, Brought to You by MTV

Microsoft may never be able to match the experience that millions of iPod buyers have had downloading music from Apple's iTunes Store. But you can't blame the Redmond company for trying.

URGE, shown in Figure 18, is a new music service featured in WMP 11 that has its roots in the American video cable channels MTV, VH1, and CMT. The parent corporation, MTV Networks, imbues URGE with a music library that's said to be two million songs strong (which should be enough to keep you entertained for at least a few weeks). The service, available only in the United States at this writing, provides unlimited listening for a monthly subscription fee, or you can buy individual tracks, similar to iTunes.

Figure 18: The URGE music service. The best of MTV, VH1, and CMT is available for download via WMP 11.

Besides the usual 99-cent music downloads, URGE offers over 6,000 music videos, more than 500 playlists by genre, and some 130 commercial-free radio stations in a wide variety of styles.

If you can't find what you want on URGE, WMP 11 still boasts partnerships with several other online audio stores. These include the selections of Audible.com, Napster, XM Satellite Radio, Microsoft's own MSN Music, and so on (see Figure 19).

cross
ref   Chapter 10 goes into detail on Windows Media Player 11.

Figure 19: Pick your online music store. WMP 11 integrates with a fistful of downloadable audio sources.

Movie Maker and DVD Maker

Audio files don't get all the action in Vista. Windows Movie Maker makes anyone with a camcorder downright dangerous.

In case you like to subject your friends and family to your video masterpieces, Movie Maker enables you to edit your raw video down into a more bearable length—say, 30 seconds? If you insist on your film noir running longer, however, you'll find a variety of special effects and transitions that can make almost any of your original content truly ghastly (see Figure 20).

Although they're two separate applications, Vista's DVD Maker complements Movie Maker. After you've edited your video to your liking, burn it to one or more DVDs for posterity. DVD Maker publishes your work in MPEG-2 format, which means it's theoretically possible to burn DVDs straight from your camcorder. That assumes, of course, that your material wouldn't first benefit from a little, ahem, editing (see Figure 21).

cross ref   Chapter 12 discusses Movie Maker and DVD Maker in more detail.

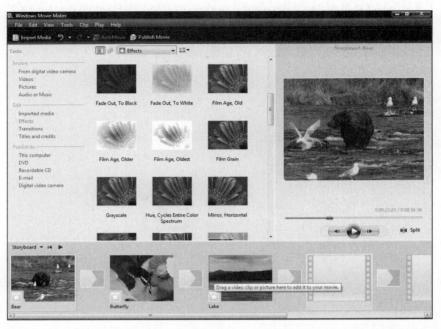

Figure 20: Movie Maker. Microsoft's video-editing tool includes titles and other special effects you can add to raw video.

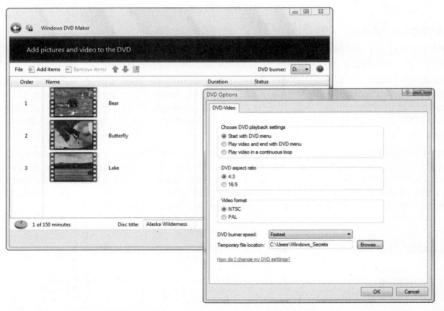

Figure 21: DVD Maker. You may not win an Oscar, but you can try by burning as many DVDs as you want.

Windows Photo Gallery

Despite all the glamour of audio and video media, Microsoft hasn't forgotten plain old still photographs. Windows Photo Gallery is a built-in tool you can use to organize, tag, enhance, and print photos from cameras, cell phones, and other digital devices (see Figure 22).

A new thumbnail slider — a user-interface widget that's revealed by clicking the maginfying glass near the bottom of the window — enables you to quickly zoom your photo collection up and down to fit as few or as many images onto the screen as you may desire.

Photo Gallery includes several basic sliders that enable you to fix (or ruin) your original photos in your own particular ways. For example, you can manually adjust the brightness, contrast, and color of a photo. A fix red-eye control is included for those pics that suffer from a wee bit too much flash (see Figure 23).

When you've got your photos the way you want them, Photo Gallery can turn your selected images into slide shows, screen savers, e-mail attachments (with five levels of compression), and prints, or burn them onto CDs or DVDs. For those of you who like to edit your videos in Movie Maker (discussed previously), you can import videos into Photo Gallery. It displays each video as a thumbnail so you can mix and match video material with your stills.

> **tip**
> **Undo your fixes, no matter how many steps you took.** In case your heavy-handed tweaks don't look so good, Photo Gallery retains the state your image started in. Simply click the Revert to Original icon to switch back to the picture the way it was before your "improvements."

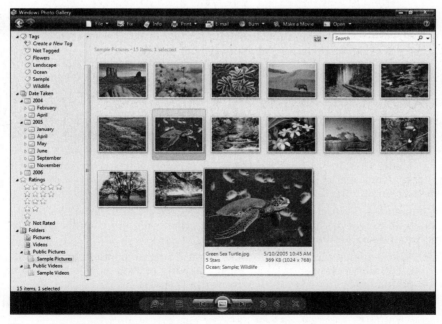

Figure 22: Windows Photo Gallery. You can organize and tag your photo collections in numerous ways.

Figure 23: Editing in Photo Gallery. Sliders enable you to enhance your photos — or not.

cross
ref

Chapter 11 includes more details on Windows Photo Gallery.

Windows Media Center

In those Vista versions that support it, Windows Media Center turns a PC into a DVD player and digital video recorder all in one. (Media Player is included in Vista Home Premium and Ultimate editions.)

In Vista, Media Center has been developed to support widescreen and high-definition monitors. It works fine on older 4:3 displays but takes full advantage of greater capabilities when present in the hardware found on a system (see Figure 24).

PCs that include a TV tuner enable users to watch, record, and pause live programming. With multiple tuners, it's possible to watch a program on one channel while recording another program on a different channel.

Besides TV and motion pictures, Media Center also supports audio files and still photography. You can direct slide shows and music playlists as well as watch live or recorded video programming.

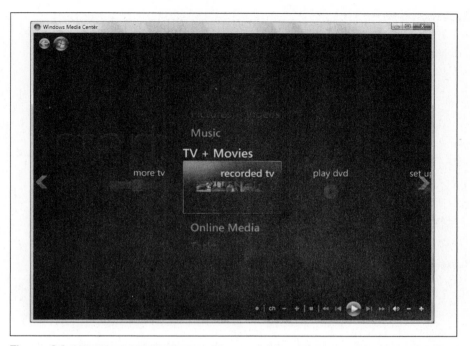

Figure 24: **Windows Media Center.** Vista supports widescreen and high-definition programming with the appropriate hardware.

cross
ref

See Chapter 13 for the latest on Windows Media Center.

There's Much More

We've barely scratched the surface of the changes you'll find in Vista, compared with the capabilities of Windows XP. Numerous improvements, large and small, show themselves in features as home-oriented as DVD burning and as business-oriented as Internet Protocol version 6; as silly as Microsoft's XPS portable document format (which no computer other than Windows Vista and XP can read) and as serious as screen magnification for users with impaired vision.

Most of the new and improved applications are relatively easy to understand and are adequately described in their Help systems.

Those that have secrets we can reveal are covered in the following chapters.

Join us as we explore the inner workings of Vista.

Part I

Surviving Setup

Selecting the Right Vista Version

Chapter

1

◆ ◆

In This Chapter

The basic differences between the Vista versions

Why you probably won't need Vista Starter or Vista N

Using the 32-bit and 64-bit versions of Vista

Determining the best Vista version for you

Choosing between the home and business versions

Choosing between Home Basic and Home Premium

Choosing between Vista Business and Vista Enterprise

Features available in all Vista versions

Choosing Vista Ultimate

◆ ◆

If you haven't purchased Vista yet—or you'd like to know whether or not it's worth upgrading to a more-capable version of Vista—this chapter is for you. A step-by-step procedure leads you through the ins and outs of selecting the right version of Vista for you.

A Quick Overview of All the Versions

It seems like Windows Vista has a lot more versions than Microsoft has ever offered before. But that isn't quite true. The Redmond company years ago split Windows XP into almost as many versions as we have today with Vista.

---

tip   You may occasionally hear Vista's versions referred to as SKUs. This term stands for Stock Keeping Unit. We'll use the more common terms *version* and *product version* throughout this book instead.

Here's a review of the major Windows XP versions (roughly in order of increasing power), which we'll compare with Vista's versions:

1. Windows XP Starter Edition (less-developed countries only)
2. Windows XP Home Edition N (European Union only)
3. Windows XP Home Edition
4. Windows XP Media Center Edition
5. Windows XP Tablet Edition
6. Windows XP Professional Edition N (European Union only)
7. Windows XP Professional Edition
8. Windows XP Professional x64 Edition

As we'll explain later, you may not have heard much about Windows XP Starter Edition because it was only preinstalled on PCs in emerging countries to offer a lower price point. The N editions (which do not include Windows Media Player) were sold only in Europe to satisfy antitrust requirements there. All Windows XP product versions, except Windows XP Professional x64 Edition, were available only in 32-bit versions.

All versions of Windows Vista, except Vista Starter, come in 32-bit and 64-bit versions. If we ignore for a moment the differences between 32-bit and 64-bit processing, the Starter edition, and the N editions, Windows Vista can be categorized into as few as five different flavors:

1. Vista Home Basic
2. Vista Home Premium
3. Vista Business
4. Vista Enterprise
5. Vista Ultimate

In a moment, we'll take you through a simple, step-by-step process that'll help you decide which version you need (or which version you might want to upgrade to, if you have a less-capable version). First, let's dispense with Vista Starter, N, and 32-bit versus 64-bit.

If You're Reading This, You Don't Need Starter

Windows Vista Starter is limited to 32-bit processors, supports only the basic Vista user interface, and will address a limited amount of RAM. It's designed only as a loss leader to get Windows' pricing down to a level that's competitive in less-developed countries.

Unless you're buying a PC in one of these countries, you probably won't hear much more about Vista Starter. And if you are buying such a PC, your computing needs are pretty basic, so it's unlikely that you're ready for this book just yet.

The N Editions Aren't For You, Either

Whatever Vista versions are being offered in Europe with an N moniker to satisfy the European Union's antitrust rulings, you also probably won't need them. The EU in 2004 began requiring Microsoft to offer versions of Windows without the Windows Media Player included. The requirement for a separate version of Windows was intended to enhance competition in the market for media players, such as the downloadable RealPlayer application.

Microsoft has (as of this writing) always sold its N versions for the same price as its full-featured Windows, so demand for the N versions never materialized. Until there's a big price difference, consumers will continue to interpret N to mean not interested.

If Your PC Is 64-Bit Ready, Run 64-Bit Vista

The differences between 32-bit Vista (usually referred to as the x86 version in honor of the 32-bit architecture of Intel's 80386, 80486, and Pentium processors) and 64-bit Vista are more complex. The good news is that, if you're buying a new PC with Vista preinstalled, it will probably come with 32-bit or 64-bit processing already enabled, depending on the chipset that powers your machine.

Any new 64-bit PC that's sold with Vista preinstalled will almost certainly come from the factory with 64-bit drivers and anything else that might be needed to support 64-bit processing. Since this is a chapter on selecting from among the five primary versions of Vista, we'll leave a full discussion of 32-bit versus 64-bit for another day.

A Few Simple Questions to Determine the Best Vista Version for You

If you're trying to decide which version of Windows Vista to buy for the first time, simply step through the following Q and A:

1. **Will your PCs need to log on to an in-house network server?**
   a. If not, and your PCs will only need (at most) to access each other's files and printers via peer-to-peer networking, you only need a Home version of Vista. Go to Question 2.
   b. If your PCs need to log on to a network domain, you need a non-Home version. Go to Question 3.

2. **(To determine which Home version): Do you have a tablet PC, do you want to burn DVDs, or do you want to record and playback video content with Windows Media Center?**

   a. If not, you can get by with Vista Home Edition.

   b. If you need any of the above features, you need Vista Home Premium.

3. **(To determine which non-Home version): Does your company have a Volume Licensing deal with Microsoft?**

   a. If yes, get Vista Enterprise, which enables you to create a centralized installation routine for Vista.

   b. If not, get Vista Business, which is available at retail and has most of the features of Vista Enterprise (as described later in this chapter).

4. **(To determine whether you need Vista Ultimate): Do you need some features that are found only in Home Premium and some other features that are found only in the Business or Enterprise versions of Vista?**

   a. If you need, for example, Windows Media Player (which is available only in Home Premium) and BitLocker drive encryption (only in Enterprise), get Vista Ultimate.

   b. If you don't need such a comprehensive mix of features, save your money and buy a version of Vista that's cheaper than Vista Ultimate.

---

tip

Prices for the various versions of Vista can change at any time, and the list prices we show in this chapter will surely be discounted online. Before you select a version of Vista to buy, enter the search term **_windows vista_** into a price-comparison engine such as Shopping.com or PriceGrabber.com. Don't overspend to get a version of Vista that has features you'll never need.

Your decision on which version to purchase will be influenced by the cost difference of the more capable versions. We're showing in Table 1-1 the U.S. list prices for different Vista versions, even though better prices will certainly become available. The relative positioning of each version, however, is very likely to remain in the order shown here.

Table 1-1: U.S. List Prices for Different Vista Versions

Windows Vista Home Basic	
Windows Vista Home Basic _Full_	$199.00
Windows Vista Home Basic _Full_ (additional license only, no disc)	$179.00
Windows Vista Home Basic _Upgrade_	$99.95
Windows Vista Home Basic _Upgrade_ (additional license only)	$89.95
Windows Vista Home Premium	
Windows Vista Home Premium _Full_	$239.00
Windows Vista Home Premium _Full_ (additional license only)	$215.00
Windows Vista Home Premium _Upgrade_	$159.00
Windows Vista Home Premium _Upgrade_ (additional license only)	$143.00

Windows Vista Business	
Windows Vista Business *Full*	$299.00
Windows Vista Business *Full* (additional license only)	$269.00
Windows Vista Business *Upgrade*	$199.00
Windows Vista Business *Upgrade* (additional license only)	$179.00
Windows Vista Ultimate	
Windows Vista Ultimate *Full*	$399.00
Windows Vista Ultimate *Full* (additional license only)	$359.00
Windows Vista Ultimate *Upgrade*	$259.00
Windows Vista Ultimate *Upgrade* (additional license only)	$233.00

Although not every Vista version correlates exactly with an XP product version, the pricing is in line with XP pricing. For example, XP Home is currently USD $189.00, compared to $199.99 for Vista Home Basic, whereas XP Home Upgrade is $89.97, just two cents off from the Vista Home Basic Upgrade. Upsells won't be particularly expensive, either: Pricing for the much more capable Vista Home Premium is just $40 to $60 higher than that of Home Basic.

Pricing in countries other than the United States will vary, but should adhere to the relative positioning shown in Table 1-1. At this writing, Microsoft's web site in Canada states that Windows Vista Ultimate will list for CAD $450 in that country, compared with USD $399 in the United States. Those two prices are about the same when currency exchange rates are factored in.

Secret

If you're buying a retail copy of Vista, and you already own a previous version of Windows, such as XP, don't buy a full version of Vista. Find out what Microsoft's current requirements are to qualify for an upgrade version, which is much cheaper. To successfully load an upgrade version, you usually must be installing onto a machine that has the old version installed, or you must have the old version on a CD (which you insert briefly during the installation of the new OS as proof). Microsoft can change these requirements at any time, so confirm this before whipping out your plastic.

Taking Advantage of Your Ability to Upgrade Vista

Table 1-2 shows how flexible Vista is in allowing you to upgrade to a more powerful version. It also describes some of the limitations of the various versions.

Windows Anytime Upgrade

Unlike previous versions of Windows, Vista installs itself with the capability to upgrade from a weaker version to a more-capable version at any time. You simply run the Anytime Upgrade applet, select a source to purchase an upgrade license from, and your PC is quickly enhanced with the more powerful version you've selected.

- **Vista Home Basic** can be upgraded in this way to Home Premium or Ultimate.
- **Vista Home Premium** and **Vista Business** can be upgraded to Ultimate.

At this writing, it doesn't appear that the Home versions of Vista can be upgraded in this way to Vista Business or Enterprise. It also doesn't seem likely that the Enterprise version will allow an easy upgrade path to Vista Ultimate. Purchasing a more capable version of Vista at retail and installing it over a lesser version may be the only way to migrate in these cases.

RAM Limitations of Vista Versions

The Home versions of Vista suffer from some stricter limitations on available main memory and peer-to-peer networking than the non-Home versions. We'll summarize these limits as follows:

- **32-bit Vista versions** will always be limited to 4 GB of RAM, due to limitations of x86 processors.
- **64-bit Vista versions** have dramatically different limitations in the various editions:
  - **Home Basic** is limited to 8 GB or RAM.
  - **Home Premium** is limited to 16 GB of RAM.
  - **Business, Enterprise,** and **Ultimate** can access over 128 GB of RAM.

Peer-to-Peer Networking Limitations

Peer-to-peer networking, called SMB (for small-to-medium business) networking by Microsoft, is also artificially restricted:

- **Home Basic** can support only 5 peer-to-peer connections;
- **All other Vista version**s can support 10 peer-to-peer connections.
- **Business, Enterprise,** and **Ultimate** can support many more connections, of course, with users logging on to one or more network servers.

Table 1-2: Version Limitations and Upgrade Paths

	Home Basic	Home Premium	Business	Enterprise	Ultimate
Comparison of version limitations:					
Maximum RAM supported with 32-bit system	4 GB	4 GB	4 GB	4 GB	4 GB
Maximum RAM supported with 64-bit system	8 GB	16 GB	128+ GB	128+ GB	128+ GB
Simultaneous SMB peer network connections	5	10	10	10	10
Windows Anytime Upgrade:					
Upgrade to Home Premium or Ultimate	Yes	—	—	—	—
Upgrade to Ultimate	—	Yes	Yes	—	—

The home versions of Vista are more limited than the business versions in general, but they also include some multimedia functionality that's not available to Vista Business users. If the restrictions of a lesser version prevent you from using a feature you need in a more capable version, it's easy to upgrade Vista's Home and Business versions to Vista Ultimate. To do so, you can use the built-in Anytime Upgrade applet (see Figures 1-1 and 1-2).

Figure 1-1: **Anytime Upgrade.** This applet, found in Home Basic, Home Premium, and Business versions of Vista, makes it easy for Basic users to upgrade to Premium. Users of Basic, Premium, and Business versions can also upgrade to Vista Ultimate.

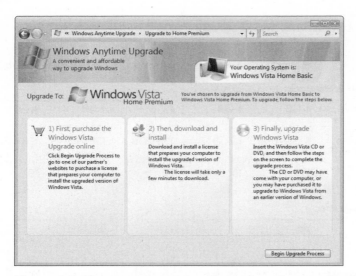

Figure 1-2: Choose your partner. Microsoft sends users of its Anytime Upgrade applet to other authorized dealers of Windows, where you purchase a license for a more capable version of Vista.

Choosing Between Home Basic and Home Premium

Table 1-3 shows the distinct features that differ between the Basic and Premium versions of Vista for home users. If you've decided that a Home version of Vista is all you need, Table 1-3 will help you decide which of the two available versions will best suit you.

♦ **Choose Home Basic** if you don't need Media Center capabilities, the ability to burn DVDs, or any of the other features shown in Table 1-3 that come with Home Premium.

♦ **Choose Home Premium** if you have a tablet PC (actually, it'll be hard to buy a tablet PC that doesn't have at least Vista Premium installed on it) or if you need the more extensive multimedia features of the premium version.

tip The list prices for the upgrade versions of Home Premium are about 60 percent higher than the same versions of Home Basic. But the full versions are only 20 percent higher. So, if you find yourself buying a retail copy of the full version of Vista Home, paying a little extra to get Home Premium seems like a pretty easy decision.

Table 1-3: Comparing Home Basic and Home Premium

	Home Basic	Home Premium	Business	Enterprise	Ultimate
Only Home Basic, Home Premium, and Ultimate:					
Parental controls	Yes	Yes	—	—	Yes
Windows Movie Maker	Yes	Yes	—	—	Yes
Only Home Premium and Ultimate:					
Themed slide shows	—	Yes	—	—	Yes
Windows Media Center	—	Yes	—	—	Yes
Windows Media Center — high-definition TV	—	Yes	—	—	Yes
Windows Media Center — CableCard support	—	Yes	—	—	Yes
Support for Media Center Extenders, incl. Xbox 360	—	Yes	—	—	Yes
Windows DVD Maker	—	Yes	—	—	Yes
In all versions except Home Basic:					
Windows Aero user interface	—	Yes	Yes	Yes	Yes
Windows Tablet PC with touch-screen support	—	Yes	Yes	Yes	Yes
Windows SideShow	—	Yes	Yes	Yes	Yes
Windows Movie Maker HD	—	Yes	Yes	Yes	Yes
Backup of user files to a network device	—	Yes	Yes	Yes	Yes
Scheduled backup of user files	—	Yes	Yes	Yes	Yes
Network Projection	—	Yes	Yes	Yes	Yes
Presentation Settings	—	Yes	Yes	Yes	Yes
New premium games	—	Yes	Yes*	Yes*	Yes
Windows Meeting Space	View only	Yes	Yes	Yes	Yes

*Feature is optional

Choosing Between Vista Business and Enterprise

Table 1-4 shows the features that are present in the Business and Enterprise versions of Vista but not the Home versions, and a few features Enterprise has that Business doesn't. Vista Ultimate, as we'll discuss later in this chapter, also supports all of Vista's non-Home features.

◆ **Both the Business and Enterprise versions,** unlike the Home versions, support domain networking. This enables users to log on to a network server using Microsoft's Active Directory (AD) technology and share centrally managed resources.

◆ **Enterprise supports a few additional features,** which might be crucial for your business:

- **BitLocker drive encryption** enables you to securely encrypt files and folders. You can require that users must have a physical token to decrypt and access these resources, protecting them from view if a PC is stolen or otherwise used by an unauthorized person.

- **Applications written for Unix** can run under Vista Enterprise. This can greatly expand the number of programs your company can run on a given system.

- **Virtual PC Express** enables you to run one virtual computer session in Vista Enterprise. This session could host a different operating system — Windows XP or even Windows 95, for example — in which you might run a legacy program that isn't compatible with Vista.

Table 1-4: Comparing Vista Business and Vista Enterprise

	Home Basic	Home Premium	Business	Enterprise	Ultimate
Only Business, Enterprise, and Ultimate:					
Support for processors in two sockets	—	—	Yes	Yes	Yes
Windows ShadowCopy	—	—	Yes	Yes	Yes
System image–based backup and recovery	—	—	Yes	Yes	Yes
Encrypting File System	—	—	Yes	Yes	Yes
Desktop deployment tools for managed networks	—	—	Yes	Yes	Yes
Policy-based quality of service for networking	—	—	Yes	Yes	Yes
Windows Rights Management Services (RMS) client	—	—	Yes	Yes	Yes
Control over installation of device drivers	—	—	Yes	Yes	Yes

	Home Basic	Home Premium	Business	Enterprise	Ultimate
Network Access Protection Client Agent	—	—	Yes	Yes	Yes
Pluggable logon authentication architecture	—	—	Yes	Yes	Yes
Integrated smart card management	—	—	Yes	Yes	Yes
Wireless network provisioning	—	—	Yes	Yes	Yes
Domain join for Windows Server	—	—	Yes	Yes	Yes
Domain join for Windows Small Business Server	—	—	Yes	Yes	Yes
Group Policy support	—	—	Yes	Yes	Yes
Offline files and folder support	—	—	Yes	Yes	Yes
Client-side caching	—	—	Yes	Yes	Yes
Roaming User Profiles	—	—	Yes	Yes	Yes
Folder Redirection	—	—	Yes	Yes	Yes
Centralized power management via Group Policy	—	—	Yes	Yes	Yes
Windows Fax and Scan	—	—	Yes	Yes*	Yes*
Internet Information Server	—	—	Yes*	Yes*	Yes*
Only Business and Ultimate:					
Small Business Resources	—	—	Yes	—	Yes
Only Enterprise and Ultimate:					
Windows BitLocker drive encryption	—	—	—	Yes	Yes
All 36 worldwide UI languages available	—	—	—	Yes	Yes
Simultaneous install of multiple UI languages	—	—	—	Yes	Yes
Subsystem for Unix-based applications	—	—	—	Yes	Yes
Virtual PC Express	—	—	—	Yes	Yes
Only Ultimate:					
Windows Ultimate Extras	—	—	—	—	Yes

*Feature is optional

As you can see, most of the features of Enterprise are also in Business, except BitLocker, multilanguage support, Unix capabilities, and virtual-machine support.

Features Available in All Vista Versions

For completeness's sake, features that exist in all versions of Vista are listed in Table 1-5, in no particular order. If this table offers you all the Windows features you'll ever want, then Vista Home Basic may be enough for you.

This would particularly be true if you plan to use Vista solely to browse the Web and occasionally check your e-mail. In that case, the improved Internet Explorer 7 and Windows Mail programs — present in all Vista versions — might be adequate to serve your needs.

Microsoft, of course, hopes that the features of Home Basic are, well, too basic for you. If so, you'll have to pony up a higher amount for one of the pricier versions. We hope we've presented in this chapter all the details you need to make an informed decision.

Table 1–5: Features Present in All Five Major Vista Versions

	Home Basic	Home Premium	Business	Enterprise	Ultimate
Remote Desktop	Client only	Client only	Client and host	Client and host	Client and host
Windows Mobility Center	Partial	Partial	Yes	Yes	Yes
Windows Vista basic user interface	Yes	Yes	Yes	Yes	Yes
Windows Security Center	Yes	Yes	Yes	Yes	Yes
Windows Defender	Yes	Yes	Yes	Yes	Yes
Windows Firewall	Yes	Yes	Yes	Yes	Yes
Windows Update	Yes	Yes	Yes	Yes	Yes
Internet Explorer 7 with Tabbed Browsing	Yes	Yes	Yes	Yes	Yes
Internet Explorer 7 RSS Feed Support	Yes	Yes	Yes	Yes	Yes
Internet Explorer 7 Protected Mode	Yes	Yes	Yes	Yes	Yes
Internet Explorer 7 Fix My Settings	Yes	Yes	Yes	Yes	Yes
Anti-phishing in Internet Explorer 7	Yes	Yes	Yes	Yes	Yes
Anti-phishing in Windows Mail	Yes	Yes	Yes	Yes	Yes
Service Hardening	Yes	Yes	Yes	Yes	Yes
User Account Control	Yes	Yes	Yes	Yes	Yes
Performance self-tuning and hardware diagnostics	Yes	Yes	Yes	Yes	Yes
Next-generation TCP/IP stack	Yes	Yes	Yes	Yes	Yes
IPv6 and IPv4 support	Yes	Yes	Yes	Yes	Yes
Windows ReadyDrive	Yes	Yes	Yes	Yes	Yes

	Home Basic	Home Premium	Business	Enterprise	Ultimate
Windows Display Driver Model (WDDM)	Yes	Yes	Yes	Yes	Yes
Windows Easy Transfer	Yes	Yes	Yes	Yes	Yes
Windows SuperFetch	Yes	Yes	Yes	Yes	Yes
Windows ReadyBoost	Yes	Yes	Yes	Yes	Yes
64-bit processor support	Yes	Yes	Yes	Yes	Yes
Fast Startup, Fast Shutdown, Sleep	Yes	Yes	Yes	Yes	Yes
Ad hoc backup and recovery of user files and folders	Yes	Yes	Yes	Yes	Yes
Instant Search	Yes	Yes	Yes	Yes	Yes
Automatic content organization via properties/tags	Yes	Yes	Yes	Yes	Yes
Support for WinFX	Yes	Yes	Yes	Yes	Yes
Low-priority I/O	Yes	Yes	Yes	Yes	Yes
Automatic hard disk defragmentation	Yes	Yes	Yes	Yes	Yes
Windows Mail	Yes	Yes	Yes	Yes	Yes
Windows Calendar	Yes	Yes	Yes	Yes	Yes
Windows Sidebar	Yes	Yes	Yes	Yes	Yes
Windows Photo Gallery	Yes	Yes	Yes	Yes	Yes
Windows Media Player 11	Yes	Yes	Yes	Yes	Yes
Games Explorer	Yes	Yes	Yes	Yes	Yes
Updated games	Yes	Yes	Yes	Yes	Yes
Speech Recognition	Yes	Yes	Yes	Yes	Yes
Accessibility Settings and Ease of Access Center	Yes	Yes	Yes	Yes	Yes
Windows Welcome Center	Yes	Yes	Yes	Yes	Yes
XPS Document support	Yes	Yes	Yes	Yes	Yes
Network Center	Yes	Yes	Yes	Yes	Yes
Network Diagnostics and troubleshooting	Yes	Yes	Yes	Yes	Yes
Windows HotStart	Yes	Yes	Yes	Yes	Yes
Sync Center	Yes	Yes	Yes	Yes	Yes
Universal game controller support	Yes	Yes	Yes*	Yes*	Yes

*Feature is optional

With the exception of the Remote Desktop and the Mobility Center for portable PCs—both of which are limited in the Home versions—most of the features of Windows Vista are the same in all versions.

Secret

One big feature you don't get with Windows Vista Home Basic is the beautiful Windows Aero user interface, which we'll look at in detail later in the book. If you want the absolute best graphical experience, don't pick Home Basic.

Choosing the Whole Enchilada — Vista Ultimate

You can use Tables 1-2 through 1-5 to compare those features of the lesser Vista versions that come together in Microsoft's priciest product: Vista Ultimate. To get it, you'll pay a list price of $60 to $100 more than Vista Business or $100 to $160 more than Home Premium. Without knowing what your specific needs may be, it's impossible for us to say whether you'll want or need this enormous package.

As we stated previously, the only serious reason to pay extra to get Vista Ultimate is if you absolutely must have two features, one of which exists only in Home Premium (such as Windows Media Center) and the other of which can only be obtained in Business or Enterprise (such as domain login).

At the time of this writing, Microsoft promises to release a number of add-ons called the Windows Ultimate Extras. These weren't well defined at all, however, when we went to press. You'll have to be the judge of whether these extras are worth anything to you or your business.

Of course, you might purchase Vista Ultimate just because you want everything Microsoft has to offer, and cost is no object. If so—*enjoy!*

Summary

Windows Vista certainly offers a lot of choice when it comes to picking a product version, but with a little know-how, you will be able to make the right choice, one that matches both your needs and your budget. We've given you what you need to know to match a Vista version to your needs. Now, you just need to figure out how much the upgrade is going to cost. Remember that it's often much cheaper to acquire a new Windows version with a new PC, so if you're going to be buying a new PC, be sure to get the right Vista version at that time. We'll look this option in Chapter 2.

Installing and Upgrading to Windows Vista

Chapter
2

◆ ◆ ◆ ◆ ◆ ◆ ◆ ◆ ◆ ◆ ◆ ◆ ◆ ◆ ◆ ◆ ◆ ◆ ◆

In This Chapter

Acquiring Windows Vista with a new PC

Performing a clean install of Windows Vista

Upgrading to Windows Vista

Dual-booting with Windows XP and Windows Vista

Using Windows Vista's deployment tools to create a custom install image

◆ ◆ ◆ ◆ ◆ ◆ ◆ ◆ ◆ ◆ ◆ ◆ ◆ ◆ ◆ ◆ ◆ ◆ ◆

So you want to install Windows Vista? Well, we'll walk you through all the various ways you can acquire Windows Vista in this chapter, including a clean install, where Windows Vista is the only operating system on your PC; an upgrade, where you upgrade an existing version of Windows to Windows Vista, leaving all of your data, settings, and application intact; and a dual-boot, where you leave Windows XP on your PC but install Vista to a different hard drive.

Taking the Easy Way Out: Acquiring Windows Vista with a New PC

The simplest way to get a completely working copy of Windows Vista is to buy a new PC. Wait, we're serious: Even though PC makers tend to fill their machines with oodles of useless utilities, add-on programs, and other sludge, the one thing you can always be sure of when you buy a new PC is that Windows Vista is going to work out of the box. That is, all of the hardware that comes as part of your new PC purchase will work without any additional effort on your part. You won't have to step through the various setup-related issues we discuss later in this chapter. In fact, if you did purchase a PC with Windows Vista preinstalled, most of this chapter won't apply to you at all (well, except for the deployment discussion at the end of the chapter, assuming you got a Vista DVD with the new PC). You should be able to simply turn your new PC on and get to work.

Secret

One thing that PC purchasers should know about is how to *restore* their system, or return it to the state in which it was in when new. Virtually all new PCs sold today include a means by which you can do this. Most of the time, you can restore your PC using a special hidden partition on your hard drive. Other PC makers actually include what's called a restore disk, or restore DVD, with the system. Check your documentation to be sure that you know how to restore your system if you need to. And when you're removing all of that junk that the PC maker installed on your previously pristine Windows Vista installation, be sure you don't remove anything you'll need to recover your system.

Interactive Setup

If you purchased a copy of Windows Vista on DVD at a retailer or online store, you can install Vista using Microsoft's new Interactive Setup application, which guides you through a series of steps while installing Vista. There are three primary ways to install Windows Vista using Interactive Setup: A clean install, where Windows Vista will be the only operating system on the PC; an upgrade, where you upgrade an existing operating system to Windows Vista, replacing the old with the new; and a dual-boot, where you install Windows Vista alongside your old operating system and use a boot menu to choose between them each time you reboot. We'll examine all three methods in this chapter.

Clean Install

A *clean install* of the operating system is our preferred method for installing Windows Vista. Although it's possible to upgrade to Windows Vista from certain previous Windows versions (see the next section), this path is perilous and can often result in a Frankenstein-like system where only some of your applications work properly. In our opinion, it's best to start with a clean slate when moving to a new operating system, especially a major release like Windows Vista.

caution   Be sure to back up your critical data before performing a clean install. Typically, you will wipe out your PC's entire hard drive during a clean install, so any documents, e-mail, and other data will be destroyed during the process. Also, make sure you have all the installation disks for the applications and hardware drivers you'll need to reinstall after Vista is up and running.

Step-by-Step: Windows Vista Interactive Setup

In this section, we're going to walk you through the entire Windows Vista Setup process, using Microsoft's interactive Setup application. This application was completely overhauled for Windows Vista, and it's much more streamlined, simplified, and faster-moving than the version used in Windows XP.

Follows these steps to install Windows Vista as a clean install:

1. Insert the Windows Vista DVD in your PC's optical drive and reboot. After the BIOS screen flashes by, you may see a message alerting you to Press any key to boot from the CD or DVD. If so, press a key. Some systems, however, do not provide this warning and will instead boot from the DVD by default.

Secret   If your system does not boot from the DVD, you may need to change the system's boot order so that the optical drive is checked before the first hard drive. To do this, you will have to consult your PC's documentation, as each PC handles this process a little differently.

A black screen with a progress bar and the text "Windows is loading files" will appear, as shown in Figure 2-1.

2. Eventually, the screen will display a multicolored drape effect and the initial Setup window appears, as shown in Figure 2-2. Here, you can preconfigure the language, time and currency formats, and keyboard or input method you'll use during Setup.

Figure 2-1: From inauspicious beginnings such as these come great things.

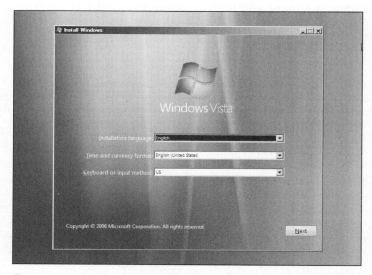

Figure 2-2: These settings apply only to Setup, not the eventual Windows Vista installation.

3. Click Next. The Install Now window appears, as shown in Figure 2-3. To continue with Interactive Setup, click Install Now.

Figure 2-3: This window jumpstarts Setup and the Windows Vista recovery tools.

Secret

This window also provides a way to access Windows Vista's new recovery tools. If you run into a problem with Windows Vista later, such as not being able to boot into Windows for some reason, you can boot your system with the Setup DVD and use these tools to help fix the problem.

4. In the next window (shown in Figure 2-4), enter your Windows Vista product key. This is a 25-digit alphanumeric string — in blocks of 5 separated by dashes — that you will find on a bright yellow product key sticker somewhere in your Windows Vista packaging. You can also optionally choose to have Windows Vista automatically activate for you.

Secret

Do not lose this product key or give it away to anyone. Each Windows Vista product key is valid for exactly one PC. After you've installed Windows Vista and activated it — which ties the product key to your hardware — you won't be able to use this number again on another PC, at least not easily. Note, however, that you will have no problems reinstalling Windows Vista on the same PC using this same product key. If for some reason you are unable to electronically activate Windows later, Vista will provide a phone number so you can do it manually.

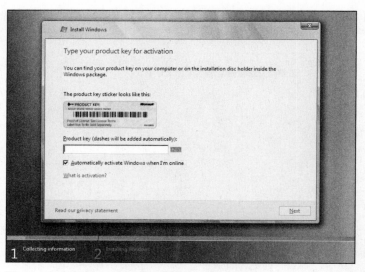

Figure 2-4: Spread 'em. This is where Microsoft ensures you're genuine.

5. In the next window, you must agree to the End User License Agreement (EULA). Although very few people actually read this document, you should take the time as it outlines your legal rights with regards to your usage of Windows Vista. Our understanding of the legaleze in this document is that Microsoft exerts certain rights over your first born and soul. In Figure 2-5, you can see the EULA window.

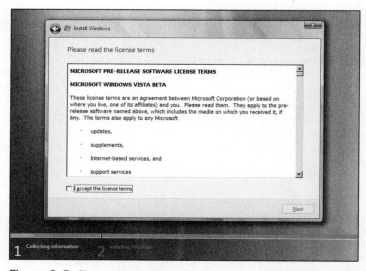

Figure 2-5: Sign over all your rights simply by clicking a single check box.

6. In the next window, select the partition, or disk, to which to install Windows Vista. On a clean install, typically, you will be installing Windows Vista to the only disk available, as shown in Figure 2-6.

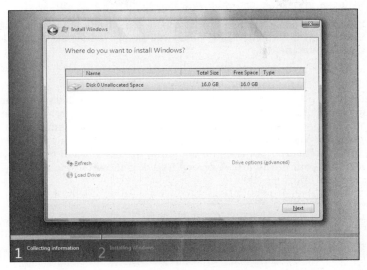

Figure 2-6: New to Vista Setup is a more graphic disk configuration phase.

7. Typically, you will see a link called More Options on this window. Clicking this link brings you to a screen where you can delete, format, or extend the current disk, if possible, or create a new partition if the hard drive is brand new and unformatted. This window is shown in Figure 2-7.

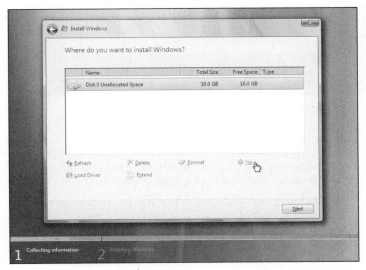

Figure 2-7: Here, you can perform various disk-related tasks, including resizing partitions.

Secret

If you are performing a clean install on a previously used machine, we advise you to format the disk during this step to ensure that none of the cruft from your previous Windows installation dirties up your new Windows Vista install.

You don't actually need to format a new disk. If you attempt to install Windows Vista on an unformatted disk, Setup will simply format the disk to its maximum capacity, automatically.

8. After you've selected the disk and formatted it if necessary, you can walk away from your computer for 20–45 minutes, depending on your hardware. During this time, Setup will copy the various files it needs for installation to the hard drive, expand the Vista image file from the DVD, install Windows Vista and any included software updates, and complete the installation by attempting to load drivers for your hardware. A screen like that shown in Figure 2-8 will display during this entire process.

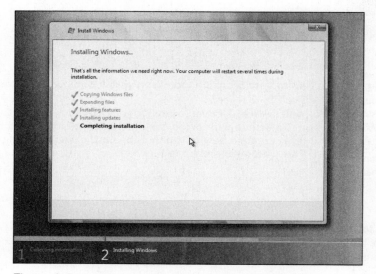

Figure 2-8: Grab lunch while Setup installs Windows Vista.

9. A reboot or two later, and your PC will launch into the second, and final, interactive phase of Setup. In the first screen, shown in Figure 2-9, you are prompted for a user name (typically a short name like Paul or Brian and not a full name like Ferris Bueller), password, and display picture. If you don't choose a picture, you get the flower by default. (You've been warned.)

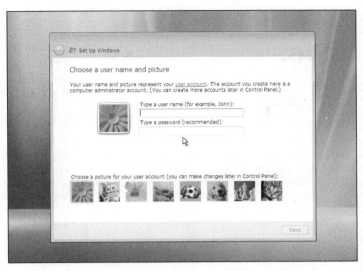

Figure 2-9: Here, you specify the account you'll typically use in Windows Vista.

Secret

A few notes about this initial user account. Unlike Windows XP, Windows Vista does not create a visible Administrator account automatically for security reasons. Nor are you allowed to create up to five user accounts, as you were in XP. Instead, you can create a single user account during Setup. That user account will be given administrator privileges.

Subsequent user accounts — created in Windows Vista using the User Accounts Control Panel — are given limited user privileges by default, but that's easy enough to change. We look at creating and modifying user accounts in Chapter 9.

caution   Be sure to use a password, please. It's unclear to us why Microsoft even makes this optional, but using a strong password is one of the most basic things you can do to keep your system more secure.

10. Type a name for your PC and choose a desktop background (see Figure 2-10). By default, Setup picks a PC name that is based on your user name. This is probably not a great name for your PC, but you're free to change it.

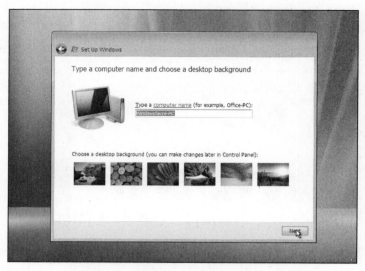

Figure 2-10: Here, you configure computer-related options.

Secret

Setup provides you with only six potential background images for some reason. To change your background to another image or a solid color after Setup is complete, right-click the Desktop, choose Personalize, and then Desktop Background. You'll see many more choices there.

Secret

Setup doesn't let you specify a workgroup name, or join an Active Directory-based domain, as did the Windows XP Setup routine. To change this after Setup is complete, open the Start Menu, right-click Computer, and choose Properties. Then, click the Change Settings link in the Computer name, domain, and workgroup settings section of the resulting window. The dialog box that appears is very similar to the one you're used to from Windows XP.

11. Choose whether to enable Automatic Updates, as shown in Figure 2-11. You can use the recommended settings, in which Windows automatically downloads and installs all updates, can install only important updates, or can choose to be prompted later.

Figure 2-11: In this part of Setup, you configure Automatic Updates.

Secret

This behavior is far more aggressive than the similar Setup screen that Microsoft added to Windows XP with Service Pack 2. Note that you can't choose to download but not install updates. Our advice is to choose the Ask Me Later option for now, even if you completely trust Microsoft. Then, you can configure Automatic Updates later using the new Windows Update utility. From that interface, you can use the more traditional options, including downloading but not automatically installing.

12. Configure the time zone, date, and time as shown in Figure 2-12.

Secret

Even if you're not particularly careful about setting the time correctly here, Windows Vista will eventually adjust to the correct time automatically, because it is configured out of the box to synchronize with an Internet time server. That said, you should at least make an effort to ensure that the time is reasonably correct to avoid problems with this process.

Setup announces when Interactive Setup is complete and you're ready to start (see Figure 2-13).

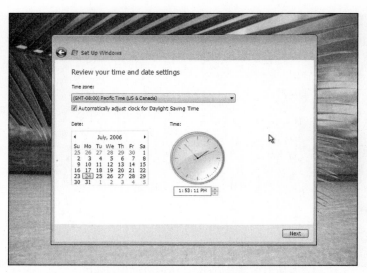

Figure 2-12: Curious that the time zone defaults to Pacific Time.

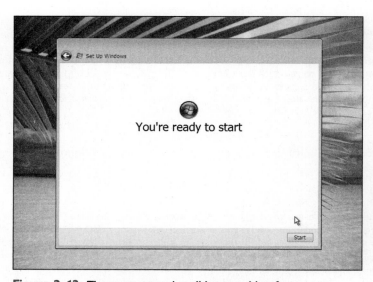

Figure 2-13: The moment we've all been waiting for.

Before the Windows Vista desktop appears, Setup takes a final bow by testing your system's performance characteristics. We'll look at what that means in the next section, but during this time, you'll see a screen like that shown in Figure 2-14. This process generally takes about 30 seconds to 2 minutes, depending on the speed of your PC.

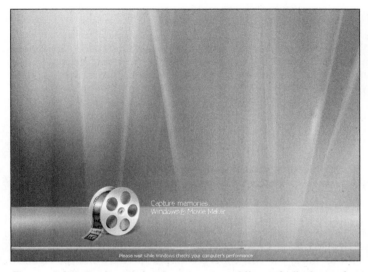

Figure 2-14: During the performance test, Microsoft displays a few small Windows Vista advertisements.

Post-Setup Tasks

With the performance test out of the way, Setup finally quits, leaving you staring at your new Windows Vista desktop. A few things will occur immediately:

1. The Welcome Center window opens, as shown in Figure 2-15, providing you with a glimpse at your system details, performance rating, and a list of 6 to 12 tasks you might want to perform now that you're up and running. You can safely close this window. We'll guide you through all of the post-setup tasks you'll need to perform.

Figure 2-15: Welcome Center isn't particularly interesting, but it does provide links to a lot of useful information and functionality.

Secret

The first time the Welcome Center appears, there's no indication that it's going to appear on your next reboot, but it will. From then on, however, Welcome Center will display an option on the bottom of its window titled, Run at startup. Clear this option if you want Welcome Center to stop being so welcoming.

tip

If you do disable Welcome Center, you can always access it at any time by navigating to All Programs ⇨ Accessories ⇨ Welcome Center in the new Start Menu.

2. If your PC includes a network card (wireless or otherwise) that was properly detected and installed during Setup, you will be prompted to configure that network connection. When you click the prompt, you will see the window shown in Figure 2-16. From here, you can choose whether the network you're accessing is private (your home network), work, or public (such as at a library, coffee shop, or airport). Windows will configure networking differently in each case.

Figure 2-16: This handy window makes sure you are as secure as you need to be, depending on which type of network you're using.

Okay, now it's time to finish configuring Windows Vista so you can begin using it. The first step is to check out your hardware driver situation: Ideally, all of the hardware connected to your PC has been detected, and Setup has installed drivers for each of your devices. To see whether this is the case, you need to open a tool called Device Manager. There are a number of ways to access Device Manager, but the quickest is to open the Start Menu, right-click Computer, and then choose Manage. This causes the Computer Management window to appear. In the tree view on the left, choose Device Manager, as shown in Figure 2-17.

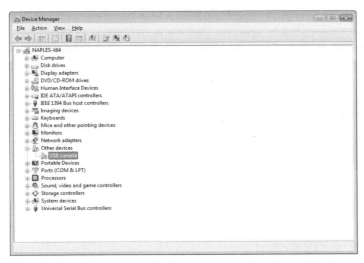

Figure 2-17: Device Manager tells you at a glance which hardware devices are connected and properly configured for your PC.

If any of the entries, or nodes, in the Device Manager tree view are open, displaying a device with a small yellow exclamation point, or *bang*, then you're going to need to install some drivers. There are four basic ways to install drivers in Windows Vista, listed below in opposite order of preference:

♦ **Automatically:** Right-click the unsupported device and choose Update Driver Software. Windows will search the local system, including any setup disks, to find the appropriate driver. In our experience, this method almost never works but it's worth trying.

♦ **Manually:** As before, you right-click the unsupported device and choose Update Driver Software. This time, however, you must supply the driver files via a setup disk or other means.

♦ **As an executable setup disk or download:** Many drivers come in self-contained executables where you run a setup routine just as you would for an application program. If possible, be sure to use a Windows Vista–compatible setup application: These should work just fine. However, Windows XP drivers often work as well, albeit with a little grumbling on the part of Windows Vista.

◆ **With Windows Update:** This is the best way to install drivers, and it's the first place to visit if you discover that Windows Vista Setup didn't install all of your hardware. The hardware drivers found on Windows Update aren't always as up-to-date as those supplied directly from the hardware manufacturers. That said, Windows Update–based drivers have been tested extensively and should always be your first choice. Note that Vista will likely connect to Windows Update automatically if you have a configured network adapter, grabbing any device drivers it can, within minutes of booting into the desktop for the first time.

tip

To find drivers on Windows Update, open the Start Menu and choose All Programs ⇨ Windows Update. Then, click the Check for updates link in the upper-right corner of the Windows Update application, as shown in Figure 2-18.

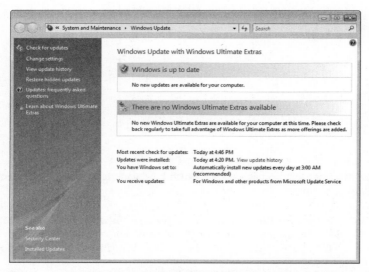

Figure 2-18: In Windows Vista, Windows Update can update your operating system, hardware drivers, and many Microsoft applications.

You should repeat the preceding processes until all of your hardware devices are up and running. If you did run Windows Update during this time, you will likely have seen a number of Windows Vista product updates as well. You should install those updates before moving on to the next step.

Now, it's time to install your applications. Install them one at a time and reboot if necessary after each install as requested. This process can often take a long time and is mind-numbingly boring, but the good news is you should only have to do it once.

With your applications installed, it's time to restore any data that you might have backed up from your previous Windows install. Or, if you have installed Windows Vista to a brand-new PC, you can transfer user accounts, music, picture, and video files, documents, program settings, Internet settings and favorites, and e-mail messages, contacts, and messages, from your old PC to Windows Vista using an excellent new Vista utility called Windows Easy Transfer. Located in Start Menu⇨All Programs⇨Accessories⇨System Tools, this utility is a wizard-like application, shown in Figure 2-19, that you can install and run on your previous OS as well.

Figure 2-19: Windows Easy Transfer makes short work of transferring your old data, documents, and custom settings from Windows XP to Vista.

Upgrading

When we discuss upgrading to Windows Vista, we are typically referring to what's called an *in-place upgrade*. When you perform an in-place upgrade of Windows Vista, you replace your existing version of Windows with Windows Vista. An in-place upgrade, hopefully, will bring with it all of your applications, documents, and settings.

Hopefully.

The reality is that in-place upgrades often don't work as planned. For this reason, we don't typically recommend upgrading from your current Windows version to Windows Vista. If you simply must perform such an upgrade, behave as if you were doing a clean install just in case, and back up all of your crucial documents and other data ahead of time. That way, if something does go wrong, you won't be stranded.

Before even attempting an upgrade, you should understand what kinds of upgrades are even possible. Windows Vista ships in a wide range of product editions, most of which don't have direct relations in Windows XP. Put simply, only certain versions of Windows can upgrade to certain versions of Windows Vista. From a licensing perspective, only certain Windows versions are eligible for a Windows Vista upgrade. That is, you can't purchase and install an Upgrade version of Windows Vista unless you're using a supported Windows version now.

If you're running Windows 95, Windows 98 (or Windows 98 Second Edition), Windows Millennium Edition, or Windows NT 4.0, you are out of luck. You cannot purchase an Upgrade version of Windows Vista, and you cannot perform an in-place upgrade from your current operating system to any Windows Vista product edition. Instead, you must purchase the Full version of the Windows Vista product edition you want, and perform a clean install, as specified earlier in this chapter.

If you're running Windows 2000 or Windows XP Professional x64 Edition, you are eligible to purchase an Upgrade version of the Windows Vista product edition you desire. However, you cannot perform an in-place upgrade. Instead, you will need to perform a clean install, as we discussed previously, using the Upgrade version.

The only Windows versions that both qualify for a Windows Vista Upgrade version and can be upgraded, in-place, to Windows Vista, are Windows XP Home, Professional, Media Center, and Tablet PC Editions. However, within this set of operating systems, there are still some restrictions. To help simplify your options, Table 2-1 summarizes which versions of Windows can be upgraded in-place to which Windows Vista versions.

Table 2-1: Which Versions of Windows Can Upgrade In-Place to Which Versions of Windows Vista.

Windows Version	Vista Home Basic/Home Basic N	Vista Home Premium	Vista Business/ Business N	Vista Ultimate
Windows 2000 Professional	No	No	No	No
Windows XP Home Edition	Yes	Yes	Yes	Yes
Windows XP Professional Edition	No	No	Yes	Yes
Windows XP Media Center Edition	No	Yes	No	Yes
Windows XP Tablet PC Edition	No	No	Yes	Yes
Windows XP Professional x64 Edition	No	No	No	No

note   **You might notice that Windows Vista Starter and Windows Vista Enterprise are not represented on this chart. That's because neither of those Windows Vista product editions supports upgrades at all. Windows Vista Starter is aimed at emerging markets, whereas Windows Vista Enterprise is a volume-licensed version of Windows that is only provided to corporations.**

Step-by-Step: Upgrading to Windows Vista

If you're undaunted by the process of upgrading of your copy of Windows XP to Windows Vista, in-place, then you've come to the right place. In this section, we'll tell you how it's done.

Most of the process is virtually identical to the steps we outlined for performing a Clean Install earlier in the chapter.

1. The first difference is that you will typically launch Windows Vista Setup from within Windows XP. To do so, simply insert the Windows Vista Setup DVD into your PC's optical drive. The Setup routine should auto-run, and you'll see the window shown in Figure 2-20.

Figure 2-20: When upgrading from Windows XP to Windows Vista, you will typically run Setup from within Windows XP.

2. Click Install Now to continue. In the next step, you'll be asked if you want to go online to get the latest updates for installation. You should always do so, because Microsoft will be improving Windows Vista over time and there will certainly be some updates available by the time you read this. Setup will search for and download any updates.

3. Setup will proceed as it does during a clean install, and you'll enter the product key, agree to the EULA, and so on. When you get to the "Which type of installation do you want?" screen, it's time to step back a second and recoup. This is where we're going to veer off into new territory.

4. Instead of choosing Custom, you will choose Upgrade. First, Setup runs a compatibility check to determine whether any of your hardware or software will need to be reinstalled — or will work at all — after the upgrade is completed. After scanning your system, Setup will present you with a Compatibility Report, as shown in Figure 2-21. What you see here will depend on how old and weather-beaten your system is. The more stuff you've installed, the bigger the chance that there will be problems.

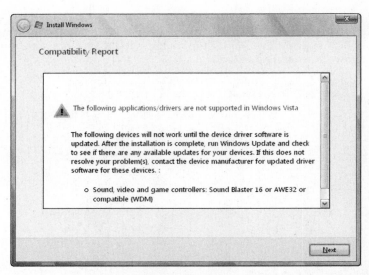

Figure 2-21: Cross your fingers: If you're lucky, nothing important will be unsupported in Windows Vista.

After that, Setup will continue exactly as it does during a clean install. And we mean exactly: Unlike previous Windows versions, Windows Setup literally backs up your settings, data, and application information, performs a clean install of the operating system, and then copies everything back in a way in which it should all work as it did before. But this is why the upgrade process is so dicey: If anything goes wrong, you've taken a perfectly usable Windows Vista install and mucked it up with all the garbage from your Windows XP install.

In any event, after Setup is complete, the system will reboot. Unlike with the other setup types, an in-place upgrade skips over a few steps, including those where you configure your user name, password, display picture, desktop background image, and machine name, because you've presumably set up all of those options in your previous Windows version. Instead, Setup jumps right to the Automatic Updates phase described in the clean install section of this chapter and then the time and date settings (which, frankly, should have been correctly configured previously as well). After that, you click the Finish button (no "You're ready to start" message, sorry), and Windows Setup tests your system performance and then loads the Welcome Screen.

So what's the end result? If everything went well, you should be able to log on to your previously established user account and access a desktop that looks reasonably like the one you had configured in Windows XP, as shown in Figure 2-22.

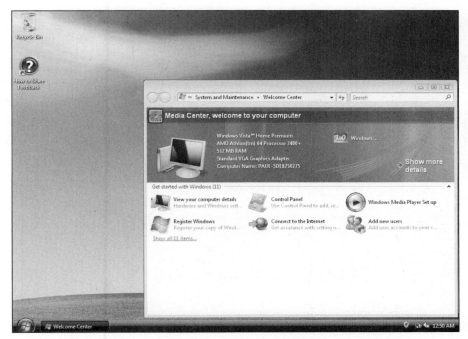

Figure 2-22: Look familiar? This desktop was upgraded from Windows XP.

The big mystery, of course, is your data and applications. You should spend some time testing each application to see if everything works. In Figure 2-23, you can see the Firefox web browser, previously installed and configured in Windows XP, up and running just fine after an upgrade to Windows Vista.

caution   Because of the potential for problems, we recommend backing up any crucial data and settings before performing any operating system upgrade.

Dual-Booting with Windows XP

With a radically different operating system such as Windows Vista, you may want to test the waters a bit before diving headlong into the future. Or, perhaps you need to run certain applications that still don't work properly in Windows Vista. Or you're a software or web developer, and you need to test your creations in both Windows XP and Windows Vista. For these and other reasons, Microsoft has long supported the notion of dual-booting, where you install two or more operating systems on the same PC, choose between them using a boot menu when you turn on or reboot the PC, and then run one or the other.

Figure 2-23: If all goes well, your previously installed applications should still work.

tip   Windows NT 4.0, Windows 2000, Windows XP (all versions), and Windows Vista all support dual-booting natively. Although it's possible to dual-boot between most of these operating systems and an older Windows version like Windows 98 or Me, those DOS-based versions of Windows are no longer supported by Microsoft and therefore won't be discussed in this chapter. If you need to run a legacy operating system, or a particular legacy application, we recommend a software virtualization environment like Microsoft's Virtual PC 2007, which is designed specifically for Windows Vista.

We're going to assume you already have Windows XP installed on your PC and are looking to add Windows Vista to the mix. We don't do this for our own benefit: Because Windows XP was developed years before Windows Vista and has no native understanding of Vista's boot loader and boot menu, it's best to simply install Windows XP first. Windows Vista was designed with knowledge of XP's boot loader and boot menu, and therefore can safely be added to a PC after Windows XP.

Before proceeding, there are two major issues to consider.

◆ You need to add a second hard drive or partition to your computer into which you will install Windows Vista. We'll look at ways to do this in the next section.

Secret

Do not, under any circumstances, try to install Windows XP and Windows Vista to the same partition or hard drive. While you might be able to pull this off, both operating systems use many identically named folders and you will run into problems.

◆ You need to decide how you are going to initiate the dual-boot install of Windows Vista. You have two choices: While in Windows XP, insert the Windows Vista Setup DVD and begin Setup from there. Or, reboot your system, boot from the Setup DVD, and begin Setup that way. What's the difference, you ask?

Secret

On a typical PC with two hard drives or partitions, one dedicated to Windows XP, and one dedicated to Windows Vista, you will typically end up with XP on the C: drive and Windows Vista on the D: drive when you initiate Windows Vista's Setup routine from within Windows XP. But when you reboot the system and boot with the Windows Vista Setup DVD, something magical occurs. After both operating systems are installed, Windows XP will be on C: and Windows Vista will be on D: while you're using Windows XP. But when you're using Windows Vista, the system will report that Windows Vista is on C: and Windows XP is on D:. This is vastly preferable to the former method, because most people are used to seeing the operating system partition located on the C: drive. For this very simple reason, we recommend that you always install Windows Vista in a dual-boot scenario by booting the system with the Vista Setup DVD and launching Setup from there.

Okay, let's not get ahead of ourselves. First we need to figure out how to make space for Windows Vista.

Adding a Drive or Partition for Windows Vista

There are two ways to make space for Windows Vista on your existing PC. You can either add a second hard drive, using the new hard drive exclusively for Windows Vista, or you can *partition* your existing hard drive, creating two logical hard drives, or partitions, one for Windows XP and one for Windows Vista.

The former method is the preferable one because it doesn't require you to deal with messy partitioning software and potentially endanger whatever data you already have on the C: drive. On the other hand, you do have to go through the effort of installing the hard drive, which can be dicey if you don't know your way around the innards of a PC. And of course, some desktop PCs and most notebook PCs can't be upgraded to support an additional hard drive. In such cases, you'll need to partition the only hard drive you've got.

If you're going to install a second physical hard drive, there's not much to say: Follow the manufacturer's instructions, and you should be all set. Modern hard drives are quite capacious and will present no problems during setup.

If you're going to partition your existing hard drive, life isn't so simple. Most partitioning tools, like the ones built into Windows, are what's known as *destructive* partitioning tools—that is, they literally destroy whatever was on the disk while partitioning. What you're looking for is a *non-destructive* partitioning tool, one that will let you slice an existing hard drive or partition into two or more partitions, while leaving all the data—and the operating system and applications—intact on the first.

There are various commercial partitioning solutions out there. We use and recommend Norton PartitionMagic, which has always been reliable. But there are various free partitioning solutions out there as well. Just be careful: This is your data you're messing with, and if the partitioning solution you use accidentally makes your hard drive inaccessible, don't say we didn't warn you.

tip   Also, you need to be sure to defragment your hard drive before partitioning in order to save time later (partitioning tools will defrag for you as needed, but aren't as efficient or fast as dedicated partitioning tools). Finally, make sure you create a partition with enough space on it to install Windows Vista. Microsoft specifies that Windows Vista requires 15 GB of free space for the premium versions of the operating system (Home Premium and Ultimate). But remember you're going to want to install applications and so forth. So the more space you can spare the better.

caution   To make it easier on yourself, preemptively name the new partition Vista or something similar, so you can more easily recognize it during Setup. You don't want to accidentally wipe out your XP install.

Step-by-Step: Installing Windows Vista in a Dual-Boot Setup

Assuming you have an additional free hard drive or partition, you can follow the steps outlined in the clean install section earlier in the chapter when performing a dual-boot installation: Boot with the Windows Vista DVD, choose Install, enter your product key, agree to the EULA, and so on. Where you're going to have to pay attention is when Setup reaches the screen that asks, "Which type of installation do you want?" This is shown in Figure 2-24.

Choose the Custom (advanced) install type and click Next. Then, examine the next screen, which should resemble Figure 2-25. In this screen, be sure to choose the empty partition that's been set aside for Windows Vista and not your XP partition. If you followed our advice in the previous section, you gave this partition an easy-to-recognize name like Vista ahead of time.

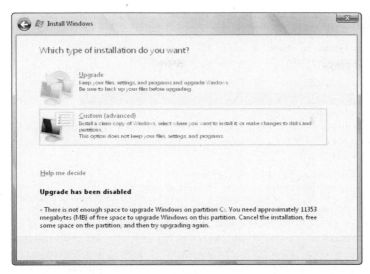

Figure 2-24: Heads-up. In this phase of Setup, you want to be sure to make the right choices.

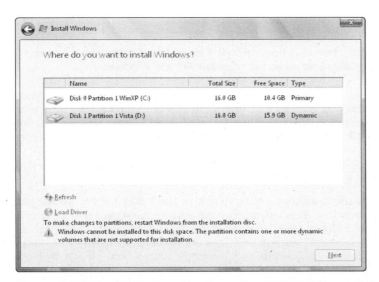

Figure 2-25: Careful: You want to choose the empty partition, not the XP partition.

After that, Setup will proceed, again, exactly as it does during a clean install. After Windows Vista is installed, however, you will notice one difference: When you reboot the PC, a boot menu, like the one shown in Figure 2-26, appears, letting you choose between your previous operating system (Earlier Version of Windows) and Windows Vista.

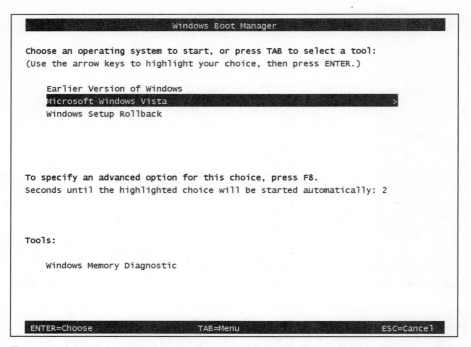

Figure 2-26: Microsoft's new dual-boot menu lets you choose between your previous operating system (typically some version of Windows XP) and Windows Vista.

You might notice that the boot menu uses a fairly lengthy 30 second countdown during which time it waits for you to choose an operating system. That's a long time to wait, and if you're not sitting there waiting to make a choice, your system will waste a lot of time waiting to boot. Good news: If you think 30 seconds is too long, there's a way to change this behavior.

To do so, open the Start Menu, right-click Computer, and choose Properties. This will display the new System Information window, as shown in Figure 2-27.

Now, click the "Advanced system settings" link in the Tasks list on the left side of the System Information window. This will display the System Properties dialog, which is quite similar to the System Properties dialog from Windows XP. Navigate to the Advanced tab and click the button labeled Settings that appears in the Startup and Recovery section. This, finally, will display the Startup and Recovery dialog box, shown in Figure 2-28, where, yes, you can configure startup options.

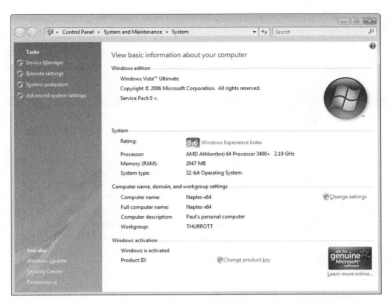

Figure 2-27: The default System Information window is much more detailed than the version in Windows 2000 or XP.

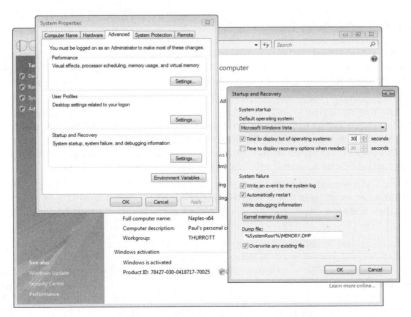

Figure 2-28: It's buried deep, but this dialog box can be used to configure the boot menu and other boot options.

Here, you can make a number of choices, but the relevant ones are:

◆ Determine which operating system is the default choice. Windows Vista is the default choice, by default.

◆ Determine how much time will elapse while the boot menu is displayed before the system boots into the default operating system.

We like to set the timer to a small value like 3 or 5 seconds so that Windows Vista boots quickly but we have enough time to make a choice if we want to.

Secret

We've been referring to Windows Vista's dual-boot capabilities throughout this chapter, but the reality is that Windows Vista (and previous NT-based Windows versions like Windows 2000 and XP) support *multi-booting*. That's right: With the right partitioning scheme, gobs of hard drive space, and plenty of time on your hands, you can configure your PC to boot between two, three, four, or more operating systems. Such a setup is conceptually interesting but of little use in the real world, at least for most people. As the saying goes, people who are dual-booting aren't getting anything done.

Deploying Windows Vista: A Power User's Toolkit

If you're an enterprise administrator faced with the prospect of rolling out Windows Vista to hundreds or thousands of desktops around the world, take heart: Microsoft has finally upgraded its deployment tools in dramatic fashion, taking advantage of the componentized architecture of Windows Vista. But these deployment tools aren't just advantageous to the world's biggest corporations. If you're a power user, a tinkerer, or someone who ends up having to reinstall Windows fairly regularly, you might just be interested to discover that Vista's newfangled deployment tools are going to prove quite enticing to you as well.

Here's what happened. With Windows Vista, Microsoft has completely rearchitected Windows for the first time since, well, Windows 95, breaking the system down to core pieces, called modules, which are as non-dependent on each other as possible. Before, each version of Windows included a foundational module that was based on the English language. If Microsoft, a PC maker, or an IT administrator wanted to create, say, a French version of Windows, they would have to add the French language on top of Windows.

Now, Windows Vista is language independent. The core foundational module of Windows is much smaller as a result, and it will now be easier for Microsoft — and IT administrators — to roll out patches because they won't need different ones for all of the languages Windows supports.

Microsoft also changed Windows Vista to a file-based disk imaging model. In the past, Windows Setup would spend a lot of time copying thousands of files from the Windows install media (typically a CD) or a network-based file share (when installed by corporations). These file operations were time consuming because each file had to be expanded and copied to a particular directory structure on the fly. With an image-based model, Windows Vista ships as a single image file containing just the most basic components required to get the OS up and running. During installation, Windows Setup simply copies this single image file to the hard drive and then expands it, creating a simple Windows installation. After that, custom features are added and the OS is installed. Simple.

Finally, Microsoft improved its Windows deployment answer file, a text-based file that literally contains the answers to the questions you answer during interactive Setup when you do a clean install, upgrade, or dual-boot. These questions include such things as "What is your product key?" But the beautiful thing is that the answer file can contain answers to questions that aren't asked during Setup at all. In this way, we can create custom Windows install images that will install a version of Windows Vista that isn't possible to obtain using just interactive Setup.

But wait, there's more: Even if all you want is a standard Windows install, creating your own answer file is still a good idea, because you can use that file to run what's called an automated Windows install, where you don't have to babysit the install process. It literally automates the whole thing.

The key to all of this is something Microsoft calls Windows Automated Installation Kit (WAIK). This free software kit includes a number of tools, including the User State Migration Tool (USMT), for migrating settings from Windows 2000 and XP to Vista; XImage, for editing Vista image files; Windows System Image Manager, for configuring custom Windows Vista images and creating unattended installaton files; and Windows PE (Preinstallation Environment), a simple Windows boot environment designed primarily to bootstrap Windows Vista installation and prepare a disk for the new operating system.

As noted earlier, these tools are designed for enterprises, which typically need to roll out Windows Vista to large numbers of PCs in an automated fashion. But you can use these tools to create custom Vista install images, burn them to blank DVDs using the third-party disk burning software of your choice, and then install the version of Windows Vista *you* want. Unfortunately, the Windows Vista version of WAIK wasn't completed in time for this book. But you can find complete instructions for creating custom Windows Vista install DVDs on the SuperSite for Windows (**www.winsupersite.com**).

Summary

Although Windows Vista Setup is dramatically simpler than the Setup routine used by Windows XP, there are still many options to understand and features you'll need to go back and configure manually after Setup is complete. Depending on which Vista version you purchased and your needs, you can clean install Vista as the sole OS on your PC, upgrade an existing Windows XP installation to Vista, or dual-boot between XP and Vista on the same machine. For the truly daring, you can also use Microsoft's enterprise-oriented deployment tools to create your own custom-built Vista deployment image, ensuring that when you install the OS, you're only installing exactly what you want.

Vista
Compatibility

Chapter
3

◆ ◆

In This Chapter

Choosing not to install Vista over an older operating system

Recognizing the conditions where you may have to install Vista over an older OS

Using the Vista Upgrade Advisor to catch problems in advance

Taking action if the Vista Upgrade Advisor says an updated driver "isn't available"

Resolving driver issues with a third-party web site

Reviewing XP drivers that work fine, but were left out of Vista

◆ ◆

Installing Windows Vista over a copy of XP or another, older version of the operating system poses problems that you may not want to face. In this chapter, we discuss the issues you could face.

Upgrading to Vista

With all of the new features of Windows Vista, there'll be a mighty temptation for you to buy a copy of the operating system in a store and immediately install it over your existing instance of Windows XP, 2000, Me, or 98.

Before you do, you should consider some of the following cautions:

◆ Your old PC may not be up to the challenge of running Vista. You may need substantial investments in additional RAM, a more capable video card, a larger hard drive, or all of the above to get adequate performance from Vista.

◆ Some of your hardware, such as printers and networking adapters, may not work at all after you install Vista — unless you update the drivers they need to versions that are Vista-compatible.

◆ Even if you find that one or more of your drivers needs to be updated, the vendor of your hardware may not make a Vista-compatible version available for months, years, or ever. (It's happened before with previous versions of Windows.)

Secret

Avoid Installing Vista over Another Version of Windows

We do recommend that you get Windows Vista preinstalled when you're buying a new PC. But you may be surprised to learn that we *don't* recommend that you install Vista over XP or an older version of Windows.

The reason is that installing Vista on top of another version of Windows may cause incompatibility problems that you might not be able to easily fix. When you buy a PC with Vista preinstalled, it's almost certain that the components in the PC will have been selected for their compatibility and will have the latest driver software. If you install Vista to an older machine yourself, however, you may find that your printer, networking adapter, or some other vital component no longer works because the version you have of its driver is incompatible.

In general, you shouldn't consider installing Vista over an older version of Windows unless the following conditions are true:

• You need a feature of Vista that you can't add to XP; or

• You need an application that requires Vista; and

• You can't afford even the least expensive new PC that comes with Vista preinstalled

Even if one of the above cases *is* true, you may be better off burning your old data to a CD, formatting the old PC's hard drive, and doing a clean install of Vista. This avoids the possibility that some components of the old OS will hang around to cause conflicts. If you've never before backed up and formatted a hard drive, however, don't try to learn how on any PC that's important to you.

A clean install, however, isn't a panacea. Your old PC may not have enough memory, disk space, video performance, or CPU performance to run Vista satisfactorily.

If you do decide to install Vista over an older version of Windows, at least run Microsoft's Vista Upgrade Advisor, described in this chapter, to see which drivers you may need to update first.

XP Users Can Try the Vista Upgrade Advisor

To help you determine whether a particular PC has the performance characteristics and the current hardware drivers it needs to work well with Vista, Microsoft provides the Vista Upgrade Advisor.

We recommend that you run the Upgrade Advisor on your current, non-Vista PC, if only to be humbled when you see the many aspects of your system that may need you to shell out some bucks for complete Vista compatibility. Even if you never install Vista on an older PC, you may find that upgraded drivers are available that will give you better performance on your current system.

The Upgrade Advisor is a short and simple test that you access on Microsoft's web site. It runs only on PCs that have Windows XP installed.

As Microsoft states on the site, "In general, PCs purchased within the last two years have a better chance of being able to run Windows Vista as-is or with affordable improvements to the system hardware." That leaves out a lot of PCs that were built when Windows 2000, Me, or 98 were the leading operating systems.

tip
> Visit Microsoft's 'Get Ready' Web page. At the time of this writing, the Vista Upgrade Advisor was available from Microsoft at www.microsoft.com/windowsvista/getready.
>
> That page also has useful information about the exact hardware requirements for Vista. This includes a description of Windows Vista Capable PCs (which can run all Vista applications) and Windows Vista Premium Ready PCs (which can also run the slick Aero user interface).

The Vista Upgrade Advisor

For those who want to upgrade a Windows XP machine to Vista, starting with the Vista Upgrade Advisor is a good first step.

Getting Ready for the Upgrade Advisor

When you start the Upgrade Advisor from Microsoft's site, a small application is downloaded to your PC. When you run this app, you see the dialog box shown in Figure 3-1.

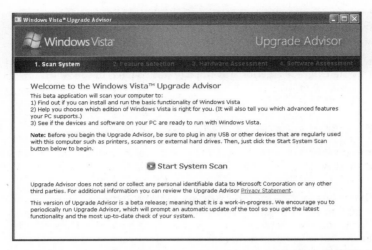

Figure 3-1: After you download and start the application, you'll be prompted to plug in any printers, scanners, external hard drives, or other devices that might need driver updates to work well with Vista.

The advisor is designed to test two different kinds of hardware compatibility:

◆ Whether your hardware is fast enough and modern enough to run Vista satisfactorily

◆ Whether your device drivers are compatible with Windows

The advisor's initial dialog box suggests that you plug in any devices you may want to use with Vista. It's easy to forget some, but this is absolutely the time you want them to be checked out. So here's a short list to jog your memory about gizmos you'll want to make sure are plugged in to your PC and powered on before you start the advisor's system scan:

◆ Printers and scanners (make sure they're *powered on,* not just plugged in)

◆ External hard disk drives, backup devices, and USB drives of all kinds

◆ An extra USB hub that you seldom use — plug it in anyway to check it

◆ Spare USB keyboards and mice that you may have forgotten

◆ iPod or other MP3 player, even if you seldom synchronize it to your PC

◆ Headphones and ear buds (they may require audio drivers that won't be tested unless the devices are jacked in to an audio port)

When you've checked for all of the preceding and you feel that you've plugged in and turned on everything you might want to test, click the Start System Scan button in the advisor.

Can Your PC Run the Core Experiences?

The Upgrade Advisor first tests a PC's hardware, looking for signs that the system has all the chops it needs to handle essential disk, memory, and CPU functions. As you can see in Figure 3-2, the Advisor will tell you whether these hardware features are up to the task of running Vista's core experiences, which are basic features.

Figure 3-2: On most PCs built since 2005, the Upgrade Advisor will report that the hardware will run the *core experiences* of Vista. If a PC fails this test, don't even think about installing Vista on the machine without investing in more serious hardware upgrades.

If the Upgrade Advisor reports "No action required" for your hardware, you can breathe a sigh of relief. This all-clear doesn't necessarily mean that Vista will run acceptably fast on that particular machine, but it does mean that the advisor found no show-stoppers that would necessitate expenditures on your part for new PC components.

If you decide at this point to install Vista on this particular PC, and it proves to be too slow for you, you can still upgrade your RAM, video board, disk drive — possibly even swap out your motherboard for a new model — to improve the situation. You may not have that luxury if you install Vista on a PC that the Upgrade Advisor reports isn't capable of handling it.

Are Your Drivers Capable of Vista?

After the core experiences test of your hardware, the Upgrade Advisor moves on to test the software drivers that are crucial for the various components of your system and peripherals that may be attached.

Assuming that the PC you're testing has passed the basic compatibility test, you may find that the driver test poses challenging obstacles for you. There are three possible situations that the advisor will report to you about your drivers.

    ◆ You may need to manually update certain drivers after Vista is installed.

    ◆ Certain devices may simply not be supported by Vista at all.

◆ Vista may simply support your devices with native Windows Vista drivers. In that case, you obviously won't need to do anything to make those drivers work with Vista.

We look at the other two cases in the sections that follow.

Drivers That Need Manual Updating

Drivers that need manual updating are updated versions of drivers that are compatible with Vista, but for some reason, Microsoft hasn't included them in the shipping version of Vista. That means Vista can't install the newer drivers. You'll have to find them and install them yourself — *before* you try to install Vista over XP.

Drivers you need to manually update are shown in the first section of Figure 3-3, with the exclamation-point-in-a-triangle icon. The details of which drivers are involved aren't shown in this figure.

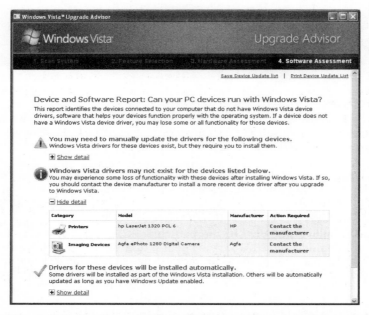

Figure 3-3: The Upgrade Advisor sorts your drivers into three categories — Vista-compatible drivers that you need to obtain and install yourself, drivers that are incompatible and have no newer version, and Vista-compatible drivers that Vista itself will install for you.

This may pose a dilemma for you. If Microsoft can't include the new drivers in Vista in such a way that it can install them for you, why does Microsoft think you'd like to search the Web for the right software and install it yourself?

That's exactly what you'll need to do, though, if you expect Vista to work properly when you install it over your older operating system. Fortunately, the Upgrade Advisor has at least told you what to look for.

Our advice, if the advisor tells you to manually install new drivers, is to start your search with the web site of the vendor of the hardware that needs a driver upgrade. You're most likely to get the latest and most compatible driver version directly from the maker. Some upgrade sites on the Web don't actually offer the latest versions of the drivers you need.

tip

If you don't know how to find drivers on a particular vendor's web site, you may be better off using DriverAgent.com. This site is run by the Touchstone Software Corp., a Massachusetts company that has developed CheckIt Diagnostics and several other well-known utility programs.

At the site, you can click Scan to find which drivers may be outdated on your system and how to obtain new drivers, whether your system is running Windows XP, 2000, Me, or 98. Don't install drivers that are labeled as *beta* unless you're willing to take a chance on these drivers' readiness for widespread use.

If newer drivers are available, the site will download them for you if you pay a fee of $29.95 for a one-year membership. This fee might save you some valuable time. If you don't want to pay, at least the scan will show you which of your drivers have newer versions available. For more details, see www.DriverAgent.com.

Drivers That May Not Have a Vista-Compatible Version

Drivers on your system that are incompatible with Vista, and Microsoft doesn't know of Vista-compatible versions, show up second in the Upgrade Advisor's software report.

In Figure 3-3, you can see that the advisor calls for new drivers for the HP LaserJet 1320 printer and the Agfa ePhoto 1280 camera. The printer, in particular, is a fairly odd omission in Vista's stable of drivers, since the LaserJet 1320 is one of HP's most popular small-office peripherals.

If the advisor says that a particular driver you need may not exist, the first place to start your search — as with the drivers Microsoft says you must manually install — is the site of the hardware vendor. New drivers are released every day, so the one you need may have just come out.

If your search doesn't reveal an updated driver that specifically says it's Vista-compatible, your next step is to enter the world of tech-support hell. That's right, you'll need to find someone in the company who'll pay attention to your e-mail, phone call, or letter and tell you when a Vista-specific driver will be released.

Good luck on making that happen. Fortunately, major manufacturers tend to quickly release drivers that work with new Windows versions. That may mean drivers that come out at almost the same time as Vista or only two or three months later.

Smaller companies and those who no longer support a particular model of hardware, however, may never spend the time to develop a Vista-ready driver. In that case, you may have no choice but to purchase newer hardware that does have a driver you can use in Vista. In such a case, there's always the question about what to do with the hardware that won't work with Vista — eBay, anyone?

Microsoft's Obscure Stash of Legacy Drivers

Even if the Vista Upgrade Advisor tells you that you need new drivers, and that they aren't known to be available, you still may have something that will work.

That something is called an XP driver. Yep, a driver that works fine under Windows XP may also work fine under Vista, even though the Upgrade Advisor doesn't say so.

Table 3-1 shows *scores* of drivers that Microsoft developers refer to as "XP drivers for legacy devices which we believe to function well on Windows Vista." These drivers, however, won't be included with Vista and the Upgrade Advisor may or may not say that they're compatible, in case your system already has one or more of them.

Sources within Microsoft report that, "For various reasons, these drivers will not be 'in the box' for the final version of Vista." If you're having trouble getting Vista to work well with a particular piece of hardware, and you can't find a Vista-specific driver for it, you could try locating and installing an XP driver as a last resort.

To install an XP driver, you'll need to download it from a manufacturer's site or have a copy of the driver on a CD, a USB drive, or some other medium. You can then use Vista's Add Hardware control panel to try to write the new driver to your hard disk.

> **caution** Be sure to copy the old driver to a safe location, such as a USB drive, in case the new driver works worse than the old one did and you need to switch back.

The list in Table 3-1 includes drivers for a lot of Ethernet cards and Wi-Fi adapters, for some reason. If your PC can't connect to a wired network or can't see your wireless router after installing Vista, this list of XP drivers that Microsoft developers believe will work under Vista could help you find software to correct the situation.

Our thanks to Wendy Stidmon of Microsoft for assembling the list of XP drivers that work in Vista.

Why Didn't Microsoft Include These Drivers in Vista?

At the time of writing, we haven't been able to get a good answer to the question of why Microsoft didn't include in Vista the hundreds of XP drivers that were found to work well on the new OS.

It appears to us that the omission of these drivers in Vista is due to licensing issues that couldn't be resolved prior to Vista's release to manufacturing (RTM). There doesn't seem to be anything inherently wrong with the drivers in Table 3-1.

As indicated previously, Table 3-1 shows XP-generation drivers that Microsoft experts "believe to function well on Windows Vista." The list is sorted by manufacturer name, although some of the descriptions of the components are very generic. The manufacturer name is followed by a hardware ID, a unique key that identifies a specific driver.

Table 3-1: XP-Generation Drivers That Should Function on Windows Vista

Product Name	HWID
3Com 10/100 Mini PCI Ethernet Adapter	PCI\VEN_10b7&DEV_9200&SUBSYS_700010B7
3Com 10/100/1000 PCI	PCI\VEN_14e4&DEV_16A6&SUBSYS_110010B7
3Com 10/100/1000 PCI	PCI\VEN_14e4&DEV_16C6&SUBSYS_110010B7
3Com 3C1000 Gigabit NIC	PCI\VEN_14e4&DEV_1645&SUBSYS_100710B7
3Com 3C918 Integrated Fast Ethernet Controller (3C905B-TX Compatible)	PCI\VEN_10b7&DEV_9055
3Com 3C920 Integrated Fast Ethernet Controller (3C905C-TX Compatible)	PCI\VEN_10b7&DEV_9200
3Com 3C920 Integrated Fast Ethernet Controller (3C905C-TX Compatible)	PCI\VEN_10b7&DEV_9200&SUBSYS_012A1028
3Com 3C920 Integrated Fast Ethernet Controller (3C905C-TX Compatible)	PCI\VEN_10b7&DEV_9200&SUBSYS_00C81028
3Com 3C920 Integrated Fast Ethernet Controller (3C905C-TX Compatible)	PCI\VEN_10b7&DEV_9200&SUBSYS_00E31028
3Com 3C920 Integrated Fast Ethernet Controller (3C905C-TX Compatible)	PCI\VEN_10b7&DEV_9200&SUBSYS_00D51028
3Com 3C920 Integrated Fast Ethernet Controller (3C905C-TX Compatible)	PCI\VEN_10b7&DEV_9200&SUBSYS_1246103C
3Com 3C920 Integrated Fast Ethernet Controller (3C905C-TX Compatible)	PCI\VEN_10b7&DEV_9200&SUBSYS_00D41028
3Com 3C920 Integrated Fast Ethernet Controller (3C905C-TX Compatible)	PCI\VEN_10b7&DEV_9200&SUBSYS_01221028
3Com 3C920 Integrated Fast Ethernet Controller (3C905C-TX Compatible)	PCI\VEN_10b7&DEV_9200&SUBSYS_00F31028
3Com 3C920 Integrated Fast Ethernet Controller (3C905C-TX Compatible)	PCI\VEN_10b7&DEV_9200&SUBSYS_1247103C
3Com 3C920 Integrated Fast Ethernet Controller (3C905C-TX Compatible)	PCI\VEN_10b7&DEV_9200&SUBSYS_00B81028
3Com 3C920 Integrated Fast Ethernet Controller (3C905C-TX Compatible)	PCI\VEN_10b7&DEV_9200&SUBSYS_000A1854
3Com 3C920 Integrated Fast Ethernet Controller (3C905C-TX Compatible)	PCI\VEN_10b7&DEV_9200&SUBSYS_3500107B
3Com 3C920 Integrated Fast Ethernet Controller (3C905C-TX Compatible)	PCI\VEN_10b7&DEV_9200&SUBSYS_00041854

(continued)

Table 3-1 (continued)

Product Name	HWID
3Com 3C920 Integrated Fast Ethernet Controller (3C905C-TX Compatible)	PCI\VEN_10b7&DEV_9200&SUBSYS_00051854
3Com 3C920 Integrated Fast Ethernet Controller (3C905C-TX Compatible)	PCI\VEN_10b7&DEV_9200&SUBSYS_C002144D
3Com 3C920 Integrated Fast Ethernet Controller (3C905C-TX Compatible)	PCI\VEN_10b7&DEV_9200&SUBSYS_C005144D
3Com 3C920 Integrated Fast Ethernet Controller (3C905C-TX Compatible)	PCI\VEN_10b7&DEV_9200&SUBSYS_00031854
3Com 3C920 Integrated Fast Ethernet Controller (3C905C-TX Compatible)	PCI\VEN_10b7&DEV_9200&SUBSYS_00061854
3Com 3C920 Integrated Fast Ethernet Controller (3C905C-TX Compatible)	PCI\VEN_10b7&DEV_9200&SUBSYS_00071854
3Com 3C920 Integrated Fast Ethernet Controller (3C905C-TX Compatible)	PCI\VEN_10b7&DEV_9200&SUBSYS_00081854
3Com 3C920 Integrated Fast Ethernet Controller (3C905C-TX Compatible)	PCI\VEN_10b7&DEV_9200&SUBSYS_00091854
3Com 3C920 Integrated Fast Ethernet Controller (3C905C-TX Compatible)	PCI\VEN_10b7&DEV_9200&SUBSYS_001314C0
3Com 3C920 Integrated Fast Ethernet Controller (3C905C-TX Compatible)	PCI\VEN_10b7&DEV_9200&SUBSYS_00B91028
3Com 3C920 Integrated Fast Ethernet Controller (3C905C-TX Compatible)	PCI\VEN_10b7&DEV_9200&SUBSYS_00E41028
3Com 3C920 Integrated Fast Ethernet Controller (3C905C-TX Compatible)	PCI\VEN_10b7&DEV_9200&SUBSYS_00F41028
3Com 3C920 Integrated Fast Ethernet Controller (3C905C-TX Compatible)	PCI\VEN_10b7&DEV_9200&SUBSYS_012B1028
3Com 3C920 Integrated Fast Ethernet Controller (3C905C-TX Compatible)	PCI\VEN_10b7&DEV_9200&SUBSYS_1101144D
3Com 3C920 Integrated Fast Ethernet Controller (3C905C-TX Compatible)	PCI\VEN_10b7&DEV_9200&SUBSYS_1248103C
3Com 3C920 Integrated Fast Ethernet Controller (3C905C-TX Compatible)	PCI\VEN_10b7&DEV_9200&SUBSYS_211914A4
3Com 3C920 Integrated Fast Ethernet Controller (3C905C-TX Compatible)	PCI\VEN_10b7&DEV_9200&SUBSYS_303C1462
3Com 3C920 Integrated Fast Ethernet Controller (3C905C-TX Compatible)	PCI\VEN_10b7&DEV_9200&SUBSYS_802A1043
3Com 3C920B-EMB Integrated Fast Ethernet Controller	PCI\VEN_10b7&DEV_9201
3Com 3C920B-EMB Integrated Fast Ethernet Controller	PCI\VEN_10b7&DEV_9201&SUBSYS_12B8103C

Product Name	HWID
3Com 3C920B-EMB Integrated Fast Ethernet Controller	PCI\VEN_10b7&DEV_9201&SUBSYS_233C1106
3Com 3C920B-EMB Integrated Fast Ethernet Controller	PCI\VEN_10b7&DEV_9201&SUBSYS_B00F144D
3Com 3C920B-EMB-WNM Integrated Fast Ethernet Controller	PCI\VEN_10b7&DEV_9202
3Com 3C940 Gigabit LOM	PCI\VEN_14e4&DEV_1645&SUBSYS_100810B7
3Com 3C996 10/100/1000 Server NIC	PCI\VEN_14e4&DEV_1644&SUBSYS_100010B7
3Com 3C996 Gigabit Fiber-SX Server NIC	PCI\VEN_14e4&DEV_1645&SUBSYS_100410B7
3Com 3C996B Gigabit Server NIC	PCI\VEN_14e4&DEV_1645&SUBSYS_100610B7
3Com 3CRWE777A AirConnect Wireless LAN PCI Card	PCI\VEN_10b7&DEV_1f1f
3Com EtherLink 10/100 PCI Combo NIC (3C905B-COMBO)	PCI\VEN_10b7&DEV_9058
3Com EtherLink 10/100 PCI For Complete PC Management NIC (3C905C-TX)	PCI\VEN_10b7&DEV_9200&SUBSYS_100010B7
3Com EtherLink 10/100 PCI TX NIC (3C905B-TX)	PCI\VEN_10b7&DEV_9055&SUBSYS_905510b7
3Com EtherLink 100 PCI Fiber NIC (3C905B-FX)	PCI\VEN_10b7&DEV_905A
3Com EtherLink PCI Combo NIC (3C900B-COMBO)	PCI\VEN_10b7&DEV_9005
3Com EtherLink PCI Fiber NIC (3C900B-FL)	PCI\VEN_10b7&DEV_900A
3Com EtherLink PCI TPC NIC (3C900B-TPC)	PCI\VEN_10b7&DEV_9006
3Com EtherLink PCI TPO NIC (3C900B-TPO)	PCI\VEN_10b7&DEV_9004
802.11b Wireless LAN PCI Card	PCI\VEN_1562&DEV_0001&SUBSYS_00010001
802.11b/g Wireless LAN Card	PCI\VEN_11AB&DEV_1FA6&SUBSYS_138E1043
802.11b/g Wireless LAN Card	PCI\VEN_11AB&DEV_1FA7&SUBSYS_138E1043
82562EH based Phoneline Network Connection	PCI\VEN_8086&DEV_1035
82562EH based Phoneline Network Connection	PCI\VEN_8086&DEV_1036
Agere Wireless Mini PCI Card	PCI\VEN_11C1&DEV_AB10
Agere Wireless Mini PCI Card	PCI\VEN_11C1&DEV_AB10&SUBSYS_AB1011C1&REV_00

(continued)

Table 3-1 *(continued)*

Product Name	HWID
Agere Wireless Mini PCI Card	PCI\VEN_11C1&DEV_AB11
Agere Wireless Mini PCI Card	PCI\VEN_11C1&DEV_AB11&SUBSYS_AB1111C1&REV_00
Agere Wireless Mini PCI Card	PCI\VEN_11C1&DEV_AB30
Agere Wireless Mini PCI Card	PCI\VEN_11C1&DEV_AB30&SUBSYS_201014CD&REV_00
Agere Wireless Mini PCI Card	PCI\VEN_11C1&DEV_AB30&SUBSYS_201214CD&REV_00
Agere Wireless Mini PCI Card	PCI\VEN_11C1&DEV_AB34
Agere Wireless Mini PCI Card	PCI\VEN_11C1&DEV_AB34&SUBSYS_201014CD&REV_00
ASUS 802.11b/g Wireless LAN Card	PCI\VEN_11AB&DEV_1FA7&SUBSYS_138F1043
ASUS 802.11b/g Wireless LAN Card	PCI\VEN_11AB&DEV_1FA6&SUBSYS_108F1043
ASUS 802.11b/g Wireless LAN Card	PCI\VEN_11AB&DEV_1FA6&SUBSYS_128F1043
ASUS 802.11b/g Wireless LAN Card	PCI\VEN_11AB&DEV_1FA6&SUBSYS_138F1043
ASUS 802.11b/g Wireless LAN Card	PCI\VEN_11AB&DEV_1FA7&SUBSYS_108F1043
ASUS 802.11b/g Wireless LAN Card	PCI\VEN_11AB&DEV_1FA7&SUBSYS_128F1043
ASUS SpaceLink WL-120 WLAN Mini-PCI Card	PCI\VEN_1260&DEV_3873&SUBSYS_38731043
Broadcom 570x Gigabit Integrated Controller	PCI\VEN_14e4&DEV_16A6&SUBSYS_81261028
Broadcom NetLink (TM) Gigabit Ethernet	PCI\VEN_14e4&DEV_16DD
Broadcom NetXtreme 57xx Gigabit Controller	PCI\VEN_14e4&DEV_1600&SUBSYS_01A71028
Broadcom NetXtreme 57xx Gigabit Controller	PCI\VEN_14e4&DEV_1600&SUBSYS_01A81028
Broadcom NetXtreme 57xx Gigabit Controller	PCI\VEN_14e4&DEV_1600&SUBSYS_01AD1028
Broadcom NetXtreme Gigabit Ethernet	PCI\VEN_14e4&DEV_16A6
Broadcom NetXtreme Gigabit Ethernet	PCI\VEN_14e4&DEV_1645
Broadcom NetXtreme Gigabit Ethernet	PCI\VEN_14e4&DEV_1600
Broadcom NetXtreme Gigabit Ethernet	PCI\VEN_14e4&DEV_1600&SUBSYS_0215107b
Broadcom NetXtreme Gigabit Ethernet	PCI\VEN_14e4&DEV_1600&SUBSYS_0280107b
Broadcom NetXtreme Gigabit Ethernet	PCI\VEN_14e4&DEV_1600&SUBSYS_0460107b
Broadcom NetXtreme Gigabit Ethernet	PCI\VEN_14e4&DEV_1600&SUBSYS_0604107b
Broadcom NetXtreme Gigabit Ethernet	PCI\VEN_14e4&DEV_1600&SUBSYS_108B1734
Broadcom NetXtreme Gigabit Ethernet	PCI\VEN_14e4&DEV_1600&SUBSYS_3010103c
Broadcom NetXtreme Gigabit Ethernet	PCI\VEN_14e4&DEV_1600&SUBSYS_3011103c

Product Name	HWID
Broadcom NetXtreme Gigabit Ethernet	PCI\VEN_14e4&DEV_1600&SUBSYS_3012103c
Broadcom NetXtreme Gigabit Ethernet	PCI\VEN_14e4&DEV_1600&SUBSYS_3013103c
Broadcom NetXtreme Gigabit Ethernet	PCI\VEN_14e4&DEV_1600&SUBSYS_3014103c
Broadcom NetXtreme Gigabit Ethernet	PCI\VEN_14e4&DEV_1600&SUBSYS_3016103c
Broadcom NetXtreme Gigabit Ethernet	PCI\VEN_14e4&DEV_1600&SUBSYS_5047107b
Broadcom NetXtreme Gigabit Ethernet	PCI\VEN_14e4&DEV_1600&SUBSYS_5048107b
Broadcom NetXtreme Gigabit Ethernet	PCI\VEN_14e4&DEV_1601
Broadcom NetXtreme Gigabit Ethernet	PCI\VEN_14e4&DEV_1644
Broadcom NetXtreme Gigabit Ethernet	PCI\VEN_14e4&DEV_1644&REV_21
Broadcom NetXtreme Gigabit Ethernet	PCI\VEN_14e4&DEV_1644&REV_22
Broadcom NetXtreme Gigabit Ethernet	PCI\VEN_14e4&DEV_1644&SUBSYS_00d11028
Broadcom NetXtreme Gigabit Ethernet	PCI\VEN_14e4&DEV_1644&SUBSYS_01091028
Broadcom NetXtreme Gigabit Ethernet	PCI\VEN_14e4&DEV_1644&SUBSYS_010A1028
Broadcom NetXtreme Gigabit Ethernet	PCI\VEN_14e4&DEV_1644&SUBSYS_102814e4
Broadcom NetXtreme Gigabit Ethernet	PCI\VEN_14e4&DEV_1646
Broadcom NetXtreme Gigabit Ethernet	PCI\VEN_14e4&DEV_16C6
Broadcom NetXtreme Gigabit Fiber	PCI\VEN_14e4&DEV_1644&SUBSYS_000214e4
Broadcom NetXtreme Gigabit Fiber	PCI\VEN_14e4&DEV_1644&SUBSYS_000314e4
Broadcom NetXtreme Gigabit Fiber	PCI\VEN_14e4&DEV_1645&SUBSYS_000714e4
D-Link Air DWL-510 Wireless PCI Adapter	PCI\VEN_1186&DEV_3300&SUBSYS_33011186
D-Link Air DWL-520 Wireless PCI Adapter	PCI\VEN_1317&DEV_8201&SUBSYS_35031186
D-Link Air DWL-520 Wireless PCI Adapter (rev.E)	PCI\VEN_1260&DEV_3873&SUBSYS_37001186
D-Link Air DWL-610 Wireless Cardbus Adapter	PCI\VEN_1186&DEV_3300&SUBSYS_33001186
D-Link Air DWL-650 Wireless Cardbus Adapter	PCI\VEN_1317&DEV_8201&SUBSYS_35021186
D-Link AirPlus G DWL-G510 Wireless PCI Card	PCI\VEN_11AB&DEV_1FA6&SUBSYS_3B091186
D-Link AirPlus G DWL-G630 Wireless Cardbus Adapter	PCI\VEN_11AB&DEV_1FA6&SUBSYS_3B081186
D-Link AirPlus G DWL-G630 Wireless Cardbus Adapter	PCI\VEN_11AB&DEV_1FA6&SUBSYS_1FA411AB
D-Link AirPlus G+ DWL-G520+ Wireless PCI Adapter	PCI\VEN_104C&DEV_9066&SUBSYS_3B041186

(continued)

Table 3-1 *(continued)*

Product Name	HWID
D-Link AirPlus G+ DWL-G650+ Wireless Cardbus Adapter	PCI\VEN_104C&DEV_9066&SUBSYS_3B051186
D-Link DFE-528TX PCI Adapter	PCI\VEN_1186&DEV_1300&SUBSYS_13031186
D-Link DFE-530TX+ PCI Adapter	PCI\VEN_1186&DEV_1300
D-Link DFE-530TX+ PCI Adapter	PCI\VEN_1186&DEV_1300&SUBSYS_13011186
D-Link DFE-530TXS FAST Ethernet 10/100 Adapter	PCI\VEN_1186&DEV_1002&SUBSYS_10401186
D-Link DFE-550FX 100Mbps Fiber-optics Adapter	PCI\VEN_1186&DEV_1002&SUBSYS_10031186
D-Link DFE-550TX FAST Ethernet 10/100 Adapter	PCI\VEN_1186&DEV_1002&SUBSYS_10021186
D-Link DFE-580TX 4 Port Server Adapter	PCI\VEN_1186&DEV_1002&SUBSYS_10121186
D-Link DFE-680TX/TXD CardBus PC Card	PCI\VEN_1186&DEV_1540&SUBSYS_15401186
D-Link DFE-680TX/TXD CardBus PC Card	PCI\VEN_1186&DEV_1541&SUBSYS_15411186
D-Link DFE-680TX/TXD CardBus PC Card	PCI\VEN_13D1&DEV_AB02&SUBSYS_15401186
D-Link DFE-680TX/TXD CardBus PC Card	PCI\VEN_13D1&DEV_AB02&SUBSYS_15411186
D-Link DGE-530T Gigabit Ethernet Adapter	PCI\VEN_1186&DEV_4C00&SUBSYS_4C001186
D-Link DL10050-based FAST Ethernet Adapter (generic)	PCI\VEN_1186&DEV_1002
Dynex DX-E101 PCI adapter	PCI\VEN_1186&DEV_1300&REV_10
Dynex DX-E201 CardBus PC Card	PCI\VEN_1186&DEV_1340&SUBSYS_13401186
Dynex DX-E201 CardBus PC Card	PCI\VEN_1186&DEV_1340&SUBSYS_13951186
High Rate Wireless LAN Mini-PCI Adapter with Modem II	PCI\VEN_1260&DEV_3873&SUBSYS_25138086
IEEE 802.11b Wireless MiniPCI Card 7007	PCI\VEN_11C1&DEV_AB34&SUBSYS_7007144F&REV_00
INPROCOMM IPN2220 Wireless LAN Card	PCI\VEN_17FE&DEV_2220&SUBSYS_7072144F
Intel(R) PRO/100 VE Network Connection	PCI\VEN_8086&DEV_1056
Intel(R) PRO/100 VE Network Connection	PCI\VEN_8086&DEV_1057
Intel(R) PRO/100 VE Network Connection	PCI\VEN_8086&DEV_106A
Intel(R) PRO/100 VE Network Connection	PCI\VEN_8086&DEV_106B

Product Name	HWID
Intel(R) PRO/Wireless 2011b LAN 3A Mini PCI Adapter	PCI\VEN_1260&DEV_3873&SUBSYS_25108086
Intel(R) PRO/Wireless 5000 LAN 3A Mini PCI Adapter	PCI\VEN_168C&DEV_0007&SUBSYS_25018086
Intel(R) PRO/Wireless 5000 LAN Cardbus Adapter	PCI\VEN_168C&DEV_0007&SUBSYS_25008086
Intersil PRISM Wireless LAN PCI Card	PCI\VEN_1260&DEV_3873&SUBSYS_116910CF
Intersil PRISM Wireless LAN PCI Card	PCI\VEN_1260&DEV_3873&SUBSYS_201310CF
Intersil PRISM Wireless LAN PCI Card	PCI\VEN_1260&DEV_3873&SUBSYS_7000144F
LAN-Express IEEE 802.11 PCI Adapter	PCI\VEN_1260&DEV_3873&SUBSYS_02001468
LAN-Express IEEE 802.11 PCI Adapter	PCI\VEN_1260&DEV_3872&SUBSYS_02021468
LAN-Express IEEE 802.11 PCI Adapter	PCI\VEN_1260&DEV_3873&SUBSYS_02011468
LAN-Express IEEE 802.11 PCI Adapter	PCI\VEN_1260&DEV_3872&SUBSYS_02001468
LAN-Express IEEE 802.11 PCI Adapter	PCI\VEN_1260&DEV_3873&SUBSYS_00001260
LAN-Express IEEE 802.11 PCI Adapter	PCI\VEN_1260&DEV_3873&SUBSYS_38731260
LAN-Express IEEE 802.11 PCI Adapter	PCI\VEN_1638&DEV_1100&SUBSYS_11001638
LAN-Express PSM IEEE 802.11g MiniPCI Adapter	PCI\VEN_1260&DEV_3890&SUBSYS_02101468
Linksys EG1032 v2 Instant Gigabit Network Adapter	PCI\VEN_1737&DEV_1032&SUBSYS_00151737
Linksys EG1064 v2 Instant Gigabit Network Adapter	PCI\VEN_1737&DEV_1064&SUBSYS_00161737
Linksys EtherFast Integrated 10/100 CardBus PC Card(PCM200)	PCI\VEN_13D1&DEV_AB03
Linksys EtherFast Integrated 10/100 CardBus PC Card(PCM200)	PCI\VEN_1737&DEV_AB09&SUBSYS_AB091737
Marvell Libertas 802.11b/g Wireless	PCI\VEN_11AB&DEV_1FA6
Marvell Libertas 802.11b/g Wireless	PCI\VEN_11AB&DEV_1FA7
Marvell Libertas 802.11b/g Wireless	PCI\VEN_11AB&DEV_1FA4
Marvell Libertas 802.11b/g Wireless	PCI\VEN_11AB&DEV_1FA6&SUBSYS_108F1043
Marvell Libertas 802.11b/g Wireless	PCI\VEN_11AB&DEV_1FA6&SUBSYS_128F1043
Marvell Libertas 802.11b/g Wireless	PCI\VEN_11AB&DEV_1FA6&SUBSYS_138F1043
Marvell Libertas 802.11b/g Wireless SoftAP	PCI\VEN_11AB&DEV_1FA6
Marvell Libertas 802.11b/g Wireless SoftAP	PCI\VEN_11AB&DEV_1FA7

(continued)

Table 3-1 *(continued)*

Product Name	HWID
Marvell Libertas 802.11b/g Wireless SoftAP	PCI\VEN_11AB&DEV_1FA7&SUBSYS_2A1B103C
Microsoft(R) Notebook Adapter MN-120	PCI\VEN_1414&DEV_0001&SUBSYS_00011414
Microsoft(R) PCI Adapter MN-130	PCI\VEN_1414&DEV_0002&SUBSYS_00021414
NETGEAR MA311 PCI Adapter	PCI\VEN_1260&DEV_3873&SUBSYS_41051385
NETGEAR WG311v2 802.11g Wireless PCI Adapter	PCI\VEN_104C&DEV_9066&SUBSYS_4C001385
NETGEAR WG511 54 Mbps Wireless PC Card	PCI\VEN_1260&DEV_3890&SUBSYS_48001385
NETGEAR WG511 54 Mbps Wireless PC Card	PCI\VEN_1260&DEV_3890&SUBSYS_00001260
Nortel Networks e-mobility 802.11b Wireless LAN PCI Card	PCI\VEN_126c&DEV_1f1f
ORiNOCO PCI Card	PCI\VEN_11C1&DEV_AB20
Symbol LA-41x3 Spectrum24 Wireless LAN PCI Card	PCI\VEN_1562&DEV_0001
Symbol LA-5030 Wireless Networker 802.11a/g CardBus Adapter	PCI\VEN_1562&DEV_0002&SUBSYS_00001562
Symbol LA-5033 Wireless Networker 802.11a/g PCI Adapter	PCI\VEN_1562&DEV_0003&SUBSYS_00001562
Wireless Cardbus Card Model 1102	PCI\VEN_11C1&DEV_AB11&SUBSYS_AB1211C1&REV_01
Wireless Cardbus Card Model 1102	PCI\VEN_11C1&DEV_AB11&SUBSYS_AB1211C1&REV_02
Wireless Cardbus Card Model 1106	PCI\VEN_11C1&DEV_AB11&SUBSYS_AB1511C1&REV_02
Wireless CB54G3/MP54G3 Wireless LAN Card	PCI\VEN_17FE&DEV_2220&SUBSYS_68551462
Wireless CB54G3/MP54G3 Wireless LAN Card	PCI\VEN_17FE&DEV_2220&SUBSYS_68631462
Wireless Mini PCI Card Model 0506	PCI\VEN_11C1&DEV_AB30&SUBSYS_AB3011C1&REV_00
Wireless Mini PCI Card Model 0508	PCI\VEN_11C1&DEV_AB34&SUBSYS_AB3411C1&REV_00
Wireless Mini PCI Card Model 0509	PCI\VEN_11C1&DEV_AB10&SUBSYS_AB1011C1&REV_00
Wireless Mini PCI Card Model 0509	PCI\VEN_11C1&DEV_AB10&SUBSYS_AB1011C1&REV_01
Wireless Mini PCI Card Model 0511	PCI\VEN_11C1&DEV_AB11&SUBSYS_AB1111C1&REV_00

Product Name	HWID
Wireless Mini PCI Card Model 0511	PCI\VEN_11C1&DEV_AB11&SUBSYS_AB1111C1&REV_01
Wireless Mini PCI Card Model 0512	PCI\VEN_11C1&DEV_AB11&SUBSYS_AB1311C1&REV_01
Wireless Mini PCI Card Model 506	PCI\VEN_11C1&DEV_AB30&SUBSYS_AB3011C1&REV_00
Wireless Mini PCI Card Model 508	PCI\VEN_11C1&DEV_AB34&SUBSYS_AB3411C1&REV_00
Wireless Mini PCI Card Model 509	PCI\VEN_11C1&DEV_AB10&SUBSYS_AB1011C1&REV_01
Wireless Mini PCI Card Model 511	PCI\VEN_11C1&DEV_AB11&SUBSYS_AB1111C1&REV_02
Wireless Mini PCI Card Model 512	PCI\VEN_11C1&DEV_AB11&SUBSYS_AB1311C1&REV_02
Wireless Mini PCI Card Model 516	PCI\VEN_11C1&DEV_AB11&SUBSYS_AB1611C1&REV_02
Wireless PCI Adapter Model 0901	PCI\VEN_11C1&DEV_AB21
Wireless PCI Adapter Model 0901	PCI\VEN_11C1&DEV_AB21&SUBSYS_AB2111C1&REV_00
Wireless-B PCI Adapter	PCI\VEN_17FE&DEV_2120&SUBSYS_00201737
Wireless-G Notebook Adapter v.2.0	PCI\VEN_104C&DEV_9066&SUBSYS_00331737
Wireless-G Notebook Adapter ver.4.0	PCI\VEN_17FE&DEV_2220&SUBSYS_00291737
Wireless-G Notebook Adapter with SRX	PCI\VEN_17CB&DEV_0001&SUBSYS_00371737
Wistron NeWeb 802.11b Wireless LAN PCI Card	PCI\VEN_1260&DEV_3873&SUBSYS_107B17C0

Summary

Windows Vista constitutes, in many ways, a break with the past, but that doesn't necessarily mean you have to make a break with your existing hardware just yet. Using Microsoft's Windows Vista Upgrade Advisor, you can determine whether your current PC is powerful enough to run Windows Vista and, if so, which of your existing hardware devices will work properly after the upgrade. Then, using the secrets discussed in this chapter, you can often get even unsupported hardware working properly with Vista. If none of that works, well, what can you do? Windows Vista is an entirely new operating system after all.

Part II

Understanding the Windows Vista User Experience

What's New in the Windows Vista User Interface

◆ ◆

In This Chapter

Exploring the various Windows Vista user experiences

Understanding what you need to run Windows Vista Aero

Examining the Windows Vista shell with Explorer

◆ ◆

Gazing upon Windows Vista for the first time, you will immediately be struck by how different everything looks when compared to older Windows versions such as Windows XP and Windows 2000. Now, windows are translucent and glass-like, with subtle animations and visual cues. This new interface leaves no doubt: Windows Vista is a major new Windows version, with much to learn and explore. In this chapter, we'll examine the new Windows Vista user interface, called Aero, and explain what you need to know to adapt to this new system.

Understanding the Windows Vista User Experience

When the first PC hit the streets over 20 years ago, users were saddled with an unfriendly, nonintuitive user interface based on the MS-DOS command line and its ubiquitous C:\ prompt. Since then, computer user interfaces have come a long way, first with the advent of the mouse-driven graphical user interface (GUI) on the Macintosh and later in Windows, and then with the proliferation of Internet connectivity in the late 1990s, which blurred the line between local and remote content.

Over the years, Microsoft has done much to evolve the state of the art of computer GUIs for the masses. Windows 95 introduced the notion of right-clicking on objects to discover context-sensitive options. Windows 98 introduced a shell, Explorer, that was based on the same code found in Internet Explorer. And Windows XP began a trend toward task-oriented user interfaces, with folder views that changed based on the content you were viewing or selected.

In Windows Vista, the Windows user interface, or as Microsoft likes to call it, the Windows user experience, has evolved yet again. Assuming you are running the proper Vista product edition (Windows Vista Home Basic and Starter editions need not apply) and have the right kind of display hardware, you'll be presented with a translucent, glass-like interface that takes the Windows user interface metaphor to its logical conclusion. That's right: In Windows Vista, windows actually appear to be made of glass just like real windows.

At a higher level, however, it may be comforting to understand that much in Windows Vista has not changed. That is, you still press a Start button to launch the Start Menu, from where you can perform tasks such as launching applications, accessing the Control Panel, networking features, and other related functionality, and turn off the system. A taskbar still runs along the bottom of the Windows Vista desktop, containing buttons for each open window and application. A system tray still sits in the lower-right corner of the screen, full of notification icons and the system clock. The desktop still contains icons and shortcuts. Windows still appear to float above this desktop, and all of your familiar applications and documents will still work. The high-end Windows Vista Aero user experience is shown in Figure 4-1.

Figure 4-1: If the Windows Gods allow it, you'll see this high-end user experience in Windows Vista.

Secret

What you see in Windows Vista depends largely on the version of Vista you're using, the hardware that's in your system, and your own personal preferences. More confusing, perhaps, is that you likely won't see options for all four of the user experiences Microsoft offers in Vista. However, the method you use for changing between these experiences is the same for all Vista product editions except for Starter edition: You need to access the classic Appearance Settings dialog box, which will look familiar if you're used to previous Windows versions. To access this dialog box, right-click the desktop and choose Personalize. Then, click the Visual Appearance link in the Personalize appearance and sound effects control panel window that appears. Then, click the link titled Open classic appearance properties. (Whew!)

This dialog box enables you to switch between what Microsoft still calls, disconcertingly, color schemes (see Figure 4-2). Windows Vista Aero is the high-end user experience, and the one you'll likely want (it's not available in Vista Home Basic or Starter). Windows Vista Basic is the simplest version of the new user interface, and it is available to all Vista editions, including Starter. Windows Vista Standard (not to be confused with the Windows Standard color scheme) is available only in Windows Vista Home Basic, so many readers will not see this choice. And Windows Classic is available to all Vista editions. All of the color schemes except for Windows Vista Aero, Windows Vista Standard, and Windows Vista Basic actually utilize the Classic user experience.

continues

continued

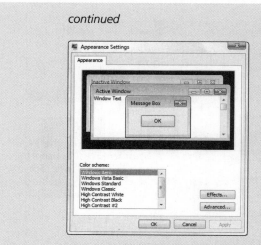

Figure 4-2: The Appearance Settings dialog box is pretty well hidden, but it's the secret to switching between various user experience types.

Table 4-1 summarizes the different user experiences and which product editions you'll need to access them.

Table 4-1: Which User Experiences Work in Which Windows Vista Product Editions

User Experience	Available in which Windows Vista product editions
Windows Vista Classic	All
Windows Vista Basic	All
Windows Vista Standard	Home Basic only
Windows Vista Aero	Home Premium, Business, Enterprise, Ultimate

There are other requirements for some of these user experiences, however. In the sections that follow, we'll highlight the different user experiences that Microsoft has included in Windows Vista, and explain how and when you might see them.

Windows Classic

Like Windows XP, Windows Vista includes a user experience called Windows Classic that resembles the user interfaces that Microsoft shipped with Windows 95, 98, Me, and 2000 (it most closely resembles Windows 2000). This interface is available on all Windows Vista product editions, including Starter edition. Classic is included in Windows Vista almost solely for businesses that don't want to undergo the expense of retraining their employees to use the newer user experiences.

Secret

Even though Microsoft markets Windows Classic as being identical to the Windows 2000 look and feel, the truth is that there are numerous differences, so users will still require some training when moving to Windows Vista and Classic mode. For example, the Start Menu and Explorer windows still retain the layouts that debuted with Windows Vista, and not the styles you might be used to in Windows 2000. However, you can fix this somewhat. To use the old Start Menu, right-click the Start button and choose Properties. Then, select the option titled Classic Start menu and then click OK. It's a bit more complicated to use a Windows Explorer look and feel that is closer to that of Windows 2000. To do so, open Computer from the Start Menu and then press the Alt key to display the Classic menu (which is disabled by default in Windows Vista). Select Folder Options from the Tools menu to display the Folder Options dialog. Then, select the option titled Use Windows classic folders and click OK. *Voilà!* Your system should now look a bit more like Windows 2000, as seen in Figure 4-3.

Figure 4-3: Windows Classic lets Vista users enjoy the Windows 2000 user interface.

Secret If you work in the IT department of a business that is considering deploying Windows Vista, you can actually roll out a feature called Classic Mode via Group Policy (GP) that does, in fact, configure Windows Vista to look almost exactly like Windows 2000. Classic Mode essentially combines the Classic user experience with the secrets mentioned previously.

Windows Vista Basic

Windows Vista Basic is the entry-level desktop user experience in Windows Vista and the one you're going to see on Windows Vista Home Basic or in other editions if you don't meet certain hardware requirements, which we'll discuss in just a bit. From a technological perspective, Windows Vista Basic renders the Windows desktop in roughly the same way as does Windows XP, meaning it doesn't take advantage of Vista's new graphical prowess. That said, Vista Basic still provides many unique Vista features such as integrated desktop search — available via a search box in the upper right corner of every Explorer window — and Live Icons, which show live previews of the contents of document files. The Windows Vista Basic user experience is shown in Figure 4-4.

Secret Windows Vista Basic isn't as attractive as Windows Vista Aero, but there are actually advantages to using it. For starters, it does perform better than Aero, so it's a good bet for lower-end computers. Notebook and Tablet PC users will notice that Vista Basic actually provides better battery life than Aero, too. So if you're on the road and not connected to a power source, Vista Basic is a thriftier choice if you're trying to maximize runtime.

On the flipside, Windows Vista Basic has a few major if non-obvious disadvantages. Because it uses XP-era display rendering techniques, Windows Vista Basic is not as reliable as Aero and could thus lead to system crashes and even Blue Screen crashes because of poorly written display drivers. Aero display drivers are typically far more reliable, and the Aero display itself is inherently superior to that offered by Basic.

Secret Even if you are running Windows Vista Aero, you may still run into the occasional issue that causes the display to flash and suddenly revert back to Windows Vista Basic. For example, some applications (like Apple QuickTime Player 7) aren't compatible with Windows Vista Aero; when you run such an application, the user experience will revert to Windows Vista Basic. When you close the offending application, Aero returns. In other cases, certain applications that use custom window rendering will actually display in a Windows Vista Basic style, even though all of the other windows in the system are utilizing Aero. These are the issues you have to deal with when Microsoft makes such a dramatic change to the Windows rendering engine, apparently.

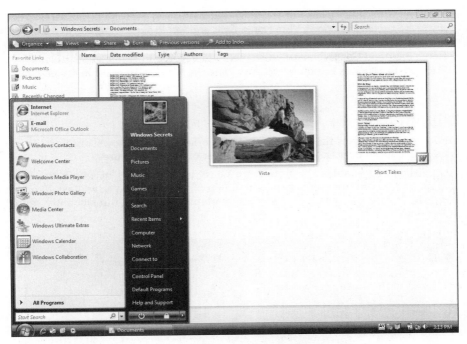

Figure 4-4: Even Windows Vista Basic is capable of displaying Live Icons.

Windows Vista Standard

This oddball user experience is designed specifically for Vista Home Basic users and is an olive branch, of a sort, to those who have the hardware required to run Vista Aero but cannot do so because that user experience is not included in Home Basic.

Secret

Windows Vista Standard has the same hardware requirements as Aero, which we'll examine in the next section.

Vista Standard is essentially a compromise between Vista Basic and Vista Aero. That is, it combines the look and feel of Vista Basic with the underlying display technologies utilized by Aero. Put another way, Vista Standard provides the glitch-free rendering and reliability users will experience with Aero, but using the less attractive Windows Vista Basic UI.

tip If you are running Windows Vista Home Basic and would like to upgrade to Aero, you'll need to utilize Vista's unique Windows Anytime Upgrade service — available to Vista Home Basic and Home Premium customers — to upgrade to Windows Vista Home Premium or Ultimate Edition. We discuss Windows Anytime Upgrade in Chapter 2.

Windows Vista Aero

Windows Vista Aero is the premium user experience in Windows Vista and the one most users will want to access. It provides a number of unique features.

First, Vista Aero enables the new Aero Glass look and feel in which the Start Menu, taskbar, and all onscreen windows and dialog boxes take on a new glass-like translucent sheen. In Figure 4-5, you can see how overlapping objects translucently reveal what's underneath.

Figure 4-5: The Aero Glass effect provides a heightened sense of depth and a more professional looking user experience.

Aero Glass is designed to move the visual focus away from the windows themselves and to the content they contain. Whether that effort is successful is open to debate, but it's certainly true that window borders lose the vast, dark-colored title bars of previous Windows versions and provide a softer-looking container around window contents. Compare Windows XP's My Computer window to Windows Vista's Computer window in Figure 4-6.

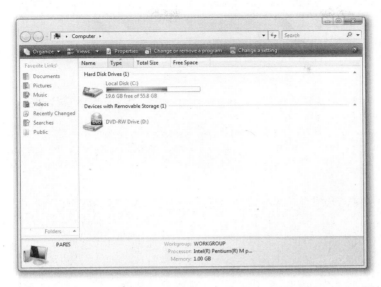

Figure 4-6: In Windows XP, too much of the visual focus is on the title bar, whereas the software window chrome in Windows Vista puts the focus on the contents of the window.

tip When you have a lot of Aero windows open onscreen, it's often hard to tell which one is on top, or has the focus. Typically, that window will have a bright red Close window button, while lower windows will not.

When you utilize the Windows Vista Aero user experience, you will receive other benefits. Certain Windows Vista features, for example, are available only when you're using Aero. Windows Flip and Flip 3D, two new task-switching features, are available only in Aero. Windows Flip 3D is shown in Figure 4-7.

Secret Windows Flip and Flip 3D are made available via keyboard shortcuts. To use Windows Flip, hold down the Alt key and tap the Tab key to cycle between all of the running applications and open windows. To use Flip 3D, hold down the Windows key and tap the Tab key to cycle between these windows.

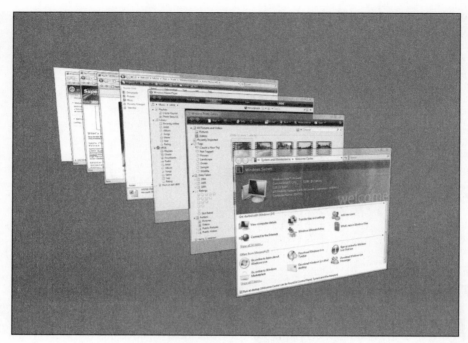

Figure 4-7: Flip 3D lets you visually inspect all of the running tasks and pick the window you want.

Aero also enables dynamic window animations, so that when you minimize a window to the taskbar, it subtly animates to show you exactly where it went. This kind of functionality was actually first introduced in Windows 95, but it has been made more subtle and fluid in Windows Vista. Additionally, Aero enables Live Taskbar Thumbnails: When you mouse over buttons in the taskbar, a small thumbnail preview will pop up, letting you see the window without having to actually activate it first, as shown in Figure 4-8.

Figure 4-8: Live Taskbar Thumbnails make it possible to preview windows without maximizing or bringing them to the forefront.

In addition to its obvious visual charms, Windows Vista Aero also offers lower-level improvements that will lead to a more reliable desktop experience than you might be used to with previous Windows versions. Thanks to new graphics architecture that's based on DirectX videogame libraries, Windows Vista can move windows across the screen without any visual tearing or glitches that were common in Windows XP. The effect is most prominent in windows with animated content, such as when you're playing a video in Windows Media Player (WMP). But it's not just about looks. Windows Aero is simply more reliable than the other user experiences. To understand why that's so, we'll need to examine Aero's strict hardware and software requirements.

Windows Vista Aero requirements

As noted earlier, you have to be running an activated version of Vista Home Premium, Business, Enterprise, or Ultimate Edition in order to utilize Windows Vista Aero. Here, *activated* refers to the Product Activation feature that's included in Windows Vista, whereby each Windows Vista installation is guaranteed, via a service called Windows Genuine Advantage, to be legitimate and not pirated. Most copies of Windows Vista that are preinstalled on new PCs come pre-activated, so this is a step that many users won't have to worry about. However, if you purchase a retail version of Windows Vista, you'll need to activate it.

cross ref   **We discuss this process in Chapter 2.**

Next, your display adapter must meet certain technical requirements. It must support DirectX 9.0 with Pixel Shader 2 in hardware and be supported by a new Windows Display Driver Model (WDDM) driver. The WDDM driver requirement is part of the reason Aero is so much more reliable than other Vista user experiences: To become WDDM certified, a driver must pass certain Microsoft tests aimed around making these drivers of higher quality.

Additionally, your graphics card must have enough dedicated memory (RAM) to drive your display. Table 4-2 explains how much video RAM you'll need to run Windows Vista Aero at particular screen resolutions.

Table 4-2: How Much Video RAM You'll Need to Drive Certain Resolutions

Video RAM	Display resolution
64 MB	Lower than 1280×1024 (fewer than 1,310,720 pixels)
128 MB	1280×1024 to 1920×1200 (1,310,720 to 2,304,000 pixels)
256 MB	Higher than 1920×1200 (more than 2,304,000 pixels)

Secret

Microsoft makes these requirements sound so difficult. But the truth is, virtually every single 3D graphics card on the market, as well as Intel's Graphics Media Accelerator 950 integrated graphics chipset, is capable of running Windows Vista Aero. And most of today's graphics cards come with at least 128 MB of RAM. Note, however, that most older integrated graphics chipsets, such as those found on most notebooks and Tablet PCs sold before 2005, are not compatible with Vista Aero. Furthermore, in order to obtain Aero on a system with integrated graphics, at least 512 MB of system RAM must be available after the integrated graphics reserves whatever it needs.

Configuring Windows Vista Aero

If you're not a big fan of the translucent glass effects provided by Windows Vista Aero but would still like to take advantage of the other unique features and reliability offered by this user experience, take heart. Microsoft has nicely provided a handy configuration utility to Aero that enables you to fine-tune how it looks.

This functionality is available via the Personalization section of the Control Panel. The quickest way to get there is to right-click a blank area of the desktop, choose Properties, and then select Windows Color and Appearance from the Personalize appearance and sound effects control panel. This window, shown in Figure 4-9, enables you to change various aspects of Aero's visual style.

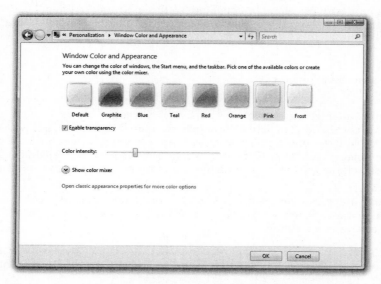

Figure 4-9: Change the color scheme or transparency of Aero windows with this utility.

First, you can pick between preset color choices by selecting one of the color scheme swatches shown at the top of the window. You can also disable transparent glass (really translucency) or vary the intensity of the translucency to meet your liking. Finally, you can expand the Show color mixer option and apply varying levels of color, saturation, and brightness to achieve just the look and feel you want.

---

tip

In our experience, most of the preset color choices just make Aero windows look dirty. The exception is Frost, which is very clean looking. You might also find some success with varying the intensity of the translucency effect or by just disabling it all together.

Exploring with the Windows Vista Explorer Shell

Regardless of which user experience you choose, you're going to notice a number of visual and functional changes as you begin navigating around Windows Vista at first. In this section, we'll highlight the most important changes you should be aware of and help you find some old favorites that have been lost in the transition.

Start Menu

The Start menu, shown in Figure 4-10, has been enhanced since Windows XP to make it easier to use and better looking. Like its predecessor, you access the Start Menu by pressing the Start button, which now resembles a rounded Windows flag, and does not include the word Start.

Figure 4-10: The Windows Vista Start Menu.

As with the Windows XP Start Menu, the Vista Start Menu is divided vertically into two halves. On the left half are a list of your most-recently used applications; on top of that, two application types—Web browser and e-mail—are pinned so that they're always accessible. On the right is a list of special shell folders and other system locations and tasks that you might need to access frequently.

Secret

You can modify the upper-left portion of the Start Menu in two ways. First, you can determine which web browser and e-mail application appear in these special locations. To do so, right-click the Start button, choose Properties, and then click the Customize button in the Start Menu Properties dialog box. In the Customize Start Menu dialog box that appears, pick the web browser and e-mail applications you prefer from the drop-down lists next to Internet link and E-mail link, respectively. Or, deselect either or both options if you don't want them to appear on the Start Menu.

You can also drag your favorite applications into this area and "pin" them permanently. To do so, select the shortcut you want to pin from the Start Menu and drag it up above the line that separates the Internet and email links from the most recently used application list. To remove a shortcut from this area, right-click it and choose Remove from this list.

Accessing All Programs

At the bottom of the most recently used applications list, you'll see the familiar All Programs link. However, in Windows Vista, this link behaves quite differently than does the All Programs link in Windows XP, which launches a cascading series of menus when clicked. Now, in Windows Vista, this link expands the Start Menu's All Programs submenu directly within the Start Menu itself. As with XP, you don't have to click the link to make it happen. Instead, you can simply mouse-over it. In Figure 4-11, you can see how the All Programs submenu opens up inside of the Start Menu, temporarily replacing the most frequently used application list.

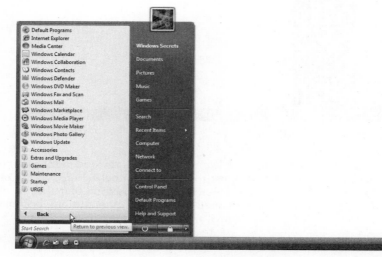

Figure 4-11: No more fumbling with cascading menus.

Secret

There are a couple reasons why this change was made. First, it eliminates the some-times maddening pause that would occur in Windows XP when you clicked or moused-over the All Programs link. Secondly, many users found the cascading menu system used previously to be hard to navigate. How many times have you expanded submenu after submenu, only to inadvertently move the mouse cursor off the menu, only to cause the whole thing to shut down? It's happened to the best of us.

To navigate through the various submenus linked to from All Programs, you simply have to click various folders. When you do so, the menu expands, in place, and scroll bars appear so you can moved around within the menu structure. As you can see in Figure 4-12, sub-menus that expand within the current view are easier to navigate than cascading menus.

Figure 4-12: With the new Start Menu, you never have to worry about losing your place.

Secret

Keyboard users can easily navigate the new Start Menu as well. To do so, click the Windows key or the Ctrl+Esc keyboard shortcut to open the Start Menu. Then, press the Up Arrow key once to highlight All Programs. To expand All Programs, press the Right Arrow key. Then, use the arrow keys to navigate around the list of shortcuts and folders. Anytime you want to expand a submenu (indicated by a folder icon), press the Right Arrow key. To close, or contract, a submenu, press the Left Arrow key.

Searching for Applications

One of the most important new features in Windows Vista is its integrated search functionality. Although you might think that this feature is limited only to finding documents and music files, you can actually use it for a variety of things, and depending on where you are in the Vista interface, those searches will be context sensitive. So when you search from the Start Menu's new Search box, located on the left side of the menu underneath All Programs, you will be typically searching for applications. You can also use this functionality to quickly launch applications, when you know their names.

Secret

The Search Menu's search feature doesn't just search applications. You can also use it to search Internet Explorer Favorites or History. Alternatively, you can search the Internet or the local file system. To do so, type in a search query and then click either the Search the Internet or Search the computer links that appear. Search results from these searches will appear in separate windows (Internet searches in your default Web browser and computer searches in a Windows Explorer window). To find out more about searching the file system and constructing your own saved searches, please refer to Chapter 5.

Here's how it works. When you open the Start Menu and begin typing, whatever you type is automatically placed in the search box. So let's say you want to run Notepad. You could always click the Start button, expand All Programs, expand Accessories, and then click on the Notepad icon. Or, you could tap the Windows key and just type **notepad**. As you type, applications that match the text appear in a list, as shown in Figure 4-13. When you see the application you want, use the arrow keys (or mouse cursor) to select it, and then Notepad will start normally.

Figure 4-13: New integrated search feature makes short work of finding the application you want.

Secret

Microsoft thinks that this new search feature will replace the old Run command that appeared in previous versions of the Start Menu. And for the most part they're right. But it's possible that some users would prefer to use the old Run command, which brings up a small dialog box and maintains a history of previously accessed commands. Good news: You can turn it on. To enable the Run command, right-click the Start Menu, choose Properties, and then click the Customize button. Scroll down the list until you see the Run command option and then select it. Click OK and then OK again, and you'll see that the Run command is back where it belongs.

Accessing Special Shell Folders and System Locations

On the right side of the Start Menu, you'll see a list of commands that are vaguely similar to what appeared on the XP Start Menu. However, many of the names have changed. For example, My Documents is now Documents, My Pictures is now Pictures, My Music is now Music, My Computer is now Computer, and My Network Places is now Network. There are some new items, too, as well as some missing items that were present in XP.

The first thing you may notice in this area is the addition of a new command, which has the same name as your user account. If you're logged on as Sally, the first link on the right side of the Start Menu will also be named Sally. When you click this link, it will open an Explorer window displaying the contents of your user folder, which contains folders such as Documents, Pictures, Music, and so on. It's unclear to us why you would ever need to access this folder, except in rare circumstances. For this reason, you may simply want to remove it from the Start Menu and replace it with a more frequently-needed command. We cover Start Menu customization in the next section.

The Games link is also new to Windows Vista. This opens the new Games Explorer, which provides access to both games that came with Windows and those you might purchase separately.

**cross
ref**

We examine Vista's Games functionality in Chapter 14.

tip

One feature some people might miss with the new Start Menu is the ability to quickly cause the system to shut down, restart, sleep, or hibernate using just the keyboard. In Windows XP, you could tap the Windows key, press U, and then U for shutdown, R for restart, S for sleep, or H for hibernate (the latter of which was a hidden option). Because of the new integrated search feature in the Windows Vista Start Menu, these shortcuts no longer work. However, you can still perform these actions with the keyboard in Windows Vista. Now, however, you have to tap the Windows key and then press the Right Arrow key three times to activate the Lock this computer submenu, which provides options for the aforementioned options as well as Switch User, Log Off, Lock, and, if you have a notebook computer with a docking station, Undock.

Start Menu Customization

While the Windows Vista Start Menu is a big improvement over its predecessor, you will likely want to customize it to match your needs. We've already discussed how you access this functionality: Right-click the Start button, choose Properties, and then click the Customize button. Table 4-3 summarizes the options that are available to you.

Table 4-3: Start Menu Customization Options

Start Menu Option	What It Does	Default Value
Computer	Determines whether the Computer item appears as a link or menu, or is not displayed. This was called My Computer in Windows XP.	Display as a link
Connect To	Determines whether the Connect To item appears. If you have a wireless network adapter, this item will trigger a submenu.	Enabled
Control Panel	Determines whether the Control Panel item appears as a link or menu, or is not displayed.	Display as a link
Default Programs	Determines whether the Default Program item appears. This item was called Set Program Access and Defaults in Windows XP with Service Pack 2. In Windows Vista, it launches the new Default Programs control panel.	Enabled
Documents	Determines whether the Documents item appears as a link or menu, or is not displayed. This was called My Documents in Windows XP.	Display as a link
Enable dragging and dropping	Determines whether you can drag and drop icons around the Start Menu in order to change the way they are displayed.	Enabled
Favorites menu	Determines whether the Favorites menu item appears.	Disabled
Games	Determines whether the Games item appears as a link or menu, or is not displayed.	Enabled
Help	Determines whether the Help item appears. This item launches Help and Support.	Enabled
Highlight newly installed programs	Determines whether newly installed applications are highlighted so you can find them easier.	Enabled
Local User Storage	Determines whether the User Name item appears as a link or menu, or is not displayed.	Enabled
Music	Determines whether the Music item appears as a link or menu, or is not displayed. This was called My Music in Windows XP.	Enabled
Network	Determines whether the Network item appears as a link or menu, or is not displayed. This was called My Network Places in Windows XP.	Enabled

Start Menu Option	What It Does	Default Value
Open submenus when I pause on them with the mouse pointer	Determines whether mousing over a submenu (like All Programs) will cause that submenu to open (or expand).	Enabled
Pictures	Determines whether the Pictures item appears as a link or menu, or is not displayed.	Enabled
Printers	Determines whether the Printers menu item appears.	Disabled
Run command	Determines whether the Run command item appears.	Disabled
Search	Determines whether the Search item appears. This item launches a Windows Explorer search window.	Enabled
Search box	Determines whether the Start Menu's integrated search box appears.	Enabled
Search Communications	Determines whether the Start Menu's integrated search box searches for communications (e-mail, contacts, instant messaging messages).	Enabled
Search Files	Determines whether the Start Menu's integrated search box searches for files and, if so, whether to search all files or just the current user's files.	Enabled
Search Programs	Determines whether the Start Menu's integrated search box searches for applications.	Enabled
Sort All Programs menu by name	Determines whether the All Programs submenu is organized alphabetically.	Enabled
System Administrative Tools	Determines whether the System Administrative Tools item appears on the All Programs menu, on the All Programs menu and the Start Menu, or is not displayed.	Disabled
Use large icons	Determines whether the left side of the Start Menu renders large icons. Otherwise, small icons will be used.	Enabled

Advanced Start Menu Customization

One of the features of the Start Menu that's not immediately obvious is that it is composed of items from the following two different locations, both of which are hidden by default:

◆ **Within your user profile:** By default, C:\Users*Your User Name*\AppData\Roaming\Microsoft\Windows\Start Menu

◆ **Inside the profile for the Public user account that is common (or public) to all users:** Typically, C:\ProgramData\Microsoft\Windows\Start Menu

If you navigate to these locations with Windows Explorer, you can drill down into the folder structures and shortcuts that make up your own Start Menu. What's odd is that these two locations are combined, or aggregated, to form the Start Menu you access every day.

tip You can also access these folders by right-clicking on the Start button. To access your own private portion of the Start Menu, choose Open from the right-click menu. To access the Public portion of the Start Menu, choose Open All Users.

So why would you want to access these locations? Although it's possible to customize the Start Menu by dragging and dropping shortcuts like you might have done with Windows XP, that can get tedious. Instead, you could simply access these folders directly, move things around as you see fit, all while opening the Start Menu occasionally to make sure you're getting the results you expect. For example, you might want to create handy subfolders such as Digital Media, Internet, and Utilities, rather than accept the default structure.

Secret

Be careful when you customize the Start Menu this way. Any changes you make to the Public Start Menu structure will affect any other users that log on to your PC as well.

Desktop

At first glance, the Windows Vista desktop looks very similar to that of Windows XP. Well, looks can be deceiving. In fact, Microsoft has made some much-overdue and quite welcome changes to the Windows desktop, although of course with these changes comes a new set of skills to master.

For the most part, you access desktop options through the pop-up menu that appears when you right-click an empty part of the Windows desktop. In Windows XP, this menu had options such as Arrange Icons By, Refresh, Paste, Paste Shortcut, Undo, New, and Properties. In Windows Vista, naturally, this has all changed.

At the top of the right-click menu is a new submenu, called View, which is shown in Figure 4-14. This submenu enables you to configure features Windows users have been asking about for years: You can now switch between Large Icons, Medium Icons, and Classic Icons. You can also select auto-arrange and alignment options, and hide the desktop icons all together, as you could in XP.

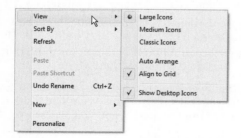

Figure 4-14: Something old, something new: Microsoft changes menus arbitrarily again, but this time at least we get some new functionality.

The Sort submenu is similar to the top part of the Windows XP Arrange Icons By submenu. Here, we get sorting options for Name, Size, File extension (previously called Type) and Date modified. The Refresh, Paste, Paste Shortcut, Undo, and New items all carry over from XP as well.

At the bottom of the right-click menu, however, is another new option, dubbed Personalize. This replaces the Properties option from XP and now displays the Control Panel's Personalization section when selected. From here, you can access a wide range of personalization options, only some of which have anything to do with the desktop.

Secret

One of the big questions you likely have, of course, is what the heck happened to the familiar Display Properties dialog box that's graced every version of Windows from Windows 95 to Windows XP? Sadly, that dialog box is gone, but pieces of it can be found throughout the Personalization control panel if you know where to look. In Table 4-4, we'll show you how to find the different sections, or tabs, of the old Display Properties dialog box, which have been effectively scattered to the winds.

It's unclear whether Windows Vista's approach is better, but if you're looking for XP Display Properties features, you really have to know where to look.

Table 4-4: Where to Find Old Display Properties Tabs in Windows Vista

Display Properties Tab	Where It Is in Windows Vista
Themes	Control Panel, Personalization, Themes
Desktop	Replaced by the new Desktop Background window, found at Control Panel, Personalization, Desktop Background
Screen Saver	Control Panel, Personalization, Screen Saver
Appearance	Control Panel, Personalization, Visual Appearance, Open classic appearance properties
Settings	Control Panel, Personalization, Display Settings

Secret

The Desktop tab of the Display Properties dialog box in Windows XP had a Customize Desktop button that launched a Desktop Items dialog box from which you could configure which icons appeared on the desktop and other related options. But in Windows Vista, the Desktop tab has been replaced with the new Desktop Background window, which does not provide a link to this functionality. To access the Desktop Icon Properties dialog box, as it's now known, you must open Control Panel, choose Appearance and Personalization, Personalization, and then choose Change desktop icons from the Tasks list on the left. Some functionality, however, is missing. You can no longer run the Desktop Cleanup Wizard or place Web items on your desktop, as you could in XP.

Taskbar

In Windows Vista, the system taskbar works similarly to the way it did in Windows XP. Every time you open an application or Explorer window, you will see a new button appear in the taskbar. When you click one these buttons, the selected window comes to the forefront. If that window was already at the forefront, it will be minimized. If you have numerous open windows from the same application—like you might with Internet Explorer—the taskbar will group these buttons into a pop-up list, just like it did in Windows XP. And when you right-click a taskbar button, you see a menu that is identical to that in XP.

Other features carry over from XP as well. When you right-click a blank area of the taskbar, you get a pop-up menu with links to enable toolbars, arrange desktop windows in various ways, show the desktop, access the Task Manager, toggle taskbar locking, and access the Taskbar and Start Menu Properties dialog box, from which you can configure various taskbar options. This dialog box is shown in Figure 4-15.

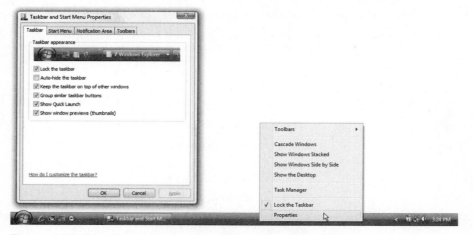

Figure 4-15: From here, you can customize certain taskbar features.

What's new is that you can get Live Thumbnail Previews when you mouse over taskbar buttons, which was shown back in Figure 4-8. To enable this feature, the option Show Thumbnails must be enabled, which it is by default. Note, too, that the Notification area options have been moved to a new tab of this dialog in Windows Vista. Not coincidentally, we'll look at this feature next.

Secret

Though the taskbar sits on the bottom of the Windows desktop by default, you can actually drag it to any of the other three screen borders should you so desire. To do so, right-click the taskbar and uncheck Lock the Taskbar. Then, simply use your well-honed drag-and-drop skills to drag the taskbar to a screen edge—you can also resize it as you see fit, so that it occupies multiple lines vertically, or is whatever width you like horizontally. Recheck the Lock the Taskbar option to ensure that you don't accidentally move it again.

Notification Area and System Clock

Way back in Windows 95, Microsoft introduced a number of user interface conventions that still exist in Windows Vista. These include, among others, the Start button and Start Menu, the taskbar, the Windows Explorer windows, and the notification area, which sits at the right end of the taskbar by default. You'll typically see two types of items here: The system clock and various notification icons. Some of these icons are installed by default with Windows, such as the volume control, the network icon, Safely Remove Hardware, and others. Other icons can be installed by third-party applications. For example, Apple's QuickTime Player and many security applications install tray icons.

As the name suggests, the tray is designed for notifications and shouldn't be used as a taskbar replacement although some developers try to use it that way for some reason (some applications inexplicably minimize to the tray rather than to the taskbar as they should). Applications like Windows Live Messenger and Microsoft Outlook, which need to alert the user to new instant messages, e-mails, or online contacts, also use the tray, and display small pop-up notification windows nearby.

Despite early plans to remove the notification area and replace it with a Sidebar panel, Microsoft has pretty much left this feature intact in Windows Vista. Not much has changed: You can now configure various notification area features—such as which system icons are displayed by default, and the display behavior of any notification icon on your system—from a new Notification Area tab in the Taskbar and Start Menu Properties dialog box. But that's about it.

One thing that has changed demonstrably is the system clock. In Windows Vista, this feature is now dramatically better than its XP relation. At first glance, it's not obvious what's changed. The clock displays the time, as you'd expect. And if you mouse over the time display, a yellow balloon tip window appears, providing you with the day and date.

In Windows XP, you could access the system's Date and Time Properties dialog box by double-clicking the clock. This doesn't work in Windows Vista. Instead, you can single-click the clock to display a new pop-up window, shown in Figure 4-16, which provides a professionally formatted calendar and analog clock. And there's an option to display the new Date and Time Properties window.

Figure 4-16: Windows Vista includes a nice looking calendar and clock display that doesn't require you to open a dialog box.

When you click Date and Time Settings, you'll see the new Date and Time Properties window, as shown in Figure 4-17. Here, you can configure options you'd expect, such as date, time, and time zone. But you can also configure additional clock displays, which is an excellent feature for travelers or those who frequently need to communicate with people in different time zones.

Figure 4-17: The Date and Time Properties dialog box has been completely overhauled.

From the Additional Clocks tab of this dialog box, you can add up to two more clocks. Each clock gets its own time zone and optional display name. What's cool about this feature is the way it changes the clock displays. Now, when you mouse over the clock, you'll see a pop-up that lists data from all of your clocks, as shown in Figure 4-18.

Figure 4-18: You can configure up to three clocks in Windows Vista.

And when you click the clock, you'll see the nice display shown in Figure 4-19.

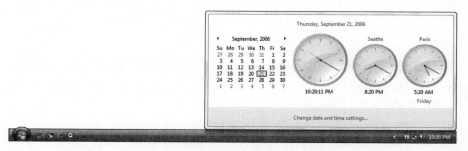

Figure 4-19: This handy and speedy time and date display can also handle up to three clocks.

Windows Vista Explorers

No discussion of the Windows Vista user experience would be complete without a look at the ways in which Microsoft has evolved Windows Explorer in this release. Windows Explorer first appeared in Windows 95, replacing the many horrible manager programs (File Manager, Program Manager, and so on) that plagued previous versions. It was a grand idea, but then Microsoft made the mistake of combining Internet Explorer with the Windows shell. Starting with an interim version of Windows 95, the Windows Explorer shell has been based on IE, and since then we've suffered through a decade of security vulnerabilities and the resulting patches.

In Windows Vista, that integration is a thing of the past. Windows Explorer has been completely overhauled, and although it's arguably better than the Explorer shell in Windows XP, it's also quite a bit different. Microsoft has also introduced some new terminology into the mix, just to keep us on our toes. So as My Documents is renamed to Documents in Windows Vista, Microsoft now refers to that window as the Documents Explorer. Likewise with all the other special folders: There are now explorers for Pictures, Music, applications, devices, and other objects.

From a usability perspective, much has changed since XP. Let's examine a typical Explorer window, as seen in Figure 4-20. The menu bar is gone, replaced by a hidden Classic Menu, which can be dynamically triggered by tapping the Alt key. The main toolbar is also gone, replaced by Back and Forward buttons, the new enhanced Address Bar, and the new integrated search box.

Figure 4-20: Like many user interface pieces in Windows Vista, Explorer windows have changed fairly dramatically.

Below those controls is a new user interface construct called the command bar, which includes context-sensitive commands, that replaces the old task pane from Windows XP Explorer. On the bottom is a new preview pane.

In the center of the window, you'll see a Navigation pane with collapsing Folders view, a large icon display area, and, optionally, a Reading pane. Let's see what all of these features do.

Classic Menu

One of the guiding principles in Windows Vista is simplification. In previous Windows versions, virtually every system window and application included a top menu structure. In Windows Vista, however, these menus are typically either nonexistent or are hidden. So the menu system is hidden by default. To display it temporarily, simply tap the Alt key. Or, you can enable it permanently by choosing Folder Options from the Tools menu, navigating to the View tab of the Folder Options dialog box, and enabling the option titled Always show Classic Menus. There's precious little reason to do this, however.

tip   The Classic Menus in Explorer are virtually identical to their XP counterparts. One major exception is that the Favorites menu does not appear in Vista, because IE is no longer integrated with the Windows shell.

Enhanced Address Bar

For the first time since Windows 95, the address bar gets a major overhaul in Windows Vista. Now, instead of the classic address bar view, the address bar is divided into drop-down menu nodes along the navigation path, making it easier than ever to move through the shell hierarchy. This is referred to as the *breadcrumb bar*.

To see how this works, open the Documents Explorer by clicking the Documents item in the Start Menu and observing the address bar. It is divided into three nodes, a folder, a node representing your user profile (Doris or whatever), and Documents. Each has a small arrow next to it, indicating that you can click there to trigger a drop-down menu.

To navigate to a folder that is at the same level in the shell hierarchy as the Documents folder, click the small arrow to the right of your user name. As you can see in Figure 4-21, a drop-down menu appears, showing you all the folders that are available inside of your user account folder. You can click any of these to navigate there immediately. Note that doing this in XP would require two steps. First, you'd have to click the Up toolbar button; then, you'd have to double-click the folder you wanted.

To simply move back up a level, click the node that is to the left of the current location. In this example we would click the node that is denoted by your user name.

Secret

To see the classic address bar, simply click a blank area of the enhanced address bar.

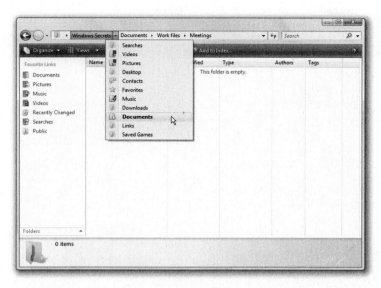

Figure 4-21: The new address bar makes it easier to move through the shell hierarchy.

Command Bar

The new command bar combines the functionality of XP Windows Explorer's toolbar and task panes in a new, less real estate–intensive place. Like the task pane in XP, portions of the command bar change depending on what items you are viewing or have selected. That is, the command bar is context sensitive.

That said, the following portions of the command bar will remain constant regardless of what you're viewing:

- ◆ **Organize button:** Appears in all Explorer windows and provides you with a drop-down menu from which you can perform common actions like create a new folder; cut, copy, paste, undo, and redo; select all; delete; rename; close; and get properties.
- ◆ **Layout submenu:** Enables you to determine which user interface elements appear in Explorer windows. These elements include Classic Menus (off by default), Search Pane (off by default except in the Search window), Preview Pane (on by default), Reading Pane (off by default), and the Navigation Pane (on by default).
- ◆ **Views button:** Lets you change the icon view style.

cross ref   This option is explored in Chapter 5.

The other options you see in the command bar will depend on the view and selection. For example, Figure 4-22 shows how the command bar changes in the Documents window when you select a document file.

Figure 4-22: The command bar provides options that are specific to what you're doing.

Instant Search

Windows Vista has search in the Start Menu, search in Internet Explorer, a new Search window, and it even has an instant search box in every Explorer window. The reason this is useful is that the instant search box is context sensitive. Sure, you could search your entire hard drive via the Search option in the Start Menu. But if you're in a folder, and you know that what you're looking for is in there somewhere, maybe in one of the subfolders, then the instant search box is the tool to use.

To search for a document or other file in the current folder or one of its subfolders, just click the search box and begin typing. Your results will begin appearing immediately. When the search results list is complete, you can also click a link titled Search for 'search query' in Index that will let you search the entire hard drive.

Navigation Pane

On the left of every Windows Explorer window by default is a new area called the Navigation pane. This pane features a list of common shell locations (like Documents, Pictures, Music, and the like) as well as any saved searches that are relevant to the current view. For example, The Documents folder includes a search folder called Recently Changed that will let you view only those documents that have recently been edited in some way.

At the bottom of the Navigation pane, you'll see a small panel named Folders. If you click the small arrow to the right, the Folders pane will expand into the Navigation pane, providing you with a traditional file explorer view.

Live Icons and Reading Pane

In Windows Vista, document icons are "live" and can provide you with a rich preview of their contents depending on which view style you're using. But even when you're using one of the smaller view styles, you can get live previews: Simply enable the Reading pane, and as you select individual documents, you'll see a preview in the Reading pane.

Preview Pane

By default, every Windows Explorer window includes a Preview pane at the bottom that provides a list of properties about the currently selected file or document. Previously, you would have to open the file's Properties sheet to view this information.

More to Come . . .

There's so much more to know about the Windows Vista Explorers, including various changes to the special shell folders, icon view styles, and saved searches. We will look at all of those features in the next chapter.

Secret

Although the Aero windows are pretty and translucent, they still include the same window controls we've come to expect from previous Windows versions. This is true of the window button, which used to be found to the left of the window title bar in previous Windows versions, where you could trigger a drop-down window with restore, move, size, minimize, maximize, and close options, or double-click it to close the window. It's there in Windows Vista. You just need to know where to click as shown in Figure 4-23.

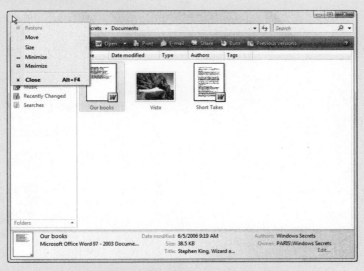

Figure 4-23: Yep, the window control button is still there.

Summary

Anyone who uses Windows Vista will need to deal with its user interface, which is both brand new in many ways and also extremely familiar to any who has used Windows XP. Like its XP predecessor, Windows Vista features a Start button and Start Menu, a taskbar, a tray notification area, and a desktop. But Vista goes beyond XP by improving each of these features while adding other unique features, new user experiences such as Windows Vista Basic and Standard and Windows Aero.

Where's My Stuff? Finding and Organizing Files

Chapter

5

◆ ◆ ◆ ◆ ◆ ◆ ◆ ◆ ◆ ◆ ◆ ◆ ◆ ◆ ◆ ◆ ◆ ◆

In This Chapter

Working with the Windows Vista file system

Understanding virtual folders

Finding the documents and files you want

Creating and using Search Folders

◆ ◆ ◆ ◆ ◆ ◆ ◆ ◆ ◆ ◆ ◆ ◆ ◆ ◆ ◆ ◆ ◆ ◆

Windows Vista includes an updated version of the Explorer file system that appeared in Windows XP. Like its predecessor, Windows Vista supports the notion of *special shell folders* where you can access such much-needed data files as documents, digital photos, digital music, and videos. However, Vista adds a number of new Explorer constructs, such as virtual folders called Search Folders, which are confusing but powerful when used correctly. In this chapter, you will explore the Windows shell and learn how to take advantage of the new features Microsoft added to Windows Vista.

Understanding Special Shell Folders

Most *Windows Vista Secrets* readers are probably familiar with basic computer file system concepts like files, folders, and drive letters. But you may not realize that certain locations in the Windows shell—that is, Windows Explorer, the application with which you literally explore the contents of your PC's hard drives—have been specially configured to work with particular data types. In Windows XP and previous Windows versions, these locations were called *special shell folders*, and they included such locations as My Documents, My Pictures, and My Music.

In Windows Vista, these special shell folders still exist, but now most of them have different names and are accompanied by a number of new members. These special shell folders are listed in Table 5-1.

Table 5-1: Special Shell Folders

Home	This special location is named after your user name. If you chose the user name Jan, for example, your Home folder will be named Jan as well. This folder is available as the top choice on the right-hand, fixed part of the Start menu. Although it was never obvious, every user actually had a Home folder in previous Windows versions. For example, your Home folder in Windows XP is typically located at C:\Documents and Settings\user name.
Contacts	A new addition to Windows Vista, Contacts acts as a central database for Vista's centralized contacts management, which is used by Windows Mail and can be used by any third-party application. We examine Contacts in Chapter 18.
Documents	A replacement for My Documents. This folder is specially configured to handle various document types, such as Word documents, text files, and the like. As with its predecessor, Documents is the default location for the Save and Save As dialog boxes in most applications.
Downloads	New to Windows Vista, this folder is the default location for files downloaded from the Web with Internet Explorer.
Favorites	A central repository for your Internet Explorer Favorites (or what other browsers typically call Bookmarks). The Favorites folder has been in Windows for several years.
Saved Games	A new addition to Windows Vista, the Saved Games folder is designed as a place for Vista-compatible game titles to store saved game information. We discuss Vista and video games in Chapter 14.
Pictures	A replacement for My Pictures. The Pictures folder is designed to handle digital photographs and other picture files.

Table 5-1: Special Shell Folders

Music	A replacement for My Music. The Music folder is designed to work with digital music and other audio files. If you rip music from an audio CD or purchase music from an online music service such as the Apple iTunes Music Store or MTV URGE, those files will typically be saved to your Music folder by default.
Searches	New to Windows Vista, this folder contains built-in and user-created saved searches. We examine this functionality later in this chapter.
Videos	A replacement for My Videos. This folder is designed to store digital videos of any kind, including home movies.

Each of the special shell folders in Windows Vista shares certain characteristics. First, they are all *physical folders* in the sense that they are represented by a specific location in the Windows shell hierarchy. For example, your Home folder is now found at C:\Users*username* by default. Likewise, Documents can be found at C:\Users*username*\Documents.

> **tip**   **In Windows XP, you had to run Windows Movie Maker once before the My Videos folder would appear. This is no longer the case in Windows Vista, where the new Videos folder is always available under each user's Home folder.**

Also, you might notice that the name of most of the folders (Saved Games is a curious exception) — and indeed the names of the folders above each of them in the shell path — has been stripped of spaces. That is, each folder is now a single word (*Documents* instead of *My Documents*). That's because of a renewed commitment to shell scripting in Windows Vista, an environment in which it's simply harder to deal with spaces. (See Chapter 22 for more information about Vista's scripting capabilities.)

Finally, many of the special shell folders is represented somewhat differently in the Windows shell than are other folders, which you might think of as normal physical folders. The Documents, Favorites, Music, and Pictures folders are all colored blue-green now instead of the normal yellow folder color. And although you can create a folder almost anywhere you'd like in the Windows Vista shell — assuming you have the security credentials to do so — special shell folders are typically only found in their preset locations within the file system.

Secret   Using tools such as TweakUI, it's possible to change the location of special shell folders. So, for example, you might redirect Videos to a separate hard disk to which you've dedicated space specifically for video content. For more information about TweakUI, see the Windows Secrets Web site (www.windowssecrets.com). Advanced users can also use Regedit to change special shell folder locations. With Regedit, navigate to HKEY_CURRENT_USER\Software\Microsoft\Windows\CurrentVersion\Explorer\Shell Folders. You'll see a variety of special shell folders listed there, including Personal (Documents), My Music (Music), My Pictures (Pictures), and My Video (Videos). To change the location of one of these special folders, simply double-click in Regedit and add the new location to the Value data field in the dialog that appears.

tip   You can see some of Vista's special folders in your Start Menu, but if you'd like a better idea of how they're laid out in the file system, simply launch Windows Explorer, and enable the classic left-mounted folder hierarchy, which is now found in the bottom-left corner of the window.

In addition to the new special shell folders in Vista, there are also some differences in the way that preexisting special shell folders are organized now. For example, folders such as My Pictures, My Music, and My Videos were physically arranged below (and logically contained within) the My Documents folder in previous Windows versions. But in Windows Vista, the new versions of these folders are found directly below each user's Home folder, alongside Documents. This won't impact typical users, who will likely access special shell folders like My Documents and My Pictures only from the Start Menu, but more advanced users will want to be aware of the changes.

tip   The new Home folder layout is actually quite similar to that used by Unix versions, including Apple's Mac OS X. Vista even follows the same naming conventions these competitors utilize.

Visualization and Organization: How the Windows Vista Shell Works

In each Windows version, there are a number of shell view styles you can utilize, each of which presents the files and folders you're looking at in slightly different way. These view styles — and the ways in which you access and configure them — have changed dramatically in Windows Vista.

By comparison, Windows XP offered six Explorer view styles — Thumbnails, Tiles, Icons, List, Details, and, for folders containing digital pictures, Filmstrip. There were also ways you could arrange the files folders, such as by name, type, or total size, or in groups, where icons representing similar objects would be visually grouped together. All of these options could be configured in a number of ways, including via buttons in the Explorer window toolbar, by right-clicking inside of an Explorer window, or from the View menu. Maddeningly, Windows XP would often forget its view styles, either on a per-window or systemwide basis. This is one of the few areas in which Windows XP was inferior to its predecessors.

In Windows Vista, you'll have to relearn many of your shell skills because the user interface has changed so much. Microsoft has not only changed the layout of the Explorer window user interface elements and menu items from which you configure view styles, but many of the view styles and arrangement options themselves have changed.

In Windows Vista, you can choose from seven view styles, as described in Table 5-2 and demonstrated in Figure 5-1.

Table 5-2: Explorer View Styles

Extra Large Icons	An absolutely gigantic view style that takes full advantage of Vista's near photographic quality icons, which are rendered at 256×256 pixels.
Large Icons	Similar to the Windows XP Large Icons view, this view style provides 128×128 icons laid out in a conventional grid.
Medium Icons	A new style that's unique to Windows Vista, Medium Icons are similar in style to Large Icons, but smaller.
Small Icons	A blast from the past: Small icons appeared in Windows 95, Windows 98, Windows Me, and Windows 2000, but were exorcised from Windows XP for some reason, much to the chagrin of many users. Rejoice, it's back.
List	A columnar version of Small Icons view, with the same size icons but a more linear look.
Details	A columnar view style that uses the same icon size as Small Icons but presents them in a more regulated fashion. Details view is quite prominent in Windows Vista, in sharp contrast to previous Windows client versions.
Tiles	A relatively new view style — it debuted in Windows XP and is the standard view style for most Explorer windows in that Windows version — Tiles view presents information about each folder and file to the right of the icon, as with Small Icons and Details, but utilizes a much larger icon (it's the same icon used by Medium Icons view). Because of the extra space available, Tiles view can present more than just the icon's name. What you see will depend on the file type. Microsoft Word documents, for example, include both the name of the file and the notation "Microsoft Word Document." And digital photos include the name and the date the picture was taken.

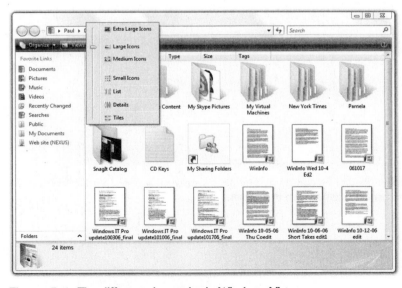

Figure 5-1: The different view styles in Windows Vista.

You can access these styles in manners that are similar to those in Windows XP, via the Views button in an Explorer window toolbar, via the View submenu on the menu that appears when you right-click a blank area of the current Explorer window, or if you have the Classic Menus option enabled, via the View Menu.

tip Unlike previous Windows versions, Windows Vista—finally—enables you to choose different icon view styles for the Desktop as well as for normal Explorer shell windows. To access these view modes, right-click a blank area of your Desktop and choose View. You'll see three view styles here: Large Icons, Medium Icons, and Classic Icons. (Details, Extra Large Icons, Small Icons, and Tiles are not available on the Desktop.)

What's interesting is that these shell view styles are not your only view style options. You can also access intermediary view styles between each of those stock settings using a new slider control that pops down when you click the small arrow on the right side of the Views toolbar button, as shown in Figure 5-2. This control enables you to fine-tune the look and feel of individual Explorer windows, so you can arrive at a view style that matches your preferences and system capabilities. For example, on a large widescreen display, you might prefer larger icons, whereas a smaller notebook display might look better to your eyes in Details view. It's up to you.

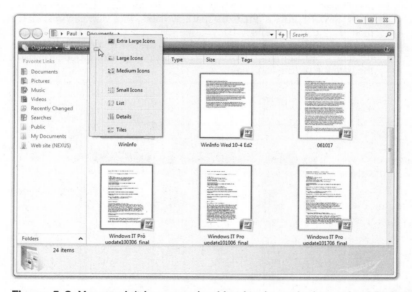

Figure 5-2: You needn't be constrained by the six stock view styles; Vista enables you to select styles that fall somewhere between the presets.

Sorting the Vista View Styles

So what else has changed? Well, you may recall that the Windows XP Details view provided columns by which you could sort the contents of the current window. In Windows Vista, every view style can be sorted by these columns, even if you can't see them. To see this in action, open a Windows Explorer window and repeatedly click the Views button. Each time you do so, the icon view style changes. But what remains is the list of column headings that you typically associate with Details View. The column headings you see will vary from window to window, depending on the content. In the Document window, you'll see column headings for Name, Data Modified, Type, Size, and Tags. But the Pictures folder has column headings for Name, Date taken, Tags, Size, and Rating.

These column headings aren't just for show. As with previous Windows versions (in which the column headings were available only in Details view), you can click any column heading in order to sort the currently viewed content by that criteria. For example, if you click the Name column heading, the folders and files in the current folder will be sorted alphabetically by name, from A to Z. If you click the Name column heading a second time, the sorting is reversed, and the folders and files are listed from Z to A. Each column heading works in a similar fashion.

What's changed is that the column headings now have a drop-down list box associated with each of them. These list boxes provide you with a wealth of sorting options. To trigger the list box, you'll first need to find it. Mouse over a column heading (like Name) and you'll see an arrow appear on the right side of the column heading. If you click this arrow, the drop-down list box appears. The various gadgets and doohickeys you see in the list box might be initially confusing, so take a closer look.

At the top of the list box you will see two or three of the following options, depending on which column heading you choose:

◆ **Sort:** Works just like clicking the column heading normally does; it sorts the folders and files in the current window accordingly. However, it does provide a bit of a visual cue, which can be handy: If the little arrow to the left of Sort is pointing down, as shown in Figure 5-3, then clicking the Sort option will result in a reverse sort (for example, Z to A in the case of the Name column heading). If the arrow is clicking up, the items will be sorted normally (A to Z for Name).

Figure 5-3: New sorting and grouping options ensure that your Explorer windows always look the way you want them to.

♦ **Stack:** This option does not appear with the Name column heading. It is brand new to Windows Vista and is the result of years of user interface testing. According to Microsoft, as hard drives get bigger and bigger, and users store more and more data on those drives, it's getting harder and harder to find the information you need. Stacks are one way to present lots of information in a simpler fashion. Like most computer user interface metaphors, Stack comes from a traditional desktop, where you might stack related papers together, creating a literal stack of content. In the real world, you might stack documents for a specific trip, project, or other relationship together. And now you can do so in Windows Vista as well. However, because Stacks don't actually appear in the current folder, but instead open a search results window, we'll examine this functionality more closely later in this chapter when we look at Vista's search features.

♦ **Group:** Enables you to group folders and files into related groups, as you would when using the Windows XP Tiles view. But now you can group files and folders regardless of the view style. You can group by name, date modified, keywords, author, type, and other criteria, and your grouping options will depend on the contents of the folder you're currently viewing. In a typical folder full of documents, the default is Date Modified. But you can choose other grouping types by right-clicking the current folder and choosing Group By and then the criteria you want.

> **tip**
>
> The Group option is most famous for its use in the default view of My Computer in Windows XP, which grouped tiled icons by Type. Interestingly, this is exactly the same in Windows Vista, as well, so open up My Computer now to see how a grouped view can look. You can see an example in Figure 5-4. (Note, however, that the types of items displayed in the Windows Vista version of My Computer are a bit different.)

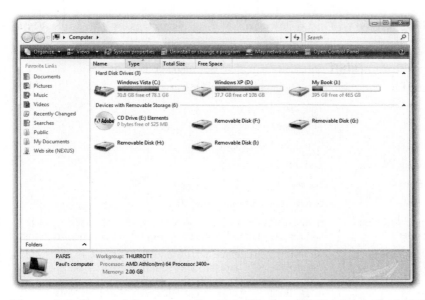

Figure 5-4: Grouped tiles were such a hit in Windows XP that they're back as the default view for Computer in Windows Vista as well.

Below the Search box, what you will see will depend on the column heading you've clicked. For example, the Date Modified column heading includes a mini calendar control that lets you specify a date or even a date range from which to filter the current folder. Like the search functionality mentioned previously, the results of this filter are displayed in a new view that actually contains search results, so we'll save this for later discussion as well.

Finally, at the bottom of the drop-down list box, you will see a number of preset Stack settings, which naturally vary according to which column heading you've chosen. The Name column heading, for example, includes preset Stacks such as 0–9, A–M, and N–Z (the actual letter ranges you see will be based on the names of the files and folders you're viewing). What's interesting about these preset Stacks is that they're, ahem, stackable. That is, you can check any number of these preset Stacks to filter the view (which, yes, returns a search result). So you can filter the view to contain files and folders that begin (or end) with both numbers from 0–9, say, and the letters A–M.

Other column headings offer different preset Stacks. You might see Last week and Today under the Date Modified heading, for example, or Jan and unspecified under Author. As is often the case in Windows Vista, of course, the choices will be based on your particular system. That is, you won't see a Jan choice unless one of the documents in the current folder was actually authored by someone named Jan.

Where Is It Now?

One of the challenges facing anyone moving to Windows Vista is that Microsoft chose to change the location of many user interface elements, which might make it hard for you to navigate around the shell in some instances. In Table 5-3, we summarize some of the changes you can expect to see, and how to work around them.

Table 5-3: Where to Find Common XP Shell Features in Windows Vista

My Documents	This folder was renamed to Documents.
My Recent Documents	This Start menu item was renamed to Recent Items.
My Pictures	This folder was renamed to Pictures.
My Music	This folder was renamed to Music.
My Video	This folder was renamed to Videos.
My Computer	Renamed to Computer.
My Network Places	Renamed to Network.
Control Panel	Location unchanged from Windows XP.
Connect To	Unchanged from Windows XP.
Set Program Access and Defaults	Renamed to Default Programs and made part of the Control Panel. It can be found in Control Panel⇨Programs⇨Default Programs.
Printers and Faxes	Removed from default Start Menu. Printers can be configured in Control Panel⇨Hardware and Sound⇨Printers. Faxing can be configured in the new Windows Fax application, which is found only in the Business and Ultimate editions of Windows Vista.
Help and Support	Location unchanged from Windows XP.
Search	Location unchanged from Windows XP.
Run	Removed from the default Windows Vista Start Menu. To achieve a similar effect, type the name of an application into the Start Menu's Start Search text box. Or, you can customize the Start Menu to include the old Run item.
Windows Explorer and Folders View	Rather than use separate My Computer and Explorer view styles, all shell windows in Windows Vista now incorporate an optional and expandable Folders panel in the bottom-left corner.
Explorer Menu System	Renamed to Classic Menus and hidden by default, but you can view it by pressing the Alt key. To permanently enable the menu, click the new Configure this Explorer's Layout button and select Classic Menus.
Folder Options	Although Folder Options is still available from the Tools menu of the hidden Explorer menu (see previous item), only the General and View tabs are available from the resulting dialog box. To access the File Types item, navigate to Control Panel⇨Programs⇨Default Programs⇨Associate a file type or protocol with a program. To access Offline Files, utilize the new Sync Center.
Explorer Status Bar	Replaced by the Preview Pane, which now sits at the bottom of all shell windows by default. Curiously, you can still enable the old Status Bar by tapping Alt and choosing Status Bar from the View menu.
Map/Disconnect Network Drive	Still accessible via the Tools menu, which is hidden by default. Press the Alt key to view this menu (see Explorer Menu System, mentioned previously in this table).

Search Folders, Saved Searches, and Virtual Folders

Early in the several-year development lifecycle of Windows Vista, Microsoft began talking up a new file management system that's based on a new user interface construct called a *virtual folder*. As the name suggests, virtual folders are a special kind of folder, one that does not actually represent a physical location in the file system. You may recall that the constructs we call folders and special shell folders do, in fact, correspond to discrete locations in the shell namespace. That is, they are what we might call *real* folders. Virtual folders are not the same as real folders. That is, they do not actually contain files and other folders. Instead, virtual folders contain *symbolic links*, or shortcuts, to real files and folders. And the way virtual folders are created might surprise you: They're really just the physical embodiment of a file search. That's right: Virtual folders contain search query results. For this reason, Microsoft has elected to name virtual folders as Search Folders. And Search Folders, naturally, contain saved searches.

Secret

Virtual Folders — A Short History Lesson

Let's step back a bit before diving too deeply into potentially confusing territory. In order to understand Vista's virtual folders, it's important to first understand the thinking that went into this feature. And since this is the ever-delayed Windows Vista we're talking about, it might also be helpful to know about Microsoft's original plans for the Vista shell and virtual folders and compare the plans with what eventually happened.

You see, Microsoft originally envisioned that it would not include in Vista a traditional file system with drive letters, physical file system paths, and real folders. Instead, the software giant wanted to virtualize the entire file system so that you wouldn't need to worry about such arcane things as "the root of C:" and the Program Files folder. Instead, you would just access your documents and applications, and not ever think about where they resided on the disk. After all, that sort of electronic housekeeping is what a computer is good at, right?

This original vision required a healthy dose of technology. The core piece of this technology was a new storage engine called WinFS (short for Windows Future Storage), which would have combined the best features of the NTFS file system with the relational database functionality of Microsoft's SQL Server products. As of this writing, Microsoft has been working on WinFS, and its predecessors, for about a decade.

There was just one problem: The WinFS technology wasn't even close to being ready in time for Windows Vista. So Microsoft pulled WinFS out of Vista and began developing it separately from the OS. Then, it completely cancelled plans to ship WinFS as a separate product. Instead, WinFS technologies will be integrated into future Windows versions and other Microsoft products.

Even though WinFS was out of the picture, Microsoft figured it could deliver much of that system's benefits using an updated version of the file system indexer it has shipped in Windows for years. And for about a year of Vista's development in 2004–05, that was the plan. Instead of special shell folders like Documents, users would access virtual folders such as All Documents, which would aggregate all of the documents on the hard drive and present them in a single location. Other special shell folders, like Pictures and Music, would also be replaced by virtual folders.

continues

continued

Problem solved, right? Wrong. Beta testers found the transition from normal folders to virtual folders to be extremely confusing. In retrospect, this should have been obvious. After all, a virtual folder that displays all of your documents is kind of useful when you're looking for something. But where do you save a new file? Is a virtual folder even a real place for applications that want to save data? And do users need to understand the differences between normal folders and virtual folders? Why are there both kinds of folders?

With the delays mounting, Microsoft stepped back from the virtual folder scheme, just as it had when it stripped out WinFS previously. So the file system you see in Windows Vista is actually quite similar to that in Windows XP and previous Windows versions. That is, the file system still uses drive letters, normal folders, and special shell folders like Documents and Pictures. If you're familiar with any prior Windows version, you should feel right at home in the Vista shell.

There's just one major difference, although it's not particularly obvious. Even though Microsoft has decided not to replace special shell folders with virtual folders in this release, the company is still shipping virtual folder technology in Windows Vista. The idea is that users will get used to virtual folders now, and then perhaps a future Windows version will simply move to that system, and eventually we'll reach some nerdvana where all the silly file system constructs we use today are suddenly passé.

So virtual folders are somewhat hidden in Windows Vista. That makes them a power user feature and, for readers of this book, inherently interesting. Most people won't even discover virtual folders and their contained shared searches. In fact, if you want to harness some of the most awesome technology in Windows Vista, this is the place to start. And heck, the skills you learn now will give you a leg up when Microsoft finally gets around to retiring the current file system. It's only a matter of time.

Understanding Search Folders

Search Folders contain the saved results from a search query. They are built using Vista's indexing engine and stored in an XML file format that developers will be able to easily access, modify, and extend. There are two types of saved searches: Those that are built into the system itself and are thus exposed in the shell and those that you build yourself. In the following sections, we'll examine both kinds of saved searches.

Using Prebuilt Search Folders

Microsoft provides a small number of useful saved searches for you, and they're available as soon as you begin using Windows Vista. There are two ways to discover these saved searches:

◆ You can open an Explorer window, which contains a single search folder, called Recently Changed, in its navigation pane.

◆ Navigate to the Searches folder, a copy of which is found in each user's Home folder (typically C:\Users*username*\ Searches). The Searches folder is shown in Figure 5-5.

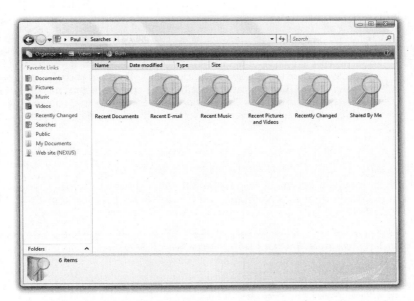

Figure 5-5: The Saved Searches folder contains prebuilt and user-made Search Folders.

Table 5-4 lists the prebuilt Search Folders that Microsoft provides in Windows Vista.

Table 5-4: Prebuilt Search Folders

Recent Documents	Finds any document files you've accessed recently, including Word documents, text files, and locally saved HTML files.
Recent E-mail	Finds any Windows Mail–based e-mail you've received recently.
Recent Music	Finds any music files that you've played in Windows Media Player 11 recently.
Recent Pictures and Videos	Finds any digital photos or videos you've viewed recently.
Recently Changed	Finds data files of any kind that you've changed recently, including documents, music files, digital photos, and digital videos.
Shared By Me	Finds folders that are configured as shared folders (and can thus be accessed by other people on your local network if networking is configured for that functionality).

Although Search Folders appear and act like normal folders, they are actually specially formatted XML files that use a .search file extension. So the Search Folder named Attachments is actually a file named Attachments.search. If you'd like to edit one of these saved searches, simply right-click it in the shell and choose Open With and then Notepad. **DANGER:** Be careful not to leave the check box named *Always use the selected program to open this kind of file* checked (selected), however. If you do that, your Search Folders will revert into normal text files and won't work properly any more.

Looking at the Code for a Search Folder

Take a look behind a typical Search Folder called Shared By Me. If you open this saved search in a text editor like Notepad, you'll see that it's composed of XML code, as shown in Listing 5-1.

Listing 5-1: Example Source Code from a Saved Search

```xml
<?xml version="1.0"?>
<persistedQuery version="1.0">
  <viewInfo viewMode="details" iconSize="16">
    <visibleColumns>
      <column viewField="System.ItemNameDisplay"/>
      <column viewField="System.DateModified"/>
      <column viewField="System.Keywords"/>
      <column viewField="System.SharedWith"/>
      <column viewField="System.ItemFolderPathDisplayNarrow"/>
    </visibleColumns>
    <frequentlyUsedColumns>
      <column viewField="System.Author"/>
      <column viewField="System.Kind"/>
      <column viewField="System.Size"/>
      <column viewField="System.Title"/>
      <column viewField="System.Rating"/>
    </frequentlyUsedColumns>
    <sortList>
      <sort viewField="System.SharedWith" direction="descending"/>
    </sortList>
  </viewInfo>

  <query>
    <conditions>
      <condition type="andCondition">
        <condition type="leafCondition" property="System.IsShared"
          operator="eq" value="true"/>
        <condition type="leafCondition" property="System.FileOwner"
          operator="eq" value="[Me]"/>
      </condition>
    </conditions>
    <kindList>
```

```
          <kind name="item"/>
        </kindList>
        <scope>
          <include knownFolder="{5E6C858F-0E22-4760-9AFE-EA3317B67173}"/>
          <include knownFolder="{DFDF76A2-C82A-4D63-906A-5644AC457385}"/>
        </scope>
      </query>

  </persistedQuery>
```

You don't have to be a programming guru to understand what's going on here. There are a few main parts to the saved search file: **viewInfo** (which includes a single subpart called **sortList**) and **query**, the latter of which includes the **scope** and **visibleInList** subparts.

The **sortList** subpart in the **viewInfo** part clearly defines how the saved search will be displayed: By date modified in descending order. The **scope** subpart inside the **query** part is interesting: It specifies three folder locations that this query will search. Those huge strings of letters and numbers are known as a Globally Unique Identifier (GUID). The idea is that each GUID identifies a unique location. When you create your own Search Folders (see later in this chapter), one or more scope subparts will be used, and will be filled with normal shell location strings, such as C:\Users\Jan.

Editing a Search Folder

If you're an XML expert, it's possible to hand-edit any saved searches, including the ones that Microsoft ships with Windows Vista. However, this isn't necessarily a great idea unless you really know what you're doing. Any text editor, including Notepad, will let you change the contents of a saved search in addition to simply letting you view them.

Creating Your Own Search Folders

Although the built-in saved searches can be handy, the real power of these virtual folders is that you can make your own. As you use Windows Vista, you may find yourself occasionally performing the same search over and over again. If that's the case, you can simply save the results as a Search Folder, which you can then access later as if it were a normal folder.

Like the built-in Search Folders, any Search Folder that you create yourself is dynamic, meaning that it can change every time you open it (and cause its underlying search query to run). For example, if you create a Search Folder that looks for all Microsoft Word (***.doc** and ***.docx**) files, you may produce a search results list in which there are 125 matches. But if you add a new Word document to your Documents folder and re-open the Search Folder, you'll see that you now have 126 matches. The point here is that Search Folders aren't static, and they don't cease being relevant after they're created. Because they literally re-query the file system every time they're run, saved searches will always return the most up-to-date possible results.

Searching for Files

To create a Search Folder, you must first search your hard drive for some kind of file. In a simple example, you might simply look for any files on your hard drive that contain your full name. To do so, launch Windows Vista search by choosing Search from the Start menu. This displays the Search tool, as shown in Figure 5-6.

You can also bring up the Search tool by pressing WinKey+F.

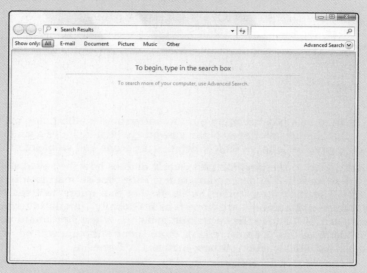

Figure 5-6: The Windows Vista Search tool is a standard Explorer window. Simply type the word or phrase you are looking for into the Search box.

Searching is context sensitive. If you bring up the Search tool as described before, Windows Vista will search the most common locations that documents might be stored in the file system. However, if you use the Search box in any Explorer window, Vista will search only the current folder (and its subfolders).

In the Search window, select the Search box in the upper-right corner of the window and begin typing your search query. As you type, Windows Vista queries the index of files contained on your hard drive and returns results in real time. This feature is called *as-you-type-search* or *word-wheeling*. Contrast this with most search tools, in which you type a search query and then press Enter or a user interface button in order to instantiate the actual search. The reason Vista performs search queries as you type is that the information it's looking for is instantly available: On a typical PC, there's no performance penalty.

As Vista displays the search results, a green progress bar will throb through the Search window's address bar. When the query has completed, the progress bar will disappear.

Secret

Although you're probably familiar with file and folder searching using the Find function in previous Windows version or a third-party tool like Google Desktop or MSN Desktop Search, you may not be familiar with some commonly used wild card characters, which can help fine-tune your searches. For example, the character * stands for one or more letters, whereas the ? character is used to represent any one letter.

Filtering the Search Results

A search query that is as general as your name can result in hundreds of hits, so it's more useful to filter the search results down a bit to make the search more specific. You do this by using the Show Only toolbar in the Search window. Here, you can specify which file types you'd like to search — All, E-mail, Documents, and some others. By default, Search will search the entire computer, but you can also force it to search all drives and devices, the current user's Home folder, or you can specify exactly where to search. For that, however, you'll need to access Advanced Search, as denoted by the button on the right of the toolbar. We'll get to that in just a bit.

When you specify a file type, such as Document, the search results list is trimmed down, often significantly, as shown in Figure 5-7. But what happens when you want to display results that include two or more file types or perform more powerful searches?

Figure 5-7: A filtered search results list is typically more relevant.

At the right side of the Show results for toolbar is the Advanced Search button. Click this button, which resembles a downward pointing arrow, and you'll be presented with the Advanced Filters pane, in which you can specify more filter types or specify another file type for which to search. This is shown in Figure 5-8.

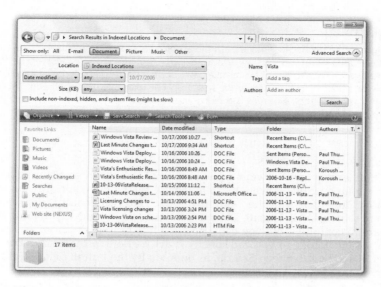

Figure 5-8: With the Advanced Filters pane, you can really fine-tune your searches.

With this pane, you can filter by location, date modified, size, filename, tags, authors, and other criteria.

Saving a Search

Secret

After you've created a search, especially a fairly complicated one that you may need to repeat in the future, it's a good idea to save it. Curiously, there's no obvious way to do this, unless you've enabled the Classic Menu. To save a search, type Alt+F to bring up the menu, and then select Save Search. This displays a standard Save As dialog box, where you can provide a name for your saved search. By default, saved searches are saved, naturally enough, to your Searches folder, but you can change the location if you'd rather save a search to your desktop, Documents folder, or other location. You can also drag any saved search over to the Favorite Links section of the navigational pane in Windows Explorer so you can access it easily later.

Configuring Search Options

For performance reasons, Windows Vista only indexes the Users folder (and all subfolders, including each user's Home folder) and certain other locations (like Offline Files) so that when it performs file searches, the results are returned quickly. However, you can change the default indexing locations if you'd like. For example, maybe you prefer saving documents and other files to a specific hard drive or partition. In such a case, it would make sense to ensure that Vista is indexing that location as well.

To configure the way Windows Vista indexes and searches, you need to locate the Indexing and Search Options tool, which is found in Control Panel⇨System and Maintenance. Shown in Figure 5-9, this tool enables you to include or exclude shell locations from indexing.

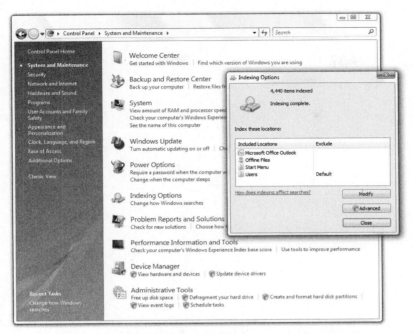

Figure 5-9: Indexing and Search Options lets you add or remove locations from the list of locations that Vista indexes for searching.

The Advanced button is particularly useful. Here, you can determine whether Vista indexes encrypted files, which file types are indexed, and where the index is stored.

tip	**If you want the absolute best performance, consider moving the index to your fastest hard drive. To do this, open Indexing and Search Options and click the Advanced button.**

Summary

Microsoft may have removed its WinFS technology from Windows Vista, but you'd never know it based on the amount of searching technologies that are still built into this system. The integrated search functionality in Windows Vista is a huge improvement over Windows XP, with numerous entry points in the OS, including the Start Menu and every Explorer window, and intelligent results based on where the search was instigated. Best of all, the Windows Vista search functionality includes one of the system's best power-user features: The ability to save searches as dynamic virtual folders you can access again and again as if they were normal shell folders.

Using Windows Sidebar

With the proliferation of local and global digital information since the advent of the public Internet, Microsoft has been working on ways to integrate the data you need most often in a seamless way with the Windows desktop. Early in the development of Windows Vista, the company created a feature called Windows Sidebar, which would sit on the edge of the PC display and provide a centralized and standardized area for Windows, third-party applications, and web services to provide notifications and alerts. Although the original Sidebar was scrapped partway through Vista's development, a new version of the Sidebar, based on web standards and partially integrated with Microsoft's Live.com web site and the Sideshow feature on modern portable computers, was eventually created. In this chapter, we'll examine this optional new feature of the Windows shell and demonstrate how you can use the Sidebar to keep valuable information at your fingertips.

What Is Windows Sidebar?

Back when Microsoft shipped Windows 98, it added a debatably useful feature called Active Desktop that provided an HTML layer on top of the traditional desktop. Active Desktop was an attempt to capitalize on the then-emerging trend of users wanting to combine live data from the Web with their PC operating system. The term for this, at the time, was *push technology*. The idea was that although you could use a Web browser to manually find, or pull down, data from the Web, a push technology client like Active Desktop could *push* data to the user automatically with no interaction required.

Ultimately, most users found Active Desktop to be confusing and undesirable, and although the feature was never really removed from Windows, it was deemphasized in subsequent Windows versions, such as Windows XP. As shown in Figure 6-1, however, it's still possible to add web content to your XP desktop via Active Desktop if you really want to.

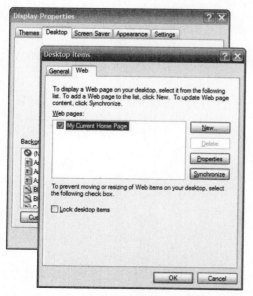

Figure 6-1: Like a vestigial tail, the Active Desktop feature lives on, largely unused, in Windows XP.

Active Desktop may have failed, but the underlying benefits of push technology are still valid today. You can see that newer versions of this functionality exist in such technologies as RSS (Really Simple Syndication), which in fact, attempts to solve essentially the same problem as Active Desktop: Rather than force users to manually search for the content they want, that content is delivered automatically to them using a unique kind of client (in this case, an RSS client). One such RSS client is included in Windows Vista as part of Internet Explorer 7, which we discuss in Chapter 17.

In Windows Vista, Active Desktop is finally gone forever. But integrated push technology lives on with a brand-new feature called Windows Sidebar. Like Active Desktop, Windows Sidebar is available by default and is running when you start up your PC, unless you configure it not to do so. But Windows Sidebar solves one of the major problems with Active Desktop by moving the main user interface to the side of the screen where it won't typically be hidden under your open applications and other windows.

Secret

Windows Sidebar is actually not displayed by default on all PCs. If the resolution of your PC's screen is 1024×768 or less, for example, Windows Sidebar will not display by default. To enable Windows Sidebar on such a system, follow the instructions in "Launching Windows Sidebar," below. Then, right-click the Sidebar and choose Properties. In the Windows Sidebar Properties dialog that appears, check the box titled Start Sidebar when Windows starts if you'd like it enabled by default.

For others, however, Sidebar might not be a desirable feature. To disable Windows Sidebar, right-click the Sidebar tray icon and choose Exit. (Do not right-click the Sidebar itself and choose Close; that simply hides the Sidebar.) Then, uncheck the option box asking whether you'd like to run Sidebar automatically when the system reboots.

Put simply, Windows Sidebar is a panel that sits at the edge of your screen and houses small *gadgets*, or mini-applications, each of which can provide specific functionality, as shown in Figure 6-2. Gadgets typically connect to data somewhere, be it on your PC or on the Internet. Windows Vista ships with a variety of these gadgets, but you can download many more online, and if you're familiar with Web technologies like HTML (HyperText Markup Language), DHTML (Dynamic HTML), and JavaScript, you can even build your own gadgets.

Because Windows Sidebar does take up a small portion of vertical real estate on your screen, this feature is more useful for those with widescreen displays. That said, Windows Sidebar appears under other windows by default so that users with normal square-shaped screens can use it as well. We'll examine this behavior in just a bit.

Figure 6-2: Active Desktop lives: Windows Vista's new Windows Sidebar feature lets you access Web-based information from your desktop.

Launching Windows Sidebar

Windows Sidebar should launch automatically when you boot into Windows Vista. If you disable the Windows Sidebar's autorun functionality, you'll have to go digging for it in the Start menu. It's somewhat hidden in Start⇨All Programs⇨Accessories, as shown in Figure 6-3. This is made all the more confusing because Microsoft has changed the way the Start menu expands; instead of the submenu system employed in previous versions, the submenu expands and contracts in place right within the Start menu now.

When Windows Sidebar starts, you'll see a subtle black shadow appear on the right side of the screen, as shown in Figure 6-4. Additionally, a blue Sidebar icon appears in the tray notification area next to the system clock. Depending on how your system is configured, you should also see one or more gadgets, or mini-applications, displaying in the Sidebar itself.

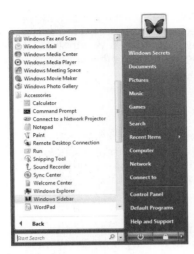

Figure 6-3: Windows Sidebar is buried pretty deeply in the Start menu.

Figure 6-4: At first you might think there is something wrong with your display, but that's just Windows Sidebar subtly appearing onscreen.

If you move the mouse cursor over to the right side of your screen, the Windows Sidebar will fade into the foreground slowly, and you'll see that it is, in fact, a translucent panel of sorts, and not a screen defect. That shadow appears only when Windows Sidebar is configured to autohide, which it is by default. We discuss this and other configuration options in the next section.

Configuring Sidebar

It's highly unlikely that you'll want to use Windows Sidebar in its default form. Thankfully, Windows Sidebar includes a number of configuration options. You can change the way this panel displays, where it displays, which gadgets it will display, and other related options. And, of course, you can determine whether it appears at all when Windows Vista first boots.

Configuring the Sidebar Display

Many Windows Sidebar features can be configured directly from the Windows Sidebar Properties dialog box. To access this dialog box, move the mouse over to the Sidebar, right-click, and choose Properties. As shown in Figure 6-5, this dialog box enables you to change how the Sidebar displays on your screen.

Figure 6-5: The Sidebar Properties dialog box enables you to configure Sidebar display features.

Using Sidebar Properties

Here, you can determine whether the Sidebar appears under other windows (the default), or is shown on top of other windows. If you select to display Sidebar on top of other windows, Sidebar will appear as a solid, glass-like panel and will lose the subtle shadow and translucency effects. Additionally, floating windows—applications, dialog boxes, and so on—will visually appear below the Sidebar. There is an additional behavior associated with this mode, however: When you maximize any window, that window will treat the innermost edge of the Sidebar as the new edge of the screen. As you can see in Figure 6-6, this creates a strange effect when both floating and maximized windows are displayed with the Sidebar.

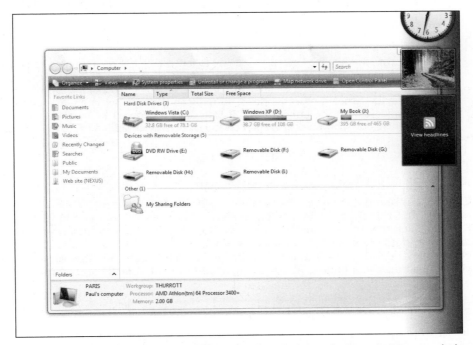

Figure 6-6: When Sidebar is configured to appear in front of other windows, maximized windows treat Sidebar as the edge of the screen, but floating windows can still display below Sidebar.

To make Sidebar appear when you log on to Windows, select the option titled Start Sidebar when Windows starts. (This option is obviously applicable on a user-by-user basis; enabling Sidebar to autostart for one user will not cause Sidebar to appear for other users.)

You can also configure Sidebar to appear on the right or left of the screen (but not on the top or bottom). And, if you have multiple computer displays, you can choose which monitor you'd like to use for Sidebar.

The View list of running gadgets enables you to examine which gadgets you've configured to run in the Sidebar. We'll look at this feature in the next section.

Other Sidebar Configuration Options

In addition to the Sidebar Properties dialog box, there are other ways in which you can configure various Sidebar features. For example, when you right-click the Sidebar surface, you'll see a number of options. To hide the Sidebar—not to be confused with autohide—select Close Sidebar. When you do this, the Sidebar disappears from the screen. To make it reappear, click (or right-click) the Sidebar icon in the tray and choose Open.

tip

All of the menu options you see when you right-click the Sidebar are available from the Sidebar icon in the tray. This enables you to easily access various Sidebar features when the Sidebar is hidden or cannot be seen under other windows. The Sidebar icon's menu is available only when you right-click the icon. If you just click it, nothing will happen.

Secret

If you use the Alt+Tab keyboard shortcut to task switch between running applications and windows, and choose the option for Desktop, all of your running applications and other displayed windows will minimize or hide, including Sidebar if it is configured to display underneath other windows. To redisplay Sidebar, select another application or window from the task switcher. If Sidebar is configured to always be on top of other windows, however, it will not disappear when you task switch to the Desktop.

Adding Gadgets to the Sidebar

The Sidebar isn't particularly interesting by itself. But Sidebar is really just a container for gadgets, and it is these gadgets that make Sidebar truly useful. To add gadgets to the Sidebar, click the Add Gadgets button at the top of the Sidebar, which resembles a plus mark. (Or, right-click the Sidebar — or the Sidebar icon — and choose Add Gadgets.) This causes the Add Gadgets window to appear, as shown in Figure 6-7. This window provides you with a number of built-in gadgets, which you can add directly to the Sidebar surface.

Figure 6-7: With Add Gadgets, you get a menu of gadgets from which to choose.

To add a gadget to the Sidebar, you either double-click the gadget in Add Gadgets, or you can simply drag and drop a gadget onto the Sidebar surface, as shown in Figure 6-8.

Secret

You can add multiple copies of any gadget to the Sidebar if you'd like. This is handy for certain gadgets, such as Clock, each instance of which can be set to a different time zone, Slide Show, or Weather.

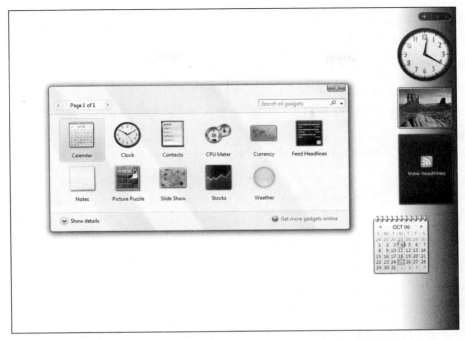

Figure 6-8: You can drag gadgets around just like you do files on the Windows desktop.

Looking at the Built-In Gadgets

Table 6-1 summarizes the gadgets that ship with Windows Vista.

Table 6-1: Built-In Windows Sidebar Gadgets

Gadget	What It Does
Calendar	Provides a handy onscreen calendar
Clock	A clock that can be configured to show the time in any time zone or city worldwide
Contacts	A gadget-based version of Windows Contacts
CPU Meter	A set of gauges that tracks the load on your PC's microprocessor and RAM

(continued)

Table 6-1 *(continued)*

Gadget	What It Does
Currency	A simple currency converter.
Feed Headlines	An RSS client that integrates with the RSS feeds to which you've subscribed in Internet Explorer
Notes	A cute little note pad, perfect for jotting down reminders
Picture Puzzle	A game in which you move tiles around until the picture displayed on the front of the tiles is complete
Slide Show	A photo slideshow gadget
Stocks	An electronic stock ticker
Weather	A weather gadget that can be configured for any town and can display the temperature in Fahrenheit or Celsius

Some of these gadgets are obviously just for fun, but some are truly useful, especially for serious multitaskers. We especially appreciate the Clock and Weather gadgets, which can be used in multiple instances for different locations, and the Calendar.

Configuring Gadgets

When you have one or more gadgets displayed on the Sidebar, you'll probably want to configure them in some way. Although each gadget exposes a slightly different Settings window based on the needs of the gadget itself, the way you access this information is identical for any gadget. If you move the mouse cursor over a gadget, you'll see a few common elements. First, many gadgets visually change in some way to let you know that hey're ready to be configured. Additionally, two small user interface items appear in the top-right corner of all gadgets, as shown in Figure 6-9: A small close button (resembling an x) and a small wrench.

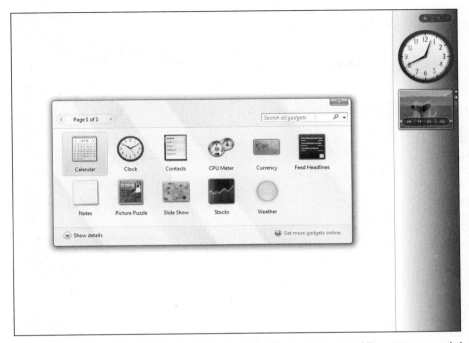

Figure 6-9: When you mouse over a gadget, you'll see some new UI appear around the edges.

If you click the close button, the gadget will close and disappear from the Sidebar without any warning dialog box. But if you click the wrench, the gadget will display its Settings window. Each gadget will display a different set of Settings options. Figure 6-10 shows the Settings option for the Clock gadget.

In addition to configuring individual gadgets, you can also rearrange gadgets on the Sidebar surface using your well-developed drag-and-drop skills. Simply grab a gadget with the mouse and move it up and down the Sidebar surface until it's positioned where you want it. Note that this feature works best when there are multiple gadgets. If you only have a few gadgets displayed on the Sidebar, they will be arranged only at the top of the Sidebar. You cannot arbitrarily move them down onto unused portions of the Sidebar's bottom area. If you try to, the bottom-most gadget will simply slide right back up so that it is on the bottom of the stack of gadgets.

Figure 6-10: From the Clock Settings window, you can select a clock name, the time zone, and optionally show the clock's second hand.

To access other gadget options, you can right-click any gadget. This displays a pop-up menu from which you can control the opacity, or translucency, of the gadget and access other options.

Moving Gadgets to the Windows Desktop

Surprisingly, you can also move gadgets directly to the Windows desktop if you'd like, making Sidebar and its gadgets work a lot more like the old Active Desktop. To do so, simply drag and drop a gadget from the Sidebar onto an empty area of the Windows desktop, as shown in Figure 6-11.

> tip   You can also move a gadget to the desktop by right-clicking it in the Sidebar and choosing Detach from Sidebar.

When you drag a gadget onto the desktop in this fashion, you'll notice that it actually grows a bit bigger than it was when displayed on the Sidebar itself.

To move a gadget back to the Sidebar, simply drag and drop the Sidebar. Or, you can right-click a floating gadget and choose Attach to Sidebar.

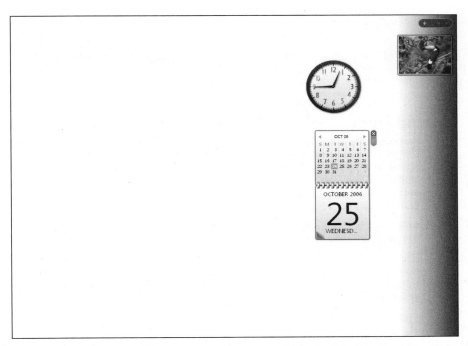

Figure 6-11: Sidebar gadgets aren't locked into the Sidebar. You can put them on the desktop as well.

Secret

If you move gadgets to the desktop, Sidebar will still need to be running in order for them to display. However, you can close (really, hide) the Sidebar if you'd like. When you do so, floating gadgets will still appear. However, if you quit Sidebar, the floating gadgets will disappear from the desktop as well.

You can also add gadgets to your desktop by opening the Add Gadgets dialog box and dragging a gadget from there directly to the desktop, and not to the Sidebar.

Gadgets remember where you left them. If you have some gadgets on the desktop and some on the Sidebar and you quit Sidebar and then restart it, each of the gadgets will reappear exactly where you left them. (This includes multiple monitor setups as well, which is nice.) Additionally, Sidebar will remember how it was configured when you quit. If you quit Sidebar while it is hidden, Sidebar will start up next time hidden as well.

tip

Finally, you might be wondering if there's any easy way to access floating gadgets that have been hidden by other application windows. There is, assuming the Sidebar is visible: Simply right-click the Sidebar (or click the Sidebar tray icon) and choose Bring Gadgets to Front. This will display any floating gadgets on top of your other windows.

Removing Gadgets

To remove a gadget from the Sidebar or desktop, simply right-click it and choose Close Gadget. Or, mouse over the gadget and click the small close button that appears. This will not delete a gadget from your system, of course. You will be able to re-add any removed gadgets later from the Add Gadgets window.

Secret

Advanced Sidebar Configuration Options

Although the Sidebar configuration user interface is fairly complete, there are a few things you can't easily do. Behind the scenes, however, the Windows Sidebar utilizes special configuration files named settings.ini to determine all of its configuration possibilities. If you don't mind taking a small risk by editing these files with a text editor such as Notepad, you can perform various configuration tasks that are impossible with the standard Sidebar UI.

Be sure to back up any files you'll be editing before making changes. You'll also want to quit Sidebar before editing these files.

There are two versions of settings.ini. The first is devoted to system-wide configuration options and default settings and is located in C:\Program Files\Windows Sidebar by default. If you right-click this file and choose Edit, you'll see the contents of this file, which should resemble the following:

```
[Root]
SettingsVersion=00.00.00.01
SidebarShowState=Imploded
SidebarDockSide=2
Section0=1
Section1=2
Section2=3
SidebarDockedPartsOrder=0x1,0x2,0x3
[Section 1]
PrivateSetting_GadgetName=%PROGRAMFILES%\windows
sidebar\gadgets\RecycleBin.gadget
PrivateSetting_Enabled=true
[Section 2]
PrivateSetting_GadgetName=%PROGRAMFILES%\windows
sidebar\gadgets\Launcher.gadget
PrivateSetting_Enabled=true
[Section 3]
PrivateSetting_GadgetName=%PROGRAMFILES%\windows
sidebar\gadgets\SlideShow.gadget
PrivateSetting_Enabled=true
```

A second version of the Sidebar settings.ini file is available for each user. This file is located in C:\Users\[*your user name*]\AppData\Local\Microsoft\Windows Sidebar by default. This file has a similar structure, but could be much longer depending on how much you've configured Windows Sidebar. Here's an example of what it could look like:

```
[Root]
SettingsVersion=00.00.00.01
SidebarShowState=Imploded
SidebarDockSide=2
SidebarDockedPartsOrder=0x2,0x3,
SidebarAlwaysOnTop=true
SidebarDockMonitor=0
PickerPosX=386
PickerPosY=233
Section0=1
Section1=2
Section2=3
[Section 1]
PrivateSetting_GadgetName=C:%5CProgram%20Files%5CWindows%20Sidebar%5CGad
gets%5CworldClock.Gadget
PrivateSetting_Enabled=true
PrivateSetting_GadgetTopmost=false
PrivateSetting_SidebarDockedState=Not%20Docked
clockName=Eastern%20Time
clockText=
timeZoneIndex=13
timeZoneBias=0
dayToNight=True
secondsEnabled=False
SettingExist=True
PrivateSetting_GadgetDropLocationX=1078
PrivateSetting_GadgetDropLocationY=179
[Section 2]
PrivateSetting_GadgetName=C:%5CProgram%20Files%5CWindows%20Sidebar%5CGad
gets%5CRSS.Gadget
PrivateSetting_Enabled=true
PrivateSetting_SidebarDockedState=Docked
PrivateSetting_GadgetDropLocationX=257
PrivateSetting_GadgetDropLocationY=859
rssFeedPath=Internet%20Explorer%20Team%20Blog
rssFeedUrl=http:%2F%2Fgo.microsoft.com%2Ffwlink%2F%3FLinkId=58643
```

continues

continued

```
PrivateSetting_GadgetTopmost=false
[Section 3]
PrivateSetting_GadgetName=C:%5CProgram%20Files%5CWindows%20Sidebar%5CGad
gets%5CRSS.Gadget
PrivateSetting_Enabled=true
PrivateSetting_SidebarDockedState=Docked
PrivateSetting_GadgetDropLocationX=1433
PrivateSetting_GadgetDropLocationY=420
rssFeedPath=Internet%20Explorer%20Team%20Blog
rssFeedUrl=http:%2F%2Fgo.microsoft.com%2Ffwlink%2F%3FLinkId=58643
PrivateSetting_GadgetTopmost=false
```

Let's examine a few of these settings. The SidebarShowState option is set to Imploded in the code example. This means that the Sidebar will be displayed normally, and not in front of other windows. SidebarDockSide is set to 2, which is the right side of the screen. If you change this number to 1, the Windows Sidebar will display on the left.

In addition to the options you see here, there are a few other undocumented options. For example, if you'd like a certain gadget to never appear in the Add Gadgets windows, you could simply find the gadget in C:\Program Files\Windows Sidebar\Gadgets and delete it, but what if you wanted it to be available to other users? In this case, you could simply add a line like the following to your user's version of settings.ini:

```
PickerDefaultPackageSkipList=SlideShow.Gadget,worldClock.Gadget
```

This particular code would only make the Clock gadget unavailable. Obviously, there are many more settings possibilities. It's also likely that an enterprising software developer will come up with a TweakUI-style application that will provide the same functionality. We'll report on any such developments on the Windows Secrets web site (www.windowssecrets.com).

Finding New Gadgets

In order to make it easy for users to find new gadgets that will run on both the Windows Sidebar and desktop, Microsoft has created a few Web communities. The first is called, appropriately enough, Microsoft Gadgets (**http://microsoftgadgets.com/**). The second, which is available from the link Get more gadgets online in the Sidebar's Add Gadgets window, is called Gadgets for Windows Vista (**http://gallery.microsoft.com/Results.aspx? vista=landing&rdm=113828&l=1&ti=2**)

Actually, you can get three different kinds of gadgets from these web sites, as Microsoft has chosen to port these mini-applications to three distinct environments: Sidebar and the Windows desktop, Live.com (a web portal that's part of Microsoft's Windows Live initiative), and Sideshow, an external display that is beginning to appear on new notebook computers and Tablet PCs.

Secret

Unfortunately, the three environments are not entirely compatible, so you can't just create one gadget that works in all three. If you wanted to get a gadget that would display your e-mail, for example, you would need different versions for Sidebar, Live.com, and Sideshow. That said, gadgets for all three environments would be built using the same HTML, DHTML, and JavaScript technologies and could share some code.

On the Microsoft Gadgets web site, shown in Figure 6-12, you can find galleries of downloadable gadgets, a blog written by the Microsoft employees that maintain the site, forums for providing gadget feedback, and other information.

Figure 6-12: Microsoft Gadgets is a web community for finding Sidebar gadgets.

Microsoft Gadgets is also an excellent resource for developers wanting to build their own gadgets. The site includes a wealth of information and documentation about building gadgets that work in any or all of the supported environments. If you are a developer, you'll appreciate the fact that Sidebar is essentially a graphic script hosting environment: All of your skills writing web applications and web sites are transferable to gadget design and development.

There are other online resources for Sidebar gadgets as well. The aforementioned Live.com web portal (**http://www.live.com**) offers some Sidebar gadgets, although most of that site's gadgets are obviously designed for Live.com, not Sidebar. And there are many, many third-party gadget sites on the Web. There are Google search gadgets, dictionaries, and virtually everything imaginable out there.

Where Have I Seen This Before?

Although Sidebar is a new feature that's unique to Windows Vista, you may be familiar with the fact that mini-applications called gadgets or something similar have been with us since the earliest days of computers. Back when PCs lacked graphics cards and were constrained to just 640K of RAM, Terminate and Stay Resident (TSR) mini-applications provided the same basic functionality as today's gadgets (minus the Web connections of course), letting users run small utilities and even personal information management applications alongside WordPerfect, dBASE, and Lotus 1-2-3. Even the earliest Macintosh computers supported a suite of mini-applications called Desk Accessories, which provided such utilities as calculators and text editors on a system that, technically speaking, could not multitask.

More recently, a wide range of gadget-type environments have cropped up, and it would be irresponsible to suggest that Microsoft wasn't influenced in some ways by these tools. Environments such as Stardock's DesktopX (**www.stardock.com/products.asp**) were among the first to provide handy Web-connected utilities that run on the Windows desktop. A Mac tool called Konfabulator (**http://widgets.yahoo.com/**) was such a hit that Yahoo! purchased it, and Apple included a pretty obvious copy of it in Mac OS X, which it called Dashboard.

All of these environments share the same basic principles, although each comes with its own differences, advantages, and limitations. (Apple Dashboard, for example, uses mini-applications called widgets that cannot be easily placed on the computer's desktop, as can Sidebar gadgets.) The question, of course, is whether any of these alternatives outshine Sidebar enough to consider installing them on Windows Vista. (Dashboard, obviously, runs only on the Mac.)

In our opinion, the answer is no. Assuming you're even interested in using gadgets, the way that Sidebar integrates into Windows and is supported by such a wide-ranging set of third-party gadgets outweighs any small advantages that other environments might have. Installing yet another gadget-type environment would bring little advantage, but would clutter up your desktop in an unnecessary way. Chances are, if you need a particular kind of gadget, there's one available for Windows Sidebar. And in the end, that is likely the biggest consideration any potential user should entertain.

Secret

Earlier Sidebar Iterations

If you followed the development of Windows Vista, you might be familiar with earlier versions of a Windows Sidebar that were quite different from the Sidebar found in the finished product. Early on, Microsoft had hoped to replace Vista's tray notification area, which dates back to the release of Windows 95 in 1995, with a feature called the Sidebar. This early version of the Sidebar would have been the system's central location for alerts and notifications, and it included such things as a clock, a search box, a synchronization center, a media player, and a list of contacts. It might have even replaced the Windows taskbar, as evidenced by early prerelease versions of Windows Vista, which then went by the code name Longhorn.

The original version of Sidebar was influenced by work done at the MSN business unit at Microsoft, which had created an Internet client called MSN Premium that included a feature called Dashboard. Like the original Sidebar, Dashboard sat at the edge of the screen and included a list of contacts, a clock, and other useful at-a-glance information. The idea was to take this sort of functionality and make it part of the underlying operating system.

So what happened? When Windows Vista's development schedule veered wildly out of control in 2004, Microsoft decided it was time to start over from scratch, so it dumped a number of features that were not considered core to the success of this release. About a year later, Microsoft created the Platforms Incubation Team in order to foster an environment where smaller Windows applications could be developed quickly and updated regularly. This team resuscitated Sidebar and is responsible for the Windows Sidebar you see in Windows Vista today, including the decision to utilize web standards instead of Vista-specific technologies that would have been more difficult for developers to learn. They also created the Windows Calendar application, which we discuss in Chapter 20.

Summary

Windows Sidebar is a highly visual and obvious change in Windows Vista. Whether it's something you're going to want to leave running on your PC will depend on your own preferences, of course. We feel that Windows Sidebar can be a valuable addition to your desktop if you're using a widescreen display, are a natural multitasker, and find a handful of gadgets that you simply can't live without. However, a certain percentage of Windows Vista users will simply be unimpressed. For those people, it's not particularly easy, but you can at least turn it off.

Fonts

Chapter

7

◆ ◆

In This Chapter

Examining which characters are supported in different Windows fonts

Reviewing how fonts differ and accessing the letters and symbols you need

Taking advantage of the new Unicode characters included with Windows

Entering special characters using the keyboard or application shortcuts

Identifying which fonts you have

Making fonts in Vista look smoother

Using web-safe fonts in your HTML pages

Learning which fonts are for various language groups (it's not obvious)

Getting the best free fonts

Finding the best scientific and programmer's fonts

Getting the best deal if you have some money to buy commercial fonts

Understanding font utilities that can make sense of your collection

◆ ◆

Windows Vista may offer you a wealth of fonts — but finding them and discovering the hidden features of each one is a challenging task.

Windows Has a Lot of Strange Characters

Windows Vista gives you *The Joy of Fonts*. Vista makes it easier than ever to use fonts in your documents and make them look the way you want them to look.

It's hard to conceive today, but as recently as the 1980s, you could only get computer printouts using heavy line printers that output in ALL CAPS or daisywheel printers that were slow and noisy.

Even when Windows 3.0 became wildly popular in 1990, it was tough to get printouts from it that looked good. Laser printers had become available by then, but they cost several thousand dollars and typically offered only rough, 300-dpi resolution. Worse, Windows users actually had to purchase and run their own font-generating utilities.

To print a document in a typeface other than the basic Courier-style fonts burned into the firmware of those early HP LaserJet printers, you generated a different font file for each desired size. These files, in turn, had to be painstakingly downloaded into the printer every time it was turned on.

Those bad old days are lo-o-ong gone. Ever since Windows 3.1 was released in 1992, every copy of Windows has come with TrueType fonts. These fonts print out on any printer pretty much the way they look on screen.

Still, you can't print a document without using a font. You're looking at a font right now. Someone selected it and styled this font, just as you do with your own documents. If the impressions your documents make on other people mean anything to you, learning to use Vista fonts in the best way possible can pay you great dividends.

Windows Vista can be very frustrating, however. It includes more fonts than ever before. But there's no place in Vista to see all those fonts arrayed together, no **Print Font Listing** command. And finding out which characters you can insert into your documents means a time-consuming hunt through little-known Control Panel applets.

We're here to give you control over your fonts. You can't use them unless you know what's available. In the next few pages, we'll give you the font guide that Microsoft forgot to provide.

You Can Never Have Enough Glyphs

Before we jump into all of the characters and fonts you have available to you under Windows Vista, we need to be clear on a few definitions:

- **Character:** A letter or symbol in a particular language group. The letter a, in Western languages, can be represented as roman, bold, italic, or bold italic, like so: a, **a**, *a*, ***a***. All four of these weights are the same character: the letter A.
- **Glyph:** A specific graphical shape of a character. The character A and the character a are different glyphs.
- **Typeface or face:** A collection of characters sharing the same general design. Arial and Times New Roman are different typefaces. All the different weights of a typeface — bold, italic, bold italic, condensed, expanded, and whatever other

variations may have been created—considered together are sometimes called a *typeface family*.

◆ **Font:** Originally meant one particular size and weight of a typeface. For example, 10 pt. Arial was considered a different font than 12 pt. Arial. Today, however, almost no one uses the word in this manner. In this book, we define *font* as a computer file that contains a typeface that can be scaled to different sizes.

How Windows Jumped from 224 Glyphs to 652 to 100,000

When Microsoft incorporated TrueType font technology into Windows 3.1, a particular set of 224 characters was present in almost every font that shipped with the operating system. This was known as the Windows ANSI character set. Installed for users in the United States and Western Europe, these characters met most Westerners' word-processing needs (when used with an appropriate keyboard, for example, U.S., U.K., French, and so forth).

These 224 characters, however, were frustrating for most of the rest of the people in the world. Many characters that are essential to write Eastern European languages were missing from the English install of the operating system. And speakers of Asian languages, such as Japanese, Chinese, and Korean, were even more at a loss to use Windows for communication in the languages they were familiar with.

Microsoft and other software companies tried to fill this gap with various add-on products. Ultimately, Windows had to expand its character set.

Beginning with Windows 95, and continuing with more fervor in Windows 98, Microsoft started including fonts that contained 652 characters. This expanded set of glyphs was called WGL4—the Windows Glyph List 4. It was considered a PanEuropean character set, because each font contained characters needed by Eastern European, Greek, Turkish, and Cyrillic language groups as well as speakers of Western European languages. Most keyboards still bore the same number of keys. But users of non-Western European languages could purchase localized keyboards and easily configure Windows to use the appropriate character set.

Beginning in Windows 2000, and continuing through Windows XP and Windows Vista, Microsoft began to build a much larger character set into Windows. This is known as Unicode, a movement with its own international standards bodies. Unicode was originally conceived to support up to 65,000 glyphs, allowing thousands of Asian ideograms to have their own place in the standard. This set of glyphs is known as the Basic Multilingual Plane or, for short, Plane 0.

Even this wasn't enough—scholars have identified more than 1 million unique glyphs used by all the world's people at one time or another—so Unicode was expanded to handle an additional 16 planes of 65,000 characters each (Supplementary Planes 1 through 16). Today, 100,000 or so glyphs have places reserved for them in official Unicode documentation, though no font yet exists that is capable of rendering them all.

Making Progress in International Communications

An overview of Windows' evolution in fonts shows a continuous increase in the size of the language groups the operating system can support.

Windows ANSI

Windows 3.1's original character set is called *Windows ANSI*, although the specification was never formally made a standard by ANSI (the American National Standards Institute).

The new 224-character range was an improvement on *US-ASCII*, a 7-bit code used by older computers, which offered only 96 printable characters out of a possible 128. The first 32 positions were reserved for control codes (such as Tab and Line Feed). Windows ANSI also retains the same 32 control codes, leaving 224 printable characters available out of the 256 that are possible in an 8-bit scheme.

Windows ANSI was designed by Microsoft as a superset (some would say an incompatible set) of *ISO-8859-1*, a specification of the International Standards Organization that ANSI did at one time adopt. ISO-8859-1 reserved 32 positions in the middle of its 8-bit series for control codes (such as CCH, cancel character). Microsoft Windows fonts instead used these positions for printable characters, such as the trademark symbol (TM) and curly quotes. This conflict of character codes still haunts Windows users, as we'll discuss later in this chapter.

Windows ANSI is also known as Windows-1252 (one of several code pages that are used to define the character encoding used in an HTML document) and Latin-1 (because it includes many of the characters of the Latin or Roman alphabet that's used in Western countries).

WGL4: Windows Glyph List 4

Windows Glyph List 4, which Microsoft's fonts began to support in Windows 95 and 98, includes 652 characters. (Around this time, Microsoft also started developing OpenType, which integrates PostScript information into TrueType fonts.) This set incorporates the following code pages, each of which defines a different language grouping:

- **Latin 1 (code page 1252):** Western European languages, such as English, French, German, Spanish, Portuguese, Swedish, Danish, Dutch, and many others, plus some languages far from Europe, including Afrikaans and Indonesian.
- **Latin 2 (1250):** Eastern European languages, such as Polish, Czech, Slovenian, Romanian, Hungarian, Slovak, and Albanian.
- **Greek (1253):** The language of Greece, which includes many glyphs that are used today in mathematical formulae by people who don't speak a word of Greek. These characters are included in Windows' Symbol font, but this font is being rendered unnecessary by Unicode.
- **Turkish (1254):** The language of Turkey.
- **Baltic (1257):** A character set used in the Estonian, Latvian, and Lithuanian languages.
- **Cyrillic (1251):** Characters used in Russian, as well as in several other languages, including Belarusian, Bulgarian, Macedonian, Serbian, Ukrainian, and others.

No one ever bought a 652-character keyboard in order to type all of these languages on the same PC. Instead, Microsoft has always made available a variety of keyboard layouts—software that users can switch among to access the characters of different language groups.

Unicode: One Font to Rule Them All

The answer to the confusion over which characters are available in Windows—and whether all Windows users can see those characters when viewing and printing a document prepared by someone using a different PC—is *Unicode*. This project, which attempts to collect and standardize every character that every language group in the world uses, is a massive effort.

According to David McCreedy, who manages the **TravelPhrases.info** web site and maintains a huge font list, there are more than 1,100 fonts available that contain at least some multilingual Unicode characters. None of these fonts, however, includes every possible glyph.

Lucida Sans Unicode, which has been included in every Microsoft operating system since NT 4 and Windows 95, includes about 1,776 glyphs, surpassing WGL4. Microsoft's *Arial Unicode MS*, which is included with Office 2000/XP/2003/2007, comes close to covering the Unicode range with more than 50,000 glyphs, McCreedy says. Meanwhile, these and other fonts seem to add to their character sets every day (as we'll describe later in this chapter).

How can you use all these characters? Think about it. Perhaps you really should be including a copyright or a trademark symbol in your documents. Hmmm, these characters don't appear on your keyboard. We'll show you how to master this challenge and much more.

How to Enter ANSI Characters from the Keyboard

Figure 7-1 shows you all of the characters in the Windows ANSI character set. The characters are numbered 32 through 127 and 0128 through 0255. The numbers above 127, representing characters that don't appear on a U.S.-style keyboard, required you in previous versions of Windows to enter a leading zero to access them via the numeric keypad. (More on this shortly.) The leading zero is no longer necessary if you're using the keypad to enter these characters in Vista.

The first glyph in each row represents the character you'll see when an ordinary text font, such as Arial or Times New Roman, is selected. The second glyph is visible if Windows' Symbol font is selected. The third glyph is from Wingdings, a whimsical dingbats font Microsoft threw into the mix to add some spice to its first rollout of TrueType.

If you're using a version of Windows from Windows 3.1 on up, and it has a Western code page configured, then you have these characters. They aren't much. U.S. users don't even see a way on their keyboards to type a symbol for the pound currency (£) or a registered trademark (®).

But they're there, and they do the job if you're writing a document in a major Western European language. Many useful characters besides letters and numbers are in there, too. And they're not so hard to use, if you know the secret.

One way to enter characters not found on your keyboard:
1. Make sure NumLock is on.
2. Hold down the Alt key.
3. Type the character number on the numeric keypad.
4. Release the Alt key.

32				64	@	≅	✎	96	`	—	♊
33	!	!	✏	65	A	A	✌	97	a	α	♋
34	"	∀	✂	66	B	B	✆	98	b	β	♌
35	#	#	✄	67	C	X	☜	99	c	χ	♍
36	$	∃	✑	68	D	Δ	✍	100	d	δ	♎
37	%	%	✆	69	E	E	☞	101	e	ε	♏
38	&	&	▣	70	F	Φ	☟	102	f	φ	♐
39	'	∋	☎	71	G	Γ	✐	103	g	γ	♑
40	(	(	☎	72	H	H	✌	104	h	η	♒
41	)	)	☏	73	I	I	☝	105	i	ι	♓
42	*	*	✉	74	J	ϑ	☺	106	j	φ	℮
43	+	+	✉	75	K	K	☻	107	k	κ	&
44	,	,	✉	76	L	Λ	☹	108	l	λ	●
45	-	—	✉	77	M	M	✺	109	m	μ	○
46	.	.	✉	78	N	N	☠	110	n	ν	■
47	/	/	✉	79	O	O	☡	111	o	o	□
48	0	0	📁	80	P	Π	☢	112	p	π	□
49	1	1	📂	81	Q	Θ	✈	113	q	θ	□
50	2	2	📄	82	R	P	✿	114	r	ρ	□
51	3	3	📄	83	S	Σ	●	115	s	σ	◆
52	4	4	📄	84	T	T	✾	116	t	τ	◆
53	5	5	🖫	85	U	Y	✞	117	u	υ	◆
54	6	6	⌛	86	V	ς	✟	118	v	ϖ	❖
55	7	7	⌨	87	W	Ω	✠	119	w	ω	◆
56	8	8	🖰	88	X	Ξ	✡	120	x	ξ	⊠
57	9	9	🖱	89	Y	Ψ	✢	121	y	ψ	⊡
58	:	:	🖥	90	Z	Z	☽	122	z	ζ	⌘
59	;	;	▭	91	[	[	☯	123	{	{	⌬
60	<	<	🖫	92	\	∴	ॐ	124	|	|	❀
61	=	=	🖴	93	]	]	✺	125	}	}	"
62	>	>	⊘	94	^	⊥	♈	126	~	~	"
63	?	?	✍	95	_	_	♉	127			▯

Figure 7-1: The Windows ANSI character set. This chart shows all the characters in the three major font types that are present in every release of Windows going back to version 3.1.

Text character set
  Symbol character set
    Wingdings character set

Character Number → 98   b   β   ℨ

Num	Text	Sym	Wing	Num	Text	Sym	Wing	Num	Text	Sym	Wing	Num	Text	Sym	Wing
0128	€		⓪	0160			·	0192	À	ℵ	⌚	0224	à	◊	→
0129			①	0161	¡	ϒ	○	0193	Á	ℑ	⌚	0225	á	⟨	↑
0130	,		②	0162	¢	′	●	0194	Â	ℜ	⌚	0226	â	®	↓
0131	ƒ		③	0163	£	≤	●	0195	Ã	℘	⌚	0227	ã	©	↖
0132	„		④	0164	¤	⁄	◉	0196	Ä	⊗	⌚	0228	ä	™	↗
0133	…		⑤	0165	¥	∞	◎	0197	Å	⊕	⌚	0229	å	∑	↙
0134	†		⑥	0166	¦	ƒ	○	0198	Æ	∅	⌚	0230	æ	⎛	↘
0135	‡		⑦	0167	§	♣	▪	0199	Ç	∩	⌚	0231	ç	⎜	←
0136	ˆ		⑧	0168	¨	♦	□	0200	È	∪	⌚	0232	è	⎝	→
0137	‰		⑨	0169	©	♥	▲	0201	É	⊃	⌚	0233	é	⎡	↑
0138	Š		⑩	0170	ª	♠	✦	0202	Ê	⊇	⌚	0234	ê	⎢	↓
0139	‹		⓿	0171	«	↔	★	0203	Ë	⊄	✾	0235	ë	⎣	↖
0140	Œ		❶	0172	¬	←	✳	0204	Ì	⊂	✳	0236	ì	⎡	↗
0141			❷	0173		↑	✲	0205	Í	⊆	℘	0237	í	⟨	↙
0142	Ž		❸	0174	®	→	✺	0206	Î	∈	ℜ	0238	î	⎣	↘
0143			❹	0175	¯	↓	❋	0207	Ï	∉	ℜ	0239	ï		⇐
0144			❺	0176	°	°	⊕	0208	Ð	∠	℘	0240	ð		⇒
0145	'		❻	0177	±	±	✛	0209	Ñ	∇	ℜ	0241	ñ	⟩	⇑
0146	'		❼	0178	²	″	✦	0210	Ò	®	ℜ	0242	ò	∫	⇓
0147	"		❽	0179	³	≥	⌘	0211	Ó	©	ℜ	0243	ó	⌠	⇔
0148	"		❾	0180	´	×	◈	0212	Ô	™	ℜ	0244	ô	⎮	⇕
0149	•		❿	0181	µ	∝	✪	0213	Õ	∏	⌧	0245	õ	⌡	⬁
0150	–		✿	0182	¶	∂	☆	0214	Ö	√	⌧	0246	ö		⬂
0151	—		✿	0183	·	•	⌚	0215	×	·	◀	0247	÷		⬃
0152	˜		✿	0184	¸	÷	⌚	0216	Ø	¬	▶	0248	ø		⬄
0153	™		✿	0185	¹	≠	⌚	0217	Ù	∧	▲	0249	ù		□
0154	š		✿	0186	º	≡	⌚	0218	Ú	∨	▼	0250	ú		□
0155	›		✿	0187	»	≈	⌚	0219	Û	⇔	☚	0251	û		✗
0156	œ		✿	0188	¼	…	⌚	0220	Ü	⇐	☞	0252	ü		✓
0157			✿	0189	½	│	⌚	0221	Ý	⇑	☜	0253	ý		☒
0158	ž		·	0190	¾	—	⌚	0222	Þ	⇒	☝	0254	þ		☑
0159	Ÿ		•	0191	¿	↵	⌚	0223	ß	⇓	←	0255	ÿ		▦

Figure 7-1 *(continued)*

We'll start with the most universal way to access ANSI characters from the keyboard and move on to other methods that are more application-specific.

Alt+Number Works in All Windows Apps

Every Windows application that supports TrueType fonts can handle the so-called *Alt+number* method of entering ANSI characters. This is often cryptically referred to in computer manuals using shorthand such as, "To enter a copyright symbol, type Alt+0169." Here's the routine:

1. Make sure your NumLock key is on (NumLock light is lighted).
2. Hold down your Alt key.
3. Type the character number shown in Figure 7-1 on the numeric keypad. (On laptops, this can be done by turning on the NumLock key, even though the numerals may share alphabetical characters on the keyboard.). In Vista, it's not necessary to type a leading zero (0) for characters above 127.
4. Release the Alt key. The desired character should instantly appear.

Of course, if you're trying to insert a Wingdings symbol into your document, it won't look right unless you previously switched the current font in your application to Wingdings. That's okay, though. You can format the character with your desired font either *before* or *after* you enter it.

> **tip**
>
> If you don't know a particular character's number, and you don't have Figure 7-1 handy, you can use Windows' CharMap utility to visually search for characters. To do this, use the Start menu to run **Charmap.exe**. This little applet lets you select any Windows font and scroll through its character set until you see something you want. Make a note of the character's location so you don't need to launch CharMap every time.

The "Dead Key" Method Is the Fastest

Americans who want to include accented characters and other foreign-language symbols in documents should take advantage of shortcuts that are built into their applications. Microsoft Word for Windows includes a series of "dead keys" for this purpose. These are Ctrl+key combinations you press, followed by an ordinary letter that's present on every U.S. keyboard.

In Word, pressing and releasing Ctrl+' (Ctrl+Apostrophe) and then pressing the letter *e* inserts into your document an é with an acute accent, as in résumé. The Ctrl+' key combination is the "dead key" that turns any vowel you subsequently type into its acute-accent equivalent.

Figure 7-2 shows the 12 kinds of characters you can insert into documents using Word's built-in dead keys. Many other programs also support these shortcuts.

To insert	Examples	Press	
Grave accent	à è ì ò ù À È Ì Ò Ù	Ctrl-` (backquote)	then the letter
Acute accent	á é í ó ú ý Á É Í Ó Ú Ý	Ctrl-' (apostrophe)	then the letter
Eth	ð Ð	Ctrl-' (apostrophe)	then d or D
Cedilla	ç Ç	Ctrl-, (comma)	then c or C
Circumflex	â ê î ô û Â Ê Î Ô Û	Ctrl-Shift-^ (caret)	then the letter
Tilde	ã ñ õ Ã Ñ Õ	Ctrl-Shift-~ (tilde)	then the letter
Umlaut or dieresis	ä ë ï ö ü ÿ Ä Ë Ï Ö Ü Ÿ	Ctrl-Shift-: (colon)	then the letter
Aring	å Å	Ctrl-Shift-@	then a or A
Ligatures	æ Æ œ Œ	Ctrl-Shift-&	then a, A, o, or O
Sharp s	ß	Ctrl-Shift-&	then s
O with stroke	ø Ø	Ctrl-/	then o or O
Inverted marks	¿ ¡	Alt-Ctrl-Shift-? *or* Alt-Ctrl-Shift-!	

Figure 7-2: It's easy to enter accented characters into documents using the 12 "dead key" shortcuts that are built into Microsoft Word and many other applications.

When All Else Fails, Head for the Symbol Menu

As a last resort, you can search for and insert most special characters using dialog boxes that are built into many applications. In Microsoft Word 97/2000/2002/2003, for example, you do this by clicking Insert⇨Symbol.

Word's Symbol dialog box shows you a scrolling window containing every character in Windows' Symbol font, or any other font you select. You can also insert special characters from Windows' middle ANSI character range of characters numbered 128 through 159, such as an em dash (—) or trademark sign (™).

Watch out for these latter symbols, however. Word, especially older versions, is notorious for its misuse of these characters, as handy as they might be. See the accompanying Secret about the proper way to access 128 through 159.

Secret

Characters 128 to 159 Are Bad for You

The middle ANSI positions numbered 128 to 159 were reserved by standards bodies years ago for control codes, as explained previously. The symbols that Microsoft put in these positions don't show up correctly when your document is opened on a Mac or Linux system, or if you paste the text into a Web form or HTML document.

Unfortunately, many versions of Microsoft Word automatically convert commonly typed expressions into symbols numbered 128 to 159. Word's so-called AutoCorrect feature silently turns ordinary ASCII characters such as (tm) and quotation marks into gylphs such as ™ and curly quotes. These characters may not display or print correctly when your document is opened by computer users whose equipment varies from yours.

To avoid this problem, make sure the middle ANSI characters are always entered using their decimal or hex Unicode values. A conversion chart for the characters between ANSI 128 and 159 is shown in Figure 7-3. You must, of course, also select a font that contains these Unicode positions for these characters to display and print. All of Windows' fonts that support WGL4 do contain these characters in the correct Unicode positions.

continues

continued

If you need to distribute your document, you must save your fonts with the file so they display and print for other computer users. "The document you save could be your own" tip later in this chapter explains how to do this.

If you can't save the fonts within a file you're going to distribute, avoid using ANSI characters 128 through 159. Use plain-text ASCII equivalents instead, such as (TM) in regular parentheses and straight quote marks.

To make sure this problem never bites you, consider turning off Word's AutoCorrect feature entirely. In Word 2000/2002/2003, for instance, click Tools⇨AutoCorrect and turn off all the check boxes you find in the resulting dialog box.

ANSI	Dec	Hex		ANSI	Dec	Hex	
0128	8364	20ac	€	0144			
0129				0145	8216	2018	'
0130	8218	201a	,	0146	8217	2019	'
0131	402	0192	ƒ	0147	8220	201c	"
0132	8222	201e	„	0148	8221	201d	"
0133	8230	2026	…	0149	8226	2022	•
0134	8224	2020	†	0150	8211	2013	–
0135	8225	2021	‡	0151	8212	2014	—
0136	710	02c6	^	0152	732	02dc	~
0137	8240	2030	‰	0153	8482	2122	TM
0138	352	0160	Š	0154	353	0161	š
0139	8249	2039	‹	0155	8250	203a	›
0140	338	0152	Œ	0156	339	0153	œ
0141				0157			
0142	381	017d	Ž	0158	382	017e	ž
0143				0159	376	0178	Ÿ

Figure 7-3: Don't use ANSI values for characters 128 to 159, if possible. Instead, select a WGL4 or Unicode font and use these characters' decimal or hex Unicode values. Ways to enter these values are explained in the Unicode section of this chapter.

How to Spell Words Good

That heading caught your attention, didn't it? For a moment, you weren't sure whether we were joking or just ignorant of proper grammar.

We want to make an important point here. Since most English words don't bear accents, many English speakers mistakenly believe it's not important to ever use them.

Au contraire, mon frère. Try this thought-experiment to see if that assumption is really true.

Imagine that you advertise for a new assistant to help you, say, with your chain of ski resorts. Soon, a talented young man applies for the job and seems to have promise. But, for some reason, he insists on preparing documents using a font that omits the dot over every *i* and *j*. He sends you letters that look like Figure 7-4.

When you ask about this, he says, "The little marks over the *i* and *j* aren't important, so I don't use them."

If he persisted in this, you'd never hire him. You couldn't trust him to represent you and give your company a good reputation in others' eyes. His work would always look, well, just wrong somehow.

This openıng ıs ıdeal, ın my opınıon, for someone wıth my ıdeas and ınsıghts ınto the skııng ındustry.

Figure 7-4: Think those little marks are unimportant? You'd never hire someone who treated the dot over the *i* with such carelessness. People who use languages other than English instinctively notice any missing diacritical marks in misspelled words.

When English speakers run roughshod over accents in, for example, people's names, the reaction is often just as negative as your disappointment in the brash young man. Not just Old World names, but also many English words—yes, there are some—are properly spelled with accents.

It never helps, and it can definitely hurt, if you spell *résumé* without its accents or drop diacritical marks from names such as Zoë and Chloë.

(It's clear that Chloë's name, spelled correctly with an accent, rhymes with *snowy*. If you mangle it as Chloe, you're suggesting that her name rhymes with *crow*, which isn't very flattering.)

Secret

Work Around Accents, Don't Simply Drop Them

There are actually some situations in which it's correct to spell a word or a person's name without using its accented letter—if you know the secret.

In German, for example, it's considered acceptable spelling to add an *e* if an umlaut letter is not available on a typewriter or computer keyboard. As an example, the city *Düsseldorf,* named after the Düssel River, can be spelled *Duesseldorf.*

Ignoring the umlaut over the *ü* and changing it to *u* is taken as a sign that the writer is a poorly educated foreigner. *Dusseldorf* literally translates as "dimwit village"—a bit of an insult to your business acquaintances there.

This convention of changing umlaut letters by adding an *e* to them developed long before computers. Old German buildings, for example, often use *OE* instead of *Ö* when words are carved in all capitals on a façade. But the practice came in handy when Europeans began using early IBM mainframes. Only nonaccented characters were available in the ASCII or EBCDIC standards used in those machines, so the conversion became more common.

In Hungarian, Turkish, and Scandinavian languages, however, *ö* is a separate letter of the alphabet. It's not considered proper to convert *ö* to *oe*. (In Swedish, *Ö* means island, but *Oe* doesn't.)

It's a lot easier to simply enter accented characters correctly in the first place rather than learning all these rules.

To help you avoid such *faux pas*, we've shown you in the past few pages how to insert accented characters into your document using even such crippled tools as the U.S.-English keyboard. And we provide Figure 7-5, which shows the correct spelling for some—but by no means all—words and place names that bear accented characters.

But what if you need a character that isn't on your keyboard—*and* it isn't found in the limited Windows ANSI character set. That's when you turn to WGL4 or, better yet, Unicode.

Words and Phrases:

à la carte	déjà vu	naïveté
à la mode	déshabillé	negligée
adiós	discothèque	passé
appliqué	divorcé (male)	pâte (moist clay)
après ski	divorcée (female)	pâté (meat paste or pastry)
attaché	doppelgänger	pâté en croûte
bête noire	émigré	pièce de resistance
café	entrée	pied à terre
cause célèbre	exposé	piña colada
coup d'état	fête	protégé
coup de grâce	fête champêtre	raison d'être
crème de cacao	fiancé (male)	répondez s'il vous plaît (RSVP)
crème de la crème	fiancée (female)	résumé
crème de menthe	fin de siècle	risqué
crème fraîche	habitué	roman à clef
crêpe	jalapeño	sautéed
crêpes Suzette	lamé	smörgåsbord
débridement	lèse-majesté	soufflé
déclassé	maître d'hôtel	tête-à-tête
décolletage	mañana	très chic
décolleté	moiré	vicuña
décor	naïf	vis-à-vis
découpage	naïve	voilà!

Company Names:

Condé Nast	Estée Lauder	Les Misérables
Crédit Suisse	Hermès	Moët & Chandon
Crédit Lyonnais	Lancôme	Nestlé
Dom Pérignon	Lazard Frères & Co.	Plaza Athénée

Major Place Names:

Ascunción, Paraguay	Düsseldorf, Germany	Québec, Canada
Belém, Brazil	Guantánamo Bay, Cuba	San José, Costa Rica
Bogotá, Colombia	Medellín, Colombia	São Paulo, Brazil
Brasília, Brazil	México	Tiranë, Albania
Córdoba, Argentina	Montréal, Canada	Valparaíso, Chile
Curaçao, Lesser Antilles	Perú	Zürich, Switzerland

Figure 7-5: Some common words that are spelled with accents. This list is by no means complete. Always include accents when they appear in people's names. (There are too many accented first and last names to include them all here.)

Unicode: One Font to Rule Them All

Unicode, when fully implemented as explained earlier, will ensure that computer users can reliably exchange documents created on different systems. Unicode support is surprisingly strong, even among zealots of such competing platforms as Windows, Macs, and Linux. This makes it only a matter of time before universal, standardized character positions are used by most applications that support fonts.

WGL4 Represents a Temporary Solution, at Best

What about WGL4? This set of characters, which supports most language groupings in the Americas and Eastern and Western Europe, is certainly convenient in countries where the use of Windows was previously difficult.

But WGL4 was a stopgap measure. Aware of Unicode's coming ascent, Microsoft encoded all the extra, non-ASCII characters in WGL4 to the positions they would eventually occupy in the Unicode standard. This means you can refer to every upper-level character in WGL4 by using its Unicode number (if the glyph doesn't appear on your keyboard).

Windows users in places like Estonia and Romania have good Windows support for their national languages—and already own keyboards with a variety of European characters printed right on the keytops—thanks to the introduction of WGL4. These languages don't need a printed chart of these character sets, any more than native speakers of English need an A to Z poster on the wall in front of them.

So we're not including in this book a chart of the WGL4 character set. Instead, we've developed for your reading pleasure a listing of major Unicode characters. This includes WGL4 and much, much more.

tip

For listings and charts of WGL4 characters, including a breakdown of the language groupings represented within the set, see Microsoft's "Character sets and code pages" documentation at http://www.microsoft.com/typography/unicode/cscp.htm.

For an excellent table showing the decimal and hex values of characters in the WGL4 range, see www.alanwood.net/demos/wg14.html. You can use the numerical values in Alan Wood's table to enter WGL4 characters the same way we'll soon explain how to enter Unicode values.

The Top 1,000 Characters of All Time

Entire books have been written on Unicode—more like small encyclopedias, actually—filled with every glyph known to humanity, literally. Even some fictional languages, such as Klingon from the *Star Trek* movies, has entries, although they're limited to private-use locations and aren't considered official.

It's impossible for us to duplicate the thousands of pages that have been written to document Unicode. Fortunately, we don't have to.

Figure 7-6 shows our pick of 1,062 Unicode characters. These are the glyphs that are the most likely for speakers of Latin and Roman languages to ever encounter.

If you're some kind of linguistics scholar, you may feel compelled to know the Unicode assignments of every script from Etruscan to Sumerian. But if you're someone who just needs to be able to spell that scholar's name correctly, do we have the characters for you.

Entering Unicode Characters from the Keyboard

If you frequently write documents in more than one language, you probably already own a keyboard that supports the characters you need. For example, many Canadians use the French-Canadian keyboard and Windows' software keyboard layout for it. Both the hardware and the software work together to produce the characters commonly used in both English and French, Canada's two official languages.

You may occasionally find, however, that you need to enter a character from the Unicode range that isn't on your keyboard. In that case, you have a few options.

In Windows 2000, XP, and Vista, Unicode values can be entered from the keyboard using either decimal or hexadecimal numbers. Figure 7-6 shows decimal numbers without leading zeros, if a leading zero need not be typed in earlier versions of Windows. All hex numbers are shown in Figure 7-6 as four digits, including leading zeros.

Application Support for Special Characters

As knowledge of Unicode becomes more prevalent among Windows users, applications will increasingly provide keyboard shortcuts or menu options to enter extra characters. If your application supports such shortcuts, they'll be the fastest way to enter such text.

Alt+X Method for Windows XP and Vista

Windows XP and higher supports using *Alt+X* to insert any Unicode character from the keyboard in some (but not all) applications:

1. The status of NumLock doesn't matter using the Alt+X method.

2. Using the main keyboard, type the hex value of your desired character directly into the visible text of your document. You can type the four-digit hex value or **U+** followed by the four-digit hex value. For example, you could type **03c0** or **U+03c0** to specify the Greek letter *pi* (π).

3. With your insertion point immediately to the right of the hex value, press Alt+X.

4. The value you typed is immediately transformed into your desired character, if the current font includes that character. You can always change the font at a later time, if you want.

5. Pressing Alt+X again at the same location *should* change the Unicode character back into its hex-value equivalent. But some applications and fonts don't support this kind of reversal. So don't save your document until you know whether or not you can toggle back and forth.

Dec	Hex		Dec	Hex		Dec	Hex		Dec	Hex		Dec	Hex		Dec	Hex	
0161	00a1	¡	0205	00cd	Í	0248	00f8	ø	299	012b	ī	350	015e	Ş	488	01e8	Ǩ
0165	00a5	¥	0206	00ce	Î	0249	00f9	ù	300	012c	Ĭ	351	015f	ş	489	01e9	ǩ
0166	00a6	¦	0207	00cf	Ï	0250	00fa	ú	301	012d	ĭ	352	0160	Š	496	01f0	ǰ
0167	00a7	§	0209	00d1	Ñ	0251	00fb	û	304	0130	İ	353	0161	š	500	01f4	Ǵ
0168	00a8	¨	0210	00d2	Ò	0252	00fc	ü	305	0131	ı	354	0162	Ţ	501	01f5	ǵ
0169	00a9	©	0211	00d3	Ó	0253	00fd	ý	308	0134	Ĵ	355	0163	ţ	508	01fc	Ǽ
0170	00aa	ª	0212	00d4	Ô	0255	00ff	ÿ	309	0135	ĵ	356	0164	Ť	509	01fd	ǽ
0171	00ab	«	0213	00d5	Õ	256	0100	Ā	310	0136	Ķ	357	0165	ť	711	02c7	ˇ
0172	00ac	¬	0214	00d6	Ö	257	0101	ā	311	0137	ķ	360	0168	Ũ	713	02c9	ˉ
0173	00ad		0215	00d7	×	258	0102	Ă	313	0139	Ĺ	361	0169	ũ	728	02d8	˘
0174	00ae	®	0216	00d8	Ø	259	0103	ă	314	013a	ĺ	362	016a	Ū	729	02d9	˙
0175	00af	¯	0217	00d9	Ù	262	0106	Ć	315	013b	Ļ	363	016b	ū	730	02da	˚
0176	00b0	°	0218	00da	Ú	263	0107	ć	316	013c	ļ	364	016c	Ŭ	733	02dd	˝
0177	00b1	±	0219	00db	Û	264	0108	Ĉ	317	013d	Ľ	365	016d	ŭ	768	0300	̀
0178	00b2	²	0220	00dc	Ü	265	0109	ĉ	318	013e	ľ	366	016e	Ů	769	0301	́
0179	00b3	³	0221	00dd	Ý	266	010a	Ċ	321	0141	Ł	367	016f	ů	770	0302	̂
0180	00b4	´	0223	00df	ß	267	010b	ċ	322	0142	ł	368	0170	Ű	771	0303	̃
0181	00b5	µ	0224	00e0	à	268	010c	Č	323	0143	Ń	369	0171	ű	772	0304	̄
0182	00b6	¶	0225	00e1	á	269	010d	č	324	0144	ń	372	0174	Ŵ	774	0306	̆
0183	00b7	·	0226	00e2	â	270	010e	Ď	325	0145	Ņ	373	0175	ŵ	775	0307	̇
0184	00b8	¸	0227	00e3	ã	271	010f	ď	326	0146	ņ	374	0176	Ŷ	776	0308	̈
0185	00b9	¹	0228	00e4	ä	274	0112	Ē	327	0147	Ň	375	0177	ŷ	778	030a	̊
0186	00ba	º	0229	00e5	å	275	0113	ē	328	0148	ň	376	0178	Ÿ	779	030b	̋
0187	00bb	»	0230	00e6	æ	276	0114	Ĕ	332	014c	Ō	377	0179	Ź	780	030c	̌
0188	00bc	¼	0231	00e7	ç	277	0115	ĕ	333	014d	ō	378	017a	ź	803	0323	̣
0189	00bd	½	0232	00e8	è	278	0116	Ė	334	014e	Ŏ	379	017b	Ż	807	0327	̧
0190	00be	¾	0233	00e9	é	279	0117	ė	335	014f	ŏ	380	017c	ż	817	0331	̱
0191	00bf	¿	0234	00ea	ê	282	011a	Ě	336	0150	Ő	381	017d	Ž	824	0338	̸
0192	00c0	À	0235	00eb	ë	283	011b	ě	337	0151	ő	382	017e	ž	864	0360	͠
0193	00c1	Á	0236	00ec	ì	284	011c	Ĝ	338	0152	Œ	461	01cd	Ǎ	865	0361	͡
0194	00c2	Â	0237	00ed	í	285	011d	ĝ	339	0153	œ	462	01ce	ǎ	913	0391	Α
0195	00c3	Ã	0238	00ee	î	286	011e	Ğ	340	0154	Ŕ	463	01cf	Ǐ	914	0392	Β
0196	00c4	Ä	0239	00ef	ï	287	011f	ğ	341	0155	ŕ	464	01d0	ǐ	915	0393	Γ
0197	00c5	Å	0240	00f0	ð	288	0120	Ġ	342	0156	Ŗ	465	01d1	Ǒ	916	0394	Δ
0198	00c6	Æ	0241	00f1	ñ	289	0121	ġ	343	0157	ŗ	466	01d2	ǒ	917	0395	Ε
0199	00c7	Ç	0242	00f2	ò	290	0122	Ģ	344	0158	Ř	467	01d3	Ǔ	918	0396	Ζ
0200	00c8	È	0243	00f3	ó	292	0124	Ĥ	345	0159	ř	468	01d4	ǔ	919	0397	Η
0201	00c9	É	0244	00f4	ô	293	0125	ĥ	346	015a	Ś	482	01e2	Ǣ	920	0398	Θ
0202	00ca	Ê	0245	00f5	õ	296	0128	Ĩ	347	015b	ś	483	01e3	ǣ	921	0399	Ι
0203	00cb	Ë	0246	00f6	ö	297	0129	ĩ	348	015c	Ŝ	486	01e6	Ǧ	922	039a	Κ
0204	00cc	Ì	0247	00f7	÷	298	012a	Ī	349	015d	ŝ	487	01e7	ǧ	923	039b	Λ

Figure 7-6: Some important characters and symbols in Unicode. You can enter these characters in Windows XP and Windows Vista by holding down the Alt key, typing the decimal number on the numeric keypad (with NumLock on), and releasing Alt. Leading zeros in the hex numbers are optional.

Dec	Hex		Dec	Hex		Dec	Hex		Dec	Hex		Dec	Hex		Dec	Hex	
924	039c	Μ	978	03d2	ϒ	1065	0429	Щ	1108	0454	є	1273	04f9	ӹ	7766	1e56	Ṗ
925	039d	Ν	981	03d5	ϕ	1066	042a	Ъ	1109	0455	ѕ	7682	1e02	Ḃ	7767	1e57	ṗ
926	039e	Ξ	982	03d6	ϖ	1067	042b	Ы	1110	0456	і	7683	1e03	ḃ	7768	1e58	Ṙ
927	039f	Ο	988	03dc	Ϝ	1068	042c	Ь	1112	0458	ј	7684	1e04	Ḅ	7769	1e59	ṙ
928	03a0	Π	1008	03f0	ϰ	1069	042d	Э	1113	0459	љ	7685	1e05	ḅ	7770	1e5a	Ṛ
929	03a1	Ρ	1009	03f1	ϱ	1070	042e	Ю	1114	045a	њ	7690	1e0a	Ḋ	7771	1e5b	ṛ
931	03a3	Σ	1025	0401	Ё	1071	042f	Я	1115	045b	ћ	7691	1e0b	ḋ	7776	1e60	Ṡ
932	03a4	Τ	1026	0402	Ђ	1072	0430	а	1119	045f	џ	7692	1e0c	Ḍ	7777	1e61	ṡ
933	03a5	Υ	1028	0404	Є	1073	0431	б	1122	0462	Ѣ	7693	1e0d	ḍ	7778	1e62	Ṣ
934	03a6	Φ	1029	0405	Ѕ	1074	0432	в	1123	0463	ѣ	7696	1e10	Ḑ	7779	1e63	ṣ
935	03a7	Χ	1030	0406	І	1075	0433	г	1138	0472	Ѳ	7697	1e11	ḑ	7786	1e6a	Ṫ
936	03a8	Ψ	1032	0408	Ј	1076	0434	д	1139	0473	ѳ	7710	1e1e	Ḟ	7787	1e6b	ṫ
937	03a9	Ω	1033	0409	Љ	1077	0435	е	1140	0474	Ѵ	7711	1e1f	ḟ	7788	1e6c	Ṭ
938	03aa	Ϊ	1034	040a	Њ	1078	0436	ж	1141	0475	ѵ	7712	1e20	Ḡ	7789	1e6d	ṭ
939	03ab	Ϋ	1035	040b	Ћ	1079	0437	з	1217	04c1	Ж	7713	1e21	ḡ	7804	1e7c	Ṽ
945	03b1	α	1039	040f	Џ	1080	0438	и	1218	04c2	ж	7714	1e22	Ḣ	7805	1e7d	ṽ
946	03b2	β	1040	0410	А	1081	0439	й	1232	04d0	Ӑ	7715	1e23	ḣ	7806	1e7e	Ṿ
947	03b3	γ	1041	0411	Б	1082	043a	к	1233	04d1	ӑ	7716	1e24	Ḥ	7807	1e7f	ṿ
948	03b4	δ	1042	0412	В	1083	043b	л	1234	04d2	Ӓ	7717	1e25	ḥ	7808	1e80	Ẁ
949	03b5	ε	1043	0413	Г	1084	043c	м	1235	04d3	ӓ	7718	1e26	Ḧ	7809	1e81	ẁ
950	03b6	ζ	1044	0414	Д	1085	043d	н	1238	04d6	Ӗ	7719	1e27	ḧ	7810	1e82	Ẃ
951	03b7	η	1045	0415	Е	1086	043e	о	1239	04d7	ӗ	7720	1e28	Ḩ	7811	1e83	ẃ
952	03b8	θ	1046	0416	Ж	1087	043f	п	1244	04dc	Ӝ	7721	1e29	ḩ	7812	1e84	Ẅ
953	03b9	ι	1047	0417	З	1088	0440	р	1245	04dd	ӝ	7728	1e30	Ḱ	7813	1e85	ẅ
954	03ba	κ	1048	0418	И	1089	0441	с	1246	04de	Ӟ	7729	1e31	ḱ	7814	1e86	Ẇ
955	03bb	λ	1049	0419	Й	1090	0442	т	1247	04df	ӟ	7730	1e32	Ḳ	7815	1e87	ẇ
956	03bc	μ	1050	041a	К	1091	0443	у	1250	04e2	Ӣ	7731	1e33	ḳ	7816	1e88	Ẉ
957	03bd	ν	1051	041b	Л	1092	0444	ф	1251	04e3	ӣ	7734	1e36	Ḷ	7817	1e89	ẉ
958	03be	ξ	1052	041c	М	1093	0445	х	1252	04e4	Ӥ	7735	1e37	Ḷ	7818	1e8a	Ẋ
959	03bf	o	1053	041d	Н	1094	0446	ц	1253	04e5	ӥ	7742	1e3e	Ḿ	7819	1e8b	ẋ
960	03c0	π	1054	041e	О	1095	0447	ч	1254	04e6	Ӧ	7743	1e3f	ḿ	7820	1e8c	Ẍ
961	03c1	ρ	1055	041f	П	1096	0448	ш	1255	04e7	ӧ	7744	1e40	Ṁ	7821	1e8d	ẍ
962	03c2	ς	1056	0420	Р	1097	0449	щ	1262	04ee	Ӯ	7745	1e41	ṁ	7822	1e8e	Ẏ
963	03c3	σ	1057	0421	С	1098	044a	ъ	1263	04ef	ӯ	7746	1e42	Ṃ	7823	1e8f	ẏ
964	03c4	τ	1058	0422	Т	1099	044b	ы	1264	04f0	Ӱ	7747	1e43	ṃ	7824	1e90	Ẑ
965	03c5	υ	1059	0423	У	1100	044c	ь	1265	04f1	ӱ	7748	1e44	Ṅ	7825	1e91	ẑ
966	03c6	φ	1060	0424	Ф	1101	044d	э	1266	04f2	Ӳ	7749	1e45	ṅ	7826	1e92	Ẓ
967	03c7	χ	1061	0425	Х	1102	044e	ю	1267	04f3	ӳ	7750	1e46	Ṇ	7827	1e93	ẓ
968	03c8	ψ	1062	0426	Ц	1103	044f	я	1268	04f4	Ӵ	7751	1e47	ṇ	7831	1e97	ẗ
969	03c9	ω	1063	0427	Ч	1105	0451	ё	1269	04f5	ӵ	7764	1e54	Ṕ	7832	1e98	ẘ
977	03d1	ϑ	1064	0428	Ш	1106	0452	ђ	1272	04f8	Ӹ	7765	1e55	ṕ	7833	1e99	ẙ

Figure 7-6 (continued)

Dec	Hex		Dec	Hex		Dec	Hex		Dec	Hex		Dec	Hex		Dec	Hex	
7840	1ea0	Ạ	8315	207b	⁻	8486	2126	Ω	8560	2170	ⅰ	8637	21bd	↽	8718	220e	∎
7841	1ea1	ạ	8316	207c	⁼	8487	2127	℧	8561	2171	ⅱ	8638	21be	↾	8719	220f	∏
7864	1eb8	Ẹ	8317	207d	⁽	8490	212a	K	8562	2172	ⅲ	8639	21bf	↿	8720	2210	∐
7865	1eb9	ẹ	8318	207e	⁾	8491	212b	Å	8563	2173	ⅳ	8640	21c0	⇀	8721	2211	∑
7868	1ebc	Ẽ	8319	207f	ⁿ	8492	212c	ℬ	8564	2174	ⅴ	8641	21c1	⇁	8722	2212	−
7869	1ebd	ẽ	8320	2080	₀	8496	2130	ℰ	8565	2175	ⅵ	8642	21c2	⇂	8723	2213	∓
7882	1eca	Ị	8321	2081	₁	8497	2131	ℱ	8566	2176	ⅶ	8643	21c3	⇃	8724	2214	∔
7883	1ecb	ị	8322	2082	₂	8498	2132	Ⅎ	8567	2177	ⅷ	8644	21c4	⇄	8725	2215	∕
7884	1ecc	Ọ	8323	2083	₃	8499	2133	ℳ	8568	2178	ⅸ	8646	21c6	⇆	8726	2216	∖
7885	1ecd	ọ	8324	2084	₄	8501	2135	ℵ	8569	2179	ⅹ	8647	21c7	⇇	8727	2217	∗
7908	1ee4	Ụ	8325	2085	₅	8502	2136	ℶ	8570	217a	ⅺ	8648	21c8	⇈	8728	2218	∘
7909	1ee5	ụ	8326	2086	₆	8503	2137	ℷ	8571	217b	ⅻ	8649	21c9	⇉	8729	2219	∙
7922	1ef2	Ỳ	8327	2087	₇	8504	2138	ℸ	8572	217c	ⅼ	8650	21ca	⇊	8730	221a	√
7923	1ef3	ỳ	8328	2088	₈	8531	2153	⅓	8573	217d	ⅽ	8651	21cb	⇋	8731	221b	∛
7924	1ef4	Ỵ	8329	2089	₉	8532	2154	⅔	8574	217e	ⅾ	8652	21cc	⇌	8732	221c	∜
7925	1ef5	ỵ	8330	208a	₊	8533	2155	⅕	8575	217f	ⅿ	8653	21cd	⇍	8733	221d	∝
7928	1ef8	Ỹ	8331	208b	₋	8534	2156	⅖	8592	2190	←	8654	21ce	⇎	8734	221e	∞
7929	1ef9	ỹ	8332	208c	₌	8535	2157	⅗	8593	2191	↑	8655	21cf	⇏	8736	2220	∠
8211	2013	–	8333	208d	₍	8536	2158	⅘	8594	2192	→	8656	21d0	⇐	8737	2221	∡
8212	2014	—	8334	208e	₎	8537	2159	⅙	8595	2193	↓	8657	21d1	⇑	8738	2222	∢
8216	2018	'	8407	20d7	⃗	8538	215a	⅚	8596	2194	↔	8658	21d2	⇒	8739	2223	∣
8217	2019	'	8450	2102	ℂ	8539	215b	⅛	8597	2195	↕	8659	21d3	⇓	8740	2224	∤
8220	201c	"	8451	2103	℃	8540	215c	⅜	8598	2196	↖	8660	21d4	⇔	8741	2225	∥
8221	201d	"	8457	2109	℉	8541	215d	⅝	8599	2197	↗	8661	21d5	⇕	8742	2226	∦
8224	2020	†	8459	210b	ℋ	8542	215e	⅞	8600	2198	↘	8666	21da	⇚	8743	2227	∧
8225	2021	‡	8461	210d	ℍ	8544	2160	Ⅰ	8601	2199	↙	8667	21db	⇛	8744	2228	∨
8230	2026	…	8462	210e	ℎ	8545	2161	Ⅱ	8602	219a	↚	8669	21dd	⇝	8745	2229	∩
8242	2032	′	8463	210f	ℏ	8546	2162	Ⅲ	8603	219b	↛	8672	21e0	⇠	8746	222a	∪
8243	2033	″	8464	2110	ℐ	8547	2163	Ⅳ	8614	21a6	↦	8674	21e2	⇢	8747	222b	∫
8244	2034	‴	8465	2111	ℑ	8548	2164	Ⅴ	8617	21a9	↩	8704	2200	∀	8748	222c	∬
8245	2035	‵	8466	2112	ℒ	8549	2165	Ⅵ	8618	21aa	↪	8705	2201	∁	8749	222d	∭
8246	2036	‶	8467	2113	ℓ	8550	2166	Ⅶ	8619	21ab	↫	8706	2202	∂	8750	222e	∮
8247	2037	‷	8469	2115	ℕ	8551	2167	Ⅷ	8620	21ac	↬	8707	2203	∃	8756	2234	∴
8304	2070	⁰	8471	2117	℗	8552	2168	Ⅸ	8622	21ae	↮	8708	2204	∄	8757	2235	∵
8308	2074	⁴	8472	2118	℘	8553	2169	Ⅹ	8624	21b0	↰	8709	2205	∅	8764	223c	∼
8309	2075	⁵	8473	2119	ℙ	8554	216a	Ⅺ	8625	21b1	↱	8710	2206	∆	8765	223d	∽
8310	2076	⁶	8474	211a	ℚ	8555	216b	Ⅻ	8630	21b6	↶	8711	2207	∇	8768	2240	≀
8311	2077	⁷	8475	211b	ℛ	8556	216c	Ⅼ	8631	21b7	↷	8712	2208	∈	8769	2241	≁
8312	2078	⁸	8476	211c	ℜ	8557	216d	Ⅽ	8634	21ba	↺	8713	2209	∉	8771	2243	≃
8313	2079	⁹	8477	211d	ℝ	8558	216e	Ⅾ	8635	21bb	↻	8715	220b	∋	8772	2244	≄
8314	207a	⁺	8484	2124	ℤ	8559	216f	Ⅿ	8636	21bc	↼	8716	220c	∌	8773	2245	≅

Figure 7-6 *(continued)*

Dec	Hex		Dec	Hex		Dec	Hex		Dec	Hex		Dec	Hex		Dec	Hex	
8775	2247	≇	8835	2283	⊃	8883	22b3	⊳	8937	22e9	⋩	9351	2487	⒇	9392	24b0	(u)
8776	2248	≈	8836	2284	⊄	8884	22b4	⊴	8938	22ea	⋪	9352	2488	⒈	9393	24b1	(v)
8777	2249	≉	8837	2285	⊅	8885	22b5	⊵	8939	22eb	⋫	9353	2489	⒉	9394	24b2	(w)
8778	224a	≊	8838	2286	⊆	8890	22ba	⊺	8940	22ec	⋬	9354	248a	⒊	9395	24b3	(x)
8781	224d	≍	8839	2287	⊇	8891	22bb	⊻	8941	22ed	⋭	9355	248b	⒋	9396	24b4	(y)
8784	2250	≐	8840	2288	⊈	8892	22bc	⊼	8942	22ee	⋮	9356	248c	⒌	9397	24b5	(z)
8785	2251	≑	8841	2289	⊉	8896	22c0	⋀	8943	22ef	⋯	9357	248d	⒍	9415	24c7	®
8786	2252	≒	8842	228a	⊊	8897	22c1	⋁	8944	22f0	⋰	9358	248e	⒎	9416	24c8	Ⓢ
8787	2253	≓	8843	228b	⊋	8898	22c2	⋂	8945	22f1	⋱	9359	248f	⒏	9585	2571	╱
8790	2256	≖	8846	228e	⊎	8899	22c3	⋃	8960	2300	⌀	9360	2490	⒐	9586	2572	╲
8791	2257	≗	8847	228f	⊏	8901	22c5	⋅	8968	2308	⌈	9361	2491	⒑	9632	25a0	■
8799	225f	≟	8848	2290	⊐	8902	22c6	⋆	8969	2309	⌉	9362	2492	⒒	9633	25a1	□
8800	2260	≠	8849	2291	⊑	8903	22c7	⋇	8970	230a	⌊	9363	2493	⒓	9651	25b3	△
8801	2261	≡	8850	2292	⊒	8904	22c8	⋈	8971	230b	⌋	9364	2494	⒔	9652	25b4	▴
8802	2262	≢	8851	2293	⊓	8905	22c9	⋉	8988	231c	⌜	9365	2495	⒕	9653	25b5	▵
8804	2264	≤	8852	2294	⊔	8906	22ca	⋊	8989	231d	⌝	9366	2496	⒖	9654	25b6	▶
8805	2265	≥	8853	2295	⊕	8907	22cb	⋋	8990	231e	⌞	9367	2497	⒗	9657	25b9	▹
8806	2266	≦	8854	2296	⊖	8908	22cc	⋌	8991	231f	⌟	9368	2498	⒘	9661	25bd	▽
8807	2267	≧	8855	2297	⊗	8909	22cd	⋍	8994	2322	⌢	9369	2499	⒙	9662	25be	▾
8808	2268	≨	8857	2299	⊙	8910	22ce	⋎	8995	2323	⌣	9370	249a	⒚	9663	25bf	▿
8809	2269	≩	8858	229a	⊚	8911	22cf	⋏	9001	2329	〈	9371	249b	⒛	9664	25c0	◀
8810	226a	≪	8859	229b	⊛	8912	22d0	⋐	9002	232a	〉	9372	249c	(a)	9667	25c3	◃
8811	226b	≫	8861	229d	⊝	8913	22d1	⋑	9332	2474	(1)	9373	249d	(b)	9674	25ca	◊
8812	226c	≬	8862	229e	⊞	8914	22d2	⋒	9333	2475	(2)	9374	249e	(c)	9711	25ef	◯
8814	226e	≮	8863	229f	⊟	8915	22d3	⋓	9334	2476	(3)	9375	249f	(d)	9733	2605	★
8815	226f	≯	8864	22a0	⊠	8916	22d4	⋔	9335	2477	(4)	9376	24a0	(e)	9824	2660	♠
8816	2270	≰	8865	22a1	⊡	8918	22d6	⋖	9336	2478	(5)	9377	24a1	(f)	9825	2661	♡
8817	2271	≱	8866	22a2	⊢	8919	22d7	⋗	9337	2479	(6)	9378	24a2	(g)	9826	2662	♢
8818	2272	≲	8867	22a3	⊣	8920	22d8	⋘	9338	247a	(7)	9379	24a3	(h)	9827	2663	♣
8819	2273	≳	8868	22a4	⊤	8921	22d9	⋙	9339	247b	(8)	9380	24a4	(i)	9830	2666	♦
8822	2276	≶	8869	22a5	⊥	8922	22da	⋚	9340	247c	(9)	9381	24a5	(j)	9837	266d	♭
8823	2277	≷	8870	22a6	⊦	8923	22db	⋛	9341	247d	(10)	9382	24a6	(k)	9838	266e	♮
8826	227a	≺	8871	22a7	⊧	8924	22dc	⋜	9342	247e	(11)	9383	24a7	(l)	9839	266f	♯
8827	227b	≻	8872	22a8	⊨	8925	22dd	⋝	9343	247f	(12)	9384	24a8	(m)			
8828	227c	≼	8873	22a9	⊩	8928	22e0	⋠	9344	2480	(13)	9385	24a9	(n)			
8829	227d	≽	8874	22aa	⊪	8929	22e1	⋡	9345	2481	(14)	9386	24aa	(o)	**Space Characters**		
8830	227e	≾	8876	22ac	⊬	8930	22e2	⋢	9346	2482	(15)	9387	24ab	(p)	0160	00a0	nbsp
8831	227f	≿	8877	22ad	⊭	8931	22e3	⋣	9347	2483	(16)	9388	24ac	(q)	8194	2002	ensp
8832	2280	⊀	8878	22ae	⊮	8934	22e6	⋦	9348	2484	(17)	9389	24ad	(r)	8195	2003	emsp
8833	2281	⊁	8879	22af	⊯	8935	22e7	⋧	9349	2485	(18)	9390	24ae	(s)	8196	2004	⅓em
8834	2282	⊂	8882	22b2	⊲	8936	22e8	⋨	9350	2486	(19)	9391	24af	(t)	8197	2005	¼em
															8198	2006	⅙em

Figure 7-6 *(continued)*

Alt+Number Works for Unicode as well as ANSI

If you need to enter just a few special characters, the Alt+number method that was described earlier for ANSI characters also can be used to enter Unicode characters in almost any Windows application.

One difference is that Windows Vista supports *two* Alt+number methods. One uses decimal numbers from 161 and higher. The other uses hexadecimal numbers from 00a1 on up. We'll first explain the *Alt+decimal* method.

1. Make sure the NumLock key is on (NumLock light is lighted).
2. Hold down the Alt key.
3. On the numeric keypad, type the decimal number of the character you desire. You don't need to include a leading zero in front of character numbers 256 and higher.
4. Release the Alt key. If your insertion point is formatted in a font that includes the Unicode character you entered, that character immediately appears. If not, you can change the font at any later time.

If the Alt+number method doesn't work, your input language or code page may be interfering. If so, try the Alt-+Alt-hex method, described in the following section.

Alt+Plus, Alt+Hex Method for Windows 2000, XP, and Vista

You may prefer to enter a Unicode character from the keyboard using hexadecimal numbers rather than decimal. If so, there's what we call an *Alt+Plus, Alt+Hex* method that works in some applications. It's a bit more convoluted and time-consuming than the Alt+decimal method.

1. The status of NumLock doesn't matter using the Alt+Plus, Alt+Hex method.
2. Hold down the Alt key throughout this process.
3. Press the plus sign (+) on the numeric keypad. Nothing will noticeably change.
4. Using the main keyboard, type the letters and digits of the hex code for the character you desire. You can include leading zeros or omit them. For example, typing **03c0** or just **3c0** specifies the Greek letter *pi* (π), if your selected font has one.
5. Release the Alt key. If your insertion point is formatted in a font that includes the Unicode character you entered, that character immediately appears. If not, you can change the font at a later time.

Secret

Registry Hack May Be Required for Alt+Plus, Alt+Hex

The Alt+Plus, Alt+Hex method won't work in Windows or any application if a certain key in the Registry isn't set correctly. This could happen if the key was inadvertently changed or was never switched *on*. If Alt+Plus, Alt+Hex doesn't work, take the following steps:

1. Use the Start menu to run RegEdit.exe.
2. Expand HKEY_Current_User to /Control Panel/Input Method. Find the key (or create a new string value) called EnableHexNumpad. If you create this string value, it should have the REG_SZ type.
3. Right-click and modify EnableHexNumpad to give it a value of 1. Close RegEdit.

tip

Enter special characters using input locales. An *input locale* is a software feature of Windows that defines a particular keyboard layout and other localized setting. Once you've set up two or more, you can quickly switch from one layout to another so you can, for example, write in different languages using the same keyboard.

For more information, see Microsoft's FAQ on locales and languages at http://www.microsoft.com/globaldev/DrIntl/faqs/locales.mspx#E6E.

Who Has Which Fonts?

We've now dispensed with *how you get at* all of the characters that you may have hidden away within your fonts. So we turn to an equally important question: How do you know *which fonts you have?*

And just as important is this: Which fonts do other computer users have? This issue is crucial to whether you can send a document file to someone else and have them correctly see it the way you do on your screen and printer. If you post a document on the Internet, does it look fine to those who read and print it, or does it look like your cat was walking across your keyboard at the time?

These aren't easy questions to answer. We've spent a ridiculous amount of time researching every font name that ever shipped with Windows or other major Microsoft products. Now we're ready to announce who has which fonts!

Love at First Sort, or Baby, You're My Type

To make this information understandable, we first need to let you in on which versions of Windows—and therefore which users—have which fonts. A font that first reached Windows users only with the release of Vista will be present on far fewer systems than a font that's been around since clay tablets.

It turns out that many things are actually sorted kind of randomly when you put them into alphabetical lists. That's more true of font lists than almost anything else.

So we're not presenting you in this chapter with the frustrating avalanche-page-of-fonts that's found in the typical alphabetical listing. Instead, it makes the most sense to understanding the Windows fonts if we sort them from those that are the most prevalent to those that have just seen the light of day and are still rare.

In brief, these are:

- ◆ **Fonts that all Windows users have:** These are the TrueType fonts that you find wherever Windows is booted up. That's because these fonts have been in the product since before Bill Gates was born. That means they were installed by default in Windows NT 4, Windows 95, Windows 98, and on up the ladder. These fonts are like cockroaches; you'll never be able to get rid of them.

- ◆ **Fonts that practically all Windows users have:** These include the fonts that come with Windows 98/Me (which are practically the same operating system), Windows 2000, and everything since then. There aren't that many Windows users who are still running NT or Win95 nowadays. And even *they* probably received this group of fonts while in the process of installing Microsoft Office, an IE upgrade, or the like. Combined with the fonts from Group 1, these are the fonts that nearly all Windows users and most Mac users can be counted on to have.

◆ **Fonts that most users have, since they have W2K, XP, or Vista:** The sweet spot in the installed base, as this book is published, is Windows 2000/Windows XP. These operating systems represent the vast majority of PCs in use today. Some of Microsoft's once famous Core Fonts for the Web were first bundled into Windows 2000 (although they were available before that). This group of fonts, therefore, is very widely installed, but by no means can you expect that *all* Windows users have them.

◆ **Fonts that were first shipped with Vista:** Windows XP wasn't much on the font front, so that left it to Vista to ship with a whole new gaggle of fonts at no extra cost. This is a fascinating category of fonts that have many attractive features, but most Windows users don't have them installed yet.

---

tip

We've assembled the lists in this chapter by referring to a Microsoft mini-search engine on the Web. This form catalogs every font the Redmond company has shipped with any of its software products in history. If you'd like to see which packages you might be able to purchase to obtain particular fonts, query the form at **www.microsoft.com/ typography/fonts/default.aspx.**

Displaying Font Samples the Fastest Way

First of all, let us explain the meaning of the following cryptic sentence, which you'll find in the font listings that follow:

Mr. Jock, TV quiz Ph.D., bags few lynx.

This is the shortest grammatically correct sentence that uses every letter in the English alphabet at least once. Actually, it's tied for shortest (more on that in a moment). There can't be one that's shorter, because the sentence above uses each of the 26 letters exactly once.

William Gillespie, who collects these *isogrammatic pangrams* — nonrepeating sentences that use every letter — explains that the sentence above was discovered by one Clement Woods. As a phrase, the pangram could be interpreted to mean, "Jock has no time for hunting game animals because he's busy showing off his doctoral degree on game shows" (see **www.spinelessbooks.com/table/forms/pangram.html**).

We'll be the first to admit that, although it may be a perfect pangram, it isn't necessarily an ideal way to display font samples. But it *is* blessedly short. That allowed us to make each font as large as possible and still fit on a single line across the page.

And it's a more coherent sentence, you'll have to admit, than the alternatives that were presented to us at Gillespie's site (**http://rinkworks.com/words/pangrams.shtml**) and elsewhere:

XV quick nymphs beg fjord waltz.
Blowsy night-frumps vex'd by NJ IQ.

Now, without further ado, let's find out which fonts people actually have.

The Fonts Everyone Has

In the remainder of this chapter, we're going to catalog those fonts that have been introduced in a particular version of Windows and have stayed in Windows ever since. Most Windows systems have a far greater number of fonts installed than we show here. But if a font appeared in, say, Windows 2000 and wasn't included in future versions of Windows, it's not a very good candidate for a font that you can assume all Windows users have.

Figure 7-7 illustrates those fonts that you can say with confidence, "Every Windows user has these fonts."

Fonts installed on all Windows PCs (NT 4, 95, 98, Me, 2000, XP, and Vista)

Arial (with bold, italic, and and bold italic)
Mr. Jock, TV quiz Ph.D., bags few lynx.

Courier New (with bold, italic, and bold italic)
```
Mr. Jock, TV quiz Ph.D., bags few lynx.
```

Lucida Console
```
Mr. Jock, TV quiz Ph.D., bags few lynx.
```

Lucida Sans Unicode
Mr. Jock, TV quiz Ph.D., bags few lynx.

Marlett

Symbol
Μρ. ϑοχκ, Τς θυιζ Πη.Δ., βαγσ φεω λψνξ.

Times New Roman (with bold, italic, and bold italic)
Mr. Jock, TV quiz Ph.D., bags few lynx.

Wingdings

Figure 7-7: The fonts everyone has. Have you seen these fonts? Sure. Windows has included a nice basic variety for many years. There are solid sans-serif and serif fonts, two monospaced fonts, an early Unicode font, and *three* pictorial (symbol) fonts.

Arial and *Times New Roman* are well known as the most widely used fonts in Windows.

Lucida Sans Unicode is, in truth, the most interesting font in this bunch. The version installed in Windows XP contains more than 1,700 characters.

That pales in the face of *Arial Unicode MS*, which can render more than 50,000 glyphs. This font, unfortunately, has never been included in any version of Windows, only as part of Microsoft Office 2000 and higher, which not everyone owns.

Arial Unicode MS also wasn't included in beta copies of Windows Vista, although Microsoft could always change its mind and add it in. We think Microsoft should widely and freely distribute this font so most people will eventually have it installed.

Until then, if you want to be sure your readers can see some little-used character from the WGL4 set, Lucida Sans Unicode probably has the glyph—*and* you know the font is installed everywhere.

The Fonts Virtually Everyone Has

Figure 7-8 shows several fonts that were first installed by default in Windows 98. More important, they've been able to stick around in the operating system ever since that time.

Fonts installed on almost all Windows PCs (98, Me, 2000, XP, and Vista)

Arial Black

Mr. Jock, TV quiz Ph.D., bags few lynx.

Comic Sans MS (with bold)

Mr. Jock, TV quiz Ph.D., bags few lynx.

Impact

Mr. Jock, TV quiz Ph.D., bags few lynx.

Tahoma (with bold)

Mr. Jock, TV quiz Ph.D., bags few lynx.

Verdana (with bold, italic, and bold italic)

Mr. Jock, TV quiz Ph.D., bags few lynx.

Webdings

Figure 7-8: The fonts almost everyone has. Since there are hardly any boxes running Windows 95 any more, the list in this figure, plus the ones in Figure 7-7, can be considered to comprise a universal set of fonts that all Windows users, and most Mac users, have installed.

Several other fonts have made an appearance in one version of Windows or another, only to disappear without a trace thereafter. (Remember Century Gothic? Four complete weights appeared in Windows 98/Me and then went missing in every future version. Licensing snafus? Greedy font owners? Cheapskate software billionaires? Who knows.)

Tahoma was introduced as the user-interface font for Office 97, continuing that role in Office 2000/XP/2003. It became the user interface font for Windows 98, too, and has held that position until Vista came out.

Verdana is the sleeper in this group. It's a slightly expanded version of Tahoma and has attracted many adherents among Webmasters, who believe it's more readable on-screen than Arial. Actually, Verdana does have wider lowercase characters, which look much better on-screen at 8 pt. than does Arial. The old stalwart Arial, however, prints more gracefully than Verdana and looks better on-screen as well, at sizes of 10 pt. and above.

Arial Black and *Impact* are Microsoft's ugliest fonts. The idea behind Impact is good—a truly extrabold font—but the typeface is unreadable on-screen at anything less than billboard-size.

The Fonts Most, But Not All, Users Have

Figure 7-9 rounds out our list of fonts that the majority of Windows users have installed. Windows 2000, and especially Windows XP two years later, established *Georgia* and *Trebuchet MS* as fonts that will have long lives and large installed user bases.

These two faces were part of the "Core Fonts for the Web" package, 11 families of type (most with four full weights) that Microsoft freely distributed at that time. This was designed to encourage Webmasters to specify more legible fonts on their pages. It seems to have worked quite well, since many now use some new-core font, especially Georgia, with Times as a fall-back selection.

By contrast, *MS Sans Serif* is uninteresting. It has no WGL4 characters, not even the "middle ANSI" set, and it has no weights other than roman.

Fonts installed on most Windows PCs (2000, XP, and Vista)

Georgia (with bold, italic, and bold italic)
Mr. Jock, TV quiz Ph.D., bags few lynx.

Microsoft Sans Serif
Mr. Jock, TV quiz Ph.D., bags few lynx.

Palatino Linotype (with bold, italic, and bold italic)
Mr. Jock, TV quiz Ph.D., bags few lynx.

Trebuchet MS (with bold, italic, and bold italic)
Mr. Jock, TV quiz Ph.D., bags few lynx.

Figure 7-9: The fonts most Windows users have. Systems running Windows 2000, XP, and Vista include these fonts.

The other Core Fonts for the Web—Arial, Arial Black, Comic Sans, Courier New, Impact, Times New Roman, Verdana, and Webdings—are files that most Windows users already have and don't need to download again. Microsoft gave these faces away primarily to expand the installed base of these fonts to Apple users (OS X supports both TrueType and OpenType fonts) and Windows 95/98 users who'd never received the fonts by upgrading to Internet Explorer (IE) 5.

tip

The most purely practical face in the Core Fonts for the Web group is *Andale Mono*. This font has a minor cult following among Windows developers, who prize it for its fixed monospacing and the dot inside its numeral 0. (This makes it easy to distinguish from the letter O when plowing through dense thickets of code.)

Strangely, Andale Mono was included with the standalone Internet Explorer 5 download and the Core Fonts, but it's done a disappearing act since then. It's never been included in any version of Windows, despite the font's usefulness as a super-legible font.

See "You Can Still Get the Core Fonts That MS Pulled" elsewhere in this chapter to find font samples and current download locations for Andale Mono.

Secret

You Can Still Get the Core Fonts That Microsoft Pulled

Microsoft withdrew the 11 type families of the Core Fonts for the Web from its site in 2002. If you have a computer that lacks any of the fonts in this set, however, you can still download them from the Internet for free.

SourceForge.net, a hub of open-source development activity, noted that the license agreement of the Core Fonts states that the fonts can be freely distributed along with any programming project. SourceForge is a giant programming project (perhaps not exactly what Microsoft had in mind, though). So all 11 families are packaged up as self-extracting executables ready for installation at http://sourceforge.net/project/showfiles.php?group_id=34153&package_id=56408&release_id=105355.

To look at samples of the fonts before downloading them, go to www.serbski-institut .de/wgl4fonts.htm.

caution

Don't install these 2000-era fonts if you already have them installed in your font list. Windows XP and Vista have newer versions of these fonts, which include slightly better character sets, hints, and so forth. Install these font packages *only* if you don't already have a certain typeface family, as would be the case for some users of Windows 95/98/Me, Mac, and Linux.

The New Vista Font Collection

Windows Vista introduces a rather high number of new fonts for a new release of Windows.

It isn't the champ. According to Microsoft's font query form that we mentioned earlier, Windows 2000 added 90 new font files (counting bold, bold italic, and other weights as separate files) that had never before appeared in Windows. Vista adds only 44 new files.

But many of the new fonts in Windows 2000 were dedicated to particular language groups, such as Simplified Arabic, Rod (Hebrew), and SimHei (Asian), which most Windows users in Europe and the Americas will never need.

Windows Vista, by contrast, includes ten—count 'em, *ten*—new font families, most with a complete set of weights, that are specifically designed for Western users.

Figure 7-10 shows these ten new font families. Learning the best way to take advantage of these new faces will pay off for any Windows user who wants his or her documents to look attractive and distinctive.

We've taken the liberty of listing the fonts slightly out of alphabetical order in Figure 7-10. This allows us to place together the serif, sans-serif, and user interface fonts.

Western fonts that are new to Vista

Cambria (with bold, italic, and bold italic)

Mr. Jock, TV quiz Ph.D., bags few lynx.

Constantia (with bold, italic, and bold italic)

Mr. Jock, TV quiz Ph.D., bags few lynx.

Calibri (with bold, italic, and bold italic)

Mr. Jock, TV quiz Ph.D., bags few lynx.

Candara (with bold, italic, and bold italic)

Mr. Jock, TV quiz Ph.D., bags few lynx.

Corbel (with bold, italic, and bold italic)

Mr. Jock, TV quiz Ph.D., bags few lynx.

Consolas (with bold, italic, and bold italic)

Mr. Jock, TV quiz Ph.D., bags few lynx.

DaunPenh

Mr. Jock, TV quiz Ph.D., bags few lynx.

Segoe UI (with bold, italic, and bold italic)

Mr. Jock, TV quiz Ph.D., bags few lynx.

Segoe Print (with bold)

Mr. Jock, TV quiz Ph.D., bags few lynx.

Segoe Script (with bold)

Mr. Jock, TV quiz Ph.D., bags few lynx.

Figure 7-10: Important new fonts for Latin and Roman language groups in Windows Vista. Not shown here are Meiryo (Japanese and Latin) and Cariadings, a symbol font.

The New C Fonts

By far the most important of the new fonts are six typeface families, the names of which all begin with the letter C.

The development of these new type families was a fairly big deal within Microsoft. The project took two years, from January 2003 to November 2004, according to the company.

The design goal was to develop fonts from the ground up that would take maximum advantage of *ClearType*. ClearType is a technique, enabled by default in Vista, that makes the edges of type look smoother on digital LCD screens. (This has its downsides; see the Secret section titled "Vista's New Fonts Aren't Hinted" later in this chapter.)

Microsoft contracted with a variety of type designers to create the C families and two other new fonts:

- **Calibri and Consolas** — Lucas de Groot, The Netherlands
- **Cambria** — Jelle Bosma, The Netherlands
- **Candara** — Gary Munch, U.S.
- **Constantia** — John Hudson, Canada
- **Corbel** — Jeremy Tankard, U.K.
- **Meiryo (Japanese)** — Eiichi Kono, Takehary Suzuki, and Matthew Carter
- **Cariadings (dingbats)** — Geraldine Wade, a ClearType program manager

A healthy visual balance among Latin, Greek, and Cyrillic characters was a significant objective in the development of the C fonts. Characters from the three different language groupings are intended to appear in proportion with each other when displayed together on the same page. This isn't always the case for fonts that weren't designed with such compatibility in mind.

Similarly, the Meiryo font is designed for visual harmony when Japanese and Latin characters are mixed on the same line (see Figure 7-11).

Sources within Microsoft tell us that naming all the C fonts with the same initial letter was a conscious decision. It would be easier for Vista users to find the new fonts, it was felt, if scrolling to C in a Fonts drop-down box displayed the new fonts in close proximity.

In reality, giving all these fonts names that are so similar makes it very hard for people to remember which font is which. Follow with us, then, as we explain how to tell these fonts apart and how to put them to their best use.

The Serif Fonts

Cambria and *Constantia* are the two new serif fonts. Cambria is a bit more like Times New Roman in design, whereas Constantia tends more toward Palatino.

We help ourselves remember which of the two C fonts are the serif ones using this doggerel phrase: "I drove my Camry to Constantinople."

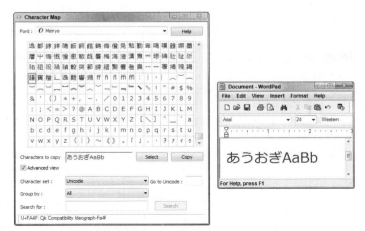

Figure 7-11: Meiryo was designed so that Japanese and Latin glyphs, when used together, are visually in balance, as shown in the WordPad window at right. You can use CharMap.exe, shown at left, to find which glyphs are located at which positions in any TrueType or OpenType font.

The Sans-Serif Fonts

Calibri, *Candara*, and *Corbel* are the three new sans-serif fonts.

- ◆ **Calibri** is the most like Arial.
- ◆ **Candara** is more like Optima, with strokes that slightly curve or flare when viewed at larger sizes. We remind ourselves that Candara has flared strokes by thinking: "Candara is tapered like a candle." (Its strokes are tapered in, not out like a candle, but still.)
- ◆ **Corbel** is the sans-serif font that may have the greatest application on Web pages and in small sizes. It's the most like Verdana in this respect.

  Corbel has wide, open letterforms. This is especially true in the open tail of the lowercase g, which doesn't close as in most other fonts, and the lowercase u, which has no final downward stroke on its right side but merely curls upward, like a bowl. Characteristics such as these should make this font clean and readable onscreen, even when used in relatively small footnotes and the like.

DaunPenh, the Graceful Font

DaunPenh is a graceful serif face that would be ideal for long blocks of text, as in a book-length work. It's more like the writings of a calligraphic pen (Penh, get it?) than any of the other Vista fonts.

Unfortunately, DaunPenh (as of this writing) is available only in roman in its Vista incarnation, with no italic or bold weights. This severely reduces its usefulness in documents. Unless Microsoft provides these additional forms of emphasis, DaunPenh is likely to remain a typographical curiosity and won't be widely used.

The Segoe Fonts

Segoe UI is the new user-interface font in both Windows Vista and Microsoft Office 2007. Unlike the UI fonts that were previously employed in Windows XP and Office, Segoe UI supports bold, italic, and bold italic weights. This means you might use this font in documents, like any other font.

Segoe is pronounced *see-go*. This name appears to be a nod to the font's use in Windows Vista and Office menus. (See and go.)

Segoe Print and *Segoe Script* are slightly slanted fonts that resemble hand printing and handwriting, respectively.

These pen-drawn fonts have nothing visually in common with Segoe UI. It was a terrible mistake to give these whimsical fonts such similar names to Vista's no-nonsense user-interface font.

However, aside from the confusion over the names, Segoe Print and Script (and their bold weights) are likely to replace Comic Sans MS as Windows users' favorite handwriting-imitation fonts. For one thing, Segoe Print and Script look a lot more as though someone might actually have written the words by hand. Like Comic Sans MS, Segoe Print and Segoe Script have bold weights but no italic or bold italic weights.

Secret

Vista's New Fonts Aren't Hinted

The new Windows C fonts and the Segoe UI user interface font are welcome additions. But they may look blurry to you on screen because they don't use black-and-white or grayscale hints like Microsoft's previous TrueType fonts. Instead, they're designed to look best on an LCD screen with the ClearType feature of XP and Vista turned on.

Microsoft insiders say the new Vista fonts weren't hinted because it's very expensive, and the company didn't want to spend the money. In addition, the fonts wouldn't have been ready to ship with Vista because of the time required for hinting, these sources say. Microsoft extensively hinted such TrueType stalwarts as Arial, Times New Roman, and Verdana in years past when widespread adoption of these new fonts was a top priority for the company.

ClearType is best at making fonts look clearer on screen only if all of the following are true:

- The display is an LCD screen, not a CRT.
- The LCD is using a digital, not an analog, interface.
- The LCD is running at its native resolution, not higher or lower.
- The display is using true color (24-bit or higher, not 16-bit or 8-bit).
- ClearType is tuned to the LCD's resolution, striping format, and gamma value.
- ClearType is enabled (ClearType on a fresh install defaults to *on* in Vista and *off* in XP; it's unavailable in Windows NT, 2000, 95, 98, and Me).

If any of these conditions is not met, ClearType fails to function with no warning to the user. In that case, fonts that depend on ClearType smoothing, and are not hinted, simply look worse.

The effect of ClearType seems to vary from person to person. Some people love it and some hate it. If you find that fonts look fuzzy in Vista, try enabling and disabling ClearType. In Vista, you do this by running the Customize Colors control panel.

To tune ClearType, and for more information, visit Microsoft's ClearType Tuner page, **www.microsoft.com/typography/ClearType/tuner/Step1.aspx** (requires Internet Explorer).

If these steps don't help, you may need to configure Vista to use a font other than Segoe UI for its user interface. At this writing, it's unclear (no pun intended) to what extent Vista and Office 2007 will allow that. As a last resort, you can move the Segoe UI font files from C:\Windows\Fonts to another folder you create, such as C:\Windows\UnusedFonts. (You may need to move the fonts in a command prompt window, since Vista doesn't allow moving fonts in the Control Panel.) Without deleting the fonts, moving them makes them unusable by Windows, in which case menus may fall back to a TrueType font that is well-hinted, such as Arial or Verdana.

Microsoft provides the following greatly magnified illustrations (Figure 7-12 and Figure 7-13) of how hinting and ClearType smoothing work:

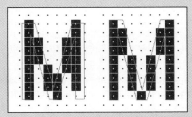

Figure 7-12: TrueType hinting is a form of grid fitting. The outline of each TrueType character is adjusted so the strokes fall more directly on a screen's grid of pixels. This makes letters more symmetrical and easier to read.

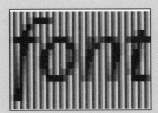

Figure 7-13: ClearType smoothing uses subpixel addressing. An LCD screen is made up of vertical stripes of red, green, and blue. Tiny sectors of each stripe, smaller than a pixel, can be lightened or darkened to make characters look smoother.

More information on hinting and ClearType is provided at **www.microsoft.com/ typography/TrueTypeHintingIntro.mspx** and **www.microsoft.com/typography/ ClearTypeInfo.mspx**.

What If Your PC Doesn't Have the Vista Fonts?

Microsoft hasn't exactly said at this writing how computer users other than users of Windows Vista will be able to get the new C and Segoe fonts. Since they're ordinary TrueType/OpenType fonts, however, they'll work on any flavor of Windows from version 3.1 up, any recent version of Apple Macs, and any build of Linux that supports the **ttmkfdir** command (which displays a file directory of any TrueType fonts that are installed).

Secret

Moving TrueType Fonts

If you have a Windows Vista machine and a licensed copy of a previous version of Windows on any other machine, you can move the new Vista fonts from one machine to the other.

If the two PCs are on a local area network, open the Fonts control panel on the PC that doesn't have the fonts. Select Install new font, then click the Network button, and navigate to the C:\Windows\Fonts folder of the Vista machine. Select the C and Segoe fonts, then click Install. The fonts should immediately become available.

If the two PCs aren't networked, you can move the individual font files from the Vista machine to a USB Flash drive or writable CD. Do this at a command prompt if it's not possible in the Fonts control panel or Windows Explorer. Insert the drive or CD into the other machine, then select Install new font in the Fonts control panel to install the files to the C:\Windows\Fonts folder of that machine.

For example, the files for Calibri (including bold, italic, and bold italic) are named Calibri.ttf, Calibrib.ttf, Calibrii.ttf, and Calibriz.ttf. Installing these files to the Fonts folder should make them immediately available, without a system reboot or even closing and reopening any applications. Just pull down a Fonts menu to see that the new fonts are there.

Moving TrueType fonts to a folder other than C:\Windows\Fonts (if you ever need to do this) makes the fonts immediately unavailable to Windows and all applications.

At this writing, the capability of Vista's Fonts control panel to move fonts (as opposed to installing them from a separate location) was in flux. For more details, see http://blogs.msdn.com/michkap/archive/2006/08/27/726378.aspx.

Who's Running Which Versions of Windows?

Now that you know which fonts are included in each version of Windows, you can do a simple calculation to see which fonts are installed on most people's computers.

A study by AssetMetrix of businesses in the United States and Canada in June 2005 found that companies were using the various flavors of Windows in the proportions shown in Table 7-1.

Table 7-1: About 85 Percent of PCs Used in Business Had Windows 2000 or XP Installed in Mid-2005

Version	Usage
Windows 2000	48 percent
Windows XP	38 percent
Windows NT	10 percent
Windows 95, 98, or Me	5 percent

These figures suggest that the vast majority of business users were running Windows 2000 or XP before Vista became available. Since Microsoft's support for Windows 2000 has expired since the study was done, XP has replaced Win2K in many businesses.

What about consumers, however? To measure the use of different operating systems by all individuals, TheCounter.com monitors the different operating systems used by people to browse to a variety of web sites. The proportions found in March 2006 are shown in Table 7-2.

Table 7-2: About 82 Percent of All Internet Users Had Windows XP Installed in 2006

Operating System	Usage
Windows XP	82.12 percent
Windows 2000	7.96 percent
Windows 98	5.97 percent
Mac	2.12 percent
Unknown	1.04 percent
Windows NT	0.28 percent
Linux	0.25 percent
Windows 95	0.10 percent
Windows 3.x	0.09 percent
Unix	0.04 percent
WebTV	0.02 percent
Windows Me	0.01 percent

Remember, the figures are derived from people browsing the Web. Servers and other serious workstations are not commonly used for web surfing. It's likely, for example, that there are many times more Unix computers than devices running Microsoft's obsolete WebTV, but TheCounter.com's figures show only twice as many Unix machines. For the latest figures, see **www.thecounter.com/stats/**.

Knowing that the figures aren't exact, we still think it's safe to make the following statement:

> *If you're distributing a document that will be viewed or printed by other people, use the fonts that are found in Windows 98 and Macs. This means your fonts will be visible to about 98 percent of computer users.*

That boils down to the fonts we show in Figures 9-7 and 9-8. It's an okay selection but not, frankly, a great selection.

What if you'd like to prepare and distribute documents using fonts that are a bit more exciting and updated? See "The document you save could be your own" tip.

---

tip

The document you save could be your own.

You can make sure your word-processing .doc files and other documents can be viewed and printed with the fonts you selected intact if you follow these rules:

Case 1. *You're the only person who'll be editing, viewing, and printing the document.* If you're just planning to print copies of a document and distribute hard copies of it to others, use any dang fonts you want. If it looks okay to you on-screen and it prints okay, you're fine.

Case 2. *You're going to distribute the file only within your department.* Let's say you want the file you create to be viewed, edited, or printed by people other than yourself. If those people are all close co-workers, and you know they all use at least Windows XP or Vista, go ahead and use in the document any of the fonts that are found in XP.

You could also save your document using the new Windows Vista XML Paper Specification (XPS) format. If anyone in your department doesn't use Vista, they'll need Windows Server 2003 or XP SP2 and higher and must install Microsoft's WinFX viewer (www.microsoft.com/whdc/xps/default.mspx).

Case 3. *You're going to distribute the file widely.* If the file will be viewed or printed by people you may not know, you can't guarantee which fonts they'll have installed. Therefore, you need to save the document with the fonts intact. (This is called *embedding* the fonts.) Many applications support a command to do this. In Microsoft Word and PowerPoint, for example, click Tools⇨Options. On the Save tab, turn on **Embed TrueType fonts.** Most TrueType fonts are embeddable. (In the worst case, a document using embedded fonts can be viewed and printed by recipients but not edited.) You can check fonts in advance using the Embedding tab in Microsoft's free Font Properties Extension (www.microsoft.com/typography/TrueTypeProperty21.mspx).

Case 4. *You're going to distribute the file on the Internet.* To make sure a document that will be accessible worldwide will use the fonts you selected, you'll need to save it as a PDF file using Adobe Acrobat or a compatible program. Anyone can open and print the file using the free Adobe Reader, which runs on Windows, Macs, Linux and other computers (www.adobe.com/products/acrobat/readstep2_allversions.html).

Which Fonts Are Web-Safe Fonts?

Using only fonts found in Windows 98 and higher may help ensure that most everyone who tries to view or print your document will have the same fonts. But what if you want to save a document in HTML and post it as a Web page?

For several years, the Web-development site CodeStyle.org has surveyed computer users to find out which fonts they actually have installed (as opposed to which fonts they *should* have installed).

This Web-based survey asks visitors to look at a specific font sample and compare it to their default browser font. If the two look different, the user clicks a box saying, "Yes, the font is installed."

This kind of survey has all of the problems that are typical of asking people's opinions (rather than, say, simply spying on them without their knowledge). But it's a start toward defining a minimum set of TrueType fonts that virtually all web surfers can be assumed to have.

We've assembled in Figure 7-14 a list of every font that the CodeStyle.org survey found in mid-2006 was reported to be installed by more than 90 percent of Windows, Mac, or Linux users. The columns show the percentage of each group who say a particular typeface is present on their systems. In the figure, the faces are sorted in descending order of the three columns' average.

Typeface family	Windows Users	Mac Users	Linux Users
Courier New (Courier on Mac/Linux)	94%	95%	91%
Arial (Helvetica on Mac/Linux)	94%	95%	77%
Arial Black	95%	96%	52%
Verdana	94%	93%	54%
Comic Sans MS	94%	92%	49%
Times New Roman (Times on Linux)	78%	88%	67%
Trebuchet MS	91%	91%	47%
Impact	93%	86%	49%
Georgia	84%	91%	51%
Tahoma	93%	71%	*too few*
Lucida Console	93%	*too few*	*too few*

Figure 7-14: Web-safe fonts. More than 90 percent of all Windows, Mac, and Linux users surveyed by CodeStyle.org say they have Courier or Courier New installed. "Too few" means not enough users reported having a font for it to show up in the survey's results.

Looking at Figure 7-14, it's clear to us that Times New Roman (which is almost universally installed in every version of Windows) is way under reported in the survey. This probably because many people use it as the default font in their web browsers. They wouldn't see a difference between CodeStyle.org's font sample and their default, so they might not report that Times New Roman is installed (although many users would correctly guess that it actually was present).

The Most Web-Safe Font Is Courier (Yuck)

Folks, we have a winner! Based on the figures from CodeStyle.org's web survey, the most web-safe font you can specify on HTML pages is Courier New, with Courier specified as a fallback. (A very similar font that uses the shorter name Courier is more prevalent in Mac and Linux systems than Courier New.)

Unfortunately, we can't recommend that you use Courier or Courier New as the primary text font on a web page you care about—even if Courier was the only typeface on Earth.

Courier New is such a lightweight typeface that it's very hard to read. An old story goes that Microsoft originally got the design by copying an IBM Selectric typewriter ball. But without the spreading of ink that occurred when the metal ball hit a piece of paper, all that was copied was a very thin, spindly set of strokes. It's probably not true, but it's a great story.

So forget about using Courier for the text of your Web pages. Instead, specify the following web-safe fonts if you need sans-serif, serif, or monospaced fonts. (Remember, HTML allows you to specify a series of font names. Every browser will go through the list, displaying the first font that a user actually has installed.)

Web-Safe Sans-Serif Fonts

To specify a sans-serif font for your Web pages in HTML, use the following list, specified in this order:

> Arial
> Helvetica
> Verdana
> Trebuchet MS
> sans-serif

Many people think that all sans-serif fonts look alike. But Verdana and Trebuchet give a web page a sharply different look than do Arial/Helvetica (which are, in fact, very similar).

If you want, feel free to specify Verdana or Trebuchet as first in your list. But be sure to look at sample pages using each of these fonts first. You might or might not like the effect of an entire web page set in either of these fonts.

In HTML, specifying *sans-serif* as the last font in the list ensures that a user's default sans-serif font will be used to display your page, if none of your named fonts are installed. You may think that's unlikely, with fonts that are as widely installed as Arial and Helvetica. But you never know for sure.

Web-Safe Serif Fonts

To specify a serif font in HTML, use the following list:

> Times New Roman
> Times
> Georgia
> serif

Again, feel free to specify Georgia as your first choice, if desired. Just test a few sample pages first.

Web-Safe Monospaced Fonts

To specify a monospaced font in HTML, which is useful when including a snippet of programming code for your readers to peruse, use the following list:

Lucida Console
Courier New
Courier
monospace

What?! We've gone and broken our own rule of specifying as your first choice the font that's the most prevalent among all kinds of computer users.

That's because Courier New is so ugly, ugly, ugly, and hard to read. And did we mention that it's ugly?

Lucida Console is a much stronger font, with an even tone that makes fixed-pitch material more pleasant to read. It may not be present on a lot of Mac and Linux users' machines. But they can fall back to Courier in their browsers and still read the monospaced section of your page just fine.

> **tip** For a list of the number of glyphs present in different Windows fonts, and the language groupings that each font supports, visit David McCreedy's Gallery of Unicode Fonts at www.travelphrases.info/gallery/views/all_fonts.html.

Don't Use the Symbol Font in HTML

You may be tempted to specify one of the Windows symbol fonts, such as Symbol or Wingdings, in an HTML document on the Web. Don't do it.

Some people who are putting together a web page say to themselves, "I need to display a symbol for some beta software, so I'll use the Greek letter *beta* that's in the Symbol font." Then they write something like the following in their code (HTML 4.01 is shown):

```
<font face="Symbol">b</font>
```

This might work in Internet Explorer on a Windows box. But it's likely *not* to work in Internet Explorer on the Mac, or in Mozilla, Firefox, Netscape, Opera, or other browsers that support web standards. As likely as not, your page will show a blob or nothing at all where you've indicated a "Symbol b."

What you're saying to standards-based browsers with an HTML line like the preceding one is this: "Give me LATIN SMALL LETTER B and look for it in the font named Symbol, if the user has it."

Unfortunately for you, the Windows Symbol font doesn't include a shape known as LATIN SMALL LETTER B. That's why you sometimes get results you don't like on your page.

The Symbol font does include a shape known as GREEK SMALL LETTER BETA. To make browsers display that glyph, which is the Greek beta symbol you want, you should specify it in your HTML code using its decimal Unicode number. In HTML 4.01, that looks like this if your page uses Arial as its text font:

```
<font face="Arial">&#946;</font>
```

The ampersand, hash sign, the number, and the semicolon tell browsers exactly what glyph you want. There are many other ways to specify the same thing and get it to work. But this isn't a book on coding in HTML, it's a book on using Vista. Since so many Windows users build their own Web pages, however, we wanted to alert you to this confusing bit of HTML lore.

You can look up the decimal number for many Unicode characters in Figure 7-6 earlier in this chapter. Or you can check Alan Wood's detailed Web listings of the Unicode equivalent for every character in Windows' Symbol font at **www.alanwood.net/demos/symbol.html**. A separate page provides the Unicode positions for many of the dingbats found in Windows' Wingdings font: **www.alanwood.net/demos/wingdings.html**. Every special Wingdings character isn't represented in Unicode yet, but a lot of them are. You can display these symbolic characters much more reliably in your web pages by specifying a font that includes Unicode's range of symbols and punctuation.

tip

Unicode supports thousands of such symbols — far more than Windows' Symbol, Wingdings, and Webdings fonts combined. To see charts filled with them, visit the Unicode Consortium's page on symbols and dingbats, www.unicode.org/charts/symbols.html.

cross
ref

For a list of the most useful Unicode symbols, see Appendix A.

What Are the Fonts with the Funny Names For?

Vista includes dozens of fonts that aren't mentioned in the previous sections. These fonts have unfamiliar names such as Andalus, Iskoola Pota, KaiTi, and Narksim.

These fonts are included in Vista primarily to support language groups other than Latin, Greek, and Cyrillic (in other words, other than Western and Eastern European).

For the first time with the release of Vista, users don't have to select individual language groups when installing the operating system in order to get the fonts needed to render every language that Windows supports. Multilingual support is automatically installed.

Unfortunately, this makes for a very long font list in the drop-down boxes of Vista and applications running on Vista. Finding the font you want may be a frustrating exercise in scrolling.

The Mac has for years had font suitcase capabilities that allow users to bundle fonts together into frequently used and infrequently used groups. Windows still has nothing like this. Unless you purchase or download a specialized suitcase utility for Windows, you'll need to scroll down a long set of options whenever you want a particular font.

We were, thank heavens, able to obtain from Microsoft a list of which fonts support which language groups (Table 7-3). At least you can look through our list and mentally eliminate those fonts that don't really fit your desired language group — until Microsoft provides font-suitcase capabilities in Windows.

caution	Many of the fonts that support non-Latin languages do include all of the ASCII characters that you might use in English-language documents — A to Z, 0 to 9, and so forth. But multilingual fonts such as SimSun (a widely used Chinese font) may not give ASCII characters the spacing and look of Latin characters that you're accustomed to. Don't select a specialized non-Latin font for your document unless you closely examine the results. Most speakers of European languages will need to use only the fonts listed in the Latin/Greek/Cyrillic and Symbols categories of Table 7-3.

Why does Vista need, say, 14 Thai fonts? Just as the Latin alphabet is supported by thousands of different fonts, Windows users in language groups around the world have used many different fonts to create documents. To ensure that these documents will display and print in Vista the same way they did in older versions of Windows, Microsoft must include all of the older fonts.

Table 7-3: Which Vista Fonts Are Designed for Which Language Groups

Latin/Greek/Cyrillic Fonts

Font Name	Primary Scripts	Other Scripts
Arial	Latin, Greek, Cyrillic	Hebrew, Arabic
Arial Black	Latin, Greek, Cyrillic	
Calibri	Latin, Greek, Cyrillic	
Cambria & Cambria Math	Latin, Greek, Cyrillic	Math
Candara	Latin, Greek, Cyrillic	
Comic Sans MS	Latin, Greek, Cyrillic	
Consolas	Latin, Greek, Cyrillic	
Constantia	Latin, Greek, Cyrillic	
Corbel	Latin, Greek, Cyrillic	
Courier New	Latin, Greek, Cyrillic	Hebrew, Arabic
Franklin Gothic Medium	Latin, Greek, Cyrillic	
Georgia	Latin, Greek, Cyrillic	
Impact	Latin, Greek, Cyrillic	
Lucida Console	Latin, Greek, Cyrillic	
Lucida Sans Unicode	Latin, Greek, Cyrillic	Hebrew, Math, Symbols
Microsoft Sans Serif	Latin, Greek, Cyrillic	Hebrew, Arabic, Thai
Palatino Linotype	Latin, Greek, Cyrillic	
Segoe Print	Latin, Greek, Cyrillic	
Segoe Script	Latin, Greek, Cyrillic	
Segoe UI	Latin, Greek, Cyrillic	

(continued)

Table 7-3 (continued)

Latin/Greek/Cyrillic Fonts (continued)

Font Name	Primary Scripts	Other Scripts
Tahoma	Latin, Greek, Cyrillic	Hebrew, Arabic, Thai
Times New Roman	Latin, Greek, Cyrillic	Hebrew, Arabic
Trebuchet MS	Latin, Greek, Cyrillic	
Verdana	Latin, Greek, Cyrillic	

Symbol Fonts

Font Name	Primary Scripts	Other Scripts
Marlett	Symbols	
Symbol	Symbols	
Webdings	Symbols	
Wingdings	Symbols	

Arabic Fonts

Font Name	Primary Scripts	Other Scripts
Andalus	Arabic	
Arabic Transparent	Arabic	Latin
Arabic Typesetting	Arabic	Latin
Majalla UI	Arabic	Latin
Microsoft Uighur	Arabic	Latin
Simplified Arabic	Arabic	Latin
Simplified Arabic Fixed	Arabic	Latin
Traditional Arabic	Arabic	Latin

Chinese, Japanese, and Korean Fonts

Font Name	Primary Scripts	Other Scripts
FangSong_GB2312	Chinese, Simplified	Latin, Greek, Cyrillic, Hiragana, Katakana
KaiTi	Chinese, Simplified	
Microsoft YaHei	Chinese, Simplified	Latin, Greek, Cyrillic, Hiragana, Katakana
MS Hei	Chinese, Simplified	
MS Song	Chinese, Simplified	
SimHei	Chinese, Simplified	Latin, Greek, Cyrillic, Hiragana, Katakana
Simsun, NSimsun	Chinese, Simplified	Latin, Greek, Cyrillic, Hiragana, Katakana
Simsun-ExtB	Chinese, Simplified	Latin
DFKai-SB	Chinese, Traditional	Latin, Greek, Cyrillic

Font Name	Primary Scripts	Other Scripts
Microsoft JhengHei	Chinese, Traditional	Latin, Greek, Hiragana, Katakana
MingLiU, PMingLiU, MinLiU_HKSCS	Chinese, Traditional	Latin, Greek, Hiragana, Katakana
MingLiU-ExtB, PMingLiU-ExtB, MingLiU_HKSCS-ExtB	Chinese, Traditional	Latin
Meiryo	Japanese	Latin, Greek, Cyrillic
MS Gothic, MS PGothic, MS UI Gothic	Japanese	Latin, Greek, Cyrillic
MS Mincho, MS PMincho	Japanese	Latin, Greek, Cyrillic
Batang, BatangChe, Gungsuh, GungsuhChe	Korean	Latin, Greek, Cyrillic, Hiragana, Katakana
Gulim, GulimChe, Dotum, DotumChe	Korean	Latin, Greek, Cyrillic, Hiragana, Katakana
Malgun Gothic	Korean	Latin, Greek, Cyrillic, Hiragana, Katakana

Hebrew Fonts

Font Name	Primary Scripts	Other Scripts
Aharoni Bold	Hebrew	Latin
David	Hebrew	Latin
David Transparent	Hebrew	Latin
Fixed Miriam Transparent	Hebrew	Latin
FrankRuehl	Hebrew	Latin
Gisha	Hebrew	Latin
Gisha Bold	Hebrew	Latin
Levenim MT	Hebrew	Latin
Miriam	Hebrew	Latin
Miriam Fixed	Hebrew	Latin
Miriam Transparent	Hebrew	Latin
Narkisim	Hebrew	Latin
Rod	Hebrew	Latin
Rod Transparent	Hebrew	Latin

Indic Fonts

Font Name	Primary Scripts	Other Scripts
Vrinda	Bengali	Latin
Mangal	Devenagari	Latin

(continued)

Table 7-3 *(continued)*

Indic Fonts (continued)

Font Name	Primary Scripts	Other Scripts
Shruti	Gujarati	Latin
Raavi	Gurmukhi	Latin
Tunga	Kannada	Latin
Kartika	Malayalam	Latin
Kalinga	Oriya	Latin
Iskoola Pota	Sinahalee	Latin
Latha	Tamil	Latin
Gautami	Telugu	Latin

Thai Fonts

Font Name	Primary Scripts	Other Scripts
Angsana New	Thai	Latin
AngsanaUPC	Thai	Latin
Browallia New	Thai	Latin
BrowalliaUPC	Thai	Latin
Cordia New	Thai	Latin
CordiaUPC	Thai	Latin
DilleniaUPC	Thai	Latin
EucrosiaUPC	Thai	Latin
FreesiaUPC	Thai	Latin
IrisUPC	Thai	Latin
JasmineUPC	Thai	Latin
KodchiangUPC	Thai	Latin
Leelawadee	Thai	Latin
LilyUPC	Thai	Latin

Fonts for Other Language Groups

Font Name	Primary Scripts	Other Scripts
Sylfaen	Armenian, Georgian	Latin, Greek, Cyrillic
Plantagenet Cherokee	Cherokee	Latin
Nyala	Ethiopic	Latin
DaunPenh	Khmer	Latin
MoolBoran	Khmer	Latin

Font Name	Primary Scripts	Other Scripts
DokChampa	Lao	Latin, Thai
Mongolian Baiti	Mongolian	Latin
Estrangelo Edessa	Syriac	
MV Boli	Thaana	
Microsoft Himalaya	Tibetan	Latin
Euphemia	Unified Canadian Aboriginal Syllabics	Latin
Microsoft Yi Baiti	Yi Syllables	Latin

How to Get the Best Free Fonts

Despite all the new fonts included with Windows Vista, you can give your documents a fresh look if you investigate and employ other fonts that are out there that most Vista users *don't* have.

Unfortunately, if you query a search engine for **free fonts,** you're likely to get a huge list of web sites that have truly horrible products. These include decorative, novelty, and fantasy typefaces that might be useful once in a rare while—a haunted house party, for example—but should never be used in most documents. There's nothing wrong with novelty fonts, if they're well done—but most such fonts aren't.

What you should look for, even in free fonts, are typefaces with at least four weights: roman, bold, italic, and bold italic. These fonts should be hinted so they look good on screen and when printed on an ordinary inkjet or laser printer.

Avoid fonts that don't have a full complement of weights or seem to be hasty rip-offs of professional typeface families. There are many good-quality free fonts to be had. If you need to buy commercial, licensed fonts, there are many affordable options for sale (as we explain later in this chapter).

The 20 Best Free Fonts

Vitaly Friedman compiles what is arguably the best list, complete with sample images, of high-quality TrueType and OpenType fonts that are free for the downloading.

Friedman's lists fluctuates over time between about 20 and 25 winners, as he periodically adds new fonts and deletes fonts that turn out to be stolen copies of commercial fonts. It's fascinating to visit his list every few months and watch the ebb and flow of type designs, which Friedman treats as his personal friends.

At this writing, Friedman's No. 1 font selection is named Delicious, shown in Figure 7-15. This is a graceful and professionally drawn font by Jos Buivenga of the Netherlands. Delicious has all the attributes you want in a free font (or any font): a full range of weights—even an extrabold, heavy weight—and characters that are well-formed enough to work in small sizes, such as a document's footnotes.

The font also has the unusual characteristic that a word or sentence is always the same length, whether the roman, bold, or heavy weight is selected (as shown at the bottom of Figure 7-15). This can be useful if you want to make certain lines of a document bold or nonbold, depending on other variables, without any of the line breaks changing.

AaBbCcDdFfGgHhIiJjKk
LlMmNnOoPpQqRrSsTt
UuVvWwXxZz!?(&%*€)

Roman *Italic* **BoldItalic**
Bold Heavy SMALLCAPS

How long is this line?
How long is this line?
How long is this line?

Figure 7-15: A Font named Delicious. This typeface family, which can be downloaded free, shows the qualities that make a font worth having (unlike many free fonts, which are garbage).

Friedman's list of the best free fonts is at **www.alvit.de/blog/article/20-best-license-free-official-fonts**. Buivenga's site, which also offers another free sans-serif font named Fontin, is at **www.josbuivenga.demon.nl/delicious.html**.

Other Free Font Lists

Some other collections of high-quality free fonts—many of which are linked to from Vitaly Friedman's site—include the following.

   ◆ **Manfred Klein's Fonteria**—**http://moorstation.org/typoasis/designers/klein03/index.htm**
   ◆ **Designer in Action**—**www.designerinaction.de/fonts/show.php?art=fonts**
   ◆ **Typemotion**—**www.typemotion.de/_typographie/lacuna.php**
   ◆ **Apostrophic Laboratories**—**http://apostrophiclab.pedroreina.net/**
   ◆ **Identifont**—**www.identifont.com/free-fonts.html**

Some of the best type design work in the world is done outside the United States. As a result, a few of the sites in the preceding list use languages other than English. These sites, however, are so easy to use—all you really need to do is select a font and click a button to download it—that you should have no trouble whether or not you understand the rest of the text on a site.

Identifont, the last site shown in the list, provides a very useful fonts-by-appearance service. If you're trying to match a font you've seen, but you don't know its name, how can you obtain the font? The answer is to click the fonts by appearance tab at Identifont, specify which characters you have a sample of, and answer a few simple questions.

These questions include the shape of the lowercase letters, the thickness of horizontal and vertical strokes, and so forth. The site then displays a few fonts that match your answers. Even if the exact font you want isn't in the results, one of the alternatives may perfectly fit your needs.

The Best Free Scientific Fonts

If you write scientific or mathematical papers, you probably need a specialized font with characters that aren't natively found in Windows Vista, even with its vast collection of symbols in the Lucida Sans Unicode font.

The answer to this problem is STIX Fonts, a project of the nonprofit Scientific and Technical Information Exchange. Organizations that belong to this consortium include the IEEE (Institute of Electrical and Electronics Engineers), the American Institute of Physics, and others that publish scientific journals.

STIX Fonts include more than 5,000 glyphs, all of which use the numbering convention established by Unicode.

For more information and to download fonts, see **http://stixfonts.org**.

The Best Programmer's Fonts

Software developers are wild about monospaced fonts. These are fonts in which every character—even *i* and *w* and all of the uppercase letters—are exactly the same width.

You might think that proportional fonts—in which *i* and *w* are different widths—would be easier for developers to read. But the fixed-width of characters in code can help developers to spot misspelled variables, which may be longer or shorter than expected.

More importantly, developers crave monospaced fonts in which there are distinct differences between characters that look confusingly similar in, say, Arial. This usually means, among other things, that a font designed for use by programmers must add a slash or a dot to the numeral zero (0) to make it clearly different from the letter O.

Trevor Lowing, a software engineer and Navy reservist, defines these differences as follows (we paraphrase):

  ◆ Crisp, clear characters
  ◆ Extended character set
  ◆ Good use of white space
  ◆ Easy to distinguish the one (1), the lowercase "el" (l), and the uppercase "eye" (I)
  ◆ Easy to distinguish the zero (0), the lowercase "oh" (o), and the uppercase "oh" (O)
  ◆ Easily distinguished quote marks, apostrophes, and back-quote marks
  ◆ Clear punctuation characters, especially braces {}, parentheses (), and brackets []

Fortunately for programmers everywhere, Lowing has tested numerous monospaced fonts and rates them on his site: **www.lowing.org/fonts**.

At this writing, Lowing's No. 1-rated developer's font is Bitstream Vera Sans Mono. This is a free monospaced font created by the well-known Bitstream typeface foundry. See Figure 7-16 for a sample.

For more information, visit **www.gnome.org/fonts**.

Another site that rates developers' fonts is maintained by Keith Devens, a PHP programmer: **http://keithdevens.com/wiki/ProgrammerFonts**.

Finally, if you need a font that's been rated highly on several developers' lists as clear and legible, and you're willing to pay a few dollars, get Andalé Mono WGL. (The name is pronounced ON-da-LAY, Spanish for "let's go!"). The Ascender Font Store offers a five-user license for this font for only $30 USD. See **www.ascenderfonts.com/**.

```
+++++++++++++++++++++++++++++++++++++++++++++++++++++++++++++++++++
+   Font: ter-914n               +  ell '1', one '1'  +  Zero "0",       +
+                                +  little eye 'i',   +  little oh "o"   +
+   Crisp Characters & Whitespace +  big eye "I"      +  big oh "O"      +
+++++++++++++++++++++++++++++++++++++++++++++++++++++++++++++++++++
+   // If you need more than     +     l 1 i I        +     0 o O        +
+   // 3 levels of indentation,  +                    +                 +
+   // you're screwed anyway,    +                    +                 +
+   // and should fix your       +                    +                 +
+   // program. - Linus Torvalds +                    +                 +
+   // <>&%$#@!+-_[](){}\/        +                    +                 +
+   // .,:;                      +                    +                 +
+                                +                    +                 +
+   class foo {                  +                    +                 +
+        function do_foo () {     +                    +                 +
+              echo "Doing foo."; +                    +                 +
+        }                        +                    +                 +
+   }                             +                    +                 +
+   $bar = new foo;               +                    +                 +
+   $bar->do_foo();               +                    +                 +
+++++++++++++++++++++++++++++++++++++++++++++++++++++++++++++++++++
SUPPORTED CHARACTERSETS: Universal Character Set (UCS-2)
SUPPORTED SIZES: 10.5, 21, 31.5, 42, 52.5, 63
```

Figure 7-16: Bitstream Vera Sans Mono. This monospaced font has been judged as one of the best for programmers because of its fixed pitch and clearly differentiated characters.

tip

Try the free Windows Vista Consolas font. Before you download a free monospaced font or purchase a commercial one, try the Consolas font family that's included in Windows Vista. It not only has useful distinguishing features, such as a slash though the zero, but it also has all of the four weights commonly needed in documents: roman, bold, italic, and bold italic. Lucida Console, which is included in every version of Windows since NT 4, is an alternative if you need to share documents with others who may not have Vista's fonts. (Lucida Console, however, doesn't make its zero look different from its letter O.)

How to Get the Best Commercial Fonts

There's nothing wrong with paying for fonts. Sometimes, the perfect font isn't available for free but only in commercial collections. And professional graphic designers, of course, must keep their designs fresh by constantly purchasing the latest typefaces.

If you're not a design professional—you just want access to a broad selection of excellent fonts—then a commercial bundle of high-quality fonts is the answer.

Arguably the best value in commercial fonts today is the Cambridge Collection CD by Bitstream. This disc provides 202 fonts in both TrueType and PostScript formats for only USD$199. That's less than a dollar per font. And these aren't useless, novelty fonts, either (although many are headline-style fonts). Most are workhorse text fonts in a full range of weights that work well in business and personal documents of all kinds.

For more information, see **www.myfonts.com/products/bitstream/cambridge**.

What About a Condensed Font?

Windows Vista, and every Windows version in years past, has lacked a good set of condensed fonts. These are fonts that are narrower than typical fonts, which means you can fit more words on a line, in a spreadsheet cell, and so forth.

One of the most versatile condensed fonts that Microsoft has ever shipped is named Arial Narrow. This font, which is a rendition of the normal Arial font, but slightly compressed, coordinates well with other sans-serif faces. Used sparingly, only where necessary, a table of figures set in Arial Narrow may look no different to the layperson's eye than the same table set in Arial (which would be too wide).

Unfortunately, Microsoft has never included Arial Narrow in any build of Windows, not even Vista. The font — with a full range of four weights — has shipped only with Microsoft Office.

If you have Office installed, and Arial Narrow is one of the fonts available to you, be of good cheer. If not, you may need to purchase it commercially.

The best price we've found for Arial Narrow is at Fonts.com, a subsidary of Monotype Imaging. Monotype is the foundry responsible for Arial Narrow, so perhaps it makes sense that the best deal on Arial Narrow resides there. Even so, the cost to purchase all four weights in Windows OpenType format is $104 at this writing (see **www.fonts.com/findfonts/detail.asp?pid=243201**).

What About Font Utilities?

Now that you have all the fonts you need, you may some day want to look inside them, catalog them, and easily pluck characters from them.

That's what font utilities are good for. The following sections list a few of our favorites.

TrueType Viewer Tool

The TrueType Viewer Tool is a free utility developed by Rogier van Dalen (see Figure 7-17). It opens TrueType and OpenLayout fonts and reveals everything there is to know about a font. That includes its TrueType instructions, control points, and other technical details.

For more information, see **http://home.kabelfoon.nl/~slam/fonts/truetypeviewer.html**.

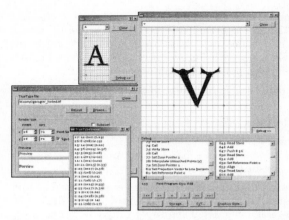

Figure 7-17: TrueType Viewer Tool. Rogier van Dalen's free utility exposes the internals of Windows fonts for close inspection.

Typograf

Among the ranks of commercial font utilities, Typograf has won kudos for its type management skills.

Whereas Vista provides no facilities to print sample output of all your installed fonts, Typograf not only prints samples, but it can also find any uninstalled fonts you may happen to have on your hard drives, DVDs, CDs, or other media.

The program is available for a 30-day free trial. During this period, watermarks are included on any printouts you make and a dialog box occasionally suggests that you get a paid registration. At this writing, the cost was USD$35. See **www.neuber.com/typograph**.

PopChar

As a replacement for Windows' limited CharMap utility, PopChar is a strong contender. The program has a resemblance to CharMap in that you can select special characters from any installed font and insert them into your documents. But PopChar does much more.

PopChar remains in your System Tray, waiting for you to click on it. When its window appears, you click the special character you want and it immediately appears in the document you were just working in. No copying and pasting needed with PopChar.

The current price is USD$29.99. See **www.ergonis.com/products/popcharwin/**.

Summary

In this chapter, we've tried to pull the curtain back from the mysteries of the fonts that ship with Windows Vista. Hopefully, you'll now be able to find and use any specialized characters that your documents may require.

Part III

Security

Windows Vista Security Features

Chapter
8

◆ ◆

In This Chapter

Using Windows Security Center to monitor the health of your PC

Using tools like Windows Defender, Windows Firewall, and Windows Update to keep your PC secure

Browsing the Web securely with Internet Explorer 7

Preventing physical loss with BitLocker Drive Encryption

Getting the best security with an x64 version of Windows Vista

◆ ◆

Although the Windows Vista Aero user interface is the most obvious change to Windows Vista, some of the more important, if less obvious, changes in this new operating system regard security. In this chapter, we examine the various new security features in Windows Vista.

Security and Windows Vista

It's been a tough decade for Windows users. As Microsoft's operating system entered the dominant phase of its existence, hackers began focusing almost solely on Windows, since that's where all the users are. As a result, various Windows versions have suffered through a seemingly neverending series of electronic attacks, security vulnerabilities, and high-profile malware breakouts.

In 2003, Microsoft halted development of its major operating system and application products and began an internal review of its software development practices. The company went back and re-examined the source code to its then-current projects and developed a new software engineering approach that is security-centric. Now, the software giant will not release any software product that hasn't undergone a stringent series of security checks. Windows Vista is the first client operating system shipped since that time that's been developed from the get-go with these principles in mind. It has been architected to be secure from the beginning.

Is Windows Vista impenetrable? Of course not. No software is perfect. But Windows Vista is demonstrably more secure than its predecessors. And although we will no doubt face awesome security threats in the future, Microsoft at least has the lessons it learned from the mistakes of the past to fall back on. There's little doubt that the security enhancements in Windows Vista will prove to be a major reason many people will upgrade to this version. It's not a misplaced desire.

Windows Vista's security features extend all the way through the system, from the high-profile applications, applets, and control panels you will deal with every day to the low-level features most Windows users have never heard of. In this chapter, we'll highlight most of Vista's new security features, starting with those you will likely have to deal with as soon as you begin using Microsoft's latest operating system.

Windows Security Center

When Microsoft shipped Windows XP Service Pack 2 (SP2) in the wake of its 2003 code review, one of the major and obvious new features it added to the operating system was the Security Center, a dashboard or front end of sorts to many of the system's security features. In Windows XP SP2, Security Center was designed to track the system's firewall, virus protection, and Automatic Updates configuration to ensure that each were enabled and as up-to-date as possible. If any of these features were disabled or out of date, Security Center would warn the user via a shield icon in the notification area near the system clock, or via pop-up warning balloons.

In Windows Vista, Security Center has been dramatically updated in order to support new security features in this Windows version. Shown in Figure 8-1, Vista's Security Center looks superficially similar to the XP SP2 version, but there's actually a lot more going on there once you begin examining its new functionality.

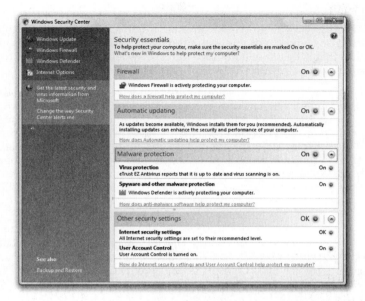

Figure 8-1: Windows Vista's Security Center now tracks far more security features.

The basic way that Windows Security Center works hasn't changed. Security Center still tracks certain security features and ensures that they're enabled and up-to-date. If they're not, Security Center will display its shield icon and alert you via pop-up balloons. But as you can see by looking at Figure 8-1, Security Center now tracks far more security features than before. Here's what Security Center is monitoring:

- ◆ **Firewall**: Security Center ensures that Windows Firewall is enabled and protecting your PC against malicious software that might travel to your PC via a network or Internet.

- ◆ **Automatic Updates**: Like Windows XP, Windows Vista includes an Automatic Updates feature that can automatically download and install critical security fixes from Microsoft the moment they are released. Security Center ensures that Automatic Updates is enabled.

- ◆ **Antivirus protection**: Although Windows Vista doesn't ship with any antivirus protection, Security Center still checks to ensure that an antivirus service is installed and up-to-date. Modern antivirus solutions are designed to integrate with Security Center so that the system can perform this monitoring function.

- ◆ **Spyware and other malware protection**: New to Windows Vista is Windows Defender, Microsoft's antispyware and antimalware tool. Windows Security Center ensures that Windows Defender is enabled, active, and using up-to-date spyware definitions.

- ◆ **Internet security settings**: New to Windows Vista, Security Center ensures that Internet Explorer 7 is configured in a secure manner. If you change any IE security settings, Security Center will warn you constantly about this issue.

◆ **User Account Control**: Security Center ensures that the User Account Control (UAC) technology, also new to Windows Vista, is active. Described more fully in Chapter 9, User Account Control is one of the many security technologies in Windows Vista that is designed to ensure that the system is running with the minimum exposure to electronic threats.

If all of the features Security Center is monitoring are enabled and up-to-date, you won't ever see Security Center unless you manually navigate to it. (You can find Security Center in Control Panel⇨Security⇨Security Center.) However, if one or more of these features are disabled, misconfigured, or out of date, Security Center will provide the aforementioned alerts. It will also display its displeasure with red-highlight sections in the main Security Center window. In such a case, you can expand the offending section and resolve the issue using a button in the windows. For example, if you disabled User Account Control, you'll see a Turn it on now button that will immediately enable that feature and return your system to a more secure state.

---

tip

One new Security Center feature in Windows Vista enables you to configure how Security Center alerts you when a security feature is not working properly. Open Security Center and click the link titled Change the way Security Center alerts me to see the dialog box shown in Figure 8-2. This way, you can optionally disable the pop-up alerts if you'd like.

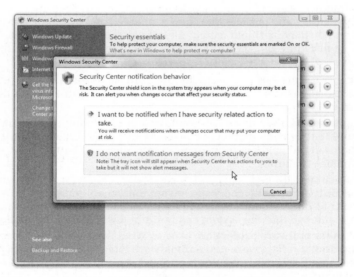

Figure 8-2: Now you can disable Security Center pop-ups.

The Security Center also provides handy links to the various security features it monitors, including Windows Update, Windows Firewall, Windows Defender, and Internet Options.

Windows Defender

Over the years, hackers have adapted and come up with new and inventive ways to attack PCs. Recently, spyware, one of the most pervasive and difficult forms of malware yet invented, has become a serious issue. For this reason, Windows Vista includes an integrated antispyware and antimalware package called Windows Defender. Unlike some security products, you won't typically see Windows Defender, as it's designed to work in the background, keeping your system safe. However, if you'd like to manually scan your system for malware or update your spyware definitions, you can do so by loading the Windows user interface, available through the Start Menu.

Shown in Figure 8-3, Windows Defender features a simple interface. You can trigger a malware scan, view the history of Defender's activities, or access various tools and options.

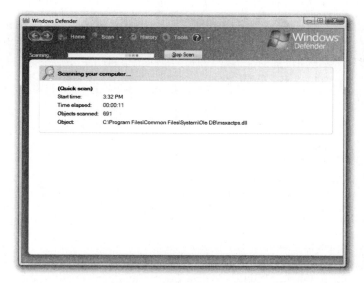

Figure 8-3: It runs silently in the background and works well. What more could you ask?

Secret

Security researchers almost unanimously agree that no one antispyware product is enough to completely protect your PC from malware attacks. For this reason, we recommend that you always run at least two antispyware products at the same time. See the Windows Secrets Web site (www.windowssecrets.com) for a list of recommended antispyware solutions.

> **tip** Windows Defender is also available for Windows XP. If you have other XP-based PCs, you might want to consider downloading Windows Defender for those systems as well.

> **tip** Curiously, Windows Vista does not include an antivirus solution, which we feel is a major omission. You can find a list of Vista-compatible antivirus products on the Microsoft web site **www.microsoft.com/security/partners/antivirus.asp.**

Secret

One of the best features in Windows Defender is hidden a bit in the application's user interface. The Software Explorer—found in Tools⇨Software Explorer—lists the applications that run at startup (you can also change the display to list currently running applications, network-connected applications, and other features). Best of all, you can actually remove or disable startup applications. In previous versions of Windows, you would use the System Configuration utility (msconfig.exe) for this functionality; System Configuration is still available in Windows Vista, but Windows Defender's Software Explorer feature is arguably a better solution because it provides so much information.

Windows Firewall

Back when Microsoft first shipped Windows XP in 2001, it included a feature called Internet Connection Firewall (ICF) that could have thwarted many of the electronic attacks that crippled that system over the ensuing several years. There was just one problem: ICF was disabled by default, and enabling and configuring it correctly required a Master's degree in Rocket Science. Microsoft wised up and shipped an improved ICF version, renamed as Windows Firewall, with Windows XP SP2.

Now, in Windows Vista, you get an even better Windows Firewall. Unlike the SP2 version of Windows Firewall, the version in Windows Vista can monitor certain outbound network traffic as well as inbound network traffic. And because it's integrated so deeply into the system, it can prevent Windows components from sending data out over the network if they're not designed to do so. This should prevent problems that arise when certain Windows components are replaced by malicious code.

Secret

There's some confusion about how the Windows Firewall is configured in Windows Vista. Although it is indeed enabled to monitor both inbound and outbound network traffic, it is configured differently for each direction. Windows Firewall, by default, is configured to block all incoming network traffic that is not part of an exception rule, and allow all outgoing network traffic that is not blocked by an exception rule.

The Windows Firewall user interface is simplicity itself. Shown in Figure 8-4, Windows Firewall is initially configured to block any unknown or untrusted connections to the PC that originate over the network. You can enable exceptions to this behavior on the Exceptions tab. Typically, you just leave it alone of course.

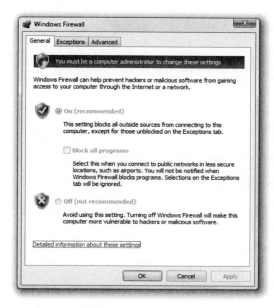

Figure 8-4: Windows Firewall.

Secret

The Windows Firewall interface described previously is quite similar to that found in Windows XP with Service Pack 2. But Microsoft also includes a second, secret interface to its firewall that presents far more options. It's called Windows Firewall with Advanced Security, and you can access it via the also-hidden Administrative Tools that ship with all mainstream Windows Vista versions. To find it, navigate to Control Panel and turn on Class View. Then, navigate into Administrative Tools and then Windows Firewall with Advanced Security. As shown in Figure 8-5, the tool loads into a Microsoft Management Console (MMC).

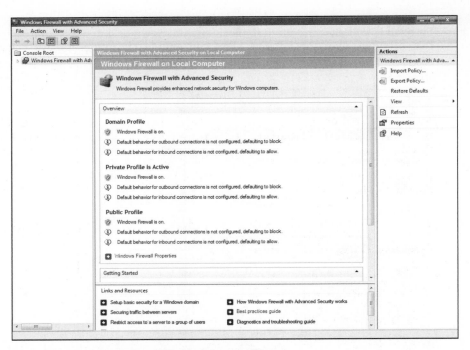

Figure 8-5: Windows Firewall with Advanced Security.

Here, you can inspect and configure advanced firewall features, such as inbound connection rules and outbound connection rules, and so on. This tool is almost identical to the one Microsoft will ship with the next Windows Server version and should be of interest to advanced users.

Secret

As good as Vista's firewall is, you should absolutely use a third-party firewall instead if you're using a security software suite. In such cases, the security suite will typically disable Windows Firewall automatically and alert Windows Security Center that it is now handling firewalling duties. Unlike with antispyware applications, you should never run two firewalls at the same time, as they will interfere with each other.

Windows Update

In previous Windows versions, Microsoft offered a Web-based service called Windows Update that provided software updates to Windows users. That service has since been superseded by Microsoft Update, which also provides updates to many other Microsoft software products. But Windows Update lives on in Windows Vista, albeit in a brand-new form.

As shown in Figure 8-6, Windows Update is now a client application that you can access from the Start Menu. From here, you can check for and install new updates, hide updates you don't want to be alerted about any more, and view the history of updates you've already installed. You can also click a link to enable Microsoft Update functionality, allowing Windows Update to download and install updates for other Microsoft applications, like Microsoft Office.

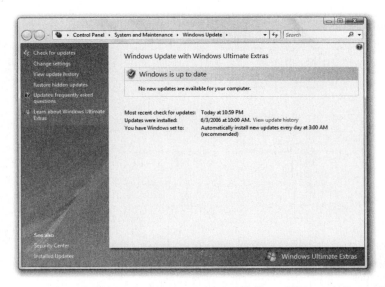

Figure 8-6: Windows Update is reborn in Windows Vista as a client-side application.

Secret

Users of Windows Vista Ultimate can also access Windows Ultimate Extras from Windows Update. These extras include exclusive applications, services, and collections of tips and tricks. Windows Ultimate Extras appear in Windows Update whenever there are new updates to download.

Curiously, Windows Update doesn't offer any links to Automatic Updates, the Windows feature that automatically downloads critical security fixes. Furthermore, you can't access Automatic Updates from its old location in the System Properties dialog box as you could in Windows XP. That's because Automatic Updates has been replaced by a new feature of Windows Update that's logically named automatic updating. Configured when Windows Vista is first set up, automatic updating allows Windows Update to behave like the old Automatic Updates tool. To configure automatic updating, open Windows Update and click on the Change Settings link. You'll see the window shown in Figure 8-7. This window also enables you to configure whether Windows Update will connect to the Microsoft Update service, which provides updates for Microsoft applications, as well as Windows itself.

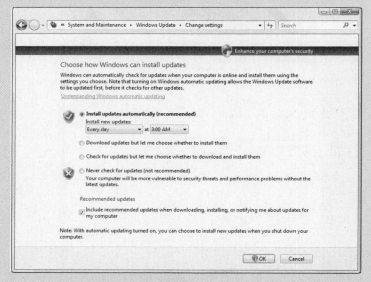

Figure 8-7: Automatic updating is now a feature of Windows Updates and not a separate tool.

User Account Security Features

Windows Vista includes two major technologies that help protect different types of user accounts against outside threats. Dubbed User Account Control and Parental Control, these technologies are discussed in Chapter 9.

Internet Explorer 7 Security Features

The version of Internet Explorer included with Windows Vista includes a number of advanced security technologies that make this the safest version of IE yet. In this section, we'll examine the many security features Microsoft added to Internet Explorer 7. And let's face facts, these features were necessary: Ever since Microsoft integrated Internet Explorer with the Windows shell beginning in the mid-1990s, Internet Explorer has been a major avenue of attack against Windows. With Windows Vista, finally, Microsoft has decoupled IE from the Windows shell and introduced advanced security controls that make IE safer.

cross ref

We cover the functional aspects of Internet Explorer 7 in Chapter 17.

ActiveX Opt-In

Initially developed as a lightweight version of COM (Component Object Model) — executable code modules that would be small and fast enough to work over the Internet — Microsoft's ActiveX technology has been maligned by security experts as being one of the most insecure technologies ever created. ActiveX controls literally litter every Windows system in existence, and hundreds of thousands of them are available online. Unfortunately, some of the controls — which can take various forms, such as browser helper objects, toolbars, and so on — are malicious and designed to hurt PCs.

In previous Internet Explorer versions, Microsoft didn't differentiate between ActiveX controls that were designed expressly for the Web — such the Adobe Reader add-on — and those that were really designed to be used locally on the PC only (Microsoft includes many such controls with Windows). With Internet Explorer 7, a new feature called ActiveX Opt-In automatically disables entire classes of ActiveX controls, including those that were not designed specifically for use over the Internet. Now, when you visit a Web page that tries to activate an ActiveX control on your system, the Internet Explorer 7 Information Bar prompts you so you can decide whether or not to proceed, as shown in Figure 8-8.

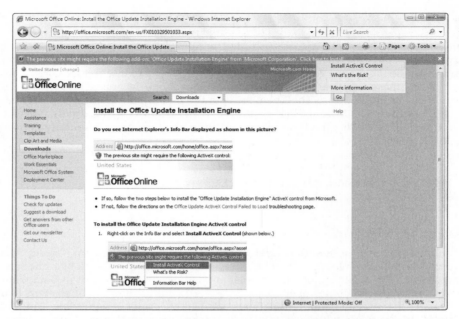

Figure 8-8: ActiveX Opt-In protects you against potentially malicious use of ActiveX controls.

If you know a particular control is safe, the Information Bar lets you enable the control and proceed.

Protected Mode

Available only in Windows Vista, Internet Explorer Protected Mode ensures that Internet Explorer 7 runs with even lower security privileges than a standard user account.

cross ref See Chapter 9 for information on the standard user account type.

This ensures that automated electronic attacks cannot succeed against Internet Explorer 7, and since the browser is restricted from accessing any part of the user's hard drive other than the Temporary Internet Files folder, Internet Explorer is effectively sandboxed from the rest of Vista. The net result is that should an attack succeed somehow, any malicious code that is injected into the system will find itself in a part of the system that is isolated from the rest of the file system. Furthermore, the code will simply be deleted when Vista reboots.

Fix My Settings

In the past, it was sometimes necessary to temporarily change Internet Explorer's security settings in order to run a certain Web application or access certain online features. But once you did that, it was hard to tell what you needed to do to get Internet Explorer back to its default state. If you are forced to change Internet Explorer 7's security settings in a way that lowers Vista's security prowess, the browser will begin prompting you with its Information Bar. Then, you can access a simple new feature called Fix Settings for Me to return IE to its default security settings.

As shown in Figure 8-9, this feature simply requires you to click the Information Bar and select Fix Settings for Me. You'll be prompted with a confirmation dialog box, and Internet Explorer reverts to its default settings. It's easy and effective.

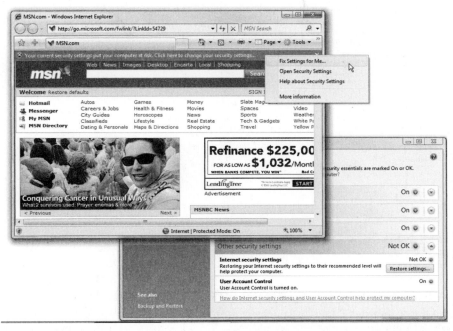

Figure 8-9: Fix Settings for Me enables you to back away from an insecure Internet Explorer 7 setup.

Phishing Filter

Internet Explorer 7 includes an integrated Phishing Filter that can help prevent you from being a victim of identity theft. These so-called phishing attacks are described in Chapter 18.

> **tip**
>
> Curiously, the Phishing Filter is optional in Internet Explorer 7. We cannot stress this strongly enough: You should enable this feature the first time you run Internet Explorer 7 (you'll be prompted). If you didn't do so and would like to enable it now, click the Tools button in the IE command bar and select Phishing Filter and then Turn On Automatic Website Checking.

Delete Browsing History

In previous Internet Explorer versions, it was difficult to delete various data related to Web browsing, such as temporary Internet files, cookies, web history, saved form data, or saved passwords. In Internet Explorer 7, this information can all be deleted from a single dialog, either individually or all at once. Shown in Figure 8-10, Delete Browsing History is available from the Tools button in the IE command bar.

Figure 8-10: Delete Browsing History is a godsend for the security conscious and truly paranoid.

Other Internet Explorer Security Features

The list of Internet Explorer 7 security features is vast, although you won't likely run into most of them unless you're truly unlucky. IE 7 integrates with Windows Defender to provide live scanning of web downloads to ensure you're not infecting your system with spyware, and it integrates with Vista's parental controls (see Chapter 9) to make sure your children are accessing only those parts of the Web you deem as safe. IE 7 provides International Domain Name (IDN) support so that hackers can't construct malicious web sites that mix character sets in order to fool unsuspecting users. And there are various low-level changes that prevent cross-domain or -window scripting attacks.

Secret   Should Internet Explorer 7 somehow be compromised, there's even a way out. A new Internet Explorer mode called Add-ons Disabled mode loads IE with only a minimal set of add-ons so you can scrub the system of any malicious code. You access this mode by navigating to All Programs⇨Accessories⇨System Tools⇨Internet Explorer (No Add-Ons) in the Start Menu.

BitLocker Drive Encryption

In Windows XP and previous NT-based versions of Windows, Microsoft offered a feature called Encrypting File System (EFS) that enabled users to encrypt important folders or files. This prevents thieves from accessing sensitive data should your computer be physically stolen: If the thief removes your hard drive and attaches it to a different computer, any encrypted files cannot be read. EFS has proven to be a popular feature with businesses that have many roaming executives with laptops, with IT administrators, and the security conscious.

EFS is still present in Windows Vista and works as before, but it's been augmented by a new technology called BitLocker. Like EFS, the new BitLocker feature in Windows Vista lets you encrypt data on your hard drive to protect it in the event of physical theft. But BitLocker offers a few unique twists.

⬥ First, BitLocker is full-disk encryption, not per-file encryption. If you enable BitLocker, it will encrypt the entire hard disk on which Windows Vista resides, and all future files that are added to that drive are silently encrypted as well.

⬥ Second, BitLocker protects vital Windows system files during bootup: If BitLocker discovers a security risk, such as a change to the BIOS or any startup files (which might indicate that the hard drive was stolen and placed in a different machine), it will lock the system until you enter your BitLocker recovery key or password (discussed shortly).

⬥ Third, BitLocker works in conjunction with new Trusted Platform Module (TPM) security hardware in some modern PCs to provide a more secure solution than is possible with a software-only encryption routine. BitLocker may not be theoretically impregnable, but in the real world the chances are that no hacker will ever defeat a BitLocker-protected PC.

tip   **BitLocker is available only to users of Windows Vista Enterprise and Ultimate editions.**

There isn't a heck of a lot of configuration you can do for BitLocker. It's either on or it's not, and you either have TPM hardware or you don't: If your system does have TPM hardware, BitLocker will use it. Otherwise, you must use a USB memory drive as a Startup Key. This key will be required to boot the system. If you don't have the key, or you lose it, you will need to enter a recovery password to access the drive. Here's where things get tricky: You can print out the recovery password and store it in a safe place, like a physical safe or safety deposit box. Or you can store it on a different computer in a text file, perhaps in an encrypted folder or encrypting ZIP file. However you store the recovery password, you can't lose it. If you lose both the startup key (either in the TPM hardware or on a USB memory key) and the recovery password, the data on the BitLocker-protected hard drive is gone for good. There is literally no other recovery option available.

Still undaunted? You enable BitLocker by navigating to the BitLocker Drive Encryption tool in Control Panel. This is located in Control Panel⇨Security⇨BitLocker Drive Encryption. Shown in Figure 8-11, there's not much to it. To enable BitLocker, simply click the Turn On BitLocker option.

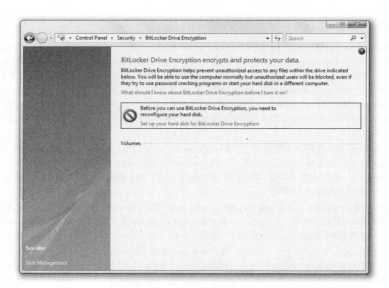

Figure 8-11: BitLocker is one of those exceedingly easy features. It's either on or it's off.

If you have the appropriate TPM hardware, BitLocker will save its encryption and decryption keys in that hardware. Otherwise, you'll be prompted to insert a USB memory key, which you'll need to insert in the machine every time it boots up. Optionally, you can also create a startup key or PIN to provide an additional layer of protection. The PIN is any number from four to 20 digits. The startup key and PIN can only be enabled the first time you enable BitLocker.

When BitLocker is enabled — which takes quite a bit of time, incidentally, because it must encrypt the contents of the drive — you don't have to do much configuration-wise. You'll see a new Manage Keys link in the BitLocker Drive Encryption control panel, and you can create a recovery password from there. If you choose to print the password, be sure to save it in safe place. Seriously.

Low-Level Security Features

Windows Vista includes a vast array of low-level security features. One of the most dramatic is service hardening. Because of the modular architecture of Windows Vista, the system has been created in such a way that the components that make up the system are as isolated from and independent of each other as is possible. Furthermore, Microsoft has gone over each of these components to ensure that they are running under the lowest possible security privileges. This protection extends to the system services that run silently in the background. While none of these features are particularly configurable, it's fair to say that Windows Vista is the most secure Windows version ever made, thanks to the sum of these many security enhancements.

Secret

To get the absolute best security with Windows Vista, run one of the *x*64 versions of the operating system. (See Chapter 1 for information about choosing between *x*64- and *x*86/32-bit versions of Windows Vista.) That's because the *x*64 versions of Windows Vista include a few unique security features that are not available or as effective in the 32-bit versions of the operating system. These include:

- A new feature called Address Space Layout Randomization (ASLR) that randomly loads key system files in memory, making them harder to attack remotely.
- A hardware-backed version of Data Execution Protection (DEP) that helps prevent buffer overflow-based attacks.
- *x*64 drivers must be digitally signed, which suggests (but doesn't ensure) that *x*64 drivers will be more stable and secure than 32-bit drivers, which are often the cause of instability issues in Windows.

Of course, *x*64 versions of Windows Vista have their own compatibility issues, both with software and hardware. The tradeoff is yours to make: Better security and reliability or compatibility.

Summary

Although much is made of Vista's new user interface, its new security features are, beyond a doubt, the number one reason to consider upgrading to this new operating system. Here's why: Although it's possible to duplicate many of the end user features in Windows Vista, its many security improvements are only available to those who upgrade. Security isn't something that's easy to sell, per se, and certainly vulnerabilities will crop up over time. But make no mistake: Vista's security improvements are as dramatic as they are important.

New User
Account Features

Chapter

9

✦ ✦ ✦ ✦ ✦ ✦ ✦ ✦ ✦ ✦ ✦ ✦ ✦ ✦ ✦ ✦ ✦ ✦ ✦

In This Chapter

Understanding the types of user accounts you can create in Windows Vista

Using User Account Control to protect your system

Disabling and configuring User Account Control

Applying and configuring parental controls for your children

Seeing how parental controls work and how you can override settings

✦ ✦ ✦ ✦ ✦ ✦ ✦ ✦ ✦ ✦ ✦ ✦ ✦ ✦ ✦ ✦ ✦ ✦ ✦

By now, most Windows users are probably used to the notion of user accounts and how each user on a PC can have his or her own individual settings, documents, and other features. In Windows Vista, Microsoft has simplified the user account types down to just two, and locked them down to make the system more secure. Using new Windows features such as User Account Control and parental controls, it's possible to modify Vista's user-related security features. In this chapter, we'll examine both of these new features.

Understanding User Accounts

Starting with Windows XP, Microsoft began really pushing the concept of user accounts to consumers. That's because XP, unlike previous Windows versions, was based on the Windows NT code base, and NT was developed to be a mission-critical competitor to business operating systems such as Unix. Previously, consumer Windows products like Windows 95 and Windows Me had provided only the barest possible support for discrete and secure user accounts because those systems had been architected for single users only.

Windows Vista, like Windows XP, is based on the NT code base. And that means that versions of Vista are being marketed to both individuals and businesses, and that Vista will retain—and enhance—the notion of each user having his or her own user account through which they access the PC. What we're concerned with primarily is how user accounts have changed in Windows Vista.

Okay, maybe a short review is in order. When you installed or configured Windows XP for the first time, you were prompted to provide a password for the special Administrator account and then create one or more user accounts. Administrator is what's called a built-in account type. The Administrator account is typically reserved for system housekeeping tasks and has full control of the system. Theoretically, individual user accounts—that is, accounts used by actual people—are supposed to have less control over the system for security reasons.

In Windows XP, that theory was literally a theory. Every user account you created during XP's post-setup routine was an administrator-level account, and virtually every single Windows application ever written assumes that every user has administrative privileges. It was an ugly chicken-and-the-egg situation that has resulted in several years of security vulnerabilities, because malicious code running on a Windows system runs using the privilege level of the logged on user. If the user is an administrator, so is the malicious code.

In Windows Vista, everything has changed. Sure, you still create user accounts, hopefully with passwords. And you log on to the system to access applications, the Internet, and other services. But in Windows Vista, user accounts—even those that are graced with administrative privileges—no longer have complete control over the system, at least not by default. Microsoft, finally, is starting to batten down the virtual hatches and make Windows more secure. And although there are ways to counteract these moves, the result is a more secure operating system than previous Windows versions, one that hackers will find more difficult to penetrate. Let's see what's changed.

Creating the Initial User Account

When you install Windows Vista for the first time, or turn on a new computer that has Windows Vista preinstalled, you will eventually run into the so-called out-of-box experience (OOBE), where Vista prompts you for a few pertinent bits of information before presenting you with the Windows desktop. Unlike with XP, an Administrator account is not created by default. Instead, you are prompted to create a first user account during the OOBE, and that account is granted administrative privileges.

Understanding Account Types

Windows Vista, unlike XP, supports just two account types.

◆ The first, *administrator*, is exactly what it sounds like, and is the same as the administrator account type in Windows XP. Administrators have complete control of the system and can make any configuration changes they need to, though the method for doing so has changed somewhat since XP.

◆ The second user account type is called *standard user*. A standard user can use most application software and many Windows services. Standard users are, however, prevented from accessing features that could harm the system. For example, standard users cannot install applications, change the system time, or access certain Control Panel applets. Naturally, there are ways around these limitations, which we'll discuss in a bit.

Microsoft would like most people to run under a standard user account. And although this would indeed be marginally safer than using an administrator account, we can't recommend it. That's because Microsoft has actually locked down the administrator account in Windows Vista, making it safer to use than before. More important, perhaps, you'll ultimately find an administrator account to be less annoying than a standard user account. To find out why that's so, we need to examine a new security feature in Windows Vista called User Account Control.

User Account Control

In order to make the system more secure, Microsoft has architected Windows Vista such that all of the tasks you can perform in the system are divided into two groups, those that require administrative privileges and those that don't. This required a lot of thought and a lot of engineering work, naturally, because the company had to weigh the ramifications of each potential action and then code the system accordingly. What they've arrived at is a decent compromise, and although some of the security controls in Windows Vista will likely cause fits in certain circles, many users will understand that they're in place to keep the system more secure and will learn to live with them. Our feeling is that anyone who's been bitten by a worm, virus, Trojan, or other bit of malicious code will gladly and willingly accept the new restrictions.

Here's how it works. Every user, whether configured as a standard user or administrator, can perform any of the tasks in Windows Vista that are denoted as not requiring administrator privileges, just as they did in Windows XP. You can launch applications, change time zone and power management settings, add a printer, run Windows Update, and perform other similar tasks. However, when you attempt to run a task that does require administrative privileges, the system will force you to provide appropriate credentials in order to continue. The experiences differ a bit, depending on the account type.

Standard users receive a User Account Control credentials dialog box, as shown in Figure 9-1. This dialog box requires you to enter the password for an administrator account that is already configured on the system. Consider why this is useful. If you've configured your

children with standard user accounts, they can let you know when they run into this dialog box, giving you the option to allow or deny the task they are attempting to complete.

Figure 9-1: Standard users attempting to perform admin-level tasks will be confronted by the
User Account Control credentials dialog box.

Administrators receive a simpler dialog box, called the User Account Control consent dialog box, which is shown in Figure 9-2. Because these users are already configured as
administrators, they do not have to provide administrator credentials. Instead, they simply
need to click Continue to keep going.

Figure 9-2: Administrators receive a slightly less annoying dialog box.

Secret

By default, administrators using Windows Vista are running in a new execution mode
called Admin Approval Mode. This is the reason you see consent dialog boxes appear
from time to time. You can actually disable this mode, making administrator accounts
work more like they did in XP, without any annoying dialog boxes popping. However,
you should realize that disabling Admin Approval Mode could open up your system
to attack. If you're still interested in disabling this feature, or disabling User Account
Control, we will discuss ways to do so at the end of this section.

Conversely, administrators who would like Windows Vista to be even more secure can also configure the system to prompt with a User Account Control credentials dialog box — which requires a complete password — every time they attempt an administrative task. This option is also discussed shortly.

The presentation of both of these dialog boxes can be quite jarring. If you attempt to complete an administrative task, the screen will flash, the background will turn black, and the credentials or consent dialog will appear in the middle of the screen. You cannot continue doing anything else until you have dealt with these dialog boxes one way or the other.

For the record, there's actually a third type of User Account Control dialog box that will appear occasionally regardless of which type of user account you have configured. This dialog box appears whenever you attempt to install an application that has not been digitally signed or validated by its creator. These types of applications are quite common, so you're likely to see the dialog box shown in Figure 9-3 fairly frequently.

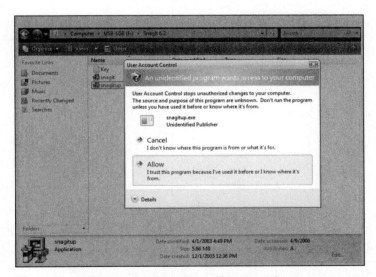

Figure 9-3: This colorful dialog box will appear whenever you attempt to execute an application installer from an unknown source.

By design, this dialog box is more colorful and in-your-face than the other User Account Control dialog boxes. Microsoft wants to make sure you really think about it before continuing. Rule of thumb: You're going to see this one a lot, but if you just downloaded an installer from a place you trust, it's probably okay to go ahead and install it.

Disabling and Configuring User Account Control

As we mentioned previously, many people are going to be annoyed by User Account Control and will want to simply disable it. This is easily done, but it's not recommended. You can also configure various User Account Control features using a hidden management console. In this section, we'll describe both of these options.

Disabling User Account Control

You can disable User Account Control across the board for all users of a given PC by navigating to the User Controls section of the Control Panel (in Control Panel⇨User Accounts and Family Settings⇨User Accounts) and selecting the option titled Change security settings. This will load the Change Security Settings window shown in Figure 9-4. To disable User Account Control, simply uncheck the option titled Use User Account Control (UAC) to help protect your computer and then click the OK button. Note that you will have to reboot your computer for the changes to take affect.

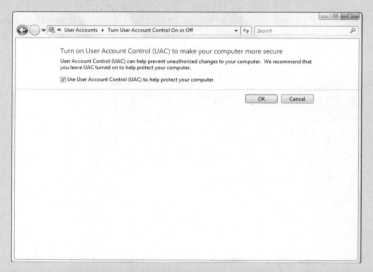

Figure 9-4: Disabling User Account Control is simple, but it affects all users.

If you want to disable User Account Control for just a single user, you simply need to select a single check box in the User Accounts Control Panel. The quickest way is to open the Start menu and click the picture that's associated with your user account. Then, in the User Accounts window that appears, click Turn User Account Control on or off. You'll see the required check box in the next window.

Secret

Configuring User Account Control

Microsoft makes a number of User Account Control settings available through the hidden Local Security Settings management console. To launch this console, open the Start menu and type **secpol.msc** and then tap Enter. This displays the console shown in Figure 9-5.

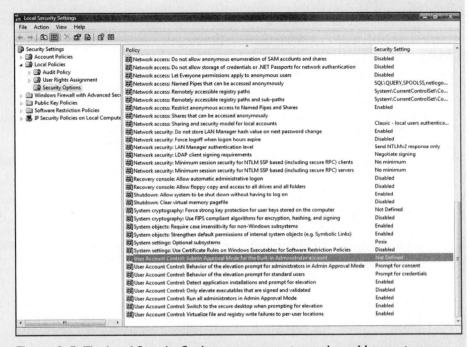

Figure 9-5: The Local Security Settings management console enables you to configure various security features, including User Account Control.

To access the User Account Control options, you will need to expand the Local Policies and Security Options nodes in the tree view under Security Settings in the left pane of the management console. When you do so, the right pane will fill up with a list of security options. Scroll to the bottom and you will see eight security options related to User Account Control. Table 9-1 highlights these settings and explains what each does.

tip   The Local Security Settings management console should be used only on PCs that are not centrally managed by a Windows Server–based Active Directory (AD)-based domain. Unless you work for a large company, it's unlikely that your PC is centrally managed in this way.

Table 9-1: User Account Control Features That Can Be Customized.

Security Option	What It Does	Default Setting
User Account Control: Admin Approval Mode for the Built-in Administrator Account	Toggles Admin Approval Mode for the built-in administrator account only.	Not defined
User Account Control: Behavior of the elevation prompt for administrators in Admin Approval Mode	Determines what type of prompt admin-level users will receive when attempting admin-level tasks. You can choose between a consent dialog box, a credentials dialog box, and no prompt.	Prompt for consent
User Account Control: Behavior of the elevation prompt for standard users	Determines what type of prompt standard users will receive when attempting admin-levels tasks. You can choose between a consent dialog box, a credentials dialog box, and no prompt.	Prompt for credentials
User Account Control: Detect application installations and prompt for elevation	Determines whether application installs trigger a User Account Control elevation dialog box.	Enabled
User Account Control: Only elevate executables that are signed and validated	Determines whether only signed and validated application installs trigger a User Account Control elevation dialog box.	Enabled
User Account Control: Run all administrators in Admin Approval Mode	Determines whether all admin-level accounts run in Admin Approval Mode, which generates User Account Control consent dialogs for admin-level tasks.	Enabled
User Account Control: Control Switch to the secure desktop when prompting for elevation	Determines whether the Secure Desktop environment appears whenever a User Account Control prompt is initiated by the system.	Enabled
User Account Control: Virtualize file and Registry write failures to per-user locations	Determines whether User Account Control virtualizes the Registry and file system for legacy applications that attempt to read or write from private parts of the system. Do not disable this option.	Enabled

Parental Controls

Although Windows XP was the first version of Windows to make user accounts truly usable, Windows Vista is the first to make them safe for children. Now, it's possible to apply parental controls on your children's accounts that will keep them away from the bad stuff online and off, and give you peace of mind that was previously lacking when the kids got on a computer. Vista's parental controls are available on a per-user basis, and you might be surprised by how well they work.

> **tip** Parental controls are available in Windows Vista Home Basic, Home Premium, and Ultimate, but not Business or Enterprise.

Configuring Parental Controls

To set up parental controls, you first need to configure one or more user accounts as standard user accounts. Then, from an administrator account, you can configure parental controls. To do so, navigate to Control Panel⇨User Accounts and Family Safety⇨Parental Controls. Then, select the user to which you'd like to add parental controls. You will see the window shown in Figure 9-6.

Figure 9-6: Parental controls enable you to configure various restrictions for your children.

> **tip**   You can only configure parental controls on one account at a time. If you have three children to which you'd like to apply identical parental controls, unfortunately, you will have to repeat these steps for each of your children's accounts. Also, note that you cannot apply parental controls to an administrator account.

By default, parental controls are not configured for any standard user accounts. When you enable parental controls, you can configure the features discussed in the following sections.

Activity Reporting

When this feature is enabled, your children's parental control-related activity is recorded and presented to you periodically in report form. The reports are available from this Parental Controls window and include such things as top 10 web sites visited, most recent 10 web sites visited, logon times, applications run, instant message conversations, link exchanges, web cam usage, audio usage, game play, file exchanges, and SMS messages, e-mails received and sent, and media (audio, video, and recorded TV shows) played. A sample report is shown in Figure 9-7.

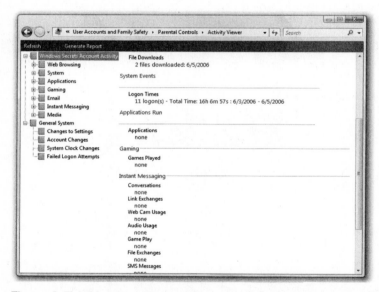

Figure 9-7: With parental controls, you can view reports that summarize your children's recent activities on the PC.

Reports are available for each standard user account. There's also a different report type, called General System, that logs such things as when parental control settings, accounts, or the system clock are changed, or when users fail to log on correctly because of entering an incorrect password (or when attempting to log on during a time period that is forbidden because of parental controls).

Web Restrictions

The web restrictions parental controls determine what web content your children can access. As shown in Figure 9-8, this control gives you fine-grained control over web access. You can block web content using web restriction levels (plain English ratings like Low, Medium, and so on) or by content type (block sites related to alcohol, bomb making, gambling, hate speech, and other categories). You can also completely block all file downloads.

Figure 9-8: Windows Vista's web restrictions will keep your children safe online.

Time Limits

The time limits parental control uses a graphical grid to let you configure exactly when your kids can use the computer. By default, Windows Vista users can use the PC on any day at any time. But by dragging your mouse around the grid shown in Figure 9-9, you can prevent your children from using the computer at specific hours, such as late at night or during school hours.

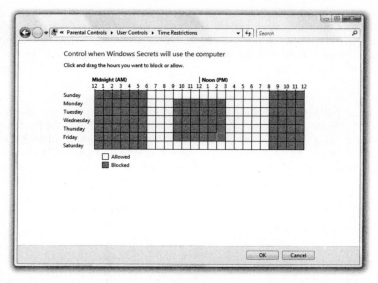

Figure 9-9: This simple and effective interface helps you configure when your kids can and cannot use the PC.

Games

The games parental control determines whether your children can play games on the PC and, if so, which games they can access. By default, standard account holders can play all games. However, you can fine-tune that setting using the screen shown in Figure 9-10, which appears when you click Set game ratings.

Figure 9-10: With the games restrictions, you can control which games your kids play.

Here, you can set acceptable game ratings using the Entertainment Software Ratings Board's (ESRB) rating system, or block games based on content (online, blood and gore, drug reference, and so on). You can also block or allow specific games, which is surprisingly helpful because many Windows games do not digitally identify their ESRB rating.

Allow and Block Specific Programs

This final setting lets you manually specify specific applications that you do or do not want your child to use. By default, standard users can access all of the applications installed on the system. However, using the interface shown in Figure 9-11, it's possible to fine-tune what's allowed. If you don't see an application in the list, click Browse to find it.

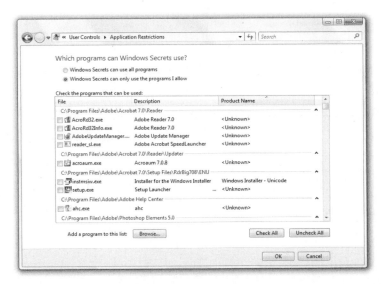

Figure 9-11: Choose the applications your children can access from this list.

Secret

One of the most unique features of Windows Vista's parental controls is that they don't need to be used only with children. Indeed, many security-conscious users will find that it's actually worth setting up a standard user account for themselves, applying various parental controls to it, and then using that account for their normal PC operations. Why would you want to do such a thing? Well, you might want to protect yourself from some of the nastier things that happen online for starters. Something to think about.

Running as Standard User with Parental Controls

You may be wondering what the experience is like running a standard user account to which parental controls have been applied. For the most part, it's just like running a standard account normally. However, certain actions will trigger parental control blocks, depending on how you've configured parental control restrictions. For example, if the user attempts to log on to the system during a time period in which the parent has restricted that, you will be prevented from doing so. And if you try to run an application that is not explicitly allowed by parental controls, you will see the dialog box shown in Figure 9-12.

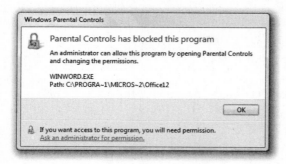

Figure 9-12: No Microsoft Word for you. Sorry, but this application is being blocked by Vista's parental controls.

Note that you can ask for permission to run individual blocked applications. When you choose this option, the User Account Control credentials dialog box appears, giving the parent a chance to come over to the machine, review what is happen, and decide whether to give their permission.

The Web experience is similar. If you use Internet Explorer to browse to a type of site that is forbidden via parental controls, IE will display the page shown in Figure 9-13. Again, you can click the Ask an administrator for permission link to get an override. When you do so, the User Account Control credentials dialog box appears as you might expect.

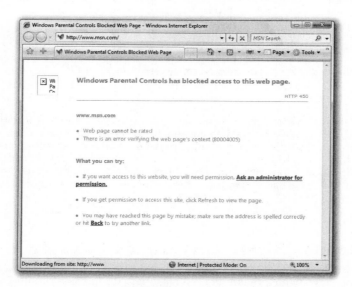

Figure 9-13: Web restrictions work in a similar manner thanks to parental control integration with Internet Explorer 7.

If you attempt a web download, and web downloads are restricted with parental controls, you'll see the dialog box in Figure 9-14. In this case, there is no administrator override: Downloads have been explicitly restricted with parental controls.

Figure 9-14: When downloads are prevented, there's no way to get an override.

Summary

Windows Vista, for the first time, makes it possible for users to run the system in more secure ways, thanks largely to advances in the way that user accounts are handled. Although features like User Account Protection will often seem annoying, the alternative is worse, as evidenced by the past half-decade of Windows security vulnerabilities. Vista's parental controls, meanwhile, finally extend a measure of safety to your children, whether they're using local applications or browsing the Web.

Part IV

Digital Media and Entertainment

Windows Media Player 11

Chapter

10

◆ ◆

In This Chapter

Using Windows Media Player 11

Understanding the new visual user interface

Working with digital music, photos, videos, and recorded TV

Ripping and burning CDs

Synchronizing with portable media devices, including the iPod

Sharing your media library with other PCs, devices, and the Xbox 360

Accessing online music services

◆ ◆

Give Microsoft a little credit: When it launched its first all-in-one media player—Windows Media Player 7, with Windows Millennium Edition (Me) in 2000—the company made it clear that this product would be about more than just music: Today, Windows Media Player 11, the version that ships with Windows Vista, is dramatically improved, with support for music, videos, photos, recorded TV shows, streaming Internet media, and more. It really is an all-in-one solution for virtually all of your digital media needs—well, with one major exception: Windows Media Player 11 doesn't natively support Apple's dominant iPod, the best-selling portable MP3 player on the planet. In this chapter, we'll show you how to get the most of Windows Media Player 11. We'll even show you how to make it work with the iPod.

Media Player Basics

As is the case throughout this book, we assume you're familiar with basic operations in Windows and its many bundled applications. And Microsoft has included a very simple media player in Windows for over a decade, and a full-featured, all-in-one player since Windows Me.

That said, Windows Media Player 11 can be fairly complicated if you don't understand what it's doing. So we'll get started by examining this new Media Player and its core functionality.

Setting Up Windows Media Player 11

The very first time you launch Windows Media Player 11, you're forced to step through a quick wizard that enables you to configure various privacy options and optionally configure MTV's URGE, an online music service that we discuss later in this chapter. Don't just click Next here. Instead, you will want to very carefully read through the options that Microsoft presents. It's possible to configure these options after the fact, of course, but it's better to do so now, as you'll see in a moment.

Secret   On the first page of the wizard, you're asked to choose between Express and Custom set-up choices. Always choose Custom. Express may be quicker, but it doesn't give you access to the most important Windows Media Player 11 configuration options and instead chooses defaults that benefit Microsoft, not you.

After you choose Custom, you'll be presented with the window shown in Figure 10-1, which is very similar to the initial dialog box that Windows Media Player 10 users saw on Windows XP. Here, you pick various privacy options.

Figure 10-1: Be sure to read through the options here very carefully. Don't accept the default values.

In the Enhanced Playback Experience section, you will want to weigh the second option very carefully. If you have a finely crafted media library, in which you've lovingly downloaded and applied album art for all of your ripped music files, you will definitely want to clear the Update My Music Files by Retrieving Media Information from the Internet check box. If you don't, you will find that your media library will, over time, become a jumbled mess as Media Player changes your nicely formatted music files to match what a third-party library on the Internet says are the correct song, album, and artist names, often with disastrous results. On the other hand, if you're just starting out and intend to use Windows Media Player 11 to rip your CDs to the PC, leave this option checked.

The other options should be pretty self-explanatory and none are as potentially destructive as the option just discussed. You can leave the default options selected as is.

When you click Next, you're presented with a window that is new to Windows Media Player 11, allowing you to place Media Player shortcuts on the desktop and Quick Launch toolbar. If you think those shortcuts will be valuable, check the appropriate boxes and continue.

The next window, too, is new to Windows Media Player 11. Here, you can choose to make Windows Media Player 11 the default music player for all of the media types it supports, or you can choose the exact file types that it will play. Obviously, this phase of setup is aimed at experts, and for the most part you should simply choose the first option, Make Windows Media Player 11 the default music and video player. However, if you have strong feelings about using a different media player for specific file types, you can choose the second option. If you do so, you'll be presented with a new Windows Vista feature: the Set associations for a program section of Control Pane shown in Figure 10-2. Here, you can configure which media file types will be associated with Windows Media Player 11.

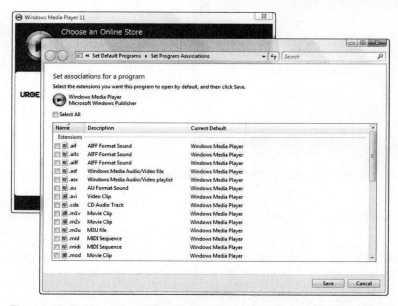

Figure 10-2: In previous Windows versions, this information was buried in the system and configured through Windows Media Player.

Finally, you will be asked if you'd like to set up the URGE online music service. Select no. You can set up URGE at a later time if you want, and we'll examine how to do this later in this chapter if you're curious.

> **tip**   You won't be prompted to install URGE if your PC is not connected to the Internet.

Understanding the Windows Media Player 11 User Interface

Shown in Figure 10-3, Windows Media Player 11 is a dramatic departure from previous Windows Media Player versions, with a more visual media library view that relies heavily on album art and photo and video thumbnails. Also, Windows Media Player 11 adopts the Windows Vista look and feel, with glass-like window borders and the new black and blue Vista color scheme.

Figure 10-3: It's not your father's media player: Windows Media Player 11 is more graphical, with rich views of your music, photos, and videos.

---

tip   Windows Media Player 11 ships with a small selection of sample music and video content, which we'll use for the examples in this part of the chapter. This lets you get started with the player even if you don't have any content of your own.

Compared to its predecessors, Windows Media Player 11 offers a number of improvements and changes. First, the player no longer uses a hokey, pseudo-rounded window that doesn't quite work correctly (maximize Windows Media Player 10 in Windows XP to see what we mean by this). Instead, Windows Media Player 11 looks and acts like many other Windows Vista applications. The toolbar has been enhanced with Back and Forward buttons, which enable you to easily move between the Media Player experiences that are listed along the rest of the toolbar: Now Playing, Library (the default view), Rip, Burn, and Sync.

Here's how Back and Forward work. If you're in the media library, denoted by a highlighted Library toolbar button, and click the Rip toolbar button, you'll find yourself transported by the Media Player music ripping experience. Now, you can press Back to get back to the previous experience you visited (i.e., the media library). And if you do navigate back to the media library, you can click Forward to go back to Rip again. In short, the Forward and Back buttons work just like their equivalents in Internet Explorer and the Windows shell.

You might notice that the Guide button is no longer available in the Media Player toolbar. You can still get to the Media Guide, however. To do so, click the small downward-pointing arrow under the Online Stores button on the far right of the toolbar and choose Media Guide from the resulting drop-down menu. This drop-down menu will appear only if you are online.

Speaking of the right side of the toolbar, this area has been cleaned up substantially this time around. In Windows Media Player 10, there were Music, Radio, Video, and Online Stores buttons. Now, there is just an Online Stores button.

Dig a little deeper, and you'll see another new bit of user interface right below the toolbar. Here, there is a breadcrumb bar that helps you navigate through the various media libraries you'll access in Windows Media Player 11—Music (the default), Pictures, Video, Recorded TV, and Other Media—buttons for layout and view options, the new Instant Search box, and a button for toggling the player's List Pane. The next sections discuss what each of these features does.

Category Button and Breadcrumb Bar

In Windows Media Player 10 (and 7, 8, and 9 for that matter), Microsoft divided up your media library by media type using an expanding tree view that many users found difficult to use. Regardless of your experience, however, the tree view was simply lousy because it made it too easy to get lost in large media libraries. Windows Media Player 11 does away with this, replacing the tree view with a breadcrumb bar (similar to what is used in the Windows Explorer address bar) that is triggered by the Category button. If you click this button, as shown in Figure 10-4, you can choose between the various media types Media Player supports and see only that part of the media library you need.

By default, you will be in Music view, since most people use Windows Media Player to play music. You'll notice that the breadcrumb bar to the right of the Category button lets you dive into your media library in various ways. For example, by default, the music portion of your media library is displaying your content by songs. But you can change this view by clicking on the various nodes in the breadcrumb bar. Say you wanted to view just the albums, and not the individual songs. To do so, click the arrow next to Library in the breadcrumb bar and select Albums. The view will now resemble Figure 10-5.

What you see in the breadcrumb bar will depend on which section of the media library you are viewing. For example, music has options for albums, artists, songs, and genres, whereas video has options for all video, actors, genre, and rating.

Figure 10-4: Media Player isn't just about music.

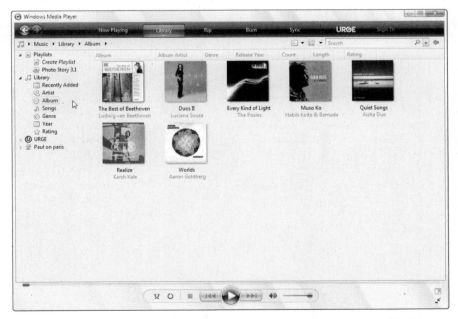

Figure 10-5: Media Player's media library view can be changed in a multitude of ways to match your preferences.

Layout Options

The Layout Options button enables you to configure various parts of the Windows Media Player 11 user interface. These parts include the Navigation pane, which is the list of information found on the left side of the player (on by default); the List pane, which was a prominent part of the Windows Media Player 10 interface, but is off by default in Windows Media Player 11; and the Classic Menus, which are off by default, as they are in so many Windows Vista applications.

Typically, you're going to want to leave the Navigation pane on. This is a handy place to access the top-most (well, right-most) items in the Media Player breadcrumb bar without having to drop down a menu. The List pane will likely be of interest in two major scenarios. First, if you're a big fan and user of previous Windows Media Player versions, you're probably used to the way those media players used temporary and saved playlists as the main way to interact with your music collection, so the List pane might be of interest. But the List pane is useful in other situations. If you're going to create a saved playlist or burn some songs to an audio CD, for example, the List pane can act as a handy holding area for the tracks you want to include.

If you enable Classic Menus, you'll see a top-mounted menu structure similar to that found in previous Windows Media Player versions. Our advice is still to skip out on Classic Menus, and enjoy the uncluttered simplicity of the Media Player interface.

Secret

To access the Windows Media Player 11 menu system without enabling Classic Menus, simply tap the Alt key at any time. You'll see a fly-out version of the Media Player menu appear, as shown in Figure 10-6.

Figure 10-6: No need to enable Classic Menus: Just tap Alt to see this menu appear.

View Options

Like the Layout Options button, the View Options button triggers a pop-out menu, but this one includes just a few options, all of which are related to the way the media library is displayed. There are three options here: Icon, Tile/Expanded Tile (depending on the content being viewed), and Details.

In Icon view, the media library displays each item as an icon. Albums appear as they do in a real music store, with album art. Artists and other groups appear as stacks, as shown in Figure 10-7, when there is more than one contained item. So, for example, if you have two more albums by Collective Soul ripped to your hard drive, the Collective Soul icon will display as a stack, not a standard square icon.

Figure 10-7: Stacks denote that the icon contains other items that can be represented by their own icons.

Stacks are cool because they are immediately obvious. They look just like a stack of paper on your desk or, in this case, like a stack of CD cases. You'll see a lot of stacks in both the Genre and Year views in the Music portion of the media library.

In Tile view, items display in a manner similar to the Tiles view in Windows Explorer. (Why there is a name discrepancy is beyond us.) That is, you will see an icon for each item — album art in the case of music — and related textual information to the right. Each item is considered a tile consisting of an icon and its related information. In some views, like Songs view in Music, Tile is replaced by Expanded Tile, which provides even more related textual information (a list of songs, in this case). Tile view is nice if you have lots of screen real estate and think you might occasionally want to edit song ratings, which is one of the bits of related info displayed on each tile.

In Details view, the media library behaves like it did in previous Windows Media Player versions (and, as it turns out, as it does in Apple's popular iTunes program): as a textual list of information only. This interface, which seems to be modeled after 20-year-old MS-DOS database applications like dBASE III+, is utilitarian, but it also performs a lot faster than the more visual Icon and Tile/Expanded Tile views. So if you have a slower computer, or a massive music collection, this might actually be your best bet from a performance perspective.

Instant Search

In keeping with one of the biggest selling points of Windows Vista, Windows Media Player 11 includes an Instant Search box so that you can quickly find the content you want. Annoyingly, the search box in Windows Media Player 11 is instant: As you type in the name of an artist, album, song, or other media information, the media library view is filtered in real time. In other words, it doesn't wait for you to press Enter; it searches as you type.

List Pane

To the right of the Instant Search box is a small right-pointing arrow that enables you to toggle the List pane, described previously. When the List pane is active, the arrow is still there, so you can turn it off again easily.

Keyboard Shortcuts for Media Player Navigation

If you're a keyboard jockey, you'll appreciate the fact that Windows Media Player includes a wealth of keyboard shortcuts related to navigating around the Media Player user interface. These shortcuts are summarized in Table 10-1.

Table 10-1: Keyboard Shortcuts for Navigating Around Windows Media Player 11

Navigation Operation	Keyboard Shortcut
Navigate backwards to the previous Media Player experience (identical to pushing the Back button)	Alt+Left Arrow
Navigate forward to the previously accessed Media Player experience (identical to pushing the Forward button)	Alt+Right Arrow
Switch to full-screen mode	Ctrl+1
Switch to skin mode	Ctrl+2
Switch to Artist view (in Music), All Pictures (in Pictures), All Video (in Video), All TV (in Recorded TV), or Other Media (in Other Media)	Ctrl+7
Switch to Artist view (in Music), Keywords (in Pictures), Actors (in Video), Series (in Recorded TV), or Folder (in Other Media)	Ctrl+8
Switch to Artist view (in Music), Date Taken (in Pictures), Genre (in Video), or Genre (in Recorded TV)	Ctrl+9
Select the Instant Search box (in Library view only)	Ctrl+E
Display Windows Media Player Help	F1

Playing Music and Other Media

As with previous Windows Media Player versions, you can easily select and play music in the media library. But the range of options you have for doing so has increased in this version, and Microsoft has finally put some often-needed playback options, like Shuffle and Repeat, right up front where they belong.

To play a single song in Media Player, simply double-click the item. It will begin playing immediately. To play a complete album, double-click the album's album art. Simple, right? Most items work this way in the media library.

Secret

There are, of course, exceptions. You can't play a stack of items by double-clicking it, for example. Instead, doing so simply opens the stack and displays the items it contains. If you want to play a stack, right-click it and choose Play.

In the bottom of the Media Player interface, you'll see the new universal media playback control, which is centered in the application window and provides simple access to the most often-needed playback features. These are, from left to right, Shuffle, Repeat, Stop, Previous, Play/Pause, Next, Mute, and a volume slider. The use of these controls should be obvious, but what might not be obvious is how you trigger these features, plus other playback controls, using the keyboard. These keyboard shortcuts are explained in Table 10-2.

Table 10-2: Keyboard Shortcuts for Controlling Media Playback in Windows Media Player 11

Playback Operation	Keyboard Shortcut
Start or pause playback	Ctrl+P
Stop playback	Ctrl+S
Stop playing a file and close it	Ctrl+W
Toggle Repeat (audio files only)	Ctrl+T
Navigate to the previous item or chapter	Ctrl+B
Navigate to the next item or chapter	Ctrl+F
Toggle Shuffle	Ctrl+H
Eject optical disk (CD or DVD)	Ctrl+J
Toggle the Classic Menus in Full mode	Ctrl+M
Fast forward	Ctrl+Shift+F
Change playback to fast play speed	Ctrl+Shift+G
Change playback to normal speed	Ctrl+Shift+N
Change playback to slow play speed	Ctrl+Shift+S
Rate the currently playing item as zero stars (not rated)	Ctrl+Windows Key+0
Rate the currently playing item as one star	Ctrl+Windows Key+1
Rate the currently playing item two stars	Ctrl+Windows Key+2
Rate the currently playing item three stars	Ctrl+Windows Key+3
Rate the currently playing item four stars	Ctrl+Windows Key+4
Rate the currently playing item five stars	Ctrl+Windows Key+5
Toggle Mute	F8
Decrease the volume	F9
Increase the volume	F10

Finding and Managing Your Music

If you already have a bunch of CDs that you've ripped to the PC, or other digital media content, and you want to make sure you can access it easily from Windows Media Player, you should take a moment to tell Media Player where that content is. By default, Windows

Media Player monitors certain folders for content. These folders include the current user's Music folder, the All Music folder, the current user's Pictures folder, the All Pictures folder, the current user's Videos folder, the All Videos folder, and, if you are using Windows Vista Home Premium or Ultimate editions, the Recorded TV folder.

Finding Your Music

You can speed media detection by telling Windows Media Player to manually search for media. This can also be helpful when you've chosen to store media in a nonstandard location.

To do this, click the small arrow below the Library button in the Windows Media Player 11 and select Add to Library from the resulting pop-down menu. This displays the Add to Library dialog box, which lets you manually find media and add other folder paths to the list of folders that Media Player monitors. By default, Add to Library displays in a super-simplified view style. Click the Advanced Options button to display the complete dialog box, as shown in Figure 10-8.

Figure 10-8: Add to Library is your one-stop center for finding media and adding it to your media library.

To add nonstandard folder locations to the monitored folders list, click the Add button. Note that you can choose to add volume-leveling information to each imported file, which slows the importing process but ensures that each media file plays back at a consistent volume level. This can be hugely important if you often shuffle songs from different sources.

When you click OK, Media Player will manually search its monitored folders list for new media.

If you want to manually add songs to the media library, you can also select them in Windows Explorer and simply drag them into Windows Media Player's media library. Behind the scenes, Windows Media Player will not add those folder locations to its monitored folders list, but will only add the dragged media to the media library.

Table 10-3 highlights the keyboard shortcuts used for managing the media library.

Table 10-3: Keyboard Shortcuts for Finding and Organizing Media in Windows Media Player 11

Media Management Operation	Keyboard Shortcut
Create a new playlist	Ctrl+N
Open a file	Ctrl+O
Edit media information on a selected item in the library	F2
Add media files to the library	F3
Refresh information in the panes	F5
Specify a URL or path to a file	Ctrl+U

Secret

Managing Your Music

As you add music to your collection, you may discover that Windows Media Player's reliance on album art as a visual means for quickly finding your music is a liability, since some music won't have the correct album art. Instead, you'll just see a black square. If this happens, fear not: It's easy to add album art to your blanked-out music. There are two ways, manual and automatic.

To manually add music to your blanked-out albums, browse to the Amazon.com web site using your web browser and then search for each album, one at a time. The Amazon.com web site is an excellent repository of album art: Simply click the See Larger Image link that accompanies each album and then drag the image from the web browser onto the blanked-out image in Windows Media Player, as shown in Figure 10-9. *Voilà!* Instant album art.

The manual approach works well if you only have a few missing bits of album art, but if you have multiple missing pieces of album art, you'll want to use a more automated method. There are many ways to do this, but Windows Media Player actually includes a Find Album Info feature that, among other things, helps you add missing album art. To trigger this feature, navigate to an album that's missing album art in the Media Player media library, right-click the offending album, and choose Find Album Info. This displays the Find Album Info window. Find Album Info is pretty simple: You just choose the correct album from the available selections, and you're off and running. But this tool has a huge problem: It works on a track-by-track basis, even when you select an entire album. And that's not automated enough.

Instead of Find Album Info, try another right-click option, Update Album Info (unless, of course, you don't want Microsoft messing with your carefully massaged media files, in which case you've probably skipped over this section anyway). Update Album Info is totally automated: If the online database that Microsoft licenses for Media Player has your album correctly listed, you should see the album art appear pretty quickly.

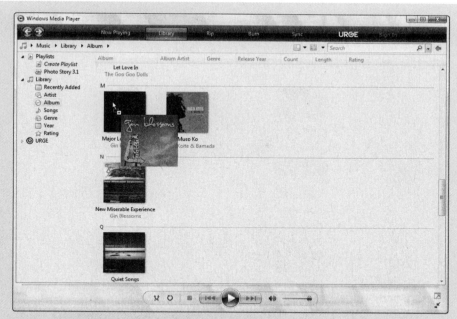

Figure 10-9: Album art is only a drag and drop away.

If neither of Microsoft's automated methods works, it's time to take matters into your own hands and try a third-party utility. One such solution is Art Fixer, which scans your media library and looks for missing album art. The application then runs through each of your albums with missing art, one at a time, and presents possible solutions. Pick the one you want and move on. You can download Art Fixer at **www.avsoft.nl/artfixer/**.

Playing with Photos, Videos, and Recorded TV Shows

In keeping with its name, Windows Media Player is about more than just music. You can also manage and access other digital media content, including photos and other pictures, videos, and recorded TV shows. For purposes of Windows Media Player, "recorded TV shows" refers to files that are stored in Microsoft Digital Video Recording (dvr-ms) format. This is the format used to record TV shows with Windows Media Center, which we examine in Chapter 13.

Accessing Photos with Media Player

Unlike its predecessor, Windows Media Player does manage your photo collection by default (in Windows Media Player 10, you had to manually enable this functionality). To access your photo collection, click the Category button and choose Pictures. This will put the media library in Pictures view, shown in Figure 10-10. By default, you will see all photos.

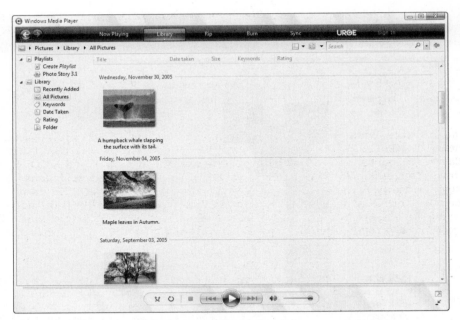

Figure 10-10: Windows Media Player in Pictures view.

When you double-click a photo in Pictures view, Media Player switches to Now Playing and displays the image in a slideshow with the other pictures around it. You can use the standard Media Player navigational controls to move through the playlist, shuffle the order, and so on. You can also click Back to get back to the media library.

Media Player's support of photos isn't fantastic, and you should probably use Windows Photo Gallery — described in Chapter 11 — to manage your photos, because it includes decent editing tools. But there's a reason Media Player supports photos: so you can synchronize them with a portable device and enjoy them on the go. We look at Windows Media Player 11's support for portable media devices later in this chapter.

Playing Videos and DVD Movies

Because of its history as an all-in-one media player, Windows Media Player 11 is an excellent solution for managing and playing videos that have been saved to your PC's hard drive. These movies can be home movies you've edited with Windows Movie Maker (see Chapter 12) or videos you've downloaded from the Internet. Windows Media Player also makes for an excellent DVD player.

Secret

As with Windows XP, Microsoft doesn't make it particularly easy in Windows Vista to access your Videos folder, which is where you'll typically store your digital movies. And like Windows XP, you can't add a shortcut to the Videos folder directly to the ride side of the Start Menu. Instead, you will need to open your user folder (the first link on the right side of the Start Menu and then open the Videos folder from there). Yes, it's dumb.

You access digital videos in Media Player by choosing Video with the Category button. Videos display as large thumbnails in the media library by default, and double-clicking them, of course, plays them.

tip   **You can make video playlists, which is actually pretty useful. Just open the List pane and drag over the videos that you want in a new playlist.**

Out of the box, Windows Media Player 11 supports a wide range of popular video formats, including MPEG-2, Windows Media Video (WMV) and WMV-HD, and AVI. But Media Player does omit support for a few popular formats, notably DivX and XViD, which are growing increasingly popular online, and QuickTime, Apple's near-ubiquitous format for movie previews. Fortunately, there are ways around these limitations. To add support for the popular DivX and XViD formats, you can simply download files that will add support for these formats from the Web. The free version of DivX is available from the DivX Web site (**www.divx.com/**), whereas XViD codecs can be downloaded from **www.xvid.org/**.

Secret   QuickTime is a bit trickier. Sure, you could download Apple's free QuickTime Player, or pony up $30 for QuickTime Pro. But neither of these would let you play back QuickTime content in Windows Media Player 11 or Windows Media Center. To gain this functionality, you'll need to turn to QuickTime Alternative, which is available on the Free Codecs Web site (**www.free-codecs.com/download/QuickTime_Alternative.htm**). This excellent bit of software enables you to play QuickTime files in Media Player, Media Center, and even your web browser. Did we mention it was free?

In previous versions of Windows Media Player, you needed to download a $10 DVD decoder in order to add movie DVD playback functionality to the player. In Windows Media Player 11, this is no longer an issue: For the first time, you can now play DVD movies in Media Player without having to go to the pain and expense of finding and purchasing extra software.

tip   **That said, Windows Media Player's support for DVDs is pretty barebones, and you don't get the wide range of functionality offered by third-party solutions such as Cyberlink PowerDVD (www.cyberlink.com/multi/products/main_1_ENU.html) or InterVideo WinDVD (www.intervideo.com/jsp/WinDVD_Profile.jsp). If you don't mind paying a bit, these products offer features like intelligent zoom for widescreen displays and various headphone output modes that simulate surround sound.**

Playing Recorded TV Shows

If you're using a Media Center PC, or a PC running Windows Vista Home Premium or Ultimate edition and a TV tuner card that's connected to a TV signal, you have the capability to record TV shows (which we discuss in Chapter 13). TV shows recorded with Windows Media Center are aggregated by Windows Media Player 11 as well, and appear in the media library when you select Recorded TV from the Categories button.

As with videos, recorded TV shows are shown in a nice thumbnail icon view by default. But if you already have Media Center on your PC, why would you want to access these shows in this fashion? Actually, there are a few reasons.

First, you might want to synchronize your recorded TV content with a portable device so you can access it during the morning commute, on a plane, or in other mobile situations. That's the primary reason this content type shows up in Media Player. But what about users with laptops? You might have Media Center on your desktop PC or Media Center PC, but if you're running a different Vista version (or a previous version of Windows) on your notebook computer, you can use Windows Media Player to access that content: Just copy the shows you want to watch to your notebook, take them on the road, watch them, and then delete them when you're done.

Secret   Seriously, delete them. Media Center content takes up massive amounts of hard drive space. Thirty minutes of recorded TV takes up almost 2 GB in Vista's version of Media Center. Yikes. Thankfully, you can make these files smaller using Windows Movie Maker. We tell you how in Chapter 12.

As you might expect, Windows Media Player supports a wide range of keyboard shortcuts that are related to videos, DVDs, and Recorded TV shows. Table 10-4 shows them.

Table 10-4: Keyboard Shortcuts for Video in Windows Media Player 11

Video Operation	Keyboard Shortcut
Zoom the video to 50 percent of its original size	Alt+1
Display the video at its original size	Alt+2
Zoom the video to 200 percent of its original size	Alt+3
Toggle display for full-screen video	Alt+Enter
Return to full mode from full screen	Esc
Rewind	Ctrl+Shift+B
Toggle captions and subtitles on or off	Ctrl+Shift+C
Fast forward	Ctrl+Shift+F
Change playback to fast play speed	Ctrl+Shift+G
Change playback to normal speed	Ctrl+Shift+N
Change playback to slow play speed	Ctrl+Shift+S
Rate the currently playing item as zero stars (not rated)	Ctrl+Windows Key+0
Rate the currently playing item as one star	Ctrl+Windows Key+1
Rate the currently playing item two stars	Ctrl+Windows Key+2

Video Operation	Keyboard Shortcut
Rate the currently playing item three stars	Ctrl+Windows Key+3
Rate the currently playing item four stars	Ctrl+Windows Key+4
Rate the currently playing item five stars	Ctrl+Windows Key+5

Ripping CDs to the PC

If you haven't yet copied your audio CD collection to the PC, Windows Media Player 11 makes doing so as painless as possible. Know, however, that ripping a CD collection—as those in the know call the copying process—can be quite time-consuming, especially if you have a large CD collection. But before you can get started, you need to make a few configuration changes.

Secret

Configuring Media Player to Use the Right Audio Format

To configure Windows Media Player 11 for CD ripping, open the Rip menu by clicking the small arrow under the Rip toolbar button and then choose More Options. This displays the Media Player Options dialog box with the Rip tab opened, as shown in Figure 10-11.

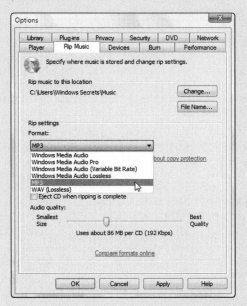

Figure 10-11: Make sure you've set up Media Player to rip music correctly before starting.

continues

continued

There are a number of options here, but we're primarily concerned with Rip settings, which determine the file format Media Player will use for the music you copy. By default, Media Player will rip music to Microsoft's proprietary Windows Media Audio (WMA) format. We cannot stress this point enough: Do not — ever — use this format.

Here's the deal. WMA is a high-quality audio format, and much more desirable from a technical standpoint than competing options such as MP3 or Advanced Audio Coding (AAC), the format Apple uses for its own music. But because WMA is not supported on some of the most popular music devices on the planet (read: the iPod), we advise against storing your entire collection in a format that could be a dead end in a few years.

So what do we recommend? We recommend the MP3 format, which is a de facto audio standard that is supported by every single audio application, device, and PC on the planet. Yes, MP3 is technically not as advanced as WMA, or even AAC for that matter. But that's okay. Thanks to today's massive hard drive sizes, you can simply encode music at a high bit rate. The higher the bit rate, the better the quality. (And, not coincidentally, the bigger the resulting file sizes. But again, who cares? Storage is cheap.)

Ripping Music

To rip, or copy, a CD to your PC, simply insert the CD into one of your PC's optical (CD, DVD) drives. An Auto Play dialog box is displayed, asking you what you'd like to do. Dismiss this dialog box immediately: Instead of choosing Rip music from CD — which is one of the choices you'll see in the Auto Play dialog box — you will want to first ensure that Media Player has correctly identified the disk.

In Media Player, click the Rip button. The CD you've inserted should show up. Examine the disk name, artist name, genre, date, and each track name to ensure that they are correct. If anything is wrong, you can edit it now before the music is copied to your computer. To edit an individual item, right-click it and choose Edit. To edit the entire album, right-click any item and choose Find Album Info.

When everything is correct, click the Start Rip button to begin the copy process. Under the Rip Status column, you'll see progress bars for each song that mark the progress of the CD copy.

Secret

Prior to Windows Media Player 10, Microsoft did not include integrated MP3 creation capabilities in its media players. But this functionality is now included at no extra cost.

Here's how you do it. From the Format drop-down box, select MP3. Then, using the Audio quality slider, change the quality to 192 Kbps or higher. Frankly, even with a compressed audio format like MP3, you're not going to notice much difference above 192 Kbps, unless you're using high-end stereo equipment. But it doesn't hurt to future-proof. We use 256 Kbps MP3 for our own CD rips.

By default, Windows Media Player 11 copies music to your Music folder. First, it creates a folder named for the group, and underneath that it will create a folder named for the album. Inside of the album folder, you'll find the individual files that make up each of the tracks in the copied album. You can change the place to which Media Player stores your songs, and the template used to name each file, in the Rip pane of the Windows Media Player Options dialog box. But for most people, the default values are just fine.

Burning Your Own Music CDs

When you have a lot of your music on the PC, you're going to want to listen to it in various ways. On the PC, you can create custom playlists of songs you really like, and if you have a Media Center PC, you can even interact with these playlists using a remote control, your TV, and (if you're really on the cutting edge) a decent stereo system. But if you want to take your music collection on the road with you, you have other options. You can synchronize music with a portable device, as described in the next section. Or you can create your own custom mix CDs, using only the songs you like. These CDs can be played in car stereos, portable CD players, or any other CD players.

As with ripping, you're going to want to configure Media Player a bit before you burn, or create, your own CD. To do this, open the Burn menu and make sure that Audio CD, and not Data CD or DVD, is chosen.

If you have a CD or DVD player that can play back data CDs or data DVDs, that option will enable you to create disks with far more music. For example, a typical audio CD can contain about 80 minutes of music maximum, but a data CD—with 700 MB of storage—can store 10 times that amount. And DVDs are even larger. Check with your CD player or DVD player's instructions to see if it is compatible with data disks.

When you're sure that you're set up for audio CD creation, insert a blank CD. Windows will display an Auto Play dialog boxes with two choices: Burn a CD (using Windows Media Player) or Burn files to disc (using Windows). You can choose the first option or dismiss the dialog box and navigate to the Burn experience in Windows Media Player by clicking the Burn button. When you do so, Media Player displays the List pane and creates an empty Burn List, which is a temporary playlist into which you can copy music to be burned to disk. To add music to this list, click on Library and navigate through your music collection. Then, drag over the songs you want on the disk.

At the top of the List pane, Media Player provides a handy progress bar and time limit gauge so you can be sure that your Burn List isn't too long to fit on the CD. Fill up the Burn List with as much music as you'd like, making sure that you don't go over the time limit. When you're ready to create the disk, click the Start Burn button at the bottom of the List pane. When you do so, the Burn experience appears, and Media Player begins burning the disk, as shown in Figure 10-12.

Figure 10-12: Burn, baby, burn: Media Player's Burn experience makes short work of custom mix CDs.

Under the Status column, you'll see progress bars appear next to each song as they're burned to disk. Unlike CD ripping, CD burning moves along pretty quickly, especially on a modern optical drive.

Synchronizing with Portable Devices

Although the iPod gets all the press these days, a growing family of Windows Media Player–compatible portable players offers better features and functionality than Apple's devices, and often at a better price. Although it's not possible here to enumerate through every single non-Apple device on the market, what you're looking for, generally, is a portable device that's labeled as PlaysForSure-compatible. PlaysForSure is a Microsoft marketing campaign aimed at educating consumers about which devices work seamlessly with Windows Media Player.

Using Windows Media–Compatible Devices

If you do go the Windows Media route, you'll find that setup and configuration are simple: Just plug the device into your Windows Vista–based PC and wait a few seconds while Vista configures drivers. Then, launch Windows Media Player 11 and get to work. You can synchronize music with all portable devices, and photos, movies, and recorded TV shows with many of them. What you'll be able to do is determined by the capabilities and capacity of the player you select.

For those with light needs — a few hundred songs but no photos or videos — a 512 MB to 2 GB flash-based device should work just fine. But even some of these small players are stepping up with video and photo support, so look for crisp color screens, even at the low end.

For the ultimate in portable entertainment, you'll want a device with a large color screen and a massive hard drive. With enough storage space, you'll have no problems storing all the photos, home movies, and recorded TV shows you want to watch.

Whichever device you choose, configuration is largely hands-free and occurs behind the scenes. If you plug the device in while Media Player isn't running, you will see an Auto Play dialog box that enables you to choose between different choices, including synchronizing with Windows Media Player. You can choose that, or close the dialog box and manually launch Windows Media Player.

When you launch Windows Media Player 11, you should see the player listed at the bottom of the Navigation pane. This entry enables you to navigate through the media in your player in the same way you would media on your PC. That's pretty interesting, in some ways, and it allows you to manually manage the content you're carrying around with you. But where Media Player really shines when it comes to devices is in its ability to synchronize content between the player and the device. Synchronizing is about more than just copying media to the device. It's about ensuring that the media on your device is always what you want and is always up-to-date.

Synchronizing with a Portable Device

You'll handle all of your device synchronization through the Sync experience in Media Player which, logically enough, is accessed through the prominently displayed Sync button in the application's toolbar. Technically, there are two kinds of synchronization: Sync (or what we might call true sync) and Shuffle. You will typically use Sync when you have a large-format portable device (that is, one with multi-gigabytes of storage, possibly hard drive–based). Shuffle is aimed a smaller players, where you can't possibly fit all of your music collection on the device.

To set up a device for Sync, select it in the Navigation pane and then click the Sync toolbar button. Then, open the Sync menu (by clicking the small arrow below the Sync button) and choose the device name in the list and then Set Up Sync. This launches the Device Setup window, shown in Figure 10-13, from where you will configure which media files you want synchronized with the device.

From this interface, you can do a few things. You can set up automatic synchronization, and, depending on the capabilities of your device, sync all of your music, photos, and videos accordingly. If the device is too small to hold all of that content, Media Player will pick which content to sync, based on criteria like ratings and so forth. (This is essentially what Shuffle does.)

Secret

Don't worry about multigigabyte video files clogging up your portable device. Windows Media Player uses a technology called *transcoding* to copy large video files (and even, optionally, high-quality music files) into smaller versions that are tailored to your device. We'll examine this capability in the next section.

Figure 10-13: Think you know what you're doing? Then choose Sync and let your media fly free.

If you're the type of person that makes a lot of hand-crafted playlists, you can use the Device Setup window to ensure that only the music you care about is synchronized with the player. It's all up to you.

Secret

One final point about Sync: We mentioned earlier that synchronization was about more than just copying. Here's why that's true. If you configure a portable device to synchronize with certain playlists, or even, say, your entire music library, the content on the device will be updated every time you make a change to those playlists or libraries. So, if you rip a new CD to your PC and then connect the device to the PC, and that device is synchronized with your entire music library, that new content will silently and automatically be copied to the device. Likewise, if you add (or remove) a song from a playlist that is synchronized with a device, the next time you connect the device, its music library will be updated to reflect the changes you made on the PC.

Using Shuffle

If you're using a small-capacity device, typically one that is based on Flash RAM and contains only a few gigabytes of storage space, you might want to configure the device to Shuffle rather than Sync. In Shuffle mode, the entire contents of the device are replaced with a random selection of songs from your music library, so you always have a fresh set of tracks. You can manually change the track list on the device by opening the Sync menu and choosing Shuffle *[device name]*.

tip Shuffle isn't an answer for many people, however. If you have a wide selection of music types in your media library, you might find it a bit jarring as your player moves from, say, classical Mozart to hard rock Van Halen to new age David Lanz. Indeed, many people use smaller Flash-based players while working out, and it's likely that such people will want a particular kind of music on their players. (David Lanz is hugely talented, but he just doesn't make good workout music.) So be sure you know what you're doing before picking Shuffle.

Managing a Portable Device in Windows Media Player

Primarily, most of your PC-to-portable device interactions will involve synchronizing content between the two (and charging the portable device). However, there are a number of ways you can configure portable devices in Windows Media Player 11, and some of these options are important if you want to get the most out of your devices.

To change the name of your device as it appears in Windows Media Player, open the Sync menu and choose *[device name]* followed by Advanced Options. In the Sync tab, you can rename the device as you'd like. If you're not using the Shuffle option, you can also use this interface to determine various synchronization options, such as how much space on the device you'd like to reserve for file storage. (Many portable devices have enough capacity that they make for excellent general purpose file storage devices as well as media players.)

In the Quality tab of the same dialog box, you can control how Media Player transcodes music, videos, and recorded TV that is synchronized with the device. The issue here is simple: A 19 GB video file might look great on your PC, but few portable devices are capable of HDTV-quality video and surround sound. So rather than waste valuable storage space on your device, Windows Media Player can make copies of these content types that are smaller and more in line with your player's capabilities.

tip Transcoding can be quite time consuming, so Windows Media Player does it in the background. If you often take your device along for the morning commute, it might be a good idea to leave Media Player on overnight so it can transcode and synchronize any new content.

You can separately configure how Media Player transcodes music and videos/recorded TV. By default, Media Player will automatically transcode content as required. Or, if you feel really strongly about file sizes and quality you can manually choose how the player will handle these media types.

Secret Audiophiles can actually use this feature to ensure that Media Player does not transcode music to lower-quality files, ensuring that what they hear on their music player is in the same quality level as the original recordings.

You can also access some portable device options from the Devices tab of the Windows Media Player Options dialog. The quickest way to access this dialog is to choose More Options from the Sync menu. In this dialog, you can select the device you'd like to configure and then click the Properties button to display the Properties dialog we described above. Or, you can click the Advanced button to display the File Conversion Options dialog box, as shown in Figure 10-14. This dialog box enables you to choose advanced transcoding options, such as whether video and audio files are converted in the background (which is recommended) and where Media Player stores temporary files.

Figure 10-14: You can really micromanage the transcoding functionality of Media Player if you'd like.

Secret

You can't use an iPod natively because Microsoft knows that if it did the engineering work to make it happen, Apple would simply launch an antitrust lawsuit. Given this limitation, you might think that getting an iPod to work with Windows Media Player 11 is a non-starter. But as it turns out, an enterprising third-party company, Mediafour (www.mediafour.com/), makes an excellent solution called XPlay that adds iPod compatibility to Windows Media Player. XPlay makes the iPod work just like any other portable music device in Windows Media Player. And as a certain overrated TV personality might say, that's A Good Thing.

Sharing Your Music Library

One of the nicest features of Windows Media Player is its *Media Sharing* functionality. This feature lets you share your Media Player 11–based music library with other PCs running Windows Media Player 11, various Media Connect–based devices, and Microsoft's multimedia game machine, the Xbox 360.

tip   If you want to share your media library with one or more PCs, Windows XP works just fine, too. Just make sure that all of the PCs are running Windows Media Player 11.

Why would you want to do such a thing? Well, with many homes having two or more PCs these days, it makes sense to save some disk space and utilize your Wi-Fi (or wired) home network to access music, photos, and videos that are stored on other PCs. In one typical scenario, you may have a desktop PC with a large hard drive on which you store all of your media content. Using a wirelessly equipped notebook, you can easily access that content from elsewhere in the house. Or you can access that content using a network-attached device such as a media receiver or Xbox 360, neither of which offers a lot of local storage.

Share and Share Alike: Setting Up Your PC for Sharing

Before you can share your Media Library content, however, you'll have to do a bit of configuration. First, the PC must be connected to your home network, and you must have configured the PC's network connection to access your network as a private network. If you haven't done this, here's the quickest way.

Right-click the network connection in the system tray and choose Network and Sharing Center. Then, in the Network and Sharing Center window that appears, click Customize below the network map. In the Set Network Location dialog box, choose Private for location type and click Next.Then Click Close.

Please note that you'll need to repeat this process on any other Windows Vista–based PCs with which you'd like to share media libraries. This step isn't required for Windows XP.

Next, you will want to configure Windows Media Player 11 for sharing. To do so, open the Media Player, open the Library menu (by clicking the small arrow below the Library toolbar button) and choose Media Sharing. This will display the Media Sharing dialog box shown in Figure 10-15.

Figure 10-15: Here, you configure the PCs and other devices with which you will share digital media content.

In Media Sharing, select the check box Find media that others are sharing, if you'd like to find other shared music libraries on your home network. If you want to share the music library on the current PC, select the Share My Media check box, and then examine the icons that represent the various PCs and devices that you can share with. Select each in turn and click the Allow button for the devices with which you'd like to create sharing relationships. As you allow devices, you will see a green check box appear on their icons, as seen in Figure 10-16.

continues

continued

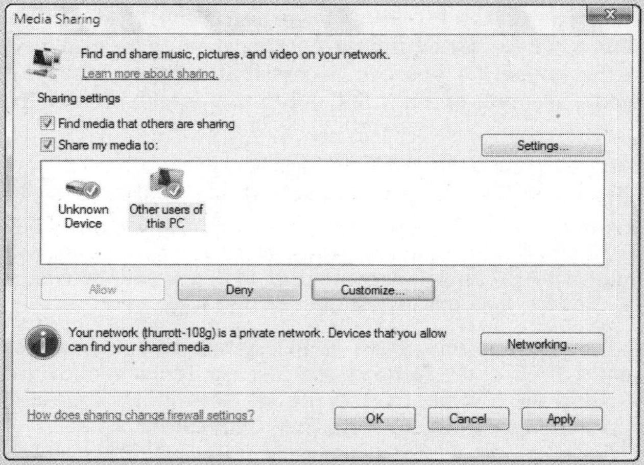

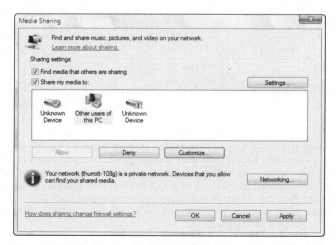

Figure 10-16: Who and what you share with is completely up to you.

If you'd like to determine the type of content you want to share, click the Settings button. You can choose between music, pictures, and videos, and choose whether to filter via star ratings or parental ratings.

Connecting to a Share Music Library with Windows Vista

When you've shared a music library on one PC, you'll be prompted to set up sharing on any other Windows Vista PCs you have in the house. As shown in Figure 10-17, you'll be prompted to establish a sharing relationship with the PC that is sharing content.

Figure 10-17: When a PC begins sharing media over the network, you'll be prompted to establish a sharing relationship.

To establish this relationship, you can click the balloon window. However, the window fades away pretty quickly (presumably because it's annoying). If this happens, you can still set up sharing: The sharing icon remains in the tray notification area. You can right-click this icon to set up sharing (Open), disable future notifications, or Exit (which will allow future sharing notifications to display. Or, simply double-click the icon to set up sharing.

In the Windows Media Player Library dialog box that appears, you can choose to Allow or Deny the other PC's request to access your shared media. You can also click a Shared settings button to access the Media Sharing dialog described in the previous section.

After you've established a connection with a shared media library, you'll see it appear in the Windows Media Player's navigation pane. You can expand and contract the list under the PC's name just as you would your own library, search for and access media, and play music and video files.

There are some limitations, of course. You can't change the contents of shared media libraries, burn them to CD or DVD, or perform any other actions that might violate the media owner's rights.

Connecting to a Share Music Library with Xbox 360

With Xbox 360 game consoles now found in tens of millions of homes worldwide, Microsoft has found a perfect way to share PC-based music libraries with a device that is probably connected to the best TV display and stereo system in the home. Thankfully, the process is incredibly simple.

1. After you've configured Windows Media Player 11 to share its media library, ensure that your Xbox 360 is connected to the home network, and then turn it on. You will see a Found Windows Media Center Extender balloon window, but you can ignore this for now (unless you're using your Windows Vista–based machine as a Media Center PC; in that case, check out Chapter 13 for more information).

2. You will also see a balloon window appear for sharing with the Xbox 360. Double-click this icon and click Allow in the resulting dialog box. Alternatively, access the Media Sharing dialog box as described previously and make sure the Xbox 360 is configured to allow sharing.

3. Access your Xbox 360 and navigate to the Media blade, as shown in Figure 10-18. This part of the Xbox 360 user interface allows you to interact with PC-based digital media, connected portable devices (like iPods and other MP3 players), and even external hard drives with stored digital media files. Right now, of course, we're just concerned with sharing media content from a Windows Vista–based PC.

4. To play shared music, select the Music option to display the Music page. Then, select Computer. If this is the first time you've done this, Xbox 360 will need to download Windows Media Connect, which is the same software many devices use to stream media from Windows Vista–based PCs. After this download is completed, Xbox 360 will search for PCs that are sharing media libraries. Select the correct PC from the list.

Figure 10-18: Xbox 360 is a multimedia powerhouse in addition to its more pedestrian video game playing capabilities.

Now you can access your PC's media library using a simple menu that consists of albums, artists, saved playlists, songs, and genres (see Figure 10-19). Xbox 360 also includes a full-featured media player for playing back this content.

As you might expect, photos and videos are accessed in a very similar manner.

Secret

If you attempt to access photos or videos from an Xbox 360 or other Windows Media Connect device and receive a "No photos found," "No videos found," or similar message, then you're not sharing any content of this type. To add photo or video content to Windows Media Player, you can either add it via Windows Photo Gallery (see Chapter 11) or use the Find Media steps described earlier in this chapter (hit F3) to manually search folders that include photo and video content.

Accessing Online Music Stores

Although Apple's iTunes Music Store is the current market leader, a host of Windows Media–compatible online music services are also available, and these services all work pretty nicely from within Windows Media Player 11. One service, however, stands out above all the rest, because of its deep integration with Media Player. It's called URGE, and we'll look at this one first.

URGE

At a very basic level, online music services all perform the same functions. They provide music for sale (so-called a la carte downloads, where you can purchase individual songs or albums) or, in some cases, provide subscription music services, which let you access all of the service's music, on a number of PCs and even portable devices, for a monthly or yearly fee. Music services also typically offer editorial content, ways to discover new music, or find out additional information about your favorite artists and albums. They often supply custom playlists, and other content.

URGE, which is owned by MTV but codesigned with Microsoft, offers all of these features. So you might wonder what the big deal is. After all, don't services such as iTunes and the various Media Player–compatible online music services described later in this chapter do the same thing?

Sort of. What makes URGE unique is its deep integration with Windows Media Player 11. By now, you should be familiar with the fact that Media Player 11 presents your media library to you visually, using new interaction points like stacks and album art. Well, URGE works the same way, and you can browse around URGE's entire music collection — well over 2 million tracks at the time of this writing — in the same way you browse your own collection. Yes, seriously.

Launching URGE

To see how this works, you need to install URGE first. To do so, simply click the URGE button in the Windows Media Player 11 toolbar. Media Player will walk you through the steps necessary to download and install URGE if you haven't already done so. Then, click the Sign In button on the toolbar to create a new account or use your existing account. From here on out, anytime you click the URGE toolbar button, you will be brought directly to URGE's main interface, shown in Figure 10-19.

Figure 10-19: Is this the future? URGE is an attempt by MTV and Microsoft to overcome the iTunes juggernaut.

Navigating the URGE Media Library

If you click around URGE, you might not see what the big deal is at first: Much of the URGE interface is very similar to other services. But to see URGE's deep integration into Windows Media Player 11, you simply have to know where to click. The easiest way to see this integration is to expand the URGE entry in the Navigation pane and then click

Genres. In the Contents pane, you will see stacks of genres, just as you would for your own media library. The difference is that URGE's genres all contain humongous collections of music, as shown in Figure 10-20. And you can dive right in, just as if URGE was stored on your own hard drive.

Figure 10-20: URGE presents its media library identically to your own local music collection.

If you double-click a genre stack, you'll be brought to a custom URGE page from which you can explore further. But you can also do some pretty crazy stuff from this interface, although you'll need to subscribe to URGE's subscription music service to hear full-length songs. For example, you can right-click on one of these stacks and choose Play to hear every single song in that genre. If you're not a subscriber, you'll only get 30-second samples. But you get the idea: If it's in URGE's collection, you have access to it, just as you do to your own music files.

You can also perform other related functions, like adding all of a genre (or other URGE collection) to the Now Playing playlist. Or, from an URGE subpage, you can use the toolbar along the bottom of the player window to navigate songs, albums, artists, and other groups just as you would your own collection. In Figure 10-21, you can see URGE's Alternative genre, sorted by artist name. Very cool.

Secret

At the time of this writing, URGE is not supported on (x64) 64-bit versions of Windows Vista. Microsoft tells us that this should be fixed by the time Windows Vista is made widely available to the public.

Figure 10-21: As you dive into URGE's music collection, you'll forget you're dealing with a music collection that exists somewhere out in the Internet.

Other Music Stores

Although URGE is pretty exciting, it isn't the only online music service game in town. To access other services that are compatible with Windows Media Player 11, you have to dig a little bit: Open the Online Services menu (by clicking the small arrow below the URGE button in the Media Player toolbar) and choose Browse All Online Stores. This will present you with options to install support for other services such as Audible.com, MSN Music, Napster, Puretracks, and XM Satellite Radio.

Frankly, if you're new to the online music service market, URGE is probably the way to go. But if you already have an account at Napster or one of the other services, they're all still available—if somewhat deprecated—in Windows Media Player 11.

Secret

You can switch between any of the Media Player–compatible online music services at any time. After you've installed and configured any of the music services that are available from within Windows Media Player 11, you can simply open the Online Services menu and pick the service you'd like to use. You'll see an entry for each configure service. Note, however, that none of the other services integrate with Media Player 11, or its Navigation pane, at least not at this time.

Summary

Windows Media Player 11 is the most full-featured version of Media Player yet, with a simpler and more visual user interface, awesome media sharing capabilities, and integration with some of the most exciting online music and video services ever offered. You can even make Windows Media Player 11 work with Apple's stunning iPod, if you really want to. There are plenty of free competitors out there, but many Windows Vista users will find everything they need right there in Windows Media Player.

Enjoying Digital Photos

◆ ◆

In This Chapter

Using the Pictures Folder to store digital photos

Using the new Windows Photo Gallery to organize your picture collection

Customizing how your pictures are displayed in Photo Gallery

Adding metadata like tags, captions, and ratings to your pictures

Importing pictures from a camera, memory card, scanner, or data disc

Editing pictures with Windows Photo Gallery and third-party applications

Sharing pictures with others in a variety of ways

◆ ◆

Windows XP took a task-based approach to digital media files, allowing you to manage digital photos, music, and videos directly in the Explorer shell. In Windows Vista, that's all changed. Although some digital media tasks are still possible from the shell, Microsoft now provides discrete applications for managing these files. For digital photos (and videos, as it turns out), the new Windows Photo Gallery application provides a handy front end to many of the tasks you need to accomplish. In this chapter, we'll examine the many ways in which the Windows shell has changed in Windows Vista with regards to digital photos, and then take an extensive look at the new Windows Photo Gallery.

Using the Pictures Folders

Like so many other conversations about Windows Vista, when discussing digital photos it's instructive to first recall how these tasks were handled in Windows XP. Several years ago, when Windows XP first shipped, Microsoft imbued the system with a number of task-centric user interface elements that made it fairly easy to work with digital media files directly in the shell. For example, the My Pictures special shell folder provided a number of picture-specific tasks, such as *Get pictures from camera or scanner*, *View as a slide show*, and *Order prints online*, among others. Windows XP also included a number of picture-specific folder views, such as Filmstrip, which made viewing pictures from Explorer reasonably pleasing. These features are both shown in Figure 11-1.

Figure 11-1: With Windows XP, digital photo management occurred directly in the Explorer shell, not within a separate application.

Other operating systems, such as Mac OS X, offer fewer shell-based digital photo management features, but Mac users have come to love the iPhoto digital photo management application, and on Windows, applications such as Google's Picasa have proven hugely popular with users. For this reason, Microsoft has stepped away from the task-centric user interfaces it developed for Windows XP and has instead created the iPhoto-like Windows Photo Gallery application for Windows Vista, which we'll describe later in this chapter.

Of course, you may be wondering at this point whether there are any picture management capabilities left in the Windows Vista shell. It's a valid question with a complicated answer. Yes, you can still manage digital photos in Windows Vista's Explorer shell, but a few things have changed.

- The My Pictures folder has been replaced by the more succinctly named Pictures folder. And instead of being a subfolder of My Documents (itself now renamed to Documents), Pictures now sits alongside Documents in your user folder (typically in C:\Users*Your User Name* by default).

- The shell-based picture capabilities have been detuned somewhat dramatically in Windows Vista. The Filmstrip view is gone, although Vista's shell does include a decent selection of view styles, all of which provide thumbnail images of pictures in those types of files. Some of the task-centric stuff is still there in slightly altered form: If you select a picture file, you'll see options for Preview, Slideshow, Print, E-mail, and Share appear in the folder's toolbar, for example.

Let's take a closer look at these changes.

Where Is It Now?

In Table 11-1, we summarize some of the picture-related changes you can expect to see in the Windows shell, and how to find similar features in Windows Vista.

Table 11-1: Where Common Picture-Related Features Are in the Windows Vista Shell

Feature	Where It Is in Windows Vista
Web Publishing Wizard (Accessed via *Publish this folder/picture to the Web* option in the folder task area)	Missing in action: Microsoft no longer offers a direct way to publish pictures to the Web in Windows Vista.
Share this folder	Replaced by a new Share toolbar button that launches the File Sharing Wizard.
Get pictures from camera or scanner	Missing, but the AutoPlay dialog box still appears whenever you plug in a digital camera or insert a memory card into a PC-connected memory card reader.
View as a slide show	Replaced by the Slide Show toolbar button.
Order prints online	You must now launch Windows Photo Gallery to access this functionality.
Print this picture/print the selected pictures	Replaced by a new Print toolbar button.
Set as desktop background	You must now launch Windows Photo Gallery to access this functionality. Alternatively, you can still right-click a picture and choose *Set as Desktop Background* from the menu that appears.
E-mail this file/e-mail the selected items	Replaced by a new E-mail toolbar button.

(continued)

Table 11-1 *(continued)*

Feature	Where It Is in Windows Vista
Preview picture	Replaced by a new Preview toolbar button, which offers enhanced functionality thanks to an attached drop-down menu that lets you choose which application to use to preview the selected image.
Edit picture	Missing, but if you select an application from the new Preview button that includes editing functionality (like Paint or Windows Photo Gallery), you can edit the picture that way.
Shell-based photo and photo folder views	Mostly missing. Now, you should use Windows Photo Gallery and its organizational view styles to view your photo collection in a variety of different ways.

Where Are the Pictures?

In Windows XP, Microsoft expected people to organize their photos in the My Pictures folder. This hasn't changed too much in Windows Vista: Now, Microsoft expects that most users will store their photos in their Pictures folder, and then manage and edit them in Windows Photo Gallery. However, with more people building simple home networks and letting multiple users create their own user accounts on single PCs, the concept of public folders — that is, folders that can be accessed by any user logged onto the PC — is gaining acceptance in Windows Vista as well.

This feature was accessed via the All Users pseudo-account in Windows XP. In that system, there was an All Users folder found in C:\Documents and Settings alongside each of the folders for actual user accounts. In Windows Vista, the layout has changed, but the idea is the same. Now, the Documents and Settings folders has been renamed to Users, and the All Users pseudo-account has been replaced by Public, which can contain data that is shared by all users who log on to the local machine. The Public folder contains its own Pictures folder, logically called Public Pictures. If you save pictures to this folder, they will be accessible to everyone that uses the PC.

tip

This is interesting for a couple of reasons, but one of the top reasons is that Microsoft provides a number of sample pictures in Windows Vista, which are accessible through the Public Pictures folder. To find them, access the Sample Pictures shortcut in your Pictures, folder, which points to C:\Users\Public\Public Picture\Sample Pictures. As shown in Figure 11-2, this folder contains a number of beautiful background images that are suitable for your desktop or enjoying in other ways.

Figure 11-2: Windows Vista comes with a number of high-quality sample pictures.

Secret

Oddly enough, these aren't the only sample pictures found in Windows Vista. Microsoft also provides a wide range of other high-quality, high-resolution images, which it intends for you to use as desktop backgrounds. But if you know where to find them, you can make copies in the Public Pictures folder (or any other folder) and access them more directly. To do so, navigate to C:\Windows\Web\. You'll notice that there is a folder called Wallpaper here. Right-click the folder, and choose Copy. Then, navigate to Public Folders, right-click a blank area of the window, and choose Paste. The Wallpaper folder contains a number of subfolders, each containing pictures in different categories, such as Black and White, Light Auras, Paintings, Textures, Vistas, and Widescreen. Most of them are quite stunning.

Organizing Photos with the Windows Vista Shell

In the Pictures and Public Pictures folder, and in any other folder that contains picture files, you can organize pictures in various ways. The Views toolbar button enables you to cycle through various shell view styles, including some like Extra Large Icons and Large Icons, which are particularly nice for viewing a folder full of pictures, as shown in Figure 11-3. (It's worth noting, however, that you can only access Extra Large Icons by clicking the More options button next to Views and selecting Extra Large Icons from the list. If you simply toggle through the various views with the Views button, Extra Large Icons will never come up.)

Figure 11-3: Some of the Windows Vista view styles are particularly nice when used with pictures.

> **tip**   **In Windows Vista and for the first time in Windows, you can now view picture thumbnails on the desktop. Previously, this functionality was available only in folder windows.**

Additionally, you can use organizational capabilities of Windows Vista to view pictures in a wide variety of new ways. As described in Chapter 5, Windows Vista includes new file organizational features such as Stacks and Groups, which can be quite handy when used in conjunction with Picture files.

To sort a folder of pictures, right-click a blank area of an open folder and choose Sort By. This triggers the submenu shown in Figure 11-4, enabling you to choose from a variety of sorting options, including Name, Date Modified, Date Taken, and others. For the most part, these options are straightforward, although the Tags and Ratings options will be described in our examination of Windows Photo Gallery later in the chapter.

The Group and Stack options are somewhat more impressive. In the same pop-up menu described above, you can choose Group By and then Name, Date Modified, Date Taken, Tag, Size, or Rating, and choose whether to group in ascending or descending order. So, for example, you might choose to group by name, which would alphabetize the list of pictures and segregate them into groups such as A-H, I-P, and Q-Z by default, as shown in Figure 11-5. If you check the Descending option, the list will sort in reverse order.

Figure 11-4: Windows Vista's file sorting options let you sort your pictures in various ways.

Figure 11-5: Group By enables you to segregate the current view into logical groups.

tip   You may have noticed there's also a More option in the Group By submenu. If you click this option, you'll be treated to a Choose Details dialog box that actually enables you to choose which items will appear in that submenu. That means you can remove some of the default choices and add such esoteric Group By options as Type, Dimensions, and more. The list is quite extensive, and of course many of the options apply only to non-picture files.

Secret

To remove a group view, simply choose a Sort option using that same pop-up menu. That will have the effect of canceling out the grouping. It's unclear why there isn't a simple None option in the Group By submenu.

To access the interesting Stack feature of Windows Vista, you follow a similar path: You choose a blank area of the current window, right-click, and choose Stack By followed by Date Modified, Date Taken, Tag, Size, or Rating. Stacked views can be quite nice. If you choose to stack the Sample Pictures by Rating, for example, you'll see three stacks indicating the pictures, which are rated as 3 Stars, 4 Stars, and 5 Stars, as shown in Figure 11-6. You can traverse into each stack as if it were a real folder: For example, the 3 Stars stack (which is really a virtual folder) contains each sample picture that Microsoft rated as 3 Stars.

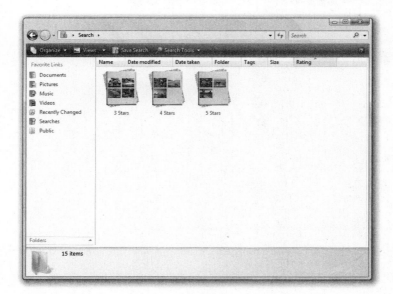

Figure 11-6: Stacks are a new user interface element in Windows Vista that enables you to organize files by category as if they were virtual stacks of paper.

If you're familiar with the virtual folder capabilities of Windows Vista, you'll recognize the Group and Stack displays as in-place searches that can be saved for later use. (Otherwise, please refer to Chapter 5 for more information.) That means you can save these views as *saved searches* and access them later whenever you want. To save a Stack By view, simply click the Saved Search button in the window's toolbar.

To view information about a picture, you can hover over a picture file with your mouse; information such as the file, type, size, date it was last modified, date it was created (or taken), and the picture's dimensions appear in a pop-up window. Also, the preview pane at the bottom of the Explorer window populates with a variety of unique information in addition to the information you see in the pop-up. These features are both shown in Figure 11-7.

Figure 11-7: In Windows Vista, selected images cough up their deepest secrets.

To find out even more information about a picture file, including such esoteric data as the make and model of the camera used to take the image, the F-number, and ISO speed, and other information, right-click an image, choose Properties, and navigate to the Details pane.

Viewing Photos in Windows Vista

To simply view an image in Windows Vista, double-click it, or click the Preview button in the window's toolbar. This launches the Photo Gallery Viewer application, which is similar to, but more powerful than, the Windows Picture and Fax Viewer application from Windows XP. Shown in Figure 11-8, Photo Gallery Viewer contains all of the picture-specific features found in Windows Photo Gallery, but none of the organizational features. Put another way, Photo Gallery Viewer is designed for working with single images only, while Windows Photo Gallery is aimed at managing your entire collection, or library, of digital images.

Figure 11-8: Photo Gallery Viewer is like Windows Photo Gallery Lite.

So what are the differences between the Windows XP Windows Picture and Fax Viewer and Windows Vista Photo Gallery Viewer? Table 11-2 shows you where to find Picture and Fax Viewer features in Windows Vista.

Table 11-2: Where Picture and Fax Viewer Features Can Be Found in Windows Vista Photo Gallery Viewer

Windows XP Picture and Fax Viewer	Windows Vista Photo Gallery Viewer
Previous Image	Previous button in navigational toolbar
Next Image	Next button in navigational toolbar
Best Fit	Not available, use Change the Display Size slider instead
Actual Size	Not available, use Change the Display Size slider instead
Start Slide Show	Play Slide Show button in navigational toolbar
Zoom In	Replaced by Change the Display Size slider in navigational toolbar
Zoom Out	Replaced by Change the Display Size slider in navigational toolbar
Rotate Clockwise	Rotate Clockwise button in navigational toolbar
Rotate Counterclockwise	Rotate Counterclockwise button in navigational toolbar
Delete	Delete button in toolbar
Print	Print button in toolbar
Copy To	Replaced by Copy option accessed via the File button
Edit	Open button in toolbar (also lets you choose which application to use)
Help	Help button in toolbar

In addition to the functionality you were used to in Windows XP, the Photo Gallery Viewer includes a number of other unique features, which we'll examine more closely in the section about Windows Photo Gallery later in the chapter.

Customizing a Picture Folder

In Windows XP, you could customize folders for pictures in a variety of ways. This functionality, alas, is largely missing in Windows Vista because Microsoft moved the picture organizational features into Windows Photo Gallery. You may recall that you could customize a folder for pictures in two ways in XP: Pictures (best for many files), which would present the folder in Thumbnail view, and Photo Album (best for fewer files), which would present the folder in Filmstrip view.

Because Filmstrip view was removed in Windows Vista, the only picture-related folder customization option is Pictures and Videos. Accessing this option is the same as it was in Windows XP: Right-click a blank area of an open folder (or right-click a folder icon) and choose Customize This Folder. This causes the folder's Properties dialog box to appear with the Customize pane displayed, as shown in Figure 11-9.

Figure 11-9: In Windows Vista, the folder customization options have been somewhat scaled back.

Managing Pictures with Windows Photo Gallery

If you were a fan of the shell-based photo management features in Windows XP, you might be somewhat disappointed that Microsoft removed a lot of that functionality from Windows Vista. But fear not: Those features—and many more—are now available in the new Windows Photo Gallery. This easy-to-use application provides a single location from which you can organize, edit, and share your digital memories. And in an interesting twist, Windows Photo Gallery can manage both photos and videos, despite its name. (It doesn't, however, provide video editing features. For that, you must use Windows Movie Maker, which is described in Chapter 12.)

Examining the Photo Gallery User Interface

Windows Photo Gallery is available from the All Programs section of the Start Menu. The application follows the increasingly familiar Windows Vista application style, with a simple top-mounted toolbar and a translucent bottom-mounted navigational toolbar, as shown in Figure 11-10.

tip   If you're familiar with Microsoft's Digital Image Suite product line, you might find that Windows Photo Gallery looks quite similar to Digital Image Suite Library. That's by design: Windows Photo Gallery offers a compelling subset of the features in Digital Image Suite, but provides those with more advanced needs with an obvious up-sell.

Figure 11-10: Windows Photo Gallery is simple but full-featured.

The Windows Photo Gallery user interface is divided into just a few main sections. Between the toolbar and navigational toolbar, you'll see three areas by default: A View By pane on the left that determines which photos you will view; a Thumbnail pane, which displays the pictures in the current view; and an Info pane, which provides information about the currently selected picture (if there is one). There is also a Choose a thumbnail view button and a search box for fine-tuning the current view.

tip A fourth pane, called the Table of Contents, can also be made to appear between the View By and Thumbnail panes. This pane provides a list of all the groups that are displayed in the Thumbnail pane and is obviously most useful if you've grouped the view in the Thumbnail pane view. We'll look at this option later in the chapter. To enable the Table of Contents, select Table of Contents from the Choose a thumbnail view button, which can be found above the Thumbnail pane and next to the search box.

Picture Files: Where and Which Ones?

You may be wondering how Windows Photo Gallery aggregates the picture files found on your PC. Does it search your entire PC for content? Actually, no. Instead, it looks only in your Pictures folder and the Public Pictures folder for picture content by default. (It also looks in Videos and Public Videos for video content.) You can add photos manually to the Windows Photo Gallery library. To do so, simply drag them from the shell into the Windows Photo Gallery Thumbnail view. However, you may simply want to add your own folders to the Windows Photo Gallery list of watched folders. We show you how in the next section.

What about picture file type support? Obviously, Windows Photo Gallery supports common image file types such as JPEG, (non-animated) GIF, PNG, TIFF, and Bitmap. But newer digital cameras support various RAW file types, which are uncompressed, and Microsoft had pledged to support RAW files in Windows Vista. Unfortunately, Windows Photo Gallery cannot edit RAW images out of the box. But if you install a compatible Windows Imaging Components (WIC) driver from a camera maker, Windows Photo Gallery will allow you to edit RAW images and export them to JPEG.

Changing How Your Digital Memories Are Displayed

Windows Photo Gallery is a fairly versatile application. In the View By pane, you can choose to filter the view of photos and videos by various criteria. The top option, or node, is called All Pictures and Videos. This option lets you view all of the photos and videos you have in the Pictures, Public Pictures, Videos, and Public Videos folders.

If you want to filter the view down a bit, you can expand and contract the various nodes found in the View By pane. For example, if you expand All Pictures and Videos, you'll see subnodes for Pictures and Videos. Choosing one of those will filter the Thumbnail pane to show only the selected content. Other nodes in the View By pane include Recently Imported, Tags, Date Taken, Ratings, and Folders.

tip
The Folders node provides you with a close approximation to the old XP-style shell management. When you expand this node, you'll see a cascading set of folders representing the folders Windows Photo Gallery watches for new content. By default, these folders include Pictures, Public Pictures, Videos, and Public Videos.

Although it's not obvious at all, you can actually add or remove folders from the list of folders that Windows Photo Gallery watches. To add a folder, simply navigate to that folder in an Explorer window and then drag it over to the Folders node. To remove a folder, including one of the default folders, right-click it inside of the Windows Photo Gallery View By pane and choose delete. When you delete a folder in this fashion, you are also deleting the original, so you will also delete the actual pictures as well. In other words, be careful.

Grouping and Arranging in Photo Gallery

The Thumbnails pane supports a number of organizational features that will be familiar to you if you've spent time playing around with similar features in the Windows shell (which are described earlier in this chapter). To access the various organizational features, you just need to click the Choose a thumbnail view button. The menu that appears enables you to choose between the following three view styles, and by grouping and arranging options, enables you to toggle the optional Table of Contents pane:

♦ **Thumbnails:** This view style is displayed in Windows Photo Gallery by default. This view style presents the images in your picture library in a manner similar to Large Icons in Explorer, except that only the thumbnails are displayed; there are no picture names cluttering up the display.

♦ **Thumbnails with Text:** This view is almost identical, but adds a text line below each thumbnail. The text you see will depend on which option is selected in the Choose a thumbnail view button's Arrange By choice. The default is Date Modified, so that's likely what you will see, unless you've changed the selection.

♦ **Tiles:** This view is perhaps the most useful. Shown in Figure 11-11, the Tiles view style provides a listing of the name, date modified, size, dimensions (resolution), rating, and caption for each thumbnail. (On the flipside, you can't see as many pictures at once because each thumbnail is accompanied by so much text.) This view style is, of course, very similar to the Tiles view style in Windows Explorer.

Figure 11-11: In Tiles view, you can see and edit important metadata information.

As with Windows Explorer windows, you can group information shown in Windows Photo Gallery's Thumbnails view by a variety of criteria, including Auto Date Taken, Month Taken, Year Taken, Occasion, File Size, Image Size, File Type, Rating, Folder, Tag, Camera, or None, in either ascending or descending order. This feature works identically to its shell-based cousin: When grouping is enabled, pictures are segregated into visual groups. So if you group by Year Taken, for example, you will see groups such as 2006, 2005, and so on.

The Arrange By option determines the order in which pictures will be arranged within groups or, if you have Group By set to None, then within the entire view. You can choose between Date Taken, Date Modified, File Size, Image Size, Rating, Caption, and File Name, and can of course sort in ascending or descending order.

If you'd like, you can also enable a unique feature called the Table of Contents, which is an optional pane that provides a list of all the groups that are displayed in the Thumbnail pane. Table of Contents is interesting if you are using the Group By feature and have an awful lot of pictures. That's because Table of Contents acts like the Table of Contents in a book, enabling you to jump from group to group quickly. Say you have grouped by Year Taken. The Table of Contents pane lists the name of each year for which you have one or more photos. Additionally, small blue meters below each year name visually hint at the number of pictures for each year. As you click year names in the Table of Contents, the Thumbnail pane scrolls down to display the corresponding group, as shown in Figure 11-12. Also, as it scrolls, a blue box appears in the Table of Contents, visually showing you which portion of your pictures you're currently viewing.

Adding Tags, Ratings, and Captions to Your Pictures

Although the Table of Contents feature is nice, if hidden, you're probably going to want a more elegant way of filtering the view of your photo collection. For example, what if you'd like to see just your vacation pictures? Or pictures that contain family members? Or any other criteria that might be important to you?

Windows Photo Gallery offers a number of ways to help you filter your photo display so that you can see just the photos you want. The problem is, you have to do a bit of work to make these features useful. If you're really into digital photography, however, we think you'll agree it will be worth the effort.

The first feature is called *tags*. Tags are unique labels that you can apply to pictures to help you identify which ones are related. By default, every picture in Windows Photo Gallery is not tagged. But you can create your own tags and then apply them to multiple pictures. You can also apply multiple tags to each picture. Tags can be as detailed or generic as you want. But you might consider tags such as Family, Vacation, Personal, Work, Home, and so on.

Figure 11-12: It ain't pretty, but Table of Contents is useful if you need to move quickly through a lot of pictures.

To create a tag, expand the Tags node in the View By pane. Then, click the Create a New Tag node. When you do so, an edit box appears, letting you create your own tag. Give it a name and then press Enter. (You can also create a tag by right-clicking an empty area of the Thumbnails pane and choosing Add Tags.) You might want to do this repeatedly until you've created all the relevant tags you can think of.

To add tags to your pictures, select the picture or pictures you'd like to tag and then drag them over to the tag name in the View By pane. You can drag pictures to multiple tags if you'd like, so, for example, some pictures might end up being tagged as Family, Vacation, and Personal.

tip

You can also add tags via the Info Pane. To do so, select a picture or set of pictures and click the Add Tag link in the Info Pane. The new tag will be added to both the pictures and the list of available tags.

To remove a tag, select the picture or pictures you'd like to affect. Then, right-click the tag name in the Info Pane and select Remove Tag, as shown in Figure 11-13.

Figure 11-13: Tags can be viewed and removed from the Info Pane.

After you've applied tags to your pictures, you can start filtering the view by this informa-tion. In the View By pane, simply select the tag you want and the Thumbnails view will change to display only those pictures that are tagged with that particular tag.

Secret

To display a view that includes more than one tag, Ctrl-click each tag name you want in the View By pane. *Voilà,* a custom view style.

You can also apply *ratings* to your pictures, on a scale from one to five stars. Pictures you really like could receive a five-star rating, whereas the duds might get one star. To give a rating to a picture, select it. Then, click the line of stars you see in the Info Pane. To give a picture a four-star rating, for example, click the fourth star, as seen in Figure 11-14.

Figure 11-14: Ratings provide a way for you to grade your pictures.

Finally, you can optionally create a unique *caption* for each of your pictures if you'd like. These labels are simply descriptive text strings, so you can be creative if you'd like. You might add text such as "Doesn't Kelly look surprised here?" or "Bob finally crested the top of the mountain!" It's up to you.

To add a label to a picture or group of pictures, select one or more pictures and then click in the Add a Caption box at the bottom of the Info Pane. Add any text you like.

---

note

Tags, captions, and ratings are what's known as metadata, which is simply data about data. Put another way, metadata is information that summarizes or explains the context of the underlying object, which is in this case a picture. Other files, including documents, music files, and video files, all include the ability to contain metadata.

Tags, ratings, and captions travel with the underlying pictures. That is, they're not limited to Windows Photo Gallery. If you rate a picture with five stars, for example, that rating will show up in Windows Media Player 11 or other applications that are compatible with this kind of metadata. Likewise, if you change the rating, tag, or caption for a picture inside of Windows Media Player, that change will reflect in Windows Photo Gallery.

Searching for Pictures in Photo Gallery

Adding metadata like tags, ratings, and captions is nice for filtering the current view, but you can also use these and other metadata to search for specific pictures from within Windows Photo Gallery in the same way that you search for documents and other files from Windows Explorer.

> **tip** Not coincidentally, this metadata also factors into shell-based searches as well from within Windows Vista. When you add metadata to a digital media file, it can be used from virtually anywhere, assuming the application or service is aware of such information.

To search for pictures in Windows Photo Gallery, simply type a search phrase into the search box located to the right of the Choose a thumbnail view button. If you tagged certain pictures with a tag such as *vacation*, for example, you could use that phrase to find all your vacation pictures. But you can also search for text in filenames and captions. In Figure 11-15, you can see a filtered view that includes the results of a search.

Figure 11-15: Searching in Windows Photo Gallery is similar to searching in the Windows Vista shell.

Importing Pictures into Photo Gallery

If you already have pictures on your PC, you can add pictures to Windows Photo Gallery by copying them into watch folders, adding their containing folders to the application's watch folder list, or by dragging them directly into the application window. But what if you need to import new pictures via a digital camera, memory card, picture CD or DVD, or scanner? Like Windows XP, Windows Vista supports image acquisition via these sources.

When you plug in a compatible camera or memory card, the Windows Auto Play function kicks in and asks you what you'd like to do. The default choice, Import Using Windows, runs a simple wizard that steps you through the process of acquiring your pictures.

> **tip** If you don't see the Auto Play dialog box appear for some reason, you can open My Computer, right-click the appropriate device, and choose Open Auto Play.

In the first step of the wizard, you can add a new tag or select an existing tag from a drop-down list. (If you'd like to add more than one tag, you'll need to do so later in Windows Photo Gallery.) Then, you click Import, and optionally choose to delete the original files from the camera or memory card.

When the import process is complete, Windows Photo Gallery loads with the Most Recently Added node displayed so you can see, organize, and edit your new pictures as needed.

> **tip** Behind the scenes, a lot of other things have happened. First, the image import wizard created a folder inside of Pictures that is constructed from the date plus the tag name you supplied earlier. So, if the date is May 29, 2006 and you used the tag *Bob's Office*, you'll see a folder called 2006-04-29 Bob's Office inside of Pictures. Each photo inside of that folder is named accordingly: You'll see Bob's Office 001, Bob's Office 002, and so on. Meanwhile, the Bob's Office tag has also been added to the list of tags found inside of Windows Photo Gallery. You can now apply this tag to other pictures, if you'd like, or add other tags to the pictures you just imported.

You can change a variety of options related to importing pictures via the Windows Photo Gallery Options dialog box. To access this dialog box, click the File toolbar button and then choose Options. On the Import tab, shown in Figure 11-16, you'll see a number of options you can change, including the folder to which imported pictures should be copied, the name that the wizard generates for the new pictures and containing folder, and so on. You can also click a link to revert to the system default settings.

Secret

The photo import functionality in Windows Vista is actually not as full-featured as that in Windows XP, which is unexpected. In Windows XP, you may recall, you could actually choose which pictures to import from the camera or memory card. In Vista, you simply import every single picture. There's no way to pick and choose.

Figure 11-16: In Windows Vista, picture acquisition is controlled from inside Windows Photo Gallery.

Secret

You can access the options for the photo import functionality by accessing the File menu in Windows Photo Gallery and choosing Options. Then, navigate to the Import tab.

Editing Pictures

When you double-click an image in Windows Photo Gallery, the application switches into its Viewer mode, which is identical to the Photo Gallery Viewer application you see when you open image files from the Windows shell. In Viewer mode, Photo Gallery replaces the View By and Thumbnail view panes (and the Table of Contents, if it's displayed) with a simpler display consisting only of the image you're viewing and the Info Pane. In this view, you'll often want to click the Fix button to display the application's image editing functions.

Editing Photos with Windows Photo Gallery

This is a big change from Windows XP, which didn't typically offer much in the way of editing functionality beyond the very basic facilities of Windows Paint. When you preview an image and then click the Fix button in Windows Photo Gallery, the display changes by replacing the Info Pane with a list of image editing features, as shown in Figure 11-17.

Figure 11-17: The editing features in Windows Photo Gallery enable you to perform several popular photo-editing tasks.

The Windows Photo Gallery image editing features are as follows:

◆ **Auto Adjust:** Evaluates the picture and performs a variety of changes based on the needs of the image. Basically, it's a best-guess estimate of what needs to be fixed, and although it's often a decent try, you'll want to carefully evaluate the changes before committing them to the file.

Secret

If you do commit to any of the changes in Fix mode, the underlying graphic file will be overwritten. Because of the compressed nature of JPEG images in particular, resaving digital photos can result in dramatic quality reduction. Be careful not to resave JPEG images too often; if you're going to edit a JPEG file, edit and save it once.

tip

If you don't like what Auto Adjust does to your picture, click the Undo button at the bottom of the Info Pane. If you've performed multiple operations, this button will pop-up a menu that lets you choose which operations to undo, or you can Undo All changes you've made.

◆ **Adjust Exposure:** Unlike Auto Adjust, this doesn't provide a single-click solution. Instead, when you click this option, the Info Pane expands to display slider controls for Brightness and Contrast. You move these sliders to the left and right to adjust these properties until you're happy with the results.

◆ **Adjust Color:** This is also a little more involved. When you select this option, another new area expands in the Info Pane, letting you use sliders to adjust the temperature, tint, and saturation of the photo.

◆ **Crop Picture:** Enables you to crop the current picture, allowing you to change its aspect ratio if needed, or simply to edit out parts of the picture that are uninteresting. A proportion drop-down box, shown in Figure 11-18, enables you to determine how you'd like the picture cropped.

Figure 11-18: The Crop Picture function provides a variety of ways for you to highlight the important parts of a picture.

After you have picked a proportion, you can use the onscreen guide lines to select the portion of the image you'd like cropped.

tip Because cropping a picture can often result in a dramatically different final image, you may want to copy, or duplicate, a picture before cropping it, just in case. To do so, select the image you want to crop and then choose Duplicate from the File button's drop-down menu.

◆ **Fix Red Eye:** Red-eye correction is one of the most often-needed features in any photo-editing package, and fortunately the one in Windows Photo Gallery works pretty well. Simply click this option and then draw a rectangle around each of the eyes you want to correct in the current picture.

Secret They're not documented, but there are some handy keyboard shortcuts you can use while editing pictures with Windows Photo Gallery. For example, you can zoom in on a picture by pressing Ctrl and the + key at the same time, and zoom out with Ctrl and -. Normally, when you're zoomed in, you can move around the picture using the small hand cursor. But in certain edit tasks, like Crop Picture and Fix Red Eye, the cursor changes for other purposes, preventing you from navigating around a zoomed picture. To return temporarily to the hand icon in these edits, hold down the Alt key and move around with the mouse. Then, release the Alt key and the cursor will return to the way it was before. By the way, Ctrl+0 zooms the picture back to its default zoom level (where the picture fills the entire viewing area).

Editing with Other Applications

Although the very basic editing features in Windows Photo Gallery should satisfy many people's needs, there are many other photo editing solutions out there, and you may want to use them to edit photos as well. If you own a third-party solution like Adobe Photoshop Elements or Google Picasa, you can use those applications to edit digital photos, and you can access them directly from within Windows Photo Gallery, which is pretty handy.

The key to doing so is the Open button on the Windows Photo Gallery toolbar. If you don't have any photo-editing applications installed in Windows Vista, you will simply see Windows Paint listed in the resulting drop-down menu when you click this button. But if you installed a third-party application, it should appear in the list as well, as shown in Figure 11-19. This way, you can edit a photo in the application you like the most, while still using Photo Gallery's excellent management capabilities to perform other photo-related tasks.

tip But what happens when your application doesn't appear in the Open drop-down menu? You can add it easily enough: Simply select Choose Program from the Open drop-down menu and then choose the program from the list, or click the Browse button to find it on your hard drive. When you've accessed a program in this fashion, it will be added to the Open drop-down list.

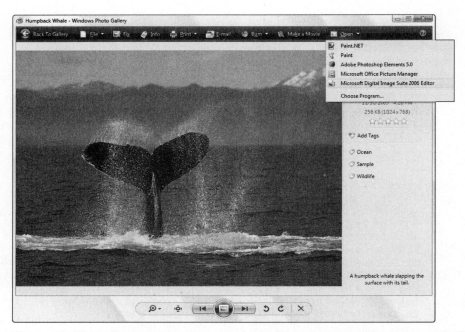

Figure 11-19: You're not stuck with the useful but limited photo-editing features Windows Photo Gallery.

Sharing Photos with Others

Although you may find the process of managing, organizing, and editing photos to be somewhat tedious, there is of course a wonderful payoff: Once you've created an extensive photo library containing your most precious memories, you can then share those photos with your family, friends, and others in a stunning variety of ways. One way to think of this situation is that Windows Photo Gallery is only the means to an end: For the most part, you'll use this application for the nitty-gritty management work, and then use its sharing features to spread the wealth.

Enjoying Photos on Your Own PC

Before we get into the various ways in which you can share your digital memories with others, let's examine a few ways in which you can enjoy your photos on your own PC. First, you can use any picture as a desktop background. There are a multitude of ways to do this, but one of the best things you can do is duplicate a favorite picture in Windows Photo Gallery, and then use the application's Crop feature to crop it to the exact resolution (or aspect ratio) of your screen. That way, you won't have to worry about stretching the picture in any way on your desktop.

Windows Vista also enables you to use animated photo slideshows as a screensaver. To access this functionality, open the Control Panel and navigate to Appearance and Personalization. The, choose Change screen saver from the Personalization section. In the resulting dialog box, choose Photos from the Screensaver drop-down menu. Then, click Settings. As shown in Figure 11-20, this dialog box enables you to choose which pictures to use in your screensaver along with various other related options. You can click Preview to see how your new screensaver looks.

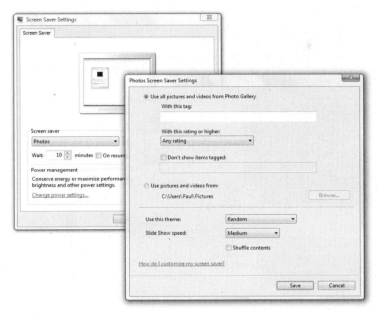

Figure 11-20: One of the coolest ways to personalize your system is to use your own photos as a screensaver.

The Windows Vista Photos screensaver doesn't just work with photos; it uses videos as well. So you can also mix home movies into your slideshow.

Printing Pictures and Order Prints

If you want to share pictures with others, one of the most obvious ways is to create traditional paper-based prints. These can be wonderful gifts, and while it's pretty clear we're in the middle of a digital revolution, not everyone has a PC or wants to enjoy pictures only with their computer. There are two ways to create picture prints in Windows Vista. You can print pictures on your own photo printer, if you have one, or you can order prints online.

To print pictures yourself, open Windows Photo Gallery, select the picture (or pictures) you'd like to print, click the Print button in the toolbar, and then choose Print from the drop-down menu. This action launches Windows Vista's excellent Print Pictures wizard, which is depicted in Figure 11-21.

Figure 11-21: You may be surprised by how many options you have for printing photos in Windows Vista.

From this deceptively simple wizard, you can customize the print job in a variety of ways, choosing what size prints to create, which printer to use, and a number of other options.

To order prints from an online photo service, select a group of photos and then choose Order Prints from the Print button's drop-down menu. This launches the Order Prints wizard, which provides a handy front end to various online printing services that have arrangements with Microsoft.

tip   You don't have to settle for the choices Microsoft provides. Bypassing the Order Prints function in Windows Photo Gallery, you can use Internet Explorer or another Web browser to discover, sign up for, and order prints from any number of web-based photo printing services. You can also bring a digital camera memory card into many pharmacies and photo printing retail kiosks and print photos from there.

Getting Creative: Adding Photos to Movies, DVDs, and Data Discs

Windows Photo Gallery also offers basic integration features with Windows Move Maker, Windows DVD Maker, and the Windows Vista CD and DVD burning capabilities to help you create movies of your photo slideshows or data discs full of your favorite pictures.

To create a digital movie of your favorite photos, select the photos you want in Windows Photo Gallery and then click the Create button on the toolbar and select Movie. Windows Movie Maker will launch and import all of the select photos into a new project, shown in Figure 11-22, which you can then edit into a finished movie. We discuss Windows Movie Maker's movie-editing capabilities — including how you can use this tool to make movies of photos — in Chapter 12.

Figure 11-22: With Windows Movie Maker, you can turn a string of photos into a compelling animated home movie.

To add a similar slideshow to a DVD movie, select the photos as before and then click the Create button on the toolbar and select DVD. This will import the pictures into Windows DVD Maker, which enables you to create DVD movies. We discuss Windows DVD Maker in Chapter 12 as well.

If you want to create backups of your photo gallery or share pictures with others electronically, Windows Photo Gallery also enables you to create data disks, in either CD or DVD format, as well. Again, you'll click the Create button on the Windows Photo Gallery toolbar, but this time, you'll choose Data Disc from the resulting drop-down menu. You'll be prompted to insert a blank CD or DVD disk into your recordable optical drive, and then Windows Vista will use its integrated disk-burning capabilities to copy the photos onto the disk.

Sharing Through E-mail

If you'd like to send a picture or group of pictures to friends or others, you can use the built-in e-mail sharing capabilities of Windows Photo Gallery. First, select the pictures you'd like to send, and then click the E-mail button in the toolbar. The Attach Pictures and Files dialog box will appear as shown in Figure 11-23. Here, you can choose how or whether to resize your images for transit, which is likely a good idea, as many of today's digital photos are quite large. After your selection, a new e-mail message will appear in Windows Mail (see Chapter 18) or whatever e-mail application you've specified as the default.

Figure 11-23: The Picture size drop-down enables you to choose from various pre-set sizes.

Network-Based Library Sharing and Portable Device Syncing

Using new functionality in Windows Vista, you can also share your photo library with other Windows Vista–based PCs on your home network, and synchronize with a compatible portable device. Links to both of these options are available via the File buttons' drop-down menu. However, these features are actually exposed through Windows Media Player 11, not Windows Photo Gallery. For this reason, we discuss this functionality in Chapter 10.

Using Photo Gallery to Manage Digital Videos

Although the name Windows Photo Gallery suggests that this application is suitable only for pictures, it can also be used to manage digital videos as well. Videos can be viewed in Windows Photo Gallery by selecting All Pictures and Videos or Videos from the View By pane, or one of the other video-related nodes. This is shown in Figure 11-24.

Figure 11-24: Videos, too, can be organized in Windows Photo Gallery.

By default, videos appear as thumbnails that provide a glimpse into the contained movie. If you double-click a video in Windows Photo Gallery, the application switches into a preview mode so you can watch the movie, as shown in Figure 11-25. (Conversely, when you open a movie file from the Windows shell, it typically opens in Windows Media Player 11.)

Even though the Windows Photo Gallery toolbar doesn't change when you view videos or video previews, some options simply aren't available with videos. For example, the Fix menu returns a simple message, "Video files can't be edited using Photo Gallery," if you try to access it.

---

tip

As with photos, Windows Photo Gallery only parses certain folders when it wants to find video content. These folders are your Videos folder (typically found in C:\Users\ *your user name*\Videos by default) and the Public Videos folder. However, you can manually add videos from other locations by simply dragging them into the Windows Photo Gallery Thumbnail View pane.

Videos are also compatible with the tag, rating, and caption metadata types that are utilized by pictures. This means that you can easily add this information to your videos, filter the view, and search for specific video content just as you do with pictures.

Figure 11-25: Videos that happen in Windows Photo Gallery stay in Windows Photo Gallery.

Summary

Although Windows Vista completely steps back from the shell-based photo management functionality that was provided in Windows XP, the new Windows Photo Gallery application more than makes up for it. Now, Windows users have a single obvious place to manage, edit, share, and otherwise enjoy digital photos (and videos). Windows Photo Gallery is one of the better end user additions to Windows Vista.

Making Movies and DVD Movies

Chapter

12

◆ ◆

In This Chapter

Learning how to manage your digital movies in a variety of ways

Using Windows Movie Maker to import content, edit video, and publish completed movies

Editing TV shows and removing commercials with Windows Movie Maker

Publishing your home movies, photo slide shows, and other videos to standard DVD movies Using Windows DVD Maker

◆ ◆

J ust a few short years ago, the notion of consumers using PCs to edit their home movies into professional-looking productions was science-fiction. But then Apple came along with iMovie and proved that it was not just possible but that high-quality video editing tools could be done elegantly and in a user-friendly fashion. At that time, Microsoft had just released its first Windows Movie Maker tool, a crippled Windows Me application that was aimed only at the low end of the market. Today, in Windows Vista, Microsoft has a variety of tools for managing, viewing, editing, and publishing digital video of all kinds. You can even edit TV shows, removing commercials, and make your own movie DVDs. Let's jump right in.

Managing Digital Movies with Windows Vista

Like Windows XP before it, Windows Vista includes a number of ways in which you can manage, view, and otherwise enjoy digital movies. You may recall that Windows XP included a special shell folder called My Videos. Actually, you will be forgiven for not remembering that—in Windows XP, the My Videos folder was curiously deprecated when compared to its My Documents, My Music, and My Pictures siblings. It didn't appear on the Start Menu by default and couldn't be added later. In fact, My Videos didn't even appear in the shell until you started up Windows Movie Maker for the first time.

In Windows Vista, the situation is only marginally different. The My Videos folder has been replaced by the new Videos folder, in keeping with Microsoft's new shell folder naming scheme. It's no longer a special shell folder, and it's not located in the file system inside of Documents, as before. Instead, it sits under your Home folder alongside Documents, Music, Pictures, and other commonly needed folders. But it still doesn't appear on the right side of Start Menu for some reason, and once again there's no way to make it appear there.

Secret

So how do you get to the Videos folder, you ask? In Windows XP, you could simply open My Documents, and there it was. In Vista, the easiest way is to open your Home folder, which is represented by your user name in the upper-right corner of the Start Menu. When you click that link, the Home folder opens in its own window, as shown in Figure 12-1. Inside, you'll see the Videos folder.

Secret

In addition to Videos, Windows Vista maintains another folder for videos called Public Videos. This was called Shared Videos in Windows XP. Public Videos, as you might expect, is located inside the directory structure for the Public user account and is shared between all of the users configured for the current PC. How do you find it? Sadly, there's no easy way. You'll have to manually navigate to C:\Users\Public\Videos (by default) to find this folder.

Figure 12-1: You'll find the new Videos folder inside your Home folder.

tip

There's also a Sample Videos folder that includes a set of short sample videos provided by Microsoft. There is a shortcut to this folder in your Videos folder, but the actual folder is located in C:\Users\Public\Videos\Sample Videos by default.

Secret

Because of the proliferation of digital cameras with video-taking capabilities, you could very likely also find videos inside of your Pictures folder. When you copy pictures from a digital camera to Windows Vista, any videos on the camera will be copied to the same location, which is typically a subfolder under Pictures.

With all these different locations for finding digital videos, you might wonder what Microsoft was thinking. Although we could never claim to offer any insight along those lines, we can tell you that video management, like that of music and photos, has changed dramatically in Windows Vista. Although it's still possible to navigate around the Windows shell and double-click movies to play them in Windows Media Player or another software tool, Microsoft actually expects that most of its users will instead use dedicated applications to manage and view digital movies. And one of those tools might just surprise you. We look at them all in the next few sections.

Watching and Managing Movies with Windows Photo Gallery

The primary movie management tool in Windows Vista, believe it or not, is called Windows Photo Gallery. Why Microsoft didn't choose to name this as Windows Photo and Movie Gallery is unclear, but the fact remains that you can organize and manage (and even play) all of the digital video on your system with this tool. Although we describe this application in detail in Chapter 11, it may be worth a short side-trip here to discuss how it works with digital movies specifically.

By default, Windows Photo Gallery enables you to manage photos and videos together, and it's designed to search the Pictures, Videos, Public Pictures, and Public Videos folders for video (and photo) content by default. (You can manually configure Windows Photo Gallery to search other locations as well; see Chapter 11 for more information.) When it comes to video, all the metadata application information works equally well with movies as it does with photos. That is, you can add tags, rating, and captions to movies, just as you can with photos.

If you want to work just with movies in Windows Photo Gallery, select the Videos entry under All Pictures and Videos in the application's View By pane. Now, you will see just videos in the Thumbnails pane, as shown in Figure 12-2.

Figure 12-2: Even video files are displayed with nice thumbnail images in Windows Photo Gallery.

As you mouse over individual videos, a pop-up window displays, showing a larger thumbnail, along with other information about the file, including its name, size, rating, and the date and time it was created. You can see this effect in Figure 12-3.

Figure 12-3: Nice flyover effects give you more information about individual videos.

Secret

If you want to discover where an individual video is located in the file system, right-click it in Windows Photo Gallery and choose Open File Location.

To play a video, simply double-click it. Curiously, videos opened in Windows Photo Gallery play in . . . Windows Photo Gallery—not Windows Media Player, as you might expect. This is undesirable for a few reasons, but the most obvious is that the video play-back window in Windows Photo Gallery is as large as the window, which is often larger than the original video, causing blurry resizing effects. As shown in Figure 12-4, Windows Photo Gallery isn't the optimal place to play video files.

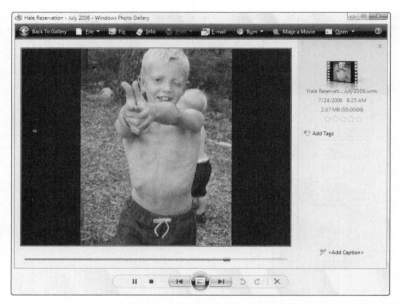

Figure 12-4: You can play videos in Windows Photo Gallery, but the application is better suited for just managing the files.

From this window, you can add rating, tags, and captioning metadata if you so desire. What you can't do is edit the movie—clicking the Fix toolbar button displays an unhelpful message. Our advice is to use Windows Photo Gallery to manage videos only, but to use Windows Media Player 11, described in the next section, for playback. We discuss editing digital movies later in this chapter as well.

Secret

You're wondering whether you can play movies in Windows Media Player from within Windows Photo Gallery, aren't you? The answer is a qualified yes. To trigger Windows Media Player playback from Windows Photo Gallery, don't double-click a video thumbnail. Instead, select the video file you'd like to play and then choose Open and then Windows Media Player from the application's toolbar. The real question, of course, is whether you can make Windows Photo Gallery do this by default. The answer, sadly, is no.

Watching and Managing Movies with Windows Media Player

Most people think of Windows Media Player as a music player, but the truth is, Windows Media Player can also work with video and photo content as well. (As we discuss in Chapter 10, however, Windows Media Player only handles these types of content so that they can be synchronized with portable media players.) This capability isn't new to Windows Media Player 11, the version that Microsoft ships with Windows Vista. However, because videos do play natively in Windows Media Player 11, it's possible that you might want to manage videos, to some degree, in the player as well. Like Windows Photo Gallery, Windows Media Player 11 is configured to automatically watch certain folders for digital media files, and those locations include, by default, your Videos and the Public Videos folders. No surprise there.

To configure Windows Media Player to display just videos, select Video from the Categories button. As shown in Figure 12-5, the display will change to show just video thumbnails.

Figure 12-5: Windows Media Player is just one of many places in Windows Vista from which you can manage digital movie files.

From here, you can rate individual videos. But that's about it. You can't add tags or captions from within Windows Media Player. What you can do, of course, is simply play videos. That's Windows Media Player's strong suit, and you can use the player's various controls to change the size of the video, display it using a nice full-screen mode, or even minimize the player to the system taskbar and watch it there while you get work done.

Secret

One nice side effect of Windows Media Player's capabilities is that you can actually create temporary or saved playlists of videos. That way you can trigger a collection of videos to play in order, or randomly. It's not possible to do that from the shell or within Windows Photo Gallery. And if you save the playlist, you can access it from Windows Media Center, described in the next section.

Watching and Managing Movies with Windows Media Center

Windows Media Center is, of course, the premium environment in Windows for enjoying digital media such as photos, music, movies, and, yes, even live and recorded TV shows. But Media Center — which we discuss in detail in Chapter 13 — isn't just for people with expensive home theater setups. There's no reason you can't use Media Center with a mouse and keyboard on your desktop PC or notebook. In fact, you may find it quite enjoyable to do just that.

Secret

Windows Media Center is not available in all Windows Vista product versions. You have to be using Windows Vista Home Premium or Windows Vista Ultimate to get Windows Media Center.

As shown in Figure 12-6, Windows Media Center is a seamless, home theater–like application that works best full screen but can absolutely be enjoyed in a floating, resizable window alongside your other applications.

Figure 12-6: Windows Media Center is a nice graphical front end to a variety of digital media experiences.

To use Media Center to manage your digital movies, navigate to the Pictures + Videos experience in the Start page and then choose Video Library. The first time you enter this area, Media Center will ask you if you'd like to choose other folders to watch for videos. If you've already configured either Windows Photo Gallery or Windows Media Player to watch particular folders, or you intend to only use the default folders for video content, you can select No; in that case, Windows Media Player uses the same database of watch folders as those other two applications.

The Video Library experience, shown in Figure 12-7, provides a horizontally oriented grid of videos through which you can navigate by either name or date. To watch a video, simply select it.

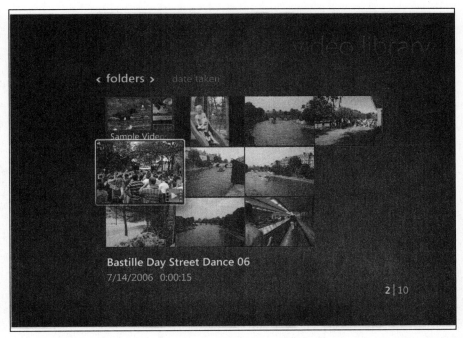

Figure 12-7: In Media Center, videos include graphical thumbnails, making for a highly visual navigation experience.

Secret

Although Windows Media Center offers tag-based navigation for music and photos, it does not do so for videos. To navigate your video collection by tag, you'll need to use Windows Photo Gallery.

In a related vein, you can't tag, rate, or add captions to videos in Media Center only. Essentially, Windows Media Center simply offers a high-end place for video consumption. If you want to interact with videos, you'll need to look elsewhere.

> **tip** And, as noted previously, Windows Media Center also works with live and recorded TV content. Although this content is technically digital video, we discuss this in more detail in Chapter 13, and later in this chapter where we talk about editing and republishing recorded TV content.

Using Windows Movie Maker

Windows Movie Maker is Microsoft's tool for creating digital videos. You can import a variety of digital media types into the application, including home movies, photos, music and other audio files, and even recorded TV shows. Then, using simple editing techniques along with professional transitions and effects, you can create completed videos that can be shared with others through PCs, e-mail, the Web, digital video tape or, in conjunction with Windows DVD maker, described at the end of this chapter, DVD movies.

Secret You may have heard of something called Movie Maker HD (where HD stands for high definition, as in HDTV). Technically, Movie Maker HD is not a separate version of Movie Maker, but is rather a description of features that Movie Maker gains in certain Windows Vista product versions. Here's how it works. All versions of Windows Vista include Movie Maker, but only the versions in Windows Vista Home Premium and Ultimate can import from and publish to HD video sources. You will need a fairly high end PC to manipulate such video, of course.

Windows Movie Maker is a relatively straightforward application, assuming you're comfortable with video editing. But even for the uninitiated, Windows Movie Maker is pretty easy to use. You just need to know your way around.

Understanding the Movie Maker User Interface

Windows Movie Maker is divided into three basic areas: The menu and toolbar at the top, the panes section in the middle, and the Storyboard/Timeline area at the bottom. As shown in Figure 12-8, these areas are clearly delineated.

Since the menu and toolbar area are similar to other Windows applications, we'll spend most of our time discussing the other two parts of the Movie Maker user interface, which are unique to this application.

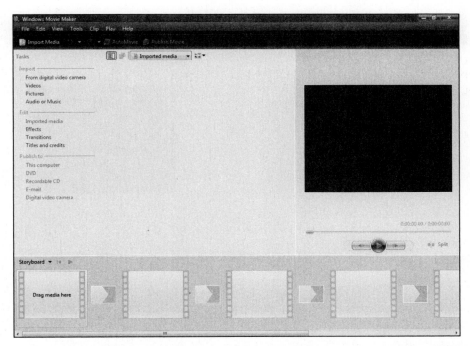

Figure 12-8: Windows Movie Maker takes digital media content in and spits out finished video after a bit of fine-tuning.

In the center of the application window, you'll see the Tasks pane, with which you can literally step through the tasks needed to bring a custom video production to life, the Imported Media pane, in which you will collect shortcuts to digital media files on your PC that will be used in the current project, and the Preview pane, where you can preview your video creation as it is developed.

At the bottom of the window is the Storyboard/Timeline pane. This area holds the edited version of your video project and can operate in two modes. Storyboard mode, which is the default, displays the digital media files that make up your video project in sequential order, and it presents small user interface slots for video effects and transitions, giving you a nice overview of the bits and pieces that make up the project. In Timeline mode, shown in Figure 12-9, you see a more literal representation of the video project, presented in a time-based display that is perfect for fine-tuning details of the presentation, such as timing. This is the mode you'll use to trim audio and video clips. We recommend staying in Timeline mode for all but the simplest video projects.

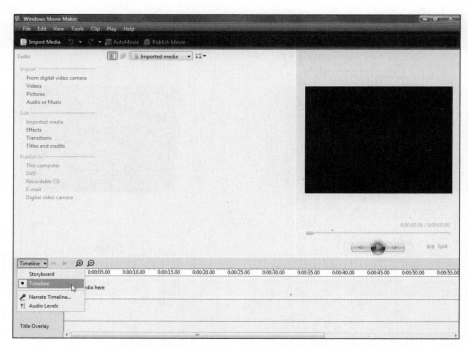

Figure 12-9: Timeline mode provides a more detailed representation of the video you're creating.

Importing Digital Media into a Project

To start a new project in Windows Movie Maker, you first need a collection of shortcuts to digital media files that will be used in your final video. Windows Movie Maker can import a variety of video, audio, and picture files, and these files can be assembled however you like in your project's storyboard/timeline. Table 12-1 highlights the formats you can use with Windows Movie Maker.

Table 12-1: Media Formats Supported by Windows Movie Maker

Movie formats	.ASF, .AVI, .DVR-MS, .M1V, .MP2, .MP2V, .MPE, .MPEG, .MPG, .MPV2, .WM, .WMV
Audio formats	.AIF, .AIFC, .AIFF, .ASF, .AU, .MP2, .MP3, .MPA, .SND, .WAV, .WMA
Picture formats	.BMP, .DIB, .EMF, .GIF, .JFIF, .JPE, .JPEG, .JPG, .PNG, .TIF, .TIFF, .WMF

Secret

The MS-DVR format is new to this version of Windows Movie Maker. This is the format Microsoft uses for its Media Center recorded TV shows. That's right: You can use Movie Maker to edit TV shows. So if you'd like to save a movie or show you've recorded, edit out the commercials, or the dead time at the beginning and end of the recording, you can now do so.

There is one caveat to this capability, however. Shows recorded on certain channels, such as HBO and Cinemax, cannot be edited (or, for that matter, copied to a different PC from that on which it was recorded). That's because these shows are protected by so-called Broadcast Flag technology, which television stations can use to restrict copying. Currently, this technology is used mostly on pay cable channels in the U.S. market, but it will become more and more common as digital video recording (DVR) solutions like Media Center and TiVo become more prevalent.

To import a movie, photo, or music file into Movie Maker, you can click the Import Media button on the Movie Maker toolbar, choose Import Media Items from the File menu, or simply drag the files into the Imported Media pane from any Explorer window. Likewise, if you want to import content from a digital video camera, select Import From Digital Video Camera from the File menu and step through the wizard.

tip   Remember that digital video imported from your digital still camera can be obtained using the normal Import wizard that appears when you connect the camera to your Windows Vista PCs. These videos will be located in your Picture folder.

In Figure 12-10, you can see a variety of media types located in the Movie Maker Imported Media pane.

Editing a Recorded TV Show or Movie

The simplest way to make a movie is just to grab any bit of media—be it music, picture, or video, though of course video works best—and take it to the Storyboard. Then, you can press Play in the Preview pane and watch your simple, unedited creation play through to completion. But typically, you're going to want to make something a bit more sophisticated. So for this section, we'll assume that you have a recorded TV show you'd like to edit. You will want to remove the dead space at the beginning and end of the show, edit out any commercials, and then save the show back to your hard drive in a high-quality format. Later, we'll even write this show to DVD, so you can watch it on any standard DVD player.

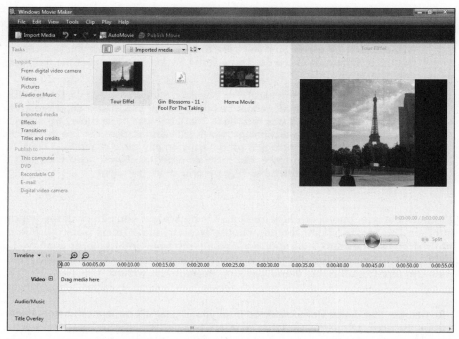

Figure 12-10: After you've assembled the pieces that will make up your video, it's time to start editing.

---

tip   If you don't have a recorded TV show, perhaps because your PC isn't connected to a TV signal through a TV tuner card, fear not. You can use one of the sample recorded TV shows that comes with Media Center, or a sample video file that ships with Windows Vista. Or, grab some of your own home video footage. It's up to you.

---

note   Recorded TV shows are stored in C:\Users\Public\Recorded TV by default. There's no Recorded TV folder under a normal user account's Home folder. That's because recorded TV shows are shared by all of the users on the PC.

Navigate to this folder and import a recorded TV show or one of the samples that Microsoft provides in **C:\Users\Public\Recorded TV\Sample Media**. It's time to start editing.

Working with the Timeline

First, you're going to want to put Windows Movie Maker in Timeline mode. To do so, click the Storyboard button in the upper-left corner of the Storyboard pane and choose Timeline from the drop-down menu that appears. Movie Maker will now resemble Figure 12-11.

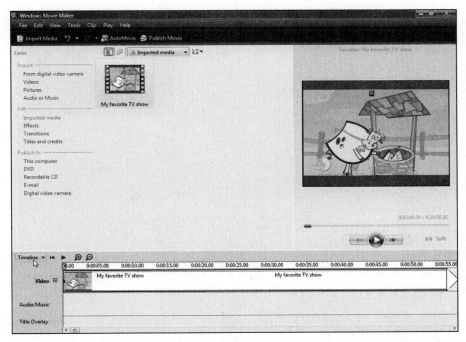

Figure 12-11: In Timeline mode, you can fine-tune the various video, audio, and title elements that make up your movie.

Drag the Recorded TV show (or movie) you want to edit from the Imported Media pane down into the timeline. When you do so, Movie Maker will now resemble Figure 12-12.

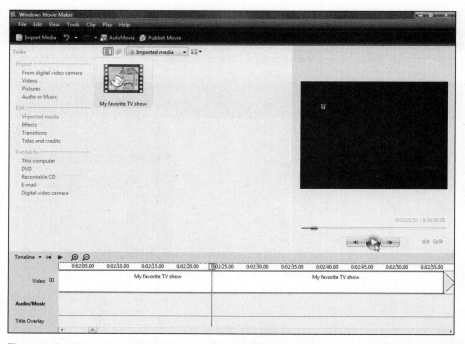

Figure 12-12: With your TV show or movie in the timeline, you can see how much time it occupies and prepare for edits.

If you're editing a recorded TV show, the first step is to remove the unrelated content at the beginning of the show. Press the Play button to play through this content and find the beginning of the bits you'd like to save. You can skip ahead, pause, and rewind to the beginning of the timeline as required. After you've found the exact moment at which the actual show begins, click Pause. If you can, try to make this pause point occur right when the image fades to black or just a hair before the actual video starts.

Now, click the Split button, which is located just below the video preview in the Preview pane. This will create a break point in the video, as shown in Figure 12-13, effectively dividing the video portion of the timeline into two sections.

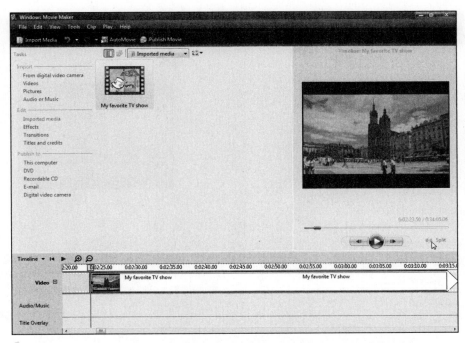

Figure 12-13: Now, you can trim off the unwanted beginning part of the video.

To trim this off the video, select the first segment of video, which will highlight in white, and click Delete. When you do so, the remainder of the video—the clip that was to the right of the split or break point—will slide left so that it starts at the beginning of the timeline.

Now, you can trim the end of the TV show or video. Using the blue pill in the scrubber bar below the video preview, move forward through the remaining video until you can pinpoint where you'd like the ending to be (see Figure 12-14). As before, use the Split button to trim off the end of the video. Then, select this ending video clip in the timeline and click Delete to remove it from the timeline.

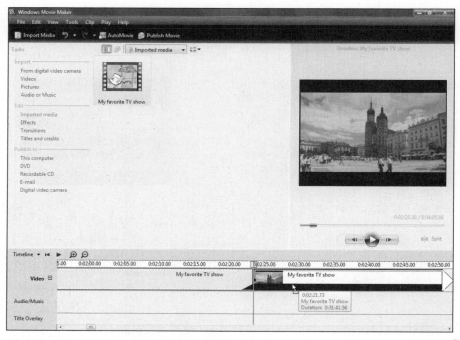

Figure 12-14: Pinpointing the end of your video.

Secret

To remove commercials from recorded TV shows, use a similar technique to locate the beginning and end of each commercial block and then remove that clip from the timeline. It may take a bit of time, but you can certainly remove any extraneous video you want with just a little effort.

Secret

You can also combine two separate video clips if you'd like to work with them as a single unit. To do so, select the first clip. Then, while holding down Ctrl key, select the second clip. Now, choose Combine from the Clip menu. For this to work, both clips must be right next to each other.

Adding Transitions and Effects

When you make hard video cuts like those described in the preceding section, the resulting video may feature sudden and jarring jumps between the clips in the timeline. You can smooth out these jumps using *transitions* and *effects*. Indeed, the simplest effects are so commonly used that they're built right into the Windows Movie Maker timeline: Just right-click the video in your timeline and choose Fade In to make the beginning of the video a bit more visually smooth. Then, right-click and choose Fade Out to do the same for the ending.

If you want to smooth the transitions between clips where you exorcised commercials in recorded TV shows, you can likewise use only the timeline. Just drag one video clip over an adjoining video clip, as shown in Figure 12-15, to make them smoothly transition into each other.

Figure 12-15: You can use your drag-and-drop skills to create transitions in the timeline.

In some cases, however, you might want to use more intricate transitions. For this purpose, Windows Movie Maker includes a huge collection of video transitions that are inspired by the transitions we see every day in TV shows and movies. To access these transitions, click the Transitions link in the Edit portion of the Task pane. The Imported Media pane will, ahem, transition into the Transitions panes and present you with numerous options, as seen in Figure 12-16.

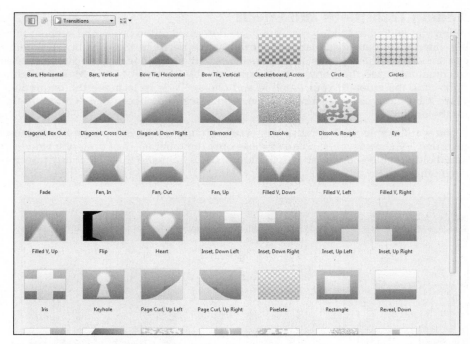

Figure 12-16: Don't be too aggressive with transitions, as they can be visually jarring, exactly the opposite effect that you're trying to achieve.

To add a transition to your video, locate a split between two video clips in the timeline. Then, find the transition you want in the Transitions pane and drag it down to the timeline, into the split between the two clips you just located.

Secret

You can preview transitions by double-clicking the icons in the Transitions pane.

When you add a transition to the timeline, it appears in the Transition well below the video. To remove a transition, right-click it and choose Remove.

You can also add special effects to your videos, although these too should be used with care. Video effects range from blurring, brightness changes, and various fades to color and hue changes and zooms. To see which effects are available to you, select the Effects link in the Edit portion of the Tasks pane, as shown in Figure 12-17.

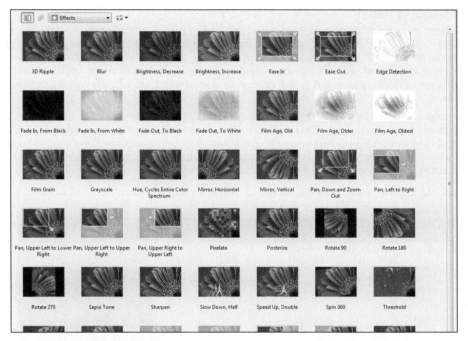

Figure 12-17: As with transitions, you're given a wide range of effects with which to play. Practice moderation if possible.

Unlike transitions, effects are added directly to a video clip, not between video clips. So pick the effect you want—after double-clicking it to preview it—and then drag it to a video clip in the timeline. Preview your changes in the Preview pane.

When you add an effect to a video clip, you'll see a small gray star icon appear on the clip. Unfortunately, it's not as easy to remove an effect as it is to remove a transition. Basically, it just involves an extra step, because you can apply more than one effect to any video clip.

Secret

Technically, you can even reapply multiple copies of an effect to any video clip. So, for example, if you added the Sharpen effect to a clip but found that it wasn't quite sharp enough, you could add it again to make it even sharper.

To remove an effect, right-click the clip in question and choose Effects. Then, in the resulting Add or Remove Effects dialog, select the effect or effects you don't want and then click the Remove button. *Voilà*.

Adding Titles

Finally, you can add titles to your video. Titles are typically added at the beginning or end (where they're often called credits) of many movies, but you can also add titles through a movie as needed. For example, if you edited a movie of your vacation to Hawaii, you could add titles at various points to describe where each scene occurred. As with transitions and effects, you want to balance your use of titles so that they don't overpower the movie.

To add a title to the beginning of your movie, click the Titles and Credits link in the Edit portion of the Task pane. This option behaves differently than most Movie Maker tasks. As shown in Figure 12-18, the application switches into a unique Titles and Credits mode, where you can add titles at the beginning of the movie, before the selected clip, or on the selected clip. You can also choose to add credits at the end.

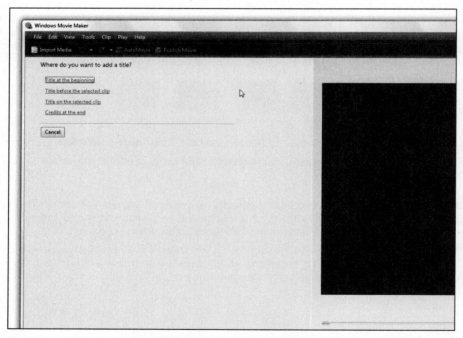

Figure 12-18: You're provided with a variety of options for adding text over the video.

Pick Title at the beginning. Then, enter the title you'd like to use into the provided text boxes. As you type, the titles you enter will be previewed in the video preview window. You can use the supplied links to change the way the title is animated — again, be careful there — or the fonts used to display the title. When you're done, click Add Title and the title will be added before the beginning of the video in the timeline. Click Play to watch your masterpiece.

At this point, you can add a transition between the title and the beginning of the video, delete the title and choose a nicer title type that is overlaid directly on the video, or add end credits. Experiment and have fun.

Secret

Titles are deleted just like video clips. Select them in the timeline and press Delete, and they're gone forever.

Sharing Your Movies with the World

The whole point of editing a home movie, TV show, or other video is to watch it and, preferably, share it with others. Fortunately, Windows Movie Maker includes a multitude of ways to share your completed videos. All of these options are located in the Publish To section of the Task pane. When you select one of those options, Windows Movie Maker will usually instantiate a version of the Publish Movie wizard, shown in Figure 12-19. This wizard will guide you through the time of movie publishing you selected.

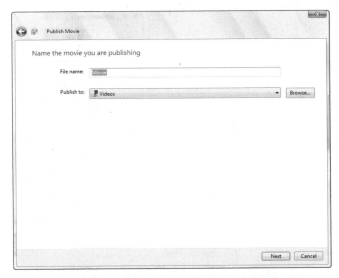

Figure 12-19: The Publish Movie wizard is typically the last thing you'll see when working with Windows Movie Maker.

Secret

There is one exception. When you choose DVD from the Publish To portion of the Tasks pane, a new application will launch as described later.

Publishing to the PC

If you'd like to save your edited movie as a digital video file that can be viewed on a PC, Media Center PC, a portable media device, or even a PDA, choose the This Computer option. Windows Movie Maker can publish movies to two different formats:

- ♦ **AVI (Audio Video Interleave):** Very high quality but requires a lot of disk space.
- ♦ **WMV (Windows Media Video):** Can be configured for a variety of quality levels and resolutions.

If you're working with a home movie that was shot with a digital camcorder, you should typically save a copy of the edited movie in the AVI format for archival purposes. But the WMV format makes a lot more sense for distribution.

In the first phase of the Publish Movie wizard, you'll be asked to give the movie a name and then choose a location to which to publish it (the Videos folder by default). Then, you can choose the quality level and resolution of the final video, as shown in Figure 12-20. In this phase of the wizard, you can choose between Best Quality (which will vary according to the performance characteristics of your PC), a special file size, or you can choose from a wide list of settings.

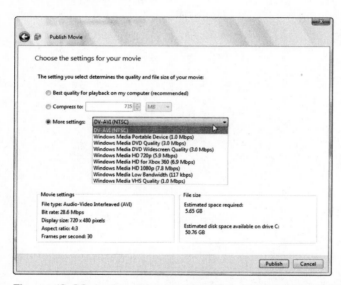

Figure 12-20: In the settings portion of the Publish Movie wizard, you determine the quality, resolution, and file size of the resulting video.

What you see in that third option will depend on which version of Windows Vista you're using. All versions of Windows Vista support the settings types described in Table 12-2.

Table 12-2: Video Settings Supported by All Versions of Windows Vista

Setting	Type	Bit rate	Resolution	Aspect ratio	Frames Per Second (FPS)	Storage space required for 30 minutes of video
Windows Media Portable Device	WMV	1.0 Mbps	640×480	4:3	30	234 MB
Windows Media DVD Quality	WMV	3.0 Mbps	720×480	4:3	30	688 MB
Windows Media DVD Widescreen Quality	WMV	3.0 Mbps	720×480	16:9	30	688 MB
Windows Media Low Bandwidth	WMV	117 Kbps	320×240	4:3	15	27 MB
Windows Media VHS Quality	WMV	1.0 Mbps	640×480	4:3	30	241 MB
DV-AVI	AVI	28.6 Mbps	720×480	4:3	30	6.44 GB

If you're running Windows Vista Home Premium or Ultimate, however, you will see additional HD video modes as well. Note that it doesn't make much sense to save a low-quality video in HD format. That is, you should only save an edited HD video in an HD format. In Table 12-3, we describe the additional HD formats that Vista Home Premium and Ultimate will see.

Table 12-3: HD Video Settings Supported Only by Windows Vista Home Premium and Ultimate.

Setting	Type	Bit rate	Resolution	Aspect ratio	FPS	Storage space required for 30 minutes of video
Windows Media HD 720p	WMV	5.9 Mbps	1280×720	16:9	30	1.36 GB

(continued)

Table 12-3 *(continued)*

Setting	Type	Bit rate	Resolution	Aspect ratio	FPS	Storage space required for 30 minutes of video
Windows Media HD for Xbox 360	WMV	6.9 Mbps	1280×720	16:9	30	1.58 GB
Windows Media HD 1080p	WMV	7.8 Mbps	1440×1080	16:9	30	1.8 GB

You don't have to be a high school AV geek to understand that bigger and more high quality video types will require more PC processing power and dramatically more storage space, especially HD video. The big question, of course, is which video setting to use?

That all depends, of course, on your source video. For a general rule of thumb, be sure to save your edited video in a format that is equivalent to, or of lower quality, than the original video. Otherwise, you're needlessly wasting space.

Secret

And understand that you can save your edited video multiple times. You can save one version in AVI format for backup purposes, another in WMV DVD quality for viewing on your Media Center PC, and yet another in WMV Low Quality for distribution on the Web.

Once you've chosen a format, click the Publish button and sit back and wait. It takes enormous amounts of time to publish video to the hard drive, especially when you're working with HD content.

Publishing to DVD or CD

If you want to publish your edited movie directly to DVD, Windows Movie Maker will prompt you to save the project (which we discuss later in the chapter) and will then open Windows DVD Maker, which we discuss later in this chapter.

Publishing to recordable CD is another story. Whereas a typical recordable DVD has space for 4.7 GB or 9.4 GB of storage space (or 1 or 2 hours of digital video, respectively), most CDs only contain about 700 MB of storage space. Thus, the quality of the resulting video will generally not be as high as is possible with a true DVD movie, unless the edited video is very short.

There's another difference. Video CDs are not the same as DVDs: Instead of creating a standard DVD movie disc that can play in any DVD player or PC, when you create a movie CD, you're essentially copying a digital video to a CD, so you can choose between the same video settings we discussed in the previous section. The resulting disc will play on some DVD players, but should work on most PCs.

Publishing for E-mail Distribution

If you'd like to send your edited video to others via e-mail, Windows Movie Maker assumes that the resulting file should occupy 10 MB or less of disk space so that it will be delivered properly by most e-mail services. You can change the size as you'd like, but be careful not to send large attachments via e-mail, as many will simply not be delivered, and even if they are, large attachments can slow down e-mail clients on either side of the conversation.

Secret

When you choose to publish your movie with the E-mail link, the Publish Movie wizard is basically providing you with a limited version of the This Computer\Publish type, where only a range of file sizes is available. You could achieve the same results by choosing This Computer, Compress To, and 10 MB in the wizard.

Writing Back to a Digital Video Camera

If you acquired a home movie via digital video camera, or have a digital video camera lying around, it makes sense to copy a perfect digital version of your edited video back to tape. Why? Well, in addition to providing you with a perfect backup of your movie, using a video tape for this purpose will save disk space. To do so, simply insert a blank video tape into your camcorder, connect the camera to the PC via a FireWire (IEEE 1394) cable, and start the wizard.

Secret

Note that publishing a movie to digital video in this fashion can be quite slow: It will require 1 minute of copying time for every 1 minute of edited video.

Saving and Working with Projects

Before moving on to the wonderful world of DVD movies, we should make one final point about Windows Movie Maker. Each time you copy material into the timeline or storyboard and begin editing it, you should save your progress as a Windows Movie Maker project. That way you can come back later, as you would with an unfinished Word document, and make additional changes.

To save a Windows Movie Maker project, simply choose Save Project from the File menu. By default, projects are saved to your Videos folder, but you're free to save them wherever you'd like. You can reopen saved projects at any time, naturally enough, by selecting File and then Open Project.

Secret

A Windows Movie Maker project is only basically just a file that points to the various digital media files you're accessing, along with whatever edits, transitions, effects, and titles you've made in the timeline or storyboard. The project does *not* contain any videos, photos, music files, or other content. If you move these files around in the file system or delete them, Windows Movie Maker will not be able to use them in a saved project later.

Using Windows DVD Maker

Windows Vista, for the first time, includes an application for *burning*, or making, DVD movies. As you might expect from a first effort, Windows DVD Maker isn't a terribly sophisticated application, so the quality and variety of DVD movies you can make are fairly limited. On the plus side, DVD Maker does deliver the most commonly wanted DVD-making features, and, as you might expect, it's especially well-suited for beginners. So if you've never made a DVD movie, take heart. This is a great place to begin.

tip

DVD Maker is only available to users of Windows Vista Home Premium and Windows Vista Ultimate. If you have a different Vista version, you will need to upgrade to one of these versions in order to use Windows DVD Maker. Or, you could purchase one of the many third-party DVD maker applications on the market. Note that any third-party package will be more sophisticated, but also more complex, than Windows DVD Maker.

Secret

There are actually several ways to start DVD Maker.

- From within Windows Photo Gallery, you can select a group of photos or videos and then select Burn and then Video DVD from the toolbar.
- From within Windows Movie Maker, you can choose DVD from the Publish To portion of the Tasks pane.
- If you saved a DVD Maker project previously, you can double-click that project's icon in the shell and pick up where you left off.
- Or, you can simply find Windows DVD Maker in the Windows Vista Start Menu and launch the application manually, and then add content to an empty project as you go.

Since the latter approach will gain you the skills necessary to explore the other options, we'll examine Windows DVD Maker as a standalone application here. But its integration with Windows Photo Gallery and Windows Movie Maker can and should be explored as well.

To start Windows DVD Maker, open the Start Menu and locate the Windows DVD Maker shortcut in the All Programs group. Windows DVD Maker is a simple wizard-based application, as shown in Figure 12-21, which steps you through the process of adding content and menus to your eventual DVD movie.

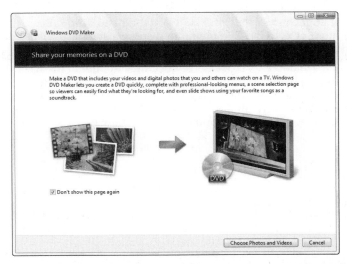

Figure 12-21: No frightening user interfaces here. DVD Maker is the definition of simplicity.

Secret   Like Windows Movie Maker, Windows DVD Maker works with something called a project, that is, a file you can save and reload later that describes the DVD you're making. Unlike Windows Movie Maker, there is no obvious way to save a project while you're compiling your DVD. However, if you look close, you'll see a single menu item, File, in most of the Windows DVD Maker screens. When you click this menu, you'll see options for saving, loading, and making new projects. You can also save your project by clicking the more prominent Cancel button. This will close Windows DVD Maker, but the application will prompt you to save the current project first.

note   DVD Maker projects are saved in your Videos folder by default.

Secret   Only one instance of DVD Maker can be running at a time.

Adding Photos and Videos to Your DVD Project

As noted previously, Windows DVD Maker is a wizard-based application in which you move through a limited set of steps and end up, hopefully, with a nice-looking DVD movie that will play on virtually any DVD player. In the first step of the wizard, you add the content you'd like on the DVD. This content consists of pictures and video. You can drag items to the DVD Maker application using your standard drag and drop skills. Or, you can click the Add Items button, next to the File menu, to display a standard Vista File Open dialog. Use this dialog to navigate to the content you'd like on your DVD movie.

When you add videos to a Windows DVD Maker project, they appear in the wizard as you might expect. Pictures are a little different. If you drag one or more image files into Windows DVD Maker, the application will create a folder called Slide Show as shown in Figure 12-22. From this point on, any photos you add to the project will be added to this one folder. And they will be displayed as an animated slide show in the finished DVD.

You can't have two or more photo slide shows on a single DVD. Only one is allowed.

You also cannot add videos to the Slide show folder. If you try to add a video, it will be added to the root of the project instead.

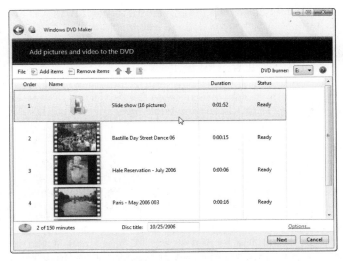

Figure 12-22: The Slide show folder will contain any pictures you add to your DVD project.

You can navigate inside of the Slide show folder in Windows DVD Maker if you'd like. To navigate back out to the root of the DVD, click the small Back to Videos toolbar icon, as shown in Figure 12-23.

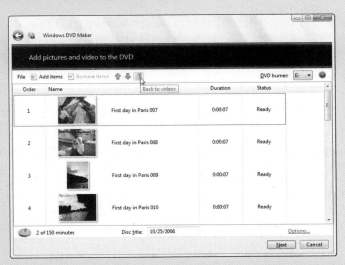

Figure 12-23: Yet another nearly hidden user interface feature lets you escape from the Slide show folder.

To remove a video, picture, or the Slide show folder, select it in Windows DVD Maker and click the Remove Items button. Alternatively, click Delete or right-click the item and choose Remove.

About DVD Storage Issues and Formats

One issue you should be concerned about is how much content will fit on the DVD. Windows DVD Maker works with standard recordable DVDs, so the storage capacities are based on the media you use. With a standard *single-layer* recordable DVD, you can have up to 60 minutes of video. With a standard *dual-layer* recordable DVD, you can store up to 120 minutes of video.

Secret

Another issue, of course, is that there are several recordable DVD types out there. To create a DVD movie that will work in virtually any DVD player in the world, use write-once DVD-R or DVD+R media. Both work well, though DVD-R seems to have better compatibility with older DVD players if that's an issue. Avoid rewriteable DVD formats, like DVD+RW or DVD-RW, because they won't work with most standalone DVD players (though they're fine for testing and PC-based use). If you see the acronym DL used, that describes dual-layer, a technology that doubles the capacity of a recordable DVD's storage space. Note that you might also be confined by the capabilities of your DVD writer. If your hardware is only compatible with, say, DVD+R, then obviously you will need to use DVD+R recordable disks. But if you have a multi-format DVD writer, it's your choice.

Arranging Content

When you've added two or more items to your Windows DVD Maker project, you can start thinking about the order in which they will appear on the final DVD movie. While DVD Maker doesn't offer a huge selection of DVD menu layout choices, it does let you reorder items. You'll notice that the list of videos and photo slide shows in the wizard has an explicit order, as noted by the Order column heading. You can easily reorder items in the following ways:

- **Drag and drop:** Using the skills you've no doubt honed over the years in Windows, simply grab an item in the list and drag it to the position in the order you'd like it to appear.
- **Move up and Move down buttons:** In the Windows DVD Maker toolbar, there are two arrow-shaped buttons, Move up and Move down, that will enable you to reorder the selected item as indicated. This is shown in Figure 12-24.
- **Right-click method:** You can also right-click any item and choose Move Up or Move Down from the resulting pop-up menu.

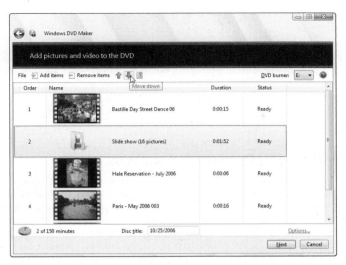

Figure 12-24: While customization is limited, you can at least change the order of items.

Previewing Content

If you'd like to play a video or preview a photo that's in your DVD Maker project, simply double-click that item. Videos play back in Windows Media Player by default, while photos are previewed in Windows Photo Gallery.

Secret

Note that you cannot play the Slide show folder. You can only open the folder and view the files inside.

Naming Your DVD Movie

Under the content list of this window, you'll see a small and easily missed text box called Disc title. By default, it's set to the current date in M/D/YEAR format, where M is a one- or two-number representation of the month (1), D is a one- or two-number representation of the day (30), and YEAR is a four-number representation of the year (2007).

You will want to change this title to something descriptive, because it will be used on the DVD's menu as the title of the DVD movie. A home movie DVD, for example, might be called Our Summer Vacation or similar.

Secret

You can pick whatever title you want, but only 32 characters are allowed.

Understanding DVD Movie Options

In keeping with the user interface minimalism of Windows DVD Maker, you access the application's DVD Options dialog box via a small Options link in the lower-right corner of its window (and not via a Tools⇨Options menu as you might expect). When you click this link, the DVD Options dialog box opens, as shown in Figure 12-25. Note that these options are related to the DVD you're creating and not to the Windows DVD Maker application per se.

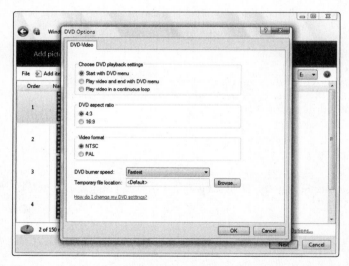

Figure 12-25: DVD Options lets you configure a small number of settings related to the DVD you're creating and not to the application itself.

The following options are available:

- ◆ **DVD playback settings:** You can configure your DVD movie to play its content in one of three ways:
    - • **Start with DVD menu:** Indicates that your DVD will behave like a typical Hollywood DVD and will display a DVD menu on first start.
    - • **Play video and end with DVD menu:** Causes the DVD movie to play through the DVD content first and then display the menu only after the content is complete.

- **Play video in a continuous loop:** Simply plays the DVD content repeatedly, in a loop. Users will still be able to access the DVD menu, however, by pressing the Menu button on their DVD remote control or player.

◆ **DVD aspect ratio:** Enables you to configure whether the DVD's video playback and menu display in a narrow 4:3 aspect ratio (which is not really square per se) or in widescreen 16:9 aspect ratio. The choice you make here should be based on the aspect ratio of the screen on which you think the DVD will be accessed, and on the aspect ratio of the content you're using. Today, most video content is created in a 4:3 aspect ratio. But many television sets are now widescreen. The choice is yours, and you can certainly make a version of the DVD in both formats, though that will be time consuming.

◆ **Video format:** Enables you to choose whether the DVD will be created in the NTSC or PAL video format. You should choose the format that is used in your locale. For example, the NTSC format is correct for the United States, but PAL is used in countries like France and the United Kingdom.

◆ **Other DVD settings:** In the bottom of the DVD Options dialog box, you can set options for the DVD burner speed and the location at which the application will store its temporary files during the DVD creation process. Typically, you will want to leave the DVD burner speed at the fastest setting, but if you run into problems burning DVDs, you can change it to a slower speed (such as medium or slow). This will increase the amount of time it will take to create your DVD movie but will result in a more reliable burn experience. Too, most will want to leave the temporary file location setting untouched. However, if one of your hard drives is faster or has much more space available, you can use this setting to change the location where temporary files are stored and, possibly, speed up the DVD creation process.

Secret

You will need a hard drive or partition with at least 5 GB of free space in order to create a single-sided DVD movie. Dual-layer (DL) DVDs require at least 10 GB of hard drive space. Do not attempt to create a DVD movie on a hard disk that is slower than 5400 RPM. Faster drives — 7800 RPM and 10,000 RPM, for example — running on modern hard drive interfaces (SATA, or Serial-ATA, instead of IDE/ATA, for example) will get better results.

Working with DVD Menus

After you've selected the content that will be included on the DVD movie and have set the DVD options, you can move on to the next step in the Windows DVD Maker wizard and select a menu style. As shown in Figure 12-26, this second and final step in the wizard can be skipped altogether if you like the default menu style: Simply click Burn and off you go.

Figure 12-26: In the curiously named Ready to Burn stage of the DVD Maker wizard, you can pick menu styles.

Secret

When you click the Next button to move to the second phase of the DVD Maker wizard, you will notice that there is no corresponding Back button. That's because Windows DVD Maker adheres to the silly new Windows Vista application style: A graphical Back button is illogically located in the upper-left corner of the application window. It resembles the Back button in Internet Explorer (that is, it's a blue arrow). Why it's not next to a similar Next button is quite unclear.

It makes sense to spend a bit of time here and experiment with the built-in menu styles, since you might not be too excited by the default choice. Besides, there are a number of other things you can do here, including previewing the DVD, changing the menu text, customizing the menu, and adding music to and changing options for the photo slide show. We'll look at those options in the next section.

Along the right side of the application window, you will see a list of menu styles, each presented with a visual thumbnail to give you a rough idea of how it will appear in your DVD. Windows DVD Maker comes with roughly 20 DVD menu styles, and if the application proves a hit with users, one might expect enterprising third-party developers to come up with more.

To select and preview a different style, simply select it in the list. After churning for a few moments, the DVD menu preview will change to reflect your selection, as shown in Figure 12-27.

Figure 12-27: Windows DVD Maker includes a decent selection of menu choices.

Each menu style is different. Some offer an animated video preview running behind the menu text, while others offer multiple video previews, running simultaneously, or even animated menu text that flies in from the sides of the screen.

Changing Other DVD Options

To fully configure your DVD movie, and appreciate what effect the various DVD menu choices will have on the finished product, you'll need to preview the movie and access the other options that are available in this step of the wizard.

Previewing the DVD Movie

Even if you don't think you'll need to make any changes, you should always preview your DVD before committing it to disc. You do so by clicking the Preview toolbar button, which brings up a Preview Your Disc view with a virtual DVD player, complete with DVD controls such as Menu, Play, Pause, and so on. This is shown in Figure 12-28.

Here, you might discover that the font used for the menu text is ugly, you made a bad decision about how the menu comes up, or you might want to change to a different menu style all together. To make any changes, click OK (or the Back button) and get back to work.

Figure 12-28: While previewing your DVD movie, you can see how it will behave and look in a real DVD player.

Secret

And yes, you can also go back from the Ready to Burn Disc phase to the first step of the DVD Maker wizard. The application will remember the settings you configured regardless of which direction you go in the user interface.

note   Each scene in the DVD menu correlates to a video or photo slide show you imported into the Windows DVD Movie Maker project.

Changing the Menu Text

To change a variety of options related to the DVD menu text, click the Menu Text button. Here, as shown in Figure 12-29, you can change the font (including color and bold and italic attributes, but not, curiously, the size), the disc title, the text used for the Play, Scenes, and Notes links, and you can write a block of Notes text that will appear on a sub-page of the main DVD menu.

Figure 12-29: Here, you can change a variety of menu text options and add an optional block of Notes text.

Secret

By default, the Notes link and corresponding Notes text will not appear. You have to add the text first. You can add up to 256 characters in the Notes block. The previews on the right side of the window will show you what the optional Notes page will look like, and of course, you can also see it in the DVD preview described previously.

Customizing the Menu

To customize the appearance of the DVD menu, click the Customize Menu toolbar button. Curiously, you can change some font properties here again, duplicating the functionality of the menu text options described in the previous section. However, the rest of the disc menu options shown here are unique, as seen in Figure 12-30. You can change the videos that display in the foreground and background (the layout and appearance of which vary from menu style to menu style), the audio that plays over the menu (its silent by default), and the style of the menu links, or buttons.

Secret

The video and audio used in the DVD menu don't even have to be related to the media files you chose for inclusion in the DVD movie itself. For example, you could select two movies and a photo slide show for the DVD itself, and separate third and fourth movies for the title if you want.

Figure 12-30: In addition to picking general menu styles, you can also configure various aspects of the DVD menu layout and presentation.

If you make enough changes, or want to reuse the customizations you made, you can actually save them as a brand-new style. When you do this, a new entry called Custom Styles is added to the drop-down above the list of menu styles in the right of the application window. Now, you can choose between Menu Styles and Custom Styles.

Configuring the Photo Slide Show

If you've included a photo slide show in your DVD movie, you can customize it by clicking the Slide Show button in the DVD Maker toolbar. In the Change Your Slide Show Settings window, shown in Figure 12-31, you can add one or more songs (music files) to the slide show, alter the length of time each photo displays, choose a transition type (cross fade is the default), and decide whether to use pan and zoom effects, which will provide a nice animation effect.

---

tip	Adding music and animation effects to a photo slide show dramatically improves its effectiveness, so spend some time playing around with these options.

Figure 12-31: Here, you can configure a nice range of options for your photo slide show.

Writing the Movie to Disc

When you're satisfied with the DVD movie, it's time to burn it to disc. Click the Burn button to proceed.

If there is no writeable DVD in the drive, Windows DVD Maker will prompt you to insert one. You should use the lowest capacity disc possible (4.7 GB for one hour or less of video), since those discs tend to be less expensive than the dual-layer versions.

If your PC does not have a DVD burner, Windows DVD Maker will tell you that a DVD burner is required and recommend that you connect one before continuing. Optionally, you could save the project instead and install a DVD burner later. What you can't do easily is copy the DVD Maker project to a different PC with a DVD burner and then create the DVD there. The reason is that the project will look for the content needed to create the DVD in file paths relative to where they were on the original PC. In order to make this work, you would have to copy the content for the project to the same locations on the second PC as they were on the first.

After you're inserted a blank recordable DVD in the drive, DVD Maker will begin the creation process. This can be a lengthy process, depending on the amount of content you've included. While DVD Maker is creating the DVD, the application window closes and a small Burning dialog appears in the lower-right corner of your screen, as shown in Figure 12-32, charting its progress.

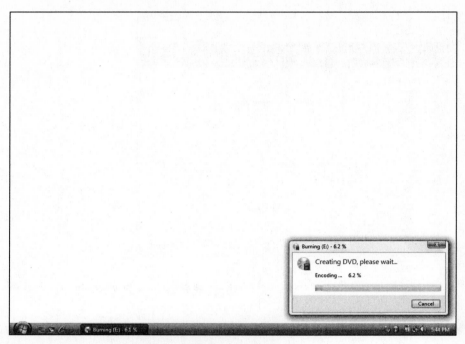

Figure 12-32: Finally, a finished DVD is on the way.

When the DVD is completed, Windows DVD Maker ejects the DVD drive tray so you can go try it in a DVD player. You're also prompted to create another copy of the disc if you'd like. Click Close to cancel that choice and return to the main DVD Maker application.

Summary

The digital video capabilities in Windows Vista are vastly superior to those offered in Windows XP. You can manage your digital movie collection in a variety of ways, including the Windows shell, Windows Photo Gallery, Windows Media Player, and Windows Media Center. You can use Windows Movie Maker to edit and distribute your home movies, recorded TV shows, and other video-related content, including HD content, and can output the results in HD-compatible glory if you're so inclined. Using Windows DVD Maker, you can even publish movies and photo slide shows to standard DVD movies that will work in virtually any DVD player in the world.

Digital Media in the Living Room: Windows Media Center

Chapter

13

♦ ♦

In This Chapter

Understanding how Media Center has evolved over the years

Seeing how Media Center has changed in Windows Vista

Configuring Windows Media Center extensively

Touring the new user interface

Accessing the Media Center TV, movie, photo, and video experiences

Extending Media Center into other rooms with Xbox 360 and other extenders

Synchronizing Media Center with portable devices

Using Media Center to burn your own CDs and DVDs

♦ ♦

Although Microsoft has been criticized for taking so long to bring Windows Vista to market, the truth is that the software giant wasn't idle during the several-year wait between Windows XP and Windows Vista. One of the most innovative technologies Microsoft added to Windows during this time period is Media Center, a wonderful, remote control–accessible front end to all of your digital media content—live and recorded TV, videos, photos, and music—that is equally at home in your living room or bedroom as it is in the home office. In Windows Vista, the Media Center environment has been made available in two mainstream versions of the operating system and will thus reach a far wider audience than it did previously. In this chapter, we examine Microsoft's answer for the living room, Media Center.

A Short History of Media Center

In January 2002, shortly after the release of Windows XP, Microsoft announced that it was working on software, then code-named Freestyle, that would extend the reach of Windows into the living room. Freestyle, which was eventually renamed to Windows XP Media Center Edition, was really just Windows XP Professional with a Media Center application and various Media Center–related services added on top. Media Center, the application, was and is a user interface designed for use with a remote control (although it works fine with a mouse and keyboard too) and what Microsoft calls the ten-foot user interface. (If you're curious, Microsoft refers to the standard way of interacting with a PC as the two-foot interface.)

The original Media Center version included all of the basic features we've come to associate with Media Center in the intervening years. It supported a simple menu-based user interface with options for recording TV, watching live TV, controlling cable set-top boxes via a so-called IR blaster, and enjoying digital media experiences like music, pictures, videos, and DVD movies (see Figure 13-1). Windows XP Media Center shipped in October 2002 and was available only with select Media Center PCs. Not surprisingly, the software was well received by reviewers, but it didn't sell very well because Media Center PCs were relatively expensive, and setting up TV tuner cards to work with cable signals was difficult.

The second version of Windows XP Media Center Edition, code-named Harmony, shipped a year later as XP Media Center Edition 2004. This version was also available only with new PCs and added support for FM radio tuner cards, online services, and functionality that Microsoft had previously left to the two-foot experience, like CD ripping. As you might expect, the product also included various UI and performance improvements as well.

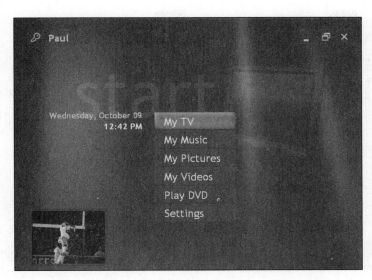

Figure 13-1: The original Windows XP Media Center Edition

In late 2004, Microsoft shipped the most extensive Media Center update, Windows XP Media Center Edition 2005, code-named Symphony. This version sported dramatic user interface improvements with a scrolling main menu with a pop-up for most-recently accessed items, a much simpler setup experience, vastly improved TV picture quality with fewer MPEG-2 compression artifacts, and support for up to three TV tuners, one of which can be an over-the-air (OTA) HDTV tuner. Microsoft also added support for Media Center Extenders, hardware devices that resemble set-top boxes and allow you to remote the Media Center experience via your home network to other TVs in the house: That way, you can be watching a live TV show on one TV, with an Extender, and watching a recorded TV show on a different TV, using the Media Center PC. Media Center 2005 supported up to five Extenders, depending on the capabilities of the hardware on which the system resided. Microsoft also shipped Media Center Extender software for its Xbox video game console, allowing that device to be used like a dedicated Media Center Extender.

Although late 2005 didn't see a major Media Center release, Microsoft did ship a Media Center update that year, ignominiously named Windows XP Media Center Edition 2005 Update Rollup 2 (UR2). This free update added support for the Xbox 360 and its Media Center Extender functionality, a feature called Away Mode that let newer Media Center PC models with modern power management features move quickly between on and off states that more closely resemble TV sets than PCs, DVD changer support, a new DVD burning utility, and support for up to four TV tuners (two of which can be standard definition, and two of which can be OTA HDTV tuners). UR2 also added a wonderful new Zoom feature that helps make 4:3 TV pictures look better on wide-screen displays, support for digital radio, and various bug fixes and performance improvements. XP Media Center Edition 2005 UR2 is shown in Figure 13-2.

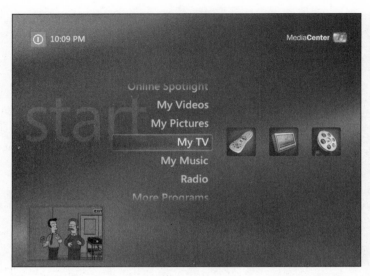

Figure 13-2: Windows XP Media Center Edition 2005 with UR2 was fast, stable, and clean looking.

Aside from the actual products that were rolled out over these years, Microsoft made some of its biggest improvements to Media Center from a marketing standpoint. Although the Media Center software was never released as a standalone add-on for all Windows users, Microsoft dropped the price of this XP version and stopped requiring PC makers to ship it only with new PCs that included TV tuners. Thus, over the years, Media Center quickly became one of the best-selling XP versions, and it's now installed on millions of PCs worldwide. Many Media Center users don't use the TV functionality at all, in fact, but use the software just to view digital media. Today, Media Center is a mature product that's benefited greatly from years of feedback.

Media Center in Windows Vista

With Windows Vista, Microsoft has made some big changes to Media Center. First, the software is no longer available only in a single special Windows Media Center product, although unfortunately, you still can't purchase Media Center separately from Windows. Now, you get Media Center with two different Windows Vista versions: Windows Vista Home Premium and Windows Vista Ultimate.

Secret

If you're using Windows Vista Home or Business editions, you can upgrade to a Media Center–compatible version of Windows Vista by using the Windows Anytime Upgrade service. We discuss this service in Chapter 1.

The second and less obvious change is this—the version of Media Center that ships with Windows Vista is only a half-realized version of where Microsoft hopes to take Media Center in the future. That is, while much of the Media Center interface has changed dramatically in Windows Vista, many of the subpages you'll navigate through while using this system have not really changed since Windows XP Media Center Edition 2005, aside from a few theme changes to make these pages look more like the Vista version. We'll discuss these weird throwbacks to XP Media Center 2005 as they come up throughout the chapter, but here's something you should know: Microsoft will be releasing an update to Media Center sometime in the holiday 2007 time period that will finish the transition to the new user interface. How this update will be delivered, at this point, is still a mystery.

In any event, from a high-level standpoint, Media Center has been changed in Windows Vista to be more intuitive and obvious. If you're used to previous Media Center versions, the changes will be a little jarring. But Microsoft hopes the new user interface will help users find the content they want more quickly, with less navigating (and remote control button pushing). At a low-level, Media Center has been architected to be more scalable, so that Microsoft's partners can more easily extend Media Center to do more. This will result in more and better online experiences, applications, and other software that works both with and within Media Center.

Third, Media Center now supports a technology called CableCard which, although not widely available at the time of this writing, will allow specially manufactured Media Center PCs to directly control cable systems without a jury-rigged IR blaster and cable set-top box. What CableCard does is replace a cable box with a card that is plugged directly into the computer. It's a great idea, especially for anyone who's had to suffer through the performance issues incurred by IR blasting.

Finally, there's a fourth major change. The version of Media Center in Windows Vista will not work with first-generation Media Center Extender devices, including the software-based version that shipped for the original Xbox. Instead, you will need to use an Xbox 360 or a new lineup of second-generation Extender-enabled devices, including set-top boxes, televisions, and DVD players. We'll examine Media Center's Extender capabilities later in this chapter.

Microsoft doesn't like to talk about it, but a number of features have been removed from Media Center, and first-generation Extender support is only the beginning. In this version, Windows Messenger and MSN Messenger integration was removed because the Messenger interfaces no longer ship as part of the operating system. (Thanks a lot, U.S. Department of Justice!) Caller ID has also been removed. This feature used to enable users to connect their phone line through the PC; when a phone call arrived, the Caller ID information would pop-up onscreen so you could decide whether to pause TV or whatever before getting off the couch to grab the phone. Fortunately, there are all kinds of Caller ID add-ons for Media Center available online. To find one you like, try http://search.msn.com/results.aspx?q=caller+id+media+center&FORM=QBHP.

Configuring Media Center

Before you do anything in Media Center, you should configure it to work with your PC's display and sound system, Internet connection, and, if present, your TV signal. Unlike any other Windows Vista feature, Media Center configuration is a bit time consuming and requires you to be prepared. Unless you've done this before, plan on spending about an hour configuring Media Center the first time.

The first time you launch Media Center, you will see a Media Center–style dialog box — as shown in Figure 13-3 — asking you whether you'd like to configure these features via an Express or Custom method. You can also optionally choose to run setup later.

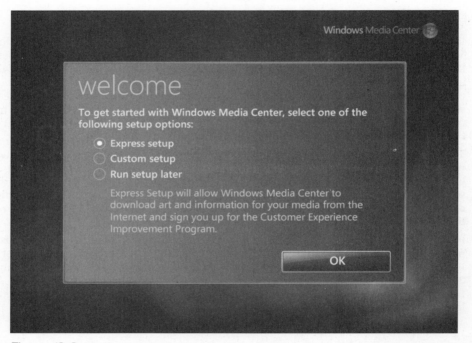

Figure 13-3: Media Center's notification dialog boxes aren't really separate windows, but are instead part of the underlying display. However, you still need to deal with these alerts before moving on and doing anything else in Media Center.

Express setup will utilize the default settings. Generally speaking, we do not recommend allowing Microsoft to configure any of its software with the company's default settings, so our advice is to skip this option. If you do choose the Express setup, Media Center will be configured to download media information from the Internet and perform other Internet-based tasks you may not approve of.

If you choose the Custom setup — which roughly lines up with the Setup experience used by previous Media Center versions — you will need to step through the Media Center Setup Wizard manually. We recommend you choose this option: Even if you ultimately choose the options Microsoft would have configured for you automatically in Express options, at least this way you know exactly what happened.

tip Media Center will actually enable you to skip the configuration stage and configure Media Center settings later. To do so, click the Setup Later button.

Running the Setup Wizard

To configure Media Center correctly, choose Custom in the Welcome to Media Center dialog we described in the previous section. This launches the Media Center Setup Wizard, which runs in full-screen mode, as shown in Figure 13-4.

Figure 13-4: Media Center Setup will guide you through many of the configuration tasks you'll want to complete before using Media Center.

The wizard steps you through the various options Media Center needs to run correctly, including your Internet connection (which includes a Join Wireless Network Wizard if you utilize a wireless connection), whether you'd like to join Microsoft's Customer Experience Program to help the company improve Media Center, and so on. We'll explain these steps as you continue in this chapter.

There are two parts of the wizard you'll want to pay special attention to. The first is the page that asks about the Customer Experience Program (Help Improve Windows Media Center). In this phase of Setup, Microsoft is asking you to have your computer automatically send anonymous reports about Media Center performance and reliability to the company over the Internet. In general, this is a nice thing to do because your Media Center experience will be aggregated with that of other Media Center users around the world to help find and fix issues with the software. But if you're a privacy aficionado and not particularly trusting of Microsoft, you may want to simply choose No Thank You and move on.

Right after the Customer Experience Program phase, you'll see a Get The Most From Windows Media Center screen. Here, you will be asked whether you'd like to let Media Center connect automatically to the Internet to automatically download music informa-tion, album art, and other data. Back in Chapter 10, you may recall that we recommended being very careful about allowing Microsoft to do this, and that advice applies here as well: If you have carefully crafted your ripped CD metadata, you might want to select No here. If, however, your digital media files are in need of some help—that is, you don't have album art associated with each of your ripped CD albums—you might want to choose Yes. Media Center's interface is very visual in Windows Vista, and it relies on displaying graphical representations of your digital media.

After this, you'll be told that the required components have been set up. Now, it's time to move on to the optional phase of setup. Here, you will configure your tuners, TV signal and program guide (if your PC has one or more TV tuners installed), and your display, speakers, and media libraries. Our advice here is simple: If you are going to be using Media Center at all, especially for watching and recording TV, you really need to take the time to go through each of these steps.

Configuring TV

If your PC includes at least one TV tuner card that is connected to a TV signal of some sort, refer to your Media Center PC's or TV tuner card's documentation for information on setting up the required hardware. Then you can configure Media Center to access and record televisions shows, as follows:

1. Configure the TV signal, and the wizard will initially ask you to confirm the region in which you live (United States in our cases). At that point, Media Center downloads TV setup options that are specific to your region.

Secret

In case it's not obvious, yes, that means you must have a live Internet connection in order to configure TV within Media Center. In fact, Media Center relies on an Internet connection to keep its program guide, through which it displays the available TV shows at any given time, up to date. Although it's possible but not advisable to turn off the PC's Internet connection once you've configured its TV features, you will absolutely have to be connected to the Internet to complete this part of Setup.

2. Choose between automatic and manual TV signal configuration. In our experience, automatic configuration works best when you're connected to a TV signal via a cable set-top box and are using IR blasting in order to control the box's channel changing functionality. Meanwhile, manual configuration works better for a direct TV connection, where a TV cable comes out of the wall and connects directly to your TV tuner card (that is, there is no set-top box). Since the manual method always works, we'll cover that here. Choose the I Will Manually Configure My TV Signal option, and then click Next.

3. In the next screen, you choose what type of TV signal you get: Cable, Satellite, or Antenna. If you choose Cable or Satellite, you're asked whether you have a set-top box. If you do, Setup will walk you through a series of steps in which you configure the system to control your set-top box so that you can change channels, raise and lower the volume, and perform other actions from within Media Center and using the Media Center remote control. If you don't have a set top box, you can simply skip that part.

4. After configuring the system to use a set-top box, choose whether to use the program guide, which provides always-updated TV program listings that are specific to your cable system. Because using the guide requires Media Center to connect to Microsoft servers, you must okay this choice. Unlike some of the other Media Center options, this one is a no-brainer: If you are going to use Media Center for TV, you absolutely must enable this feature. We'll look at the program guide later in this chapter.

5. Next, configure Media Center to work with your particular TV system. After you enter your ZIP code (in the United States), Media Center downloads a list of TV providers that match the type of TV signal you selected earlier. Pick the one that matches the service you receive and then Media Center will download the program guide for that service.

Media Center downloads about two weeks' worth of program guide at a time. The first time you do this, it will take a few minutes. But in the future, the guide download will occur in the background, and you won't even be aware it's happening. In this way, the program guide will always be up to date.

Configuring the Display

In the Display Configuration phase, you will optimize Media Center for your display. Media Center natively supports these display types:

- ◆ **PC Monitor:** For a CRT monitor connected via a VGA cable
- ◆ **Built-In Display:** For a notebook computer
- ◆ **Flat Panel:** For a flat panel monitor connected via a VGA or DVI cable
- ◆ **Television:** For any type of TV connected via composite, S-video, DVI, VGA, HDMI, or component cable
- ◆ **Projector:** For a dedicated projector connected via composite, S-video, DVI, VGA, HDMI, or component cable

Choose the correct connection type, based on how your system is physically connected to the display. Consult your Media Center PC's documentation if you're not sure which display and connection types are employed. This step is important, because Media Center will attempt to optimize the video output based on which choices you make.

Ensure that you're using the highest-quality connection type. In rough order of quality, from worst to best, the choices are composite, S-Video, VGA, DVI, HDMI. If you're using a built-in display, like that on a notebook computer, you really don't have any options.

After you've chosen the display and connection types, the wizard will prompt you to choose the Display Width (really, the aspect ratio) of your display. You have two choices: Standard (4:3) and Widescreen (16:9). Again, if you're not sure what to choose here, consult your display's documentation. The wizard will then check the system and prompt you about the resolution of the display. You can accept the value it provides (which you should do if it is correct) or select No. If you choose the latter option, you will be presented with a list of possible display resolutions, based on the capabilities of your display and whether you're using a wide-screen aspect ratio.

tip **On a high-end HDMI-based HDTV display, for example, you might see choices like 1920×1200, 1080p (59.95Hz), 1680×1050, 1440×900, 1360×768, and so on. In general, you should choose the highest resolution your display supports in order to get the best picture quality.**

Next, you can optionally configure your display's controls, including calibrating the display's onscreen centering and sizing, aspect ratio, brightness, contrast, and RGB color balance. These controls are less important on VGA, DVI, and HDMI connections, but analog connections like composite and S-Video will often benefit from some fine-tuning.

Configuring Sound

In the third part of the optional phase of Media Center Setup, you will configure the number of speakers you have and test your setup to ensure all of the speakers are working correctly. Vista's version of Media Center supports three speaker configurations: two speakers (stereo), 5.1 surround sound (two front speakers, two rear speakers, and a center speaker), or 7.1 surround sound (two front speakers, two rear speakers, two side speakers, and a center speaker). Choose the configuration that most closely matches your hardware, click Next, and then click Test to test the speakers. If you don't hear the test sound in some or all of the speakers, the wizard will help you troubleshoot.

Secret **Media Center's speaker setup is quite a bit more limited than the speaker configuration options you get in Windows Vista's Control Panel. There, you can configure mono, stereo, quadraphonic, 5.1, and 7.1 speaker setups. You configure your speakers in Control Panel by opening the Start Menu and navigating to Control Panel⇨ Hardware and Sound⇨Audio Devices and Sound Themes⇨Manage audio devices (see Figure 13-5).**

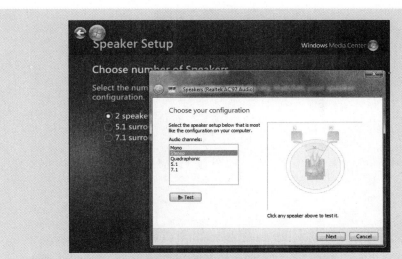

Figure 13-5: Media Center and Windows Vista both have their own ways of configuring sound.

Configuring Your Digital Media Libraries

In the next phase, you can configure your Music, Pictures, and Videos libraries. More specifically, you configure which shell folders that Media Center will watch or monitor for content. Media Center actually monitors the same folders you configure as Monitor Folders in Windows Media Player 11, which we discuss in Chapter 10. So if you configured Monitor Folders in Windows Media Player, there's no reason to do it here as well.

Secret

Folders you configure as Monitor Folders in Windows Media Player are watched by Media Center as well. But the reverse is also true: If you configure Media Center to watch certain folders, those changes will be reflected in Windows Media Player, too.

Configuring Media Center Features after Setup

After you're done configuring Windows Media Center with the Setup Wizard, you'll be presented with the Media Center menu system or, as we like to call it, Start screen. This is shown in Figure 13-6.

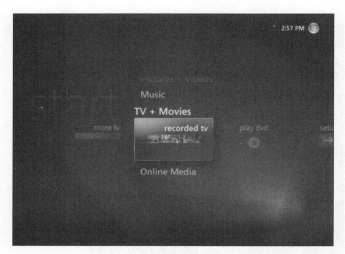

Figure 13-6: The Media Center Start screen is your home base for all of Media Center's experiences.

We examine the finer points of this user interface in the next section. But for now, we'd like to discuss how you can configure Media Center after completing the Setup Wizard. Some of the configuration information you'll see directly corresponds to features you configured in the wizard (or even runs part of the wizard in some cases). But you can access many more Media Center features from outside the wizard. For this reason, it's important to step through the Media Center Settings feature to make sure the system is configured exactly the way you want it.

You can actually access Settings from virtually anywhere in Media Center, but the simplest method is to navigate to the Start screen (press the Start button on the screen or the remote) and then choose Tasks and then Settings. Shown in Figure 13-7, Settings includes links to several major areas.

Figure 13-7: From here, a world of customization.

There's little need to walk you through each and every feature. Instead, in the Secrets that follow we'll highlight new options, those options that contain unlikely benefits and the options you should absolutely consider changing.

General

If you are using Media Center as the main interface to your TV in the living room, do the following:

1. Navigate into General⇨Startup and Window Behavior.
2. Select the Windows Media Center Window Always On Top option.
3. Select the Start Windows Media Center When Windows Starts option.
4. Disable Show Taskbar Notifications, because you'll likely never see the Windows taskbar anyway.

Got kids? Use the Parental Controls feature to access a suite of excellent ratings-based limitations that will prevent your children from viewing TV shows, DVD movies, or movies that surpass your limits. You input a four-digit code to unlock these shows for yourself. Parental controls can be found in General⇨Parental Controls.

Media Center includes an unintentionally hilarious but useful optimization kludge: In General⇨Optimization, you can configure Media Center to reboot every morning at 4:00 a.m. (or any other time). This clears out any problems and is especially useful for people who use a Media Center as their TV interface. No, it's not elegant, but it does work wonders for stability.

TV

If you're hearing impaired, you can enable Closed Captioning, which was significantly improved in this version, in TV, Closed Captioning. Closed Captioning can be on, off, or on when muted. Naturally, the quality of the actual captioning is dependent on the content creators who, unfortunately, have no federal requirements related to accuracy.

Picture

Be sure to change at least two options in the Picture settings. First, enable Show Pictures In Random Order for better slide shows. Then, consider changing the transition time from 12 seconds to something smaller, like 5 seconds.

A Somewhat New User Interface

Prior to Windows Vista, Media Center presented most of its menus using lists of text that were formatted to be readable on TV displays. In keeping with more visual style of Windows Vista, however, the new Media Center version is more graphical and takes better advantage of the onscreen real estate offered by wide-screen displays such as HDTV sets. This interface may be a bit jarring if you're used to using previous Media Center versions, but others should find themselves able to adopt the new user interface fairly easily.

The main Media Center menu, or Start screen, was shown back in Figure 13-6. From here, you scroll up or down to access primary options like TV + Movies, Music, Pictures + Videos, Tasks, Shutdown, and Online Media. But you also scroll left and right to access subchoices within each primary option. For example, if TV + Movies is selected, you can move left and right to access options like More TV, Recorded TV, Live TV, Guide, Movies Guide, Play DVD, and Search. (If TV is not configured, you might see a Setup TV option as well.)

Throughout the Media Center interface, you will run into these types of horizontally scrolling menu choices, so it's a good idea to get used to them by experimenting with the Start screen. How you navigate through the interface will depend on whether you're using the keyboard, mouse, or Media Center remote control (which you might have gotten with your PC). Each can be used. In Table 13-1, we summarize how you access the most common Media Center navigational options with each controller type.

Table 13-1: How to Get It Done in Windows Media Center

Media Center Action	Keyboard	Mouse	Remote Control
Open Windows Media Center or return to the Windows Media Center Start screen.	Press the Windows key+Alt+Enter.	Select Media Center from the Start Menu or click the Media Center logo while in Media Center.	Click the Start button.
Close Windows Media Center.	Press Alt+F4.	Select Shutdown and then Close from the Start screen.	Select Shutdown and then Close from the Start screen.
Select the highlighted option.	Press Enter.	Click the highlighted option.	Click OK.
Go back to the previous screen.	Press Backspace.	Click the Back button.	Click Back.
Go to the first item in a list.	Press Home.	Scroll to the top of the list with the mouse's scroll wheel.	Press the Page Up button until you reach the top of the list.
Go to the last item in a list.	Press End.	Scroll to the bottom of the list with the mouse's scroll wheel.	Press the Page Down button until you reach the bottom of the list.

Media Center Action	Keyboard	Mouse	Remote Control
Move left.	Press the left arrow.	Move to the left side of the menu and click the left arrow that appears; or, press left on a tilting scroll wheel-equipped mouse.	Click the Left button.
Move right.	Press the right arrow.	Move to the right side of the menu and click the right arrow that appears; or, press right on a tilting scroll wheel-equipped mouse.	Click the Right button.
Move up.	Press the up arrow.	Move to the top of the menu and click the up arrow that appears; or, scroll up on a scroll wheel-equipped mouse.	Click the Up button.
Move down.	Press the down arrow.	Move to the bottom of the menu and click the down arrow that appears; or, scroll down on a scroll wheel-equipped mouse.	Click the Down button.
Toggle full screen mode.	Press Alt+Enter.	Click the Maximize button.	n/a

One feature you can access only with the mouse is the new controls overlay that appears when you move the mouse around while Media Center displays. Shown in Figure 13-8, these controls provide you with access to the Back and Start buttons plus a nice set of playback controls perfect for music, TV, videos, or other multimedia content.

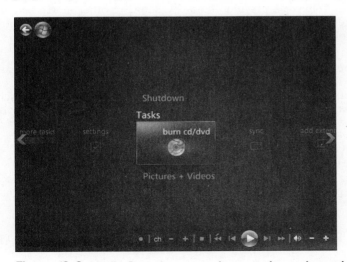

Figure 13-8: Media Center's new overlay controls are elegant looking and easy to use.

Previously, we mentioned that some screens in Media Center were new to this version while others were carry-overs from Windows XP Media Center Edition 2005. You might be wondering what actually changed.

The Start screen is all-new in Windows Vista Media Center. When TV, video, or a DVD movie is playing (but not, oddly, a photo slide show), and you return to the Start screen, the Start screen is overlayed over the video, as shown in Figure 13-9. Previously, the video would be seen playing back in a small picture-in-picture (PIP)-type window in the lower left of the screen.

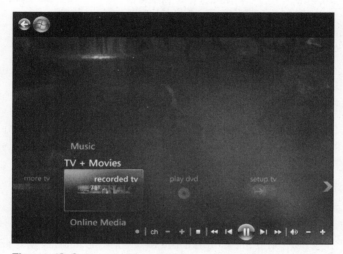

Figure 13-9: New to Vista: Movies and TV shows can be overlayed by the Start screen.

What's odd is that many subpages revert to the old way of doing things. For example, if you access the Program Info for a playing video, TV show, or other movie content (by right-clicking the screen and choosing Program Info, or clicking the More Info button on the Media Center remote), you'll see that the video pops into a PIP window and isn't over-layed by the screen, as shown in Figure 13-10.

You'll find inconsistencies like that throughout Media Center. Remember, Microsoft has only partially realized its vision for the next generation Media Center. Updates are coming in the ensuing years that will use the video overlay style in all Media Center screens. As for now, there are only two places to see this overlay: The Start page and the Program Guide.

Figure 13-10: Blast from the past: Some screens revert to the picture-box approach used by previous Media Center versions.

Exploring the Media Center Experiences

Media Center offers a rich and exciting way to access live and recorded television shows and movies, digital photos, home videos, digital music, and other digital media content, and it works equally well on a notebook, your desktop PC, or via an HDTV display in your living room. In this section, we'll examine the various digital media experiences offered by Media Center.

TV and Movies

The television experience sits up front and center in Windows Media Center, although it's likely that many Windows Vista users will not have a TV tuner card installed in their system, let alone one that is connected to and controlling their TV source (cable, satellite, or whatever). That's too bad: Although much of Media Center is exciting, its TV capabilities are the most impressive and quite superior to competing digital video recording (DVR) solutions like TiVo. Let's take a look.

Live TV

Assuming you went through the TV signal wizard described earlier in this chapter, you should be able to click the Live TV button on your remote (or select Live TV from the TV + Movies entry on the Media Center Start screen) and begin watching live TV immediately. Using your remote, you can change channels, view a program guide (see the section "TV and Movie Guides" later in this chapter), pause, rewind, and restart live TV, and perform all the other options you'd expect from a normal television.

tip One caveat: If you're using an IR blaster to control your cable box or satellite dish, you may notice that some operations, like changing channels, are quite a bit slower than they were when you accessed these devices directly. That's because Media Center has to translate the commands you press on the remote, send the control codes for the device via IR, and then wait while the device performs whatever action you requested. Because of this slowness, you won't be able to quickly move through the channels to see what's on. No big loss, however: The integrated Program Guide and recording functionality largely eliminates this need.

One very cool feature of the TV, movie, and video experiences in Media Center is that playing content will continue to play in the background of the screen if you navigate back to the Start screen or the program guide. The effect is somewhat stunning. To return to Live TV, press Back or the Live TV button.

Recorded TV

Live TV is neat, but it's so twentieth century, and as you begin using Media Center, you'll quickly discover that it's so much better to record television and then watch it at your own convenience. Doing so has three big benefits when compared to live TV.

- ◆ You can skip over commercials and watch just the show itself.
- ◆ You can pause live TV if interrupted by the phone or some other annoyance.
- ◆ You can watch the show on your schedule, not the TV networks. Forget must-see TV. You can watch what you want, when you want.

And like live TV in Media Center, you can, of course, pause, rewind, and fast forward recorded TV.

There are many, many ways to record TV shows in Media Center. But the best way is to use Media Center's search capabilities to locate the shows you want. Then, you can configure it to record individual shows (like when you want to record a movie) or a series (for popular shows like *Lost* or *The Office* where you don't want to miss a single show).

1. To search for a show to record, navigate to the Start screen, TV + Movies, and then Search. As shown in Figure 13-11, you'll see a variety of ways to search, including by title, keyword, categories, movie actor, or movie director.
2. For TV shows, the title is often the way to go. Choose Title and then type in the beginning of the show title until you see the show you want, as seen in Figure 13-12.
3. Select the show name from the list and you'll be brought to a screen where you will see all of the times that show is on.

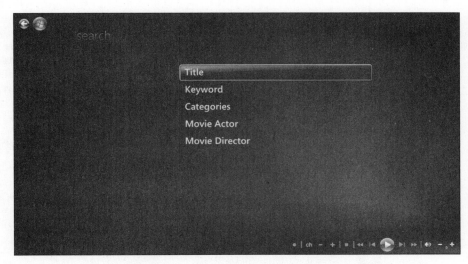

Figure 13-11: Media Center's searching functionality has improved dramatically in Windows Vista.

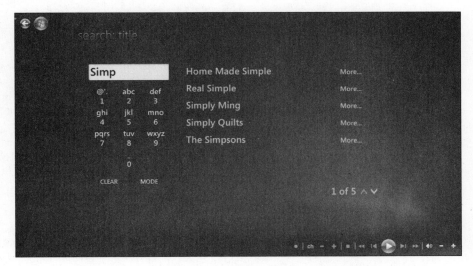

Figure 13-12: Keep typing until you've whittled the search results down to a manageable list.

Some popular syndicated shows, like "The Simpsons," are on multiple times a day on multiple channels. Newer shows, meanwhile, that are running for the first time, will usually be on less frequently and only on one station. One exception to this rule: Many TV providers now supply two versions of local TV stations, one in standard definition and one in high definition (HD). Typically, it's advisable to record HD shows on the HD version of the station on which it appears. And vice versa.

- To record an individual show, select it from the list and click the Record button on your remote. (Alternatively, right-click the show title and choose Record.) You'll see a red circle appear next to the show, indicating that the show will record.
- To record a series, press the Record button twice (or right-click and choose Record Series). As shown in Figure 13-13, multiple red circles will appear next to the show, and possibly next to other episodes shown in the list.

Figure 13-13: When you record a series, you'll see this unique recording graphic.

For series recordings, you're going to want to make sure that you're recording exactly what you want. To do this, right-click one of the episodes that is marked with multiple red circles, and then choose Series Info (or select and click More Info on the remote). On the Series Info screen, you'll see the list of episodes that is currently scheduled to record. Click Series Settings to configure how the series will record.

On the Series Settings screen, you can choose when the recording will stop (on time, or some number of minutes after it's scheduled to end); which recording quality level to use (always choose Best); how long to keep each episode (until space is needed, until I watch, until I delete, and so on); how many recordings to keep at a time; which channels to record from; when to record; and which types of shows to record (first run only, or first run and rerun). You will want to spend some time configuring these options, both in general (via TV in Settings) or for individual shows. For example, if you know that a particular show always runs three minutes late, be sure to configure it to record late in Series Settings.

tip You can view and configure various recorded TV shows and features from the Recorded TV screen. Just choose View Scheduled to see a list of shows that will be recorded in the future, view all of the series you're recording, and see a list of the shows you recorded in the past.

TV and Movie Guides

Media Center has always provided a free program guide, which shows you a listing of the shows available on your TV provider. You can use this guide to view what's on right now, and what's coming up. It's also a handy way to find shows to record: If you happen to get a high-quality HDTV station, for example, you can scroll through the timeline on just that station and see what's coming up, marking shows and movies to be recorded as you go.

tip To discover more about an individual show, select it in the guide and choose More Info. To watch a show that is on right now, simply select it. You can also filter the guide to show only the types of shows you want to see: To do, click the Guide button while in the guide (or click the Categories bar at the left of the guide) and then select Most Viewed, Movies, Sports, Kids, News, or Special. As shown in Figure 13-14, this can be a huge boon for sports fans, or anyone else who wants to filter through the programming chaff and come up with only those shows that interest them.

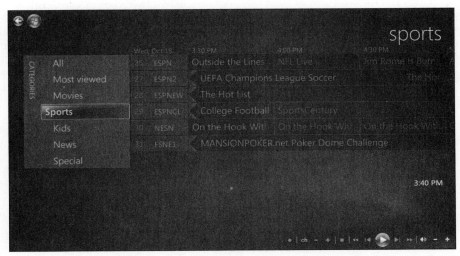

Figure 13-14: Sports fans rejoice: See only sports-related shows in the program guide.

Although Media Center's program guide is nothing new, there is a new Movie Guide in this version that's worth exploring. It replaces the Movies functionality from Media Center 2005; that feature was pretty cool, but it was buried deep in the My TV section of the user interface. The Movie Guide provides a handy front end to all the movies that are available now and in the near future on your cable system or other TV source. Shown in Figure 13-15, this feature is hugely graphical, using DVD box art to help you visually navigate through the list of available choices.

Figure 13-15: Movie Guide is a great way to find movies to watch or record.

DVDs

As you might expect, Media Center is an excellent DVD player too, offering virtually all of the functionality of a standalone DVD player. When you insert a DVD movie into the PC while Media Center is running, it will start immediately. From there, you can use the DVD button on your remote to return to the DVD's main menu, or the remote-based or onscreen playback controls to, well, control playback.

Secret

Whether you're watching TV, a movie, a video, or a DVD, be sure to experiment with Media Center's excellent Zoom feature, which cycles between four different zoom modes: Normal (1), Zoom (2), Stretch (3), and Smart (4). Users with widescreen displays will want to check out smart zoom, because it intelligently zooms standard definition 4:3 content in such a way that it fills the entire screen without making people onscreen look stretched.

Pictures and Videos

In previous versions of Media Center, Picture and Videos were separate experiences. For some reason, Microsoft has lumped them together in the Windows Vista version, and we feel that's a mistake, as pictures (typically digital photos) and videos (which can be home movies, certainly, but really any kind of digital video) are two entirely different things.

Opinions aside, they're represented together now under the Pictures + Videos menu off the Start screen. You'll see two main items there, Picture Library and Video Library, as well as a few other options like Play All and More Pictures.

Pictures

The Pictures experience in Windows Media Center is accessed via the Pictures Library item in the Start screen. As shown in Figure 13-16, it's sorted by name by default and includes nice-looking thumbnails of the subfolders and pictures contained in your Pictures folder. You can choose to sort the library by date, as well, or run a slide show of all of your pictures from this screen.

Figure 13-16: The new Pictures experience is even more graphical than its predecessor, with horizontally scrolling content.

When you navigate into a folder that contains individual photos, you'll see that the options remain the same: You can navigate horizontally through the collection of pictures, sort by name or date, or start a slide show.

Secret

To access the hidden Pictures options, right-click (or press the More Info remote button) on any selected photo or folder. You'll see a number of options, including Burn (covered later in this chapter), View Small, Library Setup, and Settings.

- View Small will change the thumbnail images to smaller icons, which may make it easier to find content when there are many files being displayed.
- Library Setup brings you to the watch folder wizard that we discussed previously in Configuring Your Digital Media Libraries earlier in this chapter.
- The Settings option navigates you to Media Center Settings. Here, you can choose Pictures and modify how slide shows work, as shown in Figure 13-17.

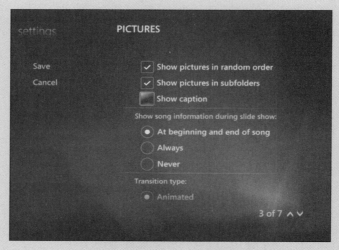

Figure 13-17: Be sure to change the settings for slide shows before launching one.

tip

You should really change some of those slide show settings. For example, you might want the pictures to display randomly and might find the default display time of 12 seconds to be quite a bit too long.

Videos

The Videos experience in Windows Media Center is inconveniently accessed via the Video Library item in the Pictures + Videos section of the Start screen. Video Library is sorted by folders by default (or date taken, optionally) and includes nice-looking thumbnails of the subfolders and movies contained in your Video folder. When you click on a video, it begins playing immediately, as shown in Figure 13-18. You can use the onscreen controls (in 2-foot mode) or the playback controls on your remote control to pause, fast forward, and perform other playback-related functions.

Figure 13-18: Videos behave much like TV shows, and offer the same controls.

Secret

Curiously, there are no video-related options in the Media Center Settings screen. Despite this, you can right-click anywhere in Video Library and choose Settings. From there you can set various settings for other Media Center features, but not videos.

Music

Media Center's Music experience is accessed via the Music item in the Start screen. From here, you can access the Music Library (that is, the songs and albums you've purchased online or ripped from CD to your hard drive) or Radio, which enables you to access Internet-based radio stations.

The Media Center's Music Library organizes the digital music you're storing on your PC in an attractive, horizontally organized way, using album art information to identify each item. By default, Music Library is organized by album, as shown in Figure 13-19.

But unlike other Media Center experiences, you can choose to view your music in a wide variety of ways, including by artist, genre, song, playlist, composer, year, or album/artist. What's interesting here is that some of these views—like Artist, as shown in Figure 13-20— are displayed in a textual, not graphical, format.

Figure 13-19: The Music Library album view is graphical and fun to navigate, especially if you have lots of music.

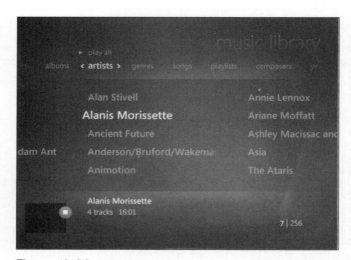

Figure 13-20: Sadly, other parts of the Music experience aren't so graphical.

As with other parts of the Media Center interface, you can navigate around, dive right in, and play any music at any time. But because of the concept of the Now Playing list, you can also add music, on the fly, to a temporary playlist called Now Playing. To do so, right-click an item and choose Add to Queue. In this way, you can construct a playlist for an event, like a party, or to later synchronize with a portable device.

After you've collected a selection of music you like, you might want to save it as a permanent playlist. To do so, select the album art in the lower-left corner of the display, or go to the Start screen and navigate to the newly added Now Playing + Queue item. On the Now Playing screen, choose View Queue and then Save As Playlist. You can also change various playback options from this screen, including shuffle and repeat.

Secret

One of the coolest features of Media Center is the ability to play photo slide shows that are accompanied by music. To do this, play some music. Then, navigate into your photo library and choose the photos you'd like to view. This is a fantastic way to enjoy pictures from a recent vacation, birthday party, or other family event. As seen in Figure 13-21, you'll see nice overlays describing the current song as it begins and ends. Underneath that: You're photo animated slide show.

Figure 13-21: One of the most enjoyable Media Center experiences: A photo slide show accompanied by music.

Accessing Media Center Away from the PC

Beginning with Windows XP Media Center Edition 2005 in late 2004, Microsoft and a handful of its hardware partners began shipping devices (or, in the case of Microsoft's solution, a software add-on for the original Xbox) called Media Center Extenders. These Extenders were set-top boxes, much like DVD players or cable boxes, which you would place on or near a TV somewhere in your house. They could then connect wirelessly, if you had a wireless network, or via Ethernet cabling to your home network and thus to your Media Center PC. The idea is that Extenders can literally extend the reach of your Media Center, its stored multimedia content, and even live TV to other TVs around your home.

It was a good idea in theory. The problem is that first-generation Media Center Extenders weren't very good in practice. They were expensive, for starters, and lacked key features like built-in DVD players (as DVD content couldn't be extended from the PC to an Extender for copyright reasons). And because they were based on low-end, Windows CE–based chipsets, the Extenders were not capable of some of Media Center's nicer graphical effects. We don't think many Extender users missed some of the user interface–based animations per se, but Extenders were incapable of animating photos and transitions during photo slide shows. That was rather inelegant.

With the version of Windows Media Center in Windows Vista, Microsoft has cut off the first-generation Media Center Extenders. So if you have a hardware Extender or an Xbox with Microsoft's Media Center Extender software, they won't work with Windows Vista. Instead, you will need to get an Xbox 360 — which includes second-generation Extender software — or a second-generation Extender device. These devices are all powerful enough to render the graphical effects that first-generation Extenders could not, and unlike first-generation Extenders, the devices themselves are better all-around solutions. Instead of empty boxes with Extender chipsets built in, it's now possible to get Extender functionality in certain DVD players, TV sets, and other devices.

Because the Xbox 360 video game console is so much more prevalent than these devices in the market place at this time, we'll focus on the Xbox here. But using a device-based Extender is almost identical, although, of course, only the Xbox 360 can play blockbuster video games as well.

But using an Extender isn't the only way to get content from your Media Center out into the world. In this section, we'll also examine how you can use Media Center to interact with portable devices and to burn your own audio CDs and movie DVDs.

Using an Xbox 360 or Media Center Extender

The Xbox 360 is an interesting synthesis of video gaming, online services and communities, person-to-person interaction, and multimedia. It is, in other words, everything the first Xbox was plus a whole lot more. While it doesn't make sense to cover the Xbox 360 in depth here, suffice to say that Microsoft's next generation video game console is actually a multifunction device with impressive non-gaming capabilities.

If you do have an Xbox 360 (or have just purchased a Media Center Extender–capable device of any kind), connecting it to your Media Center PC is relatively straightforward. You'll want a 100 Mbps wired home network for best performance, especially if you intend to stream live or recorded TV. But a 54 Mbps wireless network (802.11g or 802.11a) should suffice as well, assuming you're not doing a lot of other high-bandwidth networking activity while using the Extender.

tip   **An 11 Mbps 802.11b network is completely inadequate for this functionality.**

Your Xbox 360 includes instructions on connecting the device to your home network. Assuming you're up and running — you should be able to log on to the free Xbox Live service, for example — you're ready to link the Xbox 360 to your Media Center. To do, simply turn on the Xbox 360, being sure to eject whatever game DVD happens to be in the tray. Then, turn on Media Center on your PC if you haven't yet done so.

If the two machines are connected to the same network, you will see a Windows Media Center Extender dialog box appear in Media Center, as shown in Figure 13-22. Click Yes to begin the setup process.

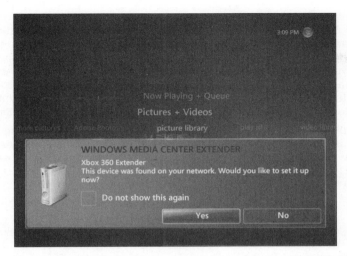

Figure 13-22: Media Center will prompt you to connect with the Xbox 360 or other Extender if it can detect it.

At this point, a wizard will walk you through the process of configuring the Xbox 360 (or other Extender) to work with your Media Center PC. Note that the Xbox can be configured to work with only one Media Center PC at a time. (However, each Media Center PC can be linked to up to five different Extenders.)

The only tricky part of this process is that you will need to enter an 8-digit Setup Key in the Media Center Setup Wizard to link the two machines. When Media Center prompts you for this key, walk over to the Xbox 360 with a pen and piece of paper so you can write down the number generated on the Xbox. Then, return to the PC and enter the Setup Key to continue, as shown in Figure 13-23.

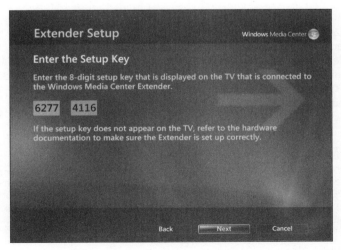

Figure 13-23: The Setup Key links an Extender to a single Media Center PC.

Most of the rest of the wizard involves a lot of waiting around while Media Center does its thing. It will need to change a few firewall rules in Windows Vista to allow the two devices to communicate, configure power settings so that Xbox 360 can turn on the Media Center PC if needed when someone wants to access Media Center functionality from another TV, and get your permission to access the media folders you currently use for local Media Center content. After that, the wizard configures settings on both the PC and Extender and connects to the Extender. On the Extender side, any necessary software updates will be downloaded as well. The whole process usually takes a few minutes.

Once the wizard completes, the Media Center Extender software will load on the Xbox 360. From that point, using Media Center Extender via the Xbox 360 should be virtually indistinguishable from using it on the PC, albeit with possible lag time due to network slowness. You can use the Xbox 360's hand controller as a remote control, or you can even purchase an Xbox 360 Media Remote; there are several available.

Secret   You can even use a Media Center PC remote with the Xbox 360, and we've found this to be the best approach, since these remotes tend to be more full-featured than the ones offered specifically for the Xbox 360. To use a Media Center PC remote with Xbox 360, you'll need to configure the machine first: Navigate to the System blade and choose Console Settings and then Remote Control. From this user interface, choose All Channels (which enables you to use both Media Center PC remotes and Xbox media remotes).

After configuring an Xbox 360 or other Extender for use with Media Center, you can visit Settings and then Extenders to add other Extenders, configure a single Extender-related option (whether notifications are displayed when an Extender is connected), and view information about the Extenders that are already connected. From here, you can tune the network for best performance — which we recommend — and reconfigure, disable, or uninstall an Extender.

tip   Note that the Xbox 360 will also appear twice in Network in the Windows Vista shell after you've configured it as a Media Center Extender, once simply as Xbox 360 and again as Xbox 360 Media Center Extender. If you double-click the Xbox 360 icon, you'll see the Windows Media Player Media Sharing window displayed. But if you double-click the Xbox 360 Media Center Extender icon, Media Center will load with the Xbox 360 Setup screen displayed.

Secret   When you configure any Media Center Extender device, Windows will silently create a new user account, with a name like Mcx1, that is used by the Extender to access your PC's media resources. Mcx1 will appear in the User Account control panel, but you shouldn't try to change it in any way, because doing so will break the connection between the Extender and Media Center.

Synchronizing with Portable Devices

If you're using a portable MP3 player or other portable multimedia device, you may want to synchronize it with your digital media content using Windows Media Player 11, as we discuss in Chapter 10. This is the recommended approach if the system you're using is a typical PC, where you interact with the machine using the mouse and keyboard while sitting at a desk.

If, however, you utilize Windows Media Center via a remote control in your living room, bedroom, or other non-home office location, you might want to use Media Center to synchronize with a portable device. And as you might expect, Microsoft supports this scenario fully.

To synchronize content between Media Center and a portable device, plug in the device and ensure that it's fully supported by Windows Vista. That is, if Windows Vista doesn't automatically recognize the device and install drivers, you might have to consult with the device's documentation and install the drivers manually, perhaps with a setup CD.

When that's done, launch Media Center and navigate to Settings and then Sync from the Start screen. Media Center will pop-up an alert asking if you'd like to synchronize media content with the device, as shown in Figure 13-24.

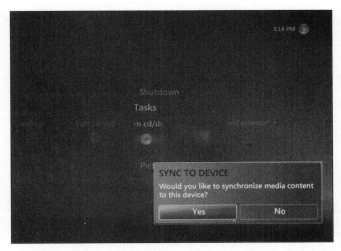

Figure 13-24: It's possible to manage a portable device completely from within Media Center.

When you click the Yes button, the Manage List screen will appear, as shown in Figure 13-25. From this screen, you can determine which content from your Media Center PC will be synchronized with the device. By default, the Manage List screen will display a list of the built-in playlists, such as Music Rated At 5 Stars, Music Added In The Last Month, and so on. For many people, those options will not be exactly what they're looking for. The alternative is to quit out of this screen and create custom playlists that will hold the content you'd like copied to the device. Or, you can click the Add More option on the left side of the Manage List screen and navigate through a list of content, checking the types you'd like synchronized.

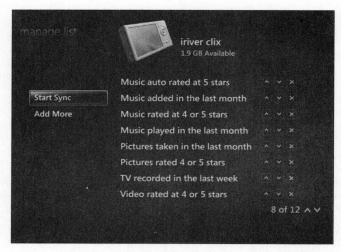

Figure 13-25: The Manage List screen determines which content is synchronized with a device.

Depending on your needs, you might want to simply remove all of the playlists shown in the Manage List screen (by pressing the small delete button, shaped like an x that's to the right of each item). Then, you can use Add More to add only the content you want, or create your own custom playlists. It's up to you.

When you've determined which content to synchronize, press the Start Sync option. A Sync Progress dialog box will appear while the content is synchronized between the PC and device. You can do other things in Media Center while this happens: Just click the OK button to move along. When the sync process is completed, a Sync to Device notification will appear, alerting you.

Secret

What if you have more than one portable device? When you select Sync from the Settings menu, you'll be presented with a screen that enables you to choose which device to access.

Secret

When you synchronize a device with Media Center, that device is added to the Windows Vista Sync Center as well, and you'll see a new icon in the system tray that enables you to open Sync Center, shown in Figure 13-26, or perform various synchronization-related activities right from the Windows shell. When you unplug the device, the Sync Center icon disappears (unless there are other syncrhonizable devices attached).

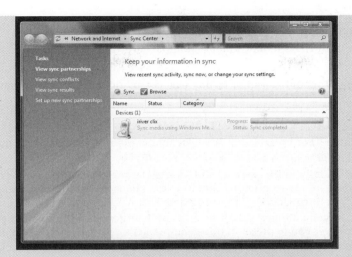

Figure 13-26: Sync Center is a centralized location in Windows Vista for managing portable devices of all kinds, including PDAs, phones, and MP3 players.

Burning a DVD Movie or Music CD

The version of Windows Media Center in Windows Vista now includes native CD and DVD burning capabilities. This means that you can create your own audio CDs, data CDs (containing pictures, photos, TV shows, or whatever), DVD movies (typically of TV shows), or DVD data disks.

Creating an Audio CD

To create an audio CD:

1. Select the artist, album, playlist, genre, or whatever song list from within Media Center's music library, right-click it (or press the More Info button on the remote) and choose Burn.

2. If you haven't already inserted compatible writeable optical media, Media Center will prompt you to do so. Choose Audio CD in the next screen and then provide a name for the CD (Media Center will default to the name of the media you previously selected).

Secret

Although it's possible you're going to want to recreate a CD you already ripped to the hard drive, it's more likely that will you want to create what's called a mix CD, a CD of various content that you've hand-picked. For this reason, it's much easier to create a playlist first, add the songs you want to that playlist, and then start the audio CD creation process when you're done. Be mindful of the limits of a typical CD, which can store about 80 minutes worth of music.

3. In the next screen, Review & Edit List, click Add More and repeat the preceding steps until you've filled the CD or added everything you want.

4. Click Burn CD. Media Center will make sure you want to proceed and then burn the CD.

The resulting CD should work fine in any CD player, including in-car, home, and portable CD players.

Creating a Data CD or DVD

To create a data CD or DVD—that is, a disc that contains the underlying media files, one that will not play back in a normal CD or DVD player:

1. Select an item in the appropriate Media Center experience, right-click (or press the More Info button on the remote), and choose Burn (for pictures, videos, and music) or Burn CD/DVD (for recorded TV).

2. If you haven't already inserted compatible writeable optical media, Media Center will prompt you to do so. In this example, let's assume you insert a blank CD-R.

3. In the next screen, choose Data CD (and not Audio CD) and then click Next.

4. Pick a name for the disc; Media Center will auto-select the name of the media you initially selected as the default.

5. In the next screen, Review & Edit List, click Add More and repeat the preceding steps until you've filled the CD or added everything you want.

6. Click Burn CD. Media Center will make sure you want to proceed and then burn the CD. Since CDs are relatively small, from a storage perspective, burning a CD does not take a lot of time.

The resulting CD will work only in a computer, for the most part.

Secret

However, many car and home CD players are now compatible with MP3 and WMA formats. If this is the case, you can use this functionality to create a data disc of music files, and it should play just fine in such a player.

Creating a DVD Movie

To copy a recorded TV show to a DVD movie:

1. Open Recorded TV (in TV + Movies, Recorded TV) and select the movie you'd like to copy to DVD.

2. Right-click (or press the More Info button on the remote) and choose Burn CD/DVD.

3. If you haven't already inserted compatible writeable optical media, Media Center will prompt you to do so.

4. In the next screen, select Video DVD and click Next.

5. Pick a name for the DVD movie; Media Center will auto-select the name of the TV show as the default, as shown in Figure 13-27.

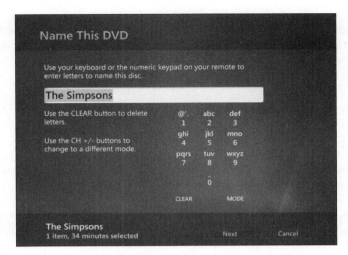

Figure 13-27: Media Center tries to guess which name you want for the DVD movie.

6. In the next screen, Review & Edit List, you can perform a number of actions. If the TV show you selected is the only one you want on the DVD, simply click Burn DVD to commit the movie to disc. Otherwise, click Add More and repeat the preceding steps.

Secret

Note that you can only add Videos and Recorded TV to DVD movies from Media Center in this fashion. If you want to add a photo slide show, you'll need to use Windows DVD Maker, which is covered in Chapter 12. Photos can be added only to data DVDs from within Media Center.

Secret

Some recorded TV shows cannot be burned to DVD. For example, shows on pay stations like HBO and Cinemax are referred to as *protected content* in Media Center. That means that Microsoft is respecting the so-called broadcast flag technologies these channels are using to protect the content. The end result is that HBO (which owns Cinemax too) and other channels have made the decision that they don't want users copying their content. This means that you can't copy a Media Center–recorded version of an HBO show to a portable device or other PC as well, incidentally. It just won't work.

> **tip** If you select too much content, Media Center will warn you that the TV shows (or videos) must be burned at a lower-quality level in order to fit everything on the disc. You can choose to remove a TV show or video or accept the lower quality.

7. When you do finally set about actually burning the DVD, be prepared for a wait. DVD burning takes a long time, especially for video content. A. Really. Long. Time.

> **tip** You can do other things in Media Center when a DVD is burning, but the burning process will take even longer in such a case. You've been warned.

When the DVD is completed, it should work just fine in any DVD player, including the set-top box you probably use on your TV, portable DVD players, in-car DVD players, and laptops.

Summary

Windows Media Center is a wonderful environment for enjoying digital photos, music, videos, TV shows, and other digital media content. If you're lucky enough to be using this system via a Media Center PC or any Xbox 360's Media Center Extender functionality, that's even better — the best features of Media Center come to life when accessed via an HDTV set and remote control. But Media Center isn't just for TVs. Even on a lowly portable computer, Media Center provides a highly visual way of enjoying digital media content. For many users, this program will be reason enough to upgrade to Windows Vista Home Premium or Ultimate.

Having Fun: Games and Vista

◆ ◆

In This Chapter

Discovering the games that Microsoft supplies with Windows Vista

Utilizing the new Games special shell folder

Installing and configuring other games

Utilizing game controllers and other game-related hardware

◆ ◆

Although the experts may extol the many productivity enhancements in Windows Vista, the truth is, we all need to relax sometimes. And sure enough, since the earliest versions of Windows, Microsoft has been including a number of games with its operating system, from classics like Minesweeper and Solitaire to lamented lost titles like Pinball. In Windows Vista, Microsoft has provided users with a totally refreshed and modernized set of game titles as well as a centralized Games shell folder that aggregates all of your game titles and related hardware devices, such as game controllers. In this chapter, we'll have a bit of fun, Windows Vista style.

Games You Get with Windows Vista

If you were a fan of Minesweeper, Freecell, or any of the classic games from Windows past, get ready for a fun surprise: In Windows Vista, many of these games have been completely overhauled with new graphical treatments that take advantage of the underlying 3D graphics capabilities of Microsoft's latest operating system. Table 14-1 summarizes the games you'll find in Windows Vista.

Table 14-1: Games Included with Windows Vista

Game	What It Is	Included with Which Vista Editions
Chess Titans	A 3D chess title	Home Premium, Business (optional install), Enterprise (optional install), Ultimate
FreeCell	A variation of the Solitaire card game, sometimes called Klondike	Home Premium, Business (optional install), Enterprise (optional install), Ultimate
Hearts	A classic card game; a variation of whist	Home Premium, Business (optional install), Enterprise (optional install), Ultimate
Inkball	A Tablet PC-based title in which you use the stylus to push onscreen balls into holes in a maze	Home Premium, Business (optional install), Enterprise (optional install), Ultimate
Mahjong Titans	A curiously addictive Chinese tile game	Home Premium, Business (optional install), Enterprise (optional install), Ultimate
Minesweeper	The classic, updated for Windows Vista, in which you must uncover all of the spots on a grid that do not include a hidden bomb	Home Premium, Business (optional install), Enterprise (optional install), Ultimate
Purble Palace	A children's game title that is new to Windows Vista	Home Premium, Business (optional install), Enterprise (optional install), Ultimate
Solitaire	The classic single player card game in which you try to rearrange a shuffled deck of cards	Home Premium, Business (optional install), Enterprise (optional install), Ultimate
Spider Solitaire	A two-deck variant of Solitaire	Home Premium, Business (optional install), Enterprise (optional install), Ultimate

Using the Games Folder

Although the built-in games were relegated to the All Programs portion of the Start menu in previous Windows versions, Windows Vista now includes a special shell folder called Games and has elevated that folder to a position on the permanent, right-most side of the main Start menu display, as shown in Figure 14-1.

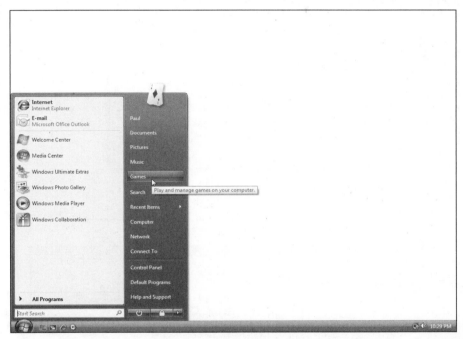

Figure 14-1: Apparently, games are as important in Windows Vista as the computer and the network.

When you select this option, you're shown the Games special shell folder, as referenced in Figure 14-2. Games is a handy front end to the games that are included with Windows Vista as well as a number of other game-related features.

As you select any of the built-in game titles, a preview of the game and its Entertainment Software Rating Board (ESRB) rating is displayed in the Reading Pane, which is found on the right side of the Games window.

> **tip** Depending on how you've installed or acquired Windows Vista, you may see additional games in the Games folder. For example, PC makers often include their own selection of game titles. And if you've upgraded from Windows XP, many of the games you had previously installed in that system should show up here as well.

To launch a game, simply double-click its icon. Or, select the icon and click the Play toolbar button. As you can see in Figure 14-3, the games included with Windows Vista are significantly more attractive than the games in previous Windows versions.

Figure 14-2: The Games special shell folder.

Figure 14-3: Looking good: Although none of these games will give *Halo 3* a run for its money, they're a lot better looking than the games that used to come with Windows.

As a special shell window, Games is customized in certain ways. The toolbar includes links to Games options, game-related tools, and Vista's parental controls, which provides a way for parents to restrict which games their kids can play (among other related functionality). If you select a game from the list of available titles, the toolbar will change to include a Play menu and a Community and Support button that links to the web site of the company, Oberon Games, which supplied the updated game titles in Windows Vista. We'll examine these features in the next few sections.

Secret   Some of these options appear only for built-in games. If you select a game you installed previously, for example, you will see a Play menu, but not the Community and Support button.

Game Updates and Options

Various Games options can be configured via the Set up Games options dialog box, which you can access via the Options button on the toolbar in the Games folder. Shown in Figure 14-4, this dialog box enables you to configure the few options that are directly related to Games.

Figure 14-4: Here, you can determine how the Games folder behaves.

Rating Your System's Performance

One of the more interesting features in Windows Vista is the new Performance Information and Tools functionality. Using a simple interface, you can let Windows Vista test your system, determine its overall performance rating on a scale from 1 to 5, and then get advice about ways to improve performance. This tool isn't just useful for game playing, but it should be quite interesting to gamers and anyone else who wants to ensure that their system is running as efficiently as possible.

To access this user interface, click the Tools button and then choose Performance Information and Tools from the drop-down menu. (Alternatively, you can find this tool in Control Panel⇨System and Maintenance⇨Performance Information and Tools.) Shown in Figure 14-5, this control panel gives you an idea of how fast your overall system is and rates individual components such as processor, memory, primary hard disk, graphics, and gaming graphics.

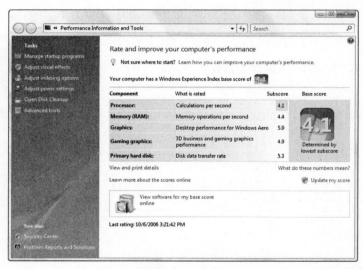

Figure 14-5: Performance Information and Tools puts your system to the test.

Typically, your PC's performance is tested and given a rating during initial setup. However, if you don't see a score — called the Windows Experience Index — or perhaps if you'd like to retest the system because you've made a hardware change, you will see a button titled Rate this computer. Press the button to run the test, which takes a few minutes and then returns a score. If you've already run the test, you can click the link titled Refresh this rating now to run the test again at any time.

| tip | Based on the scores your PC and individual components receive, you may want to make some upgrades. For example, a score below 3 in any one category should be a warning sign to any dedicated gamer. There's also a performance issues section that lists a number of general issues that could affect overall system performance. You can scan through the list and click any that you'd like to fix. This will cause a Solutions dialog box to appear, which steps you through the steps needed to fix the problem. |

Managing Your Game Controllers and Other Game-Related Hardware

In addition to working with actual games, you can manage your game-related hardware from the Games folder as well. If you click the Tools button in the toolbar, you'll see a number of items in the drop-down menu that are related to hardware gaming:

◆ **Hardware:** This option launches the Hardware and Sound Control Panel, from which you can perform such tasks as access configuration information for printers, audio devices, mouse, scanners and cameras, keyboard, and other hardware devices. Hardware and Sounds is shown in Figure 14-6.

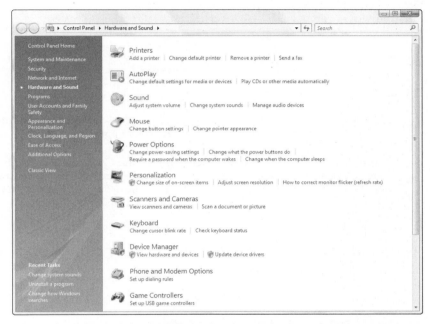

Figure 14-6: Hardware and Sounds is a handy front end to all of your hardware devices.

---

tip   This is also a handy place for accessing the Windows Device Manager, which can tell you whether you need updated drivers for any of your hardware devices. You'll see Device Manager in the list of options in the Hardware and Sound Control Panel.

◆ **Display Devices:** This option launches the Display Settings dialog box, as shown in Figure 14-7. What you see here will depend largely on your hardware, but the dialog box generally includes information about the displays and video cards attached to your system, and the screen resolution and color depth.

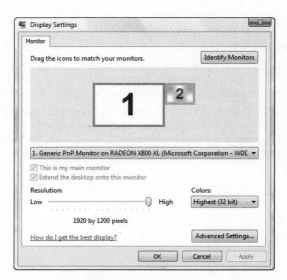

Figure 14-7: From Display Settings, you can access configuration information about your display devices, screen resolution, and color depth.

♦ **Input Devices:** This option launches the Game Controllers dialog box, which provides access to configuration information about any game controllers, such as the Microsoft Xbox 360 Controller for Windows, that you may have attached to your PC. The Game Controllers dialog box is shown in Figure 14-8.

Figure 14-8: Game Controllers lets you configure settings for your gaming controllers.

tip Most people actually play PC-based video games with the mouse and keyboard. You can access the properties for both of these devices from the Hardware and Sound Control Panel described previously.

◆ **Audio Devices:** This option launches the Sound dialog box, which provides access to the new sound device customization features included in Windows Vista. As you can see in Figure 14-9, this dialog box provides access to all of the sound-related hardware attached to your system and provides a separate tab for sound events and themes.

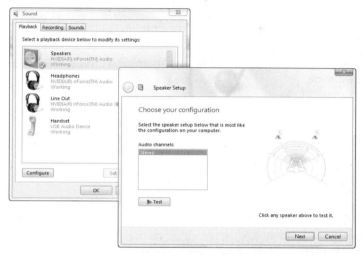

Figure 14-9: Audio Devices and Sound Themes is new to Windows Vista.

If you double-click an audio device in the list, you can deep-dive into its unique abilities. For example, the Volume Control playback device lets you configure how many speakers you have attached to the PC, various default volume levels, and much more.

There are also links for Firewall and Programs and Features, as follows:

◆ **Firewall:** This entry is important because some games require specific network ports to be open so that you can play against other people online.

◆ **Programs and Features**: The Control Panel applet that is your primary interface for uninstalling or changing applications.

Installing and Playing Third-Party Games

Windows Vista's built-in games are attractive and even occasionally addictive, but real gamers will want to install their own games. One of the big questions with Windows Vista concerns compatibility: How compatible will this system be with the mammoth Windows software libraries out there? The question is particularly problematic for games, because they tend to take more advantage of low-level hardware features that are typically hidden from within Windows.

Using Legacy Games with Windows Vista

In our testing of fairly recent and even several-year-old game titles (hey, someone has to do it), we've found Windows Vista to be reasonably compatible with so-called legacy game titles. In some cases, such as Valve's epic *Half-Life 2*, which is a modern 3D shooter, there's no work to be done at all: You simply install the game as before — albeit with the occasional User Account Protection (UAP) silliness. (See Chapter 9 for more information.)

Other games, especially older games, will require a bit of prodding. In some cases, Windows Vista includes compatibility information about certain problematic game titles. For example, when we installed Microsoft's classic *Halo: Combat Evolved*, we were presented with the dialog box shown in Figure 14-10: Halo has known compatibility issues with Windows Vista.

Figure 14-10: Microsoft knows there are issues running certain games on Windows Vista and tries to help.

Secret

This won't be a problem for *Halo 2*, which should ship around the same time as Windows Vista and be released exclusively for that operating system on the PC. That's right, you'll need Windows Vista to run *Halo 2*.

If you expand the See Details widget on this dialog box, you'll discover that *Halo* developer Bungie (a subsidiary of Microsoft) has released a Vista-compatible patch. The dialog box provides a link to download that patch so you can get back to the game. Prepare for another round of UAP foolishness, however. Just copying the two patched files you download into the Halo directory will require a mind-numbing series of UAP confirmation dialog boxes. Isn't security fun?

Adding Games to the Games Folder

Although this isn't documented anywhere, it's quite possible to add games you've installed on your PC to the Games special shell folder, so you can access them as you do the built-in games. Presumably, next-generation game titles will do this automatically so that they can integrate more closely with the games-related infrastructure Microsoft created in Windows Vista.

To add a third-party game title to the Games folder, simply drag a shortcut to the title into the folder. As you can see in Figure 14-11, legacy games such as *Halo* and *Half-Life 2* can be added directly to Games. Many games will be added automatically, however, so check before dragging and dropping.

Figure 14-11: You can add your own games to the Games folder, too.

Any games in the Games folder, including built-in games and third-party games, can be customized in very limited ways. If you look at the Play button in the Games toolbar, you'll see that it has a drop-down menu associated with it, with one choice: Customize. Click this option and the Customize dialog box is displayed, as shown in Figure 14-12.

What this does is let you create numerous shortcuts for a single game title. This is handy for a number of reasons. For example, some games come with different shortcuts for launching single player and multiplayer versions of the game. So this would be an obvious place to add a shortcut for the secondary version, which you could then access from the Play button's drop-down list. Other games enable you to add command-line options to access special game features. As any dedicated gamer knows, these options can often be used to unlock new features or even cheat.

Figure 14-12: With the Customize dialog box, you can create multiple launch points for each game.

Problems with *x64* Versions of Windows Vista

If you think the process of installing and playing older games in Windows Vista is difficult, then you'll want to avoid the *x64* versions of Windows Vista for a while. If you purchase a copy of Windows Vista at retail and install it on *x64*-based hardware — that is, a PC that includes an AMD or Intel microprocessor that includes the 64-bit *x64* processor instruction set — you will be able to install either the 32-bit or 64-bit version of Windows Vista. Our advice is simple: With very few exceptions, you're going to want to install the 32-bit version, not the *x64* version.

Here's why. Although the *x64* versions of Windows Vista will enable you to use more than 4 GB of RAM, very few people will have a need for such a thing during the lifetime of this OS version. The downsides to *x64*, however, are daunting. First, the *x64* versions of Windows Vista cannot utilize any of the thousands of 32-bit device drivers out there. So you'll have to make sure that you have a 64-bit driver for each and every hardware device you are, or will be, using. And right now, there are plenty of instances where 64-bit drivers aren't — and maybe never will be — available.

Second, software compatibility is more problematic in the *x64* versions of Windows Vista. Although Microsoft tried to engineer these versions of the OS to run 32-bit software — that is, virtually every single bit of Windows software produced before 2007 — many software packages refuse to install or run. And yes, you've guessed it, games are among the worst offenders. If you're a gamer, you will want to stick with the normal 32-bit Vista versions.

That said, some games will work find in the *x64* versions of Windows Vista, and some game makers are actually creating *x64* versions of their game titles so early adopters can experience next-generation computing. Over time, of course, this situation will get better and better. But for now, we believe that *x64* is just too problematic for most Windows users.

Downloading More Games for Windows Vista

In addition to the games that come with Windows Vista, the vast library of legacy game titles out there, and the unique Windows Vista game titles that developers will be creating, there's one more avenue for adding games to Windows Vista: Microsoft will be offering a variety of entertainment-related downloads via both Windows Updates and, for Ultimate edition users, the unique Windows Ultimate Extras.

Shown in Figure 14-13, Windows Ultimate Extras is a special benefit of using the most advanced Windows Vista edition. Ultimate edition users will gain access to a number of special features via this interface, including unique applications and services, and even tutorials. Some of these applications will be games, of course.

Figure 14-13: Windows Ultimate Extras is a special bonus that customers get for buying the most expensive Vista version.

Secret

Although Microsoft is tight-lipped about exactly which games it plans to ship in the months after Windows Vista is finally released, we do know that certain locales will gain access to a special version of the Texas Hold 'Em poker game that's quite popular these days. Apparently, Microsoft won't be happy unless we never leave the house.

Summary

There's no doubt about it: Windows Vista will be the ultimate operating system for gamers, and a better destination than even the Xbox 360 or Sony's Playstation 3. With its array of nicely spiffed-up built-in games, parental controls aimed at helping keep children away from inappropriate games, stellar support for gaming hardware, and a handy Games explorer that works nicely with third-party games, Vista has it all. And if you're lucky enough to own Windows Vista Ultimate, you can look forward to some extra perks as well.

Part V

Mobility

Computing to Go: Windows Vista Mobility Features

◆ ◆

In This Chapter

Managing the Windows Vista user interface settings for optimal performance and battery life

Discovering new power management features

Creating and using your own power plans

Utilizing the new Windows Mobility Center

Exploring new features aimed at presentations

Accessing files and folders while disconnected from the network

Holding ad hoc meetings with others over your own wireless network

Using Windows SideShow

◆ ◆

Windows Vista is the ultimate version of Windows for users on the go. Whether you use a notebook computer, Tablet PC, or Ultra-Mobile PC, you won't get a better mobile experience than what's available in Microsoft's latest operating system. This time around, Microsoft has fortified Windows with new user interface, power management, and presentation capabilities, along with a suite of mobile-oriented applications and utilities that tie it all together. We'll examine each of these features in this chapter.

Windows Vista on the Road

Over the years, Microsoft has steadily improved Windows to better take advantage of the unique hardware features and capabilities offered by portable computers such as notebooks, laptops, and Tablet PCs (including a new generation of tablet devices called Ultra-Mobile Personal Computers, or UMPCs). For the most part, using Windows Vista on a notebook computer or other portable PC is just like using it on a desktop PC. That is, a notebook computer can do anything a desktop PC can, and Windows Vista doesn't offer a limited feature set when you're using a portable PC.

That said, you may want to approach Windows Vista a bit differently when using a notebook computer. Certain operating system features, such as the user interface or power management plan you select, can impact both performance and battery life when you're not connected to power, for example. And Vista includes special presentation, security, and networking features that are often specific to portable computers or at least work somewhat differently when you're using a portable PC.

---

tip   In this chapter, we're going to use terms like *portable PC, portable computer, notebook, laptop,* and even, occasionally, *Tablet PC* to describe mobile computers running Windows Vista. For the most part, these terms are largely interchangeable in the context of this chapter unless specifically stated otherwise.

Working with the Vista User Interface

One of the most obvious improvements in Windows Vista is the Windows Aero user interface, which we discuss in Chapter 4. Windows Aero offers several unique features compared to the other user interface options available in Windows Vista, including translucency, various special effects, and even access to certain Windows features, such as Windows Flip 3D. On the other hand, Windows Aero is hardware intensive and thus can result in poorer battery than the other user interface choices. Thus, the decision whether to use Windows Aero — shown in Figure 15-1 — should come down to how you feel about battery life, performance, and usability.

Before we get to that, however, you should also be aware that many portable computers simply don't include enough graphical processing power to even run Windows Aero. If this is the case, you will typically see the Windows Vista Basic user interface instead. Windows Standard offers an enticing middle ground between the beauty of Windows Aero and the power management thriftiness and performance of Windows Classic, the low-end user interface that is designed to resemble the user interface from Windows 2000.

Figure 15-1: Windows Aero is gorgeous looking but can drain a notebook's battery more quickly than other Windows Vista user interface choices.

So depending on your hardware, your choice might already be made: If you install Windows Vista on a portable PC, and the user interface is set as Windows Vista Basic and not Windows Aero, then you're out of luck: Your system is not capable of displaying Vista's highest end user interface.

Secret

Okay, that's not strictly true. There is a chance that Windows Vista simply didn't install the very latest driver for your display hardware. Before diving into despair, consult the documentation for your notebook, find out exactly which display hardware it uses, and then visit the hardware maker's web site and obtain the very latest driver to see if that makes a difference.

tip

In order to run Windows Aero, you need a DirectX 9–compatible 3D video card with 64 MB or more of discrete graphics RAM, depending on the resolution of your display (64MB is adequate for a 1024x768 display, but you'll need 128 MB or more for higher resolutions). Virtually all integrated graphics chips — the types that share RAM with the system and are more common on notebooks — are not capable of displaying Aero. The one exception at the time of this writing is Intel's GMA 950. This integrated chipset works just fine with Aero.

Assuming your machine is powerful enough to display Windows Aero, you might still want to opt for the Windows Basic user interface, because of its thriftier power management. However, Windows Aero is more stable and reliable than other user interfaces because of the way it interacts with the underlying system and signed drivers from hardware makers. Like all trade-offs, the decision is not an easy one. Our advice is to test how your particular system behaves on battery power while using both user interfaces. If the battery life difference between the two is negligible, go with Windows Aero.

To change the user interface, right-click the desktop and choose Personalize from the resulting pop-up menu. This displays the Personalization Control Panel window. The first option, Windows Color And Appearance, lets you choose between user interface types. If you click this option and see the dialog shown in Figure 15-2, then you're running Windows Vista Basic, and there's no way to enable Windows Aero short of contacting the notebook maker and finding a Vista-capable driver.

Figure 15-2: If you see this dialog box, you're running Windows Vista Basic.

If, however, you see the window shown in Figure 15-3, then you're running Windows Aero, the high-end user interface.

From here, you can make two changes that will impact the performance and battery life of Windows Vista.

◆ First, you can turn off Windows translucency by unchecking the Enable Transparency option. Translucency is a fun feature, but it doesn't really aid productivity, so this is an obvious candidate for change.

◆ The second option is to use Windows Vista Basic instead of Aero. To do so, click the Open Classic Properties For More Color Options link at the bottom of the window. This will display the dialog box shown back in Figure 15-3. Select the Windows Vista Basic option (and not the confusingly named Windows Standard option) to invoke Windows Vista Basic.

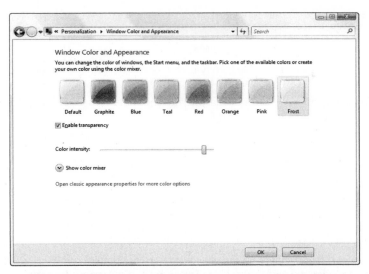

Figure 15-3: This window signifies that you're running Windows Aero.

Secret

Early in Windows Vista's development, Microsoft promised that the OS would seamlessly move between Windows Aero, while attached to power, and Windows Basic, while the machine was untethered and running on battery. This feature, sadly, was never added to the final version of Windows Vista, forcing users to manually switch between user interface modes. Curiously, Vista will, however, automatically move between the two environments if you launch an application that is incompatible with Aero. Such applications include many games, but also productivity applications like Microsoft Virtual PC 2004 and Apple QuickTime 7.

Power Management

Although even desktop-based computers running Windows Vista support various power management features, this functionality is so much richer and varied on portable computers, which is the reason we're discussing it here in this chapter. Windows Vista's power management functionality can be accessed throughout the user interface in various ways, but the easiest way to think of power management in Vista is that it comprises three basic areas: A new notification area-based icon, a Power Options control panel, and a newly simplified set of power plans. We'll examine each of these features in this section.

Updated Battery Meter

Mobile computing users are quite familiar with the battery meter that's been in the tray notification area since Windows 95. This handy icon has been significantly updated in Windows Vista and can appear in various states, which change the look of the icon. The state you see will depend on whether the machine is connected to a power source, and how well the battery is charged. Table 15-1 summarizes the various icon types you can expect to see.

Table 15-1: Windows Vista Battery Meter States

Icon	State	What It Means
	Charged, plugged in	The battery is completely charged and the system is plugged into a wall outlet.
	Charging, plugged in	The battery is charging while the system is plugged into a wall outlet.
	On battery power	The battery is discharging because the system is operating on battery power.

Secret

Although the new battery meter now offers far more functionality than before, you may find it all a bit bewildering. That's because the new battery meter offers a completely different experience depending on how you decide to interact with it. Here are the various actions you can perform with the battery meter:

- **Mouse-over:** If you move the mouse cursor over the battery meter, it will display the pop-up shown in Figure 15-4. This pop-up summarizes the state of the battery and provides a link to access the system's power plans.

Figure 15-4: This handy pop-up provides you with an at-a-glance look at the state of power management for your system.

- **Single-click:** If you click the battery meter icon once, you'll see the larger pop-up shown in Figure 15-5. This pop-up provides the same information as the mouse-over pop-up, but it also enables you to select from one of three preset power plans — we discuss power plans in the next section — and access other power management–related OS features.

Figure 15-5: This pop-up offers a wealth of power management functionality in a relatively small space.

- **Right-click:** If you right-click the battery meter, you'll see the pop-up menu shown in Figure 15-6. From this menu, you can access Power Options (discussed later), Windows Mobility Center (discussed later in this chapter), or click an option curiously titled Show System Icons, which brings up the Taskbar and Start Menu Properties window's Notification Area tab. From this dialog box you can turn off the battery meter (identified as Power) if you'd like. Our advice: Leave it on if you're using a mobile computer.

Figure 15-6: This pop-up menu offers a way to access the Windows Vista mobile and power management features.

tip   Curiously, if you double-click the battery meter, nothing happens.

Power Plans

Microsoft has simplified the power plans in Windows Vista. These power plans are used to manage your PC's use of its power resources, both while attached to power and battery. There are three preconfigured power plans, but you can modify each of them to suit your needs, and you can even add your own power plans if you'd like.

tip   Confusingly, your PC maker might make its own machine-specific power plans as well, so if you purchased a notebook with Windows Vista preinstalled, you could see additional plans listed.

The three built-in power plans are discussed in the following sections.

Balanced

This default plan balances power management between power consumption and performance. It does this based on how you're using the computer at the time. If you begin playing a game or accessing Vista's multimedia features, Windows Vista will automatically ratchet up the processor speed to make sure you don't experience any slowdowns. But if you're just browsing the Web or reading text documents, Vista will slow the processor down as much as possible, conserving battery power.

By default, the Balanced power plan turns off the display after 60 minutes of inactivity, and turns off the hard drive after 20 minutes of inactivity while the machine is plugged in. After 2 hours of inactivity, the computer will go to sleep. Under battery power, Windows will turn off the display after 15 minutes of inactivity, and will turn off the hard drive after 10 minutes of inactivity. Windows puts the PC to sleep after 60 minutes of inactivity while on battery power.

Power Saver

This plan sacrifices performance for better battery life. It should be used only by those with light computing requirements that are trying to maximize uptime while on the road.

Here's how Power Saver affects your power management settings. Even when plugged in, Windows Vista aggressively decreases the processor speed and display brightness. After 20 minutes of inactivity Windows turns off the display and hard drive, and then puts the computer to sleep after an hour. On battery power, Windows Vista will turn off the display after 3 minutes and the hard drive after 5 minutes. Then, Windows will put the PC to sleep after 15 minutes of inactivity.

High Performance

The High Performance plan provides the highest level of performance by maximizing the system's processor speed at the expense of battery life. This plan is aimed at those who spend most of their time playing modern video games or working in graphic-intensive applications.

Under the High Performance plan, Windows Vista will turn off the display and hard drive after 20 minutes of inactivity, but the computer is never put to sleep. On battery power, the PC's display and hard drive are turned off after 20 minutes, and the computer is put to sleep after 1 hour.

Secret Desktop PCs utilize power plans as well. So even though you likely won't see a battery meter icon in the tray notification area on such a system, it's worthwhile to navigate into Control Panel⇨Hardware and Sound⇨Power Options, to ensure that the High Performance power plan is selected. That's absolutely the most relevant preset power plan for a desktop-bound PC.

Scanning through the power plans, it's likely that you'll find a plan that at least somewhat matches your expectations. But you don't have to accept the Microsoft default settings. You can easily modify any of the existing plans and even, optionally, create your own power plans. We'll look at those possibilities in the very next section.

Power Options Control Panel

Windows Vista's power options are, go figure, configured via the Power Options Control Panel applet, which is available in Control Panel⇨Mobile PC⇨Power Options on a notebook computer, or Control Panel⇨Hardware and Sound⇨Power Options on a desktop PC. Shown in Figure 15-7, this Control Panel initially presents a choice of the three power plans mentioned previously.

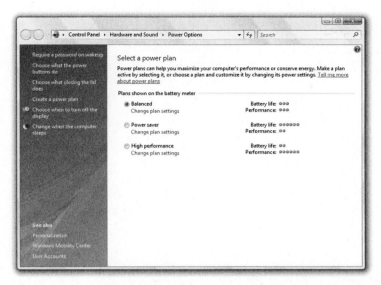

Figure 15-7: Power Options is your central management console for the Windows Vista power management features.

There's a lot more going on here, however. On the left of the window, you'll see a number of power management related tasks. If you're using a mobile computer of any kind, you're going to want to navigate through each of these options to ensure your system is configured exactly the way you want it.

> **tip** Some of the options listed there are available from the Mobile PC or Hardware and Sound page in Control Panel as well.

Requiring a Password on Wakeup

The first option, Require a password on wakeup, can differ a bit depending on the capabilities of your system, and there's a lot more going on here beyond the password option hinted at in the link. On a typical desktop PC, this Control Panel page will resemble Figure 15-8.

But when you view this page on a typical notebook computer, you'll see more options, as shown in Figure 15-9. These options are directly related to the additional hardware buttons and features that you get with mobile computers.

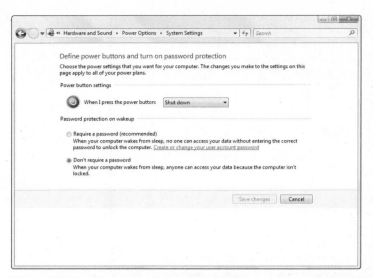

Figure 15-8: Desktop PCs don't have many power management options related to hardware features.

Figure 15-9: Notebook computers and other mobile PCs offer power management options related to the lid and other hardware features.

Here, you can modify how Windows Vista reacts when you press the power button, press the sleep button, or, on portable computers configured with a lid-based display, what happens when you close the lid. Each of these choices has different settings for when the system is operating on battery power and plugged in.

In keeping with the Require a password on wakeup task referenced on the previous page, this dialog box also includes a single wakeup-related option that determines whether you need to logon again each time the system wakes up after being in the sleep state. By default, Windows Vista does require you to logon again to unlock the computer as a security measure. We strongly advise leaving this feature configured as is, especially if you're a mobile computer user who often accesses the PC on the road.

Choosing What the Power Button Does

Humorously, this option triggers the same dialog as described previously. The top half of the dialog relates to this option.

Choosing What Closing the Lid Does

This option, which is available only on portable computers with a lid, also brings you to the same dialog described previously.

Creating a Power Plan

When you click this option, you're brought to the Create A Power Plan page, which is a short wizard you can use to create your own power plan.

1. In the first step, you choose the preset power plan—Balanced, Power Saver, or High Performance—that you would like to base your plan on. Then, you give the plan a name and press Next.

2. In the next phase of the wizard, shown in Figure 15-10, you determine when the system will turn off the display and put the system to sleep, on both battery power and when plugged in. (Desktop PC users will only see options for plugged in.)

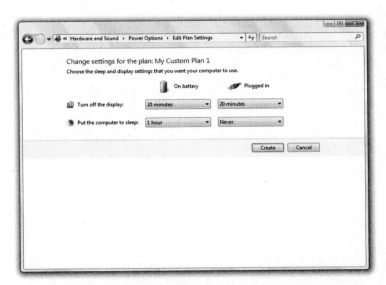

Figure 15-10: Curiously, you don't get options for turning off the hard disk.

3. Click the Create button to create your plan. You'll see that your power plan has been added to the list of available plans, as seen in Figure 15-11.

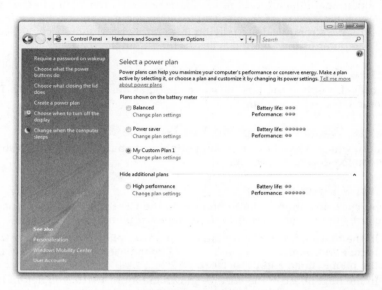

Figure 15-11: Custom power plans replace the plan on which your plan was based, but the old default plans are still available.

This is all well and good, but the short wizard we just used doesn't really provide access to all of the power management options that are available. To modify your custom plan, or an existing preset plan, click the Change Plan Settings link below the plan name. This brings you to a dialog that resembles the second phase of the wizard just described, but with one difference: There's now a Change Advanced Power Settings link. Click that link to modify other settings. Doing so opens the Advanced Settings dialog box, shown in Figure 15-12.

Figure 15-12: From this rather complicated dialog box, you can handcraft your power plan using every single power management option available to Windows Vista.

Secret

It would require an entire book to document every option found in this nasty, tree control-based dialog box. But here are a few options we've found to make a huge difference.

- **Hard disk:** Configure the hard disk to wind down after a period of time to preserve battery life. On battery, you want this time to be reasonably low, say, 10 minutes.

- **Sleep:** Newer PCs support a new type of Sleep mode called Hybrid Sleep, which lets the machine appear to turn off and on almost immediately, like a consumer electronics device. If you have a mobile PC manufactured after mid-2006, it might support this feature, so experiment with enabling Hybrid Sleep. Alternatively, you might want to enable Hibernation, which was a major power management feature in Windows XP. Hibernation is faster than turning on and off the PC, but it also preserves the state of the system so you can get back up and running with your applications more quickly.

- **Processor power management:** If you have a modern Intel or AMD microprocessor, you can fine-tune how much processor power is used under certain states. This one is for power users only, and it replaces a nifty utility Intel used to ship for its mobile microprocessors.

- **Search and indexing:** Windows Vista's integrated search functionality is wonderful, but it can be a real drag on system performance, especially when it's indexing content. To minimize the impact on your system, especially consider reducing the load that search and indexing can occupy on battery power.

- **Battery:** The battery in a Windows Vista–based mobile PC is configured to warn you or perform certain actions at specific times, such as when the battery is low or critically low. You can configure these features here.

Choosing When to Turn Off the Display

This option triggers the same dialog as described previously.

Changing When the Computer Sleeps

This option also triggers the same dialog as described previously in the "Requiring a Password on Wakeup" section.

Windows Mobility Center

If you've ever owned a mobile PC, you've probably marveled (and not in a good way) at the cruddy utility applications that PC makers seem compelled to ship with their hardware. Microsoft feels your pain. So in Windows Vista, for the first time, the software giant has taken the first steps toward creating a centralized management console called Windows Mobility Center for all of this functionality, and it has preloaded the thing with all of the utilities a mobile user could want. Best of all, PC makers are free to extend Mobility Center with their own notebook-related utilities. We can't guarantee they'll be any good, but at least they'll be easily located if the PC maker develops them correctly.

Shown in Figure 15-13, Windows Mobility Center is available only on mobile computers. You won't see it on desktop PCs.

Figure 15-13: Windows Mobility Center looks nothing like any other Windows Vista applications.

Curiously, Windows Mobility Center in no way resembles any of the other applications that Microsoft bundled with Windows Vista. Instead, a set of mobile-related options are arrayed in cubes across an unadorned window that cannot be resized or formatted in any way. These options include Volume, Battery Status, Wireless Network, External Display, Sync Center, and Presentation Settings.

Basically, each of these cubes launches a setting that mobile PC users need fairly often. Click the icon in the Volume cube, for example, and the Audio Devices and Themes dialog box appears. Or, you can set or mute the system volume from directly within Mobility Center.

Secret

With one exception, all of the options made available in Mobility Center are available elsewhere in the Windows Vista user interface. That one exception is Presentation Settings, which we look at in the next section.

tip   Remember, you might see additional cubes here that were installed by your PC maker.

Presentations A-Go-Go

Although not a particularly glamorous lifestyle, many mobile users cart their notebooks around the globe, set them up in an unfamiliar location, and attempt to give a presentation using Microsoft PowerPoint or a similar presentation package. Notebooks are perfect companions for such users because of their portability. But until Windows Vista, they weren't particularly accommodating if the presentation was being given on battery power. In Windows Vista, Microsoft has added two major features related to giving presentations, one of which solves the problem mentioned above.

Presentation Settings

An obscure but useful feature, Presentation Settings lets you temporarily disable your normal power management settings and ensures that your system stays awake, with no screen dimming, no hard drive disabling, no screensaver activation, and no system notifications to interrupt you. In other words, with one click of the mouse (well, a few anyway), you can set up your mobile PC to behave exactly the way you'd want it to while giving a presentation.

To enable Presentation Settings, run Mobility Center as described in the previous section and click the projector icon in the Presentation Settings cube. Presentation Settings is shown in Figure 15-14.

Select the I Am Currently Giving A Presentation option to enable Presentation Settings. Optionally, you can turn off the screen saver (the default), turn off the system volume, and temporarily change the desktop background. Presentation Settings also provides a handy way to configure connected displays, including network projectors.

tip   You can also enable Presentations with a single click by clicking the Turn On button in the Presentation Settings cube in Windows Mobility Center. Regardless of how you enable this feature, the Presentation Settings cube will change to read Presenting, and the projector icon will change to an On state.

Figure 15-14: Presentation Settings is a boon to anyone who's had to struggle with Windows getting in the way of a presentation.

Using a Network Projector

If you're going to show a presentation via a modern network-based projector, Windows Vista includes a Connect to a Network Projector utility that automatically configures firewall settings and searches for nearby projectors. To run this utility, find Connect to a Network Project in Start Menu⇨All Programs⇨Accessories. You can search for a projector automatically or enter the projector's IP address.

Other Mobile Features

In addition to the major new mobility-related features mentioned previously, Windows Vista ships with a host of other technologies that will benefit mobile workers. In this section, we'll highlight some of these features and explain how you can best take advantage of them.

Offline Files and Folders

In Windows XP, Microsoft introduced a feature called Offline Files and Folders that allowed mobile users to mark network-based files and folders so that they would be cached locally, using space on the mobile computer's hard drive. When the mobile PC is connected to the network, the local and remote versions of the files and folders are synchronized so that they are always up to date. When the user works away from the network—which can be a corporate network based on Active Directory or just a simple wireless home network—they can access these remote resources even when in a disconnected state, just as if they were connected.

Offline Files and Folders is a wonderful idea, and it's been made even better in Windows Vista. It works almost exactly as before, as we'll outline, but now Windows Vista uses Delta Sync technology, first developed by Microsoft's Windows Server team, to speed synchronization. Delta Sync works on the sub-file level: If a user changes part of a document, for example, only the changed parts of the document need to be synced to the server. Previously, the entire document would need to be synchronized.

To set up Offline Files and Folders for the first time, use the new Network Explorer to navigate to a location on your network that contains files or folders you'd like to cache locally. Then, right-click the items you'd like to cache and choose Always Available Offline. When you do so, the Always Available Offline dialog box is displayed, as shown in Figure 15-15, and synchronize the content to your hard drive.

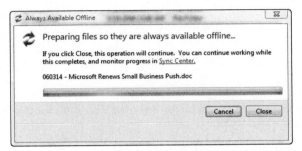

Figure 15-15: You can configure network-based data to be available even when you're not connected to the network.

When the synchronization is complete, you'll see a small sync icon overlay appear on top of the lower left of the folder or file you just synced. This icon overlay indicates that the item is available offline.

tip   **To remove this association, right-click again and uncheck Always Available Offline.**

In Windows XP, Offline Files and Folders were managed via the Folder Options window. Now, in Windows Vista, you manage these relationships in the new Sync Center, which is shown in Figure 15-16. The Sync Center is used to manage relationships between Windows Vista and portable devices (like MP3 players and PDAs) as well as offline files and folders. It does not, however, manage relationships with network-based media devices, like other PCs, Xbox 360s, and Media Center Extenders. No, we don't know why either.

Regardless of how many network-based files and folders you make available offline, you will only see one item, titled Offline Files, in the main Sync Center display. If you double-click this item, you can dive into the partnership detail, and see separate items for each network share that contains shared files and folders. Or, you can click the Sync button to manually synchronize with the server, or click Schedule to view and manage the sync schedule. The schedule is managed via a simple wizard-based application that lets you schedule synchronization at specific times or in response to certain events, such as when you log on or lock Windows, or when your computer is idle.

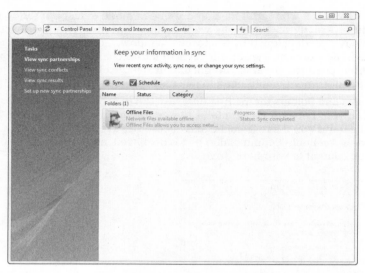

Figure 15-16: Sync Center is an almost one-stop shop for Windows Vista's relationships with other devices and network-based files and folders.

If you take your system on the road and modify network-based files and folders, they will be synchronized with the server when you return. Should there be any conflicts—such as what could happen when a file is edited both on the server and in your local cache, you'll be given the opportunity to rectify the conflict in a variety of ways, most of which are non-destructive.

Windows Meeting Space

In a nod to the peer-to-peer technologies that have been sweeping across the PC industry since the Napster phenomenon of a decade ago, Windows Vista includes a new peer-to-peer service called Windows Meeting Space that is oriented towards collaboration, not stealing music. (Presumably any technology can be used for good or evil.) Windows Meeting Space enables you to share documents, applications, or your entire desktop with other network-equipped Windows Vista users near you, and can automatically set up an ad hoc network if no wired or wireless network is available.

Secret

To use this ad hoc network, however, each user would need to have a Windows Vista–equipped machine with a properly configured wireless card. Meeting Space is most often used by notebook users for this reason, and it's useful when coworkers are together in a coffee shop, airport, meeting, or hotel and need to collaborate, even when there's no wireless network (or when the network in question requires a usage fee).

To start Windows Meeting Space, you need to first configure the new People Near Me service of Windows Vista, which helps Vista identify other users near you—both physically and on the same network subnet—that meet the technical qualifications of Meeting

Space. The first time you run Meeting Space, you'll be prompted to configure People Near Me with your name and various other options, as shown in Figure 15-17.

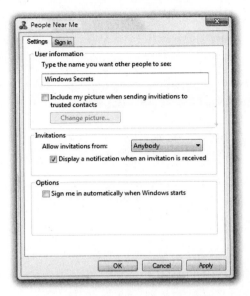

Figure 15-17: People Near Me is the Windows Vista feature that helps Windows Meeting Place find other people with which to collaborate.

After People Near Me is configured, you'll be presented with the main Windows Meeting Space application window, as seen in Figure 15-18. This window enables you to start a new meeting or find other meetings in progress nearby.

Figure 15-18: Windows Meeting Space is a peer-to-peer collaboration application.

To start a new meeting, click Start A New Meeting. Then, provide a name, passphrase, and, optionally, other meeting-related options as prompted. Then, a new Meeting Space will be shown, with panes for sharing applications or the desktop, people nearby, and handout downloads (see Figure 15-19).

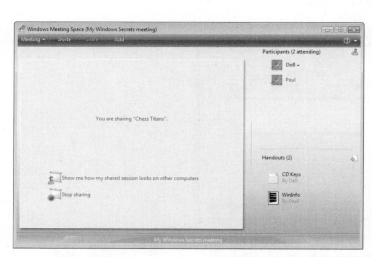

Figure 15-19: Virtual meetings can get as busy as physical meetings, with multiple participants and lots of work.

From here, the person who started the meeting—called the meeting presenter—can share applications or his or her entire desktop, and the display will be remotely routed to each participant (maximize the window for best results). You can also pass electronic notes to each other, as with an instant messaging (IM) application, and participants can copy documents into the Handouts well so that other users can download them.

Windows SideShow

A coming generation of Tablet PCs and notebook computers—and, we're told, even desktop computers and servers—will soon sport a new kind of auxiliary display that lets you access certain information on the computer, even when it's asleep. These auxiliary displays will initially be most interesting on mobile computers, and they'll come in color and black and white versions.

Here's how they work: Auxiliary displays access a feature in Windows Vista called SideShow to display small gadgets, similar to those used by the Windows Sidebar (see Chapter 6), that provide limited access to various applications and services in Windows. You'll see a Windows Media Player gadget that will let you play music in your Windows Media Player 11 media library, and an e-mail gadget that will help you read e-mail. All of these gadgets work when the laptop's lid is closed, and they require very little power, and come on instantly. And although Microsoft will no doubt include a number of gadgets in Windows itself, we can expect third parties to come up with their own gadgets as well.

The bad news about Windows SideShow is that you need very specific hardware to access this feature. You can't add on an auxiliary display, at least not elegantly, to a mobile PC. So you'll need to get a brand-new mobile device with an integrated auxiliary display in order to experience it for yourself.

Improved Support for Tablet PC Hardware

If you're using a Tablet PC computer—a notebook computer that typically comes in one of two form factors, a convertible laptop or a true slate-type tablet—or a notebook computer with Tablet PC–like hardware, such as a touch screen, digitizer screen with stylus, or a compatible external writing pad, Windows Vista includes a wide range of functionality related to handwriting recognition, pen-based input, and the like. We discuss these features in Chapter 16, which is devoted entirely to Tablet PCs and other computers that have Tablet-like hardware.

Summary

There's no doubt about it: Windows Vista is the most capable and feature-packed operating system yet created for mobile computers. Thanks to new features like Windows Mobility Center, Presentation Settings, network projector support, Windows Meeting Space, and People Near Me, and massive changes to power management, Windows Vista will keep any mobile computer humming along nicely with a wide range of new and improved functionality.

New Tablet PC Features

Chapter
16

◆ ◆

In This Chapter

Learning about the history of the Tablet PC and Microsoft's pen-enabled software

Discovering the changes to Tablet PC functionality Microsoft made in Windows Vista

Using and configuring Tablet PC features

Entering handwritten text with the Tablet PC Input Panel

Using Flicks and other gestures

Controlling your computer with speech recogition

Understanding Tablet PC–related changes to the Windows shell

Accessing Tablet PC utilities like the Snipping Tool, Windows Journal, and Sticky Notes

◆ ◆

During the lifecycle of Windows XP, Microsoft shipped two versions of that OS that were targeted specifically at Tablet PCs, a new type of mobile computer based on notebooks that added digitized screens and pens for a more natural style of interaction. Tablet PCs flopped, but Microsoft's software was, for once, widely heralded for its high quality. So with Windows Vista, Microsoft has made the Tablet PC capabilities available to a far wider range of PCs and has lifted the restrictions on how users acquire these capabilities. It's now possible to get Tablet PC functionality in most mainstream versions of Windows Vista.

A Short History of the Tablet PC

In mid-2002, Microsoft released the first version of Windows XP that was specifically targeted at a new generation of pen-based notebook computers called Tablet PCs. Logically named Windows XP Tablet PC Edition, this software wasn't, of course, the first to try to tie pens (or, really, styli) and PCs together. Indeed, as long ago as the late 1980s, innovative companies such as Go, Apple, and Palm were plying the way to a future of more ergonomic and natural interactions with computers. Even Microsoft got into the game in the early 1990s with a short-lived (and overhyped) product called Pen Windows.

But Tablet PCs were different. First, they were mainstream computers with added functionality such as displays with built-in digitizers that could not only sense pen input, but understand when the tip was pressed down harder or lighter. Second, they came in two form factors. The first was called a tablet, although it's sometimes referred to as a slate design. These machines did not include integrated keyboards and trackpads, but were instead intended to be used primarily via the pen. You could, of course, attach keyboards, mice, and even auxiliary displays to these machines.

The second was called a convertible laptop. These machines looked just like regular laptops, but with one difference: The screen could be swiveled around and rotated back onto the keyboard, giving the machine a temporary slate-like form factor. In this way, a convertible laptop could be used like a regular notebook computer — with a keyboard and trackpad — or like a slate-type Tablet, via the pen.

First-generation Tablet PCs didn't exactly take off in the market. There are many reasons for this, but for once, Microsoft wasn't to blame. In fact, the initial version of Windows XP Tablet PC Edition was surprisingly solid. It was based on Windows XP Professional, and thus could do everything that XP Pro could. It supported a variety of screen digitizer types, could perform decent handwriting recognition, could switch the display between landscape and portrait modes on the fly (to better simulate writing on a pad of paper), and included some worthwhile software, like a Windows Journal note-taking application, a Sticky Notes utility, a game, and an add-on pack for Office that gave it better Tablet capabilities. All in all, it was an excellent release. Windows XP Tablet PC Edition is shown in Figure 16-1.

So why did Tablet PCs fail in the market? For starters, they were too expensive. Partly to offset research and development costs, and partially to help pay for XP Tablet PC Edition, which carried a premium over other XP editions, PC makers priced first-generation Tablet PCs too high. The machines were also woefully underpowered, with sad Pentium III Mobile processors and horrible battery life. Many users who might have otherwise been interested in the ultimate mobile companion gave up given the prices, performance, and battery life.

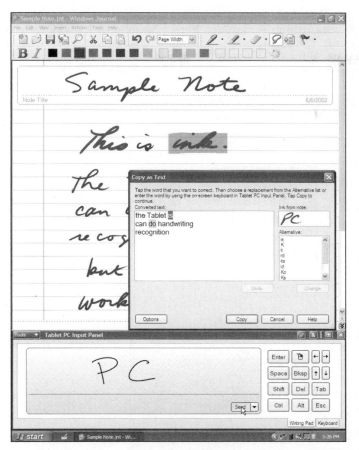

Figure 16-1: Microsoft's original Tablet PC operating system was surprisingly good, but it floundered in the market.

Microsoft trudged on, thanks in part to the involvement of Bill Gates, the company's co-founder and then the chairman and chief architect of the software firm. Gates was convinced that Tablet PCs were the future, and in late 2004 the company shipped its second version of Windows XP aimed at Tablet PCs. Dubbed Windows XP Tablet PC Edition 2005, this software benefited from the release of Intel's Centrino and Pentium-M chipsets, which offered notebook makers dramatically better performance and battery life. New Tablet PC designs showed up, with both larger and smaller form factors, giving the customer more choices. And prices came down. Now, it's possible to get a Tablet PC for little more than a comparable notebook. Some PC makers even include Tablet capabilities as an add-on option.

Windows XP Tablet PC Edition 2005 added a new version of the Tablet PC Input Panel (TIP), a pop-up window which is used to translate handwriting into non-Tablet-enhanced applications. The new TIP included real-time recognition, so that handwriting was translated on the fly, giving you the option to correct as you wrote, rather than later, after a line of text was entered. XP Tablet PC Edition 2005 was also contextually aware, so that the system could filter its handwriting recognition library based on what you were doing in order to get better results. For example, if you're entering script into a text field that only accepts numbers, the OS will only test your handwriting against numbers, not its entire library of characters. Windows XP Tablet PC Edition 2005 is shown in Figure 16-2.

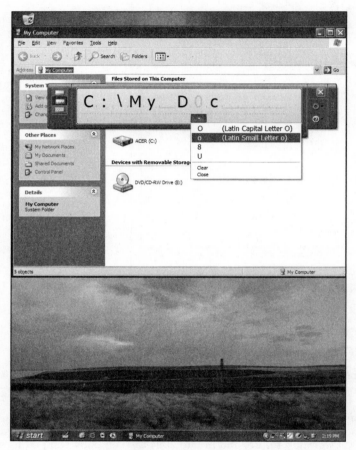

Figure 16-2: Windows XP Tablet PC Edition 2005 offered many improvements over its predecessor, including an enhanced TIP.

Like its predecessor, Windows XP Tablet PC Edition 2005 was technically excellent and, like its predecessor, it failed to make much of a dent in the market, despite a seemingly endless market of students, factory floor workers, roaming sales people, doctors, and many others that would benefit from this platform. Part of the reason for this continued lackluster success was that customers couldn't use just any PC with XP Tablet PC Edition 2005: They had to purchase a system with that software preinstalled. You couldn't use any digitizer, like the millions of available pen input systems out there, typically in use by graphic designers. And it didn't support touch screen interaction.

All these issues were addressed in Windows Vista. Indeed, the Tablet PC features in Windows Vista are the best yet.

Tablet PC Capabilities in Windows Vista

For Windows Vista, Microsoft has decided to open up the market for Tablet PC functionality dramatically. There is no Windows Vista Tablet PC Edition. Instead, users will automatically get Tablet PC functionality if they use Windows Vista Business, Enterprise, Home Premium, or Ultimate editions. The software itself has been enhanced somewhat dramatically, and you can now use it with a coming generation of touch screens, digitizers, and other devices. That's right, you don't even need a true Tablet PC. More to the point, many Tablet PC features work even if you're just using a keyboard and mouse, although of course such systems are only marginally interesting.

Using a Tablet PC

In Windows Vista, using the Tablet PC functionality is virtually identical to the way it worked in Windows XP Tablet PC Edition, but naturally with a few enhancements. Windows Journal, Sticky Notes, and the Tablet PC Input Panel (TIP) all make it over with some functional improvements, as does the Snipping Tool, a favorite Tablet PC download that Microsoft used to provide separately. In this section, we'll examine how the Tablet PC functionality has improved in Windows Vista.

Configuring Tablet PC Features

Before using your Tablet PC or tablet-equipped PC with a stylus or other pointing device, you should probably take the time to configure the Tablet PC functionality that's built into Windows Vista. If you have tablet hardware, you'll see a few items in the shell that aren't available on non-Tablet hardware, including a handy way to select multiple items with a pen, a few new tray notification icons that appear over time, and the same reordering of Control Panel items that one sees when using Windows Vista with a notebook computer. With the exception of that last item, we'll examine these features throughout this chapter.

Tablet PC features are configured via the Control Panel, through the Tablet PC Settings option in Mobile PC. This dialog box, shown in Figure 16-3, includes four tabs that help configure the system for tablet use.

Secret

If you're using a non-Tablet system, the Tablet PC features are found in a different location: Control Panel⇨Hardware and Sound⇨Tablet PC Settings.

Figure 16-3: The Tablet PC Settings dialog box is an important first stop for any tablet user.

Using Tablet PC Settings

In the General tab, you configure the Tablet PC for right- or left-handed use and determine the screen orientation (portrait or landscape). This tab also provides a link to Microsoft's Digitizer Calibration Tool, which is used to ensure that the pen hits the screen on target. Anyone who's used a Pocket PC will recognize this tool, shown in Figure 16-4.

Secret

The Digitizer Calibration Tool only supports calibrating integrated digitizers. It will not work with an external digitizer. If you're using an external digitizer, it should have come with software to help you calibrate the pen.

In the Handwriting Recognition tab, you configure two tools that help you personalize the system's handwriting recognition. The Handwriting Recognition Personalization tool helps you improve the system's handwriting recognition results by stepping you through a wizard where you provide examples of your handwriting.

To calibrate the screen, tap the crosshair each time that it appears on the screen. You can right-click anywhere on the screen to undo the last point calibrated or to cancel calibrating altogether.

Do not change your screen orientation until you have completed the calibration.

Figure 16-4: The Digitizer Calibration Tool helps you configure your pen for accuracy.

Automatic learning is an opt-in (and recommended) Tablet-based service that gathers information about the words you use regularly, and how you write them, and then skews the system's handwriting recognition so that it can be more accurate and attuned to both your writing style and word usage. Don't be alarmed by the wording Microsoft uses in the dialog box: No data is sent to the company. It's all stored right on your PC where it belongs.

In the Display tab, you configure the default screen orientation from a selection of four possible choices: Primary landscape, secondary portrait, secondary landscape, and primary portrait. You can also change the order in which these orientation choices are implemented when you press the hardware-based screen orientation button that is found on many Tablet PCs.

Consider a typical slate-style Tablet PC device, where the display takes up most of the surface of the front of the device. On such a machine, you could conceivably view the screen in any of four configurations, depending on how you're holding it. The primary landscape and primary portrait modes are the two modes that you'll use most often, based on the button layout on the device, your left- or right-handedness, and the ways that feel most comfortable to you. The secondary portrait and secondary landscape modes are less-often-used modes.

Most users will likely just need two screen orientation types, especially if they're using a convertible laptop-style Tablet PC. In normal laptop mode, when the user is accessing the system through the keyboard and mouse, the screen would be in horizontal mode. This would be Primary landscape. But when the screen is rotated so that the system is accessed like a tablet, using the stylus, this would be Primary portrait (or perhaps Secondary portrait depending on the user and the layout of the device's hardware controls). In this case, you might want to configure Primary landscape for the first and third locations in the orientation sequence, and Primary portrait for positions two and four.

On the Other tab, there's a link to Pen and Input Devices, which is a separate Control Panel applet.

tip   **You could separately navigate to Pen and Input Settings by visiting Control Panel, Hardware and Sound, and then Pen and Input Settings.**

Using Pen and Input Devices Settings

The Pen and Input Devices dialog box, shown in Figure 16-5, also offers a variety of tabs, each of which provides configuration options related to the stylus, or pen, you're using with the system.

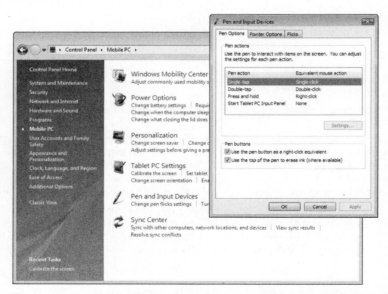

Figure 16-5: Here is where you can configure options related to your stylus and Tablet PC hardware.

The Pen Options tab enables you to configure what different pen actions and Tablet PC buttons do. By default, a single-tap is the equivalent of a single-click with a mouse button, for example, while a double-tap, naturally, emulates a double-click. You can also configure press and hold (right-click by default, although some Tablet PC styli actually include a dedicated pen button that acts as a right-click button in conjunction with a tap) and the Start Tablet PC Input Panel button, which is found on many Tablet PCs.

In the Pointer Options tab, you can configure whether Vista's new dynamic feedback for Tablet PCs is enabled, as well as a few other pointer-related options. Dynamic feedback is an excellent bit of new functionality in Windows Vista, and it's designed to provide visual feedback whenever you perform a pen action—like a single-tap, double-tap, pen button press, or right-click (pen button press plus a tap). Each of the visual feedback types are circular in nature, and you can see them in Figure 16-6.

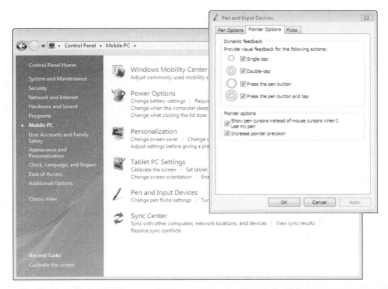

Figure 16-6: In Windows Vista, you can be sure a pen action occurred thanks to dynamic feedback.

In the Flicks tab, you can configure various options related to Flicks, which we discuss later in the chapter. Flicks are one of the major new features in the Windows Vista version of the Tablet PC software.

Tablet PC Input Panel

Back in the original version of Windows XP Tablet PC Edition, the TIP was typically docked to the bottom of the screen, just above the taskbar, and you toggled its display by clicking a TIP icon next to the Start button. In Windows XP Tablet PC Edition 2005, Microsoft enhanced the TIP by allowing it to pop up in-place, where you needed it. That is, if you wanted to input some text into the address bar of an Internet Explorer window, for example, you could tap the address bar with the pen and the TIP would appear in a floating window right under the tap point. That way you wouldn't have to move the pen up and down across the entire screen in order to enter text or other characters.

That said, the TIP was still manually launched by clicking that special icon next to the Start menu. That could be quite a distance to travel with the pen. And the TIP in Windows XP Tablet PC Edition 2005 was a pretty big bugger, occupying a large swath of onscreen real estate.

These issues are now fixed in Windows Vista. Instead of special taskbar button, the TIP is now always accessible, but mostly hidden, on the edge of the screen. As shown in Figure 16-7, only a small portion of the TIP is visible by default on the edge of the screen.

Figure 16-7: The TIP stays out of the way until you need it.

To activate the TIP, simply click it with the pen or stylus. The TIP will then appear in the center of the screen, as shown in Figure 16-8.

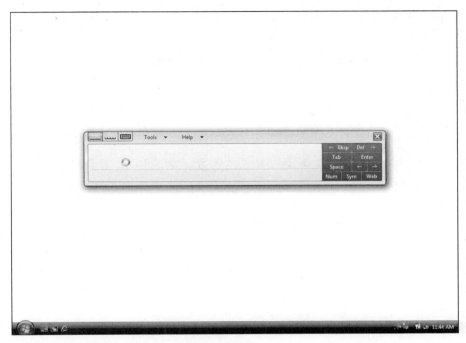

Figure 16-8: An activated TIP is a happy TIP.

So what does the TIP do? The TIP is designed to help you interact with applications that aren't Tablet PC-aware. (That is, virtually every single application on the planet.) So if you want to enter a URL in the Internet Explorer address bar, search for an application in the Windows Vista Start Menu–based search box, or perform similar actions. As shown in Figure 16-9, the TIP gives your pen the ability to work with any application.

Compared to the TIP in previous versions of Windows XP Tablet PC Edition, The Windows Vista TIP offers very similar functionality with a slightly reworked user interface. The quick launch icons for Writing Pad (the default), Character Pad, and On-Screen Keyboard have been moved to the top of the window, next to Tools and Help menus. And the right side of the TIP, which includes buttons for frequently needed actions, has been dramatically simplified. If you've used a Tablet PC before, you'll have no problems using the new TIP.

Figure 16-9: The TIP is a bridge between applications of the past and the future way we'll all interact with computers (maybe).

tip   In the previous version of Microsoft's Tablet PC operating system, the TIP included dedicated buttons for Web shortcuts like http://, www., and so on. These can now be accessed through the new web button, which expands to show these and other related options. Likewise, the Sym button expands to show various symbols (!, @, #, and so on), while the Num button expands to show numbers. The web button expands automatically when you select the address bar in Internet Explorer 7.

If you want to return the TIP to its previous behavior of docking at the top or bottom of the screen, click the Tools button and chose the appropriate option. The default (and new) behavior is called Float.

Also, be sure to spend some time meandering around the TIP's Options dialog box. The TIP supports an amazingly rich collection of configurable options, including such things as to which side of the screen it docks, whether it's configured for left- or right-handed users, and how the Writing Pad and Character Pad recognize handwriting (as you write — the default — or after you pause).

Finally, while Windows Vista does enable handwriting recognition personalization by default so that the system learns your handwriting style as it goes, you could and probably should take the time to engage in a little handwriting recognition training if you think you're going to be using a pen to interact with Vista regularly. There are various ways to trigger this training, but one handy place is right in the TIP: Click Tools and then Personalize Handwriting to launch the Handwriting Personalization wizard, shown in Figure 16-10.

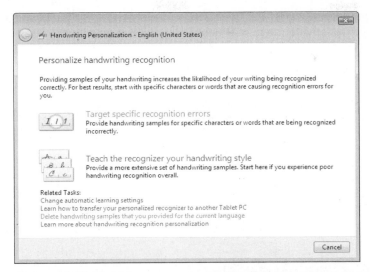

Figure 16-10: Make it your own by teaching Windows Vista how you write.

Flicks and Gestures

Flicks, called gestures in other pen-based systems, are special quick movements you can make with a Tablet PC stylus over the digitizer to navigate quickly or launch shortcuts for commonly needed functionality like copy and paste. With a Flick, you literally flick the pen in a certain way to cause an action.

Secret

Windows Vista also supports a related type of gesture called a Touch Flick, which enables you to perform similar actions using your finger on special touch screen displays.

There are two types of Flicks, navigational and editing. Navigational flicks include such things as scroll up, scroll down, back, and forward. Editing flicks include cut, copy, paste, delete, and undo. Flicks occur when you flick the pen in any of eight directions, including up, down, left, right, and the diagonal positions that are between each.

You configure Flicks via the Flicks tab of the Pen and Input Devices dialog box, which can be found in Control Panel (Hardware and Sound➪Pen and Input Settings) or accessed directly via the Pen flicks icon in the system tray. This tab of the dialog box determines whether Flicks are available, what types of Flicks are available, and how sensitive the digitizer will be to recognize Flicks. Obviously, this particular feature will be set differently on each system, based on the sensitivity of the digitizer and pen combination.

When you click the Customize button, you're shown the Customize Flicks dialog box, which enables you to set a wide range of actions for each Flick (see Figure 16-11).

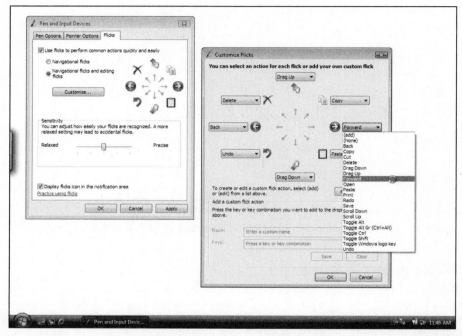

Figure 16-11: Customize Flicks enables you to determine what each of the eight possible Flicks can do.

tip   The Practice using Flicks link at the bottom of the Flicks tab of the Pen and Input Devices dialog box provides a link to a handy Pen Flicks Training application, shown in Figure 16-12, that will help get you up to speed with this productivity enhancing feature pretty quickly.

Secret   Microsoft has supported gestures on its Windows Mobile operating system for quite some time, and much of the functionality you see in Flicks comes directly from that work.

Figure 16-12: Pen Flicks Training helps you practice and learn how to use Flicks.

Password Hiding on Logon with Pen

In the Windows XP Tablet PC editions, you could log on to the PC using a stylus and the TIP in onscreen keyboard mode: All you had to do was tap your password with the stylus. The problem was that each key in the onscreen keyboard would be highlighted as you tapped, so it was possible for someone looking over your shoulder to steal your password relatively easily.

In Windows Vista, Microsoft has implemented a small but important security change: As you tap the on-screen keyboard on the TIP during logon, the keys are no longer highlighted. Thus, your password is safe — or at least as safe as it can be — from prying eyes. On the flipside, it's a little weird tapping the virtual keyboard and getting no feedback at all.

Secret

Microsoft also uses this technique whenever you need to enter a password in a secure web page.

Voice Control

One of the biggest promises with the original Tablet PC operating system was that Microsoft would one day extend the more natural user interaction techniques it was offering for that system with the ultimate in human/PC interaction: Voice control. Successfully parodied in *Star Trek IV*, voice control has long been an unattainable goal for PC users. Today, a small fraction of the population is able to put up with the training time required to make third-party voice control systems even remotely useable. But Microsoft has been working on its speech recognition technologies for several years now and you can see the fruit of its labors in Windows Vista.

tip

That said, Windows Vista's voice control features are still passable at best. To enable speech recognition, navigate through Control Panel to Ease of Access and then Speech Recognition (see Figure 16-13). There are a number of steps you'll need to perform to make this work. First, you will have to enable speech recognition. Then, you will have to set up your microphone for optimal performance using a simple wizard. Then, Microsoft has a nice speech tutorial and speech reference card to help you understand how the system works. Finally, there is a training wizard that you should spend some time with to make the system work better for you and your particular speech patterns.

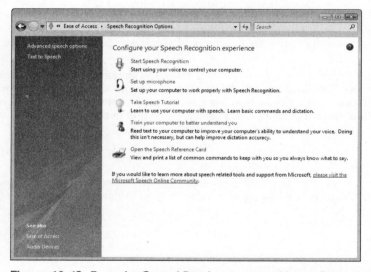

Figure 16-13: From the Control Panel, you can enable, configure, and train speech recognition so that you can control the system with your voice.

Shell Changes for Tablet PC Users

One thing you'll probably notice right away is that Windows Vista displays a new user interface element by default when it detects Tablet PC hardware on your system. It's a small check box that's available on virtually every shell item, including the desktop's Recycle Bin and every icon in Computer and the other Explorers that appears when you move the mouse cursor over the item. Shown in Figure 16-14, this check box makes it easier to select multiple items in the shell using a pen. Otherwise, you'd have to drag a selection box around, which can be difficult with a pen.

Figure 16-14: Windows Vista offers a fairly elegant way to multi-select items with a pen.

Secret

Windows Vista users can turn this feature on if they'd like. (Conversely, Tablet PC users can turn it off.) To do so, you need to find the Folder Options dialog box. (Easiest way: Open Control Panel and type **Folder Options** in the Instant Search box.) Then, navigate to the View tab and check the Use Check Boxes to Select Items option.

In addition to the check boxes, you'll see a few other small changes on a system with Tablet PC hardware. For example, Welcome Center includes a link to Tablet PC training, a Pen flicks icon appears over time in the tray notification area of the taskbar, and the Control Panel includes a top-level Mobile PC item—discussed in Chapter 15—that provides quick links to notebook and Tablet PC-based options. And of course, you'll see the tip of the TIP (ahem) sticking out on the left side of the screen by default, waiting for your pen to activate it.

tip Oddly, many Tablet PC–oriented features are installed by default even on non-Tablet systems. You'll see entries for a number of these features and related applications throughout the Start Menu and Control Panel on normal desktop and notebook computers.

Revisiting Some Old Friends

Windows XP Tablet PC Edition was always well-supported with a group of fun accessories, or mini-applications, that enable users to use the pen in fun and unexpectedly productive ways. Microsoft includes three of these accessories in Windows Vista, and they're all worth a look.

Snipping Tool

The Snipping Tool is a Windows accessory aimed at Tablet PC users that lets you circle any area of the screen and copy the encircled image to the system clipboard. You can then paste the image into email messages or any other document, and annotate it with your own handwritten notes. The Snipping Tool is particularly well suited to copying information from web pages, but it works well with just about anything.

The Snipping Tool is launched via the Start Menu (just type **snip** or look for Snipping Tool in All Programs⇨Accessories). When you first launch the application, it assumes you want to grab a screen capture, or *snip*, right away. But you can cancel that operation by clicking the Cancel button. Then, you can more closely examine this useful utility's user interface and uncover its surprisingly rich feature-set. The Snipping Tool is shown in Figure 16-15.

Figure 16-15: The Snipping Tool can be used to capture arbitrary parts of the screen.

If you just click the New button, the entire screen will fade, letting you drag the pen (or the mouse) around the screen to capture a given area. Or, you can click the small arrow next to the New button to choose other capture types, including free-form snip (the default when using a pen), rectangular snip (the default when using a mouse), window snip (to capture a single window), or full-screen snip (to capture the entire screen).

When you've captured a portion of the screen, or the entire screen, that image is hidden in the Windows Clipboard as an image. You can then paste that image into any application that supports images, including a Word document or Microsoft Paint. The Snipping Tool also opens an edit window that enables you to save the image to disk in various image formats, send the snip via e-mail, or, more interestingly, add your own handwriting-based comments to the snip (see Figure 16-16).

Figure 16-16: The Snipping Tool enables you to annotate snips with your own handwriting and then send them via e-mail, save them to disk, or copy them to the Clipboard.

> **note** The Snipping Tool first debuted as a PowerToy for Windows XP Tablet PC Edition. Microsoft shipped an updated version of the tool in the Experience Pack for Tablet PC in 2005. You can see this heritage in the design of the applet's window buttons, which are still curiously XP-like.

Secret

If you need to regularly take screenshots, the Snipping Tool is only marginally easier to use than the built-in Windows screen capture utilities, which enable you to copy the contents of the entire screen to the clipboard at any time by pressing PrtScn (Print Screen) or the top-most window by pressing Alt+PrtScn. If you need something more elegant than that, you should use a dedicated screen capture utility, like the excellent TechSmith SnagIt at www.techsmith.com/, which we both use and recommend.

Windows Journal

Windows Journal is a simple note-taking application that debuted in the first version of Windows XP Tablet PC Edition. Shown in Figure 16-17, Windows Journal works only with handwriting and cannot be used to take notes with the keyboard. It remains an excellent way to get accustomed to Tablet PC usage, if you're a beginner.

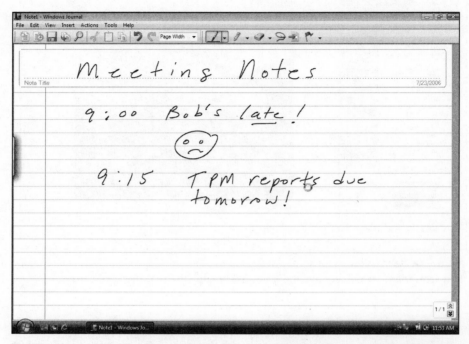

Figure 16-17: Windows Journal is designed for anyone who wants to take handwritten notes.

Windows Journal starts off with a college-ruled notebook look and feel, but you can change the style using Journal's stationary and template features. Stationary is a combination of paper size (like 8.5" by 11"), line style (college ruled, wide ruled, and so on), and other characteristics. Or, you can choose from preset templates like Blank, Dotted Line, Memo, and others. To define the default look and feel of your notes, visit Tools⇨Options⇨Note Format.

---

note   Curiously, you can draw in Windows Journal using the mouse if you want, although the results are rarely inspiring.

---

tip   Microsoft sells an excellent note-taking application called OneNote, which you can also purchase as part of the inexpensive Microsoft Office Home and Student Edition 2007. OneNote supports both pen- and keyboard-based note taking, as well as audio and video recording that can be synchronized with notes. It is much more sophisticated than Windows Journal and has been updated far more frequently.

Sticky Notes

Shown in Figure 16-18, Sticky Notes is a new Windows Vista accessory that any user can use to create short handwritten or voice notes. The application resembles a small stack of yellow notes, just like the paper-based sticky notes they're meant to represent. Sticky Notes is designed for a Tablet PC, and indeed, you'd need such a device for the hand-written note portion. But anyone can use Sticky Notes to create voice notes.

Figure 16-18: Sticky Notes is meant to emulate paper-based sticky notes.

Summary

As with Windows Media Center, Microsoft has taken the Tablet PC functionality it developed during the lifetime of Windows XP, enhanced it, and made it available to far more users in Windows Vista. Whether you have a traditional Tablet PC, a convertible laptop, a PC with a touch-based screen, or even a normal desktop or notebook computer, there's a Tablet PC feature in Windows Vista that's sure to delight. Hopefully, as this technology goes more mainstream, more people will become comfortable with an alternative form of computing that could yet change the world.

Part VI

Internet and Networking

Browsing the Web with Internet Explorer 7

Chapter
17

◆ ◆

In This Chapter

Figuring out the new Internet Explorer 7 user interface

Working with tabbed browsing and Quick Tabs

Searching the Internet

Optimizing the Internet Explorer 7 display

Printing information you find on the Web

Become more efficient with Internet Explorer 7's keyboard shortcuts

Discovering and mastering the new RSS features

◆ ◆

Windows Vista features a brand-new and much-improved version of the Internet Explorer Web browser called Internet Explorer 7. As with previous Windows versions, Internet Explorer 7 is integrated into Windows Vista, although Microsoft offers a free download of Internet Explorer 7 for Windows XP as well. But here's one reason to upgrade to Windows Vista: The version of Internet Explorer 7 found in Microsoft's latest operating system is actually much more secure than the XP version and even offers a few unique features.

What Happened

To say that Internet Explorer has an ignoble history is perhaps an understatement. Originally conceived as a minor add-on for Windows 95 and one that did not ship in the initial version of that Windows release, Internet Explorer later became the linchpin of Microsoft's strategy for competing in the dot-com era and, not surprisingly, the subject of antitrust legal battles that continue to this day.

Inexplicably, Microsoft melded Internet Explorer into Windows beginning with Windows 98, and designed the system in such a way that Internet Explorer could not be easily removed from the operating system (OS). This intermingling of web browser and OS code led to years and years of security problems, some of which eventually forced Microsoft to delay the release of Windows Vista simply so that it could ensure that its Internet Explorer–riddled operating systems were shored up with additional defenses.

Worst of all, after Microsoft won the browser wars in the early 2000s, displacing competitors such as Netscape and Opera, the company lost interest in Internet Explorer and stopped active development of the browser. It even briefly considered removing Internet Explorer from Windows Vista altogether, relegating its web browsing duties to the Explorer shell, which as you probably know is simply based on Internet Explorer code anyway.

Then a wonderful thing happened. A scrappy group of upstarts from The Mozilla Foundation (since renamed to The Mozilla Corporation) took the vestiges of the software code from Netscape's browser and reconstituted it as a small, lean, and powerful browser named Firefox. Roaring out of the gates in 2004, Firefox quickly began seizing market share from Internet Explorer, thanks to its unique new features and functionality. And suddenly, Microsoft was interested in updating Internet Explorer once again. It's amazing what a little competition can do.

Starting with the Service Pack 2 (SP2) version of Windows XP, Microsoft re-established its Internet Explorer team and began working actively on new features. Although the version of Internet Explorer 6 that appeared in Windows XP SP2 was focused largely on security features, a future version, Internet Explorer 7, would include a huge number of functional improvements, aimed at closing the gap with Firefox and giving Microsoft's customers reasons not to switch. For the first time in several years, Internet Explorer is a compelling web browser again, and it's likely that most Windows Vista users will want to use this product to browse the Web and access other web-based content.

Secret

Truth be told, we both prefer and recommend Mozilla Firefox over Internet Explorer, although we admit that the latest Internet Explorer version does indeed include a number of new and interesting features. You can find out more about Firefox from the Mozilla Web site (www.mozilla.com/).

Basic Internet Explorer Usage

Although it's unlikely that Windows Secrets readers are unaware of basic Internet Explorer features, many of you may have moved along to Mozilla Firefox or other browsers over the past few years. If that's the case, this section will serve as a nice refresher.

Starting Internet Explorer

Click the Internet Explorer icon in your Start Menu to start Internet Explorer. You can also start the Internet Explorer by clicking the Internet Explorer icon in the Quick Start toolbar.

Secret   In previous version of Windows, you could type a web address (a URL) in the Address bar of any Explorer window and press Enter to change the Explorer window into an instance of Internet Explorer. This no longer works in Windows Vista: Now, when you type a web address into an Explorer address bar and tap Enter, a new Internet Explorer window opens.

New Link, New Window

If you want to open a new window when you jump to a new site, hold down the Shift key when you click the link. (If you prefer, you can right-click the link and then click Open In New Window to do the same thing without using the keyboard.) You'll then be able to see both the target site and the source page in different Internet Explorer windows. You can also choose to use Internet Explorer's new tabbed browsing feature instead. We describe this feature later in the chapter.

Secret   You can display the Internet Explorer icon on your desktop, although the process has changed. To do so, right-click an empty area of the desktop and choose Personalize. Then, in the Personalization window, select the Change Desktop Icons link on the left side of the window. In the Desktop Icon Settings window that appears, check Internet Explorer and click OK.

Managing Downloads from the Internet

Like previous versions of Internet Explorer, Internet Explorer 7 does not provide a download manager. Instead, it provides only basic functions for downloading files from Internet servers. Each time you click a link to download a file with Internet Explorer, you get a new download dialog.

Edit on the Internet Explorer Toolbar

Unlike previous Internet Explorer versions, Internet Explorer 7 doesn't include an Edit button on its command bar by default. If you don't have the Edit button and wish you did, here's how to get it:

1. Click the Tools button in the Internet Explorer toolbar.

2. Scroll down to Toolbars and then select Customize.

3. In the Customize Toolbar dialog box, select Edit from the Available Toolbar Buttons field and then click the Add button.

4. Click Close.

The Complete AutoComplete

Internet Explorer has a feature called AutoComplete that helps you complete your entry in the address bar as soon as you type in the first few letters. For example, type **www.appl**, pause for a few seconds, and you'll get a drop-down list of sites you have previously visited that start with **www.appl**, including **www.apple.com/**. Even if there is a long list of URLs that start with the same letters that you've typed, you can easily use your mouse or arrow keys to scroll to and highlight an entry in the list, and then press Enter or Tab to jump to the site.

If you press Alt+down arrow or F4 when the address bar is active, Internet Explorer displays a drop-down list of complete addresses you've recently typed in the address bar. This is a totally different list than the AutoComplete drop-down list; it is the same list that appears when you click the down arrow at the right end of the address bar.

To enable or disable AutoComplete, choose Tools⇨Internet Options, click the Content tab, and click the Settings button in the AutoComplete section. In the AutoComplete Settings dialog box, you can choose whether to use AutoComplete for Web addresses, forms, or user names and passwords.

> **tip**
>
> You can save time when typing Web addresses by making Internet Explorer automatically preface your entry with www. and end it with the suffix .com. Just type the domain name in the address bar and then press Ctrl+Enter. For example, type **windowssecrets**, press Ctrl+Enter, and you get www.WindowsSecrets.com. This is different from actually searching on the Internet for the address; see the "Autosearch for a Web Address" section later in this chapter for more on that.

Finding Web Sites

Do you want to find a specific web site, or text from a specific web page?

In an Internet Explorer window, click the address bar, type **find**, **search**, or **?**, type a space, and then type the name of the company or organization whose site you want to find. If the name has a space in it, forget typing the **find**, **search**, or **?**, and just put double quote marks around the name. You can also just type in any word, and the search function will be started.

This will automatically start a search for the company, word in a Web page, or organization on Live.com. We discuss changing your search options later in this chapter.

Autosearch for a Web Address

Internet Explorer will automatically search on the Internet for a Web address if you ask it to. Type a fragment of an address in the Address bar, press Enter, and Internet Explorer will treat the fragment as a search term. After a minute or two, you'll see a list of URLs containing the text you typed.

You can choose to turn this feature off or change how it functions by taking these steps:

1. Click Tools➪Internet Options.
2. Click the Advanced tab and scroll down to Search From The Address Bar.
3. Select the option that you prefer — Do Not Search From The Address Bar or Just Display The Results In The Main Window — and then click OK.

tip   It isn't the default, so you might miss it. Internet Explorer will not put in placeholder borders for images yet to be downloaded. If you want this feature turned on so that the text can wrap around the images as yet unseen, you can turn it on in your Internet Options dialog box. Choose Tools➪Internet Options, click the Advanced tab, and scroll down to Multimedia. Mark the Show Image Download Placeholders check box. Click OK.

Copy and Paste Links

Wherever there's a hot link, there's a way to cut and paste it. If you receive an e-mail message in Windows Mail that contains a link, you can of course just click it to invoke an Internet Explorer window (if it's a link to a web site or an FTP address).

You can right-click a link and click Copy Shortcut. Then paste this URL into the address bar, into a text file, onto the Desktop — whatever you like. You can also click Add To Favorites instead of Copy Shortcut.

Right-click a web page name in your History Explorer bar, and you can click Copy or Add To Favorites. You can do the same with a web page name in search results displayed in the Search Explorer bar.

Toggle Internet Explorer between Full-Screen Mode and Restore

Open up Internet Explorer and press the F11 key. If you weren't before, you are now in full-screen mode. If you were maximized before, pressing F11 again will get you back there.

Favorites and Offline Web Pages

A URL (Uniform Resource Locator) is a unique identifier for a web page or other resource on the Internet. Windows maintains a list of the URLs for your favorite sites. Your *favorites* are actually shortcuts stored in the Favorites folder.

You can store whatever you like in the Favorites subfolders, but we suggest limiting what you put in these folders to shortcuts (either to URLs or to other folders or documents). You can put copies of URL shortcuts on your Desktop and start your Internet Explorer by clicking a shortcut's icon.

To create a shortcut to your favorites, open an Explorer window and navigate to Favorites in your Home folder. Right-drag and drop your Favorites folder onto your Desktop. Choose Create Shortcut(s) Here.

You can get to your favorites from the new Favorites Center as well, which we discuss later in the chapter.

URL Shortcuts

Internet Explorer keeps track of web sites using shortcuts to URLs. These shortcuts have an extension of **url** instead of the standard **lnk** extension for Windows shortcuts.

URL shortcuts store more information about the URLs than just their values. Internet Explorer uses this additional information to help you manage your shortcuts as well as to enable you to view web sites offline. You can see this information by right-clicking a URL shortcut in Windows Explorer and choosing Properties.

You can create a URL shortcut to a web site just by displaying the site in an Internet Explorer window, and clicking the new Add To Favorites button. We discuss this new functionality later in this chapter.

If you would rather put the shortcut directly on the Desktop, right-click an area on the web page that doesn't include a graphic or a link to another location and choose Create Shortcut from the context menu. You can also drag the icon at the left end of the address bar to the desktop to create a shortcut to the web page.

> **tip**
> To create a shortcut to a link (a jump to another URL) in a web page, drag the link to the desktop. You can later click this shortcut to open an Internet Explorer window and go to the indicated location on the Web.

> **tip**
> You don't have to put URL shortcuts in the Favorites folder or one of its subfolders. If you do, then the shortcuts are accessible from the Favorites Center. But you are free to put them wherever you like. You can create many folders of URL shortcuts, and place shortcuts to these folders on your desktop.

Saving Graphics off the Internet

Do you want to save a web-based graphic that you are viewing in Internet Explorer? Right-click it, choose Save Picture As (sometimes you will see Save Background As as well), and then give it a path and a name. If you don't save a graphics file as you're viewing it, you can save it later from the cache. When Internet Explorer first downloads a graphics file, it automatically caches (saves) it in the Temporary Internet Files folder. You can find the file in this folder and save it permanently by copying it to another location.

If you want to turn a graphic in a web page into wallpaper on your desktop, right-click the graphic and choose Set As Wallpaper.

Saving Complete Web Pages

Saving a web page as an HTML file in Internet Explorer usually saves only the text and layout of the page—the graphics are saved separately as links. However, Internet

Explorer does have the ability to save a web page as a single document. The MIME HTML (**.mht**) file format incorporates both the graphics and the HTML text on a web page into one file. The graphics are encoded using MIME (and Uuencoding), so everything is stored in e-mail-capable, 7-bit ASCII text characters. But Internet Explorer can decode the file on the fly and display the graphics.

This feature greatly expands the power of the Internet. If a document is displayed as one web page, you can download it and all of its associated graphic files, and save everything in one very convenient document. If you do this, you don't have to save the document as an offline page to keep it readily available.

All you do to save a web page in this format is tap the Alt key to enable the Internet Explorer menu, and then click File⇨Save As, and choose Web Archive, Single File in the Save As Type field. This secret isn't hidden, but it sure is powerful. It turns the Web into something that you can actually use as a publishing arena.

Secret

You can see the entire underlying text file if you open a file with an mht extension in WordPad. If you click View⇨Source in Internet Explorer when viewing an mht file, you'll only see the HTML code and not the encoded graphics that are in fact there in the file.

Internet Explorer also enables you to save a document as a complete web page (click File⇨Save As, and choose Web Page⇨Complete in the Save As Type field). In this case, the graphic files are not included in the HTML source text. Instead, Internet Explorer creates a subfolder in which it saves the downloaded graphics files. It rewrites the saved web page to reference the graphics files in this subfolder, and enters the Web page's URL as a comment at the top of the page. We wish Save As⇨Web Archive for Email saved the web page's URL as a comment.

Finally, you can also save web pages as a Webpage type, which includes only the text of the page along with links to the online graphics. If you choose this option and view a saved page while offline, you'll see just the text. However, if you are online, the graphics will load as normal.

Turning Your Favorites into a Web Page

The Favorites menu and submenus are fine for starters, but sometimes it is a bit of a drag to search repeatedly through all these menus. How about creating a single web page of all your favorites? Or separate web pages for different subsets of favorites?

Internet Explorer includes the Import/Export Wizard, which can export your favorites or cookies. It writes them to your disk in a format that Netscape, Mozilla Firefox, and other browsers can read. You can also use the wizard to import cookies and favorites from other browsers. The wizard writes out your favorites as an HTML file. This makes it easy to look through your favorites with Notepad and edit them if you like. You can also use the HTML file as a page in Internet Explorer, from which you can easily jump to any site on your list.

Choose File⇨Import and Export to run the wizard.

Internet Explorer 7 Is Not Your Father's Web Browser

If you're familiar with Internet Explorer 6 or previous Internet Explorer versions, you might be in for a shock when you first start Internet Explorer 7: Gone is the simplicity of the Internet Explorer you know, replaced with a more complicated user interface that mimics the look and feel of the Windows Explorer shell while providing onscreen real estate for all its new features. As shown in Figure 17-1, Internet Explorer 7 is quite a bit busier looking than its predecessors.

Figure 17-1: Something old, something new: Internet Explorer 7 is clearly a new Internet Explorer, but you may find it difficult to find features you were once used to.

So what's changed in the Internet Explorer 7 user interface? First, the menu bar is hidden and renamed to Classic Menu, similar to what happened with the menu bar in the Explorer shell. Microsoft says that it disabled the Classic Menu to reduce the clutter, but we think you'll agree that the Internet Explorer 7 user interface is still quite a bit more cluttered than that of Internet Explorer 6.

> **tip** If you don't like this design decision, you can temporarily cause the Internet Explorer 7 Classic Menu to appear by pressing the ALT key once. Or, you can simply click the new Tools toolbar icon and select Toolbars and then Classic Menus to enable this menu all the time.

Various user interface elements have also been moved around to conform to the new Windows Vista common user interface style. The Back and Forward buttons are prominently featured in the upper left corner of the window next to the top-mounted address bar, for example. The main toolbar, now called the *command bar*, is now located way over to the far right of the window, causing the Home button to be located quite a ways from its previous location, which is sure to frustrate those who have committed the location of this commonly needed button to memory.

<table>
<tr>
<td>tip</td>
<td>You can easily resize the size of the command bar if you want to ensure that you can see all of its buttons. First, ensure that the toolbars are not locked by navigating to Tools⇨Toolbars and unchecking Lock Bands (this option is unchecked by default). Then, you can drag the command bar left and right to resize it. If you make the command bar too short, a double chevron will appear at the right, indicating that you can reach the rest of its options via a drop-down menu, as shown in Figure 17-2.</td>
</tr>
</table>

Figure 17-2: Hidden command bar options can be accessed via this handy drop-down menu.

The Command Bar

Love it or hate it, the new command bar houses some of Internet Explorer's most commonly needed functionality. Table 17-1 explores the options you'll see, from left to right, in this toolbar. All of these features are described in more detail later in this chapter.

Table 17-1: Default Internet Explorer 7.0 Command Bar Buttons

Command Bar Button	What It Does
Home	Navigates the browser back to your home page (or home pages, as the case may be). This button includes an optional drop-down menu as well, which enables you to change your home page(s) and add and remove home page(s).
Feeds	Provides a handy front end to the new support of RSS feeds in Internet Explorer.
Print	Provides printing facilities that are dramatically improved when compared to previous Internet Explorer versions.
Page	This button launches a drop-down menu that provides access to options related to web pages, such as zoom and text size.
Tools	This button launches a drop-down menu that provides access to options related to the web browser itself, including security feature configuration, Internet Options, and which toolbars are displayed. Tools is similar to the Tools menu in the Classic Menu, but lacks certain options, such as Windows Update.
Help	This button launches a drop-down menu that is similar to the Help menu item in the Classic Menu.

You can also customize which buttons appear in the Internet Explorer 7.0 command bar. To customize this toolbar, right-click one of the visible toolbar buttons and choose Customize. This will display the Customize Toolbar dialog box shown in Figure 17-3.

Figure 17-3: The Customize Toolbar dialog lets you configure which buttons appear in the Internet Explorer 7 command bar.

You might use this dialog box to remove existing toolbar buttons you don't want, or you can add optional buttons that don't appear by default. Table 17-2 summarizes the optional buttons you can add to the Internet Explorer 7.0 command bar. Additionally, you can add one or more separators, which visually separate command bar buttons. Most of these features will be described later in this chapter.

Table 17-2: Optional Internet Explorer 7.0 Command Bar Buttons

Command Bar Button	What It Does
Size	Toggles the font size of the text in the current browser window between preset sizes, including Largest, Larger, Medium (the default), Smaller, and Smallest.
Read Mail	Adds a button to launch Windows Mail, or your default e-mail application.
Encoding	Provides a drop-down menu that enables you to select from the various language and locale display modes that are available on your system. Typically, you will leave this at its default value, Unicode (UTF-8), unless you are browsing the Web in an area of the world that uses right-to-left text or other text encoding methods.
Edit	Opens the currently displayed web page in your default web page editor application.
Cut	Cuts the currently selected text from the address bar and places it in the Windows Clipboard.
Copy	Copies the currently selected text from the address bar or web page and places it in the Windows Clipboard.
Paste	Pastes the contents of the Windows Clipboard at the cursor position.
Full Screen	Toggles the Internet Explorer 7.0 Full Screen mode.

tip

If you install software that adds a button to the Internet Explorer toolbar, that button will be added to the right side of the command bar now. For example, Windows Live Messenger installs a Messenger button, and Microsoft Office (2003 and newer) installs a Research button (and, if you've installed OneNote, a Send to OneNote button). You might see other similar buttons, depending on which software you've installed. Likewise, if you upgrade from Windows XP to Windows Vista, any buttons that were added to Internet Explorer 6 will show up in the Internet Explorer 7 command bar as well. You can remove these buttons via the Customize Toolbar dialog box described previously.

Where Is It Now?

Hundreds of millions of people used to Internet Explorer 6 may be asking this question. Despite IE's widespread use, Microsoft made some startling changes to the way Internet Explorer 7 works. With that in mind, Table 17-3 should help Internet Explorer 6–savvy users find their way around the new interface.

Table 17-3: Where Common Internet Explorer Features Moved in Internet Explorer 7

Feature	Where It Is Now
File menu	Now called the Classic Menu and hidden by default. Tap the Alt key to display this menu.
Back button	Now located in the upper-left corner of the browser window.
Forward button	Now located in the upper-left corner of the browser window to the right of the Back button.
Stop button	Moved to the right of the Refresh button.
Refresh button	Moved to the right of the address bar.
Home button	Moved to the command bar.
Search button	Replaced by a new Search box found in the top right of the browser window.
Favorites button	Replaced by the Favorites Center. The icon for Favorites Center is a yellow star and is found below the Back button.
History button	Missing in action. You can access the browser history by displaying the Favorites Center, however.
Mail button	Replaced by the optional Read Mail command bar button and the Send This Page option on the Page button's pull-down menu.
Print button	Now located in the command bar.
Edit button	Missing in action. To edit a web page, enable the Classic Menu by tapping Alt and then choose Edit from the File menu.
Go button	Missing in action. To load a web page whose address you've typed into the address bar, simply press the Enter key.
Status icon ("throbber")	In previous versions of Internet Explorer, an Internet Explorer E logo or Windows logo in the upper right corner of the browser indicated progress while a web page was loading. In Internet Explorer 7, this has been replaced by a standard progress bar, which is located in the middle of the status bar at the bottom of the browser window.
Address bar	Now located in the top row of controls in the browser window to the right of the Forward button.
Information bar	Hidden by default, but still located at the top of the web page display area.
Status bar	Still located at the bottom of the browser window. The status bar in Internet Explorer 7 behaves similarly to the status bar in previous Internet Explorer versions.

New Internet Explorer 7 Features and Functionality

After you get over the new look of Internet Explorer you will discover that Microsoft has added a lot of new functionality to this release. Indeed, Internet Explorer is arguably the most dramatic upgrade in the history of Microsoft's web browser. In this section, we'll examine the biggest changes.

Manage Your Favorite Web Sites with Favorites Center

In previous versions of Internet Explorer, the Favorites folder provided a place in the system where you could save links, or shortcuts, to your favorite web sites. Favorites were typically accessed in Internet Explorer via the Favorites menu. This tradition has changed somewhat in Internet Explorer 7. Now, Favorites are accessed via a new Favorites Center, which is basically an Explorer bar that can be triggered to appear on the left side of the browser window. You trigger the Favorites Center by clicking the yellow star icon, as shown in Figure 17-4.

Figure 17-4: The new Favorites Center provides a holding pen for your Favorites, browser history, and subscribed RSS feeds.

> **tip**
> The Favorites menu still exists in Internet Explorer 7, but you'll have to display (or permanently enable) the Classic Menu in order to see it. To do so, tap the Alt key and choose Favorites.

By default, Favorites Center appears in Favorites view, which displays your favorite web sites in a menu-like list. But don't be concerned that Microsoft simply duplicated the functionality of the old Favorites menu and moved it to a new location in order to fool you. The Favorites Center includes far more functionality than the old Favorites menu.

tip   Favorites Center appears as a floating panel of sorts by default, but you can attach, or pin, it to the browser window by clicking the Pin button, which looks like a small door with a green arrow on it. Curiously, to close the Favorites Center when pinned, you need to click the Close Favorites Center button, which looks like a small black x and is found above, not within, the Favorites Center panel.

To see what this means, enable the Favorites Center and mouse over the various folders and shortcuts you see in the list. If you mouse over a folder, a small blue arrow appears. If you click this arrow, you will open all of the shortcuts in that folder in their own tabs. (See the next section for more information about tabbed browsing if you don't understand what this means.) Conversely, if you mouse over a shortcut, you'll see a small red x appear. If you click this red x, the selected shortcut will be permanently deleted, with no warning dialog box. Naturally, if you click a shortcut, that shortcut will open in the current browser window. And if you click a folder, the view will expand to show you the contents of that folder, as shown in Figure 17-5.

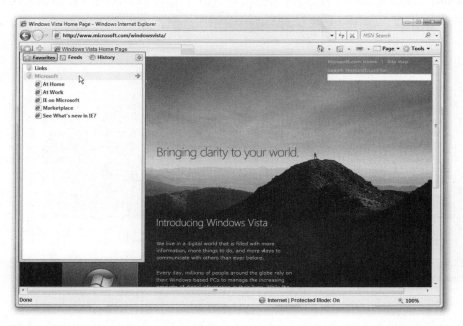

Figure 17-5: Favorites Center provides a more full-featured hub for your favorite web sites.

In addition to containing links to your favorite web sites, the Favorites Center also includes views for History (your browser history) and something called Feeds. In this way, you might think of Favorites Center as the front end to the memory of Internet Explorer 7. Here's how these two new buttons work:

- **Feeds:** Contains RSS feeds to which you've subscribed. (We examine RSS feeds in detail later in this chapter.)
- **History:** Shows you the web pages you visited in the past. When you click this button, a drop-down menu enables you to organize the list by various criteria and search your history for a previously viewed page.

Navigate the Web with Tabbed Browsing

While opinions differ on which web browser first offered tabbed browsing, a feature that optionally lets the user open new web pages within the frame of a single browser window, and access each individual page via a series of visible tabs, one thing is very clear: Internet Explorer was the last major browser to get the feature. Now that Microsoft has finally caught up and added this crucial bit of browsing functionality to Internet Explorer 7, Internet Explorer is no longer a second-class web citizen.

If you haven't had the opportunity to use tabbed browsing, chances are you'll appreciate the feature, especially if you tend to open a lot of web documents in different windows. Because you can now optionally open new web documents in a tab contained within a single browser window, you'll have fewer windows to manage and less clutter on your desktop.

Here's how tabbed browsing works. By default, Internet Explorer opens with a single document loaded, as before. But now, each document Internet Explorer displays is contained within a tab. The top of the tab — the part that looks like an actual tabbed file folder — is found at the top of the browser window, below the address bar and to the right of the Favorites Center and Add/Subscribe buttons. If you choose to never deal with tabs per se, Internet Explorer will essentially act as it did before, except that you will see that single tab there near the top of the window.

The beauty of tabbed browsing, however, is that you can open multiple tabs, which are essentially child windows of the main browser window. To open a new tab, click the New Tab button, which is the gray squared-shaped object to the right of the rightmost tab, as shown in Figure 17-6.

Secret

Although this isn't documented, you can also open a new tab by double-clicking the blank area to the right of the New Tab button.

Figure 17-6: To open a new tab, click the New Tab button.

By default, the new tab will open to a blank page and you're good to go: You can enter a web address and navigate there, go directly to your home page, or perform any other similar navigational tasks. But there are better ways to open a new tab. You can use the Ctrl+T keyboard shortcut, for starters. This will open a new tab in a manner similar to clicking the New Tab button.

But say you're doing a Google search and you want to open links to certain search results in new tabs. (This, frankly, is a great use for tabbed browsing.) To open a link in a new tab, you can right-click the link and choose Open In New Tab, or Ctrl-click the link (that is, hold down the Ctrl key on your keyboard while you click it). Alternatively, you can click the middle mouse button to open a new tab as well.

This method is particularly effective when you have a list of hyperlinks that you want to open, all at the same time. You can simply move down the list, Ctrl-clicking as you go, and then casually examine each tab in order.

That last bit brings up an interesting issue. How do you navigate between tabs? You may recall that you can navigate between open windows in Windows using the Alt+Tab key combination (or, starting in Windows Vista, the new 3D view, which is toggled by using the Windows Key+Tab key combination). In Internet Explorer 7, you can select an individual tab by clicking its tab button. But you can also use various key combinations to select tabs. To cycle through the available tabs, use the Ctrl+Tab key combination. Or, to move in reverse order, try Ctrl+Shift+Tab.

To close a tab, click the Close Tab button — which appears as a small x on the tab button of each tab. Or, use the Ctrl+W keyboard shortcut. Note that Internet Explorer will prompt you now if you attempt to close the entire browser window if two or more tabs are open: As shown in Figure 17-7, closing down multiple tabs (that is, open documents) with a single mouse click could be disastrous, so this is a nice feature.

Figure 17-7: Internet Explorer 7 will warn you if you attempt to shut down a browser window with two or more open tabs.

Quick Tabs

Although other browsers have had tabbed browsing functionality for years, Internet Explorer 7 is the first to utilize an innovative new tabbed browsing feature called Quick Tabs. Quick Tabs are a visual way of managing the open tabs you have in any Internet Explorer 7 window, and it's likely that you'll be quite taken with it.

To understand why Quick Tabs is so cool, you'll have to open a number of web pages in different tabs in Internet Explorer 7. When you are displaying two or more tabs in an Internet Explorer browser window, you'll notice that a new icon appears next to the Favorites Center and Add to Favorites icons. This icon enables you to use Quick Tabs; it resembles four squares. When you click the Quick Tabs icon, the document contained in each tab will be tiled in a thumbnail view within the main browser window as shown in Figure 17-8.

To select a particular tab from this display, simply click any of the thumbnails. That page will jump to the front and Internet Explorer will return to its normal display.

The Quick Tab icon also provides a drop-down menu. When you select this menu, you'll see a list of the available documents. You can jump to a particular tab by selecting any of the choices, and the currently displayed tab is displayed in bold type.

Figure 17-8: Quick Tabs let you quickly and visually determine which documents are loaded in each tab.

Using Multiple Home Pages

You may recall that previous Internet Explorer versions enabled you to specify any web document as your home page, which is displayed when the browser is launched. In Internet Explorer 7, you can assign multiple documents as your home page. Each document opens in its own tab. This concept is similar to that of a *tab group*, which is portrayed in the Favorites menu or Favorites view of the Favorites Center as a folder full of links. So your home page can be a single page, like before, or it can be a folder full of links, or a tab group.

To assign multiple web documents as your home page, you must first load each of the documents you want into Internet Explorer. Then, click the Tools button and select Internet Options to display the Internet Options dialog box. In the Home page section at the top of the General tab, click the Use Current button. You'll see that all of the open documents in the current browser window are added to the list.

You can also come back later and add or remove documents from the list. To add a document while keeping all of the other documents, first load the document you want to add. Then, select all of the web address in the browser's address bar and copy it to the Clipboard (by clicking Ctrl+C or right-clicking and choosing Copy). Then, select Tools and then Options, and click inside the list of web addresses you see in the Home Page section of the General tab. As shown in Figure 17-9, you can edit this list as if it were any text file. Paste the contents of the Clipboard into a new line of the list to add it to the list of home pages.

You can delete particular home pages in a similar fashion. Simply open the Internet Options dialog and edit the list, removing the pages you no longer want.

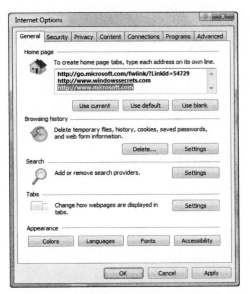

Figure 17-9: You can easily add and remove web documents from your list of home pages.

Integrated Web Search

In previous versions of Internet Explorer, Microsoft built in very basic web search features, but the company has been busy advancing the state of the art in web search in other products since Internet Explorer 6, including a variety of MSN and Windows Live toolbars, its MSN Search and Windows Live Search services, and its index-based desktop search technologies, which are included in Windows Vista. In Internet Explorer 7, Microsoft has finally added integrated web search functionality to its browser. It's pretty obvious, too: A search box sits prominently in the top-right corner of the browser window, to the right of the address bar and Refresh and Stop buttons. What's not obvious is how powerful this feature is and how easily it can be configured to your needs.

Before getting to that, think about how web search worked in Internet Explorer 6. Basically, you could navigate to a web search engine, such as Google (**www.google.com**) or, if you were savvy enough, you could utilize the autosearch feature in Internet Explorer 6 to search the Web directly from the address bar. This functionality still works in Internet Explorer 7: If you click the browser's address bar and enter text that can't be resolved as a URL, or prepend the text with a question mark (the ? character), Internet Explorer will search the Web for the text you entered. By default, it uses MSN Search, but you can configure the browser to use different search providers.

In Internet Explorer 7, you don't have to know about this secret because the search box is built right into the browser and is displayed by default. To search in Internet Explorer 7, simply select the search box, type a search query, and tap Enter (or press the Search button, which resembles a magnifying glass). The search box displays the name of the default search provider—again, MSN Search by default—in light gray text just so you know what it will use.

Specifying a Different Search Provider

But you don't have to use Microsoft's search engine. If you're a Google fan, for example, you can use Google instead. To select Google as the default search provider, click the Search Options button (the small arrow to the right of Search) and select Search Google. Now, all of your searches — including autosearch from the Internet Explorer address bar — will use Google instead of MSN Search, as shown in Figure 17-10.

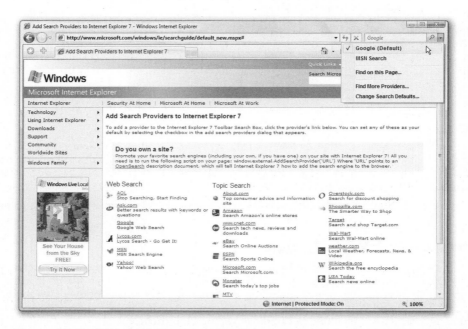

Figure 17-10: A Microsoft browser with built-in support for a competing web search service? Say it isn't so, Bill.

Microsoft also built in a way for users and other search engines to add their own providers into Internet Explorer 7 so you can use any web search service you'd like. To select from a list of search providers, click Search Options and then select Find More Providers. This will launch a Microsoft web page called the Windows Search that includes a list of search providers, including popular favorites like AOL and Yahoo!, as well as topic searches such as Amazon.com, ESPN, Wal-Mart, and even Weather.com. There's something for everyone. You can even add other providers to the site if you'd like.

Using Find in Page

In addition to searching the Web, the Internet Explorer 7.0 search functionality also enables you to search the text within a currently loaded document. This is handy when you search the Web for a specific term and then load a page that contains the text, but is quite long. Instead of reading the entire document, you can search within the document for your search string. This feature is called Find in Page.

To access Find in Page, you must first load a web document. This can be something you searched for, or it can be any web page anywhere on the Web. Then, enter a search string in the Internet Explorer search box as you would normally. However, instead of tapping Enter or hitting search, click the Search Options button and select Find In Page. This will trigger the Find dialog, which auto-fills to include the text in the search box. Click the Find Next button to begin searching.

Working with the Internet Explorer 7 Display

In previous versions of Internet Explorer, the way text was displayed in the browser was dependent on various factors, including whether you had enabled ClearType (in Windows XP only), a display mode that triples the vertical resolution of text only via a technology called sub-pixel rendering. Most people find ClearType to be hugely beneficial on LCD displays, but many complain that it makes text look fuzzy on older CRT-type monitors.

Secret   In Internet Explorer 7, ClearType is always enabled by default. However, if you find that the display is blurry on your monitor, you can turn it off. To turn off ClearType, open Internet Options and navigate to the Advanced tab. In the Settings list, scroll down to the Multimedia section. Then, deselect the option titled Always Use ClearType for HTML and restart the browser. Problem solved.

Configuring Text Size and Page Zoom

Before Internet Explorer 7, Microsoft's browsers offered only rudimentary text-sizing capabilities. Although you would typically view the text in a given web page at 100 percent magnification, Internet Explorer also offered a Text Size option that enabled you to navigate between choices such as Largest, Larger, Medium (the default), Smaller, and Smallest. These choices still exist in Internet Explorer 7, and if you're happy with them feel free to continue using them. However, they're hidden by default, since the Internet Explorer menu is hidden. To display the menu, tap the Alt key and select Text Size from the View menu.

That said, you're going to want to skip the Internet Explorer Text Size options and utilize the new Page Zoom feature instead. Unlike the Text Size options, Page Zoom works by retaining the underlying design of the web page you're viewing. That is, it doesn't just increase or decrease the size of text, which often blows away the underlying layout design. Instead, Page Zoom intelligently zooms the entire page display, including both graphics and text, all the while improving the readability of the text and retaining wonderful graphical image quality as well.

The Page Zoom user interface is located in the bottom right of the browser window, at the far right of the status bar. There, you'll see a small magnifying glass icon with the text 100% next to it (by default). When you click the small arrow to the right of this icon or text, a pop-up menu appears, as shown in Figure 17-11, letting you choose from various zoom amounts.

You can also simply click the Page Zoom icon to jump between preset page zoom values of 100 percent, 125 percent, and 150 percent. What you'll notice is that the graphics look quite good as they're resized. But the text is simply phenomenal looking. No matter how much you zoom in, the text looks impressive, as shown in Figure 17-12.

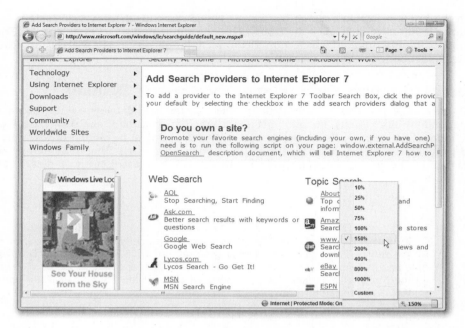

Figure 17-11: Page Zoom lets you intelligently zoom in on the current web document.

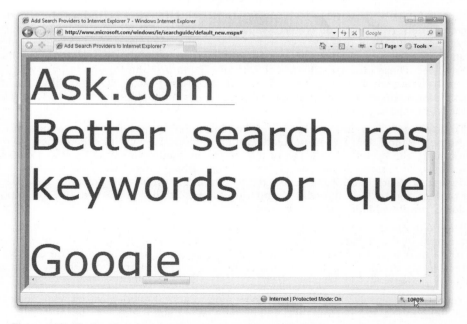

Figure 17-12: People with vision problems will appreciate the way Page Zoom makes text appear crisply and clearly.

Browsing in Full-Screen Mode

Like its predecessors, Internet Explorer 7 supports a full-screen browsing mode in which Internet Explorer covers the entire display, including the Windows Vista task bar. To enable full-screen mode, tap F11 or choose Full Screen from the Tools menu. By default, full-screen mode even hides the Internet Explorer toolbars, so you can literally use the entire system display to read the current Web page, as shown in Figure 17-13.

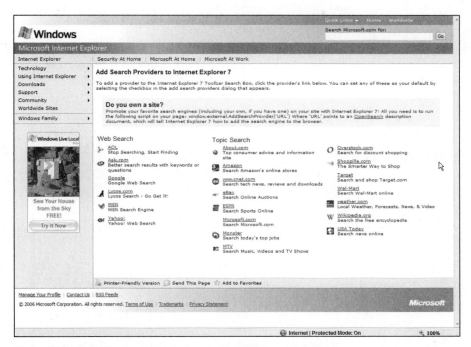

Figure 17-13: Full-screen mode is exactly what it sounds like.

tip

To display the Internet Explorer toolbars in full-screen mode, simply move your mouse to the top of the screen. The toolbars will slide in with an animated effect.

Printing

Anyone who has tried to print a web page with Internet Explorer knows how poorly that feature works. Well, take heart: Microsoft has not just fixed printing in Internet Explorer 7, removing problems that existed in previous versions, such as the way that the rightmost third of most page printouts would simply disappear off the side of the page. Now, in Internet Explorer 7, printing is actually a positive experience. It's been thoroughly overhauled.

You'll access most printing features directly through the Print button, which is found in the Internet Explorer command bar. If you just click the Print button, a standard Windows Print dialog box will appear, just as it would in any other application. From here, you can select a printer, and configure other system-wide printing options.

However, the Print button also offers a drop-down menu from which you can access additional functionality, including Print Preview and Page Setup. Both are dramatic improvements over previous Internet Explorer versions.

Using Print Preview

When you select the Print Preview option from the Print button drop-down menu, you'll see the Print Preview display shown in Figure 17-14. From here, you can switch between portrait and landscape display modes, access the Page Setup dialog, and perform other printing-related tasks.

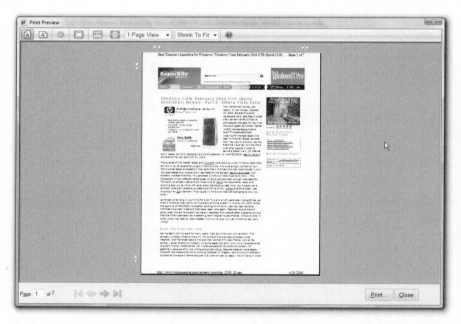

Figure 17-14: The Internet Explorer 7 Print Preview feature is a big improvement from Internet Explorer 6.

The biggest change from Internet Explorer 6 is that you can now easily toggle whether each page includes footer and headers. To see how this works, click the Turn Headers And Footers On or Off button and see how it changes the display in Print Preview. You can also display the pages to print in various ways. For example, you can display an entire page in the window, fit the display to the width of the window, or even display multiple pages as shown in Figure 17-15.

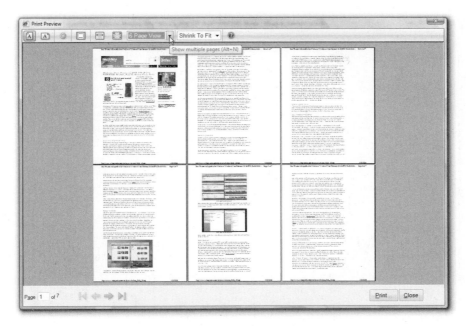

Figure 17-15: A multiple-page preview in Internet Explorer 7.

When you're ready to print, click the Print button at the bottom of the Print Preview window. Or, click Close to return to Internet Explorer.

Print Preview of Selected Content

Another truly amazing feature is that you can print, and print preview, only the content you've selected in a web page. That is, you don't have to print an entire web page. Instead, you can print that text that you've selected, or highlighted.

To see how this works, open a web document and select some text. Then, choose the Print Preview option from the Print button drop-down menu. When the Print Preview window comes up, you'll see a new Select Content drop-down menu in the middle top of the window, as shown in Figure 17-16. Open the drop-down list and choose As Selected On Screen. Now, only the selected text is ready to print.

Using Page Setup

If you want even more fine-grain control over how your web pages will print, you can use the Page Setup dialog box. This dialog box can be accessed in two ways: through the Page Setup button in the Print Preview toolbar, or through the Page Setup option in the Print button's drop-down menu. This dialog box, shown in Figure 17-17, enables you to configure the paper size and source, the margin sizes, and also the text strings used to configure the header and footer display.

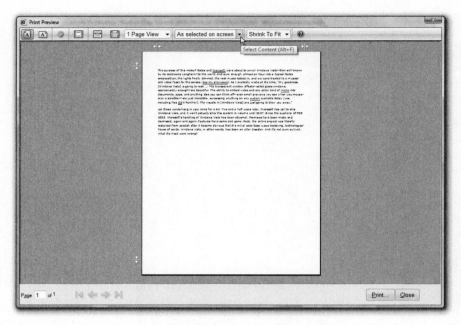

Figure 17-16: Now, you can print only those parts of a web page you want.

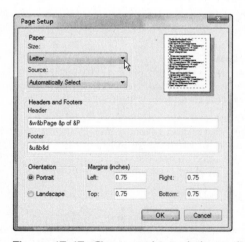

Figure 17-17: Change various printing options through the Page Setup dialog box.

By default, the Header text string is set to **&w&bPage &p of &P**, which looks like a bunch of gooblygook until you realize that each of those characters has meaning. The **&** character is used to denote a header or footer *variable*. So **&w** is a variable, which happens to stand for window title. The full range of header and footer variables is shown in Table 17-4.

Table 17-4: Page Setup Header and Footer Variable Values

Variable	*Value*
Window title	**&w**
Page address (URL)	**&u**
Date in short format	**&d**
Date in long format	**&D**
Time	**&t**
Time in 24-hour format	**&T**
Current page number	**&p**
Total number of pages	**&P**
Right-aligned text (following **&b**)	**&b**
Centered text (between **&b** and **&b**)	**&b&b**
An ampersand character (**&**)	**&&**

tip   In previous versions of Internet Explorer, you had to use the Page Setup dialog box to remove headers and footers from the printout. This method still works, though the Print Preview method described previously is simpler and quicker. To remove the header completely, simply select the Header text box and delete all of the text.

Covering Your Tracks

Although it was possible to perform housekeeping tasks such as removing temporary Internet files and cookies and deleting your browser history, and saved form data and passwords, Internet Explorer 7 now offers an incredibly handy front end for doing this all with the single click of your mouse button. The feature is called Delete Browsing History, and it's a nifty addition.

Shown in Figure 17-18, Delete Browsing History enables you to delete temporary Internet files, cookies, browser history, saved form data, or saved passwords individually or all at the same time using the Delete All button. It's a one-stop shop for covering your tracks.

Figure 17-18: Delete Browsing History is one of the best new features in Internet Explorer 7.

Here's what each of the options means.

- ◆ **Temporary Internet Files:** These are downloaded files that have been cached in your Temporary Internet Files folder, including Offline Favorites and attachments stored by Microsoft Outlook.
- ◆ **Cookies:** These are small text files that include data that persists between visits to particular web sites.
- ◆ **History:** This is the list of web sites you've visited with Internet Explorer and the web addresses you've typed in the Windows Vista Run dialog box.
- ◆ **Form Data:** Information that's been saved using the Internet Explorer's auto-complete form data functionality.
- ◆ **Passwords:** Passwords that were saved using Internet Explorer autocomplete password data functionality.

note
One feature Microsoft didn't improve in Internet Explorer 7 is its handling of web downloads. Users of other browsers, such as Mozilla Firefox, are used to more sophisticated download managers, which can pause downloads midstream and resume them later. Microsoft has pledged to improve Internet Explorer more rapidly than it did in the past, and we've been told that the company will look at including a full-featured download manager in a future Internet Explorer version.

Understanding and Using RSS

Although much of the World Wide Web is based on a rather passive system where users manually browse to the web sites they'd like to visit, a new type of web technology, called Really Simple Syndication (RSS), has turned that paradigm on its head and changed the way many people consume web-based information. In keeping with this sea change, Internet Explorer 7 supports RSS, letting Windows Vista users access web-based content in both traditional and modern ways.

So what is RSS? Basically, it's a data format, based on XML, designed for distributing news and other web-based content via the Internet. Content that is available via RSS is said to be published in RSS format, while applications (like Internet Explorer) that can access RSS content are said to subscribe to that content.

What makes RSS different from traditional web browsing is that RSS applications periodically poll the content publishers to which you've subscribed. So if you subscribe to the RSS *feed*, as such a link is called, to a particular web site, that feed will be updated on your local machine periodically, assuming you have an Internet connection. Most good RSS applications, including Internet Explorer 7, allow you to specify how often feeds are updated. Some feeds, obviously, are updated more often than others.

The Internet Explorer RSS functionality is exposed in a number of ways. The Internet Explorer 7 command bar has a prominent orange Feeds button, which provides an obvious front end to this technology. (The Feeds button is grayed out if you are currently visiting a web page with which there is no RSS feed associated, however.) So you must visit a site with an RSS feed to discover how it works.

Viewing an RSS Feed

As an example, take a look at the CNN web site. CNN, a major news site, does indeed have an RSS feed, as indicated by the orange color of the Internet Explorer Feeds button. To view the feed, simply click the button. Internet Explorer will switch to its new feed reading page, which displays the content of the CNN feed (in this case) in the vaguely pleasant, if bland, style shown in Figure 17-19.

Figure 17-19: Internet Explorer 7.0 feed reading page.

Secret

Some web sites include two or more RSS feeds. If this is the case, you can display the list of available feeds by clicking the small arrow at the right of the Feeds button. Then, simply choose the feed you want.

In the Feed Reading Page view, you can perform various actions, including searching the feed for specific text using the search box in the upper-right corner of the page, or sorting by date (the default) or title. The CNN feed publishes only the title and a small abstract for each article it lists. So if you want to view a full article, you must click on the title for the article you'd like to read. Some feeds publish entire articles directly in the feed, so you don't have to manually visit the main web site.

Subscribing to an RSS Feed

In this view, you're essentially just browsing the Web as before, albeit through a non-standard display. But the real power of RSS feeds comes when you subscribe. To subscribe to the CNN feed, you simply click the Subscribe To This Feed link at the top of the page. When you do so, the Subscribe To This Feed dialog box appears, as shown in Figure 17-20. Here, you can edit the name of the Feed, where it will be created (the Feeds folder, by default), and whether to automatically download any files that might be attached to the feed.

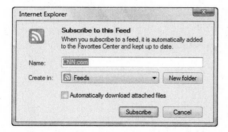

Figure 17-20: When you subscribe to an RSS Feed, it is stored in a Favorites-like database.

When you've subscribed, the feed-reading page changes to indicate that you've successfully subscribed to the feed. Additionally, you may see an alert noting that automatic feed updates are turned off. If you see this alert, your RSS subscriptions will not be updated automatically. To enable this functionality, click the Turn On Automatic Feed Updates link.

Managing RSS Feeds

Internet Explorer treats RSS subscriptions much like Favorites. However, RSS subscriptions are not stored in your Favorites folder. Instead, they are stored in a special database that is based on the RSS platform technologies built into Windows Vista.

You access your subscribed feeds through the Favorites Center. You may recall from our discussion earlier in this chapter that Feeds, like Favorites and History lists, are stored in this browser memory. If you open the Favorites Center, you'll see that CNN has been added to the Feeds view, which is shown in Figure 17-21.

Figure 17-21: The Feeds view in Favorites Center is like Favorites for Feeds.

As with your Favorites list, you can do a few interesting things with RSS feeds in the Favorites Center. When you mouse over a feed in the list of subscribed feeds, you'll see a small refresh icon appear. If you click this icon, the feed will manually be updated if there is any new content to download. If you simply click the feed name, the feed will be displayed in the feed reading page as you'd expect.

RSS Is a Platform

One of the more interesting things about the RSS support in Internet Explorer 7 is that it's based on a much wider RSS platform that is available to any application running in Windows Vista. This means that third-party applications can access the RSS feeds you've subscribed to in Internet Explorer and provide you with even more advanced functionality. To see an example of what's possible, check out the RSS Feeds gadget for the Windows Sidebar. We examine that feature in Chapter 6.

Internet Explorer 7 Keyboard Shortcuts

Keyboard shortcuts make it possible to navigate the Internet Explorer user interface without having to move a hand over to the mouse. Internet Explorer 7 supports virtually all of the keyboard shortcuts supported by Internet Explorer 6, but it also adds a slew of new shortcuts related to new functionality in this version. Table 17-5 summarizes the Internet Explorer 7 keyboard shortcuts.

Table 17-5: Internet Explorer 7.0 Keyboard Shortcuts

Keyboard Shortcut	What It Does
Alt+left arrow key	Navigate to previous page.
Alt+right arrow key	Navigate to the next page.
Esc	Stop current page from loading.
F5 or Ctrl+R or Ctrl+F5	Refresh (reload) the current page.
Alt+Home	Go to your home page.
Alt+D	Select the address bar.
Ctrl+Enter	Automatically add **www** and **.com** to what you typed in the address bar.
Spacebar	Scroll down the web page.
Shift+Spacebar	Scroll up the web page.
Alt+F4	Close the current window.
Ctrl+D	Add the current page to your Favorites list.
Alt+N	Select the information bar.
Shift+F10	Open the context menu for the currently selected item.
Shift+mouse click	Open link in a new window.
Ctrl+mouse click	Open link in new background tab.
Ctrl+Shift+mouse click	Open link in new foreground tab.
Ctrl+T	Open a new tab.
Alt+Enter	Open a new tab from the address bar.
Ctrl+Tab	Switch between available tabs.
Ctrl+Shift+Tab	Switch between available tabs in the opposite direction.
Ctrl+W	Close the current tab (or current window if there are no open tabs).
Ctrl+x (where x represents the number of the tab, as numbered from 1 to 8)	Switch to a particular tab.
Ctrl+9	Switch to the last tab.
Ctrl+Alt+F4	Close other tabs.
Ctrl+Q	Open Quick Tabs.
Ctrl+(+)	Zoom page by 10 percent.
Ctrl+(-)	Decrease page zoom by 10 percent.
Ctrl+0	Zoom to 100 percent (normal view).
Ctrl+E	Navigate to the Toolbar Search box.
Alt+Enter (from the search box)	Open search in a new window.

Keyboard Shortcut	What It Does
Ctrl+Down Arrow (from the search box)	Display the search provider menu.
Ctrl+H	Open Favorites Center to the History view.
Ctrl+I	Open Favorites Center to the Favorites view.
Ctrl+J	Open Favorites Center to the Feeds view.

In addition to these handy keyboard shortcuts, Internet Explorer 7 also supports a few helpful mouse actions, which are like shortcuts you can trigger with the mouse. These actions are detailed in Table 17-6.

Table 17-6: Internet Explorer 7.0 Mouse Actions

Mouse Action	What It Does
Click the middle mouse button	Open link in a new tab.
Click the middle mouse button on the tab	Close a tab.
Double-click the empty space to the right of the New Tab button	Open a new tab.
Ctrl + mouse wheel up	Zoom page by 10 percent.
Ctrl + mouse wheel down	Decrease page zoom by 10 percent.

Secret

It's worth noting that other browsers support a much wider range of these mouse actions, which are typically called mouse gestures, or simply gestures, outside of Microsoft. Fortunately, some intrepid developers have released a handy plug-in for Internet Explorer 7 that adds far more mouse actions to the browser. So head on over to The Code Project (www.codeproject.com/atl/MouseGestures.asp) if you think this will enhance your productivity.

cross ref

This is Internet Explorer we're talking about, so you might be wondering where you can find a discussion of Internet Explorer 7 security features. Have no fear: Internet Explorer 7 includes a huge number of security-related features, and they're all covered in Chapter 8.

Summary

Internet Explorer 7 is a huge advance over previous versions, with major functional advances. Although we might debate whether the user interface changes will make

Internet Explorer 7 harder to use, it's hard to argue the other features Microsoft has added: Tabbed browsing and Quick Tabs, Favorites Center, integrated web search, the browser's vastly improved text display and printing functionality, and its history-hiding techniques are all wonderful advancements. Internet Explorer 7 integration with RSS is also a positive sign: This standards-based web technology is sweeping across the Internet, enabling everything from blogs to podcasts. For once, Internet Explorer is on the cusp of the next big thing.

Windows Mail and Contacts

In This Chapter

Finding out about the new features in Windows Mail

Getting support for web e-mail accounts

Finding and managing new Windows Mail storage engine

Managing contacts and contact groups with Windows Contacts

Importing contacts from your previous Windows version

Back when Microsoft shipped Windows 95, e-mail was a corporate curiosity, but today, e-mail is a pervasive presence in many people's lives, both personal and professional. For years, Windows has been saddled with an almost universally loathed e-mail client called Outlook Express. Unfortunately, that e-mail client carries through to Windows Vista, albeit with a new name: Windows Mail. On the flipside, Windows Vista does introduce a dramatically improved contacts management system, based on XML technology, called Windows Contacts. We'll examine the facets of both Windows Vista features in this chapter.

Windows Mail Basics

In previous versions of Windows, Microsoft offered a bare bones e-mail and newsgroup client called Outlook Express. The name suggested that Outlook Express was somehow related to Microsoft's premier e-mail and personal information management client, Outlook, although nothing could be further from the truth. Oddly, Outlook Express includes certain functionality that was never included in Outlook—primarily support for USENET Newsgroups—whereas Outlook, of course, includes numerous features not found in Outlook Express, including Exchange Server support, calendaring and tasks, and more.

In Windows Vista, Outlook Express has been replaced by a new mail client called Windows Mail, shown in Figure 18-1. So you might be forgiven if you think that Microsoft has finally replaced the lackluster Outlook Express with something better. Unfortunately, that's not what's happened. Instead, Windows Mail is nothing more than a minor upgrade to Outlook Express, presented in a warmed-over user interface that's only barely updated to look a bit like other Windows Vista applications. In fact, Windows Mail is actually missing a few features from Outlook Express.

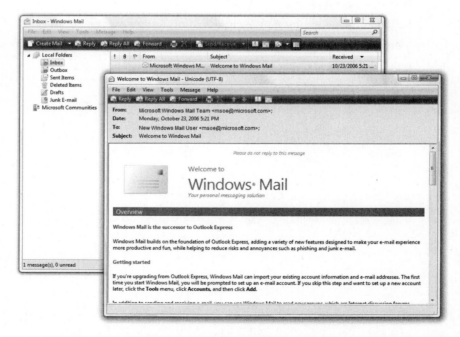

Figure 18-1: It's déjà vu all over again: Windows Mail is really just a new name for Outlook Express.

Configuring Windows Mail

To use Windows Mail with your e-mail account, you need to get the names of the SMTP and POP3 servers at your Internet service provider (ISP), as well as your e-mail address and e-mail password, your account name (user ID), and your logon password. In the Windows Mail window, choose Tools⇨Accounts, and then Add⇨E-Mail Account to start configuring your Internet mail account.

By default, Internet Explorer uses Windows Mail as the mail tool when you click an e-mail address while viewing a web page. If you want to use another e-mail client (such as Microsoft Outlook or Mozilla Thunderbird) you can change this default behavior. To do so, right-click the Start button, choose Properties, and then click Customize. In the bottom of the Customize Start menu dialog box, click the E-mail link button to pick the default client.

To read the articles (also called *messages* or *postings*) in newsgroups, you need to connect to a news server. Your ISP probably maintains a news server, but Windows Mail is already preconfigured with a newsgroup account called Microsoft Communities that provides access to Microsoft's public product support newsgroup server. You can also connect to other news servers.

To connect to a news server, choose Newsgroup Account in the New Account wizard.

Changing Windows Mail Options Right Away

We don't like the default configurations for Windows Mail—especially for the first-time user. We suggest that you make the following changes along with us:

- ◆ Choose Tools and then Options. Click the Read tab, and mark the Automatically Expand Grouped Messages check box. Now you won't have to click the plus symbol repeatedly to follow a conversation thread, at the slight cost of seeing multiple entries in a thread that you might not be particularly interested in.

- ◆ On the Signatures tab, enter at least a rudimentary signature—your name at least—or other information that will appear in the bottom of every e-mail message or newsgroup message you send. You can make additional signatures and get more elaborate as discussed later in this chapter, but we suggest that you don't get carried away. Mark the Add Signatures to All Outgoing Messages check box. You can choose Insert⇨Signature in a New Message window to insert your default signature when you write a message, but if you usually use the same signature it's easier and more consistent to let the computer do it for you.

  To automatically associate a particular signature with a mail or news account, highlight it in the Signatures list and click the Advanced button. In the Advanced Signature Settings dialog box, check all the accounts for which this signature is to be the default. For these accounts only, doing so will override the general default signature setting.

- ◆ Make sure that the Send Messages Immediately check box in the Send tab (Tools⇨Options) is marked if you work online or want to have messages sent as soon as you finish writing them. If you work offline, clear this check box, and choose Tools⇨Send And Receive when you're ready to send your mail. You can also just click the Send And Receive button in the Windows Mail toolbar to send mail from your Outbox to the mail server.

  If you are browsing the Internet online and click an e-mail address on a web page to send a message, that message will not go out right away unless the Send Messages Immediately check box is marked. Instead it will wait in your outbox until you click the Send And Receive button in Windows Mail.

More Windows Mail Features

The Windows Mail window is divided into three panes. The message header pane (the one on the top right) lists the message headers, and the preview pane (the one on the bottom right) displays the contents of whatever message you have selected in the message header pane. You can arrange these two panes either horizontally or vertically. To do this, choose View⇨Layout⇨Below Messages or Beside Messages (actually below or beside message headers).

By default, Windows Mail displays its folders in a large pane on the left, called the Folder List. Unlike its predecessor, Outlook Express, however, Windows Mail does not display the contents of your address book in a pane on the lower left. Unfortunately, there's no way to enable this old feature.

When you single-click a message header, you can view its contents in the preview pane. This works just fine most of the time. If you want to view a message in a new (and bigger) window, double-click the message header. If you want to get rid of the preview pane and only view messages in separate message windows, choose View⇨Layout and clear the Show Preview Pane check box. Typically, you'll want to leave the preview pane open, however.

tip   If you want news messages to appear in the preview pane as soon as you select them, choose Tools⇨Options, click the Read tab, and make sure the Automatically Download Message When Viewing in the Preview Pane option is selected. When this option is turned off, you have to press the spacebar after selecting a message to display its contents in the preview pane.

If you don't like the column order in the message header pane, drag the gray column header buttons to the desired position. You can also change the width of the columns by resting your mouse on the spacer line between column header buttons and dragging to the right or the left. To sort your messages by a particular column (such as the Subject column), click the column header button. To sort by the same column in reverse order, click the button again. To add or remove columns, right-click the column header and choose Columns, then check or clear the boxes for the columns you want to display.

tip   If you're using the preview pane to view your messages, you can get a little extra room by hiding the header bar at the top of the preview pane. To do this, choose View⇨ Layout⇨Show Preview Pane Header. The tradeoff is that you lose the ability to quickly open or save attachments by clicking the paper clip button in the header bar. For this reason, you should leave the header on.

If you right-click the Windows Mail toolbar and choose Customize, you'll notice that you can change its content and appearance. The toolbar gets a lot bigger and more readable if you make the icons bigger (choose Large Icons from the Icon Options list) and take out the text under the buttons (choose No Text Labels from the Text Options list). You can also get rid of the toolbar altogether by choosing View⇨Layout, and then clearing the check mark next to Toolbar.

Sadly, Microsoft removed the popular Outlook bar in this version, so that's no longer an option.

Using the Views Bar

Right-click your toolbar and you'll see a menu item named Views Bar. Click it to display a handy drop-down list of view types. Now you can easily see whether you've chosen Show All Messages, Hide Read Or Ignored Messages, or Hide Read Messsages. You can drag the Views bar below or above the regular toolbar if you'd like.

The Folder Bar and Folder List

The folder bar is a thick gray stripe under the toolbar that lists your current message folder and identity. When the Folder List pane is not displayed, you can use the folder bar to verify which folder you're in and navigate to another. Click the name of the current folder in the folder bar to display a drop-down folder list. The folders list works similarly to the Folder List pane, in that you can right-click folders in it, and use it to drag and drop.

You may decide not to display the Folder List pane, and to use the folder list instead. This gives you a wider Preview pane and makes it easier to read messages without opening them. To turn off the Folder List pane, click the Close Window button in the upper-right corner of the pane — or choose View⇨Layout, Clear Folder List, and then click OK.

If you prefer to display the Folder List pane, you might find that the folder bar takes up too much real estate in your Windows Mail window. To turn the folder bar off, choose View⇨ Layout, and clear the Folder Bar check box. If you do this, you may want to put the Folder List button on your toolbar so you can toggle the Folder List pane on and off without using the folder bar.

Working Online or Offline

If you have a constant Internet connection, you can work online all the time without wor-rying about it. But if you want to compose e-mail offline, such as when you're on a plane, you sometimes need a way to use communications applications such as Windows Mail and Internet Explorer without trying to communicate with the server.

For example, when you move from your inbox to a news folder, Windows Mail attempts to connect to that news server if you are working online. This might also happen when you highlight the header of an e-mail message that links to a web site. If you just want to look at the messages without connecting, first switch to working offline. This setting is global for all of your applications that use it, so if you are offline in Internet Explorer, you are also offline in Windows Mail.

The standard way to change your work online/work offline setting is by choosing File⇨ Work. But Windows Mail offers two other ways to both see and change your current state. One is an Offline button that you can add to your mail or news toolbar. When you are working offline, it appears to be depressed. The button's icon and text show you what will happen if you click it, *not* your current state. Some of us find this confusing.

More convenient than the toolbar button is the status bar at the bottom of your Windows Mail window. Not only does the status bar clearly indicate your current online/offline state, but in Windows Mail it toggles on and off with a simple double-click. Best of all, it's visible all the time by default.

Using a Nondefault Mail or News Account

If you have set up more than one mail account, when you start a new mail message you will see a From field at the top of the New Message window displaying your default mail account. Likewise, when you reply to a mail message, the From field in your reply will display the account to which the original message was sent, but give you the option to change the account from which your reply is sent. News messages prompt you with a dialog box to choose the account to use.

It's really easy to choose a different mail account or news server for your message. Click the down arrow to the right of the From (or News Server) field in the message header and select from the list of active accounts. When a message is in your outbox, you can look in the Account column to see which account it will use. (If you don't see that column, right-click a column header, click Columns, mark the Account check box in the Columns list, and then click OK.)

What's That Pushpin For?

You may have noticed a pushpin icon in the lower-right corner of the Send And Receive dialog box in Windows Mail. Or you may never have noticed it. The purpose of the push-pin is to tell you how the dialog box will behave. Normally, the point of the pushpin points to the left. This indicates that the dialog box will close automatically after your e-mail messages are downloaded. But if you click the pushpin, it will appear as though it's sticking into the screen, indicating that now the dialog box will stay visible after the download is complete. That can be useful if you want to review the tasks Windows Mail went through in sending and receiving messages. If Windows Mail encounters any errors, the dialog box stays visible with the Errors tab in front, even if the pushpin is out. In either case, you can just click the Hide button to send the dialog box away.

Dragging and Dropping to a Windows Mail Message

If you want to send a new message containing some text from another message or document, all you have to do is drag and drop. Windows Mail must be open for this to work, but it can be minimized as follows:

1. Highlight the text that you want to send. If the text is in a Windows Mail message, you can highlight it in either the message window or the Preview pane. If it's in another document, such as a text file or a Microsoft Word document, highlight it there.

2. Drag and drop the highlighted text onto any message folder except the outbox. If Windows Mail is minimized, hover over its Taskbar button until it opens. If the Folders pane is not displayed, hover over the folder name on the folder bar until the Folders list appears. Drop onto a mail folder for mail, or onto a news folder for news.

    A New Message window appears containing only the text you highlighted. No header information appears in the new message, and no quote characters are included.

Using Windows Mail with E-mail

Windows Mail operates in mail mode by default, but you can switch mail modes by highlighting a mail folder in the Folder List pane.

Handling Multiple E-mail Accounts

If you have multiple e-mail server accounts, you can poll a single account for e-mail manually. Just choose Tools⇔Send and Receive, and then choose the account from the submenu that appears. You can choose which e-mail accounts are polled when you click the Send And Receive button (which does the same thing as Tools⇔Send and Receive⇔Send And Receive All). Just click Tools⇔Accounts, highlight a mail account, click the Properties button, and mark or clear the Include This Account When Receiving Mail or Synchronizing check box. This also works to choose which accounts Windows Mail polls automatically.

Replies to your messages will still go to your stated e-mail address (the reply address you indicate in the General tab of each account's Properties dialog box) even though you don't necessarily send out your e-mail through the SMTP server at your e-mail address location.

Choosing Which Account to Send Your Messages Through

If you have multiple e-mail server accounts, the New Message window gives you the ability to choose which account the message will be delivered through. This is true even if you are replying to a message that may have been delivered through a different account. Each account has a specific SMTP outgoing mail server. To associate a specific account with a message, use the drop-down menu button at the right end of the From field.

If you don't specify an account, Windows Mail sends the message through your default mail server account. Because each account can have a separate Internet connection, and because you can stack mail in your outbox, it is quite possible to click the Send And Receive button and have Windows Mail call up multiple ISPs and send out mail through each of them.

Waving When the Mail Arrives

You can make your computer play a tune (play a **.wav** or Windows Media Video, **.wmv**, file) when your mail arrives. To do this, choose Tools⇔Options, click the General tab, and select the Play Sound When New Messages Arrive check box. This only makes sense if you have marked Check for New Messages Every [ ] Minute(s) in the same tab.

Windows Mail must be running for the tune to play. (And if you receive your mail from the Internet and not an Intranet, you have to be connected to the Internet as well.)

To pick the sound to play, right-click the Volume icon in the Windows Vista system tray and choose Sounds. Then, in the Program list, scroll down to New Mail Notification. Click Sounds to pick a default sound. Or, click Browse to find another sound file you'd like to use.

Leaving Mail on the Server

If you are traveling, you might want to leave mail messages on your mail server until you get back, even though you want to read them now. That way, you can download them to your office computer when you return.

To do this, choose Tools⇔Accounts, highlight your mail server, click the Properties button, click the Advanced tab, and mark the Leave a Copy of Messages on Server check box.

Converting the Mail

You can import Exchange, Outlook, Outlook Express 6, and Windows Mail 7 messages into Windows Mail format. In Windows Mail, just choose File⇨Import and then Messages.

Reading and Managing Messages

Electronic messages differ from other types of messages in several ways, but one of the most significant is the ease in composing and sending messages electronically. This ease contributes to the absolute flood of messages that many people send and receive on a regular basis. Fortunately, Windows Mail offers several ways for you to deal with all of these messages — as you'll see in the following sections.

Did You Receive the Message?

When you send an important letter the old-fashioned way, you can ask the post office to notify you when the letter is delivered. It's possible for e-mail to work the same way. Actually it's not quite the same, because there's no friendly postal carrier to hand the letter to the addressee and ask him or her to sign the receipt. Still, you can ask to be notified when someone opens a message you have sent. In the New Message window, select Tools⇨Request Read Receipt. You can set this globally for all messages you send by choosing Tools⇨Options⇨Receipts and marking Request A Read Receipt For All Sent Messages. But before you select this check box, consider: do you really want to clutter your inbox with all those receipts?

If you receive a message with a receipt request, Windows Mail will ask whether you want to send a receipt. You can set it to Always Send A Read Receipt or to Never Send A Read Receipt by marking the appropriate box on the Receipts tab of the Tools⇨Options dialog box. If you decide to always send a receipt, you will probably want to make an exception for mailing lists by marking the Always send a read receipt check box.

If you frequently send or receive digitally signed messages, it can be very helpful to verify that the message arrived free of security errors. You set the behavior for secure receipts separately from the nonsecure kind, using the same Tools⇨Options⇨Receipts dialog box.

Choosing Your Columns

You can choose which columns to display in the Message pane. To do this, right-click any column header button and click Columns (or choose View⇨Columns). In the Columns dialog box, mark the columns you want to see and clear those you don't. Use the Move Up button and the Move Down button to set the order in which columns will appear (or you can drag the column header buttons to position them). Each message folder can have different column settings.

For example, if you find the Flag column isn't useful and is just taking up space, you can turn it off. Although you will still be able to flag a message, you won't see the icons in the Message pane and will be unable to sort by flag.

tip If you have more than one incoming mail account, you might want to view the Account column. That way, you can easily see where a message came from without bothering with message rules. The Account column can also be very helpful in your Outbox.

Composing and Sending Messages

You can associate a new mail message with a specific account at the time that the message is composed. This is especially helpful if you have multiple users with different accounts on the same computer.

1. Open a New Message window by clicking Message, New Message.
2. Click anywhere in the From field to display a list of your accounts.
3. Select the mail account you want to use when sending the message.

What's the Drafts Folder For?

The Drafts folder is a place to keep messages that you're not yet ready to send. When you are composing a message and you choose File⇨Save, your unfinished message is automatically stored in the Drafts folder. If you close a New Message window without sending the message and click Yes when asked if you want to save it, the message will be stored in Drafts. To finish editing a message stored in the Drafts folder, double-click the message to open it. When you click the Send button, Windows Mail moves it from the Drafts folder to the outbox.

Quoting in Replies and Forwards

When you reply to an e-mail message, it's helpful if you can distinguish the text you write from the message text you are replying to. In plain text messages, the standard is to place a > symbol in front of each quoted line of text. Fortunately, Windows Mail does this by default. But to configure related functionality, follow these steps:

1. Choose Tools⇨Options in the Windows Mail window, and click the Send tab.
2. Make sure that the Include Message in Reply check box is marked. (This is the default.) If this option is deselected, your replies will be much harder to understand since they will not include a copy of the original message.
3. On this same tab, click the Plain Text Settings button under Mail Sending Format. Make sure Indent the Original Text with [ ] When Replying Or Forwarding is marked. Windows Mail no longer lets you use a character other than > at the beginning of each line of quoted text.
4. Click OK.

So far, so good. But this kind of quoting only works as long as you are replying to a message sent using plain text. Messages sent using MIME/Quoted Printable (such as HTML-formatted messages) don't insert line endings, so there are no line beginnings for Windows Mail to mark with >. Instead, the text is formatted in paragraphs. Even if you tell Windows Mail to reply in plain text, it will still not place a > at the beginning of quoted lines if they weren't originally composed in plain text. Instead, quoted HTML text is indented with a vertical bar along its left side.

Secret

There is a downside to marking Indent Messages on Reply, however, if you like to intersperse replies with quoted text to simulate a conversation. If you insert your reply after a section of quoted text, you'll find the new text is also indented with the vertical bar. To get rid of the indent and the bar, first place your insertion point in the quoted text where you want to insert your reply text and press Enter — this inserts a line break. Then with your insertion point in the new paragraph, click the Paragraph Style toolbar button and click Normal. Even though the drop-down list shows that the current paragraph is already Normal, this will work. Your new text will be flush left and will not have a vertical bar.

Messages Formatted in HTML

Windows Mail formats your e-mail messages and newsgroup posts using HTML by default. Choose Tools⇨Options, and click the Send tab to override the default setting for the current newsgroup post or e-mail message. Just choose Format in the New Message window, and click Rich Text (HTML) or Plain Text. If you're using HTML, you get a formatting toolbar that lets you choose the font, font size, font color, and so on.

tip

Lots of newsgroup and e-mail clients aren't able to display HTML-formatted text. If they can't, your correspondents will see the HTML tags embedded in the plain text of your messages — something that they might not appreciate.

Frankly, HTML e-mail is generally obnoxious. Our advice is to use plain text for both e-mail and newsgroup messages.

Stationery

If you do use HTML e-mail, you can configure Windows Mail to automatically start a new blank message with your chosen background color, background image, font, and margins. You can choose from among the existing stationery files, create new stationery, create stationery that is just a background color, or download new stationery from Microsoft.

To pick a default stationery type, choose Tools⇨Options⇨Compose, mark the Mail or News check box under Stationery, and click the Select button. You get to preview the stationery before you select it. After you have chosen a stationery type, clicking New Mail or New Post will open a New Message window with that stationery already included in the message.

Secret

Press Ctrl+F2 to see that the source code of the HTML e-mail file that Windows Mail uses to create the stationery has been inserted into your new message, including the name of the associated GIF file. In addition, at the top of this HTML view of your message, you'll find a reference pointing to the folder that holds the stationery's image file.

If you want to create a message with something other than the default stationery, click the down arrow to the right of the New Mail or New Post button. You can pick the stationery or choose no stationery at all.

Attachments

Here's how to handle all those incoming e-mail attachments.

Saving Attachments

To save an attachment to a message you have received, double-click the message header in the message header pane to display the message in a separate window. Then drag and drop the attachment icon from the Attach field into a folder or onto the desktop. You can also right-click the attachment icon and click Save As.

To save an attachment without opening a separate message window, click the message header, and then click the paper clip icon in the upper-right corner of the preview pane (the Show Preview Pane Header check box must be marked in the View⇨Layout dialog box). A menu listing the names of the attachments in the message appears. Click the name of the attachment you want to open. If you instead choose Save Attachments from this menu, you can browse to a folder for saving more than one at a time.

You can also just highlight the message header and choose File⇨Save Attachments.

New Features in Windows Mail

You either use Outlook Express or you don't. If you do, you might be interested in some of the few new features Microsoft actually did add to the Windows Vista version, Windows Mail. If you don't use Outlook Express, there's no reason to start now. There are much better e-mail clients out there, including Microsoft Outlook, and if you're looking for a solution that handles both e-mail and newsgroups, Mozilla's free Thunderbird client is more secure and feature-packed than is Windows Mail.

That said, there are some new features and secrets to be had. Let's take a look.

Slightly Updated User Interface

The first thing you'll notice when you fire up Windows Mail is that it's been updated subtly to conform to the new Windows Vista look and feel. It still includes a classic menu bar, but the old bulky toolbar has been replaced by a smaller blue toolbar similar to those found in other Vista applications. That said, the user interface of Windows Mail is almost identical to that of Outlook Express. There is a new Contacts button in the toolbar that replaces the old Contacts panel from Outlook Express, and various icons used throughout the Windows Mail user interface have been refreshed. But that's about it: Even the Windows Mail menu structure is virtually identical to that of its predecessor, with very few exceptions. This just isn't a brand-new application, let alone a major update.

No More Support for Web Mail

The biggest change in Windows Mail, unfortunately, is that support for web-based e-mail services, such as Hotmail and Gmail, has been eliminated. In Outlook Express, you could choose between POP3, IMAP, and HTTP mail server types; the latter was used for web mail accounts. In Windows Mail, that last option was eliminated. Only POP3 and IMAP accounts are now supported.

Why is this, you ask? After reassessing its web mail strategy during the development of Windows Vista, Microsoft began evolving Hotmail into a new service called Windows Live Mail that includes both free and paid versions. Not coincidentally, the company is also offering a new e-mail client that is designed expressly for the new service. This new client is called Windows Live Mail Desktop, and it offers support for web mail accounts. Microsoft's advice is to use this client, and not Windows Mail, if you need to access web mail accounts.

cross ref   We discuss Windows Live Mail Desktop in Chapter 19.

Secret   A better option, we think, is to use Google's free Gmail service. Gmail offers oodles of storage, and you can even access it via standard POP3 servers, which means that, yes, Gmail is fully compatible with Windows Mail even though it's technically a web mail service. Interested in Gmail? Check out www.gmail.com.

You can find out more about Windows Live Mail from the Live.com web site at **www.ideas.live.com/**.

Instant Search

Like much of Windows Vista, Windows Mail is integrated with the operating system's instant search functionality. This means that Windows Mail picks up a handy instant search box in the upper right corner of the main application window. To search the current view — be it an e-mail folder or online newsgroup — simply select the search box and start typing. Searching is instantaneous, so it will begin filtering down the list as you type. Also, instant search will search across all applicable criteria, including sender, subject line, and e-mail or newsgroup body.

tip   Interestingly, the old Find toolbar button from Outlook Express is still available in Windows Mail. Why would you need Find when Windows Mail includes instant search? Actually, there are some good reasons. When you click Find, you'll see the Find Message dialog box shown in Figure 18-2. This dialog box enables you to search in a very fine-grained way, where you can specify exactly the person, subject, or message you're looking for. More important, perhaps, you can also specify *where* to look using the Browse button. Unlike instant search, Find isn't limited to the current folder view.

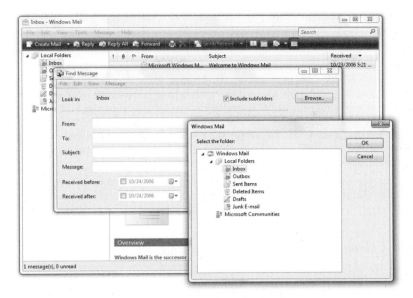

Figure 18-2: Find Message isn't as elegant as instant search, but it helps you look for what you want where you want.

Secret

You can also search your Windows Mail-based e-mail from the Start Menu's search box.

Contacts Integration

Where Outlook Express integrated with the Windows Address Book used in previous Windows versions, Windows Mail naturally integrates with the new Contacts store found in Windows Vista. We examine Contacts at the end of this chapter, but you can access Contacts from within Windows Mail through the aforementioned toolbar button, from the Tools menu, or by tapping Ctrl+Shift+C.

Automatic Spell Checking

Unlike its predecessor, Windows Mail includes built-in automatic spell checking. To get this functionality in Outlook Express, you would have had to have installed Microsoft Word or any other part of the Microsoft Office suite. That said, the Windows Mail spell checker is a bit less functional than the one included with Word or Office: It cannot suggest replacements for misspelled words.

No More Identities

Because Outlook Express was first designed to work with Windows 95 and subsequent consumer Windows products that had no real concept of individual user accounts, it used a construct called *identities* to allow users to create two or more pseudo-user accounts within the application. You could use identities in various ways. First, multiple users accessing Outlook Express from the same PC could maintain separate identities so that their e-mail accounts wouldn't comingle. Second, individual users could set up multiple identities within Outlook Express in order to separate them.

Identities no longer exist in Windows Mail. Now, users are expected to each maintain their own user account, each of which has a separate desktop, configuration settings, and so forth.

cross
ref

See Chapter 9 for more information about user accounts.

tip

If you upgrade an older computer to Windows Vista and were using Outlook Express with multiple identities, Windows Mail will run a wizard the first time it's launched that lets you import identities into your user account. You can run this wizard on each account to ensure that the correct identities are matched to the correct user accounts in Vista.

New Mail Storage

Windows Mail, finally, uses an entirely new storage engine for e-mail that is more reliable and offers better performance than that used by Outlook Express. Anyone who's been frustrated by antiquated storage issues of Outlook Express — seen most frequently when the application slows to a crawl when accessing large e-mail folders or newsgroups — will appreciate this change.

Secret

On a related note, it's now much easier to move the Windows Mail storage around because Windows Mail keeps everything — its e-mail and newsgroup folders, account information, and settings — in a single, easily accessible folder. Now, when you move the Windows Mail storage folder, everything else moves with it. This also makes Windows Mail much easier to back up. All of the Windows Mail data files can now be found in C:\Users\[User Name]\AppData\Local\Microsoft\Windows Mail by default. To back this up, simply copy this folder to a different location, like a rewriteable optical disk or removable hard drive. If you are backing up Windows Mail, back up your contacts as well. Contacts are stored in C:\Users\[User Name]\Contacts by default.

If you do want to move the Windows Mail storage folder to a new location, it's actually quite simple.

1. Navigate to Tools⇨Options⇨Advanced, and then click the Maintenance button.
2. Click the Store Folder button.
3. In the Store Folder dialog box, click the Change button and browse to the new location.

Unlike with Outlook Express, the new Browse For Folder dialog box in Windows Vista enables you to create a new folder as well, so you don't have to do that ahead of time as you did previously. Windows Mail moves all of your data to the new location automatically after you shut down the application.

tip Registry buffs should know that Windows Mail's Registry structure has changed as well. So if you've been using a favorite set of Registry scripts for Outlook Express, beware: They won't work anymore in Windows Mail.

Security Features

In keeping with the push for better desktop security in Windows Vista, Windows Mail picks up a couple of useful features that make it marginally safer than Outlook Express. (Note: You're still better off using a full-featured mail client like Microsoft Outlook.) The first is a new Junk Mail filter, which is very similar to the Junk Mail filter found in Microsoft Outlook. You can access Junk Mail options from the Junk E-mail Options dialog, shown in Figure 18-3.

Here, you can choose a level of automatic junk e-mail protection and set up Safe Senders, Safe Recipients, and Blocked Senders lists. There's also an International tab for automatically blocking mail written in languages you don't understand and e-mail from certain top-level domain names. If you're familiar with Junk e-mail protection in Microsoft Outlook, you'll be right at home here.

There's one major exception. Junk e-mail protection works only for POP3 accounts, and not IMAP accounts.

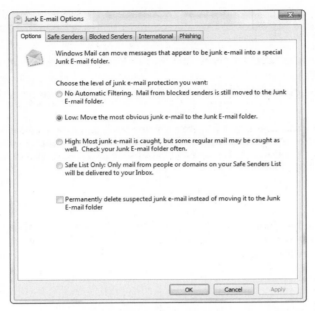

Figure 18-3: Finally, Windows Mail picks up one of the more useful features of Outlook.

Secret

While IMAP email is typically superior to POP3, you wouldn't know it by running Windows Mail. In addition to not providing junk e-mail protection to IMAP accounts, Windows Mail also does not support message rules with IMAP.

In addition to its Junk Mail feature, Windows Mail also includes a Phishing Filter, which can prevent certain e-mail–based scams. Here's how a phishing (pronounced like *fishing*) attack works. A malicious user sends out junk e-mail to random recipients that appears to come from a bank, online retailer or auction site, or other trusted institution with which you might do business. These e-mails, which are often written in such a way to suggest that there might be something wrong with an account you may have, try to get you to click embedded links and visit malicious web sites. These web sites are also masquerading as legitimate locations. They try to get you to provide valid logon information that you might use at the actual institution and then use this information for identity theft. Each year, millions of people fall victim to phishing scams.

To help prevent this, Microsoft has added antiphishing technology to both Internet Explorer 7 and Windows Mail in Windows Vista. In Windows Mail, the Phishing Filter is on by default. You can view two Phishing Filter options from the Phishing tab of the Junk

E-Mail Options dialog box if you're curious, but our advice here is simple. Don't turn this feature off under any circumstances.

Advanced Windows Mail Options

Amazingly, if you navigate through the Windows Mail menu structure and Options dialog box, you'll discover that very little has changed since Outlook Express 6 (the version that shipped with Windows XP). There is one major addition to the Windows Mail Options dialog box, however: A new Advanced tab replaces the Maintenance tab that appeared in previous versions. On this tab, shown in Figure 18-4, you can access various advanced options, as you'd expect, but you can also access the contents of the old Maintenance tab through a new Maintenance button. Clicking that button brings up a new dialog box that is identical to the old Maintenance tab.

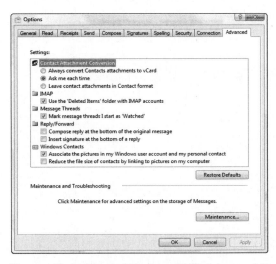

Figure 18-4: New in Windows Mail: Advanced Options.

Managing Contacts with Windows Vista

Unlike Windows Mail, the system for managing contacts has changed dramatically in Windows Vista. In previous Windows versions, Microsoft utilized an application called Windows Address Book (commonly referred to as WAB) to handle contacts. WAB was a simple application, and it integrated nicely with Outlook Express, predecessor of Windows Mail. But few other applications took advantage of WAB. So in Windows Vista, a new Windows Contacts mechanism has been architected to take advantage of new technologies that developers are more likely to embrace. Indeed, Microsoft expects Windows Contacts to eventually replace all other personal contact storage systems used in Windows, Microsoft or otherwise.

Secret

Under the covers, Windows Contacts utilizes a well-respected and widely used open technology called XML (eXtensible Markup Language). XML is also used in other places within Windows Vista. For example, the system's integrated support for RSS utilizes XML technology.

To the user, Windows Contacts are typically accessed through the new Contacts special shell folder called the Contacts Explorer, which is specially formatted for managing contacts. You can access this folder through the Start Menu as Windows Contacts. The Contacts Explorer is shown in Figure 18-5.

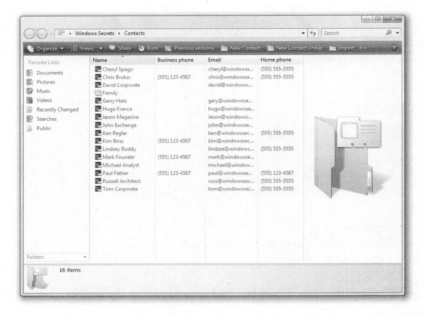

Figure 18-5: The new Windows Contacts replaces Windows Address Book in Windows Vista.

If you upgraded to Windows Vista from a previous Windows version (or ran the Windows Easy Transfer utility) and were using WAB for contacts, you should see all of your contacts in the new Contacts folder. Otherwise, Contacts will be empty.

Adding a New Contact

To add a new contact to Windows Contacts, simply click the New Contact toolbar button. This brings up a blank Contact Properties window, as shown in Figure 18-6, which is roughly analogous to a similar window in the old WAB application.

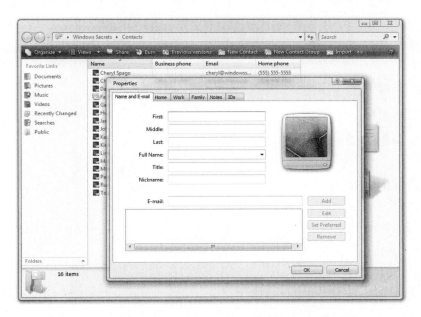

Figure 18-6: In Windows Vista, Contacts are stored using an XML back end.

One feature that's new this time around is that you can add a picture to each contact. To do so, click the picture well in the upper right of the Contact Properties window and then select Change picture from the drop-down menu. You can then browse to the picture you want. Pictures are a nice way to customize your contacts. In Figure 18-7, you can see how a few photos really spice things up, especially if you play with the Contacts Explorer's view styles.

Viewing and Editing Contacts

By default, the Reading pane is enabled in the Contacts Explorer, a rarity in the Windows Vista shell. So as you select individual contacts, you can preview much of their information directly in the Reading pane, without having to open each one in a separate window.

tip   If the Reading pane is not enabled, you can enable it by clicking the Organize button in the Contacts toolbar and selecting Layout and then Reading pane.

Figure 18-7: It's a more visual interface to your friends, family, and coworkers.

To edit a contact, simply double-click it. This displays the Contact Properties window described in the previous section.

Organizing Contacts

If you have enough contacts, you might want to organize them into logical collections called Contact Groups. To do this, you must first create a Group. For example, you may want to place your family members in a group called Family. Here's how you do it:

1. Make sure the Contacts Explorer is open and no contacts are selected.
2. Click the New Contact Group button in the Contact Explorer toolbar. This brings up the Contact Group Properties dialog box shown in Figure 18-8.
3. Pick the contacts you want to add to the group by pressing the Select Members button, or simply press OK to create the group and then drag the appropriate contacts into the group.
4. To view the contents of a group, double-click it. The Contact Group Properties dialog box now displays whatever contacts happen to be part of that group.

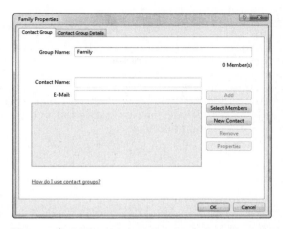

Figure 18-8: Here, you can create a logical group to contain related contacts.

Secret

Any contact can be a member of one or more Contact Groups. And if you delete a Contact Group, you won't delete the contacts it contains.

tip

Contact Groups can be accessed as a group in applications that utilize Windows Contacts, like Windows Mail. For example, if you created a Contact Group called Family, you could address an e-mail to Family, and it would be sent to every contact in that group.

Secret

Importing and Exporting Contacts

Windows Contacts includes import and export capabilities so you can copy contacts to and from this new type of storage engine. Oddly, these features are almost completely identical to the fairly weak import and export features in Outlook Express. If you find that the import options aren't good enough, here's a secret: You can also import WAB contacts by exporting them from Outlook Express in Windows XP (or previous Windows versions) to a new WAB file. Then, copy the WAB file to Windows Vista and double-click it. The contacts will be imported into Windows Contacts.

If that doesn't work, try using the Windows Easy Transfer program to copy your old contacts from your previous operating system to Windows Vista Windows Contacts.

Summary

Although Windows Mail is largely a disappointing upgrade over its Outlook Express predecessor, this application does, at least, include a few interesting new features, including a phishing filter, automatic spell checking, and better performance, so it's worth a look if you're a die-hard Outlook Express user only. Others will find better features in Windows Live Mail Desktop or Mozilla Thunderbird. The new Contacts functionality in Windows Vista, meanwhile, is similar to its predecessor but accessible through a new shell-based user interface that is both easy to use and attractive.

Using and Understanding Windows Live Services

Chapter

19

◆ ◆

In This Chapter

Discovering the various Windows Live products and services, including those not promoted in Windows Vista

Extending Internet Explorer with the Windows Live toolbar

Protecting your PC with Windows Live OneCare

Getting a better e-mail client than that offered in Windows Vista

Making cheap phone calls from your PC with Windows Live Messenger

◆ ◆

In late 2005, about a year before it completed development of Windows Vista, Microsoft announced that it was radically changing its online strategy to better compete with Google, Yahoo!, and other companies. Microsoft's strategy is simple: Because it already dominates the operating system market with Windows, it no longer needs to take the technically dubious (and antitrust unfriendly) tact of bundling online services directly in Windows, as it did in the past. Instead, Microsoft's online services are combining capabilities from both desktop software and online services to deliver the best possible user experience. More to the point, Microsoft can build off the success of Windows without truly taking advantage of its market power. Yes, most of its services will require Windows, but none will ship directly in the box with Windows.

It may seem like a subtle distinction. But after a decade of antitrust problems both in the United States and around the world, Microsoft is finally doing the right thing, both for the company itself and its customers. Previously, most of Microsoft's online services were developed through its MSN division, which used to develop the company's Internet access services. But now, that work has all been brought into the Windows Division. And not so surprisingly, the online services are now being marketed with the Windows Live brand.

Secret   You might not be surprised to discover that the various Windows Live services and desktop products are simply updated or new versions of products and services that were once being developed by MSN and were once branded with the MSN name. That is indeed exactly what happened.

note   Windows Live isn't Microsoft's only online initiative. In tandem with Windows Live, Microsoft is developing a set of online services around its Office suite of productivity applications called, naturally enough, Office Live. And the software maker already had a brilliant set of online services for gamers called Xbox Live. Together, these three sets of services are often simply referred to as Microsoft's Live services.

When Microsoft announced its strategy to enhance the Windows product line with a set of online products and services under the Windows Live umbrella, it wasn't clear exactly what form the resulting software would take. Since then, however, Microsoft has shipped an alarming amount of Windows Live products and services, almost all of which are updated regularly. Staying on top of these products and services would almost be a career in and of itself.

Because the Windows Live services are being updated so frequently, it doesn't make sense to provide an in-depth look at every single one of them. Instead, we'll first discuss the Windows Live services that Microsoft is promoting directly in Windows Vista. Then, we'll provide a laundry list of some of the other interesting Windows Live products and services that are available at the time of this writing. You might be surprised by what's out there.

Windows Live Services in Windows Vista

Microsoft is promoting Windows Live services in Windows Vista in two key areas.

◆ First, a variety of Windows Live services are advertised in the Offers from Microsoft section of the Windows Vista Welcome Center, as shown in Figure 19-1. Because this window is displayed the very first time you boot into Windows Vista, and then again by default every time you reboot, millions of customers from around the world will be tempted to download and install some of these products. Fortunately, most of the Windows Live offers are for free, high-quality products.

Figure 19-1: There are no Windows Live products or services in Windows Vista per se, but Microsoft does go to great lengths to advertise them.

◆ Second, Microsoft includes a shortcut in the default Start menu called Windows Live Messenger Download. This shortcut opens Internet Explorer 7 and navigates you to the download page for Microsoft's instant messaging (IM) application. There is also an identical shortcut in the All Programs portion of the Start menu.

Secret

Stupidly, if you do choose to install Windows Live Messenger via either one of these shortcuts, the shortcut for installing the product remains on your system. You can, of course, manually delete it by right-clicking it and choosing Delete, and then wading through the inevitable User Account Control (UAC) silliness that ensues any time you do something even remotely dangerous.

In the following sections, we'll take a look at the Windows Live products and services Microsoft is advertising in the Welcome Center.

Going Online and Learning about Windows Live

The shortcut titled "Go online and learn about Windows Live" opens Internet Explorer and brings you to a pared-down version of the Windows Live web site (**http://get.live.com/**) that includes information about just Microsoft's top-level Windows Live services, such as Windows Live Search (a Google competitor), Live.com (a web portal), Windows Live Expo (an eBay competitor), Windows Live Messenger (instant messaging), Windows Live Mail (the Hotmail replacement), Windows Live Spaces (blogging), and Windows Live OneCare (a comprehensive PC safety product).

Secret   There are, of course, far more Windows Live products and services available to Windows Vista users. For the full lists, check out the Windows Live Ideas web site (http://ideas.live.com/), which includes both beta (prerelease) and completed products and services.

Downloading Windows Live Toolbar

Anyone who's used Internet Explorer is probably familiar with the notion of helper toolbars that include such things as integrated search boxes, pop-up blockers, and a variety of other useful features. Given how advanced Internet Explorer 7 is — it includes, by default, both an integrated search box and a pop-up blocker, for example — you might think that these toolbars would be a thing of the past. That, alas, is not true. And while the Googles and Yahoo!s of the world are still offering their own brands of Internet Explorer–compatible toolbars, Microsoft has one, too. Not surprisingly, it's called Windows Live toolbar.

The Windows Live toolbar, shown in Figure 19-2, includes a number of cool features, like smart menus that let you find any location on a map simply by highlighting the address on a web page. There's a form fill function that saves commonly typed web form information (name, address, telephone number, and so on), sparing you from having to manually enter that data over and over again. The toolbar also integrates with a number of useful Windows Live online services, giving you one-click access to such things as Windows Live Spaces (blogging) and Windows Live Mail.

Signing up Online for Windows Live OneCare

There's probably a great joke just waiting to be told about the operating system company whose buggy products inspired a multibillion dollar security tools market only to see that company enter that market with a security solution designed to protect users from problems caused by vulnerabilities in its own products. Let that one sink in for a second and then get this: Windows Live OneCare, Microsoft's desktop security solution is excellent. Here's what you get.

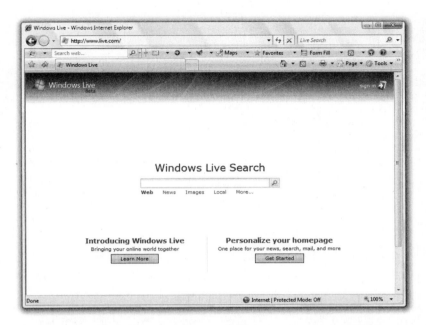

Figure 19-2: The Windows Live toolbar integrates with Internet Explorer 7 and adds a number of useful features.

Windows Live OneCare is a subscription offering that ostensibly costs $49.95 a year, but in reality can be had for much, much less (think half off or more) at various online and brick-and-mortar electronics retailers. It covers up to three PCs in your home, so you can install OneCare on multiple machines. And it provides a bevy of services, including antivirus and antispyware protection (the latter through its integration with Windows Defender, which you get with Windows Vista), a two-way firewall that's more capable than the one included with Vista, nice wizard-based file backup and restore functionality, and free technical support via phone, e-mail, or online chat, 24 hours a day, 7 days a week. It's shown in Figure 19-3.

Windows Live OneCare runs continually in the background, monitoring your system, and ensuring it's always up to date. It also runs regular PC tune-ups, to ensure the system is running at top speed. Overall, Windows Live OneCare is an excellent addition to Windows and is highly recommended unless you're already using a competing security suite such as Zone Alarm Security Suite or Symantec Norton Internet Security.

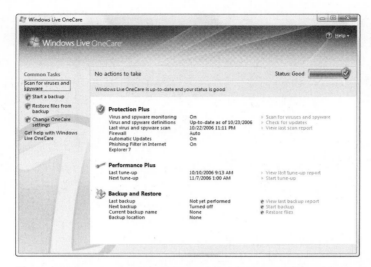

Figure 19-3: Windows Live OneCare is a complete PC health solution for Windows Vista.

Secret

The only thing missing from Windows Live OneCare, and it's a curious omission, frankly, is e-mail antispam protection. Microsoft says that most of its customers are already protected from spam via services provided by their e-mail provider (Google Gmail, Microsoft Hotmail or Windows Live Mail, and so on), their Internet service providers (ISPs), or their e-mail clients. And sure enough, if you choose to use the company's Windows Live Mail service, you do get a certain level of protection against spam, assuming you don't mind using the web-based client. Not surprisingly, both Zone Alarm Security Suite and Symantec Norton Internet Security offer e-mail anti-spam capabilities.

Downloading Windows Live Mail Desktop

Windows Vista includes a new mail client named Windows Mail that is really just Outlook Express from Windows XP with a new name and a few features removed. (We cover Windows Mail in Chapter 18.) Well, there's a new mail client in town, and if you're slumming around with Windows Mail for some reason, you might want to give it a shot. It's called Windows Live Mail Desktop, and although it's based on the same technical underpinnings as Windows Mail (that is, it's really just Outlook Express in disguise), it does offer one killer feature that's sorely lacking in Windows Mail: It can access the Web-based Hotmail and Windows Live Mail services.

There's just one catch. Unless you're paying for a premium Microsoft online service such as Hotmail Plus or MSN Premium, Windows Live Mail Desktop is advertising-supported, so Microsoft and its partners will deliver contextual ads. If you can deal with that, and honestly, it's not all that annoying, Windows Live Mail Desktop is most certainly a better e-mail client than Windows Mail. Figure 19-4 shows Windows Live Mail Desktop in action.

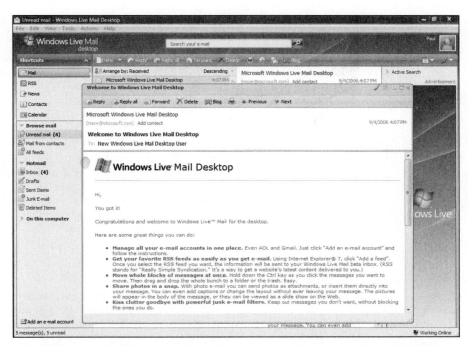

Figure 19-4: Windows Live Mail Desktop is based on the same technologies as Windows Mail, but offers many more features.

Here's what you get.

⬧ First, Windows Live Mail Desktop works with multiple e-mail accounts. That includes multiple web mail accounts, like Hotmail and Windows Live Mail, as well as multiple POP3 and IMAP accounts. It even works with AOL Mail, Gmail, and Yahoo! Mail.

⬧ Second, Windows Live Mail Desktop integrates with other Windows Live services. If you're running Windows Live Messenger, for example, Windows Live Mail Desktop can import your Messenger contacts and set them up as e-mail contacts. It will also subscribe to any RSS contacts feeds you've configured for your Windows Live Spaces blog, if you've set one up. There's also an Active Search pane through which you can launch Internet searches via Windows Live Search.

⬧ Speaking of RSS feeds, that's another advantage Windows Live Mail Desktop has over Windows Mail: It's a full-featured RSS client. We discussed RSS feeds and how that feature works in Internet Explorer 7 back in Chapter 17, but some people believe it makes more sense to read RSS feeds in an e-mail client. Now you can, with Windows Live Mail Desktop.

♦ Like Microsoft's more powerful Outlook application, Windows Live Mail Desktop also includes a Calendar component, yet another feature that's lacking in Windows Mail (though you might opt to use the elegant Windows Calendar application we describe in Chapter 20 instead, of course). The Calendar module is based on the web-based calendar that's part of Windows Live Mail, and like its e-mail brethren, anything you configure in the client will be synchronized back to the web so you can access your schedule from anywhere that has an Internet connection.

Secret

If you started off using Windows Mail before realizing there was a better solution out there, fear not: You can easily migrate your Windows Mail accounts and settings to Windows Live Mail Desktop. You'll be prompted to do so after you've installed Windows Live Mail Desktop.

Downloading Windows Live Messenger

Windows Live Messenger replaces MSN Messenger as Microsoft's mainstream instant messaging (IM) application. In truth, the term instant messaging doesn't really do this application a lot of justice. Although it can indeed be used to hold text-, audio-, and video-based chats online with your friends, coworkers, and other contacts, Windows Live Messenger is blurring the line with telephone-like functionality thanks to its integration of Voice over IP (VoIP) technologies. That means you can make long-distance and international phone calls via Windows Live Messenger for a small fraction of what you're probably being charged by the phone company. It might be time to invest in a PC headset. Windows Live Messenger is shown in Figure 19-5.

Secret

Windows Live Messenger can also be used to communicate with friends using Yahoo! Messenger, a competing instant messaging application.

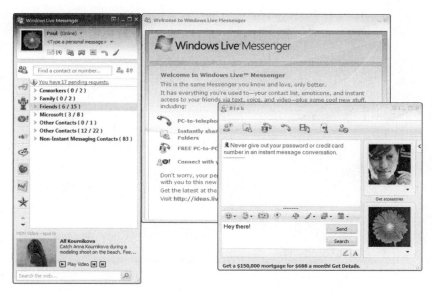

Figure 19-5: Windows Live Messenger offers IM functionality and can be used to make PC-to-phone calls.

Other Offers from Microsoft

In addition to the Windows Live services mentioned previously, the Windows Vista Welcome Center also offers two other offers from Microsoft, "Go online to Windows Marketplace" and "Sign up online for technical support."

♦ Windows Marketplace is Microsoft's shopping and download site, from which you can purchase hardware and software for your Windows Vista–based PC. It has developed into an interesting destination, especially because much of the software it offers can actually be downloaded, for instant gratification. Windows Marketplace is shown in Figure 19-6.

♦ The second option opens Internet Explorer 7 and navigates to the Microsoft Support Web site (**http://support.microsoft.com/**). From here, you can get guided help, visit the product solution center for Windows Vista, or submit support requests. It's a good place to visit if more traditional support options—such as the Vista help files, this book, or the teenaged geek down the street—aren't able to answer your questions.

Figure 19-6: Windows Marketplace showcases hardware and software that's compatible with Windows Vista.

Secret

There are other support options available to you as well, of course. For example, you might use Windows Mail or Windows Live Mail Desktop to visit Microsoft's product support newsgroups. There, you can get peer-to-peer support (from other Windows users) or even responses from the Microsoft engineers that frequent the groups. To access these newsgroups in Windows Live Mail Desktop, simply click the News shortcut and then Microsoft Communities.

A Few Other Windows Live Services

In addition to the several Windows Live products and services that Microsoft promotes from within Windows Vista, the company offers a wide range of other Windows Live services, which you can examine and download at your leisure online. Here are a few of the more valuable Windows Live services you may want to check out.

Live.com

Microsoft's newest Web portal, Live.com (**www.live.com/**), looks like a simple search page, but it's highly customizable. You can add a number of dynamic content panes containing news, sports, or entertainment headlines, weather, stock quotes, and even your Windows Live Mail e-mail. Live.com is shown in Figure 19-7.

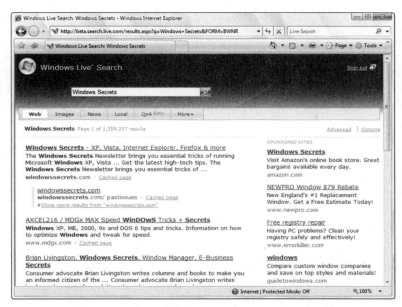

Figure 19-7: Live.com offers Web search but is also highly customizable.

Although Google has become so popular that the term *Google* is now used both as the company's name and as a verb to describe searching the Web (as in, "I need to Google Windows Vista to find out more about it"), it's not the only game in town. Live.com with its Windows Live Search is now the default homepage in Windows Vista's version of Internet Explorer 7, and the company hopes that this exposure will help it convince users to give the service a chance. Give it a shot. The customization options are quite interesting.

Secret

Like the Windows Sidebar (Chapter 6), Live.com can be customized with gadgets, small software programs that provide much more interactivity than is commonly associated with web pages. Live.com gadgets are created similarly to Windows Sidebar gadgets, so many developers will create gadgets that work in both places. To discover gadgets for Live.com (or the Sidebar), visit Windows Live Gallery (**http://gallery.live.com**).

Windows Live OneCare Family Safety

Although Microsoft does offer a Windows Live OneCare subscription product (mentioned earlier in this chapter), the company's customers told it that it would need to protect non-subscribers online if it expected them to access its various Windows Live services. So Microsoft extended the OneCare brand into a variety of other free services, including an online virus scanner (the Windows Live OneCare Safety Scanner at **http://safety.live.com**) and the Windows Live OneCare Family Safety service (**http://fss.live.com**), which provides web filtering and contacts management for parents wishing to keep their children safe online.

Windows Live OneCare Family Safety requires a small download—it also requires that you and your children all have Windows Live IDs (formerly called Passport accounts). But the effort of doing so is worth it. With this web-based service, you can monitor your children's activities online, and protect them from undesirable content and online predators. And what the heck, it's absolutely free.

Windows Live Spaces

Windows Live Spaces is Microsoft's blogging solution, software that enables anyone to publish a web site, complete with photos and interactive content, easily and without any technical knowledge. Spaces has proven quite popular—by some metrics it's the most popular blogging software in the world—and it certain does provide a friendly and welcome environment with professional looking page design and nice integration with other Windows Live services. You can find out more at the Spaces web site (**http://spaces.live.com/**). A typical Windows Live Spaces blog is shown in Figure 19-8.

Figure 19-8: Windows Live Spaces lets anyone create their own web site.

Secret

A related Windows Live product, Windows Live Writer, allows you to publish content to your Windows Live Spaces blog (or numerous other blog types, including Blogger, LiveJournal, TypePad, WordPress, and many others) using a standard Windows-based application. Windows Live Writer, shown in Figure 19-9, is nice because it works offline, letting you cache blog posts until you can get online, and it provides true What You See Is What You Get (WYSIWIG) editing. Find out more on the Windows Live Writer web site (http://windowslivewriter.spaces.live.com/).

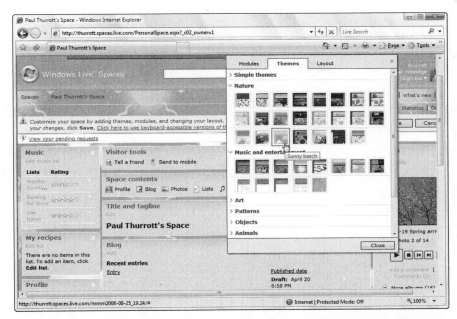

Figure 19-9: Windows Live Writer lets you use a Microsoft Word–like WYSIWYG environment for posting information to a blog.

Summary

In this chapter, we've examined Microsoft's Windows Live products and services, which augment Windows Vista with a number of useful web-based capabilities, including instant messaging, PC safety and security, e-mail, and much more. With Windows Live services, you can communicate with friends, coworkers, and loved ones, publish your thoughts and photos to web sites, and keep your PC running securely and smoothly. And unlike previous Microsoft online services, the Windows Live services integrate with Windows only when you choose to install them: They aren't simply provided for you whether you need or want them or not.

Part VII

Home Office/Power User

Managing Your Schedule with Windows Calendar

Chapter

20

⬥ ⬥

In This Chapter

Discovering PC-based calendaring

Navigating the Windows Calendar interface

Working with calendars and calendar groups

Creating and managing appointments and tasks

Sharing and synchronizing calendars

Searching for appointments and tasks

Printing calendars

⬥ ⬥

Although operating systems such as Linux and Mac OS X have offered calendaring applications for years, Microsoft has historically sold such functionality as part of its Office and Works productivity suites. Starting with Windows Vista, however, Windows users are finally getting a first-class calendaring solution as part of their favorite operating system. Dubbed Windows Calendar, this application provides attractive and full-featured calendaring features, including tasks functionality, the ability to subscribe to remote calendars, and even a way to publish your own calendars for others to use. In this chapter, we'll examine this new Windows application.

Understanding PC Calendaring

If you've ever used the Calendar component in Microsoft Outlook, then you're familiar with the notion of PC-based calendaring and scheduling. Microsoft Outlook is an extremely powerful tool, enabling you to create and manage appointments, meetings, and other events, as well as tasks and other time-based schedules. For all its strengths, however, Microsoft Outlook isn't perfect. First, you must pay a hefty sum for Microsoft Outlook unless you get a version along with other Microsoft Office applications when you purchase a new PC. Second, Outlook is designed to work primarily with Microsoft Exchange–based servers. Although it's possible to use Outlook as an individual, it's not ideal, and even the very latest Outlook version offers only very simple methods for sharing calendaring information with other people.

Meanwhile, standards-based web calendars have been gaining in popularity for the past few years, and these solutions offer features that are much more applicable to individuals than what Outlook offers. Best of all, most of these web-based calendars are free. For example, Apple Computer supplies users of its Mac OS X operating system with a calendar application called iCal that integrates very nicely with web standards for calendaring, making it possible for iCal users to share calendars with family and friends from around the world. And the Mozilla Corporation, which makes the popular Firefox web browser, is developing its own calendar application called Sunbird, offering similar functionality to Windows and Linux users.

Standards-based calendar applications offer a number of useful features. First, you can create discrete calendars in categories such as Personal, Work, Gym, or any categories you choose to imagine and overlay them as needed on the same calendar view to see how your entire schedule plays out. You can share calendars with others, via a publish and subscribe mechanism that enables you to superimpose your own calendars visually with remote calendars. Using this functionality, for example, you could find a night in which both you and your wife were free to have dinner at a restaurant together, or compare your son's soccer schedule with your own weekend plans to make sure you can get to the game.

Because these standards-based calendars are becoming so popular, many organizations and individuals publish their own schedules on the Web so that other individuals can subscribe to them. If you're a fan of the Boston Red Sox or any other sports team, you can subscribe to their schedule and always be alerted when a game is coming up. There are calendars out there for all kinds of events including regional holidays, concerts, and the like. And these calendars can be superimposed on your own calendars, if you'd like, within these calendaring applications.

There's more, of course. Standards-based calendars also support lists of tasks, which can be assigned days and times for completion and checked off as they are completed. You can print calendars in attractive styles, and use them as paper-based personal information managers during your work week or on trips. All of this is possible without having to deal with an expensive, centralized server. The Internet's enterprising denizens have gotten their hands on calendaring and rescued it from the shackles of Microsoft Exchange.

> **tip**
>
> When we refer to standards with regards to calendaring, we're referring to the iCal, or iCalendar, standard, which specifies "interoperable calendaring and scheduling services for the Internet." Rather than extend proprietary solutions like Outlook to the Internet, the iCal standard proposes that all calendars should use a single, open standard for inter-operability purposes. It's a great idea and works well in the real world. You can find out more about the iCal format on the IETF web site (**www.ietf.org/rfc/rfc2445.txt**).

Exploring Windows Calendar

Microsoft isn't blind to this change in how people are interacting online via standards-based calendars. So Windows Vista includes a standards-based calendar application called, logically enough, Windows Calendar. If you're familiar with competing solutions such as Apple iCal or Mozilla Sunbird, Windows Calendar will seem very familiar. It works with the same standards-based calendaring format, and it can publish and sub-scribe to the same sources as those solutions. However, because Windows Calendar is built into Windows Vista, it will soon become the predominant calendaring solution for individuals worldwide. For this reason, we expect standards-based calendaring to become truly mainstream during the lifetime of Windows Vista.

> **tip**
>
> Obviously, Microsoft isn't giving up on its Exchange Server and Outlook product lines. If you want a quick understanding of how these solutions are differentiated, think of it this way: Exchange and Outlook are tools for business users, while Windows Calendar is for individuals like consumers, soccer moms, and your grandparents. Put simply, Windows Calendar is for *people* not businesses.

Understanding the Windows Calendar Interface

Windows Calendar can be found in the All Programs portion of the Start menu. When you launch Windows Calendar for the first time, you'll be presented with a standard daily cal-endar view, and you'll see that Windows Calendar has created its first calendar for you, which is named after your user name (see Figure 20-1).

The Windows Calendar user interface is divided into a number of logical areas. On the top is a menu bar and toolbar. Below that, you'll see three areas, or panes, two of which are optional. On the left is the Navigation pane, which enables you to select between dif-ferent calendars and tasks. In the center of the application window is the current calendar view, which is set to Day view by default. On the right is the Details Pane. This pane will change based on what's currently selected. By default, the current calendar is selected, but you might select other items, such as an appointment or a task.

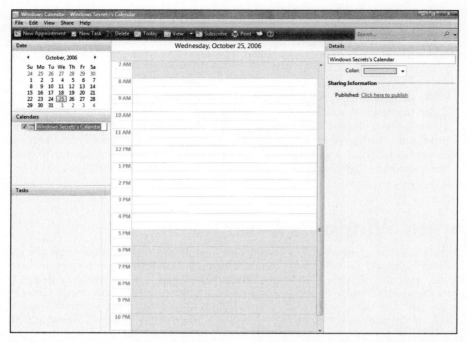

Figure 20-1: Windows Calendar shares many similarities with other standards-based Internet calendars but presented in a clean, Vista-like user interface.

Understanding Calendar Lingo

Because there are so many calendar applications out there, you might be confused about some of the language Microsoft uses to describe the various items with which Windows Calendar deals. Table 20-1 summarizes these items.

Table 20-1: Common items in Windows Calendar

Windows Calendar Item	Definition
Calendar	A collection of appointments that makes up your schedule. You can have different calendars for different purposes, and intermingle them within the Windows Calendar user interface.
Group	A logical grouping of related calendars.
Appointment	A meeting or other event. Appointments can have specific starting and ending times or be all-day or multi-day events. For example, a meeting will typically have static start and end times, whereas a vacation is a multi-day event.
Task	A to-do item that typically needs to be completed by a specific time.

Windows Calendar Item	Definition
Publish	A method by which a calendar is distributed electronically so that it might be shared with others or viewed online.
Subscribe	A method by which a published calendar is displayed locally within Windows Calendar and is updated automatically as changes are made to the original.

Working with Calendars and Groups

The first time you launch Windows Calendar, you'll see that it has created a default calendar for you with the name *[User name]'s calendar* (where *[User name]* is obviously replaced by the logon name of the current user). Each calendar gets its own name and color, and you can change either. For some people, this single calendar may be enough. But others may want to create different calendars for the different types of events they confront each day. Microsoft has also added the ability to create calendar groups, called *groups*, within which you can collect related calendars if desired.

Take a look at some ways in which you might organize your calendars within Windows Calendar. As stated previously, the default calendar you get just by running Windows Calendar might be enough for you. But some would rather organize things differently, and there are certainly many advantages to using different calendars. First, because each calendar is assigned a unique color, appointments for each calendar will stand out visually. Second, because you can arbitrarily hide and show individual calendars, it's possible to simplify the calendar view as needed, which can be handy when publishing or printing calendars. The important thing to remember is that Windows Calendar supports virtually any level of customization when it comes to calendar management. For example, you can use Windows Calendar to do any of the following:

◆ **Change the name of the default calendar:** Just select the name of the calendar in the Details pane and type a new name, as shown in Figure 20-2.

◆ **Change the calendar display color:** Click the Color drop-down bucket and choose from one of the 16 available colors.

◆ **Add multiple calendars:** Click the New Calendar button in the navigational control in the bottom of the Windows Calendar window. This is the button to the left of the Previous button. (Alternatively, you can select File⇨New⇨Calendar from the Windows Calendar menu.) When you do so, you'll see a new calendar appear in the Calendars list of the Navigation pane. Since the default name is New Calendar, you'll want to change that: Simply start typing to give it a new name. If the name becomes deselected for some reason, click the new calendar name in Calendars and then select the name in the Details pane and begin typing.

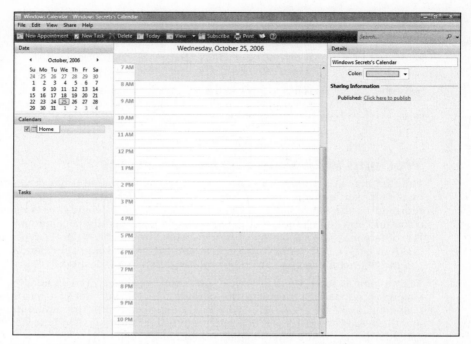

Figure 20-2: Renaming a calendar is simple: Just select the name in the Details pane and start typing.

◆ **Create new calendars and calendar groups:** You can use a calendar group to logically group related calendars. For example, you might create a group called Personal and lump calendars such as Home, Health, and Vacations inside. Or you might have a work group within which you'd create calendars called Meetings, Work Trips, or whatever.

To create a group, click the New Group button in the Windows Calendar navigational control (or, select File⇨New⇨Group from the menu system). Groups appear in the Calendars section of the Navigation pane as small folders. By default, groups will be empty. You can drag existing folders in and out of groups. But if you want to create a new calendar inside of an existing group, you can do so: Simply select the group folder first, and then click the New Calendar button. In Figure 20-3, you can see how one might organize a large number of calendars and groups.

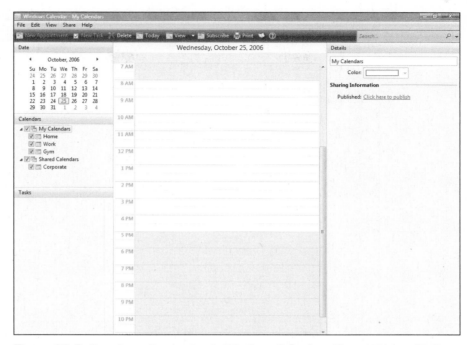

Figure 20-3: If you're really systematic, Windows Calendar will reward you with fine-grained control over calendar organization.

Secret

Here's one excellent use for groups. Later in this chapter, we discuss ways that you can subscribe to calendars that have been published online by organizations and individuals. We recommend creating groups for these subscribed calendars in order to keep them separated from your personally created calendars. For example, you might create a group called Subscribed Calendars, Sporting Events, or something similar.

Understanding Calendar Views and Navigation

Windows Calendar supports the following four basic view styles:

- ◆ **Day view:** Presents a top-down view style segregated into 30-minute slices, as shown in Figure 20-4.
- ◆ **Week view**, shown in Figure 20-5, divides the display into seven columns, one for each day of the week (compared with five for **Work Week view**) As with Day view, the view is segregated into 30-minute slices of time from top to bottom.

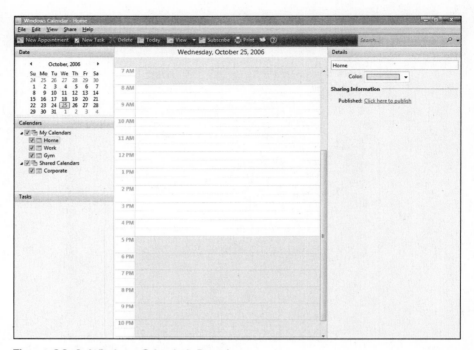

Figure 20-4: Windows Calendar's Day view.

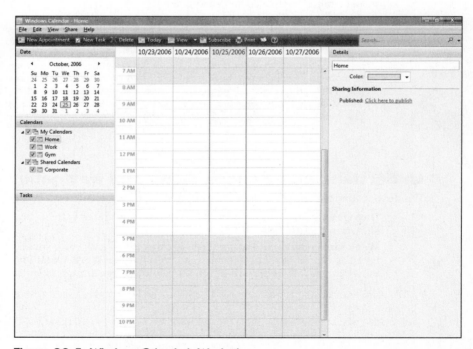

Figure 20-5: Windows Calendar's Week view.

◆ **Work Week view:** The same as the Week view, except the display is divided into five columns, one for each workday of the week.

◆ **Month view:** The central pane of Windows Calendar is divided up into a standard monthly calendar view, where each day of the month is denoted by a rectangular shape. Month view is shown in Figure 20-6.

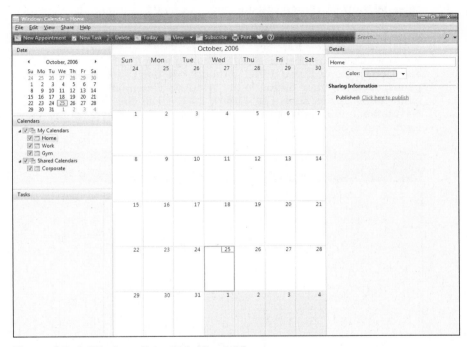

Figure 20-6: Windows Calendar's Month View.

In Week view, Work Week view, and Month view, the currently selected day is demarked by bold blue lines. By default, this day is set to the current day. If you select other days for various reasons and want to return to the default display, click the Go To Today button, which is the blue circle in the bottom center of the Windows Calendar window. When you do so, the current day is selected.

tip	If jumping directly to today isn't exactly what you're looking for, you can also cause Windows Calendar to jump to any date of your choosing. To do so, select the View menu (not the View toolbar button) and then Go To Date. Then, in the resulting dialog box, simply pick the date you want as well as the view style you'd like displayed.

tip	The little calendar found in the Date section of the Navigation Pane can be used to view different months without changing the main calendar view. If you look at this little calendar, you'll see small arrows to the left and right of the month name. Click them to navigate back and forth, respectively, from month to month.

Hiding and Viewing Calendars

When you have a number of calendars working, you may sometimes want to hide certain calendars in the main calendar view. Notice that each calendar and group has a check box next to its name in the Calendars section of the Navigation pane. When a calendar or group is checked, appointments contained within will display normally within the main calendar view. But when you uncheck a calendar or group, those items will be hidden.

Configuring Windows Calendar

Windows Calendar offers a variety of configuration options. You can hide the Navigation and Details panes if you'd like, although we don't recommend doing so. To hide these panes, click the View button in the Windows Calendar toolbar. When you do so, a short menu pops up, as shown in Figure 20-7. From this menu, you can toggle both the Navigation and Details panes (you can toggle these panes via the View menu) and perform other tasks.

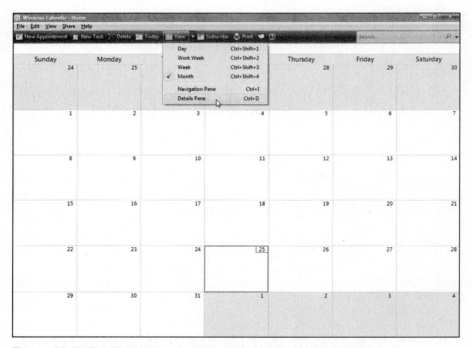

Figure 20-7: The View button lets you configure the display layout.

To access other Windows Calendar options, you'll need to visit the application's Options window, which is curiously found by navigating to File⇨Options in the menu. The Options window is shown in Figure 20-8.

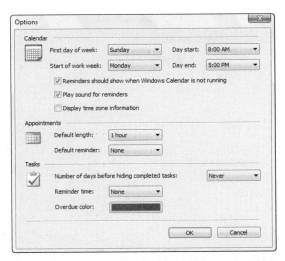

Figure 20-8: Most of Calendar's options are configurable via this simple window.

Here, you can set a variety of options related to calendars, appointments, and tasks. For example, you can determine which day is visually displayed as the first day of the week (Sunday by default), and the hours at which the day begins and ends. We'll examine the appointment and task options later in this chapter.

Working with Appointments

Within each calendar you use in Windows Calendar, you will create various *appointments*. An appointment is an event that occurs on a specific date or over a range of dates. Appointments can have static beginning and end times—like a meeting that runs from 9:00 a.m. to 10:00 a.m.—or be all-day events. Appointments also have other characteristics. For example, you might create an appointment for an event that occurs repeatedly, like a birthday or anniversary. And you can choose to be alerted when specific appointments are coming up.

There are various ways to create a new appointment in Windows Calendar, but how you do so matters little because you can change any appointment details during the creation process. Say you want to schedule a meeting for 9:00 a.m. next Monday. One way to do so would be to select the appropriate calendar and then navigate to the specific date in Day view. Then, position the mouse cursor over the time at which you'd like the appointment to begin. Now, double-click to start creating the new appointment. As shown in Figure 20-9, two things happen when you do this. First, a new appointment appears within the center calendar view and the name of the appointment is highlighted. Second, information about the new appointment appears in the Details pane.

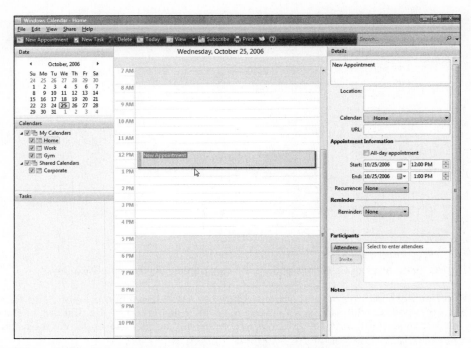

Figure 20-9: Creating a new appointment in Windows Calendar.

Examining Appointment Details

You can edit the following characteristics of the appointment:

◆ **Name:** This is how you identify an appointment. You can use any name you'd like, such as Meeting With Sarah, Car To Shop, or Flight To Phoenix.

◆ **Location:** As with the name, this entry can contain any text value. So you might use Phone for phone calls, Meeting Room 133, American Airlines Flight 133, or whatever you like.

◆ **Calendar:** Specifies the calendar to which the appointment will be attached. If you use multiple calendars, you can drop down the list and pick the appropriate calendar.

◆ **URL:** If there is a web address associated with the appointment, you can enter it here.

◆ **Appointment Information:** In this section, you specify the starting and ending times (and days) or whether it's an all-day event. You can also determine whether the appointment repeats. If it does, you can choose between Every day (as shown in Figure 20-10), Weekly, Monthly, Yearly, or Advanced. If you select the latter option, the Recurrence dialog appears letting you fine-tune its repetition characteristics.

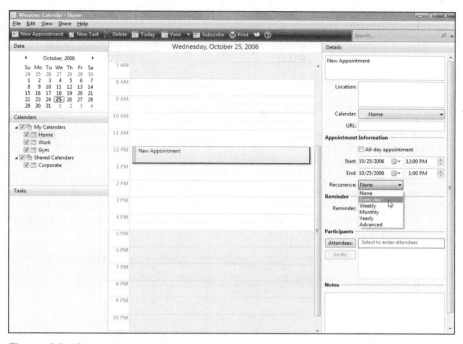

Figure 20-10: Use Recurrence to set up how often an appointment repeats.

◆ **Reminder:** If you'd like Windows Calendar to pop up a reminder dialog box at a specified interval before an appointment, this drop-down box will enable you configure it. Allowable reminder times include 0, 5, 15, and 30 minutes; 1, 2, and 4 hours; 1, 2, and 4 days; 1 and 2 weeks, or On date, the latter of which triggers a reminder at the start of the day of the appointment. When the Reminder dialog box does appear, as shown in Figure 20-11, you'll have the opportunity to snooze the reminder to a later time, dismiss it, or view the item. This dialog box is identical to the Reminder dialog used by Microsoft Outlook, incidentally.

Figure 20-11: Outlook users will find the Reminder dialog box to be somewhat familiar.

◆ **Participants:** This feature integrates with the Contacts database in Windows Vista, allowing you to add people from your address book to the appointment.

◆ **Notes:** This large text entry area enables you to write or paste in large blocks of text that may be pertinent to the appointment.

After you've edited a new appointment, you might notice small icon-like symbols in the colored blocks that represent the appointment in the calendar view. For example, if you specify a reminder, a small alarm clock icon will appear. You can get a bit more information about a particular appointment by moving the mouse cursor over it. When you do so, a small balloon help window will appear and display the name, location, and time of the appointment. This is especially useful in Month view, when you can't see start and end times for individual appointments.

Also, the display of appointments will vary according to their type. Appointments with start and end times will appear as colored rectangles in the calendar view. But all-day and multi-day events will appear in the upper well of the Day and Week views. In Month view, multi-day events will visually expand across all of the applicable days, as shown in Figure 20-12.

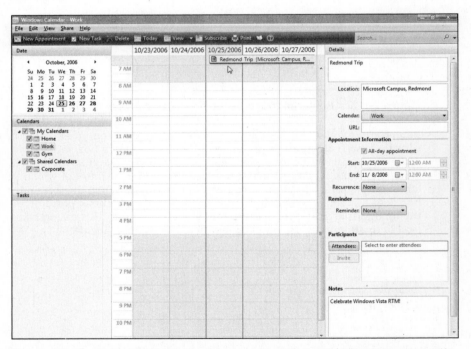

Figure 20-12: Multi-day events visually expand to include all of the days you specify.

If you'd like to view or edit an appointment at a later time, just select it in the calendar view. You'll see the appointment details appear in the Details pane.

If you just need to edit the name, simply double-click the appointment in the calendar view. The appointment name will be highlighted, enabling you to type a new name.

Configuring Appointments

You can access exactly two appointment-related options in the Windows Calendar Options dialog box, which is available via the Tools menu. In this dialog box, you can specify the starting length of new appointments (the default is one hour) and the default reminder time (the default is none). This is handy if your new appointments typically share common characteristics. If you almost always want to be reminded about an appointment one day early, for example, you could change the default reminder value to 1 day. This won't prevent you from changing this value on an appointment-by-appointment basis, of course.

Taking Calendar to Task with Tasks

In addition to scheduling appointment events, Windows Calendar also enables you to configure various tasks. As its name suggests, a task is a to-do item that you want to ensure gets completed. As with appointments, you can set reminders for tasks, and can configure individual tasks to repeat at regular intervals. When you complete a task, you can mark it as completed from within Windows Calendar.

Like appointments, tasks are associated with calendars. This makes sense if you think about it. If you do choose to organize Windows Calendar with various calendars, it's likely you'll want to associate certain tasks with home, work, or whatever other categories you may choose to use. That said, tasks are relegated to the Tasks section of the Navigation pane and don't get added to the main calendar view.

Creating Tasks

To create a new task, first select a calendar in the Calendars section of the Navigation pane. Then, click the New Task button in the Windows Calendar toolbar. (There are other ways to initiate a new task. You can right-click an empty spot in the Tasks section and choose New Task. Or, simply select File⇨New⇨Task from the Windows Calendar menu.)

However you do it, a new task will appear in Tasks with its name highlighted for editing, as shown in Figure 20-13. Additionally, information about the task appears in the Details pane so you can configure it as needed.

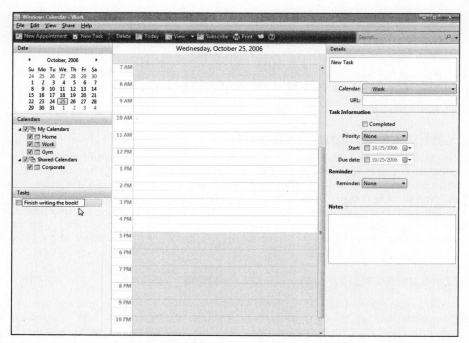

Figure 20-13: Creating a new task in Windows Calendar.

In the Details pane, you'll see a number of options for your newly created task. The following options are available:

- **Name:** This is how you identify the task. You can use any name you'd like.
- **Calendar:** This specifies the calendar to which the task is attached.
- **URL:** If there is a web address associated with the task, you can enter it here.
- **Task Information:** In this section, you specify whether the task is completed, a priority rating (Low, Medium, High, or None), and optional start and end dates (but not times). When a task is marked as completed, that task will feature a check mark in the Tasks section. If you want to be reminded of an upcoming task you need to complete, it often makes sense to set up at least a start date for the task. That way, when you enter a reminder time in the next section, it will have something to work from.
- **Reminder:** As with appointments, you can configure Windows Calendar to remind you when tasks are incomplete. These reminders behave identically to appointment reminders.
- **Notes:** This large text entry area enables you to write or paste in large blocks of text that may be pertinent to the task.

> **tip**
> So what's the difference between a task and an appointment? Appointments typically come and go at specific times, but tasks are often more open-ended and come with a completion requirement. Also, appointments can involve other people. With a task, you're on your own.

Configuring Tasks

You can configure a number of task-related features from the Options dialog box for Windows Calendar. These options include whether and when to hide completed tasks (which might otherwise clutter up the Tasks section if you're highly productive), the default reminder time, and the default color to use to mark a task that's overdue. That's right. Windows Calendar can get nasty if you don't keep on top of your tasks.

> **tip**   There's another option in the Options dialog box that's pertinent to tasks. In the Calendar section of this dialog box, you'll see an option titled *Reminders should show when Windows Calendar is not running*. For the most part, you will want to ensure that this option is enabled. Otherwise, you'd have to think to run Windows Calendar for task (and appointment) reminders to pop up. That kind of defeats the purpose of a reminder.

> **tip**   You can also change how tasks appear in the Task section of the Navigation pane. If you right-click in this area and choose Sort By, you'll see that you can sort by due date, priority, title, and calendar name.

Sharing Calendars

So far, everything we've covered in this chapter will be familiar to you if you've used an application such as Microsoft Outlook or even the calendar functionality of a web mail solution such as Hotmail or Yahoo! Mail. But what really sets Windows Calendar apart from those products is that Windows Calendar adheres to the iCal Internet-based calendaring standard. This means that it's extremely easy to share calendars with people from all over the world, as long as they too use Windows Calendar or another application (such as Apple iCal or Mozilla Sunbird) that also respects this standard.

Importing and Exporting Calendars

Previous to Window Calendar, Microsoft supported only static calendar data interoperability in its various calendar products. That is, you could *import* or *export* calendar data in specific formats so that you could move information from one calendar to another. This functionality has been added to Windows Calendar as well, and although it's not as exciting as the sharing technologies we describe later in the chapter, it's still useful.

Windows Calendar can only import (and export) to industry-standard ICS format, which is sometimes referred to as iCalendar format. This format is supported by applications like Apple iCal and Mozilla Sunbird, but not by Microsoft Outlook (though Outlook 2007 does allow you to open files in ICS format).

To export a calendar to ICS:

1. Select a calendar and then select File⇨Export.
2. Select a location to which to save the file using the Export dialog box, and then give it a description name.
3. You can now import the file into another compatible calendar application.

To import an ICS calendar into Windows Calendar, you follow a similar set of steps, although this time you'll obviously need an ICS file to import. There are a few ways to get such a file. If you have a calendar application that supports exporting into ICS, you could obviously use that. But a better example is to download one of the many ICS files that are out there on the Web. We'll look at this circumstance in the next section.

Publishing and Subscribing to Calendars

Importing and exporting is nice, but both of these operations are like slices in time because they can't help you if future changes are made to any of the calendars you've exchanged. What's needed, of course, is a way to *synchronize* data between calendars so that you can ensure that your calendar is always up to date. And this, of course, is where the iCal standard comes in. Using the publish and subscribe functionality that's built into Windows Calendar, it's possible to subscribe to any number of online calendars and even publish your own calendars.

Subscribing to Calendars

Before you can subscribe to an online calendar, you'll need to find one of course. There are a number of online calendar resources that you can peruse. One of the best is Apple's iCal Library (**www.apple.com/macosx/features/ical/library/**), because Apple was one of the first major companies to embrace the iCal standard. Apple's site includes professional sports schedules, worldwide holidays, movie openings, and much more. Another excellent resource is iCalShare (**www.icalshare.com/**), which lists even more calendars to which you can subscribe, in a bewildering list of categories.

Using either site, or a similar resource, you can browse different calendars until you find one to which you'd like to subscribe. Say you're a Boston Red Sox fan. If you search for "Red Sox" on iCalShare, you'll see a number of calendars devoted to the schedule of Boston's major league baseball team.

Secret

You might think that you could subscribe to one of these calendars simply by downloading it. Unfortunately, it's not that simple. Instead, you must right-click the link to an online calendar and copy its web address, or URL, to the clipboard. To do this with Internet Explorer, right-click and choose Copy Shortcut. Then, switch to Windows Calendar and click the Subscribe button. This displays the Subscribe wizard, as shown in Figure 20-14.

Paste the URL for the calendar into the text box and click Next. Windows Calendar will connect to the Web and discover details about the calendar. In the next phase of the Subscribe wizard, you'll see the name of the calendar (which you can change), along with options for how often it should refresh (or synchronize with) the remote calendar. If there are reminders or tasks included with the calendar, you can optionally enable them as well. This is all shown in Figure 20-15.

Figure 20-14: It's nice that you can subscribe to online calendars, but it's not very automated.

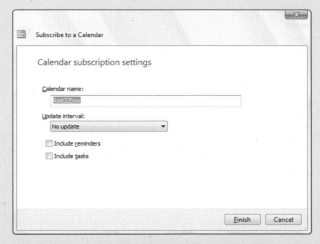

Figure 20-15: It's unlikely that you'll want to be issued reminders from a remote calendar, but it's nice to have the option.

Click Finish and you'll complete the subscription. This process is similar to that when you create your own calendars. For example, you'll see a new calendar appear in the Calendars list, along with its associated appointments, all displayed in a custom color. And you can edit the name of the calendar, delete it, or change its display color if you'd like.

continues

continued

There are key differences as well. Subscribed calendars are marked as read-only. This means you cannot add or change appointments with subscribed calendars. You can only view them (or, as noted above, change their name and color within Windows Calendar). The people who publish the calendars to which you are subscribing are free to change them, of course. If they do change a calendar you're subscribing to, you can get the changes by setting up a refresh schedule when you subscribe, or by synchronizing, which we describe below.

Publishing Your Calendars

If you have access to a web server to which you can copy an ICS file, you can publish your own calendars as well. Since this action isn't as common as subscribing, Windows Calendar doesn't include a Publish toolbar button. However, it does include a full-featured if slightly-hidden Publish Calendar wizard that steps you through the process. To find it, select a calendar and then navigate to Tools⇨Sharing⇨Publish. This displays the Publish Calendar wizard shown in Figure 20-16.

Figure 20-16: With this simple wizard, you can publish your own calendars online.

To publish a calendar directly to a web server, that server will need to be compatible with the web-based Distributed Authoring and Versioning (WebDAV) standard, a set of technologies aimed at making it easier to manage files on remote web servers. If you don't have access to such a server, you can always export your calendar to a local ICS file and then upload it to a web server using FTP or whatever uploading tool you may choose to use. However, when you do this, you lose the best feature of publishing, which is the ability to keep the remote (or published) version of your calendar up to date as you make changes to it from within Windows Calendar.

In the Publish Calendar wizard, you will first provide a name for your calendar (Windows Calendar uses the calendar name by default). Then, enter a URL where you'd like to publish the calendar. This URL is formatted just like any web address, using the HTTP prefix. If your web server is named **windowssecrets.com** and you have dedicated a remote folder for calendar sharing called **ical**, you might type in the address **www.windowssecrets.com/ical**. Then, determine whether you want the published calendar to be automatically updated when changes are made and decide whether to include Notes, Reminders, and Tasks. When you're ready, press the Publish button.

Now, Windows Calendar will publish your calendar to the web site you specified. At this point, you can continue making changes to the calendar; unpublish it, if you're not happy with the results; or announce the calendar, giving friends and family an opportunity to discover it and, hopefully, subscribe. The latter two options are available in Tools⇨Sharing.

Synchronizing Your Calendars

With the proliferation of local and shared calendars on your system, you're going to want some way to ensure that everything is up to date. Fortunately, Microsoft has included a synchronize function in Windows Calendar that performs two key functions. If you have a remote calendar to which you've subscribed, synchronizing will ensure that you have the very latest version. And if you are publishing a calendar, synchronize will ensure that the remote copy is up to date with the changes you've made locally. You can choose to synchronize only the currently selected calendar or Synchronize All, which will sync up all of your calendars, in both directions. Both options are available in Windows Calendar's Tools menu.

Searching Calendars

In keeping with the Windows Vista search-centric user interface, Window Calendar provides a handy search box in the upper-right corner of the application window, from which you search for both appointments and tasks. If you just type a term into the search box, by default, Window Calendar will search all appointment and task events and will display the results in a Search Results pane that appears at the top of the Windows Calendar window, seen in Figure 20-17.

However, you can also limit searches with certain criteria. If you look to the right of the search box, you'll see that there is a drop-down menu. This menu enables you to limit the search to today's events, the next 7 days, the next 14 days, the next 31 days, this calendar month, all future events, or the currently selected day.

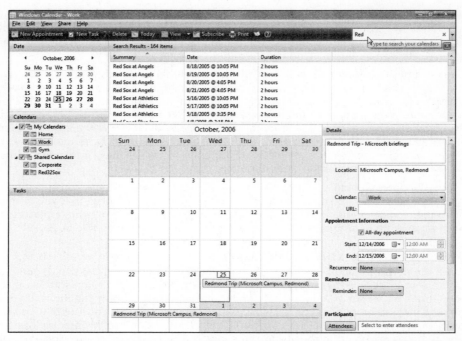

Figure 20-17: The Search feature in Windows Calendar works with both appointments and tasks.

Printing Calendars

Finally, Windows Calendar includes a nice printing component, which enables you to print your calendars in various attractive ways. This is handy for people who need a quick printout or haven't otherwise embraced the notion of personal digital assistants (PDAs) or smart phones.

Before you print, you need to decide which calendars to include in your printout. Any calendars that are selected, or checked, in the Calendars list in the Navigational pane will print. So deselect any calendars you'd like to exclude first.

Now, click the Print button in the Windows Calendar toolbar. This launches the Print window, as shown in Figure 20-18. Here, you can configure various print options.

Under Print Style, you can pick between Day, Work Week, Week, and Month print styles. You can also specify a date range and other options. The actual printouts are quite nice. They provide an attractive calendar look but none of the Details information found with each appointment.

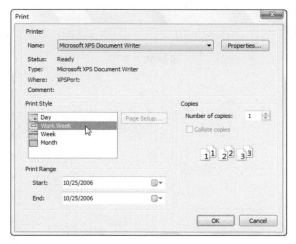

Figure 20-18: When printing calendars, you can choose between various view styles.

Secret

The printing functionality in Windows Calendar prints only appointments, not tasks.

Summary

Windows Calendar is a decent standards-based calendar, and given the fact that no such functionality existed in Windows XP, it's a welcome addition to the stable of Windows Vista applications. With Windows Calendar, you can maintain one of more calendars, subscribe to web-based calendars, and publish your own calendars so that others can keep up with your activities. Hopefully, this chapter has inspired you to discover this application's many and varied features.

Keeping Your Data Safe

Chapter
21

◆ ◆

In This Chapter

Understanding the different ways to back up and restore data

Utilizing the Backup and Restore Center

Creating and restoring data backups

Managing automatic backups with Windows Backup

Backing up an entire PC using system images

Restoring an entire PC using the Windows Recovery Environment

Using Volume Shadow Copy to recover old versions of data files

Repairing Windows with System Restore

◆ ◆ ◆ ◆ ◆ ◆ ◆ ◆   ◆ ◆ ◆ ◆ ◆ ◆ ◆ ◆ ◆ ◆ ◆ ◆ ◆ ◆ ◆ ◆

With Windows Vista, Microsoft has finally given users pervasive and reliable backup and restore solutions for both data files and the entire computer. You can use the File and Folder Backup Wizard to copy your important files and folders to a safe location, the Complete PC Backup tool to create a system image that can be used later to restore a broken PC, and the Windows Backup Utility to enable automatic data backups or restore data backups or system images. There's even a cool new feature borrowed from Windows Server that will help you recover old versions of data files if you save the wrong version, and an updated version of System Restore that can help your PC "go back in time" and remove bad drivers or applications. You may never need to turn to a third-party backup and restore utility ever again.

Different Backups, Different Goals

Now that you've moved to digital storage for your most valuable data, it's time to start thinking about creating backups, which are copies of your original data that should be kept elsewhere for safe keeping. Many people don't even consider backing up until the unthinkable happens: A hard drive breaks down, literally taking all the data with it, or there's a fire or theft. However it happens, you should be prepared for the worst. This is all the more important because many people now manage both their professional and private lives on their PCs. It's one thing to lose this week's meeting agenda, but what will you do when a hard drive crash takes away the only copies you had of five years' worth of digital photos?

Given the almost complete lack of decent backup solutions in previous Windows versions, you may be surprised to discover that Windows Vista offers an almost mind-boggling suite of backup and restore solutions, each aimed at a different need. Best of all, Vista also includes a friendly front end to all these capabilities, so that even the most non-technical person can get up to speed quickly. Before we get into that, however, let's examine the various types of data safety facilities that Windows Vista supports.

Data Backup

If you think of your Documents folder as the center of your data universe, and keep an elaborate series of folders and files there, then you'll understand the necessity of backing up these crucial files on a regular basis. To this end, Windows Vista supports both automatic and manual data backup options, enabling you to choose which files to back up and when. You can then restore your backups at any time to recover previous versions of documents, or to replace a file you may have accidentally deleted.

Complete PC Backup

There's nothing worse than discovering that you need to reinstall Windows for some reason. Not only do you have to take the time and effort to get the operating system installed, but then you have to make sure you have drivers for all your hardware, find and reinstall all the applications you use regularly, reload all your personal data, and reconfigure all of the system's options so that it's exactly the way you used to have it. Rather than go through this rigmarole, you can use a new Windows Vista feature called Complete PC Backup to create what's called a *system image* or *snapshot*. This image contains the entire contents of your PC, as it was the day you created the image. If you need to recover your entire PC, you can simply restore the system image and get right back to work.

File Recovery

Windows Vista offers the following two excellent ways to recover lost files:

◆ **Volume Shadow Copy:** If you want to recover an older version of a document, perhaps because you made an edit in error and then saved it, you can use this feature to access previous versions of the file.

◆ **System Restore:** If you make a change to your system that renders the PC unstable, such as installing a bad driver, you can use this feature to return to a previous time period, or *restore point*. When you reboot, none of your data has been changed, but the rest of your system configuration returns to that of the day and time the restore point was first made.

Add all that up, and what you have is the makings of a full-featured data recovery software suite. Amazingly, Microsoft provides all of that functionality in Windows Vista for free. Let's take a look.

Using the Backup and Restore Center

Although the various data recovery tools are available scattered through the Windows Vista user interface, there is a single application, the Backup And Restore Center, that provides a handy front end to all of them. Shown in Figure 21-1, this application helps you both back up and restore files on your PC.

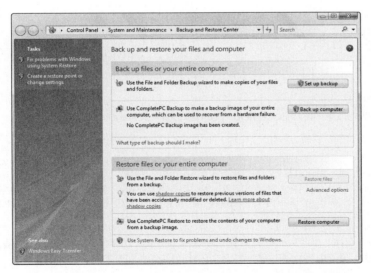

Figure 21-1: It's a one-stop shop for all your data protection needs.

Because the Backup And Restore Center basically sits in front of most of the other data recovery functions included in Windows Vista, we'll use this as the obvious starting point for most of the data, file, and system backup and restore features we discuss below.

tip   The Backup And Restore Center can be found in the Start Menu under All Programs⇨Maintenance.

Backing up Data

If you'd like to create a data backup, you can use the Back Up Files Wizard, which is available from the Backup And Restore Center. To do so, launch the Backup And Restore Center and click the Back Up Files button. This launches the wizard, shown in Figure 21-2. The wizard is a friendly interface to Backup Status And Configuration, which you can also access separately if you'd like.

Figure 21-2: The Back Up Files Wizard helps you manually create a backup of your important data files.

In the first step of the wizard, you must choose a location to store the backup. The amount of space you'll need, of course, is based on the amount of data you will be backing up. You can save a backup to an internal or external hard disk or other storage device, a recordable optical disk (typically a writeable CD or DVD), or a network share.

tip   You cannot back up to a disk or partition you are backing up. That is, if you are backing up data from the C: drive, you cannot save the backup to the C: drive.

In the second step, you select which disks (or partitions) to include in the backup. If you only have a single disk (or partition), this will be pretty simple, but many people are using multiple disks and partitions, so the wizard gives them the option to include those as well.

In the third step, you select which types of data files you'd like to back up, as shown in Figure 21-3. You can choose between picture, music, videos, e-mail, documents, recorded TV show, compressed files, and other data files.

Figure 21-3: Rather than make you step through a series of document locations, the wizard intelligently finds the data files you specify, regardless of their location.

Secret

Although the wizard doesn't offer any way to fine-tune exactly which data file types to back up, one thing you won't have to worry about is it missing anything. As long as you leave every data file type checked in this step of the wizard, Windows Backup will be overly thorough and backup all known data types plus virtually anything it can't recognize.

If you're running the wizard for the first time, it will now alert you that this first backup is what's called a *full backup*. That is, it will backup all of the data file types you specified on the drives or partitions you selected. If you'd like, you can now configure Backup Status and Configuration, via this wizard, to make regular *partial backups* that include files that have changed since the first full backup. As seen in Figure 21-4, you can determine how often these partial backups occur and on what day and time.

tip If you set up an automatic backup schedule now, Windows Vista will monitor your PC usage and prompt you to perform occasional full backups over time as well.

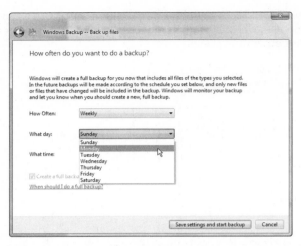

Figure 21-4: The wizard enables you to access the Backup Status And Configuration automatic backup functionality as well.

Now you're prompted to start the backup, which runs in the background. As the backup runs, a small Windows Backup icon sits in the system tray, where you can view the status of the backup's progress if you'd like.

Secret

The Backup utility in Windows Vista uses standard ZIP files to store its backups, so if you need to recover the files from a non–Windows Vista–based PC, you'll have no problems. Backups are saved to a folder on the backup device named in the form of *Backup Set–date–unique identifier*, and if you drill into those folders, you'll find a Backup Files folder full of ZIP files. These files contain all of your data backups.

tip

You can create multiple automatic data backup schedules this way if you want. For example, you may want to back up different drives or data file types at different times or with different regularity.

Managing Backups

If you want to manage the various backups you've created, you can access Backup Status and Configuration directly. You will find the Backup Status and Configuration shortcut in the Start menu: It's located in All Programs➪Accessories➪System Tools. Either way, you'll be presented with the Spartan Windows Backup interface shown in Figure 21-5.

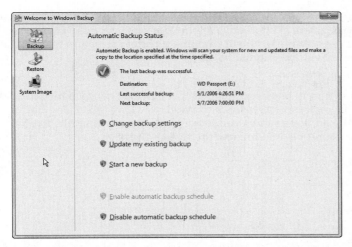

Figure 21-5: Backup Status and Configuration enables you to schedule automatic and manual backups, restore backups, and create a system image.

From this interface, you can change the backup settings for an existing backup, start a new backup, or enable and disable automatic backups all together. You can also access the restore and system image functionality that we'll examine later in the chapter.

If you click Change Backup Settings, you'll return to the Backup Files Wizard, where you can change any of the settings you previously configured. The Back Up Now link enables you to manually trigger a backup, which you may occasionally need if you make a lot of changes to data files well in advance of your next backup. Finally, the Change Backup Settings link lets you configure automatic backups or start a new full backup.

Restoring Files

To restore files you've previously backed up, access the Backup And Restore Center again, and then trigger one of the following two types of data restore operations:

- ◆ **Basic Restore:** Restores all of the files and folders you backed up previously.
- ◆ **Advanced Restore:** With this type of restore, you can perform more advanced restoration tasks, such as restoring only files from the latest backup, restoring files from a particular backup, or even restoring files from a different PC.

Follow these steps to trigger a restoration process:

1. Click the Restore Files button in the Backup And Restore Center.
2. The Restore Files Wizard appears, allowing you to choose between files from the latest backup or files from an earlier backup. If you choose the former option, you will restore the files you most recently backed up, whereas the second choice enables you to navigate through a list of the backups that have been performed and choose the one you want. Either way, you can then choose between restoring all backed up files or browsing or searching through the selected backup to find only the file or files you need.

3. Choose where to restore the files. You can restore in the original location, which is the default, or select a different location. If you select a different location, you also have the opportunity to create a unique directory structure that emulates the directory structure of the original backup.

4. Start the restore process.

If restoration will cause files to be overwritten, as it will if you choose to restore the files to their original location, you'll receive a standard Windows Copy File dialog box, as shown in Figure 21-6. This dialog box enables you to overwrite the existing file, keep the existing file, or keep the existing file and rename the restored version.

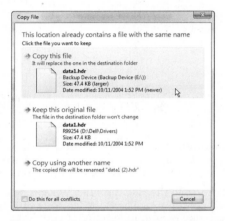

Figure 21-6: This dialog box ensures that you understand you'll be overwriting an existing file if you're not careful.

And that's all there is to it: After the copy phase, the wizard completes.

Backing up the Entire PC

Backing up and restoring data files is important and should occur on a regular basis. But over the past few years, a new type of backup utility by which entire PC systems are duplicated, or *imaged*, in the event of a hardware disaster have become quite popular. System imaging utilities aren't actually all that new; corporations have been using them for years. But now that consumer-oriented system imaging utilities have gained in popularity, Microsoft has created its own version and bundled it right in Windows Vista.

Secret

System imaging utilities typically compress the data on your hard drives so that the image file takes up a lot less space than the original installation. Various solutions use different compression schemes, but you may be interested to know that Windows Vista uses the tried and true Virtual Hard Disk (VHD) format that Microsoft also uses in its Virtual PC and Virtual Server products. That means that system images created with Windows Vista will be supported for a long time to come.

caution
System images contain complete PC environments. You can't arbitrarily restore just parts of a system image, as you can with data backups. Instead, when you restore a system image, it restores the whole PC and overwrites any existing operating system you may already have on there. That means you should be careful before restoring a system image: Any data you have on the disk will be overwritten. But you're using automatic backups, right?

To create a system image, launch Backup and Restore Center and click the Back Up Computer button. This launches the Windows Complete PC Backup Wizard, which naturally walks you through the steps needed to completely back up your PC system. You can save system images to hard disks or optical storage (like recordable CDs or DVDs).

Secret
You can only write a system image to a hard disk that is formatted with the NTFS file system. That's because system images often exceed the 4 GB file size limit imposed by the older FAT32 file system. Windows Complete PC Backup will provide an estimate for the amount of space needed to create a system image.

Secret
After you've selected a location for the image, you choose which disks (or partitions) to include in the image. Two file system locations must be included in the system image, what Microsoft refers to as the boot partition and the system partition. The boot partition is always C:\, whereas the system partition is the drive with the Windows Vista Windows directory. This is typically C:, but if you installed Vista in a dual-boot setup with a previous Windows version, the system partition might be in a different location. If you have other drives or partitions, you can optionally choose to include then in the system image as well.

Creating a system image is typically a lengthy process. For this reason, you should ensure that your system is exactly the way you want it before you start imaging the PC.

Restoring the Entire PC

Although a Restore computer option appears in Backup and Restore Center, you can't actually trigger an entire PC restoration from within Windows. Instead, you will need to reboot your system and utilize the Windows Recovery Environment, which should be installed on your system, or the Windows Vista installation DVD. The reason for this is that the recovery process literally overwrites all of the data on your hard drives. Obviously, you will want to be sure you've backed up any crucial data before attempting this process.

Follow these steps to restore your entire PC using a system image:

1. Reboot the computer.

2. After your PC has finished its BIOS sequence, hold down the F8 key. If you don't see an option for the Windows Recovery Environment, just boot up your computer with the Windows Vista DVD instead.

3. After Windows Vista Setup begins, you'll be brought to the Install Now screen. Instead of installing Vista, however, choose the System Recovery Options link.

4. You'll be guided through a series of steps. Choose your keyboard layout (US for US residents) when requested to do so.

5. Setup searches for Windows installations to repair. When you are asked what type of repair task you'd like to accomplish, select Windows Complete PC Restore.

6. The Windows Disaster Recovery Wizard launches. If you haven't already attached a hard drive or DVD containing the system image, do so now. The wizard will step you through the process of recovering the system image, rebooting, and loading your newly recovered system. As with creating a system image, this can be a very lengthy process. For this reason, you should budget an hour or more to complete this recovery.

Recovering Old Versions of Data Files

One of the most useful new features for information workers first appeared in Windows Server 2003. It's called *Volume Shadow Copy*, which silently and automatically creates backups, or snapshots, of data files every time a user makes any changes. In a managed environment like Windows Server, Volume Shadow Copy is a wonderful feature, because end users who save documents on the server can easily recover older document versions without having to summon an administrator to restore an old backup from a tape or hard drive.

With Windows Vista, Microsoft has added Volume Shadow Copy to its client operating system as well. This means that any Windows users can take advantage of this amazing bit of functionality and recover seemingly lost versions of files they've mistakenly edited.

The trade-off, of course, is disk space. Because Windows must store multiple copies of your data files, Volume Shadow Copy does eat up a bit of disk space. However, because Volume Shadow Copy saves only the parts of files that have changed, or what Microsoft calls the *delta changes*, the disk space loss is not as bad as it would be otherwise.

Unlike with Windows Server, you can't really manage how much disk space Volume Shadow Copies uses, or even the drives on which it is enabled. Instead, Microsoft enables the service across all drives, folders, and data files on a Windows Vista PC.

To access this feature, find a document that you've changed a lot recently, right-click it, and choose Properties. Then, navigate to the Previous Versions tab. As you can see in Figure 21-7, Windows maintains a number of previous versions, each of which you can restore when needed.

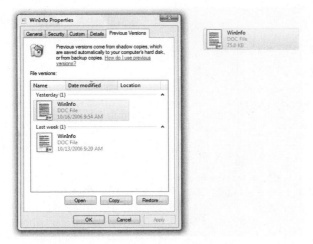

Figure 21-7: The Volume Shadow Copy service makes it possible to resurrect old versions of data files.

To restore an older version of a file, select the file version you want and then click the Restore button. As with any other file copy operation, you'll be prompted to replace the existing file, keep the existing file, or keep the existing file and rename the newly recovered version.

Using System Restore to Repair Windows

One of the best features in Windows Millennium Edition (Me) and Windows XP was System Restore, which has proved itself to be a life saver. This feature carries forward in slightly improved form in Windows Vista. What System Restore does is automatically back up key system files at opportune times, such as when you're installing a new hardware driver. That way, if a driver or application wreaks havoc with your PC, you can use System Restore to reload older system file versions and get back up and running again.

System Restore now has the following two main interface points.

♦ **System Protection:** Located in the System Properties dialog box (which is annoyingly much harder to find in Windows Vista than it was in previous Windows versions). To get to it the quickest possible way, open the Start Menu, right-click My Computer and choose Properties, and then click the Advanced System Settings link in the System window. Then, navigate to the System Protection tab.

As shown in Figure 21-8, this interface enables you to configure which disks or partitions you will protect (typically only the system volume, which is usually drive **C:**). You can also manually create a system restore point by clicking the Create button. You'll need to supply a name for the restore point.

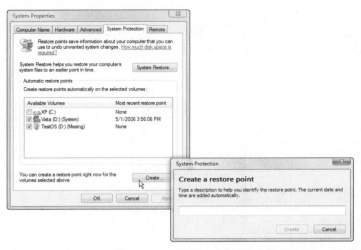

Figure 21-8: From System Protection, you can trigger a restore point manually.

◆ **System Restore Wizard:** Restores your PC's key system files to a previous point in time. To launch this wizard, open the Start menu and navigate to All Programs⇨ Accessories⇨System Tools⇨System Restore.

In the introductory page of the wizard, you can choose the recommended restore point (typically the most recent one) or optionally see a list of previously created restore points, as shown in Figure 21-9. Most of these will have been automatically created by the system and will include a description of what was going on when each restore point was created. If you manually created your own restore points from System Protection, those restore points will have the word *(Manual)* appended to the front of the name.

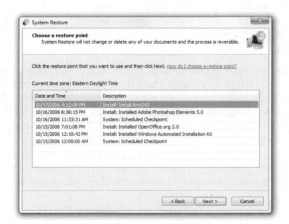

Figure 21-9: Here, you can choose the restore point you'd like to use.

When you select a restore point, Windows will move into the secure desktop and begin restoring your system to its previous state. This will require the PC to reboot. Note that any applications you've installed since that restore point will almost certainly need to be reinstalled.

Summary

Windows Vista includes a surprisingly rich set of features for backing up and restoring both specific file types and the system itself. This is one instance where Vista really distances itself from Windows XP: With Vista, you get handy file backup and restore wizards, a system imaging utiltiy that enables you to recover completely from any kind of PC calamity, and a nice front end from which to manage all of this functionality. It will be interesting to see how the third-party utility market responds to these changes.

Microsoft
PowerShell

Chapter
22

◆ ◆ ◆ ◆ ◆ ◆ ◆ ◆ ◆ ◆ ◆ ◆ ◆ ◆ ◆ ◆ ◆ ◆ ◆

In This Chapter

Working with the new **.ps1** *scripts*

Constructing PowerShell commands

Finding all available PowerShell commands

Drilling down to the specific parameters supported by each command

Exploring why Microsoft developed a new language for Windows

Downloading, installing, and running PowerShell for the first time

Providing a PowerShell Quick Reference

◆ ◆

Microsoft PowerShell is a new programming language with capabilities far beyond the older command interpreters that were included with previous versions of Windows.

Getting Used to .PS1 Scripts

Released at nearly the same time as Windows Vista, Microsoft PowerShell is an extensive script language that is far richer than the batch language included with previous versions of Windows. PowerShell can also be downloaded and run on Windows XP and Windows 2003, if these operating systems are updated to a recent service pack. This means PowerShell scripts you write can also run on most other Windows PCs in operation today.

If you think, as we do, that PowerShell is kind of a silly name, go ahead and imagine that PS stands for Microsoft's Programming Shell. Aside from the hyped-up marketing moniker, the language is quite serious.

PowerShell represents so much capability that scripts for Microsoft's Exchange 2007 e-mail application are written in it. You probably won't need to write anything that complex. But no matter the size of your project, Microsoft has built PowerShell so it has few limitations. It's worlds away from Windows' old batch language, which is run by the **Cmd.exe** command interpreter.

As just one of the features PowerShell brings to Windows that Microsoft's older command-line environments did not, you can use PowerShell commands to read from and write to hives in the Windows Registry as though they were ordinary drives. For example, you access **HKEY_LOCAL_MACHINE** through a drive named **HKLM** and **HKEY_CURRENT_USER** via **HKCU.**

PowerShell scripts normally bear an extension of **.ps1,** for PowerShell version 1. This contrasts with Windows' built-in **Cmd.exe,** which runs batch files ending in **.bat**. Presumably, if a future PowerShell version 2 is released, scripts that require the more advanced language will bear the extension **.ps2,** and so on.

Microsoft wisely avoided making **.ps1** files execute automatically if you happen to open one. Under a new Microsoft policy announced before Vista was released, a potentially harmful feature is not turned on by default unless 90 percent of Windows users would use it.

Almost everyone sends files to a printer, for example, and this isn't particularly dangerous — so printing capabilities are automatically enabled in Vista.

Running scripts, however, can silently install worms or Trojan horses if you inadvertently open one. Hacker web sites and untrustworthy e-mails will undoubtedly try to use PS scripts to slip rogue programs onto users' PCs.

To give you an idea of the problem, the **.ps1** extension sounds like it might have something to do with PostScript. You can imagine virus writers sending out mass e-mails after Vista becomes widely installed, saying things like, "See the naughty pictures in the attached PostScript file." Noticing the unfamiliar **.ps1** extension, many users might indeed assume the attachment was a harmless image file. In reality, although a racy picture might be displayed, a powerful script could also be silently launched, infecting a user's PC.

Keeping PowerShell disabled, except for those users who need such scripts and turn them on, is Microsoft's way of minimizing the damage. If you know what you're doing, enabling

PowerShell isn't particularly dangerous. If you don't need PowerShell, however, you don't need it. Viruses can't run rampant via PowerShell scripts if most Windows users have PowerShell turned off.

To run PowerShell safely if you do use it, be sure to see the Secret in this chapter on running only digitally signed scripts.

Running PowerShell Scripts Safely

Microsoft disables by default the operating system's ability to run PowerShell scripts merely by clicking or opening them. But, if you use PowerShell scripts, you should take the following three steps to protect yourself against hacked web sites or e-mails that might find ways to run them without your knowledge.

1. Obtain a digital certificate and digitally sign any scripts you develop in-house. Require that scripts you obtain from other parties be signed by them.
2. Configure PowerShell so it will run only those scripts that are signed by parties you know and trust.
3. Secure your list of trusted certificates. It doesn't do any good to restrict scripts to a list of trusted parties if a virus or Trojan horse is able to quietly add other signatures to your list.

If you don't know how to take the preceding steps, get a professional to set up your system in this way — or don't configure your system to run any scripts that happen to get opened.

Constructing a PowerShell Command

We can't adequately document the PowerShell language in this chapter — entire books deal with this subject, and we recommend that you study one if you want to become proficient. Instead, we offer here an introduction and a Quick Reference that we hope you'll find useful.

The PowerShell language draws from several older programming languages. Its grammar is based on POSIX, a character-based command language that's also called a *shell* (because it sits over the operating system *kernel*). POSIX is a subset of the Korn Shell, which is widely used in Unix environments.

PowerShell, however, is not a copy of POSIX. Instead, it adopts many of the features of the Microsoft .NET object model. In a nutshell, pardon the expression, .NET objects have properties, which are defined in well-understood ways. For example, a file object has a size in bytes, a date and time when the file was last modified, a read-only flag (which may be on or off), and so forth.

In creating the commands that would be available in PowerShell, Microsoft's developers used a *verb-noun* naming convention. Some common PS commands are:

```
Get-ChildItem
Get-Content
Remove-Item
```

In each case, the first word is a verb, followed by a hyphen and then a noun on which the verb operates. (Speaking of case, all PS commands are case-insensitive. **GET-childITEM** does the same thing as **get-childitem**. We're showing commands here with initial capital letters for the same reason Microsoft does — to improve readability.)

These commands seem awfully long—and you haven't seen anything yet. Fortunately, short versions called aliases are built in for most commands. You can also define your own aliases. The three PS commands previously shown are equivalent to the following **Cmd.exe** commands that you probably know:

```
dir
type
del
```

That's right—Microsoft has defined long, hard-to-remember commands to replace **dir** (which shows a directory listing of filenames), **type** (which displays the contents of a file), and **del** (which erases files).

Microsoft explains the length of its new PS commands by saying it helps developers understand them. It also makes it possible to get a synopsis of a group of commands by using the command **get-help.** Um, well, actually, almost everyone will use the command's short, memorable alias instead: **help**.

For example, you can see a 1-line listing of all the commands that get information:

```
help get-*

Name                          Category   Synopsis
----                          --------   --------
Get-Acl                       Command    Get the access control list ...
Get-Alias                     Command    Returns alias names ...
Get-AuthenticodeSignature     Command    Gets the signature object ...
```

You can also see those commands that operate on objects:

```
help *-object

Name            Category   Synopsis
----            --------   --------
Compare-Object  Command    Compares the properties of ...
ForEach-Object  Command    Applies script blocks to each ...
Group-Object    Command    Groups the objects that contain ...
```

Seeing All the Commands

PowerShell provides a command, known as **Get-Command**, that displays all the built-in commands that are available. Unlike the old **Cmd.exe**, which relies on external, on-disk files for most of its features, PowerShell has a wealth of internal commands. These are known as *Cmdlets*, pronounced *commandlets*.

The alias for **Get-Command** is **gcm**. In our tests, both the Cmdlet and its alias required the addition of a pipe (|) and the **more** command to keep the output from scrolling off the top of our screen. The following lines show how to use the **more** command:

```
gcm | more

CommandType   Name          Definition
-----------   ----          ----------
Cmdlet        Add-Content   Add-Content [-Path] ...
Cmdlet        Add-History   Add-History [[Input-Object] ...
Cmdlet        Add-Member    Add-Member [-MemberType] ...
```

> **note** If you often use batch commands or PowerShell scripts, you'll probably want to expand the character-based window in which the commands appear. The Layout tab of the Command Prompt Properties dialog box will enable you to do just that (see Figure 22-1).

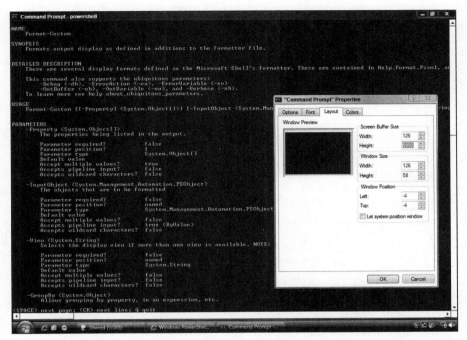

Figure 22-1: In this example, we've specified 9999 lines of height. If anything scrolls off the top of your screen, you can scroll back to see it again.

Getting Help on Commands

To find the syntax and all the parameters of a command, type **help** and the name of the command or its alias. This command automatically pages the output, so no more than one screenful appears at a time:

```
help foreach

NAME
    ForEach-Object
SYNOPSIS
    Applies script blocks to each object in the pipeline.
DETAILED DESCRIPTION
    This command allows you to process the set of objects ...
```

Why a New Language?

PowerShell has far more capabilities than the old Windows command language, **Cmd.exe**. Let's take a very simple example to see what you can do with PowerShell.

The **dir** command, as you probably know, displays a directory listing of the files in the current directory or any specified directory. The output of **dir** looks the same in both **Cmd.exe** and PowerShell, but PS enables you to do a lot more with it.

In **Cmd.exe**, the **dir** command simply lists the name, file sizes, and other attributes of the files it lists. If you wanted to see whether a particular set of files would fit onto a single CD-R, for example, you could look at the output of a **dir** command:

```
dir

Mode        LastWriteTime          Length    Name
--------    -------------------    --------  --------
-a---       12/31/2007  10:00 AM   20123456  File1.doc
-a---       12/31/2007  10:30 AM   21234567  File2.doc
-a---       12/31/2007  11:00 AM   22345678  File3.doc
```

You could then add up the length of the files in your head or on a calcuator. Or you could try to write a batch file that would accept the output of **dir**, extract the byte sizes, and then somehow add them up and display a total.

In PowerShell, determining the size of a directory in bytes can be accomplished with three lines of code. We first define a variable, **$bytesize**, and set its value to zero. Then we pipe the output of the PowerShell version of **dir** into the **foreach** alias and add up the bytes. Finally, we display the total:

```
$bytesize = 0
dir | foreach {$bytesize += $_.length}
$bytesize
```

In response to the third line of code, PowerShell displays the value of **$bytesize**:

```
63703701
```

Instead of the third line of our script, which simply puts the total on the screen, we could have fed the number into another process, written the total into a file for later analysis, or whatever. For example, if the selected files were too large for a single CD-R, a script we wrote could show us the message, "Whoa, boy! You'll need two CDs for those files," or three, or four, or whatever number had been calculated.

Notice that we used the aliases **dir** and **foreach** to make the second line of our script concise. If we'd used the longer name of each Cmdlet, the script might have looked as follows:

```
$bytesize = 0
get-childitem | foreach-object {$bytesize += $_.length}
$bytesize
```

Since a percent sign (%) is also an alias for the **for-eachobject** Cmdlet—as shown in the Quick Reference later in the chapter—we could also have made the original script even shorter:

```
$bytesize = 0
dir | % {$bytesize += $_.length}
$bytesize
```

The percent sign, in this case, doesn't have anything to do with calculating a percentage. It's just an alias for the command **foreach-object**. This use of symbols may be confusing, but it does reduce the amount of typing developers have to do (and guess who created PowerShell).

Getting PowerShell

If PowerShell isn't already installed on your computer, and you need its functions, take the following steps to obtain and run it:

1. Visit **www.microsoft.com/downloads**, search for "powershell," and download the free package that contains the installer.
2. Run the installer.
3. Click Start⇨All Programs⇨Windows Powershell to open the command-line environment.

When you start PowerShell for the first time, it may ask you, "Do you want to run software from this untrusted publisher?," referring to Microsoft. You need to answer Always Run in order for scripts signed by Microsoft to run. This includes files that are included with PowerShell, so you won't get much use of the environment if you're not willing to run Microsoft-signed scripts.

As an alternative to Step 3, you can use the Start menu to open a command prompt, which runs **Cmd.exe**. You can then type **powershell** and press Enter to start PowerShell.

To exit PowerShell, type **exit** and press Enter. This closes the PowerShell character mode window or, if you started **Cmd.exe** before starting PowerShell, returns you to **Cmd.exe**. You can exit **Cmd.exe** in the same way.

Whether PowerShell or **Cmd.exe** is running, you can also simply click the X button in the upper-right corner of the window to close the shell. There's no need to type **exit.** You can, however, put the **exit** command to good use within a script to close any window your script may have opened.

PowerShell Quick Reference

A long list of commands presented in a single block in alphabetical order is how most books document a computer language. But this, we believe, is hard for readers to grasp.

Instead, we've broken the commands into groups sorted by verb. (All PowerShell Cmdlets have a long name in the form *verb-noun*.) Understanding PowerShell's verbs makes it easier for you to then drill down and learn the details of any nouns you'll actually need to use.

Many, but by no means all, Cmdlets have shorter, built-in aliases. Where these exist, they're shown in the left-hand column. Where no alias exists, you can easily make one up using the command **Set-Alias**.

Add

The **Add** command inserts contents or entries to an object, to the console, or to the session history (Table 22-1).

Table 22-1: Add Cmdlets

Alias	Cmdlet
ac	Add-Content
	Add-History
	Add-Member
asnp	Add-PSSnapin

Clear

The **Clear** command removes contents or properties of an object without deleting the object (Table 22-2).

Table 22-2: Clear Cmdlets

Alias	Cmdlet
clc	Clear-Content
clear	Clear-Host
cls	Clear-Host
cli	Clear-Item
clp	Clear-ItemProperty
clv	Clear-Variable

Compare

The **Compare** command finds differences in the properties of objects (Table 22-3).

Table 22-3: Compare Cmdlet

Alias	Cmdlet
diff	Compare-Object

Convert

The **Compare** command changes the form of an input to a particular output format (Table 22-4).

Table 22-4: Convert Cmdlets

Alias	Cmdlet
cvpa	Convert-Path
	ConvertFrom-SecureString
	ConvertTo-Html
	ConvertTo-SecureString

Copy

The **Copy** command makes a duplicate of an object or its properties in another location (Table 22-5). (**Copy-Item** has three aliases that do the same thing, copying — so to speak — the syntax of older languages.)

Table 22-5: Copy Cmdlets

Alias	Cmdlet
copy	Copy-Item
cp	Copy-Item
cpi	Copy-Item
cpp	Copy-ItemProperty

Export

The **Export** command writes content to a file, the console, CLiXML (Constraint Language in XML), CSV (comma-separated values), and so on (Table 22-6).

Table 22-6: Export Cmdlets

Alias	Cmdlet
epal	Export-Alias
	Export-Clixml
	Export-Console
epcsv	Export-Csv

ForEach

The **ForEach** command performs actions on a series of objects (Table 22-7).

Table 22-7: ForEach Cmdlets

Alias	Cmdlet
%	ForEach-Object
foreach	ForEach-Object

Format

The **Format** command creates output with specific tabular or columnar arrangements (Table 22-8).

Table 22-8: Format Cmdlets

Alias	Cmdlet
fc	Format-Custom
fl	Format-List
ft	Format-Table
fw	Format-Wide

Get

The **Get** command fetches various objects, properties, processes, and other information (Table 22-9). Notice that **Get-ChildItem** is the same as **dir** and two other aliases.

Table 22-9: Get Cmdlets

Alias	Cmdlet
	Get-Acl
gal	Get-Alias
	Get-AuthenticodeSignature
dir	Get-ChildItem
gci	Get-ChildItem
ls	Get-ChildItem

Alias	Cmdlet
gcm	Get-Command
cat	Get-Content
gc	Get-Content
type	Get-Content
	Get-Credential
	Get-Culture
	Get-Date
	Get-EventLog
	Get-ExecutionPolicy
help	Get-Help
ghy	Get-History
h	Get-History
history	Get-History
	Get-Host
gi	Get-Item
gp	Get-ItemProperty
gl	Get-Location
pwd	Get-Location
gm	Get-Member
	Get-PfxCertificate
gps	Get-Process
ps	Get-Process
gdr	Get-PSDrive
	Get-PSProvider
gsnp	Get-PSSnapin
gsv	Get-Service
	Get-TraceSource
	Get-UICulture
gu	Get-Unique
gv	Get-Variable
gwmi	Get-WmiObject

Import

The **Import** command extracts values from an alias list or an XML or CSV file (Table 22-10).

Table 22-10: Import Cmdlets

Alias	Cmdlet
ipal	Import-Alias
	Import-Clixml
ipcsv	Import-Csv

Invoke

The **Invoke** command executes a string as an expression, executes a previously run command, or opens a file (Table 22-11).

Table 22-11: Invoke Cmdlets

Alias	Cmdlet
iex	Invoke-Expression
ihy	Invoke-History
r	Invoke-History
ii	Invoke-Item

Join

The **Join** command merges path elements into a single path (Table 22-12).

Table 22-12: Join Cmdlet

Alias	Cmdlet
	Join-Path

Measure

The **Measure** command calculates the execute time for code or computes the properties of objects (Table 22-13).

Table 22-13: Measure Cmdlets

Alias	Cmdlet
	Measure-Command
	Measure-Object

Move

The **Move** command changes the location of objects or changes the properties of objects (Table 22-14).

Table 22-14: Move Cmdlets

Alias	Cmdlet
mi	Move-Item
move	Move-Item
mv	Move-Item
mp	Move-ItemProperty

New

The **New** command sets a new property of an object or creates new objects, services, drives, and so on (Table 22-15).

Table 22-15: New Cmdlets

Alias	Cmdlet
nal	New-Alias
ni	New-Item
	New-ItemProperty
	New-Object
mount	New-PSDrive
ndr	New-PSDrive
	New-Service
	New-TimeSpan
nv	New-Variable

Out

The **Out** command determines the destination of output, such as to a file, printer, or pipeline (Table 22-16).

Table 22-16: Out Cmdlets

Alias	Cmdlet
	Out-Default
	Out-File
oh	Out-Host
	Out-Null
lp	Out-Printer
	Out-String

Pop

When you use the **Pop** command, the location determined by the latest stack entry becomes the current location (Table 22-17).

Table 22-17: Pop Cmdlets

Alias	Cmdlet
popd	Pop-Location

Push

The **Push** command places a location on the stack (Table 22-18).

Table 22-18: Push Cmdlets

Alias	Cmdlet
pushd	Push-Location

Read

The **Read** command gets a line of data from the host console (Table 22-19).

Table 22-19: Read Cmdlets

Alias	Cmdlet
	Read-Host

Remove

The **Remove** command deletes an item, object, or property; removes a drive from its location, and so on (Table 22-20). Notice that **Remove-Item** is the same as **del**, **erase**, and four other aliases.

Table 22-20: Remove Cmdlets

Alias	Cmdlet
del	Remove-Item
erase	Remove-Item
rd	Remove-Item
ri	Remove-Item
rm	Remove-Item
rmdir	Remove-Item
rp	Remove-ItemProperty
rdr	Remove-PSDrive
rsnp	Remove-PSSnapin
rv	Remove-Variable

Rename

The **Rename** command changes the name of an item or property (Table 22-21).

Table 22-21: Rename Cmdlets

Alias	Cmdlet
ren	Rename-Item
rni	Rename-Item
rnp	Rename-ItemProperty

Resolve

The **Resolve** command determines the meaning of wildcards in a path (Table 22-22).

Table 22-22: Resolve Cmdlet

Alias	Cmdlet
rvpa	Resolve-Path

Restart

The **Restart** command starts a service that had been stopped (Table 22-23).

Table 22-23: Restart Cmdlet

Alias	Cmdlet
	Restart-Service

Resume

The **Resume** command starts a service that had been suspended (Table 22-24).

Table 22-24: Resume Cmdlet

Alias	Cmdlet
	Resume-Service

Select

The **Select** command matches objects, files, or strings that have specified parameters or patterns (Table 22-25).

Table 22-25: Select Cmdlets

Alias	Cmdlet
select	Select-Object
	Select-String

Set

The **Set** command establishes a value, property, and so on, for an object, service, or the host computer (Table 22-26).

Table 22-26: Set Cmdlets

Alias	Cmdlet
	Set-Acl
sal	Set-Alias
	Set-AuthenticodeSignature
sc	Set-Content
	Set-Date
	Set-ExecutionPolicy
si	Set-Item
sp	Set-ItemProperty
cd	Set-Location
chdir	Set-Location
sl	Set-Location
	Set-PSDebug
	Set-Service
	Set-TraceSource
set	Set-Variable
sv	Set-Variable

Sort

The **Sort** command sorts objects into ascending or descending order (Table 22-27).

Table 22-27: Sort Cmdlet

Alias	Cmdlet
sort	Sort-Object

Split

The **Split** command divides a PowerShell path into individual components, such as parent path or leaf item (Table 22-28).

Table 22-28: Split Cmdlets

Alias	Cmdlet
	Split-Path

Start

The **Start** command runs a service that had been stopped, begins a period in which activities are suspended, or starts a transcript of a session (Table 22-29).

Table 22-29: Start Cmdlets

Alias	Cmdlet
sasv	Start-Service
sleep	Start-Sleep
	Start-Transcript

Stop

The **Stop** command halts processes or services, or ends a transcript that had been started in a session (Table 22-30).

Table 22-30: Stop Cmdlets

Alias	Cmdlet
kill	Stop-Process
spps	Stop-Process
spsv	Stop-Service
	Stop-Transcript

Suspend

The **Suspend** command pauses a service that had been running (Table 22-31).

Table 22-31: Suspend Cmdlet

Alias	Cmdlet
	Suspend-Service

Tee

The **Tee** command routes selected objects to two different places (Table 22-32).

Table 22-32: Tee Cmdlet

Alias	Cmdlet
tee	Tee-Object

Test

If a specified path exists, the **Test** command returns **true**; otherwise, returns **false** (Table 22-33).

Table 22-33: Test Cmdlet

Alias	Cmdlet
	Test-Path

Trace

Turns on tracing for a command line, multiple command lines, a pipeline, and so on (Table 22-34).

Table 22-34: Trace Cmdlet

Alias	Cmdlet
	Trace-Command

Update

The **Update** command changes information in format data files or PowerShell's **types.psxml** file (Table 22-35).

Table 22-35: Update Cmdlets

Alias	Cmdlet
	Update-FormatData
	Update-TypeData

Where

The **Where** command allows operations to be conducted only on objects in a pipeline that meet certain criteria (Table 22-36).

Table 22-36: Where Cmdlet

Alias	Cmdlet
?	Where-Object
where	Where-Object

Write

The **Write** command outputs a string, object, or message to the display, pipeline, and so on (Table 22-37).

Table 22-37: Write Cmdlets

Alias	Cmdlet
	Write-Debug
	Write-Error
	Write-Host
echo	Write-Output
write	Write-Output
	Write-Progress
	Write-Verbose
	Write-Warning

Summary

In this chapter, we've just scratched the surface of what PowerShell, the new scripting language, can do. It's a complete development language, and to take full advantage of it, you'll need to study one or more books dedicated to this topic. We've tried to give you in this chapter just a quick overview and a few tricks to get you started.

Now that you've read this chapter, you'll be able to access the properties of objects in ways impossible in **Cmd.exe**, understand how PowerShell commands work and how to use aliases, and use our Quick Reference to find particular commands to study further.

Vista Symbols

Vista includes more fonts and more symbols that you can insert into documents than ever before. In addition, the Arial Unicode MS font, which is preinstalled with Microsoft Office on many PCs, offers a huge assortment of symbols and character sets from around the world.

Getting the Symbols You Want

To enter graphical symbols into your documents in Vista, it's no longer necessary to switch to Symbol, an old-style font that has only about 220 distinct characters. The Windows core fonts—including Arial, Times New Roman, and Courier New—now support 1,000 to 2,000 characters. This acccomodates every European language as well as providing many pictorial symbols.

If you can't find the symbol you want in a core font, Vista provides the Wingdings, Webdings, and Lucida Sans Unicode fonts.

◆ **Wingdings** and **Webdings** have been included with the operating system since Windows 3.1 and Windows 98, respectively. These two fonts, like Symbol, also support only about 220 designs, but several of them are offbeat images that may be exactly what you're looking for.

◆ **Lucida Sans Unicode** is a wide-ranging collection of characters and symbols that has been included in the OS since Windows 95. With the introduction of Windows 2000, Lucida Sans Unicode grew to encompass some 1,776 characters. That number has risen only slightly to date, so almost anyone who's installed a version of Windows since 2000 will have the same Lucida characters that Vista users do.

For the ultimate in language and symbology support, Microsoft provides a giant font called Arial Unicode MS. This font, which is currently over 22MB in size, includes more than 50,000 shapes representing about 39,000 different characters. At this writing, Arial Unicode MS is not included with Vista but is loaded by default when you install Microsoft Office 2000 or higher. Because many PCs today come with Office preinstalled, the characters present in Arial Unicode MS are available to a large number of Windows users.

Figure A-1 shows a tiny sampling of the symbols you can insert into your documents using the Vista and Office fonts described previously.

When It's Safe to Use Your Fonts

A great deal of information about which fonts are present in different versions of Windows—and how best to use them—is presented earlier in this book in Chapter 7. In this appendix, we'll just quickly review a few rules of thumb. And we'll plunge into a few figures that show you which symbols are available to you as a Vista user.

You can safely use any font in Vista if you observe the following guidelines:

1. **Print-only documents.** If you plan to distribute only hard copies of your documents, and you don't expect anyone other than yourself to be editing the files, you can use any font and any character you wish. If you can see the character on your screen, and it prints correctly on your printer, that's all that matters.

2. **Adobe PDF files.** If you have Adobe Acrobat or an alternative program that creates PDF (Portable Document Format) files, you can also use any font or character you wish. The PDF technology automatically saves the outlines of any fonts used in a document. This makes the document display and print the same way on the computers of other people you distribute the file to. (Widely used "core" fonts, such as Arial, are exceptions that are sometimes not included in PDF files. But, at your option, you can require the inclusion of even these fonts. In Acrobat, click Advanced⇨Acrobat Distiller⇨Settings⇨Edit Adobe PDF Settings⇨Fonts⇨Embed All Fonts.)

3. **Sharing .doc files.** If you want other people to be able to edit a document that you've created using noncore fonts, you have two choices. You can make sure that your associates are all using the same version of Windows that you are. This makes it very likely that they'll also have the same fonts and characters on their PCs that you do. Or you can save all the fonts you use within the document itself so others are guaranteed to have all the same characters you do.

   To do this in Microsoft Word, click Tools⇨Options⇨Save⇨Embed TrueType Fonts. Embedding a font makes your file take up more space on disk, but it's usually worth it to prevent editing problems. (To reduce the disk-space requirements, the Embed TrueType Fonts check box allows you to save only those characters you actually use in a document. This reduced character set, however, makes it impossible for other people to edit the document and include characters you didn't use, if they don't have the same fonts installed.)

4. **Posting documents on the Web.** If you use the correct methods, you can safely include special characters in articles that you post on the Web. The trick is to specify characters above decimal 127 using an HTML feature called *numbered entities.* For example, don't insert an em dash (—) into your writing by entering character number 150. This only displays properly in Windows, not in Macs or Linux. Instead, make sure your HTML code uses the Unicode decimal value of the em dash, which is 8212, in an encoded entity like this:

   —

   All modern Web browsers, at least since version 4.0 of the Internet Explorer and Netscape browsers and version 1.0 of Firefox, will convert a numbered entity into the desired character as long as *any font present on the visitor's machine* supports that character. This means that you don't have to know every font that your visitors may have installed. As long as you use a character that's present in a core font or in Lucida Sans Unicode, 99 percent of Web surfers will be able to see it.

The preceding comments about embedding fonts into PDF and DOC files assume that the particular fonts you're using don't prohibit embedding. Fortunately, most of the fonts provided by Vista do allow embedding. If you've purchased fonts from other sources, however, check that they're "embeddable" or, even better, "editable." If not, don't assume these fonts can be saved within your PDF and DOC files.

---

tip

It's easy to check whether a given font is "editable" (it allows whoever opens the file to enter new characters from the embedded font) or merely "embeddable" (it allows whoever opens the file to see all same characters in whichever font you originally used). To do this, open the Fonts control panel, right-click a font name, click Properties, and select the Details tab. The Font Embeddability line will show you the font's status.

Symbol	Select this font	Use these decimal values
©	Arial, Times New Roman, etc.	169
®	Arial, Times New Roman, etc.	174
¼ ½ ¾	Arial, Times New Roman, etc.	188 189 190
°	Arial, Times New Roman, etc.	176
•	Lucida Sans Unicode	8226
■	Lucida Sans Unicode	9642
▶ ▸	Lucida Sans Unicode	9654 8227
¹³⁄₆₄	Lucida Sans Unicode	185 179 8260 8326 8324
€ £ ¥	Lucida Sans Unicode	8364 163 165
ˢᴹ	Lucida Sans Unicode	8480
™	Lucida Sans Unicode	8482
℗	Lucida Sans Unicode	8471
☺	Lucida Sans Unicode	9786
♠ ♣ ♥ ♦	Lucida Sans Unicode	9824 9827 9829 9830
→	Lucida Sans Unicode	8594
℞	Lucida Sans Unicode	8478
★★★☆	Arial Unicode MS	9733 9733 9733 9734

Figure A-1: **Common symbols.** To insert symbols such as these into your documents, select the recommended font in your application, and then use the Alt+number method described in this appendix to enter the decimal value of each character.

Symbol	Select this font	Use these decimal values
❶❷❸	Arial Unicode MS	10122 10123 10124
Ⓐ Ⓑ Ⓒ	Arial Unicode MS	9398 9399 9400
⌖	Arial Unicode MS	8982
⍇	Arial Unicode MS	9003
ᶜ_R ᴸ_F	Arial Unicode MS	9229 9226
♚ ♛ ♞	Arial Unicode MS	9818 9819 9822
✂	Arial Unicode MS	9985
➠	Arial Unicode MS	10408
◯	Arial Unicode MS	10061
❏	Arial Unicode MS	10063
☑	Arial Unicode MS	9745
☒	Arial Unicode MS	9746
☃	Arial Unicode MS	9731
🕐	Wingdings	183
⊞	Wingdings	255
🚭	Webdings	122
🔒 🔓	Webdings	207 208

Figure A-1 *(continued)*

Entering Special Characters

Many applications have their own unique methods that allow you to enter special characters into documents. Microsoft Word, for example, supports an Insert⇨Symbol command. This enables you to select any character you wish from within a list of all installed fonts.

The following method, however, works the same way in almost all Windows applications, regardless of who developed them. It involves holding down the Alt key while you enter a decimal number on your numeric keypad.

Entering Characters Using Alt+number

1. In your application, select a font that contains the character you wish to insert.
2. Make sure NumLock is on (the NumLock light is lighted).
3. Hold down your Alt key.
4. Type the decimal number of the character on your numeric keypad. (This even works on laptops with no numeric keypad, as long as they have a NumLock key and numerals that are printed on alphabetical characters on the keyboard.)
5. Release the Alt key. The desired character should instantly appear.

For example, to enter an em dash into text, hold down Alt and type 8212 on your numeric keypad. (This is usually written "Alt+8212.") Vista's core fonts and most of the other fonts will display a dash at your cursor location as soon as you release the Alt key.

Secret

The Leading Zero Is No Longer Needed

Windows users have long used the Alt+number method to enter special characters. Alt+0169, for example, accesses a copyright symbol in most fonts. Vista eliminates the need to enter a leading zero in front of the rest of the number. Any decimal number may now be entered by holding down Alt, typing the number on the numeric keypad, and releasing Alt. Alt+169, for example, is all that's needed to get a copyright symbol.

In previous versions of Windows, using the Alt+number method to enter a number between 128 and 255 without the leading zero resulted in the insertion of a character from the old DOS upper-ANSI character set — but no longer.

What if you forget to switch to the appropriate font before entering the character number — or it turns out that the font you selected doesn't in fact support that character? Most applications allow you to select a different font for specified text even after you've entered it.

The Alt+number method, unfortunately, is somewhat dependent on the specific *input language* that's in effect when you're typing. For example, Alt+number works in the English (United States) input language but not in every input language that can be used by Windows.

tip   **Check your input language. To find out which input language Vista is using, open the Regional and Language Options control panel. In the Keyboards and Languages tab, click the Change Keyboards button. Your default input language should be shown.**

Entering Characters Using CharMap

If the Alt+number method doesn't work for you, a technique that always works is to use CharMap.exe. This little accessory allows you to scroll through the entire character set of any installed font. You can then pick characters using the Select button, copy them to the Clipboard using the Copy button, and finally paste them into your word-processing application. Your pasted characters should retain their font information, just as they appeared in CharMap.

To launch CharMap, click Start⇨All Programs⇨Accessories⇨System Tools⇨Character Map. Or enter **charmap.exe** in the search bar.

Figure A-2 shows an example of using ChapMap to select the copyright symbol (Alt+169).

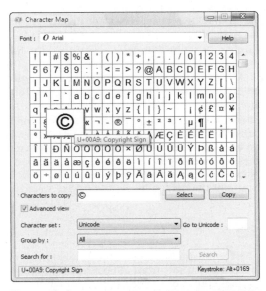

Figure A-2: Selecting characters using CharMap. Clicking a character shows an enlarged version of it. Clicking the Select button enters a character into the "Characters to copy" area. Clicking the Copy button copies the characters in this area to the Clipboard, after which you can paste the characters into documents.

Apps That Help You Pick Your Fonts

Secret

Some Vista applications will actually help you find a character you enter, if that character isn't present in your currently selected font. Try this in WordPad, for instance: Change the current font to Lucida Sans Unicode. Enter Alt+9398 to insert a circled letter "A." Without warning, WordPad switches the current font to SimSun and inserts a circled "A," because Lucida doesn't contain that symbol but SimSun does. You'll need to manually switch back to your base font if you don't want to use SimSun (a font widely used in China) for the rest of your document.

Choosing the Right Font for the Job

When entering symbols, selecting a font that's "low on the food chain" will reduce any potential problems if you want to allow others to open and edit your document.

Look for the characters you want in the following kinds of fonts, from the most prevelent to the least:

1. **Use "core" fonts first.** If you can find a desired symbol in Arial, Times New Roman, or Courier New, select one of these fonts. Almost all users of Windows, Macs, and Linux have versions of these fonts installed.

2. **Use Lucida Sans Unicode when needed.** This font has been present by default in Windows since version 98 and most Windows users will therefore have it installed. If Mac or Linux users will be receiving your document, however, they may not have Lucida available. In that case, distribute your document only with Lucida embedded when you save the file.

3. **Use Wingdings or Webdings sparingly.** Only Windows users typically have these fonts installed. So use them only if necessary, and always embed them when you do. Figures A-3 and A-4 show the symbols available in Wingdings and Webdings, respectively. If possible, use instead the characters in the Dingbats range of Unicode: hex 2700 to 27BF.

4. **Use Arial Unicode MS when necessary.** Even many Windows users don't have this font handy, because it's currently installed only by Microsoft Office 2000 and higher. Even so, others can see and edit your document—including even the most offbeat Unicode characters—if, when you save the file, you embed the characters that you used. Be aware that Arial Unicode MS is over 22MB by itself, so embedding the entire font can enormously increase the size of your files.

The Benefits of Unicode

Unicode is an international standard, first published in 1991, that now defines more than 100,000 different characters, ideograms, and symbols from almost every language group in the world. The decimal and hexadecimal values of the characters shown in this appendix are the same as the values specified in Unicode.

The standardization of these language groups' symbols—known as glyphs—is a huge boon for communication. Microsoft is a strong supporter of Unicode. Files saved in Windows are now stored using an encoding of Unicode called UTF-8. This encoding ensures that the characters in a disk file will remain stable regardless of the various input languages that may be selected on a computer at any given time.

We haven't attempted to include every known Unicode character here. Entire books that document the standard — including tens of thousands of Chinese, Japanese, and Korean ideograms — are available from the Unicode Consortium at **www.unicode.org**.

In this book, Chapter 7 includes a chart of some of the Unicode characters available in Arial and Times New Roman. In this appendix, by contrast, Figure A-5 is a chart showing useful symbols that are found in Lucida Sans Unicode and Arial Unicode MS. We show a column for each character in both of those fonts because the appearance sometimes differs notably between the two. Also, some symbols appear only in one font and not the other. This is indicated by a blank space in one font's column.

The position of a character in the Unicode scheme is often represented using a number, as follows: U+20AC, for instance, for a euro sign (decimal 8364). We simply show in our charts the decimal and hex values without tacking on the "U+" indicator. Also, the Unicode Consortium usually specifies the names of defined characters in all caps. For legibility's sake, we've written out the character names for you in upper- and lowercase, although the all-cap version is technically more correct.

In no way do we believe that we've shown here every character that might possibly be useful to you. Also, please note that the charts we've designed for this book were created using a beta version of Windows Vista. Characters that weren't included in the Vista fonts then may have become a part of those fonts by the time you read this or shortly thereafter. As always, be sure to test any characters and fonts you wish to include in a document before relying on those characters to be there.

Have fun using these characters! The only limit is your imagination.

note	**Make your own snowman.** Does a collection of all the glyphs of all the world's language groups really need a symbol of a snowman? Who knows, but there he is, top hat and all, at position U+2603. (see Figure A-5) That's funny, but some sillier things have been fended off by the Unicode Consortium. The group rejected a request to reserve character positions for Klingon, a made-up language spoken only by Star Trek devotees.

For a complete set of Vista glyphs and symbols, download *Strange Characters in Vista*, a PDF e-book, from **http://WindowsSecrets.com/vista**.

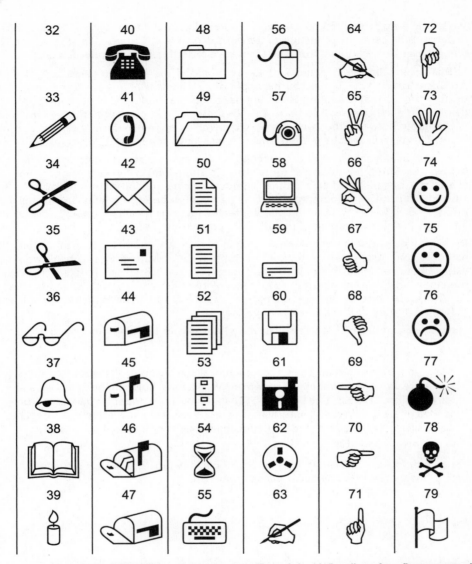

Figure A-3: The Wingdings character set. The original Wingdings font first appeared way back in Windows 3.1. Like its 1998 sibling, named Webdings, Wingdings contains approximately 220 symbols, most of which require a fairly large size to be legible.

Figure A-3 *(continued)*

Figure A-3 *(continued)*

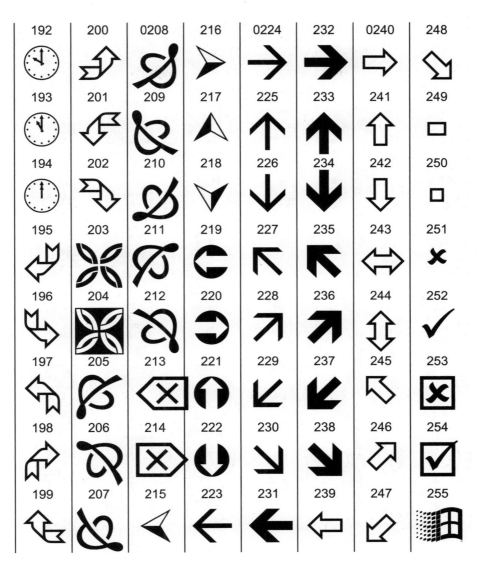

Figure A-3 *(continued)*

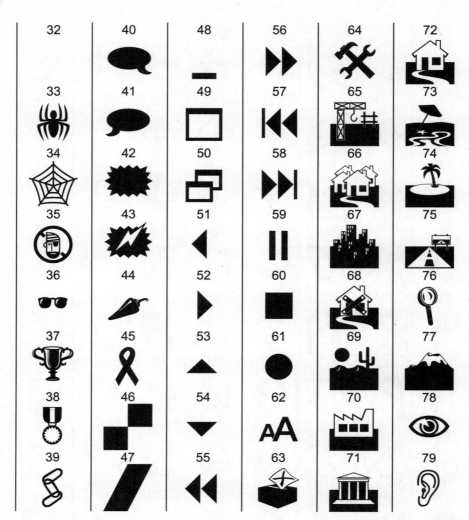

Figure A-4: The Webdings character set. The Webdings font has been included in every version of Windows since Windows 98.

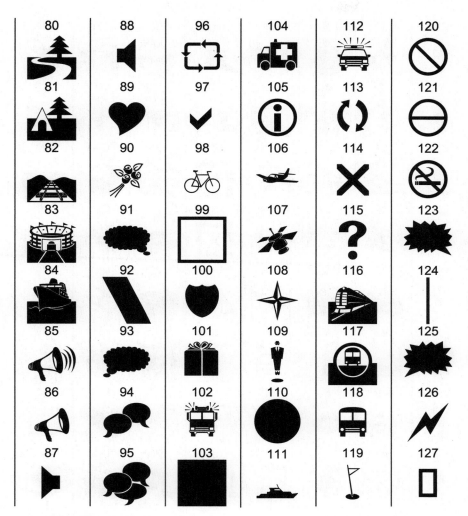

Figure A-4 *(continued)*

Figure A-4 *(continued)*

Figure A-4 *(continued)*

Superscripts and Subscripts — 2070 to 209F

Dec/ Hex	Lucida Sans Unicode	Arial Unicode MS	Description	Dec/ Hex	Lucida Sans Unicode	Arial Unicode MS	Description
8304 2070	0	0	Superscript zero (1–3 at dec. 185, 178, 179)	8323 2083	3	3	Subscript three
8308 2074	4	4	Superscript four	8324 2084	4	4	Subscript four
8309 2075	5	5	Superscript five	8325 2085	5	5	Subscript five
8310 2076	6	6	Superscript six	8326 2086	6	6	Subscript six
8311 2077	7	7	Superscript seven	8327 2087	7	7	Subscript seven
8312 2078	8	8	Superscript eight	8328 2088	8	8	Subscript eight
8313 2079	9	9	Superscript nine	8329 2089	9	9	Subscript nine
8314 207A	+	+	Superscript plus sign	8330 208A	+	+	Subscript plus sign
8315 207B	–	–	Superscript minus	8331 208B	–	–	Subscript minus
8316 207C	=	=	Superscript equals sign	8332 208C	=	=	Subscript equals sign
8317 207D	(	(	Superscript left parenthesis	8333 208D	(	(	Subscript left parenthesis
8318 207E	)	)	Superscript right parenthesis	8334 208E	)	)	Subscript right parenthesis
8319 207F	n	n	Superscript Latin small letter n				
8320 2080	0	0	Subscript zero				
8321 2081	1	1	Subscript one				
8322 2082	2	2	Subscript two				

Figure A-5: Symbols in Lucida Sans Unicode and Arial Unicode MS. These fonts support approximately 1,800 and 39,000 characters, respectively. We show on these pages a subset of the symbols in these fonts that may be most useful to you.

sixteen

Currency, Enclosed Alphanumerics — 20A0 to 20CF, 2400 to 24FF

Dec/ Hex	Lucida Sans Unicode	Arial Unicode MS	Description	Dec/ Hex	Lucida Sans Unicode	Arial Unicode MS	Description
8352 20A0	₠	₠	Euro-currency sign	9312 2460		①	Circled digit one
8353 20A1	₡	₡	Colon sign	9313 2461		②	Circled digit two
8354 20A2	₢	₢	Cruzeiro sign	9314 2462		③	Circled digit three
8355 20A3	₣	₣	French franc sign	9315 2463		④	Circled digit four
8356 20A4	£	£	Lira sign	9316 2464		⑤	Circled digit five
8357 20A5	₥	₥	Mill sign	9317 2465		⑥	Circled digit six
8358 20A6	₦	₦	Naira sign	9318 2466		⑦	Circled digit seven
8359 20A7	Pts	₧	Peseta sign	9319 2467		⑧	Circled digit eight
8360 20A8	Rs	₨	Rupee sign	9320 2468		⑨	Circled digit nine
8361 20A9	₩	₩	Won sign	9321 2469		⑩	Circled number ten
8362 20AA	₪	₪	New sheqel sign	9322 246A		⑪	Circled number eleven
8363 20AB		₫	Dong sign	9323 246B		⑫	Circled number twelve
8364 20AC	€	€	Euro sign	9324 246C		⑬	Circled number thirteen
				9325 246D		⑭	Circled number fourteen
				9326 246E		⑮	Circled number fifteen
				9327 246F		⑯	Circled number sixteen

Figure A-5 *(continued)*

Currency, Enclosed Alphanumerics — 20A0 to 20CF, 2400 to 24FF

Dec/ Hex	Lucida Sans Unicode	Arial Unicode MS	Description	Dec/ Hex	Lucida Sans Unicode	Arial Unicode MS	Description
9328 2470		⑰	Circled number seventeen	9410 24C2		Ⓜ	Circled Latin capital letter m
9329 2471		⑱	Circled number eighteen	9411 24C3		Ⓝ	Circled Latin capital letter n
9330 2472		⑲	Circled number nineteen	9412 24C4		Ⓞ	Circled Latin capital letter o
9331 2473		⑳	Circled number twenty	9413 24C5		Ⓟ	Circled Latin capital letter p
9398 24B6		Ⓐ	Circled Latin capital letter a	9414 24C6		Ⓠ	Circled Latin capital letter q
9399 24B7		Ⓑ	Circled Latin capital letter b	9415 24C7		Ⓡ	Circled Latin capital letter r
9400 24B8		Ⓒ	Circled Latin capital letter c	9416 24C8		Ⓢ	Circled Latin capital letter s
9401 24B9		Ⓓ	Circled Latin capital letter d	9417 24C9		Ⓣ	Circled Latin capital letter t
9402 24BA		Ⓔ	Circled Latin capital letter e	9418 24CA		Ⓤ	Circled Latin capital letter u
9403 24BB		Ⓕ	Circled Latin capital letter f	9419 24CB		Ⓥ	Circled Latin capital letter v
9404 24BC		Ⓖ	Circled Latin capital letter g	9420 24CC		Ⓦ	Circled Latin capital letter w
9405 24BD		Ⓗ	Circled Latin capital letter h	9421 24CD		Ⓧ	Circled Latin capital letter x
9406 24BE		Ⓘ	Circled Latin capital letter i	9422 24CE		Ⓨ	Circled Latin capital letter y
9407 24BF		Ⓙ	Circled Latin capital letter j	9423 24CF		Ⓩ	Circled Latin capital letter z
9408 24C0		Ⓚ	Circled Latin capital letter k	9424 24D0		ⓐ	Circled Latin small letter a
9409 24C1		Ⓛ	Circled Latin capital letter l	9425 24D1		ⓑ	Circled Latin small letter b

Figure A-5 *(continued)*

Currency, Enclosed Alphanumerics — 20A0 to 20CF, 2400 to 24FF

Dec/ Hex	Lucida Sans Unicode	Arial Unicode MS	Description	Dec/ Hex	Lucida Sans Unicode	Arial Unicode MS	Description
9426 24D2		ⓒ	Circled Latin small letter c	9442 24E2		ⓢ	Circled Latin small letter s
9427 24D3		ⓓ	Circled Latin small letter d	9443 24E3		ⓣ	Circled Latin small letter t
9428 24D4		ⓔ	Circled Latin small letter e	9444 24E4		ⓤ	Circled Latin small letter u
9429 24D5		ⓕ	Circled Latin small letter f	9445 24E5		ⓥ	Circled Latin small letter v
9430 24D6		ⓖ	Circled Latin small letter g	9446 24E6		ⓦ	Circled Latin small letter w
9431 24D7		ⓗ	Circled Latin small letter h	9447 24E7		ⓧ	Circled Latin small letter x
9432 24D8		ⓘ	Circled Latin small letter i	9448 24E8		ⓨ	Circled Latin small letter y
9433 24D9		ⓙ	Circled Latin small letter j	9449 24E9		ⓩ	Circled Latin small letter z
9434 24DA		ⓚ	Circled Latin small letter k	9450 24EA		⓪	Circled digit zero
9435 24DB		ⓛ	Circled Latin small letter l				
9436 24DC		ⓜ	Circled Latin small letter m				
9437 24DD		ⓝ	Circled Latin small letter n				
9438 24DE		ⓞ	Circled Latin small letter o				
9439 24DF		ⓟ	Circled Latin small letter p				
9440 24E0		ⓠ	Circled Latin small letter q				
9441 24E1		ⓡ	Circled Latin small letter r				

Figure A-5 *(continued)*

Box Drawing, Block Elements, Geometric Shapes — 2500 to 25FF

Dec/ Hex	Lucida Sans Unicode	Arial Unicode MS	Description	Dec/ Hex	Lucida Sans Unicode	Arial Unicode MS	Description
9642 25AA	■	■	Black small square	9658 25BA	►	►	Black right-pointing pointer
9643 25AB	□	□	White small square	9659 25BB	▷	▷	White right-pointing pointer
9644 25AC	▬	▬	Black rectangle	9660 25BC	▼	▼	Black down-pointing triangle
9645 25AD	▭	▭	White rectangle	9661 25BD	▽	▽	White down-pointing triangle
9646 25AE	▮	▮	Black vertical rectangle	9662 25BE	▾	▾	Black down-pointing small triangle
9647 25AF	▯	▯	White vertical rectangle	9663 25BF	▿	▿	White down-pointing small triangle
9648 25B0	▰	▰	Black parallelogram	9664 25C0	◄	◄	Black left-pointing triangle
9649 25B1	▱	▱	White parallelogram	9665 25C1	◁	◁	White left-pointing triangle
9650 25B2	▲	▲	Black up-pointing triangle	9666 25C2	◂	◂	Black left-pointing small triangle
9651 25B3	△	△	White up-pointing triangle	9667 25C3	◃	◃	White left-pointing small triangle
9652 25B4	▴	▴	Black up-pointing small triangle	9668 25C4	◄	◄	Black left-pointing pointer
9653 25B5	▵	▵	White up-pointing small triangle	9669 25C5	◁	◁	White left-pointing pointer
9654 25B6	►	►	Black right-pointing triangle	9670 25C6	◆	◆	Black diamond
9655 25B7	▷	▷	White right-pointing triangle	9671 25C7	◇	◇	White diamond
9656 25B8	▸	▸	Black right-pointing small triangle	9672 25C8	◈	◈	White diamond containing black small
9657 25B9	▹	▹	White right-pointing small triangle	9673 25C9	◉	◉	Fisheye

Figure A-5 *(continued)*

Misc. Symbols — 2600 to 26FF

Dec/ Hex	Lucida Sans Unicode	Arial Unicode MS	Description	Dec/ Hex	Lucida Sans Unicode	Arial Unicode MS	Description
9728 2600		☀	Black sun with rays	9744 2610		☐	Ballot box
9729 2601		☁	Cloud	9745 2611		☑	Ballot box with check
9730 2602		☂	Umbrella	9746 2612		☒	Ballot box with x
9731 2603		☃	Snowman	9747 2613		✕	Saltire
9732 2604		☄	Comet	9754 261A		☚	Black left pointing index
9733 2605		★	Black star	9755 261B		☛	Black right pointing index
9734 2606		☆	White star	9756 261C		☜	White left pointing index
9735 2607		☇	Lightning	9757 261D		☝	White up pointing index
9736 2608		☈	Thunderstorm	9758 261E		☞	White right pointing index
9737 2609		☉	Sun	9759 261F		☟	White down pointing index
9738 260A		☊	Ascending node	9760 2620		☠	Skull and crossbones
9739 260B		☋	Descending node	9761 2621		☡	Caution sign
9740 260C		☌	Conjunction	9762 2622		☢	Radioactive sign
9741 260D		☍	Opposition	9763 2623		☣	Biohazard sign
9742 260E		☎	Black telephone	9764 2624		☤	Caduceus
9743 260F		☏	White telephone	9765 2625		☥	Ankh

Figure A-5 (continued)

Misc. Symbols — 2600 to 26FF

Dec/ Hex	Lucida Sans Unicode	Arial Unicode MS	Description	Dec/ Hex	Lucida Sans Unicode	Arial Unicode MS	Description
9766 2626		☦	Orthodox cross	9785 2639		☹	White frowning face
9767 2627		☧	Chi rho	9786 263A	☺	☺	White smiling face
9770 262A		☪	Star and crescent	9787 263B	☻	☻	Black smiling face
9771 262B		(Ψ)	Farsi symbol	9788 263C	☼	☼	White sun with rays
9772 262C		☬	Adi shakti	9789 263D		☽	First quarter moon
9774 262E		☮	Peace symbol	9790 263E		☾	Last quarter moon
9775 262F		☯	Yin yang	9791 263F		☿	Mercury
9776 2630		☰	Trigram for heaven	9792 2640	♀	♀	Female sign
9777 2631		☱	Trigram for lake	9793 2641		♁	Earth
9778 2632		☲	Trigram for fire	9794 2642	♂	♂	Male sign
9779 2633		☳	Trigram for thunder	9795 2643		♃	Jupiter
9780 2634		☴	Trigram for wind	9796 2644		♄	Saturn
9781 2635		☵	Trigram for water	9797 2645		♅	Uranus
9782 2636		☶	Trigram for mountain	9798 2646		♆	Neptune
9783 2637		☷	Trigram for earth	9799 2647		♇	Pluto
9784 2638		☸	Wheel of dharma	9800 2648		♈	Aries

Figure A-5 *(continued)*

Misc. Symbols — 2600 to 26FF

Dec/ Hex	Lucida Sans Unicode	Arial Unicode MS	Description	Dec/ Hex	Lucida Sans Unicode	Arial Unicode MS	Description
9801 2649		♉	Taurus	9817 2659		♙	White chess pawn
9802 264A		♊	Gemini	9818 265A		♚	Black chess king
9803 264B		♋	Cancer	9819 265B		♛	Black chess queen
9804 264C		♌	Leo	9820 265C		♜	Black chess rook
9805 264D		♍	Virgo	9821 265D		♝	Black chess bishop
9806 264E		♎	Libra	9822 265E		♞	Black chess knight
9807 264F		♏	Scorpius	9823 265F		♟	Black chess pawn
9808 2650		♐	Sagittarius	9824 2660	♠	♠	Black spade suit
9809 2651		♑	Capricorn	9825 2661		♡	White heart suit
9810 2652		♒	Aquarius	9826 2662		♢	White diamond suit
9811 2653		♓	Pisces	9827 2663	♣	♣	Black club suit
9812 2654		♔	White chess king	9828 2664		♤	White spade suit
9813 2655		♕	White chess queen	9829 2665	♥	♥	Black heart suit
9814 2656		♖	White chess rook	9830 2666	♦	♦	Black diamond suit
9815 2657		♗	White chess bishop	9831 2667		♧	White club suit
9816 2658		♘	White chess knight	9832 2668		♨	Hot springs

Figure A-5 *(continued)*

Dingbats — 2700 to 27BF

Dec/ Hex	Lucida Sans Unicode	Arial Unicode MS	Description
9985 2701		✂	Upper blade scissors
9986 2702		✂	Black scissors
9987 2703		✂	Lower blade scissors
9988 2704		✄	White scissors
9990 2706		✆	Telephone location sign
9991 2707		✇	Tape drive
9992 2708		✈	Airplane
9993 2709		✉	Envelope
9996 270C		✌	Victory hand
9997 270D		✍	Writing hand
9998 270E		✎	Lower right pencil
9999 270F		✏	Pencil
10000 2710		✐	Upper right pencil
10001 2711		✑	White nib
10002 2712		✒	Black nib
10003 2713		✓	Check mark

Dec/ Hex	Lucida Sans Unicode	Arial Unicode MS	Description
10004 2714		✔	Heavy check mark
10102 2776		❶	Dingbat negative circled digit one
10103 2777		❷	Dingbat negative circled digit two
10104 2778		❸	Dingbat negative circled digit three
10105 2779		❹	Dingbat negative circled digit four
10106 277A		❺	Dingbat negative circled digit five
10107 277B		❻	Dingbat negative circled digit six
10108 277C		❼	Dingbat negative circled digit seven
10109 277D		❽	Dingbat negative circled digit eight
10110 277E		❾	Dingbat negative circled digit nine
10111 277F		❿	Dingbat negative circled number ten
10112 2780		➀	Dingbat circled sans-serif digit one
10113 2781		➁	Dingbat circled sans-serif digit two
10114 2782		➂	Dingbat circled sans-serif digit three
10115 2783		➃	Dingbat circled sans-serif digit four
10116 2784		➄	Dingbat circled sans-serif digit five

Figure A-5 *(continued)*

Dingbats — 2700 to 27BF

Dec/Hex	Lucida Sans Unicode	Arial Unicode MS	Description	Dec/Hex	Lucida Sans Unicode	Arial Unicode MS	Description
10117 2785		⑥	Dingbat circled sans-serif digit six	10136 2798		↘	Heavy south east arrow
10118 2786		⑦	Dingbat circled sans-serif digit	10137 2799		→	Heavy rightwards arrow
10119 2787		⑧	Dingbat circled sans-serif digit eight	10138 279A		↗	Heavy north east arrow
10120 2788		⑨	Dingbat circled sans-serif digit nine	10139 279B		→	Drafting point rightwards arrow
10121 2789		⑩	Dingbat circled sans-serif number	10140 279C		→	Heavy round-tipped rightwards arrow
10122 278A		❶	Dingbat negative circled sans-serif	10141 279D		→	Triangle-headed rightwards arrow
10123 278B		❷	Dingbat negative circled sans-serif	10142 279E		➞	Heavy triangle-headed rightwards
10124 278C		❸	Dingbat negative circled sans-serif	10145 27A1		➡	Black rightwards arrow
10125 278D		❹	Dingbat negative circled sans-serif	10146 27A2		≫	Three-d top-lighted rightwards
10126 278E		❺	Dingbat negative circled sans-serif	10147 27A3		≫	Three-d bottom-lighted rightwards
10127 278F		❻	Dingbat negative circled sans-serif	10148 27A4		➤	Black rightwards arrowhead
10128 2790		❼	Dingbat negative circled sans-serif	10149 27A5		↪	Heavy black curved downwards and
10129 2791		❽	Dingbat negative circled sans-serif	10150 27A6		↬	Heavy black curved upwards and
10130 2792		❾	Dingbat negative circled sans-serif	10151 27A7		▸	Squat black rightwards arrow
10131 2793		❿	Dingbat negative circled sans-serif	10152 27A8		➨	Heavy concave-pointed black
10132 2794		→	Heavy wide-headed rightwards arrow	10162 27B2		➲	Circled heavy white rightwards arrow

Figure A-5 *(continued)*

Index

Symbols and Numerics

continued

continued

G

                                        continued

continued